FERNANDO INCIARTE

FIRST PRINCIPLES, SUBSTANCE AND ACTION

STUDIEN UND MATERIALIEN
ZUR GESCHICHTE DER PHILOSOPHIE

Begründet von Heinz Heimsoeth, Giorgio Tonelli und Yvon Belaval
Herausgegeben von Bernd Dörflinger, Heiner F. Klemme und Gerhard Funke

Band 69

FERNANDO INCIARTE
FIRST PRINCIPLES, SUBSTANCE AND ACTION

2005

GEORG OLMS VERLAG HILDESHEIM · ZÜRICH · NEW YORK

FERNANDO INCIARTE

FIRST PRINCIPLES, SUBSTANCE AND ACTION
Studies in Aristotle and Aristotelianism

Edited by Lourdes Flamarique

2005

g

GEORG OLMS VERLAG HILDESHEIM · ZÜRICH · NEW YORK

Gedruckt mit freundlicher Unterstützung der Universidad de Navarra, Pamplona.

Das Werk ist urheberrechtlich geschützt. Jede Verwertung außerhalb der engen Grenzen des Urheberrechtsgesetzes ist ohne Zustimmung des Verlages unzulässig und strafbar. Das gilt insbesondere für Vervielfältigungen, Übersetzungen, Mikroverfilmungen und die Einspeicherung und Verarbeitung in elektronischen Systemen.

Die Deutsche Bibliothek verzeichnet diese Publikation
in der Deutschen Nationalbibliografie; detaillierte bibliografische Daten
sind im Internet über *http://dnb.ddb.de* abrufbar.

∞ ISO 9706
Gedruckt auf säurefreiem und alterungsbeständigem Papier
Herstellung: Druck Partner Rübelmann, 69502 Hemsbach
Umschlagentwurf: Irina Rasimus, Köln
Alle Rechte vorbehalten
Printed in Germany
© Georg Olms Verlag AG, Hildesheim 2005
www.olms.de
ISBN 3-487-12987-6   ISSN 0585-5802

TABLE OF CONTENTS

Foreword   7

PART I: FIRST PRINCIPLES AND THE THEORY OF SUBSTANCE

Chapter 1: Aristotle on First Principles and the Theory of Substance   15

Chapter 2: Aristotle's Defense of the Principle of Non-Contradiction   75

Chapter 3: Aquinas on Aristotle: Some Examples (Excluded Middle, Substance and God)   105

Chapter 4: The Unity of Aristotle's Metaphysics   125

Chapter 5: Metaphysics and Reification   159

Chapter 6: On Aristotle's Theory of Substance   183

Chapter 7: Schelling on Aristotelian Metaphysics and Kantian Criticism   219

Chapter 8: Heidegger on Hegel and Aristotle: A straight line?   245

Chapter 9: Aristotle and the reality of time   271

PART II: FIRST PRINCIPLES AND THE THEORY OF ACTION

Chapter 10: Non-Contradiction and Practical Truth   297

Chapter 11: Discovery and Verification of Practical Truth   317

Chapter 12: *Natura ad unum - ratio ad opposita*: On Duns Scotus' Transformation of Aristotelianism   359

Chapter 13: Aristotle and Scotus on Practical Truth: A Comparison ... 379

Chapter 14: Further Developments in the Problem of Practical Truth ... 395

Chapter 15: *Peccata ignota*: On moral objectivism and moral subjectivism ... 439

Afterword ... 455

Appendix to Chapter 3, Part 1:
    On the Aristotelian Principle of Excluded Third (PET) ... 467

Index of names ... 507

FOREWORD*

This book deals mainly with the relevance of the first principles to the theory of substance as well as, to a lesser extent, to that of action in Aristotle. The difference between the two parts lies not so much in the fact that more chapters are devoted to the theory of substance than to that of action but rather in the fact that the first principles are, generally speaking, more intimately connected with the realm of necessity than they are with the realm of contingency to which action more properly belongs. ("Generally speaking", for as regards the Principle of Excluded Middle, some qualifications are still to be made). For much the same reason first principles and substance are most thoroughly intertwined in the case of God as pure actuality.

As far as Aristotle is concerned, the topic of the book is closely related to that of Terence Irwin's book, *Aristotle's First Principles*, which covers even more ground but which, on the other hand, does not deal with the question of God. In a rather detailed review, I have pointed out the lines of my agreement and disagreement with Irwin's book[1]. The content of the review, though, was circumscribed by the question of foundations, and such is also the case in the present book. This is already apparent from the title of its first and lengthier part ("First Principles and the Theory of Substance"). The second part ("First Principles and the Theory of Action") likewise concentrates on foundations, as is evident from the fact that its main topic is the problem of practical truth. As regards first principles, the link between

---

* *Editor's note:* Fernando Inciarte (1929-2000) prepared and left the book as is.

[1] "Die philosophische Querelle des anciens et des modernes", *Philosophisches Jahrbuch*, 99, 1992, pp. 329-352; T. H. Irwin, *Aristotle's First Principles*, Oxford 1988; L. Honnefelder, *Scienta transcendens. Die formale Bestimmung der Seiendheit und Realität in der Metaphysik des Mittelalters und der Neuzeit (Duns Scotus-Suárez-Wolff-Kant-Pierce)*, Hamburg 1990.

the two parts of the book is given by the issue of future contingencies and, more generally, of time.

The book consists mainly of a collection of previously published articles[2]. I have, however, included neither the review alluded to above nor some articles which I have published on related topics. As a result, I have been able to add some new material. Thus Chapter 1, the first chapter to embody original material, contains the slightly modified text of three lectures delivered in July of 1993 at the University of Notre Dame along with an appendix. The conference was on St. Thomas Aquinas, but Professor Ralph McInerny, who chaired it, was kind enough to allow me to speak mainly on Aristotle. It was during this conference, incidentally, that the Dean of the School of Philosophy at the Catholic University of America, Professor Jude Dougherty, suggested the publication of my collected English papers and so indirectly also that of this book. But not having published sufficient number of papers in English I had either to add entirely new material or to translate some of the old from the original German. The second hitherto unpublished text is concerned with the Aristotelian Principle of the Excluded Third (or Middle). (The terminological hesitation is due to the fact that the appendix breaks new ground –and not purely in a terminological sense– or so it seems to me). The text was originally conceived as Chapter 3 so as to follow upon Chapter's 2 treatment of the Principle of Non-Contradiction, but for reason still

---

[2] *Editor's note*: Relation of previously published Articles: "Aristotle's Defence of the Principle of Non-Contradition", *Archiv für Geschichte der Philosophie*, 76, 1994, pp. 129-150. "Metaphysics and Reification", *Philosophy*, 54, 1979, pp. 311-327. "Heidegger, Hegel, and Aristotle: A Straight Line?", *Acta Philosophica*, 9, 2000, pp. 223-240. "Aristotle and the reality of time", *Acta Philosophica*, 4, 1995, pp. 189-203. "Discovery and Verification of Practical Truth", *Moral Truth and Moral Tradition. Essays in Honour of Peter Geach and Elizabeth Anscombe*, L. Gormally (Ed.), Dublin 1994, pp. 25-52. "Natura ad unum – ratio ad opposita. Zur Transformation des Aristotelismus bei Duns Scotus", J. P. Beckmann, L. Honnefelder, G. Schrimpf, und G. Wieland (Hrgs.*), Philosophie im Mittelalter. Entwicklungslinien und Paradigmen*, Hamburg 1987, pp. 259-273. "Peccata ignota On moral objectivism and moral subjectivism", *Humane Vitae: 20 Anni Dopo. Atti del II Congresso Internationale di Teologia Morale*, Milano 1988, pp. 583-593.

to be given is now printed as an appendix at the end of the whole book. Chapter 6 as well as Sections 2 and 3 of Chapter 3 are likewise also published here for the first time (the previously published section 1 of Chapter 3 contains a summary of the afore mentioned appendix). Those three texts are exclusively devoted to the theory of substance, but the underlying thesis is that it was not only owing to a casual editorial decision that the Books on Substance in the *Metaphysics* were placed more or less midway between Book IV on the first principles and Book XII on Theology. Finally, Chapter 13 on the concept of practical truth in Aristotle and Duns Scotus also appears here for the first time. It originated with my contribution to the International Scotus Conference held in March of 1994 at the University of Bonn and chaired by Professor Ludger Honnefelder (Bonn) and Professor Rega Wood of the St. Bonaventura Institute, N.Y. The contribution was written in German[3]. In preparing the oral presentation, which was to be given in English, and in expanding it for inclusion here I have profited from my conversations with Professor David Gallagher of the Catholic University of America.

The chapters on Aristotelianism in both parts of the book are concerned with Aquinas, Duns Scotus, Hegel, Schelling, Heidegger and, to a lesser degree, with analytical philosophy. They are partly intended to give some examples of the transformations which Aristotle's theoretical and practical philosophy have undergone in the history of Western thought, but partly also to show the possible relevance of Aristotelianism to current philosophical as well as –to a lesser degree– to theological issues. In this respect the purpose of the book is less monumental or antiquarian than it is indicative of that third ("critical") way of dealing with history specified in the first of Nietzsche's *Untimely Considerations* ("On the use and the disadvantages of history for life"). The afterword is intended to stress this point. It was written after a careful reading of H. Weidemann's

---

[3] "Scotus' Gebrauch des Begriffs der praktischen Wahrheit im philosophiegeschichtlichen Kontext", in *John Duns Scotus: Metaphysics and Ethics*, edited by Ludger Honnefelder, Rega Wood, Mechthild Dreyer, E. J. Brill, Leiden-New York-Köln 1996, pp. 523-535.

commentary on Aristotle's *Peri Hermeneias* 9 and after conversations with M. García Clavel (then at Stanford and now at the University of Madrid as Professor of Computer Sciences) during a meeting at the University of Navarra. I cannot fully assess the impact of both reading and conversations upon me, but I know for sure that the latter also corrected two mistakes in the appendix on the Principle of Excluded Middle and that the arguments of the former, who once was my student and is now successor to the chair formerly held by me at the University of Münster, have served as a foil against which I have tried in the Afterword to mark my own position. In both respects I also profited from some remarks concerning intuitionism in a letter from Michael Dummett.

One further remark might not be superfluous. Given the diverse origins of the book, some repetitions could not be avoided. Its topic, as a whole, is a difficult one, even for specialists. I once submitted one of the papers included here (as Chapter 2) to a highly specialized professional journal. It was rejected with some remarks too flattering to be repeated. The reason given for the rejection was that the paper was written with a view to professionals of only the most specialized sort. The article was, incidentally, later published without modification, except for the expansion of some footnotes and the inclusion in one of them[4] of a translation of the two Greek texts which had been interpreted in the main body of the essay. Such an experience has led me to think it appropriate, for the sake of proper balance, not to tamper too much with the text of the oral presentation of Chapter 1. It deals in a less technical way with the matters discussed in Chapter 2 as well as with the content of the appendix on the Principle of the Excluded Third, which is even more specialized. This is the reason why this appendix (originally conceived as Chapter 3) has been moved to the end of the book[5], The three Notre Dame lectures (i.e.

---

[4] Here p. 76, n. 5, Chapter 2.

[5] In view of some criticisms to which it has been subjected even before publication, it would perhaps not be superfluous to point out here once again that the "truth-tables" that appear in the appendix to this appendix, as far as the expression "not-p" (in contrast to "¬p") is concerned, are *under no circumstances* to be considered

Chapter 1) represent a general introduction to the contents of the book as a whole, whereas the appendix explains with more detail than any previous chapter of the book why, in my opinion, the genuinely Aristotelian Principle of Exclude Middle is no less important for the problem of contingency, and hence in some way or other also for the concept of practical truth, than it is for the problem of necessity. Whether in the light of the current crisis of the concept of truth as a whole the proposed reading of Excluded Middle as bearing on the contingency inherent in the concept of practical truth might be of some help and, if so, in which way, is not for me to decide here. (Chapters 5, 8 and 15 were originally also given as lectures).

For correcting my English at different stages in the preparation of the essays as well as for translating some of them I am indebted to my colleagues Gregg Beasley, José Mariano, Barry Miller, Stephen Theron and, last but by no means least, to my former research assistant at the University of Münster, Roger Wasserman. The last named also helped prepare the book for publication together with Stephanie Freiin von Beverfoerde, to whom I am also grateful for unfailing assistance over many years. Ruth Breeze was kind enough to go through the whole manuscript.

---

truth-functional tables. Together with the first section of Chapter 1 the first section of Chapter 3 (printed as section 1 and 2 of my article "Aristotle and Aquinas. The Principle of Excluded Middle" in *Logical Analysis and History of Philosophy*, 2, Paderborn 1999) may serve as introductory reading for the whole appendix.

PART I

FIRST PRINCIPLES AND THE THEORY OF SUBSTANCE

CHAPTER 1
ARISTOTLE ON FIRST PRINCIPLES AND THE THEORY OF SUBSTANCE

1

In one of the opening ἀπορίαι of Book III of the *Metaphysics* Aristotle asks whether it falls to one and the same science to deal with the first principles as well as with substance (οὐσία). I would like to show that it is his positive answer to this question which gives the Aristotelian *Metaphysics* its structural unity. Book IV to Book XII of the *Metaphysics* constitute one sustained argument, which leads from the first principles to God or from the first principles of knowledge to the very first principle of being. Although I shall be concentrating on Aristotle's theory of substance in connection with the Principles of Non-Contradiction ("PNC" in the following) and of Excluded Third ("PET" in the following), I wish to stress right from the beginning that my interpretation is in accordance with that of Aquinas. In fact, as far as the first principles are concerned, my interpretation can be viewed as an explanation of two texts by Aquinas in his commentary on Book IV of Aristotle's *Metaphysics*. I shall presently quote these two texts.

This initial remark is relevant on at least two counts. Firstly, regarding the theory of substance, especially of the substance of material things, one may detect important differences between Aristotle and Aquinas. These differences might be summed up by saying that Aquinas, unlike Aristotle, was never prepared to consider form alone (without matter) as the first substance of material things. They do not concern, though, either the interconnection between the theory of substance and the first principles or the interpretation of the first principles themselves. Secondly, and more importantly, Aquinas' interpretation of the two first principles in Aristotle is of invaluable help in overcoming two different sorts of difficulties which mar modern interpretations of the first principles, firstly with respect to their own inner consistency and secondly with respect to their bearing on Aristotle. It is here that the two texts of Aquinas I was alluding to come into play. The first one is rather general since it concerns the meaning of the two principles and their relation to each other. The second one is far more specific and refers only to PNC or, rather, to the question of its justification. I shall begin my exegesis with the first text, but before doing so I would like to quote the second one, if only to have it in reserve until the time comes to deal with it specifically.

The more specialized text of Aquinas runs as follows: "magis opponuntur esse hominem et non esse hominem quam homo et album; sed homo et album sunt diversa secundum rationem, licet sint idem subjecto; ergo et esse hominem et non esse hominem sunt diversa secundum rationem"[1]. ("To be a man and to be not a man are more opposed to each other than man and white; but man and white are different in meaning, even if they coincide in the same subject; so to be a man and not to be a man ought to be different in meaning too"). In these words "to be different in meaning" lies the quintessence of the Aristotelian justification of PNC. I shall be returning to this in due course. But first to the more general text of Aquinas. It runs as follows: "Postquam disputavit contra ponentes contradictoria simul esse vera hic disputat contra ponentes esse medium inter contradictionem: hi enim dicunt non semper alteram partem contradictionis esse veram"[2]. ("After having argued against those who say that both parts of the contradiction [p and not-p] are at the same time true, here[3] Aristotle argued against those who say that there is a middle [or third] between the contradictories [p and not-p]: for them neither part of the contradiction need be true [i.e. both parts could be false]").

As one can easily see, Aquinas' interpretation of the two principles differs significantly from the modern one. Strictly speaking, it would

---

[1] Thomas Aquinas, *In libros Metaphysicorum*, ed. Spiazzi, Taurini 1964, n. 622.
[2] Thomas Aquinas, *In libros Metaphysicorum*, n. 720.
[3] In the final chapters, 7 and 8, of *Metaphysics*, IV.

probably be false to say that it is Aquinas' own interpretation. It was, rather, the common interpretation of the Aristotelian tradition before it came to be replaced by the modern one which, following Frege, bases the first two principles on the meaning of propositional negation: if p is true, then not-p is false, and *vice versa*. As a result, since both principles can, in the modern interpretation, be deduced from the meanings of propositional negation and of propositional connectives, such as conjunction and disjunction, both can hence be transformed, *via* one of the DeMorgan Laws, into each other. By contrast, in the traditional interpretation, which extends from Aristotle to Aquinas and surely beyond, PNC and of PET were not held to be equivalent but, rather, to be complementary to each other. The first only states, as Aquinas pointed out in our second and more general text, that both members of a contradiction cannot be true, whereas the latter only states that both cannot be false. In saying this nothing has been said as to whether (on the basis of either of the two principles, taken separately) if p is true, not-p has to be false, and *vice versa*.

Historically speaking, the very first principle (namely PNC) was directed against the Protagoreans who, as can already be seen in Plato, said that everything is true, that there is no falsity, whereas the second one, i.e. PET, was directed against Anaxagoras who, according to Aristotle, said or, at least, according to lore, is said to have said that nothing can be true, that everything must be false. Later on we shall also see in some detail why it is that the Protagoreans and others, on the one hand, and Anaxagoras, on the other, were obliged to say such strange things, a revival of which we are nevertheless witnessing in our own day by those who contend that there are no principles at all. Later on we shall examine in some detail why, according to Aristotle, such things are not only strange but in themselves impossible. But the important thing to hold on to for the moment is the very fact of this incompatibility of the traditional with the modern interpretation of the first principles. This will constitute my main topic in this section.

The importance of this incompatibility lies mainly in its bearing on the interpretation of PET. This is so because no one, at least in the field of analytical philosophy, expressly denies the unrestricted validity of PNC. (The so-called "postmodern" or "poststructuralist" philosophers are, of course, a different matter altogether). But the question of whether the Principle of Excluded Middle is unrestrictedly valid is very much disputed even within analytical philosophy. As is well known, for philosophers such as Michael Dummett in England or Willard Van Orman Quine in the USA, the acceptance of the unrestricted validity of Excluded Middle or, intimately bound up with it, of Bivalence is the hallmark of realism as opposed to anti-realism or indeed idealism. Now, as we shall see, the difficulties in holding on to the unrestricted validity of the Principles of Excluded Middle and of Bivalence arise only in connection with the modern or post-Fregean interpretation of these principles, but not with the Aristotelian and traditional one as it was presented to us in our first Thomistic text. This requires some explanation.

The difficulties with the modern reading of Excluded Middle and Bivalence arise in connection with undecidable alternatives such as whether there is or is not an odd perfect number. All the perfect numbers that have so far been discovered have been even (e.g. $6 = 1 + 2 + 3$), but this does not preclude the possibility of an odd perfect number being discovered sometime in the future in much the same way that the theorem of Fermat appears to have been recently proved. Now, since there is no way of saying whether this will be the case or not, the question is thus far undecidable. Nevertheless, realists such as Frege insist that either the one or the other member of the contradictory pair (p or not-p) has to be true and, accordingly, the other false. It is precisely with this supplement "and, accordingly, the other false" that the modern interpretation of the principles parts company with the Aristotelian and traditional one, and it is this departure that accounts for the difficulties which confront the modern interpretation. For, as we heard from Aquinas, the genuine Aristotelian PET does not say anything as to whether both alternatives (e.g., there will or will not be a sea battle tomorrow) could not be true. The only thing it states is that both cannot be false, i.e., that at most one can be false and that therefore at least one must be true. In the qualification "*at least*" in "at least one must be true" one can recognize another difference between the traditional and modern interpretations.

The difference consists in the fact that whereas in the modern interpretation each of the two principles is derived from the meaning of propositional negation and neither, by virtue of this very fact, may function as a *first* principle at all, in the traditional interpretation it is the other way round. Here propositional negation is derived from a combination of the two complementary principles taken together. For if according to PET *at most* one of the two members can be false and if according to PNC *at most* one can be true, the result of combining both genuine principles is precisely propositional negation: exactly one is true and the other false. As a result both Aristotelian principles can function independently of each other as well as together, depending upon what the individual case may require. That is why Aristotle as well as Aquinas view both principles merely as complementary and not as equivalent. Now, this may be of help in solving some of the difficulties which the modern interpretation of Excluded Middle and of Bivalence cannot overcome, it being obliged by this very fact either to give up the realistic stance in metaphysics altogether, as in Dummett, or, if retaining it, as in Quine, to defend it only with serious misgivings.

Since there are plenty of contradictory pairs (we shall be referring to them generally as p and not-p) for which it is as yet or will always be undecidable which of its members is true and which false, the genuine Aristotelian PET cannot possibly be put at risk by the fact of undecidability, since it does not preclude nor indeed say anything about the possibility of both members being true. If there is any principle which has been put at risk by such undecidable alternatives, it is either post-Fregean Excluded Middle along with post-Fregean Bivalence, which, incidentally, does not coincide with the genuine Aristotelian Principle of Bivalence either, or perhaps also PNC according to which both members of a contradiction cannot be true.

Once the case for the Aristotelian PET has been put as boldly as I have just put it, one could in fact suspect that not only the modern Principle of Excluded Middle but also PNC is or has been put at risk by as yet undecidable alternatives such as whether there will or will not be a sea battle tomorrow and the like. Granted that both alternatives could already now be true, would this, one might ask, not constitute a violation, not, of course, of the Aristotelian PET, but of PNC, whether Aristotelian or modern? And would not this very fact, one might continue to ask, speak in favor of the superiority of the modern Principle of Excluded Middle (as opposed to the Aristotelian PET)? For although it is true that the latter is not endangered by the possibility, say, of future contingent events, such undecidable matters would appear rather to endanger the more fundamental PNC.

The seeming justification for this suspicion lies in the fact that, contrary to the Aristotelian PET, the modern principle of Excluded Middle operates, as a matter of fact, with the exclusive "or". For, although the corresponding connective "v" (like the Latin "vel" from which it derives) is in itself inclusive, the fact that the propositional negation ("¬") is attached to it, allows it –indeed compels it– to function like an exclusive "or". And this is why the possibility of contradiction ("p and not-p") is here banned right from the start. Contrary to this, the Aristotelian Excluded Third does not operate with an exclusive "or", since it does not preclude the fact that both members of the alternative could be true. And that is why it seems to threaten PNC or, to put it another way, that is why the fact that alternatives which are as yet or even in principle undecidable do not force us to restrict the validity of the Aristotelian but only that of the modern Excluded Middle (or, for that matter, that of Bivalence), seems instead to endanger the unrestricted validity of the seemingly more important PNC (Aristotelian or modern). Now, if things were in fact so, then, pending the discussion of PNC, they would, indeed, argue for the superiority of the modern interpretation. To save Excluded Third at the price of endangering Non-Contradiction would be to jump out of the frying pan and into the fire.

However, there is no question of that. For the "or" of Aristotelian Excluded Third (in "p or not-p") as we say, is in no way exclusive, but it is not inclusive either. To put it differently: it does not state the possibility of the contradiction, i.e., of "p" and "not-p" both being possibly true, but only the possibility of the possibility of the contradiction, which is a totally different case. For although modern modal logic operates as if "it is possible that p" (Pp) would be equivalent to "possibly it is possible that p" (PPp), it does this, understandably, with a bad conscience. Modern modal logic derives this alleged equivalence (between "it is possible that p" and "possibly it is possible that p") from that other equivalence which is alleged to hold between "it is necessary that p" and "necessarily it is necessary that p"[4], but it has to acknowledge that "this is both a disputed question and one of some obscurity... from an intuitive point of view"[5]. From an intuitive point of view, if something is necessarily necessary, it is, of course, also necessary, but not the other way around. On the other hand, if something is possibly possible, it is –again from an intuitive point of view– not therefore possible, whereas if something is possible, it is, of course, also possibly possible. Now, this would not only conform to the intuitive, as opposed to the modern, purely formal meaning of the modal operators but it would also banish at once the threat of endangering PNC instead of that of Excluded Middle.

To point out the relevance of these at first sight rather formal matters to Aristotelian metaphysics I propose to start with one text in which Aristotle, although still dealing with PNC, is already hinting at those questions which I have just been discussing in connection with Excluded Third. The text runs: "δυνάμει... ἐνδέχεται ἅμα ταὐτὸ εἶναι τὰ ἐναντία..."[6]. Here we have the double possibility. To translate literally: "With respect to possibility (δυνάμει) contraries [and *a fortiori* contradictories] *can* (ἐνδέχεται ἅμα) both at the same time be true". David Ross misses the point, when he translates[7]: "The same thing is potentially, but not actually, possessed of contrary qualities". Having dropped the double possibility (but double possibility here means weak possibility), this translation can, or indeed must, then drop "at the same time" (ἅμα) as well. In other

---

[4] Cf. G.E. Hughes and M.J. Cresswell, *An Introduction to Modal Logic*, London 1977, p. 44.

[5] *Ibid.*, p. 43.

[6] Aristotle, *Metaphysics*, IV, 5, 1009a 35.

[7] In his commentary, not in the Revised Oxford Translation (*The Complete Works of Aristotle*, Edited by J. Barnes, Princeton University Press; "ROT" in the following).

words Ross's translation follows the pattern not only of the modern but also of the Kantian interpretation of Non-Contradiction, according to which the principle is purely formal or analytical and has nothing to do with matters either of being or of contingency, of movement or indeed time.

Two remarks on this are here pertinent. First, contrary properties can be possessed by one and the same thing even at the same time –provided the attribution of those (contradictory or contrary) properties is not meant in the same sense, or, as Aquinas put it in the first text I quoted, "*secundum rationem*" ("with respect to the [same] meaning"). We shall also see how much confusion there is concerning these things in the modern analytic interpretation of Aristotle. Secondly, even in the same sense (κατά τὸ αὐτὸ) or with respect to the (same) meaning (*secundum [eandem] rationem*) contradictory properties (whether of things or propositions) can be had by the same thing at the same time –provided this "can" is understood in the sense of double or "weak" possibility, i.e., provided that what is meant with "can" is that the affirmation and negation of the same proposition ("tomorrow there will be a sea battle") be possibly possibly true, and not simply possibly true, which would amount to stating the possibility of a contradiction.

I selected this one text of Aristotle's not only because in it this double possibility with respect to a contradiction is clearly stated, but mainly because the whole course of the Aristotelian *Metaphysics* from beginning to end, i.e., from the question of the first principles in Book IV to the theory of the very first substance, God, is marked by the effort to remove that contradiction which even in the guise of a double possibility might still threaten the *unconditional* validity of PNC. In other words, only God is, as the pure act which he is, beyond any simple or even double, strong or weak possibility, however remote, of not being, which means beyond any potentiality to be and/or not to be, just as God is the only absolutely necessary being in contrast to such beings as Aristotelian heavenly bodies or –for that matter– angels, which are only non-absolutely necessary beings. This is the essence of the story I shall have to tell or, to put it more accurately, it is the end of that story, the story of the unity of Aristotelian metaphysics. So, before closing the first section I would like to give some hints as to the role that PET in particular is due to play on the long road starting from PNC and leading to God as *actus purus*.

After having shown the necessity of accepting substances as subjects of properties in the context of defending PNC against the attacks of Protagoreans and others in Book IV, Aristotle concentrates in Books VII to IX, i.e., in the so-called "Substance Books" of the *Metaphysics*, on the meaning of substance. And first he shows that to be a subject of properties cannot be the main meaning of substance or "οὐσία". Each material substance must have, for reasons still to be shown, some essential properties or an essence with which to identify itself. After this Aristotle then shows that the essence of each substance cannot contain any matter at all, sensible or intelligible. In other words, the first substance (πρώτη οὐσία), i.e., the first meaning of the οὐσία of material things, cannot be a mere subject of properties, because this would in the end be pure matter and that means something undetermined, a bare particular, as it is called nowadays. But first substance (πρώτη οὐσία) cannot be a specific essence either, like man or horse or oak, for such an essence still includes matter. (By the way, this is the point where Aquinas departs from Aristotle, but this does not impair the overall agreement). So, according to Aristotle, to be a man cannot be the first substance of Socrates, i.e., the first substance of the *Categories*. Instead the first substance must be the pure form as first actuality, e.g., the soul of Socrates.

First substance, πρώτη οὐσία, means here pure form in the sense of actuality as opposed to potentiality. That is why Aristotle has to repeat in Book VIII the analysis of substance already carried out in the notoriously difficult, but central, Book VII, but now under the general aspect of actuality and potentiality and then, in Book IX, to discuss the modal concepts of actuality and potentiality in particular. And it is in this last among the so-called "Substance Books" (in Book IX) that PET in the sense explained above again comes into play. This can be seen very clearly at the beginning of the fourth chapter of that Book IX. The passage (in the ROT) runs as follows: "...It cannot be true to say 'this is capable of being but will not be' –a view which leads to the conclusion that there is nothing incapable of being"[8], i.e., to the conclusion that nothing is impossible.

There has arisen around this passage (according to Richard Sorabji[9], "the hardest passage" of Book IX) an unending controversy. Some authors, including Ross as well as Hintikka, read the words "It cannot be true to say 'this is capable of being but will not be'" in a deterministic way, seeing in them a confirmation of the Principle of Plenitude, according to which only those things (events) are possible that will at some time or other be realized or actualized. But since it is hard to saddle Aristotle with such a deterministic Megarian view, other authors, including G.E.L. Owen and Martha Kneale, try to avoid this unlikely conclusion by forcing the plain meaning of the text. Its plain meaning, however, has nothing to do with the Principle of Plenitude nor with any form of determinism. Accordingly, it should not be changed or its meaning forced in any way whatsoever. The passage I just quoted could be interpreted as asserting or not asserting the Principle of Plenitude only on condition that it be read according to the modern, but not Aristotelian, Principle of Excluded Middle, i.e., only by not taking into account the fact that those members of a contradiction (p and not-p) which are as yet (or even in principle) undecidable cannot for Aristotle both be false, i.e., that PET or, for that matter, of Bivalence does not exclude, nor, of course, include, the possibility of both members being true, but includes only the possibility of such a possibility, which amounts to saying that p and not-p cannot both be false (non-exclusive "or").

The traditional approach to *Peri Hermeneias*, Chap. 9, which discusses future contingents, stresses the non-exclusiveness of "vel" ("or") in Excluded Third. Thus Aquinas writes in *Peri Hermeneias*: "...quae sunt de contingentibus, necesse est quod sub disjunctione altera pars contradictionis sit vera vel falsa; non tamen haec vel illa determinate..."[10]. ("With respect to [future] contingents, it is necessary that one part or the other... be true or (*vel*) false; but not this

---

[8] Aristotle, *Metaphysics*, 1047b 3 f.
[9] R. Sorabji, *Necessity, Cause and Blame*, London 1980, p. 136.
[10] Thomas Aquinas, *In Peri Hermeneias*, n. 205.

determinate part or the other one"). Without expressly, but of course very much implicitly, referring to Aristotle and Aquinas, Michael Dummett writes: "... this view seems to me to rest on a philosophical confusion"[11]. He himself formulates the view so baldly criticized as follows: "Statements about the [contingent] future are... either-true-or-false; but they do not yet have a particular one of these two truth-values. They have present truth-or-falsity, but they do not have present truth or present falsity..."[12]. So he is in fact clearly, though only implicitly, referring to and criticizing the traditional view of Aristotle and Aquinas; as is Peter Geach[13] when, in a paper entitled "The Law of Excluded Middle", he writes the following: "Sometimes they say that neither [member of "p or not-p"] need be *determinately* true; but this qualification, though it may make their doctrine easier to swallow, is quite devoid of sense". And he adds: "Oddly enough, they claim as a precedent the famous chapter 9 of Aristotle's *Peri Hermeneias*. In fact, Aristotle expressly rejects the idea of such a breakdown of our law". True, Aristotle did not admit the idea of such a breakdown (or indeed of any breakdown) of Excluded Third. So he need not take refuge in those plurivalent logics which Geach is expressly attacking when in the same context he writes: "People have tried to maintain (some appealing to three-valued logic) that of a pair of contradictory predictions relating to a future contingency neither need be true. (Sometimes they say that neither need be *determinately* true...)". Now, Aquinas too had said this. So Geach's position is somewhat paradoxical inasmuch as he wants, on the one hand, to remain faithful to Aquinas, but is implicitly criticizing his interpretation, on the other. (With this I am not, of course, throwing together Aquinas and adherents of three-valued logic, the whole difference being precisely that three-valued logic says that both members are neither true nor false whereas Aquinas, following Aristotle, says that they are neither determinately true nor false). The paradox, though, can by now be easily resolved. To say, as Aquinas literally said and as Geach

---

[11] M. Dummett, *Truth and other enigmas*, London 1978, p. 338.

[12] *Ibid.*

[13] P. Geach, *Logic Matters*, Oxford 1972, p. 81.

(arguing against those who, contrary to Aquinas or indeed Aristotle, appeal to three-valued logic) repeats, that "neither [of any pair of contradictories] need be determinately true" only runs afoul of the modern Principle of Excluded Middle, and not of the Aristotelian PET. So, the rider "not determinately true" represents a departure only from the former. According to the latter one takes the words "neither need be determinately true" not as meaning –as Dummett seems to think to be the case– "neither need be true or false", which would in fact destroy Excluded Third and indeed Bivalence, but rather as meaning "it is precluded that both be false", or "at least one need be true", i.e., "p and not-p are now, in fact must both now, be true, but not determinately true". And this is precisely the sense of the Aristotelian principle as it is also the plain sense of the allegedly "hardest passage" I just quoted from *Metaphysics*, Book IX, Chapter 4: "Obviously it cannot be true to say so and so is possible, but will not be". The passage is not excluding unactualized possibilities (*pace* David Ross, Hintikka, and others) but simply saying that both opposite propositions about future contingencies can be true, but not determinately true. This is again the "weak" possibility of Excluded Third with its non-exclusive "or". –As for Dummett's charge of *philosophical* confusion, it would be justified only if "p or not-p" were a categorical proposition. But traditional logic wisely treated it under the heading of hypothetical propositions, whose component parts need not be asserted, and in fact are not asserted, to be determinately true or false. Quotations from Saint Thomas to this effect could be multiplied indefinitely.

In his article "What Price Bivalence?" Willard Van Orman Quine writes: "Bivalence is, as Michael Dummett says, the hallmark of realism"[14]. Being, unlike Dummett, a realist, Quine writes at the end of the article: "One might then despair of bivalence and proceed disconsolately to survey its fuzzy and plurivalent alternatives in hopes of finding something viable...". Despair and disheartenment could, though, easily have been avoided, for Quine had said at the beginning of his article: "Bivalence seals" the paradoxes arising from such vague

---

[14] W.V.O. Quine, "What Price Bivalence?", *The Journal of Philosophy*, 1981, p. 91.

terms as 'heap' and 'bald' by "requiring as it does at each stage that the statement that a heap remains, or that the man is bald, be univocally true or false". As we have seen, this cannot undermine traditional Excluded Third but only post-Fregean Excluded Middle. For in this context "univocally true or false" is but another term for "determinately true or false" –which is precisely what traditional Excluded Third falls short of saying. It would also be interesting to assess the very end of Quine's article in the light of the genuine Aristotelian Principle of Bivalence. I cannot go into this, but perhaps I should quote Quine's misgivings: Bivalence –he writes– "has us positing a true-false dichotomy across all the statements that we can express in our theoretical vocabulary, irrespective of our knowing how to decide them ... what we now observe is that bivalence requires us further to view each general term, e.g., 'table', as true or false of objects even in the absence of what we in our bivalent way are prepared to recognize as objective fact. At this point, if not before, the creative element in theory-building may be felt to be getting out of hand, and second thoughts on bivalence may arise..."[15] –but not, as in accordance with my previous remarks I would like to add, on the genuine Aristotelian Principles of Bivalence or of Excluded Third. On the other hand, I have not discussed the difference between Aristotelian and modern Bivalence nor between Aristotelian Bivalence and Aristotelian Excluded Third. But I cannot go into this here. Instead I shall close this section with some remarks on the role of Excluded Third in connection with the demonstration of God's existence.

Contingency does not represent or denote, as it were, the normal state of affairs, not so much because it runs into difficulties with PET or PNC, but because the latter (not the former!) does not as it were fully apply to it[16]. That is the case for any alternative that has not yet been settled. On the other hand, contingency would run (again, not counter to PET but) counter to PNC if all things were contingent. But precisely because of the absolutely unrestricted validity of PNC (as

---

[15] W.V.O. Quine, "What Price Bivalence?", p. 94 f.

[16] Cf. again Aristotle, *Metaphysics*, 1009a 35.

well as of PET) this is impossible. Since if all things were contingent nothing at all would now be in existence, there must be something which cannot possibly not be, viz. a necessarily necessary being. This argument, reminiscent of Aquinas' *tertia via*, is a *reductio ad absurdum* as is shown by some key words in Aristotle's *Metaphysics* XII[17] in this connection. They run as follows: "...if this were so [i.e., if potentiality or contingency were prior to actuality or necessity], nothing at all would exist" (ROT). That seems to me to be a pretty strong existential statement, and an almost existentialist one at that –in the sense that from Leibniz to Heidegger it has been asked why there is something rather than nothing. Against this one might object that in saying this, Aristotle does not mean that without God nothing at all would exist but only a different order of things from ours or even no order at all: neither world nor anything true. But one can still retort that since there cannot be time without movement, that different order, or, for that matter, that disorder, would at any rate include movement, so that in this respect there would be no difference between it and our world. Now this is a fundamental respect, for it is precisely the impossibility of an everlasting movement without a necessarily necessary being which forms the basis of the Aristotelian argument for God's existence. To repeat: "... if this were so [i.e. if all things were contingent or at least in the state of local motion] nothing at all would exist". But since something exists, a pure actuality, God, must exist.

As with any *reductio ad absurdum*, the key to the argument lies in the genuine Aristotelian PET, viz. that contradictories cannot both be false. So God's existence is arrived at by a combination of the two complementary principles. The argument requires in addition –as in Aquinas' *tertia via*– the application of the Principle of Plenitude –not, of course, with respect to future contingencies where it cannot play any role at all, but with respect to events that have already been decided in the past– as in the key passage of the *tertia via: quod possibile est non esse quandoque non est*. It has been translated in a very Aristotelian way as follows: "If everything could not be, then at

---

[17] Aristotle, *Metaphysics*, 1071b 25f.

one time there was nothing in existence"[18]. Some interpreters ask how it is that Aquinas could at the same time hold on to the rational possibility of the world being eternal. However, what Aristotle in his *Physics* is continually repeating in this connection is only this, that there was no time before the world started to move or, for that matter, to be, and therefore that there was no time in which it could have started. In this sense movement and time are, of course, everlasting, but not eternal. Therefore, in Book VIII of the *Physics* (Chapter 1) Aristotle writes: "it is evident that movement is everlasting[19], and is not something which now is and now was not [ὅτε μέν ἐν, ὅτε δ'οὐ: sometimes was, sometimes was not]. Indeed to assert the opposite is very like a contradiction in terms", for it is as good as saying that there was a time when time [the measure of movement] was not[20]. The conclusion of the whole of Chapter 1 of this last book of *Physics* reads again: "Let this suffice to demonstrate that there never was nor will be a time when movement was not or will not be"[21]. In other words, Aristotelian time is not Newtonian time, it is rather Einsteinian time, but not, of course, as a fourth dimension of space –which would do away with contingencies as well as with time and the future altogether. Now it seems to me that when Aquinas was attacking Bonaventure and others in this connection, he was arguing along the same lines as when, for example, he insists that *"ex nihilo"* in *"creatio ex nihilo"* does not mean anything but *"non post aliquid"*, for there was no time before the movement of the heavens began and the world came into being. But instead of elaborating further on this let me finish by showing very briefly the importance of PET as a first principle in yet another respect. This respect relates to the distinction between substance and accident as well as to epistemology. I mean the question of universals or –to put it more precisely– the question of

---

[18] Cf. A. Llano, "Aquinas and the Principle of Plenitude", *Thomas Aquinas and His Legacy*, ed. David M. Gallagher, Washington D.C. 1994, p. 147.

[19] ἀΐδιος: mostly translated as 'eternal' –as it is in the volume of the Loeb Library on which the translation offered here is based.

[20] Cf. note in the Loeb-edition.

[21] Aristotle, *Physics*, 252b 6.

whether one should accept the Aristotelian-Thomist *distinctio rationis cum fundamento in re* (i.e., a rational or conceptual, but not real, distinction of forms which nevertheless is grounded in reality itself) or rather the Scotist-Rationalist *distinctio formalis a parte rei* (i.e., a distinction of forms or determinations prior to any abstractive intervention of reason). The *distinctio rationis* corresponds –as is well known– to a moderate realism, whereas the formal distinction *a parte rei* corresponds to some kind of exaggerated, but not necessarily Platonistic, realism. The remaining possibilities involve either a purely nominal or a purely conceptual distinction corresponding to nominalism or conceptualism respectively. The latter two also correspond to pragmatist holism as opposed to Aristotelian essentialism. In fact, if there are no distinctions whatsoever *a parte rei*, reality is in itself thoroughly undetermined as it is, for example, in both Anaxagoras and Quine.

One might ask what these distinctions have to do with PET. The easiest way for us to answer this question so far is to point to the fact that when explaining and applying PET Aristotle is always attacking Anaxagorean holism. This is the case in Book IV as well as in Book XII concerning theology. In the latter Aristotle himself associates the absurdity of there being nothing with such a holism. Now, we know that it is also *via* this *reductio ad absurdum* and the application of PET that Aristotle arrives at God. The relevant passage runs as follows: "But if this is so, then nothing at all will exist; for it is possible for things to be capable of existing but not yet to exist. Yet if we follow the mythologists who generate the world from night, or the natural philosophers who say that all things were together, the same impossible result ensues"[22]. The expression "all things were together" clearly refers to Anaxagoras. In Book IV the reference is even more explicit. Aristotle says: "The doctrine of Heraclitus, that all things are and are not, seems to make everything true while that of Anaxagoras, that there is an intermediate between the terms of contradiction, seems to make everything false; for when things are mixed [all together] the mixture is neither good nor not-good, so that one cannot say anything

---

[22] Aristotle, *Metaphysics*, 1071b 24-28.

that is true"²³. So the question of universals has very much to do with PET. The epistemological question at issue here is the question of abstraction. If *a parte rei* (in reality) nothing at all corresponds to our conceptual determinations, our concepts can evidently not be the product of abstraction but must be the result of a construction carried out in accordance with our most basic needs, such as, say, our need to ensure survival by communicating with one another. This is a nominalist or at best a conceptualist approach. At the opposite extreme lies the rationalist approach characterized by the Scotist *distinctio formalis a parte rei*. This approach is abstractionist in that according to it there is a thorough-going correspondence or isomorphism between thought and reality as in Duns Scotus and rationalism in general: *ordo et connexio idearum idem est ac ordo et connexio rerum.*

Years ago Professor Geach launched a powerful attack against abstractionism, according to which concepts simply mirror reality passively. But even if one were to reject abstractionism straight away –as I think one should– one still need not reject, as Geach seems to imply, abstraction altogether in order to preserve the active role played by the mind in concept-formation. In other words, abstractionism is not the only alternative to holistic nominalism or conceptualism or to pragmatism. The mirror- or copy-theory of knowledge would only be appropriate if the properties of things were as different from one another in reality (*a parte rei*) as they are distinct in the mind after the operation of abstraction or concept-formation, as in Duns Scotus. But to claim this would amount to mistaking properties of substances for parts. Whereas parts are not mixed together, some properties –of course, not all properties as with Anaxagoras– are, viz. those which contribute to the formation of a given substance. The property of being, e.g., white is not the stuff by virtue of which, say, a horse is white. And even if it is only, say, the forefront of the horse that is white, the property of being white in the forefront cannot be identified with the corresponding pigment (a mere part) nor can it be restricted to the forefront of the horse only. For it is the whole horse that is white

---

²³ Aristotle, *Metaphysics*, 1012a 23-28.

or has the property of being white there. In fact the whole horse is included in its property of being white there, but the whole horse is, of course, not included in that part which is the forefront of the horse, let alone in the white pigmentum of the forefront. And as long as the horse has this property, even its particular horsehood *is* white. *Equinitas* –pace Scotus– is *non equinitas tantum*, i.e., horsehood, contrary to Scotus' abstractionist thesis, *is not* horsehood alone –except after abstraction. So there is no need to attack abstraction in order to avoid nominalism, conceptualism, or even pragmatism, for abstraction does not imply abstractionism. The difference between the two was altogether clear to Geach himself when he wrote: "...the mind *makes* concepts, and this concept-formation and the subsequent use of the concepts formed never is a mere recognition or finding... In all cases it is a matter of fitting a concept to my experience, not of picking out the feature I am interested in from among other features given simultaneously"[24] –in my opinion a beautiful text. Moreover, in an appendix to *Mental Acts* Geach himself points to the *Summa Theologiae*[25] where Aquinas refers to two different interpretations of the metaphor of the *lumen intellectus agentis*. According to Averroes light is only needed to make the medium, air, transparent since the colors are already *actu visibiles* (capable of actually being seen) in things. According to the second interpretation it is needed to make the colors *actu visibiles* (capable of actually being seen) in the first place. The first alternative corresponds to the *distinctio formalis a parte rei*, the second to the *distinctio rationis cum fundamento in re*. So in order to retain realism by preserving Bivalence one can very well –and had even better– adopt a middle course between Anaxagoras and Duns Scotus, holism and rationalism. It is the middle course of *analogia entis*. In this connection two interrelated questions remain which may be examined briefly: first, what *analogia entis* could mean in the context of Aristotelian metaphysics; secondly, in what sense one can still speak of truth and falsity even in the case of *distinctio rationis cum fundamento in re*. In the case of *distinctio formalis a parte rei* the

---

[24] P. Geach, *Mental Acts*, London 1971, p. 40.

[25] Thomas Aquinas, *Summa Theologiae*, I, q79, a3 ad2.

question does not apply, it already being clear from the outset that truth and falsity are to be understood here in the sense of a conformity or non-conformity between intellect and reality. To answer the question in the other case one may think of two letters, say "A" and "B" superimposed on the same spot of a page, the superimposition symbolizing the mixing-up of determinations or forms in reality as opposed to their separatedness after abstraction. Then any proposition to the effect that there is an "A" and a "B" or any other section of the resulting shape would be true. But a proposition to the effect that there is a "C" or any section of the "C" would be false. In other words, in order for there to be a true proposition under the given conditions it is necessary and sufficient that the features picked out exist in reality, however differently (viz. mixed) they may be there. As has already been noted the question is related to that of *analogia entis*[26].

2

Whereas in the previous section I concentrated on PET, I should like to concentrate in the next two sections on PNC. Here too there are differences between the Aristotelian and the modern interpretation which it is important to take note of. The Aristotelian principle leaves open the possibility that both sides of the contradiction may be false, a possibility which is to be precluded by PET. That, of course, is not the way things look after Frege. But the consequences of departing from the traditional view are in the case of PNC not as great as they are in the case of the Principle of Excluded Middle. So in this section I will be concentrating on the Aristotelian principle itself (PNC) and especially on the way in which Aristotle justifies it. Nevertheless, there is also room in the case of PNC for controversy with respect to modern interpretations, the main difference being that modern interpreters, especially in the analytic field, often approach Aristotle in a pragmatist manner alien to Aristotle's own way of thinking. True,

---

[26] Cf. Chapter 5 below.

Aristotle's justification of PNC is thoroughly pragmatic. This means that the justification of the principle in Aristotle is neither the reason for the validity of the principle nor the reason why we should accept or believe it. Alan Code has put this aptly and succinctly as follows: "The fact that acceptance of PNC is required for significant thought is not the reason why PNC is true"[27]. So one has to distinguish very sharply between the principle itself and Aristotle's justification of it. It is not the principle itself which stands in need of justification, it is only the person who, whether sincerely or merely for the sake of argument –or, if you will, sincerely or eristically– questions the validity of PNC who himself stands in need of it. This means that the justification is to be understood as a defense of the principle against its opponents. But this does not mean that the principle must first wait upon its defense in order to be valid.

In the case of pragmatism it is the other way around: the validity of the principle is founded, or dependent upon, our own needs, above all our need to communicate with each other in order to survive as living beings or as rational beings or as scientists or in whatever capacity you choose. If we did not, or need not, communicate, especially verbally communicate, the principle, according to the pragmatist approach, would not hold. In Aristotle, on the contrary, whether someone accepts it or not is his or her own concern, and not, as it were, anything that need concern the principle itself. True, without the principle we could not communicate with each other or with ourselves, i.e., could not speak or think, let alone have any knowledge at all. But even without knowledge or communication on our part, the principle would be in force all the same. So much so that one could say: for Aristotle God is PNC turned positive [*das ins Positive gewendete Nichtwiderspruchsprinzip*]. God is for him τοιαυτη ἀρχή, that principle, ἧς οὐσία ἐνέργεια, whose substance or essence is nothing but actuality[28]. And that means that God, being his own

---

[27] A. Code, "Aristotle's Investigation of a Basic Logical Principle: Which Science Investigates the Principle of Non-Contradiction?", *Canadian Journal of Philosophy*, 16, 1986, p. 356.

[28] Aristotle, *Metaphysics*, 1071b 20.

activity, his own behavior, can under no circumstances change. ἐνέργεια ὂν ἐνδέχεται ἄλλως ἔχειν οὐδαμῶς[29]: "this can in no way be otherwise than as it is", hence he cannot not be but is necessarily (οὐδὲν ἔσται τῶν ὄντων[30]). Now, God being PNC made positive or posited as positive, no possibility (of being or not being, of being so or of being otherwise) is to be found in him. In other words, there is in him no possibility which might precede his actuality. So one could say (and Schelling, commenting on Aristotle, did, in fact, say), God is originality itself, if by originality one understands, as one should, that the possibility of which can be neither known nor believed before it is actually or really there. Besides, without him, says Aristotle[31], nothing at all would be (οὐδὲν ἔσται τῶν ὄντων). But since there is obviously something, there must also be a principle such that without it there could be nothing at all. So the Aristotelian proof of God's existence consists in the application of PNC as well as, *via reductio ad absurdum*, PET to the universe whose actual being we cannot help but recognize every day. Either there is such a positive principle or there is nothing, but there is something, so –by combination of the two first principles– there is God. In contrast to God the two principles, when taken separately, are negative. As already said in the previous section, some interpreters have been wondering how it is that Aquinas could at the same time defend the rational possibility of the world's being eternal. However, if one looks more closely at the last Book (VIII) of the *Physics* where Aristotle develops more fully the thesis of the "eternity" of the world, one realizes that what Aristotle asserts time and time again (Chapter One) amounts to only this, that there was no time before the rotating movement of the first heavens started, because there is no time without movement. It is in this sense that movement (as well as the world as we experience it) is everlasting.

So much, again, for Aristotle's theology in *Metaphysics* Book XII and in *Physics* Book VIII. The proof, though, can already be found with reference to modalities, not to time, in *Metaphysics* Book IX

---

[29] Aristotle, *Metaphysics*, 1072b 8.
[30] Aristotle, *Metaphysics*, 1072b 10.
[31] Aristotle, *Metaphysics*, 1071b 25.

which deals with actuality and potentiality (Chapter 8). It is interesting to note that Book IV is interspersed with announcements of or hints as to the pure actuality of an unchanging mover that cannot not be and without which nothing would be. So, immediately after the text I quoted in the previous section concerning the possible possibility of both members of a contradiction being at the same time true, Aristotle says: "...again we shall ask them [the opponents of PNC] to believe that among existing things there is another kind of substance to which neither movement nor destruction nor generation at all belongs"[32]; or shortly afterwards: "And again, obviously we shall make to them also the same reply that we made before; we must show them and persuade them that there is something whose nature is changeless. Indeed, from the assertion that things at the same time are and are not, there follows the assertion that all things are at rest rather than that they are in movement; for there is nothing into which they can change, since then all attributes would belong to all subjects"[33]. And in Chapter 8: "Evidently again those who say all things are at rest are not right, nor are those who say all things are in movement. For if all things are at rest, the same statements will always be true and the same always false, –but they obviously are not... And if all things are in motion, nothing will be true; everything therefore will be false. But it has been shown that this is impossible... But again it is not the case that all things are at rest or in motion *sometimes*, and nothing *forever*; for there is something which always moves the things that are in motion, and the first mover must itself be unmoved"[34].

One can easily recognize in these texts from *Metaphysics* IV as well as in the parallel texts from *Physics* VIII the interconnection between the first two principles in their traditional guise and the theory of substance. The interconnection appears already in the second among the fifteen questions reported in Book III, the book of ἀπορίαι. There Aristotle asks: "Is the science which deals with the first principles of demonstration (περὶ τῶν ἀποδεικτικῶν ἀρχῶν) the same

---

[32] Aristotle, *Metaphysics*, ROT, 1009a 36f.

[33] Aristotle, *Metaphysics*, 1010a 32ff.

[34] Aristotle, *Metaphysics*, 1012b 22-31.

one which is to deal with substance?"[35]. The answer is yes and it is from it that Aristotle's *Metaphysics* gains its momentum. The way which leads to the justification of this answer is the same one leading to the justification of PNC. So we must turn to the pragmatic (but not pragmatist) defense of PNC in Aristotle.

It is not, as I have said, the principle itself which is in need of defence, it is its opponents who are in need of enlightenment, provided they are sincerely confused about the issue. More difficult to convince are, of course, those who eristically, or from a spirit of contrariness, oppose PNC. In dealing with the latter there is but one expedient, viz. not so much to convince as to overcome them, and in the end, to silence them. For as soon as they say something meaningful, as opposed to only making noises, they have not so much declined to accept PNC as they have by this very fact already accepted it –whether they are prepared to acknowledge it or not.

The author who in my opinion has dealt most painstakingly with the main Aristotelian argument in defence of PNC is Russell Dancy. So it is not surprising that others have taken up the main lines of his argumentation[36]. At the end of his book on the subject Dancy draws the following general conclusion: "One might deny the law of contradiction for all sorts of reasons. None that I have seen strike me as good reasons. But neither do I see any reason for saying that there never *could* be good reasons for denying it"[37]. Now, since according to Aristotle anyone who says something meaningful, regardless of what it is, has already accepted the law, Dancy's conclusion means that he has not been convinced by Aristotle's argument. Has Aristotle then been unable to convince Dancy and those that follow him in his interpretation of Aristotle or have they ultimately misunderstood Aristotle? In support of the first alternative may be adduced the fact that Aristotle also failed to convince many others before Dancy and

---

[35] Cf. Aristotle, *Metaphysics*, 996b 26-37.

[36] Cf., e.g., M. Furth's "A Note on Aristotle's Principle of Non-Contradiction", *Canadian Journal of Philosophy*, 16, 1986, pp. 378 f.

[37] R. Dancy, *Sense and Contradiction: A Study in Aristotle*, Dordrecht 1975.

his followers[38]; in support of the second, the fact that in order to justify their conclusion they advance an argument that Aristotle would have seen rather as confirming his own conception, viz. that one can speak out against PNC with thoroughly meaningful words, intelligible to everyone[39]. Precisely this indisputable fact, which constitutes the heart of Aristotle's pragmatic argument, is used against him by Dancy (and others[40]). The paradox, however, can easily be explained: whoever expects too much from Aristotle's argument must eventually be disappointed by it. Expecting too much here means expecting more than a purely pragmatic defence in the sense mentioned above. Dancy projects upon Aristotle some of the fundamental features of Quine's pragmatist semantic theory[41]. Yet for Aristotle PNC itself lies behind all attempts either to refute or to defend it, as a necessary condition for the very possibility of such attempts. So according to Aristotle, no such attempt —even an attempt to refute it— could itself be meaningful, let alone true, without thereby confirming PNC. Dancy is not the only one who has consistently disregarded this.

The main mistake consists in trying to decide the case for or against PNC on the level of judgments instead of concepts, of use instead of meaning, or, to put it still differently, of use of rules instead of rules of use. According to Dancy, propositions like "The moving vehicle is and is not in the same place" (a quotation from Engels against PNC), "I love and do not love, I am mad and not mad" (a quotation from Anacreon), "Christ is man and not man" (a quotation from Kierkegaard) etc. negate PNC but are nonetheless intelligible. Each of them ascribes to one and the same subject (to this moving vehicle, to Anacreon, to Christ) mutually contradictory predicates, without the predicates uttered ("is in the same place", "is loving", "is mad", "is a man" etc.) having thereby lost their meaning.

---

[38] Cf. *ibid.*, p. 5.

[39] *Ibid.*, p. 37, 142.

[40] As, e.g., besides M. Furth, C. Kirwan, in his *Notes* in *Aristotle's Metaphysics Book* Γ, Δ, *and* E, Oxford 1971.

[41] R. Dancy, *Sense and Contradiction*, pp. 34-36.

In order to show that this does not prove any inconclusiveness on the part of the Aristotelian argument for PNC, it suffices to point out that Aristotle himself does not see anything wrong with propositions such as those quoted by Dancy. On the contrary, he expressly says that "nothing prevents the same thing from being a man and... then a thousand times not a man", namely "white and a thousand other such things", which are different from being a man[42]. Such propositions are not even false, let alone contradictory. This alone should suffice to demonstrate the serious consequences of approaching Aristotle in the spirit of pragmatism. According to pragmatism, the meaning of a word is a result of its use, but it has nothing to do with concepts, to which the word itself gives expression, let alone with the nature of things. As Quine put it, meaning is nothing more than essence once it has become divorced from things and married to words[43]. Of course, for Quine there is no such thing as meaning. That is indeed the gist of his bon mot. Now, to be able at least to understand the Aristotelian argument, setting aside the question of its soundness, the first thing to do is to turn directly to the meanings of words (or to concepts) and to consider them independently of their use in judgments. To put it more precisely, the first thing to do is to realize that, according to Aristotle, it is the question of meanings or concepts which decides the question of the contradictoriness or non-contradictoriness of a proposition or judgment and not vice versa. When applied to the allegedly contradictory propositions quoted by Dancy, this means the following: Engels would have been contradicting himself only if, in saying that the moving vehicle is at the same time there and not there (pointing to some more or less precise spot), he had managed to give the meaning (or concept) of the expression "there" the same meaning as the meaning of the expression "not there", i.e., the same meaning as the expression "here" or, say, "man" or "vehicle" or whichever word you prefer, provided these other words don't mean the same thing as

---

[42] Aristotle, *Metaphysics*, 1007a 10, 16f. 11.

[43] To quote him verbatim: "Meaning is what essence becomes when divorced from the object of reference and wedded to the word", W.V.O. Quine, *From a Logical Point of View*, Cambridge 1964, p. 22.

"there" which, as far as the English language is concerned, they do not. If *per impossibile* Engels, Dancy, or anyone else had succeeded in doing such a thing, he would have been unable to assign to the word "there" or to any other word used in the same (viz. contradictory) way a definite meaning. Words whose meaning have been made to coincide with the meaning of other words which do not have the same meaning in that language (as, e. g., in English "here" and "there" or "man" and "white" etc.) can no longer play a role in the language. They would be like parts of a machine which do not move when the other parts move, i.e., they would cease to be parts of the machine. And so the same applies to Dancy's other examples or indeed to any examples which one might adduce for rejecting, or at least doubting, the validity of PNC.

But if the counter-examples of Dancy and others are just the type that Aristotle would treat as completely harmless, then something must have gone wrong with their interpretation. And where they have gone wrong is in disregarding the following: as far as the pragmatic, as opposed to the pragmatist, approach to PNC in Aristotle is concerned, everything hangs on the assumption of a minimal distinction in meaning, without which communication would be impossible. For if one has assumed a minimal distinction in meaning (viz. that no word can signify everything[44]), then one has already assumed PNC as well. If, for example, being a man, is not the same thing as being God, being white, being educated, etc. –independently of whether there is something which is man and God, man and white, etc., i.e., independently of whether the judgment "Jesus of Nazareth is man and God", etc. is or is not true– then *ipso facto* being cannot be not being. So the justification of PNC turns on the existence of meanings or concepts as opposed to truth-values and judgments. One might with Quine or anyone else hold on to a pragmatist view of things and language, but one cannot approach Aristotle in a pragmatist way with impunity.

Aristotle himself did not tire of saying that the defence of PNC has to be conducted on the level of meaning and not of use, on the level of

---

[44] Cf. Aristotle, *Metaphysics*, 1006b 6.

concept and not of judgment. The reason is obvious. Since judgments correspond to beliefs and beliefs are held to be either true or false, to begin one's justification of PNC not with pure meaning but with judgments could easily lead to a form of question-begging. Accordingly Aristotle writes, "the starting point for all such arguments is not the demand that our opponent shall say that something either is or is not (for this one might perhaps take to be assuming what is at issue), but that he shall say something which is significant both for himself and for another"[45]. Aristotle writes this at the beginning of his justification of PNC. And he repeats it in connection with PET at the end of *Metaphysics* IV: "Against all such arguments we must postulate, as we said above, not that something is or is not, but what people mean, so that we must argue from a definition, having got what falsity or truth means"[46].

One need only read again the first text of Aquinas with which we began these lectures in this light to notice the superiority of Aquinas' interpretation to those we have just been considering. The text ran: "Magis opponuntur esse hominem et non esse hominem quam homo et album; sed homo et album sunt diversa secundum rationem, licet sunt idem subjecto; ergo et esse hominem et non esse hominem sunt diversa secundum rationem"[47]. ("To be a man and to be a not-man are more opposed to each other than man and white; but man and white are different in meaning, even if they coincide in the same subject; therefore to be a man and to be a not-man ought to be different with respect to meaning as well [*secundum rationem*]"). In these words lies the quintessence of Aristotle's argument. I would like to elaborate a little more on this.

Aquinas is here commenting on the passage in which Aristotle repeats his main argument against the opponents of PNC: "ὁ δ'αὐτὸς λόγος καὶ ἐπὶ τοῦ ἀνθρώπῳ μὴ εἶναι"[48]: The same holds good with regard to not being man. These words have generated some

---

[45] Aristotle, *Metaphysics*, 1006a 18-21. (ROT)

[46] Aristotle, *Metaphysics*, 1012b 5f. (ROT)

[47] Thomas Aquinas, *In libros Metaphysicorum*, n. 622.

[48] Aristotle, *Metaphysics*, 1006b 34 ff.

amount of confusion among interpreters. In his commentary in the Clarendon Aristotle Series Christopher Kirwan writes, "'the same argument applies' if –Aristotle apparently means– one starts by assuming a signification for 'not-man' [instead of for 'man']"[49]. Then Kirwan continues: "It is hard to see how the second sentence explains this contention..."[50]. The same perplexity is to be found in Dancy: "The primary difference here seems to be the presence of the negation. But Aristotle does not go on to give anything like a revised version of the first refutation with the negative expression ['not-man'] replacing the positive ['man']"[51]. In this connection as well Aquinas' comment hits the nail on the head. For in the repetition of the argument there is no question of replacing the positive expression 'man' with the negative one, 'not-man', but of replacing the few examples given previously of words having a different meaning than the word 'man', viz. the words 'white' (and 'educated'), with the whole range of words whose meaning is different from the meaning of the word 'man', this whole range being represented by the comprehensive negative expression 'not-man'. So in the repetition of the argument for PNC the meaning of 'not-man' does not replace the meaning of 'man', but that of 'white' (and 'educated'). And this is what Aquinas had said: "...homo et album sunt diversa [with respect to the meaning (*secundum rationem*)]...; ergo esse hominem et non esse hominem". That is to say, "...man and white are different with respect to the meaning... so also [*a fortiori*] the meaning of man and of not being a man".

The argument is in fact an argument *a fortiori*. If the meaning of 'white', which represents only one portion of the meaning of 'not-man', is different from the meaning of 'man', then this must *a fortiori* also be the case for the whole range of meanings implicitly included in 'not-man', viz. the meaning of 'white' and of 'educated', and of 'tall' and of, say, 'helicopter' or of whichever word you happen to choose. So the repetition does not offer any new argument for PNC but is only

---

[49] C. Kirwan, *Aristotle's Metaphysics Book* Γ, Δ, *and* E, p. 99.

[50] C. Kirwan, *Aristotle's Metaphysics Book* Γ, Δ, *and* E, p. 99.

[51] R. Dancy, *Sense and Contradiction*, p. 28.

intended to make the pragmatic argument in the beginning more plausible, viz. that in uttering a single meaningful word like 'man' one has already distinguished its meaning from other meanings (since a word meaning everything would not mean anything) and by implication show that not everything is indifferent or equally true –which is what PNC states. In this way the purely pragmatic character of the argument comes even more clearly into focus, i.e., simply by enlarging the range or multiplying the examples of words that do not have the same meaning as "man".

Aquinas' comment points directly to the passage in which the argument was first advanced, a passage in which, no less than in Aquinas' comment, there is still a hidden reference to substance. Aquinas says, "man and white are different in meaning, although they are true of the same subject, e.g. Socrates" (*licet sunt idem subjecto*). These words clearly refer back to a passage in Aristotle, which they only repeat in an even more plausible way. The passage runs as follows: "The meaning of 'man' cannot be the meaning of 'not-man', if 'man' signifies not only about one thing but also one thing ("εἰ τὸ ἄνθρωπος σημαίνει μὴ μόνον καθ' ἑνὸς ἀλλὰ καὶ ἕν"). Here again we have the difference between judgment and concept, belief and pure meaning. For, Aristotle continues, "by signifying one thing, we do not mean signifying-about-one-thing, since in this case 'musical' [or educated] and 'white' and 'man' [if, that is, they would all be true, e.g., of the subject Socrates] would signify one thing, so that all would be one"[52].

The argument is clearly a *reductio*. All things would be the same, viz. an Anaxagorean chaos, were all words to mean the same thing, viz. an ὁμοῦ παντα in a state of rest before things started to move and hence to be. So, one must distinguish between judgment and concept, use and meaning or, as Aristotle says here, signifying about and signifying in general. Otherwise, since 'white' and 'educated' are both true of Socrates they would have the same meaning, i.e., no meaning at all. But then argument, communication, and language would be impossible. Now the reason why Dancy, Kirwan, and others, against

---

[52] Aristotle, *Metaphysics*, 1006b 13-18.

the evidence, fail to accept, as Aquinas does, that the repetition (ὁ αὐτὸς λόγος, "the same argument") refers to precisely this passage, is that with this argumentation Aristotle has so far only proved that the contradiction is not necessary, but not –as PNC requires– that it is not possible, i.e., impossible. Lukasiewicz had brought this objection to bear against Aristotle. The objection, though, is not a sound one. True, by showing that one word, like 'man', cannot mean everything if it is to have any meaning at all and so be a useful piece of language, communication, or argumentation, Aristotle has as yet only refuted those who held the extreme opinion according to which the contradiction is necessary. However, one need do nothing other than repeat the same argument for any functioning word of the language in order to refute as well those who say, more moderately, that the contradiction is possible, and to establish thereby the impossibility of contradiction, i.e., PNC proper. Aristotle is here applying the same procedure as he did in connection with PET. In connection with the latter he, first, *via* the meaning of the word 'false', proved that not all propositions are necessarily false (this is the step leading to the Aristotelian Principle of Bivalence which I omitted in the previous section), and then –dealing with the affirmation and negation of the same proposition– he proved the impossibility of all propositions being false, which is PET. Correspondingly, this time he first proves the non-necessity and then the impossibility of all propositions being true, which is PNC.

Up until now Aristotle has only shown that we must accept a multiplicity of words with different meanings. In other words, up until now Aristotle has only shown the unavoidability of admitting different categories without specifying which ones. If one were to stop here one might come to think that Aristotle is only interested in linguistics, not metaphysics. However, this impression disappears as soon as one follows the last and more important part of his main argument for PNC or, rather, against its opponents. For it is in this last part that Aristotle goes on to show the unavoidability of admitting not only different categories, without specifying which ones, but the unavoidability above all of admitting the difference between two sorts of categories, viz. the accidental ones as well as the category of substance. And it is only by showing the necessity of accepting substances as subjects of properties, first of accidental properties, but then of essential properties as well, that Aristotle first gains, as it were, a foothold on reality beyond the realm of pure linguistics. In other words, it is only by demonstrating the unavoidability of accepting such things as substances that Aristotle enters the domain of metaphysics proper. So far he has been developing his argument only in the field of dialectics. *Nunc incipit metaphysica.* Now, in order to get a better view of the whole argument, I propose to read it as a whole starting with the repetition with which I have been dealing. In the course of this reading I shall mark the point where Aristotle goes beyond the repetition of the first argument and approaches little by little the fundamental problem of substance.

The beginning of the repetition is well known to us by now. It ran (in the ROT): "The same account holds good with regard to not being man, for 'being man' and 'being not-man' mean different things, since even 'being white' and 'being man' are different; for the former terms are much more opposed, so that they must mean different things"[53]. What follows is only an unfolding of the argument *a fortiori* hinted at here: "And if any one says that 'white' means one and the same thing as 'man', again we shall say the same as what was said before, that it would follow that all things are one, and not only opposites. But if this is impossible, then what has been said will follow, if our opponent answers our question. And if, when one asks the question simply, he adds the contradictories, he is not answering the question. For there is nothing to prevent the same thing from being both man and white and countless other things: but still if one asks whether it is true to call this a man or not our opponent must give an answer which means one thing, and not add that it is also white and large. For, besides other reasons, it is impossible to enumerate the accidents, which are infinite in number; let him, then, enumerate either all or none. Similarly, therefore, even if the same thing is a thousand times man and not-man, we must not add, in answering the question whether this is a man, that it is also at the same time not a man, unless we are bound to add also

---

[53] Aristotle, *Metaphysics,* 1006b 34-35; 1007a 1-3.

all the other accidents, all that the subject is or is not; and if we do this, we are not observing the rules of argument". The first part of the argument runs up to here. From this point on Aristotle begins to approach little by little the question of substance. The metaphysically most important text runs as follows: "And in general those who use this argument do away with substance and essence. For they must say that all attributes are accidents, and that there is no such thing as being essentially man or animal. (For if there is to be any such thing as being essentially man this will not be being not-man or not being man (yet these are negations of it); for there was some one thing which it meant, and this was the substance of something. And denoting the substance of a thing means that the essence of the thing is nothing else. But if its being essentially man is to be the same as either being essentially not-man or essentially not being man, then its essence will be something else. Therefore our opponents must say that there cannot be such a definition of anything, but that all attributes are accidental; for this is the distinction between substance and accident –white is accidental to man, because though he is white, whiteness is not his essence). But if all statements are accidental, there will be nothing primary about which they (the statements) are made, if the accidental always implies predication about a subject. The predication, then, must go on *ad infinitum*. But this is impossible; for not even more than two terms can be combined. *For an accident is not an accident of an accident*, unless it be because both are accidents of the same subject"[54]. This ("an accident is not an accident of an accident") is the key proposition in the argument. From it follows, as we shall see in the third section, the necessity of admitting substances.

This could be dubbed the transcendental deduction of the category of substance. Then Aristotle continues: "I mean, for instance, the white is musical and the latter is white, only because both are accidental to man. But Socrates is musical, not in this sense, that both terms are accidental to something else. Since then some predicates are accidental in this and some in that sense [*ens per accidens* and

---

[54] Aristotle, *Metaphysics*, 1007a 20-1007b 3. Again in the ROT; but I have introduced some minor modifications in the translation.

accidens praedicamentale], those which are accidental in the latter sense, in which white is accidental to Socrates [*accidens praedicamentale*], cannot form an infinite series in the upward direction, e.g., Socrates the white has not yet another accident; for no unity can be got out of such a sum. Nor again will white have another term accidental to it, e.g., musical. For this is no more accidental to that than that is to this, and at the same time we have drawn the distinction, that while some predicates are accidental in this sense, others are so in the sense in which musical is accidental to Socrates; and the accident is an accident of an accident not in cases of the latter kind [*accidens praedicamentale*], but only in cases of the other kind [*ens per accidens*], so that not all terms will be accidental. There must, then, even in this case be something which denotes substance. And it has been shown that, if this is so, contradictories cannot be predicated at the same time"[55]. This is a text as difficult as it is fundamental. After having transcendentally deduced the necessity of categories, Aristotle goes on here to deduce the category of substance. In the next section I shall try to explain this. But before closing I would like to anticipate some implications of the doctrine to be found in this fundamental text.

Let me concentrate on the key statement in this passage according to which there is no accident of an accident. If that statement could be justified, it would rule out, e.g., the possibility of events having properties of their own, which of course is vital to any ontology of events such as that of Quine but is irrelevant to an ontology of substances such as that of Aristotle and Aquinas. A very instructive way of viewing the difference between both kinds of ontology is to look at the question of numbers. As is well known, Aristotle himself compared substances with numbers when he said that just as a number cannot be changed in the least without destroying it, so substances do not admit of a more and a less. One must be very careful not to misunderstand the point of this comparison. It has in any case not been made in order to rule out the fact that substances as well as their essence –unlike numbers– may very well change. It has been made

---

[55] Aristotle, *Metaphysics*, 1007b 4-18.

rather in order to rule out the possibility of essential, but not of accidental, changes in substances and their essences. The only reason why this does not make itself evident in the comparison is because numbers, like accidents, cannot have accidents so that as far as they are concerned –and in marked contrast to substances– only essential changes would be possible, which of course means that numbers cannot change at all. For, if something changes essentially, it is no longer the thing it was. So, since numbers, if they could change at all, could only change accidentally, then given that there are no accidents of accidents they cannot change in any way whatsoever. By contrast, having reduced all there is to events or to accidents of the sort which Aristotle is in our texts opposing, Quine is compelled to accept accidents of accidents in the guise of properties of events. So it is not surprising that he also accepts something like changing or –as they are called by him– variable numbers.

Now one might ask why not accept them? Is it not a thoroughly natural way of speaking when we say that the number of inhabitants of Chicago varies? Is it not as natural as saying –as we do indeed say– that, e.g., the speed of the moving vehicle is changing, viz. increasing or diminishing? What else may be said to accelerate or decelerate, if not the speed? To take a quite different example, the poem "Among Children" by W. B. Yeats ends with the verse: "How can we know the dancer from the dance". The dance –or dancing– is an event or –to employ the terminology of process-theology or process-thought– a process; the dancer, a substance. Now, even conceding that there are substances like dancer and the like, is it not quite natural to say –one might surely ask– that if, say, Nureyev sweats it is because he is dancing so that it is the dancing Nureyev who sweats, just as it is the moving locomotive which speeds up, or the extended surface which is white, or, for that matter, the white Socrates that is educated? Why not accept all this along with variable numbers and accidents of accidents and properties of events and –to put it in a Quinean way– spatio-temporal slices (Nureyev now, Nureyev later, i.e., Nureyev dancing and sweating, etc.) as the fundamental unities of reality (instead of a substance called "Nureyev")? Aristotle would reject this suggestion as misleading –indeed as a fundamentally and dangerously misleading way of speaking. Just as there can be for him –as strange as it may at first sight appear– no such thing as a variable number, so there can also be for him no such thing as a dancing person who sweats. According to him, it is not the dancing Nureyev who sweats but Nureyev himself who dances and sweats and so on but in such a manner that all the accidents are *immediately* related to the substance and not *via* other accidents –just as it is not the white Socrates who receives education, but Socrates. This is a very important point, and a point related to the question of PNC. If, to take now a Platonic example, it were the sitting Theaetetus to whom we apply the predicate 'sitting' instead of Theaetetus himself, it would not be possible to say anything false, which is precisely what PNC denies. But, as is obvious from the statement "Theaetetus is flying", predicates never share in the constitution of the subject. Otherwise the statement would have to be true. The argument applies to accidental predicates –the only ones accepted by Quine and his followers– not to essential ones. And if it is merely a misleading way of speaking to say that the sitting Socrates is sitting as it is to say that the flying Theaetus flies –since otherwise no proposition with the exception of PNC would be false– then the same holds true of propositions like "the dancing Nureyev is sweating" and the like. Contrary to all appearances but in agreement with the last section of Aristotle's defence of PNC, it is not the dancing Nureyev who sweats but Nureyev, as it is Nureyev who dances but not, say, the white Nureyev.

At this point one might again ask: What might be raised in objection to this? The answer is: the same objection that must be raised against variable numbers and accelerating speeds and the like. What changes is not the speed, if by "changing" one understands the process of undergoing a modification. It is not the speed which changes in this sense but only the vehicle. And in this sense of "change" the vehicle may be said to be changing by constantly assuming different speeds which therefore do not change themselves in the least but are merely replacing one another constantly. In keeping with his defence of PNC in *Metaphysics* Book IV Aristotle had explained this in *Physics* Book V, and this, in turn, explains why in Book VII of the *Metaphysics* he is constantly insisting on the fact that in order to get at first substance one must first of all eliminate such compounds as "white man" and the like. Afterwards one must, of course, eliminate as well such essential compounds as man, since man is still form plus matter, in order to arrive at pure forms –e.g., souls– as the actualities of organic bodies and in the end to God as pure actuality. Now, inasmuch as it is not the number of inhabitants of Chicago which undergoes a process of change but Chicago itself that now has this number of inhabitants and then some other number, there are no variable numbers nor for that matter variable accidents of any kind whatsoever, i.e., accidents of accidents. And in just this respect the ontology of substances with their essential and accidental properties proves its superiority over and against the ontology of processes and events which only recognizes accidents and is by virtue of this very fact always in danger of denying PNC.

At this juncture it would be helpful to consider a text stemming from the First Analogy of Experience concerning the relationship between substance and accident in Kant's *Critique of Pure Reason*. If one disregards the fact that he is speaking of phenomenal, and not noumenal, substances, it becomes possible to recognize that Kant is making essentially the same point as Aristotle when he writes: "...we can say, using what may seem a somewhat paradoxical expression, that only the permanent (substance) is altered [or undergoes a change], and that the transitory (accident) suffers no alteration and undergoes no change inasmuch as certain determinations cease to be and others begin to be"[56]. In order to assess the adequacy of Thomas Aquinas' position in this respect another text of Kant's drawn from the same Analogy might prove to be of some help. The text runs: "The determinations of a substance, which are nothing but special ways in which it exists, are called *accidents*... if we ascribe a special kind of existence to this real [the accident] in substance (for instance, to movement as real accident of matter), this existence is entitled inherence, in distinction from the existence of substance which is entitled subsistence". But, Kant adds, "this occasions many misunderstandings", and he concludes, "it is more exact and more

---

[56] I. Kant, *Critique of Pure Reason*, A187/B230-231.

correct to describe an accident as being simply the way in which the existence of a substance is positively determined"[57].

As far as I can determine, the position Kant is here attacking corresponds to Aquinas' *analogia secundum intentionem et esse*, whereas his own position –along with the position of Aristotle– corresponds to Aquinas' *analogia secundum intentionem sed non secundum esse*. For according to the former the being of accidents is the being of substance and nothing else, i.e., there is no *inhaerentia* as the being of accidents apart from *subsistentia* as the being of substances, since, being only determinations of substance, accidents do not have their own being –just as a so-called healthy color is not healthy, but is only a sign of the health of the living being. What led me to inquire as to the exact nature of Thomas's position is the fact that in the text of the *Commentary on the Sentences* he not only distinguishes between the example of health and the example of being but separates the latter from the former, as at the beginning of the second chapter of *Metaphysics* IV Aristotle did not. St. Thomas writes: "something is said analogously in three ways: firstly, according to intention only and not according to being; and this is when one intention is applied to several things in the order of prior and posterior, which nevertheless only exists in one thing, as for example the intention of health is applied to an animal, to urine or to diet in respectively differing ways, as to prior and posterior, nevertheless not according to different beings (different realizations of health), since only animals are healthy. Secondly, something is said analogously according to being and not according to intention... Thirdly, it is thus [analogously] said according both to intention and to being, and this is when no equality obtains either in intention or in being, such as when being is predicated of substance and of accident, and of such cases it is required that the common nature have some being in any one of those things of which it is said but yet differs in the sense of being more or less fully realized as the case may be"[58]. Nevertheless, independently

---

[57] I. Kant, *Critique of Pure Reason*, A186/B229-230.

[58] "...aliquid dicitur secundum analogiam tripliciter: vel secundum intentionem tantum et non secundum esse; et hoc est quando una intentio refertur ad plura per

of the question of whether Aquinas' division was taken over in his later works, the first heading in the text just quoted ("*secundum intentionem tantum...*) is very useful in understanding why in *Metaphysics* IV, Chapter 2, as the *primum analogatum* (to retain the later terminology) of health not the animal but the meaning (*intentio*!) health itself –and analogously not the substance, but the meaning of being– is chosen. In spite of that, the question remains how deep the difference runs between Aristotle and Aquinas as regards the doctrine –again phrased in the later terminology– of *analogia entis* insofar as it bears on the relationship between substance and accidents. At least in the *Commentary on the Sentences* Aquinas seems to be taking a step away from Aristotle towards Duns Scotus, if one may put it that way. It is to be noted that in our days W. Letzl –severely critized by D. Frede– seems to have interpreted Aristotle along the lines laid down here by Aquinas, as if accidents themselves had *esse* or existence, only in a weaker form. In this respect Kant appears to be closer to Aristotle than Aquinas. However, it is not only through the Copernican revolution, but also through his not distinguishing between accidental and essential properties that Kant is really much farther away from Aristotle than Aquinas was. In the following section we must prepare the way for treating the relationship between substance and accidental, as well as essential, properties.

---

prius et posterius, quae tamen non habet esse nisi in uno; sicut intentio sanitatis refertur ad animal, urinam et dietam diversimode, secundum prius et posterius; non tamen secundum diversum esse, quia esse sanitatis non est nisi in animali. Vel secundum esse et non secundum intentionem... Vel secundum intentionem et secundum esse; et hoc est quando neque parificatur in intentione communi, neque in esse, sicut ens dicitur de substantia et accidente; et de talibus oportet quod natura communis habeat aliquod esse in unoquoque eorum de quibus dicitur, sed differens secundum rationem majoris vel minoris perfectionis"; Thomas Aquinas, *In Sententiarum*, I, d. 19, q. 5, art. 2.

3

I would like to give an overview of the entire Aristotelian argument in defense of PNC before entering into the details of what will constitute the main topic of this section and which we might in advance describe as a justification or transcendental deduction of the category of substance and hence of the fundamental categorial difference between substance and accident. In what follows it will become evident that the difference between essential and accidental properties is by implication also involved.

Properly speaking it is not until the key proposition "τὸ γὰρ συμβεβηκὸς οὐ συμβεβηκότι συμβεβηκὸς"[59] (that is: "for an accident is never accident of (or to) another accident") that Aristotle in the text I quoted towards the end of the last section begins his transcendental deduction of substance, i.e., begins the work of demonstrating the unavoidability of accepting substances. This means that in the course of his argument he has up until now been speaking neither of substances nor of accidents in the sense of *accidens praedicamentale*, i.e., in the sense of real, although contingent, properties of real things, let alone of necessary or essential properties of such real things. If he sometimes had occasion to mention substances like Socrates or Callias with their properties of being white and musical and so on, this was done only for the sake of illustration, *viz.* to make it easier to grasp the point of his argument as thus far developed. What was his point thus far? It was what we might well dub the transcendental deduction, not of substances or of the categorial difference between substance and accidents, but of categories as such, without saying for the time being which ones they are and, of course, without distinguishing for the moment between the category of substance and accidental categories.

From this it follows that when, at the beginning of the passage with which we shall for the most part be concerned here, Aristotle alludes to the difference between substance and accident (οὐσία or τί ἓν εἶναι on the one hand and συμβεβηκὸς on the other), the difference

---

[59] Aristotle, *Metaphysics*, 1007b 2-3.

(between οὐσία and συμβεβηκός) must still be understood in another sense than in the sense of *substantia praedicamentalis* on the one hand and *accidens praedicamentale* on the other. For the distinction which Aristotle here draws between substance and accident occurs before he has shown the unavoidability of admitting substances as real subjects of real properties. In what sense, then, is it to be understood? Well, as far as accidents are concerned, obviously in the only possible sense which remains when the sense of *accidens praedicamentale* is rejected as premature, *viz.* in the sense of *ens per accidens* (ὄν κατά συμβεβηκός). When taken in this sense, "*accidens*" must be understood to be in the plural. *Accidens* in the plural, *accidentia*, means nothing other than significant contents, i.e., meanings, which have nothing whatsoever in common with each other. Such is the "relation" –if one may properly deem it such– which, for example, the meaning of 'white' bears to the meaning of 'musical'; strictly speaking, they are *qua* meaning in no way related to one another. And since we cannot as yet refer to specific categories, we could also say that they belong to different categories, without having to specify which ones. But the same also holds true for the meaning of 'man' and, say, the meaning of 'white': they too are not related to each other at all, but belong to different categories, i.e., they too stand in no conceptual relation to one another and can only be thought *per accidens* to one other. Under these circumstances, one cannot as yet say that man is less accidental than white. At this stage of the argument, i.e., before the transcendental deduction of real substances and hence of real accidents has been carried out, the only thing one can say about man is that it is a significant content, i.e., that it is a meaning (if you like, a concept), which in the sense of *ens per accidens* is no more or less accidental than the conceptual content or meaning of any other word which one might happen to choose. They can only be brought into accidental relation with each other: to be a man, to be white, to be musical, etc.

The result to which the defense of PNC has thus far led could more briefly be put by saying that there is no logical space. That does not mean that one ought once again to eliminate those differences in meaning which Aristotle had thus far shown to be unavoidable, and unavoidable because all things would otherwise be one, namely chaotic, with the result that we could not utter a single significant noise or convey any meaningful token whatsoever, let alone engage in an argument or conversation. By saying "there is no logical space" what is meant is rather that one cannot stop at that stage of the argument where the necessity of accepting different meanings or categories in order to preserve the possibility of meaning, language and communication has already been shown. And the reason why one cannot stop at this stage is because in deducing the necessity of accepting different meanings (i.e., in proving that no meaningful word can mean everything, that the meaning of each word must have its own limits or boundaries) one has not yet detected any order or rules for relating one meaning to a certain other meaning rather than to yet a third or different meaning. Since such different meanings as white and color or man and biped animal are not related *per se*, let alone by definition to each other, they can only be made to stand *per accidens* to each other. But then there is as yet no reason why some meanings should be connected with certain others rather than with still others; in other words, there are as yet no rules for ordering them. That is what I meant when I said that for Aristotle there is no logical space. One could also say –with Kant– that there is no *omnitudo realitatis*, nothing which corresponds to the totality of realities or –as Kant says– *Sachheiten*, i.e., significant contents or meanings, and hence no *ens realissimum* either. On the other hand, for Aristotle God is not *ens realissimum* but rather *actus purus*; he is devoid of content and, in this sense (but only in this sense) devoid of meaning. So, in rejecting *omnitudo realitatis* as an ordered totality of signifying contents as well as *ens realissimum*, Kant was not attacking Aristotelian but rather Scotist as well as rationalist metaphysics for which the pure contents of thought, even if they do not hang together by definition, are ordered according to rules of compossibility and incompossibility, rules which we could in principle, although not always in fact, detect *a priori*. Such a logical space, which in Wittgenstein's *Tractatus* still played such a prominent role, had been rejected by Aristotle long before Kant. To claim that there is no logical space is, though, only another way of saying that without admitting real substances which could be detected *a posteriori* one could not even think or speak meaningfully.

For thinking and speaking are incompatible with thorough rulelessness.

To look back at the previous stages in Aristotle's defense of PNC before going into the key passage seems all the more advisable in the light of the fact that Aristotle himself is doing exactly the same thing at the beginning of that passage; viz. when he writes: "And in general those who use this argument [against PNC] do away with any essence or definition [τί ἐν εἶναι the correlate of definition, i.e., as abstract essence, significant meaning or content]. For they must say that all [meanings] belong accidentally [to each other] and that there is no such thing as being essentially man or animal [i.e., no such thing as man being rational –or for that matter biped animal– or animal being such and such an organic body]"[60].

The Greek text need not be translated –as in the ROT– as if Aristotle were with "οὐσία" and "τί ἐν εἶναι" referring to real substances with their real, and even, essential properties. That it is necessary to accept real substances, let alone essences of real substances, has not yet been shown. Because of this, it is far more appropriate to take the "καὶ" in "οὐσία καὶ τί ἐν εἶναι" as epexegetic or merely declarative and the whole expression as referring to as yet purely abstract essences or meanings of words. So, at this stage in his argument in favor of PNC, Aristotle has not gone beyond the preceding one in which he had merely repeated the necessity of admitting meanings which do not include each other such as man and, say, biped animal do. As long as we have not yet in the course of a transcendental deduction arrived at substances like Socrates we are not even justified in positing biped animal as the essence of man (*quid rei*) but only as the definition of the expression "man" (*quid nominis*). The time for real definitions has not yet come. The argument is still moving on the level of ideal significations. Of course, in real communication people are usually speaking of real things and real properties. That is why even in the preceding passage Aristotle had illustrated his argument by referring to them. Thus he tells us that "there is nothing to prevent the same thing [we could, for example,

---

[60] Aristotle, *Metaphysics*, 1007 21-23, ROT modified.

add Socrates] from being both man and white and countless other things: but still if one asks whether it is true to call this a man or not our opponent must give an answer which means one thing and not add that it is also white and large. For, besides other reasons, it is impossible to enumerate the accidents, which are infinite [indeterminate] in number; let him, then, enumerate either all or none. Similarly, therefore, even if the same thing is a thousand times man and not-man, we must not add, in answering the question whether this is a man, that it is also at the same time not a man, unless we are bound to add also the other accidents, all that the subject is or is not; and if we do this, we are not observing the rules of argument"[61]. Indeed, the whole argument turns on the necessity of rules of argumentation, but also of speaking in general, either to oneself, as in thinking, or to others, as when we communicate with each other (and not only with the opponent of PNC). So, the Greek ἐὰν δὲ ταὐτὸ ποιῇ οὐ διαλέγεται, could also be translated as "where there is no rule, i.e., where you can answer any question with any answer, there is no communication at all". But it is important to understand the reason why it is not permitted to answer each question with just anything –e.g., the question of whether Socrates is a man, by saying not only "yes" but enumerating all those things which Socrates happens to be besides being a man as well as all those things that he, as a matter of fact, is not nor (the climax of the *a fortiori* argument) could ever be, for all this is included in the meaning of 'not-man'. Now, the reason for this is precisely that 'man' means only one definite thing, say, biped animal, and not those other things which a real man could also be. The latter are just as little contained in the meaning of 'man' as those things which a man like Socrates could not possibly be, say, a prime number. In other words, white is just as little contained in the meaning of 'man' as prime number. This means –once again– that man must, so far, be understood to be just as accidental as white or whichever meaning you choose. All things may be arranged only *per accidens* to each other, and Socrates, had it played any essential role in the argument thus far (which it did not), is to be taken as a bare

---

[61] Aristotle, *Metaphysics*, 1007a 10-20.

particular whose attributes, including that of being a man, are all accidental to him as well as to each other. Otherwise one would not be able to understand the need for those rules whose absence would make any communication impossible.

Plato had already magisterially demonstrated this by means of an example which reflects this extended sense of συμβεβηκὸς as *ens per accidens*. And he did this in that dialogue with which Book IV of the *Metaphysics* is most intimately related, viz. in the *Theaetetus*. In the course of this dialogue, as you may recall, several answers to the question of what knowledge is are discussed: knowledge is perception as claimed by Protagoras, or opinion, as claimed by the Sophists in general, or true opinion, or grounded true opinion (δόξα ἀληθής σύν λόγῳ). But, even though all these answers are finally rejected, Plato thinks it meaningful to concern himself with them. For, though false, all these answers are nevertheless relevant to the question insofar as they might possibly answer it. Nor do they make the dialogue impossible in advance; until their inadequacy has been brought out these answers keep it going. For they are all answers which suggest themselves *prima facie*, i.e., they belong to the same category or domain as that which had been asked about, or one could at least suppose at first that they do. Only one of the answers that Theaetetus gives to the question "what does 'knowledge' mean?" (which is analogous to Aristotle's question "what does 'man' mean?") constitutes an exception. It is so much of an exception that Socrates will not even allow it as an answer, even if it is true. As an answer to the question it would make discussion just about impossible from the very outset. So, if one admitted it, it would only succeed in bringing about or maintaining an appearance of discussion. I am referring to the first answer Theaetetus gives. Usually it is passed over, I suppose not unfairly, for it is in fact quite useless with regard to the subject of the dialogue. But precisely for this reason it is important if, as in our text from *Metaphysics* IV, it is a matter of establishing the conditions for the possibility of a dialogue, argumentation or, in general, communication and in so doing of laying the foundations for metaphysics. Theaetetus' answer reads: "Knowledge seems to me to be what one can learn from Theodorus [the teacher of Theaetetus], beginning with geometry, as well as the crafts of the cobbler or other workmen"[62]. Socrates' rejection is delivered without delay: "I ask for one thing and you answer with many... whoever answers the question of what knowledge is with the name of some kind of knowledge or other makes himself ridiculous, for in citing the knowledge of someone or other he answers a question he wasn't asked"[63]. It is true that there is a knowledge possessed by geometers, cobblers, and so on. But this is accidental (κατά συμβεβηκός) to knowledge itself, i.e., to what it means to know something. "Accidental" not in the sense that the existence of cobblers and geometers would be an (real) accidental property of knowledge. Just like any other significant content, knowledge has no properties whatsoever, neither accidental nor indeed essential, it has only definitory characteristics or marks (*notae*). The converse is rather the case, since knowledge (i.e., the possession of it) could indeed be a real property of real men. But the existence of cobblers etc. attaches only accidentally (*per accidens*) to what it means to know something. Knowledge is only related *per accidens* to it. Only indirectly, i.e., *via* the existence of really existent cobblers like Sophroniskos, the father of Socrates, or real existent geometers like Theodorus, the teacher of Theaetetus, is the meaning of 'knowledge' related to the meaning of 'man'. 'Indirectly' here is but another expression for "*per accidens*". Now, insofar as one could think of infinitely many things which are related to the meaning of 'knowledge' or, for that matter, to that of 'man' –beginning with all those words whose meanings are not related *per se* with the meaning of 'knowledge' or 'man' or whatever the subject of conversation might happen to be, Theatetetus' first answer is completely arbitrary with respect to the debated issue. With the rejection of this answer, though, recourse to that which concerns any topic only accidentally (κατά συμβεβηκός) has not been completely disqualified. This rejection amounts to nothing more than the claim that whoever concerns himself in the course of some discourse with side-issues, without at the same time being aware of the fact that they are not to

---

[62] Plato, *Theaetetus*, 146 C-D.

[63] Plato, *Theaetetus*, 147 B-C.

the point, does not know what he is talking about. This is so, no matter how many true things he may say in the process. These truths lead nowhere, they only feign relevance to the discussion. Accordingly, Socrates permits himself later in the dialogue all kinds of digressions (about the difference between the philosophical and sophistical ways of life and so on), but he never forgets that they are not the issue with which he is concerned and thus he always returns to this main theme, never abandoning it permanently. Since the opponent of PNC, were he to proceed according to his theory –which he, of course, cannot– would never distinguish between central and incidental matters (οὐσία καὶ τὸ συμβεβηκός[64]), everything would become for him the main topic and, as a result, he would lose himself in sheer inconsequentialities. Supposing he were *per impossibile* to apply his theory consistently, he would not have been able to know what was being discussed. In Aristotle's words[65], he would never have a first subject to which his utterances could refer, and, thus, they would refer to everything and nothing. It is the consistent holistic negation of every rule. Inasmuch as the pragmatist Quine, despite his holism, holds on to PNC, one cannot ascribe to him the consequences of a thorough rulelessness. In fact Quine's radical pragmatism allows him to extricate himself from such consequences again and again through a calculated inconsequence[66], viz. that of renouncing the task of maintaining holism consistently. A consistent holism would lead to a form of chaos in which everything is in everything and everything is *per impossibile* true, which would be the negation of PNC as understood by Aristotle.

There are two ways of being led astray into a ruleless chaos, in which every meaning is connected in the same way (viz. holistically) to every other meaning. The first way to be led astray is by expansion, the other by contraction, as it were. The first corresponds to the negation of PNC, the other to the negation of PET. The negation of PNC leads one astray insofar as it presupposes that each word means everything, as if one could with impunity add to its meaning the

---

[64] Aristotle, *Metaphysics*, 1007a 31.

[65] According to Alexander's emendation of 1007a 34.

[66] Cf. W.V.O. Quine, *Word and Object*, Cambridge 1964, p. 3, n. 5.

meaning of any other word. By contrast, the negation of PET leads one astray insofar as it implies that each word swallows up in its meaning the meaning of every other. This latter form of holism Aristotle attributed to Anaxagoras. Both sorts of holism do away with concepts, meanings, definitions, or categories, but each for different reasons, viz. either through expanding or through contracting, adding or mixing. One might also speak of an accordion-effect. If the sharp boundaries between concepts disappear, then either one word (whether 'man' or 'knowledge' or whatever) will have its own meaning *plus* the meaning of any other word with which it is not *per se* related or, alternatively, it will, as it were, absorb the meaning of every other word. In the first case, in saying what is so and so (e.g., man) one is also saying what is not *per se* or by definition the same thing (e.g., white) and in applying any one predicate one is applying the others as well. But then the claim to truth would always be fulfilled[67]. And that is what PNC denies or asserts cannot possibly be true. Similarly in the second case, the case not of expansion but of contraction. In the corresponding passage Aristotle takes as an example of this second case the predicate 'good'. There can be no good if 'good' does not even have its own meaning. And it would not have even this, if its meaning were mixed with –or, as I have said, if its meaning had absorbed in itself– all other meanings. The mixture (μῖξις) would be neither good nor not-good. Anyone using a predicate, regardless of which one, would under such circumstances not be able to say anything true but only something false[68]. And this is the negation of PET attributed by Aristotle to Anaxagoras. For if the truth-claim of any assertion could not be fulfilled by either of the contradictories, truth would have to be sought in a third or middle between affirming and negating the same thing[69], this being, of course, impossible since there are only these two ways of aiming at or asserting truth. But now let us turn our attention specifically to the defense of PNC.

---

[67] Cf. Aristotle, *Metaphysics*, 1012a 15.

[68] Cf. Aristotle, *Metaphysics*, 1012a 27 f.

[69] Cf. Aristotle, *Metaphysics*, 1012b 26 f.

We have not yet seen why in the process of defending PNC by exposing the conditions of the possibility of language, communication, and argumentation, one has to accept not only meanings or categories which are sharply distinct from one another but even more importantly the basic categorial distinction between substance and *accidens praedicamentale*. The comparison of the Aristotelian text with a passage from Plato's *Theaetetus* could only serve to bring out even more clearly the deduction, which I have dubbed transcendental, of the categories in general. The limits of the comparison lie in the fact that for Plato the ultimate reality is not οὐσία as substance or subject of properties. That is why Aristotle denies him knowledge of true substance[70]. Nevertheless, in drawing a distinction between the essential and the incidental, Plato and Aristotle make common cause against the sophistic dissolution into pure συμβεβηκότα.

Once everything has been reduced to the accidental in the wider sense of ὂν κατά συμβεβηκὸς, then no further impediment deters us from taking the final step to the climax of the *a fortiori* argument. This last step allows not only the attribution of something true, even if only contingently true, to a subject. It also allows for the attribution of something contingently false to it; indeed it even permits the attribution of something that could never be the case. In other words it enables one to set up arbitrary cross-connections across several categories or meanings accidental to each other and to say, for example, that man or knowledge is or is not uneven, and so to connect literally everything with everything. "The predication, then", says Aristotle in the key passage whose details we ought finally to consider, "must go on *ad infinitum*. But this is impossible; for not even more than two terms can be combined". And he continues with what is the key statement in this crucial passage of our text: "For an accident is not an accident of an accident, unless it be because both are accidents of the same subject"[71]. Here we have the justification for (the transcendental deduction, or demonstration, or unavoidability of) accepting real substances as subjects of real, though still only

---

[70] Cf. Aristotle, *Metaphysics*, 1004b 10 and 1004b 17.

[71] Aristotle, *Metaphysics*, 1007b 1 ff.

accidental, properties. Take once again the example of Socrates, as Aristotle does when he goes on to write: "I mean, for instance, the white is musical [or educated] and the latter is white, only because both are accidental to man. But Socrates is musical, not in this sense, that both terms are accidental to something else"[72].

One must take care to realize what precisely has been shown by this and what has not as yet been shown. The necessity of admitting some substance as a bare particular has been shown. This means that the properties (of the chunk or bit of matter we might have in front of us and call Socrates) of being white, educated or even a man are all still on a par with one another. They are for the time being all accidental properties of Socrates and, still more important for the transcendental deduction of substance, accidental to each other. Of course, we know that for Aristotle the property of being a man is not an accidental property but an essential one. But for him to make use of this knowledge at this stage would be to run ahead of his argument. When Aristotle mentioned the properties of being white and educated, setting aside for the moment the property of being a man, this was only a concession to our knowledge of this fact. Strictly speaking he is not yet entitled to treat man as an essential property of Socrates. (In any case, substantial form or soul is no property of Socrates at all). And from the very beginning of his argument in defense of PNC he was in fact treating man as if it were just like any other conceptual content. The most important thing now to be kept in mind until the very end of the argument is that there is, as I have put it, no logical space ordering these contents; i.e., the fact that they all, unless they be connected definitionally with each other, stand *per accidens* to each other, for it is here that the key to the "deduction" of substances lies. The only thing that they all have are definitions, i.e., abstract essences, not concrete or real ones, let alone accidental properties. There can be no rule explaining why white should be connected with educated, or for that matter, with man, unless there is a subject capable of receiving simultaneously those contents (viz. as real properties) which in themselves have nothing to do with each other. Now, such a subject is

---

[72] Aristotle, *Metaphysics*, 1007b 4 ff.

what we call substance proper. But which substances we will be obliged to accept we cannot say in advance of our experience or *a priori* as rationalism would have it, but only *a posteriori*. It is from this point on that realist metaphysics in the genuine Aristotelian (not in the Scotist or Cartesian or Spinozian or Leibnizian or Wolffian) sense begins. So, if we did not accept real substances as subjects of real accidents, either we could not speak meaningfully or our discourse would be, to say the least, extremely primitive. It would consist only in giving definitions, i.e., it would be a tautological discourse. That things, though, are not so, is demonstrated by the fact that our language is again and again connecting words in such a way that, even if what it expresses is not something true, it is surely for the most part meaningful. That means: in speaking or thinking we are again and again cutting across categorial barriers we could not transgress if everything were a matter of connecting linguistic items which in themselves are not connected at all. It would punish us for making such transgressions by plunging us into a chaos without rules and thereby plunging us into a linguistic mess, i.e., in no language at all or, at most, in an extremely primitive one. Therefore, the reason why we are constrained to accept real accidents of real substances lies ultimately in the fact that, logically prior to becoming such accidents, they are in themselves accidental to each other. Of course, this is the reason why we are constrained to accept substances, not the reason why there are substances, any more than the reason why we must accept PNC is the reason for its existing. *As entia per accidens*, accidents, including among them for the time being such conceptual contents as man, can be connected with each other *ad infinitum*, but not as *entia per se*, i.e., as real accidents of real substances. Real substances are such that they, and they alone, can stop such a chaotic process from proceeding *in infinitum*, since, as Aristotle has said and will soon repeat, it is always one, and not two, let alone indeterminately many, accidents which can be related to substance at any one time. In other words, each one is directly related to it. Aristotle placed the emphasis as follows: "Since then some predicates are accidental in this and some in that way, those which are accidental in the latter sense, in which white is accidental to Socrates, cannot form an infinite series in the upward direction; e.g. Socrates the white has not yet another accident; for no unity can be got out of such a sum"[73]. To put it bluntly, it is not the speeding locomotive which accelerates but the locomotive which assumes ever different speeds in the process of accelerating. Here are included some most interesting metaphysical issues, issues Aristotle explains in Books VII to IX of his *Metaphysics* in which he develops the hints he has given in our main text.

Aristotelian metaphysics proves once again to be, as it were, the reverse of, say, Quinean pragmatism. For Quine there are no Aristotelian substances but only four-dimensional segments of them, i.e., slices of a unique spatio-temporal worm which we, as scientists and communicators, cut this way or that in order to get something more or less equivalent to Aristotelian substances. According to pragmatism it is only our need to communicate and to engage in scientific enquiry which compels us to do so, not anything out there in the reality of things, i.e., in that which is insofar as it is, in the reality of *ens qua ens*. The plausibility of such a holistic pragmatism is, however, no greater than the plausibility of assuming variable numbers or speeds that accelerate; and, of course, no greater than the plausibility of there being accidents of accidents or four-dimensional objects. It is no coincidence that Quine admits variable numbers. Inasmuch as he does not accept Aristotelian substances he can accept only Aristotelian accidents and hence accidents of accidents. The result is that "any collection of particle stages, however spatio-temporally gerrymandered or dispersed counts as a physical object. There is a physical object part of which is a momentary stage of a silver dollar sometime in 1976 and the rest of which is the temporal segment of the Eiffel Tower through its third decade"[74]. Such objects are no more plausible than variable numbers. But they are the consequence of substituting a process-ontology for the genuine Aristotelian (and Thomistic –as opposed to the Scotist and rationalist) substance-ontology. And the same thing applies to all other accidents. As Aristotle put it in Book V of *Physics*, there is no "movement of movement" "for movement is

---

[73] Aristotle, *Metaphysics*, 1007b 6 ff.

[74] H. Noonan, *Personal Identity*, London 1989, p. 107.

not a subject at all"⁷⁵. Or again: "...all this being so, the movement, or passing, clearly pertains to the log [thing] itself and not to the condition of heat or coldness; for no quality or place or magnitude either causes movement or experiences it"⁷⁶.

It is time to deal with some objections that might easily be raised. For instance: 1. What about the hierarchy of material accidents with quantity and extension as the most basic ones? 2. What about the property which all triangles share of having their angles equal to two right angles? 3. What about dancing well or badly, dancing gracefully or ungracefully? 4. And what about the relationship between *actus* and *habitus*, *habitus* and *potentiae*, *potentiae* and *anima*? Are these not all cases —except for the very last one— of accidents of accidents? As a matter of fact, they are not.

First, it is true that quantity or extension is presupposed by all other material accidents. But that does not mean that the quantity or the extension is, say, colored. These are two different things. Were it not extended the surface could not be colored either, but it is the surface (thing) which is colored, not its extension or quantity. Secondly, the property of having two right angles is a property *per se*, not *per accidens*, of the triangle; it is not its *accident praedicamentale*. Thirdly, gracefully or ungracefully is the way in which one dances, but it is not the dancing itself which is dancing, but the person. And it is she or he who is good or bad at it, not the dancing person. Fourthly, and by way of more adequately explaining the third point, *anima specificatur per potentias, potentias per habitus, habitus per actus (actus per objecta)*. "*Specificatur*" means here *actuatur* (is actualized) –the way in which *corpus*, too, is actualized (*actuatur, specificatur*) *per animam*: this is but the first, or last, member of the series. Take the relationship between *actus* and *potentiae*, or *actus* and *habitus*. All of them are accidents. Do *actus* not presuppose *habitus*, like *habitus potentias*, and presuppose them not merely in the sense of *conditiones sine quibus non* but in that of *accidentia accidentium* or, at least, of an accidental compound having other accidents –like Policletus along

---

⁷⁵ Aristotle, *Physics*, 225b 16 f.
⁷⁶ Aristotle, *Physics*, 224b 4 f.

with (= plus) his natural ability (his *potentia*) and his acquired capacity to sculpt (his *habitus*) having the accident of putting such ability and capacity into practice? Such examples seem to be all the more disturbing insofar as in their case it is not a question of an accident having accidents of an entirely different category, kind, or sort, as in the case of the white Socrates receiving education. In this latter case one can easily accept that the fact that Socrates is white has nothing to do with his receiving education. So, one can easily see here that it is only Socrates who receives education –to put it crudely, although he is also white. But what about the example of Policletus? Here the accidents involved belong to the same category, meaning, or content. So, why not accept that it is not Policletus but rather the gifted and well-trained Policletus who actually sculpted the cannon?

The same thing which seems to make such examples more disturbing to us –viz. the belonging of the involved accidents to the same contentual class, sort, or meaning– makes them in fact even more easy to resolve. For neither *actus* with respect to *habitus* nor *habitus* with respect to *potentiae* of the same class are superimposed unities, each with its own being. They are all nothing but the actualization of the former –not something, a unity, added to it. And in the end (or, rather, at bottom) they are all nothing but actualizations of a substance –e.g., of Policletus, and only of him. In the end (at bottom) there is only substance in this or that state, or condition, or whatever one wishes to call it. Similarly, if someone is dancing gracefully or ungracefully, in the end (at bottom) it is only she or he who is good or bad at it (i.e., with respect to dancing).

Accidents are not spatial parts, as we have already had occasion to observe. It is even more important to realize that material substances do not have temporal parts, although they do have spatial ones. Professor Geach once drove home against Quine the point that it is not McTaggart in 1901 who believed in Hegel's dialectic or McTaggart in 1921 who did not, but one and the same philosopher named McTaggart. Of course, in order to get rid of temporal slices one cannot stop there, since to be a philosopher is also a temporal slice of McTaggart, only a longer one than McTaggart as a believer or "disbeliever" in Hegel's dialectic. Now, whereas the whole McTaggart was not in his hand or his nose etc., the whole McTaggart was in each moment of his existence. That is what Aristotle refers to as ἐντελέχεια or *actuality*. And the being of McTaggart, his soul, was the actuality of all his acts and forms (*esse actus actuum et etiam formarum*), i.e., his one and only actuality. From beginning to end it is only substance which exists, though in ever-changing states. You can cut off a spatial part –say, the hand– of a man without killing him, but if you were to try cutting off a temporal part –past or present (future "parts" are even more obviously no parts at all)– you would end up killing him (at least in effigy, i.e., in your imagination). One cannot treat temporal parts on a par with spatial ones. There are no such temporal parts, nor for that matter spatio-temporal ones.

All this (variable numbers, accelerating speeds, in short, accidents of accidents and all of their implausible consequences) is what Aristotle is rejecting in the last words I quoted from our key text: "...for no unity can be got from such a sum". And he continues: "Nor again will white have another term accidental to it, e.g., musical" –nor, we could add, will movement or number have another term accidental to it, e.g., acceleration or variation in the sense of variable numbers. "For", Aristotle adds, "this is no more accidental to that than that is to this; and at the same time we have drawn the distinction, that while some predicates are accidental in this sense, others are so only in the sense in which musical is accidental to Socrates"[77]. And he finishes with a summary argument which forms the upshot of what I have been trying to explain: "...and the accident [he writes] is an accident of an accident not in cases of the latter kind, but only in cases of the other kind, so that not all terms will be accidental. There must, then, even in this case be something which denotes substance"[78]. Note how Aristotle emphasizes "even in this case". It is precisely the impossibility of there being only a chaotic process *in infinitum* of ideal contents accidental to each other which, according to Aristotle, compels us to accept substances and hence accidents in the other sense of *accidens praedicamentale* or real properties of substances as well.

---

[77] Aristotle, *Metaphysics*, 1007b 10 ff.

[78] Aristotle, *Metaphysics*, 1007b 15 ff.

With this the defense of PNC has reached its end: "And it has been shown that, if this is so, contradictories cannot be predicated at the same time"⁷⁹. These are the last words of the argument we have been following from the previous to the present section in defense of PNC, as is clear from the fact that the text continues with an ἔτι ("again" or "besides"), which signals the beginning of a new argument. Let me, though, quote the first words of the argument which follows, since it will permit us to see very briefly the course which Aristotle's *Metaphysics* will take up to Book XII. These words are: "Again, if all contradictories are true of the same subject at the same time, evidently all things will be one. For the same thing will be a trireme, a wall, and a man, if it is equally possible to affirm and to deny anything of anything"⁸⁰.

The interesting thing to note here is that Aristotle is referring only to terms for essential properties ("wall", "man", "trireme"). This offers a hint as to what the next step in the one sustained argument which constitutes Aristotle's *Metaphysics* as a whole will be. After having, as I have put it, transcendentally deduced substance as a mere subject or bare particular, the next step is to deduce the necessity of accepting real essential properties as opposed to accidental ones. Should one fail to take this additional step, everything that has up until now been achieved would crumble again into the chaos of an infinite regress. The reason is this: If there were only accidental, but no essential properties (or, rather, essences) as well, then there would only be one substance, one huge bare particular. But then accidents –the whole variety of contents or meanings– would still lack any rule for relating them to certain other accidents rather than to still other ones. In short, we would have been thrown back into the initial rulelessness. This means that in the transcendental deduction of substance(s) the transcendental deduction of essences is by implication already included –not only in the sense of specific essences, which would be but another set of mere meaningful contents accidentally related to one another, but also and above all in the sense

---

⁷⁹ Aristotle, *Metaphysics*, 1007b 17 f.
⁸⁰ Aristotle, *Metaphysics*, 1007b 19 ff.

of individual essences or forms (*formae substantiales* as distinguished from *formae essentiales*). This, of course, poses again the problem of the relationship between substances and their accidents, but not in the exacerbated form of the relationship between accidents and essences. This relationship is one of real identity and conceptual difference (*distinctio rationis cum fundamento in re* or *ratiocinatae*). It forces us to accept not only a constant modification of substances but of their individual essences or substantial forms too. In it there is also involved the question of the relation of specific and individual properties in general, i.e., with respect to so-called essential as well as to accidental properties. I would like to close this section with a consideration of the possible theological consequences of a specifically Aristotelian essentialism. In particular I shall be concentrating on the consequences for the doctrine of transubstantiation. By doing so one may perhaps be able to bring out in passing some important differences between the specifically Aristotelian and the specifically Thomist ontology.

It might be asked whether the specifically Aristotelian doctrine concerning the relationship between essential and accidental properties would not put the doctrine of transubstantiation in a difficult position; to put it bluntly, whether they were not utterly incompatible with one another. For since according to Aristotle there is an identity –though a contingent and often only a temporal identity– between accidents and substance, the latter being in its turn identical, and indeed necessarily identical, with its essence, transubstantiation seems to be ruled out not simply on the grounds that it is false but even more fundamentally on the grounds that it is nonsensical. Between the essence of bread and the accidents of bread Aristotle could accept only a conceptual distinction, not a real one (*distincto rationis cum fundamento in re*). Besides, the essence of man and the essence of bread, i.e., what it is for this loaf of bread to be bread and for this man to be man –and indeed what it is for the divine person Jesus Christ to be, on the one hand, man and, on the other, God– cannot be identified with each other. One essence cannot be composed of two essences, say, man and bread. So where –as in Aristotle– the accidents can only be conceptually detached from the essence, there can be no question as to the essence of bread disappearing while its accidents remain in place.

In answer to this question which has been put to me in somewhat the terms outlined above I would say: It is in fact far more difficult to explain the doctrine of transubstantiation on Aristotelian than on Thomistic terms. But even on Aristotelian terms it cannot be a question of allowing the doctrine of real presence to appear nonsensical. True, from a rationalist point of view, to be bread and to be man (or indeed God) are incompatible, i.e., are situated differently within one and the same logical space. A man-bread, then, is no less nonsensical than a chimera. But the fact is that according to Aristotle, as we have seen, there is no logical space. So there can be no question of an *a priori* incompatibility or nonsensicality of a man-bread or a God-bread. To be sure, there are, as a matter of fact, no such things as chimeras or goat-stags (*tragelaphos*) in nature. But this does not mean that they are nonsensical. It would only be nonsensical to mix the concepts or –to put it in theological language– the natures of such things as goats and stags, or women, snakes and lions, or –for that matter– man and God. But, as we also saw, to mix concepts or natures in this way is to run afoul of the Aristotelian PET. In the end, the doctrine of real presence is just as little contradictory or nonsensical on Aristotelian terms as is the doctrine of the Trinity or that of the Incarnation, which, as we saw, is not contradictory or nonsensical at all. I think that even the solution of those problems which are connected in St. Thomas with the possibility or non-possibility of a better world than the existing one lies here. Think, e.g., of the possibility of rational apes. Would a world with rational apes be a better one than, or at least a different one from, ours? Or, better still, would a rational ape still be an ape?

I think Aquinas, drawing on Aristotelian principles[81], would say: first, as regards the order of our world (*suppositis istis*) it would be worse if by means, say, of genetic engineering rational apes were to be, *per impossibile*, created: it would disturb the *ordo creationis huius mundi*. But secondly, God could have created another world with

---

[81] Cf. Thomas Aquinas, *Summa Theologiae*, I, q25, q6.

rational apes which perhaps would have been better than ours. At least there is no contradictoriness or senselessness in the idea. Thirdly, as to the question of whether a rational ape would still be an ape, the answer has been already given, viz. not in our world, but in another world which by this very fact, strange at it may sound, might perhaps be a worse one, but perhaps also a better one than ours. In addition to this one might point out that Aristotelian-Thomism is not incompatible with evolution but only with evolutionism. For it is in fact possible for an individual that was formerly an ape to become (or to have become) a man. But then it would (in our world, *rebus sic stantibus*) not remain the same individual as before –just as no number remains the same if added to another. That is (I think) the only, but important, limit placed by Aristotelian-Thomism on the so-called transformation of species –"transformation" being, of course, a very inaccurate expression, since neither the individual nor the species would in the process have been transformed but only changed in the sense that one individual or species had been substituted for the other. So one ought to be very careful in assessing the true Aristotelian theory of the invariability of species (*Artkonstanz, constantia specierum*)[82].

As far as the doctrine of transubstantiation in particular is concerned, I would like to cite in closing some words which were first uttered at a conference at Notre Dame. "It is sometimes said, e.g., in connection with discussion of the doctrine of transubstantiation, that the medieval scholastic thought of properties as being metaphysical 'skins' enveloping the objects which possess them. This is historically quite inaccurate and badly misrepresents the view they actually held and had derived from their reading of Aristotle... In this way of thinking properties are laid (by Nature) one upon another on top of an underlying bearer..."[83], i.e., on top of a bare particular. Such an

---

[82] Cf. for more on this paragraph Alejandro Llano, "Aquinas and the Principle of Plenitude", p. 147.

[83] "Analytical Thomism" by John Haldane.

"extrincesisme", as it has been called (by Gilson, Lubac, and others), is in fact thoroughly un-Aristotelian and surely thoroughly un-Thomistic as well, for *esse est actus actuum et etiam formarum.*

CHAPTER 2

ARISTOTLE'S DEFENSE OF THE PRINCIPLE
OF NON-CONTRADICTION

Aristotle's main argument in *Metaphysics* IV, 4 against the attack on the law of PNC has three parts[1]: The first ("I" in what follows) runs from 1006a 31 to 1006b 34, the middle part ("II"), which will chiefly concern us, from 1006b 34 to 1007a 20, and the third ("III") from 1007a 20 to 1007b 18. C. Kirwan[2] and above all R. Dancy[3] have painstakingly exposed the difficulties of Aristotle's text. One can learn much from both, but their interpretations are rather misleading. In this paper I wish to show three things: 1. (against Alexander of Aphrodisias as well as almost all interpreters known to me) that in II we have to do with an *a fortiori* argument[4]; 2. (*contra* Kirwan and others)

---

[1] Cf. *Aristotle's Metaphysics, Books* Γ, Δ, *and* E, translated with notes by Christopher Kirwan, pp. 93-102.

[2] *Ibid.*

[3] His book, *Sense and Contradiction: A Study in Aristotle*, is completely devoted to the argument. Besides Ross and Furth (cf. n. 10 and n. 16 below), Dancy and Kirwan are the only modern authors known to me who deal with II.

[4] One occasionally finds hints in this direction (cf. also n. 10 below). Petrus Fonseca (*In libros Metaphysicorum Aristotelis Stagiritae*, Tomus I, Coloniae MDCXV, p. 866) writes in a short parenthesis: "(quod etiam perspicue confirmatur in albo, et homine, argumento a minore sumpto)". But in contrast to Thomas Aquinas he does not once sketch the argument. Thomas (*In duodecim libros metaphysicorum Aristotelis expositio*, n. 622) writes: "Magis opponuntur esse hominem et non esse hominem quam homo et album; sed homo et album sunt diversa secundum rationem, licet sunt idem subjecto; ergo et esse hominem et non esse hominem sunt diversa secundum rationem". "*Secundum rationem*" ("according to the meaning"): in these words lie the quintessence of our interpretation. –The *argumentum a fortiori* does not contain anything that the argument in I had

that recognition of this point permits coherent interpretation of the letter of the text in II; 3. (*contra* Dancy's influential book and *contra* other authors) that in view of II the other two parts require a new interpretation[5].

---

not already proved. II is added only for the sake of greater plausibility (cf. n. 10 below). But precisely for this reason it is easier to understand the point of I in the light of II –the advantage of the *Dünnbrettbohrer* procedure.

[5] Cf. also my paper "Die philosophische querelle des anciens et des modernes", as well as Chapter 4 below, "The Unity of Aristotle's *Metaphysics*". These two articles deal mainly with III, (cf. also the end of n. 68 below), the present one with II as well as the central passage of I, to which II refers back. It would be useful to give II in full as well as the relevant part of I in the ROT:

I: "...not to have one meaning is to have no meaning, and if words have no meaning reasoning with other people, and indeed with oneself has been annihilated, for it is impossible to think of anything if we do not think of one thing; but if this is possible, one name might be assigned to this thing. Let it be assumed then, as was said at the beginning, that the name has a meaning and has one meaning, it is impossible, then, that being a man should mean precisely not being a man, if 'man' is not only predicable of one subject but also has one meaning (for we do not identify 'having one meaning' with 'being predicable of one subject', since on that assumption even 'musical' and 'white' and 'man' would have had one meaning, so that all things would have been one; for they would all have been synonymous)..."; Aristotle, *Metaphysics*, 1006b 7-18.

II: "The same account holds good with regard to not being man, for 'being man' and 'being not-man' mean different things, since even 'being white' and 'being man' are different; for the former terms are much more opposed, so that they must mean different things. And if any one says that 'white' means one and the same thing as 'man', again we shall say the same as what was said before, that it would follow that all things are one, and not only opposites. But if this is impossible, then what has been said will follow, if our opponent answers our question. –And if, when one asks the question simply, he adds the contradictories, he is not answering the question. For there is nothing to prevent the same thing, from being both man and white and countless other things: but still if one asks whether it is true to call this a man or not our opponent must give an answer which means one thing, and not add that it is also white and large. For, besides other reasons, it is impossible to enumerate the accidents, which are infinite in number; let him, then, enumerate either all or one. Similarly, therefore, even if the same thing is a thou-

1

On the beginning of II Kirwan comments: "'The same argument applies if –Aristotle apparently means– one starts by assuming a signification for 'not-man' (an 'indefinite name': *Peri Hermeneias*, 2, 16a 32). It is hard to see how the second sentence explains this contention"[6]. Compare also Dancy[7]. The perplexity is, however, unfounded.

Like Kirwan and Dancy, Alexander too[8] had understood the passage in the sense of a replacement of the positive expression "man" with the corresponding negative "not-man". Such a change, however, would destroy any trace of repetition of the argument of I within the text itself[9]. It would seem advisable therefore to see whether the

---

sand times man and not-man, we must not add, in answering the question whether this is a man, that it is also at the same time not a man, unless we are bound to add also all the other accidents, all that the subject is or is not; and if we do this, we are not observing the rules of argument" (Aristotle, *Metaphysics*, 1006b 34 - 1007a 20).

[6] C. Kirwan, *Aristotle's Metaphysics, Books* Γ, Δ, *and* E, p. 99.

[7] "The primary difference here seems to be the presence of the negation. But Aristotle does not go on to give us anything like a revised version of the first refutation with the negative expression replacing the positive" (R. Dancy, *Sense and Contradiction*, p. 28).

[8] Alexander Aphrodisiensis, *In Met.: In Aristotelis Metaphysica commentaria*, Ed. by M. Hayduck, Berlin 1891, 283, 1-5.

[9] What the wrong kind of substitution can lead to is also shown by M. Furth's. Having characterized the substitution in II in the same way as Dancy, Furth continues: Aristotle "proceeds to argue, or just asseverate, that it simply cannot be done". But then, in explaining this, Furth refers in his eight propositions exclusively to I. The real contribution of II, viz. the extension from one or two cases to all cases of 'not-man', appears only as an "interesting remark" which "follows 8. below: '...so that they must ["*a fortiori*" –Ross] mean different things' (1007a 1-4)" ("A Note on Aristotle's Principle of Non-Contradiction", pp. 371-383, pp. 378-379). But this "interesting remark", not the eight propositions, is all that the argument in II is about! (cf. Section 3 as well as n. 88 below). I take "*a fortiori*" as Furth's comment on Ross's "must" –and of course on Aristotle's text itself. On

following passages shed any light on the kind of substitution involved. To ask what Aristotle actually did is safer than to ask what he intended to say, all the more so as the resulting picture is entirely sound. What follows immediately in the text is the announcement of an *a fortiori* argument: "For if being a man and being white are different, also that which (for something) means existing in the manner of being a man, and that which (for something) means existing in the manner of being a not-man, will signify something different. For the latter is much more opposed within itself, so that it signifies something different"[10].

According to this, the argument should be repeated not –as Alexander, Kirwan, Dancy, Furth as well as Ross and many others propose– with the replacement (of the meaning) of 'man' with (the meaning of) 'not-man'. Rather, the stronger (and more explicit) opposition 'man'-'not-man' should now (in II) take the place of the more limited opposition 'man'-'white' (in I), which is a part of it. In other words, 'not-man' in the repetition should not be substituted for 'man', but for 'white' (and 'educated' and similar individual instances of 'not-man').

The real substitution, and with it the *a fortiori* argument too, are to be understood thus: in I, in order to prove the difference in meaning between 'man' and 'not-man' (viz. that which means existing in the manner of being a man cannot mean not existing in the manner of being a man or in the manner of being a not-man), Aristotle had adduced only two examples that mean not being man (or being not-

---

the other hand, *a fortiori* does not mean here "the strongest form of the impossibility of the failure of PNC" (*ibid.*), but only the strongest form of plausibility in the context of the elenchos. –The oddness of the wrong substitution appears also in Ross' commentary: "Aristotle passes from his argument derived from the necessity of a fixed meaning for 'being man' to one derived from the necessity of a fixed meaning for 'not being man' or 'being not-man'" ("As 'being man' has a fixed meaning, so has 'not being man'"). One cannot, in fact, fix the meaning of an indefinite name. 'Not-man' does not mean 'man', that's all. The *a fortiori* argument rests on this indefiniteness of 'not-man', on the fact that one cannot fix its meaning.

[10] Aristotle, *Metaphysics*, 1007a 1-4.

man). These were (the meaning of) 'white' and (of) 'educated'. That indeed is quite enough for the defense of PNC. The reason is that, whoever thinks he may answer the question what 'man' means or whether anyone is a man, not only by giving the meaning of 'man' or, where appropriate, with 'yes', but also by giving the meaning of 'white' and 'educated' or, where appropriate, with white and also educated cannot exclude any particular answer[11]. Consequently, he

---

[11] Cf. Aristotle, *Metaphysics*, 1007a 15: either all or none. Kirwan objects: "Aristotle's objections to the answer 'yes and no' are not quite fair. The opponent who appended to his answer 'and he is pale' would be adding something that does not answer the question put, but 'and he is not a man' does constitute an alternative answer" (*Aristotle's Metaphysics, Books* Γ, Δ, *and* E, p. 99 f.) Inasmuch as he sees both answers as neither equally justified nor equally unjustified Kirwan removes the basis for the *a fortiori* argument. Yet the justification for his objection depends exclusively on the accidental circumstance of how both answers (to the same question) are formulated. For, purely grammatically, I cannot answer the question "Is Callias a man?" as well with "yes and white" as with "yes and no". But the question is not whether the answers are grammatically correct but whether they are pertinent, i.e. whether they in fact answer the question put, to which again the answer is: Yes, but only because of the "yes" contained in both. The addition "and no" on the contrary may be just as true as the addition "and white"; the only thing that matters is that the former addition is just as irrelevant (though in a clearer manner) as the latter; for no question was asked about this. A single question will not bear more than a single answer, be this ever so long (cf. Socrates to Theaetetus: "I ask for one thing and you answer with many", 146 D). One can of course weigh several answers to a single question, and try them out, but not give them. Ross's translation of the passage in question hits the nail on the head (the commentary on II by contrast is less helpful): "The same thing may be man and white and many other things, but if I ask whether it is man, I ought not to get the answer, 'Yes –and white and tall'"). –Immediately after the sentence of his commentary just cited Kirwan writes further: "Nevertheless it is reasonable to insist on dealing with alternative answers one at a time". The alternative answers are "yes" and "no" ("man" and "not-man"). But it doesn't help at all to give them one after the other. For even if the corresponding sentences should be "a thousand times true" (1007a 16 f.), it would be factually impossible to run through the whole series of the meaning-content of the negative predicate. Alternatively, any selection from it would be arbitrary. Hence any attempt to give such an answer at all is improper.

would make all argument or communication impossible. The substitution in II of 'not-man' in general for 'white' and 'educated' makes this explicit. Hence the *a fortiori* character of the argument.

Whoever confuses what 'man' means with what 'not-man' means (and the meaning of 'white' as well as of 'educated' are both included in the latter) has already annulled the meaning of both. This was already shown by Aristotle in I and is repeated in II. By means of the *a fortiori* argument the same thing is simply made clearer in II. For in II reference is expressly made to the countless other cases also contained in the meaning of 'not-man' which can be predicated of man no less truly than can 'white' and 'educated'[12]. It would, however, be impossible to run through all these cases for the sake of exhausting the negative predicate "not-man" (ἀδύνατον ἄπειρά ὄντα τὰ συμβεβηκότα διελθεῖν)[13]. Thus Aristotle's conclusion reads: "even if the same thing is a thousand times a man and not a man..." (τοίνυν εἰ καὶ μυριάκις ἐστὶ τὸ αὐτὸ ἄνθρωπος καὶ οὐκ ἄνθρωπος...)[14]: to

---

[12] Cf. Aristotle, *Metaphysics*, already 1006b 13-17.

[13] Aristotle, *Metaphysics*, 1007a 14 f.

[14] Aristotle, *Metaphysics*, 1007a 16 f. What is meant is obviously: May the same thing be man and ten thousand times not man; or: May it be ten thousand times the case that the same thing is man and not-man (white, educated, large, trireme, wall, God...). Here Ross's translation easily suggests a *conditio irrealis* ("even if the same thing were man and not man") not present in the text ("ἐστὶ"). This misleading translation corresponds to Dancy's interpretation. Dancy's own translation, on the contrary, is thus far unobjectionable ("even if the same thing is a man and also not a man"). Kirwan's translation is also thus far unobjectionable. (When I say, Dancy's and Kirwan's translations are only "thus far" unobjectionable I mean that both (just like Ross's translation) suppress "ten thousand times" (= "uncountably many times"). With this the *a fortiori* aspect is also suppressed). —Where Aristotle formulates PNC in accordance with the schema ¬∃x ∃F ◊ (Fx ∧ ¬Fx) (cf. e.g. 1006a 1) one must always supply in thought the usual qualification (τὰ εἰοθότα: 1005b 28). If when he uses it the above schema be interpreted in the sense that nothing can have an individual property and at the same time also not have this individual property, then the phrase "in the same respect" is already implicitly included in it. In such a case the ascent to the meta-level of the concept or meaning is already complete. For then a predicate F will be affirmed and denied,

the question of what 'man' means or whether someone is a man there is no need to list all these (possibly true) cases, even if it were possible to do so.

To see the merit of this interpretation it is worth comparing it with what Dancy advances in support of his own conclusion against Aristotle: "One might deny the law of non-contradiction for all sorts of reasons. None that I have seen strike me as good reasons. But neither do I see any reason for saying that there never *could* be good reasons for denying it"[15]. According to Dancy, propositions like "The vehicle is and is not in the same place" (cited by Engels), "I love and do not love, am mad and am not mad" (Anakreon), "Christ is man and is not man" (Kierkegaard), etc. negate PNC but are nonetheless intelligible. Each of them ascribes to one and the same subject (to this vehicle, to "me", to Christ) mutually contradictory predicates, without the predicate expressions thereby losing their meaning. This, according to Dancy, already shows that Aristotles' defense of PNC is inconclusive. And this is Dancy's conclusion[16].

This criticism, however, leaves Aristotle untouched. Consider Dancy's last example: "Christ is man and is not man". This proposition corresponds to Aristotle's example ('man', 'not-man') not only in form as do the other propositions, but in content as well. Now, unlike Kierkegaard, the non-Christian Aristotle had no need to engage in theological questions such as whether Christ is not man *insofar* as

---

not because the subject also has other individual properties which fall under another predicate G (G not meaning the same as F) (as is quite possible), but because the subject allegedly at the same time also does not have the same individual property falling under F (which is not possible). To be succinct, the subject would then, in fact, have not to be F just *insofar* as it is F (i.e. κατά τὸ αὐτὸ), and just that is not possible. "In the same respect" belongs therefore intrinsically to every contradiction. Only then is *the same meaning* asserted as being not the same meaning or as being *a different meaning* from itself. We shall see how much depends upon attending to or neglecting the qualification "κατά τὸ αὐτὸ" (1005b 20).

[15] Besides R. Dancy, *Sense and Contradiction*, p. 142, cf. pp. 5, 12 f., 36 f., 54.
[16] R. Dancy, *Sense and Contradiction*, p. 142.

he is God, 'God' however not meaning the same as 'man'. A thousand other ways are available to him to show that a sentence like this can not only make sense, but even be true. As he says: "Even if the same thing [Christ, Socrates or Callias] is a thousand times truly a man and not a man..."[17]. If for no other reason than that Christ (or Socrates or Callias) has real contingent properties (συμβεβηκότα in the sense of an *accidens praedicamentale*, such as the property of being white), he (and Socrates and Callias) afford examples of the truth and meaningfulness of propositions with contents of the type "the same thing is man and not-man". For the meaning of 'white' is no more the meaning of 'God' than it is the meaning of 'man'. Both are cases of (the meaning of) 'not-man'. In that particular regard the fact that a man, but not God, can be white is quite irrelevant. As regards PNC all that matters is that in both cases ('God', 'white') there is a word which has a different meaning from 'man'. Compared to that the question whether a predicate is true or not of a subject (or whether it is affirmed and denied of one and the same subject) is secondary: Christ may be man and (as God or as white) not-man[18]. That does not concern PNC.

Now, if Dancy's counter-examples are just the type that Aristotle would treat as completely harmless, then something must have gone wrong with his interpretation. I will later show more exactly what that is. But already one may say: with the defense of PNC everything hangs on the assumption of a (minimal) distinction in meaning, without which (even the most primitive kind of) communication would be impossible. But if one has assumed a (minimal) distinctness in meaning (viz. that no word can signify *everything*), then one has already assumed PNC as well. If, for example, being a man is not the same as being God, being white, being educated...; in short, not the same as not being a man, then being cannot be non-being.

---

[17] Aristotle, *Metaphysics*, 1007a 17.

[18] It is not the case that Socrates is not (a) man (= no man at all) because he is white, but neither is it the case that Socrates is (a) man (= exist) because he is white. It is in the latter sense that (the meaning of) 'white' is (a part of the meaning of) 'not-man'. I am indebted to Hermann Weidemann for this point.

The difference of meaning does not, however, depend on the truth of the corresponding sentences in which communication normally (and argumentative communication always) takes place. This is crucial against Dancy as it marks the difference between Aristotelian and Quinean semantics[19]. And just as difference of meaning (or

---

[19] Dancy projects upon Aristotle some of the fundamental features of Quine's semantic theory (R. Dancy, *Sense and Contradiction*, pp. 34-36). In so doing he already places him in proximity to pragmatism. Ultimately the only ground for leaving open at least the possibility of a good reason for denying PNC (142) must be dissatisfaction with the Aristotelian defense. In his attempt to show this Dancy exhibits philosophical subtlety no less than philological acumen. Yet for Aristotle PNC itself underlies all attempts both to refute and to defend it. According to him, no such attempt could itself be meaningful, let alone true, without thereby confirming PNC. As we shall see, Dancy has consistently disregarded this. Aristotle defends PNC purely pragmatically, but that does not mean that his reasons for accepting it are also pragmatic. To endorse PNC on pragmatic grounds, i.e., because otherwise all argument or communication would be impossible, should rather be called a pragmatistic defense of PNC. For Aristotle there is no question of this. For him the validity of PNC is not relative to our needs, not even to our need for communication and argument, but is absolute. This, of course, does not prevent one from appealing *ad hoc* to these needs, whenever PNC is denied for any reason, be it thoughtlessness or stubbornness. Dancy (*op. cit.*, pp. 14-21) works out beforehand very exactly the *ad hominem* character of the argument. In the end, unfortunately, this has no influence upon his detailed interpretation. PNC being a principle, many things depend on it; but it itself depends on nothing. This point is well brought out in A. Code: "The fact that acceptance of PNC is required for significant thought is not the reason why PNC is true" ("Aristotle's Investigation of a Basic Logical Principle: Which Science Investigates the Principle of Non-Contradiction?", p. 356) - In his metaphysical realist, as opposed to Dancy's and others' pragmatist, view of Aristotle's *Metaphysics*, T. Irwin (*Aristotle's First Principles*) is surely right too (cf. n. 5). But it is precisely because PNC is valid not only with respect to human needs that its defense is required (*pace* Irwin) only on pragmatic grounds, as is apparent from II. Not surprisingly Irwin does not take II into consideration. The *ad hominem* character of the defense of PNC plays in his account even less of a role than in Dancy's, upon which Irwin in this respect relies (cf. n. 15 of Chapter 9 of his book). Section 98 in Irwin's book ("The defense of the principle of non-contradiction", pp. 181-183) deals expressly with the attribution of contradictory predicates to a subject, not with the meaning of a word

meaning as such) is not dependent upon the truth of any particular sentences, so meaninglessness is not dependent on the falsity of any sentences. Nor is it dependent on their real or supposed contradictoriness as necessary falsity. Dancy turns this (in)dependence relation on its head by foisting upon Aristotle a pragmatistic theory of meaning. But Aristotle's pragmatic defense has nothing to do with that theory. It may be stated as follows.

Suppose someone were to say: man or a man is not only such ('white', 'educated', 'tall'), but simply everything for which 'not-man' may stand, so that one can say of it without any reservation, that it (or he or she) is not-man as well. In this case, according to Aristotle, the answer to the question whether it is a man should no longer just be: yes, but he is also white (educated, large etc.). To be consistent, it must also contain (and here lies the climax of the *a fortiori*) the specification of anything else (καὶ τἆλλα[20]) which could also be given in answer –whether it belongs (or can belong) to man or not

---

(cf., against Dancy, n. 5 of Chapter 9), and hence with the principle itself rather than with its defense. The same observation applies to J. Lear [*Aristotle and Logical Theory*, Cambridge 1980, Chapter 6: "Proof by Refutation"] upon whom Irwin relies in his metacritique of Dancy's critique of Aristotle (cf. n. 5 of Chapter 9). Lear writes: "Dancy takes what a word signifies to be its sense and is thus led to make criticisms of Aristotle that I do not think are justified" (p. 108, n. 20). However, Dancy's criticism depends on his unduly ascribing to Aristotle a connection between the meaning of a word and its application in a judgment (cf. n. 49 below). To be sure, as the real referent of definition, the essence of a determined substance is more than the sense of, say, 'man'. But this difference, as well as that between substance, essence, and accidents, does not affect the defense of PNC in I or II. It only becomes relevant in III where Aristotle goes on to show the impossibility of accepting only accidents. Since there is no accident of accidents (1007b 15), without substances everything would equally belong (*per accidens*) to anything. So Irwin and Lear assume even more clearly than Dancy that Aristotle defended PNC on the basis of the truth-value of judgments instead of on the basis of the sense of words. This mistake goes back as far as Asclepius and Syrianus. Both hold, moreover, that the transition from I to II consisted in the substitution of a negative proposition for an affirmative one (cf. M. Hayduck, p. 262, 30 and Kroll, 68, 36-8).

[20] Aristotle, *Metaphysics*, 1007a 18 f.

(ὅσα ἐστὶν ἢ μὴ ἐστὶν). At this point the impossibility of carrying on a conversation has indeed become more evident. For, if it is impossible to cite everything that could apply with truth –even if purely factually– to a subject, then it is still more impossible to cite everything that might be said of a subject whether it in fact applies to it or not. Accidental properties, such as 'white' and so on, affect only the real being (*ens reale*, [ὂν κατά] τὰ σχήματα τῆς κατηγορίας[21]). But by accidental being is meant not only the *accidens praedicamentale*, but much else as well[22], including *ens per accidens*[23]. The incorporation of this further sense of συμβεβηκὸς[24] makes it all the easier to grasp the purely pragmatic (not pragmatistic!) sense of this argument[25], as distilled in the last sentence of II. That sentence reads:

---

[21] Cf. Aristotle, *Metaphysics*, 1026a 36.
[22] Cf. Aristotle, *Metaphysics*, 1007a 22, 30 f.
[23] Aristotle, *Metaphysics*, 1007b 7.
[24] Cf. the whole of III.
[25] If everything is reduced to the accidental, including this further sense of κατά συμβεβηκὸς (1007a 21 f. in connection with 1007a 30 f. and 1007a 33 f.), then nothing further obstructs the final step to the climax of the *a fortiori* argument. This last step allows not only attribution of something true, even if accidental. It also allows attribution of something false (which can only be accidental), and even permits attribution of what could never be the case. In other words it lets one set up arbitrary cross-connections across several (the more so since accidental) categories and enables one to say, for example, that knowledge is or is not uneven, and so actually to connect everything immediately (per se) with everything. The rulelessness would be perfect. Even if something (someone) is in fact white, the question of whether it is man cannot be answered by saying that it is 'white'. If one continued to do that, then any rational conversation would become impossible. This is indeed not immediately clear in the case of a single (true) predicate ('white'), the meaning of which does not coincide with the meaning of "man", nor in the case of some few (true) predicates (like 'white' and 'educated'), the meanings of which are likewise different from the meaning of 'man', since the possible answers are here correspondingly limited. But as soon as one considers –and herein lies the *a fortiori* of the argument– that for every single man there are countless (1007a 11, 16) such predicates which together make up the meaning of 'not-man', it becomes clear that one cannot conflate the meaning of 'man' with the meaning of 'not-man' without impairing discourse. One could neither go

"But if one does such a thing, then one is no longer having any discussion"[26].

---

through the whole series to exhaust the meaning-content of 'not-man', nor make a selection within this meaning-content, unless completely arbitrarily (1007a 14-15). Consequently the *a fortiori* argument only makes explicit what is true of every single predicate not of the same meaning as "man" (e.g. 'white'), namely, that its meaning is not the meaning of 'man' or that it is the meaning of 'not-man' (cf. also the end of n. 68 below).

[26] Aristotle, *Metaphysics*, 1007a 19 f. That would not mean that, whenever one lets a single word ("man") mean its negation as well, any discussion whatever would at once collapse. The discussion could not of course under these circumstances range over the word "man", but it could do so over other words. With each one of these, one could employ the same pragmatic approach as with "man", and so defend PNC generally. On this account Dancy shows himself unconvinced by Aristotle, because it is possible "to disobey these rules [namely PNC] without ceasing to think or talk articulately" (*Sense and Contradiction*, p. 142 *et passim*). That this is possible is obvious. However, Aristotle has not denied that one can in fact contradict oneself, i.e., disregard PNC (in contrast to simply denying it). In this connection he only means that one cannot think or speak meaningfully (more exactly: that one will not think or speak at all) if –*per impossibile*– one continually disregards PNC, exactly as we do not stop playing a game every time we cheat, but we would stop if we continually cheated. (I cannot go into the question here of whether this in itself would suffice to account for the fact that Aristotle often limits himself "to establish[ing] the impossibility of the assumption that *everything* is contradictory", J. Lukasiewicz, "Aristotle on the Law of Contradiction", in J. Barnes, et al., *Articles on Aristotle*, Vol. 3. *Metaphysics*, London 1979, p. 57. Cf. also section 3 and n. 68 below). To this extent it is misleading when Dancy says: "Articulate thinking and talking are not games we play" (*ibid.*). Elsewhere Dancy comes closer to the matter at hand when he asks himself what percent of contradictions one could allow oneself ("I have no idea what the least upper bounds might be", *op. cit.*, p. 37). Here however he does not mean how many words in a context, but how many occurrences of the same word in several contexts, might be indeterminate (= meaningless). These symptomatic modifications belong together with a thesis of Dancy's which will be further criticized later on (section 3). This thesis concerns a "weaker connection" than the alleged Aristotelian "rigid connection", which according to Dancy we should assume between meaninglessness and contradiction. Dancy must have recourse to this unnecessary maneuver only because he fails to bear in mind that "something is F and not-F" is only con-

The point of the pragmatic argument lies therefore in the fact that the opponent puts himself in the wrong. If he holds to his opinion he must, to be consistent, keep silent. If he were to remain silent he would perhaps be in the right. But as soon as he speaks the refutation snaps shut[27]. The opponent may, in fact, be right. As to this Aristotle needs, strictly speaking, as little as any Pyrrhonian sceptic to judge. He merely brings to the opponent's attention that he can be right only at the price of meaningful speech. If he were consistently to reject PNC he could give no meaning to his own words.

True, one is powerless should the opponent not admit defeat but speak further. But, insofar as his further speech is not completely without sense, he has already accepted PNC willy nilly, although he can still verbally deny it. In the end one can only proceed further by bringing him by force to silence. For one is always free verbally to deny the evidence. That's why some opponents, in contrast to the honestly confused, are so hard to dissuade[28].

2

In part 1 above we saw one can only take the sentence "Someone (something) is man and white" as a case of "Someone (something) is man and not-man" under the (obvious) condition that the meaning of 'man' and the meaning of 'white' are not identical. Under this condition the sentence "The meaning of 'man' is the meaning of 'white'" in fact becomes equivalent to the sentence "The meaning of 'man' is the meaning of 'not-man'". Only then (not of course if such a view were merely voiced, but if it were also endorsed) would the word "man" in fact have no meaning, since it would mean anything at all

---

tradictory for Aristotle when one accords to "F" the same meaning as "not-F", even when "F" has both times the same meaning. For then there is no longer any occasion to weaken the "rigid connection" (cf. n. 49 and p. 93 f. below).

[27] Aristotle, *Metaphysics*, 1006a 12 f.
[28] Cf. Aristotle, *Metaphysics*, 1009a 16-22.

–viz. itself and its negation. In that case, a sentence in which 'man' features could not be a possible instrument of understanding. For any question whatever relative to "man" would allow any answer.

Hence the whole matter of the pragmatic defense of PNC actually turns upon the distinction between the meanings of different words (and not on the real or supposed contradiction of any particular sentences). No distinction between meaning, no possibility of discussion. Accordingly, since distinction of meaning is a case of PNC (of being as not not-being) it is impossible to deny PNC if talking with one another is to have any sense. Every attempt to reverse this relation of dependence –apart from its implied *petitio principii*– must have fatal results for one's interpretation of Aristotle.

So far as Dancy's proffered counter-examples are concerned, the significance of what I have been saying is this: Dancy considered whether the predicates "man", "in the same place", "loves", "to be mad" and so on have a meaning or not and hence whether the corresponding sentences ("Christ is man and not-man", "the vehicle is and is not in the same place" etc.) can be means of communication. How one settles this question, he says, will depend in its turn on whether with these sentences PNC has been denied or, what for Dancy amounts to the same thing[29], misused. If what I have said is correct, however, this question is completely irrelevant.

So far as the defense of PNC is concerned, it is irrelevant that Kierkegaard believed Christ to be both man and (as God) not man, or that Engels thought that any moving vehicle both was and was not in the same place and so on. All that is relevant is whether they used the predicates "man", "in the same place" and so on with the same meaning as their negation. That is to say, did they use these words in the same sense as all other words that are not (according to modern usage) synonymous with them? Only if they had done that would meaninglessness and the impossibility of discussion be present; only so would one be faced with a real contradiction. Such would be the case if, e.g., someone were to say that *insofar* as he was man, Christ (or Callias) was also (κατά τὸ αὐτὸ) God (or white). Thus it really

---

[29] Cf. R. Dancy, *Sense and Contradiction*, pp. 36, 142.

only concerns distinctness of meaning. To neglect this would make communication altogether impossible.

If Engels had at some time so used the predicate "in the same place" that its meaning coincided with that of the predicate "not in the same place"[30] he would *eo ipso* have given it no meaning. Only in such a case would he not only have been denying PNC but also disregarding it: he would have contradicted himself[31]. What one may not do is to say with Dancy that meaninglessness depends on negation or disregard of PNC[32]. One may not say this because, in the context of defending PNC, one would be committing a *petitio principii* by doing so. More importantly, however, one may not say it because according to Aristotle, a word's meaning or meaninglessness is not dependent upon the truth or falsity, not even the necessary truth or falsity, of the sentence in which it occurs. Meaning for Aristotle has primarily to do with concept formation (abstraction), not with affirmation or denial. And for him the meaning of a concept-word does not represent or copy reality, but is reality itself in another mode[33]. Therefore Aristotle can conclude immediately[34] from the lack of difference of meaning to the identity of the things meant. He does this both in II[35] and at the place in I[36] to which he there refers.

Immediately after the sentence I cited above (at the start of section 1) Kirwan continues his commentary: "It [the second sentence from II

---

[30] This –as Aristotle expressly notes with respect to his own example (1006b 20-22)– is not simply that which one calls 'man'; one could just as well call it 'not-man'. It is rather a question of the meaning.

[31] Of course, he would also have contradicted himself if he had affirmed and negated the same proposition. But for the pragmatic argument this case is, on pain of *petitio principii*, not relevant.

[32] R. Dancy, *Sense and Contradiction*, p. 142.

[33] Cf. e.g. Aristotle, *De anima*, 2, 426a 15-17; 4, 430a 3-4; 7, 131b 17.

[34] Cf. on the contrary, R. Dancy, *Sense and Contradiction*, pp. 46-48.

[35] Aristotle, *Metaphysics*, 1007a 6.

[36] Aristotle, *Metaphysics*, 1006b 16-17.

translated above on n. 5]³⁷ would fit better with 1006b 13-18, to which it apparently refers back. But the reference is not wholly apt, because the previous passage argued to the conclusion, not that 'man' and 'not-man' signify different things, but that their signifying different things would be compatible with their signifying 'about' one thing"³⁸.

This implies that if at the passage in I referred to in II it were a matter of the difference of meaning of 'man' and ('white', 'educated' etc., therefore in general of) 'not-man', then the backwards reference in II would indeed be "wholly apt". But section 1 above has shown that it is a matter in both places of just this difference in meaning. And this interpretation will be confirmed in what follows. The backwards reference and the passage referred to complement each other perfectly.

Where the error lies appears more clearly in Dancy. In one place he writes: "...he [Aristotle] demands that Antiphasis [= the opponent of PNC] accept a distinction between signifying one thing and signifying about one thing to get Antiphasis to see that that predicate could be applied on different occasions, to different things, with the same significance"³⁹.

In Aristotle however the passage in question in I reads: "That which (for something) is called existing in the manner of being a man cannot signify that which (for something) precisely is not called existing in the manner of being a man, if 'man' signifies not only about one thing but also one thing. For by signifying one thing, we do not mean signifying-about-one-thing, since in this case 'educated', 'white' and 'man' [if, that is, they would all be true, e.g., of Callias] would signify one thing, so that all would be one"⁴⁰.

To prove that the positive and negative expressions ('man' and 'not-man') cannot have the same significance, Aristotle thus adduces instances of 'not-man' (viz. 'white' and 'educated'). That they differ

---

37 "For if being a man and being white are different... so that it signifies something different" (Aristotle, *Metaphysics*, 1007a 1-4).

38 C. Kirwan, *Aristotle's Metaphysics, Books* Γ, Δ, *and* Ε, p. 99.

39 R. Dancy, *Sense and Contradiction*, p. 126 f.

40 Aristotle, *Metaphysics*, 1006b 13-17.

in meaning from one another *as well as from 'man'* is clear to anyone, provided one does not confuse meaning with statement (use) or meaning with being true-about-something ("signifying-one thing" with "signifying-about-one thing"). Let 'white', 'educated' (and a thousand such cases) be just as true of Callias as 'man' (always or necessarily) is, their meanings will nonetheless be not only distinct from each other but also from (the meaning of) 'man'. Consequently the meaning of 'not-man', of which the meaning of 'white' is only one among infinitely many instances, is different from the meaning of 'man'.

Dancy's interpretation here turns Aristotle on his head. Where Aristotle speaks of *several predicates* and *one subject*, of which they (like 'white') may or (like 'man') must be true, Dancy, in the passage just cited, speaks on the contrary of *several subjects* and *one predicate*. With that he is indeed able forcefully to underline the difference between subject and predicate[41]. That difference is important for Plato's and Aristotle's whole struggle with the Sophists[42]. As

---

[41] Cf. R. Dancy, *Sense and Contradiction*, p. 126 f. So forcefully indeed, that he sees related difficulties when it is a case of dealing with essential predicates: "So he [Aristotle] is in no position to say that what it signifies is the same as what it is true of" (p. 127; cf. ch. V and VI in their entirety). That, contrary to all appearances, Aristotle does not confuse essential predication and statements of identity has been shown by H. Weidemann (e.g. "In Defence of Aristotle's Theory of Predicates", in *Phronesis*, 1980, 25/1, pp. 76-87, and "Τόδε τί *and* τί ἐν εἶναι", in *Hermes*, 110, 1982, pp. 175-184, with the important note 12). One can indeed assume an "identity factor in predication" (cf. H. Weidemann, "The Logic of Being in Thomas Aquinas", in S. Knuuttila and J. Hintikka (eds.), *The Logic of Being*, Dordrecht 1986, p. 188), without thereby confusing predication with statements of identity (cf. also the end of n. 33 below).

[42] Were the subject (what one is talking about) constituted by the predicate (by what one says of it), if, for example, when one said "Cleinias is ignorant" one spoke not of Cleinias but of an ignorant Cleinias, then obviously no falsity would exist. As Dancy has shown (Ch. III), Aristotle's opponent ("Antiphasis") is a mixture of the Euthydemus of the *Euthydemus* and that of the *Cratylus*. Both let the subject be constituted by the predicate. But whereas for the former contradictory statements are about different subjects (either about ignorant or about informed Cleinias), this

regards the pragmatic defense of PNC, however, it is only a means of guaranteeing the differences of meaning from one another. It is, moreover, concerned here solely with *these* differences. If, in contrast with this, the meaning- and concept-level is seen as merely secondary and dependent relative to the sentence- and judgment-level, then in the end one cannot avoid making the loss of meaning of a word dependent upon asserting the contradiction or denial of PNC, and this quite apart from whether it is a question of a real contradiction or not[43].

---

presupposition is not valid for the latter. Accordingly for the first there can exist no contradiction, while for the second all contradictions are true. The first position can, as with Dancy, be called ultra-essentialism, since the loss of any property leads to the perishing of the substance. If this is not assumed, then ultra-essentialism converts into ultra-accidentalism. It is the conception combated above all in III and does not belong, *pace* Dancy, to just a sideline of the main argument (cf. n. 49 below). - The sophistical dissolution of identical individuals into their various states finds its echo in the segmenting of individual substances into pure space-time phases (slices) in Quine. Yet Quine seems to hold on to PNC as steadfastly as Aristotle (R. Dancy, *Sense and Contradiction*, p. 35). Consequently one cannot charge him with the consequences of total rulelessness which accrue to the opponent of PNC at the theoretical level. In fact Quine's radical pragmatism allows him to extricate himself from these consequences again and again only through a calculated inconsequence, namely that one renounce the task of maintaining holism consistently (see W. V. O. Quine, *Word and Object*, § 3, n. 5). Otherwise one would have to consider each time simultaneously all questionable predicates (accidents both in the narrower sense of real predicates and in the further sense, distinguished in III, of what is said *per accidens*), i.e., simply all, which would through sheer rulelessness make one lose one's ability to speak. But for Aristotle the necessity of PNC is not positively based on this. According to him this necessity is no more merely pragmatic than it is merely semantic (see e.g. 1007b 26-29, 1010a 34, 1012b 26-31).

43 "That argument [which Dancy holds to be Aristotle's main argument, see section 3 below] would show that the predicate in any instance of a denial of the law of non-contradiction could not be significant. So it makes a rigid connection between someone's using a word significantly and his obeying the law of non-contradiction. - But that connection is too rigid... The word 'man' has significance in English, and so does the corresponding Danish word; that allows us to understand Kierkegaard, in translation or in the original, when he insists that Christ was both

2. ARISTOTLE'S DEFENSE OF THE PRINCIPLE OF NON-CONTRADICTION 93

The fundamental error of such an interpretation consists in making the meaning of a word dependent upon the sentence and its truth-conditions. As we noted earlier, however, the meaning depends for Aristotle on the forms abstracted from things and itself regulates the use of the word in the sentence, instead of being regulated (specified) by the latter. Meanings can indeed be considered in Aristotle as truth-conditions, though not because they (pragmatistically as it were) might result from the use of words in declarative sentences, but only because they determine the truth-values of those sentences. And they are only able to determine them because they, before any judgment, in an act of what was later called abstraction (ἐπαγωγή as concept formation[44]), not merely correspond with the forms of reality but are identical with them[45].

---

a man and not a man. A weaker connection seems reasonable, namely, that persistent denial of the law of non-contradiction tends to remove sense from that predicate" (R. Dancy, *Sense and Contradiction*, p. 54). In this (partial) "Summary" (54) of his central Chapter II Dancy's interpretation is both better and more succinctly expressed than in his general "conclusion" (p. 142) cited above. It also contains its fair share of mistakes. In the further course of the same "summary" Dancy writes: "Antiphasis is inclined to block the argument by making the word 'man' in some way irredeemably ambiguous, and to save his denial of the law of non-contradiction with ideas that, as Aristotle sees it, make 'a man' and 'not a man' coincide in significance" (*op. cit.*, p. 55). For Dancy, remarkably, this discussion belongs only to the "subplots" of Aristotle's argumentation. It is even "sealed off from the main line of the refutation" (*op. cit.*, p. 54). One asks oneself what else could be more important for the defense of PNC. For Dancy's answer to that and our criticism of it see section 3 above in connection with n. 68.

[44] Aristotle, *Analytica Posteriora*, B 19, 100b 4.

[45] One can only speak of a simple correspondence theory of truth if (as in the 14th century) *cognitio abstractiva* (*pro statu isto*) is opposed to *cognitio intuitiva*. From this moment on the intellect can no longer behold the forms of reality in the *phantasmata* (see e.g. Duns Scotus as against Aquinas, *Ord.* I, d.3, p. 3, q. 1, n. 292, ed. Vat. III, 239: "*Quod additur de Philosopho quod speculamur quod quid est in phantasmatibus* etc.'"), but it must produce together with this (as a further *causa partialis*) a *species intelligibilis* as *ens repraesentatum*, which merely corresponds to reality. The resulting realism, to the Scotist origin of which Peirce had referred (see e.g. 4.50, 4.507), has much in common with pragmatism, but little

Let Aristotelian semantic theory, depending on the identity of meanings and forms of reality (τί ἐν εἶναι), be howsoever primitive, one can not with impunity replace it with a completely different theory of meaning like Quine's. Quite apart from the conventional character of words, the meaning of words for Aristotle belongs primarily to the *quid rei* (τί ἐν εἶναι) and not to our linguistic custom (*quid nominis*). For him, unlike in pragmatism, this meaning is not simply the result of the propositions in which our common convictions find expression, i.e. not merely the rule of use emerging out of a linguistic community[46]. Every interpretation of Aristotle must hold fast to that. Other-

---

with Aristotle. On the other hand Scotus himself is still miles away from pragmatism, insofar as he does not make the *simplex apprehensio* dependent on the *judicium*, and sees in the former much more than in the latter (hence before any *compositio propositionis*) the possibility of contradictions through *incompossibilitates* of meaning. Consequently, Duns Scotus' semantic theory has in a weakened form the same basis, that of abstraction, as does Aristotle's. (Cf. Aristotle's *Posterior Analytics*, translated with notes by J. Barnes, Oxford 1975, p. 260 in reference to B19: "the ascent to (C4) ['a has the notion of swan'] yields any interesting results which might be extracted from (P4) ['a understands that all swans are white']". "C" stands here for "concept", "P" for "proposition". This priority of the concept vis-à-vis the judgment level still holds good for Duns Scotus). Already with Scotus, however, the weakening itself resulted in first philosophy as theory of reality becoming dissolved through *scientia transcendens* into conceptual and later on linguistic and sign analysis. To this extent the road from Duns Scotus *via* (Suarez, Wolff and) Kant to American pragmatism is a logical one (cf. on this L. Honnefelder's *Scientia transcendens. Die formale Bestimmtheit der Seiendheit und Realität in der Metaphysik des Mittelalters und der Neuzeit (Duns Scotus-Suárez-Wolff-Kant-Peirce)*, Hamburg 1990 as well as the papers referred to in n. 5 above). As for the rest, *Peri Hermeneias*, 1 should be read in conjunction with *De anima* (cf. e.g. 430a 19-20), to which it refers.

[46] The incompatibility of Aristotelian essentialism and Quine's holism shows itself nowhere so clearly as in Quine's denial that there is a difference in principle between analytic and synthetic. Herein lies already the rejection of a difference in principle between concept and judgment. For the quality of being analytic applies no less than that of being synthetic to judgments, but only to those judgments whose truth-values depend on the meaning of the constituent words and hence on concepts. Already in the sense of analytic conventions (C.I. Lewis), but even more

wise the difference between "signify" and "signify about", on which Dancy rightly sets so much value, will be relativized again in the sense that the first is made dependent upon the second, the question of meaning upon the question of truth value. And whether one assumes here a strict or a loose dependence is of no consequence[47]. In regard to the question of whether the predicates "man", "in the same place", "love", etc. do or do not have meaning, the question about the truth-values of Kierkegaard's, Anacreon's or Engels's corresponding sentences is irrelevant. What counts is whether the meanings of these predicates coincide with the meanings of their negations. In this case they would apply to everything and so be useless for purposes of communication. Sentences would be meaningless (of truth-values we need and ought not to talk) to the extent in which they contained such a word, since any question concerning it would in fact allow any answer.

That is all that Aristotle can adduce in defense of PNC, but it is enough. It means indeed that the defense is only valid *ad hoc*, only for each individual case. But it is valid for any individual case. A further comparison with Dancy's interpretation may bring this out.

3

In Dancy's interpretation the passage in I, to which the argument in II[48] refers back, appears only to raise a side issue with its distinction between "signify" and "be true of". It is a side issue which Aristotle

---

so as *necessitates de re*, meanings (and concepts) are herewith radically eliminated. That the Aristotelian position is incompatible with this is indirectly but strikingly expressed in Quine's famous *bon mot* (against C.I. Lewis, of course): "Meaning is what essence becomes when it is divorced from the object of reference and wedded to the word" (W. V. O. Quine, "Two Dogmas of Empiricism", in *From a Logical Point of View*, p. 22).

[47] See n. 49 and the end of section 3.
[48] Aristotle, *Metaphysics*, 1006b 14-17, 1007a 1 ff.

has to consider only on account of certain extreme views of his sophistical opponent[49]. Those "extravagant" views demand not only the possibility, but precisely the necessity of contradiction: (A) $\forall x \forall F$ (Fx $\wedge \neg$Fx), everything is contradictory. Now, to oppose this demand one obviously has only to show that in some case the contradiction does not apply or that PNC applies. With that one has certainly not yet shown that the contradiction is impossible: (B) $\neg \exists x \exists F \Diamond$ (Fx & $\neg$Fx)[50]. Consequently, the refutation of (A) is not enough to prove the validity of PNC (B).

Now Dancy's view is this: so far as the defense of PNC is concerned, an argument which indeed refutes (A) but does not refute (B) can only yield a subsidiary argument or a subsidiary line of the main argument. But in order to refute (A) it suffices to show that the meaning of at least one word is not the meaning of all other words (or that *one* meaning does not embrace all meanings). Consequently, the interpretation which we arrived at with the help of the *argumentum a fortiori* (viz. communication must fail as soon as one word can signify *everything*, viz. also its own contradictory) can be for Dancy only a subordinate skirmish, so far as refuting PNC's opponent is concerned. Instead of this Dancy considers as the main argument what he calls the "clincher" argument. When applied to all words having significance, this argument consists in a formal (and not pragmatic) refutation of the contradiction and results in its negation[51], i.e., has (B) as conclusion[52].

---

[49] R. Dancy, *Sense and Contradiction*, pp. 43-54.

[50] With such schemata one must understand the "usual qualifications" (1005b 28). Kirwan (*op. cit.*, pp. 89, 102 f.) draws attention to this as little as Dancy is able to do with his interpretation (see above n. 16). Dancy's difficulties prove that the following remark (about 1005b 18-32) cannot *de facto* be applied generally: "The dialectical difficulties can safely be ignored in a modern presentation of Aristotle's argument"; J. Barnes, "The Law of Contradiction", *Philosophical Quarterly*, 19, 1969, p. 306, n. 5.

[51] The reference is to the end of I (1006b 28-34).

[52] This conclusion runs in Dancy's words: "(3) It is not possible for anything to be a man and not to be a man (b 33-34)". (The wording of this conclusion, where "the usual more exact modifications" ("simultaneously", "to that extent", etc.) (1005b 27 f.) are merely tacitly assumed, has clearly misled Dancy). Aristotle comes to

2. ARISTOTLE'S DEFENSE OF THE PRINCIPLE OF NON-CONTRADICTION

To this end, however, Aristotle needs a strict notion of meaning according to which *one* meaning not only may not mean everything, but must mean something definitely statable. In other words, according to Dancy, the consistency of meaning demanded by Aristotle requires more than the impossibility of one word meaning simply anything at all. It requires that there be necessary and/or sufficient conditions for the word's use in true sentences, e.g., if something or other falls under the concept man. In short, according to Dancy, Aristotle cannot handle the extreme borderline cases[53].

---

the conclusion by means of the premise "(1) Necessarily, if anything is a man, it is a biped animal (b 28-30)", which, through the definition of "necessarily (b 31-32)" as well as the double use of the definition "(D) Biped animal is what 'man' signifies (b 30)" (here the usual main presumption of PNC (κατά τὸ αὐτὸ) is expressly mentioned!), leads firstly to "(2) It is not possible for anything that is a man not to be a biped animal (b 31)" and then to the conclusion (3). Cf. R. Dancy, *Sense and Contradiction*, pp. 29-30. (Without generalization of course (3) only amounts to the negation of (A)). - Obviously (D) must not be confused with "(S) 'man' signifies something" (*op. cit.*, p. 32) (not even with "(almost-D) 'man' signifies biped animal" (*op. cit.*, p. 33)). This is why Dancy thinks the main argument is not satisfied with just any meaning (as against 'mean everything, i.e. nothing'). Yet as *quid rei* the meaning does not always need to be known. The expression "τί ἐν εἶναι" (τηε), where the philosophical imperfect (Natorp) need not be referred back to a fixed definition, shows this sufficiently, just as does the characteristically loose example "two-footed animate being" for the τηε (cf. on the contrary Dancy (*op. cit.*, p. 33): "It (D) makes 'man' univocal"). Doubtful cases are accordingly considered by Aristotle from the beginning. Since it proceeds purely formally the "clincher" argument can of its own nature decide nothing. The opponent is free to raise an objection against the *petitio principii* and so deny (*op. cit.*, p. 41 f.) the conclusion (3). Against this it only avails to draw attention to the consequences of the lack of communication which results from the identity of meaning of "F" and "not-F", amounting to the negation of any meaning at all. M. Furth's eight propositions as alleged explanation of II (cf. n. 10 above) only reproduce Dancy's "clincher" argument.

[53] Such an extreme case arises if, for example, one cannot know whether the synthetically bred Bernie is to be addressed as human or not. Yet the only borderline case, which neither Aristotle nor anyone else (for this is his argument!) can resolve, is the most extreme case, where a word means everything, *so that* all is one

It is not surprising that Dancy takes no account of the *argumentum a fortiori*. For it is only here that the purely pragmatic (and not at all formal) character of Aristotle's method is employed to the full. Here one must decline appeal to the truth or falsity (or indeed contradictoriness) of sentences in which communication normally takes place. It is not the truth or falsity of these sentences, but only their suitability as a vehicle for communication, that can be considered without *petitio principii*. Now, communication threatens to degenerate into nonsense whenever any word can mean everything (so that, as a result of what was later called the intentional identity[54] of meaning and form, reality would be all one and the same). And it does so every time one simple word intends its own meaning as well as its negation. For this to occur, it is not enough that a predicate should be both affirmed or denied of one subject; it must also be intended that the predicate's meaning be identical with the meaning of some other (and if so, then *any*) word, which does not by chance (i.e. because of customary linguistic connections, which have nothing to do with the matter) coincide with it; therefore not, for example, if it be said "Christ is man and not man", but "'man' does not mean 'man' (or means also 'not man')". Because Dancy does not consider this in his

---

(1006b 15-18; 1007a 4-7). It is not correct that according to Aristotle "communication can only take place where there are statable necessary and sufficient conditions for the application of words..." (R. Dancy, *Sense and Contradiction*, p. 42). Even with reference to what Dancy only considers a subsidiary argument he finds that "If I am right, it [the main argument] is still not waterproof, partly because Aristotle is one of those people who sees rejection of the idea that words only have significance if there are necessary truths governing their application as tantamount to subjectivism". Dancy adds: "I think there are other alternatives" (*op. cit.*, p. 43). So does Aristotle. His supposed "subsidiary" argument pertains directly to this. But one can only see this if one treats it as the proper and only argument, as Aristotle emphasizes at the beginning of II (ὁ αὐτὸς λόγος). J. Lukasiewicz ("Aristotle on the Law of Contradiction") does not take II into account and leaves out the relevant words in his quotation of I to which II refers back (*ibid.* p. 56, (b)). This explains his difficulties with the Aristotelian elenchos (*ibid.* p. 55, (b)).

[54] Cf. n. 51 above.

interpretation, he sees himself compelled to assert two theses, both of which are made superfluous by the *a fortiori* argument and hence the purely pragmatic character of Aristotle's *main line* of argument. The first thesis, which he falsely ascribes to Aristotle, is the thesis of a rigid connection between meaninglessness and mere denial and affirmation as alleged disregard of PNC[55].

The second thesis is Dancy's own thesis against Aristotle, viz. the thesis of a weak connection between these two items, contradiction and meaninglessness. But since the first thesis is not Aristotelian, it is entirely superfluous to offer the second as a substitute for it.

Associated with the first thesis is Dancy's peculiar view that according to Aristotle a word's meaning presupposes that there is always a delimitation one can give to its true or its false use as a predicate in a sentence. "Peculiar", because, in the context of the pragmatic defense of PNC, it ignores what Aristotle never tires of emphasizing[56], viz. that in defending PNC one may not refer to the question of truth-values. In addition, the notion of a "rigid connection" results in the equally untenable claim that for Aristotle a word's meaninglessness (and hence the at least partial absence of communication) arises not only with the identity of meaning of this word (say "man") with all other words (or with some other word like "white" with a clearly different meaning), but already with particular borderline cases of this word's use as predicate[57].

According to Dancy, the thesis concerning meaninglessness as an identity of meaning with any other word is only encountered in Aristotle as an incidental side-issue arising from exceptionally extravagant opinions of some Sophists. These are that everything is contradictory (A), and hence that no meaning of a word is definable in terms of any other not conjoined definitionally with it. As our interpretation has shown and as will become more evident still, it is

---

[55] Cf. n. 49 above.

[56] Cf. e.g. Aristotle, *Metaphysics*, 1012b 6-9 with 1006a 19-21.

[57] For example in the case of the undecidability of whether the predicate "man" should be denied or affirmed of Bernie (see n. 60 above).

precisely this, and nothing else, which Aristotle opposes in the main body of his argument. Consequently, Aristotle's conception of meaning and meaninglessness should not be burdened with the absurdities (the "rigid connection" thesis) that compel Dancy to his second thesis. Dancy's second thesis pleads for a "weak connection" instead of a strong one[58]. Although he does not indeed ascribe this thesis to Aristotle, it is just as superfluous as the first. For it only arises from the needless effort to substitute a weaker thesis for the supposedly Aristotelian thesis of the rigid bond between meaninglessness and simultaneous denial and ascription of a predicate.

Since Aristotle has never asserted the strong connection, there is no ground for Dancy's weakening of it. Moreover, even where it really is a case of meaninglessness due to identity of meaning of 'F' and 'not-F' (given the same meaning of 'F' and the normal meaning of 'not'), there is just as little reason to weaken the thesis of a connection between this and a, in this case, real contravention of PNC by substituting the thesis of a gradual loss of meaning setting in through repeated use (of that identity). For the identity of meaning of 'F' and 'not-F' under the conditions just given immediately entails a violation of PNC. In this single case of real contradiction the word has from the beginning, *ex definitione* as it were, no meaning. And its meaninglessness accrues to it neither suddenly nor gradually from the assertion of a contradiction which is sometimes not even real, viz. if the ascription and denial do not occur in the same respect.

Aristotle would regard as confirming his own position precisely what Dancy himself adduces in his conclusion in order to hold the question of PNC open, viz., that one can speak out against PNC with thoroughly meaningful words in principle intelligible to everyone[59]. For *insofar as* one expresses oneself intelligibly, even if only in order to deny PNC, one has already accepted PNC. This again does not mean one could not *now and then* not only deny PNC (or dispute its validity); one could even regularly disregard it. But insofar as the

---

[58] Cf. n. 49 above.

[59] R. Dancy, *Sense and Contradiction*, p. 37.

sentences by means of which this happens have sense, one's use of them must already acknowledge the validity of PNC.

A meaninglessness which leads to the (at least partial) impossibility of discussion consequently does not, according to Aristotle, appear at the point where a word (e.g. 'man') is not used according to identifiable truth-conditions, but only when it means potentially everything. This would always be the case if it were used as a synonym (in the modern sense) for any other word which (like 'white', 'educated' etc. as against 'man') clearly had a different meaning. In other words, what Dancy considers just a subsidiary matter is already the main argument. Nor was anything else to be expected from the *argumentum a fortiori*. For it would be more than strange if Aristotle, announcing an argument at the beginning of II where he only promises a clarifying recapitulation of I, had simply intended a corollary and not the main argument of I itself. To this extent also the reference to I at the beginning of II is "wholly apt"[60].

---

[60] The objection (cf. above) that the main argument would then not affect the real negation of PNC (i.e., of (B)), but would only refute (A), drops out if one takes seriously the *ad hoc* character of any purely pragmatic argument. In any single case it can obviously only be shown *ad hoc* that the price of allowing a word to mean anything, viz. also its own negation, must be to make mutual understanding impossible (Aristotle, *Metaphysics*, 1006b 6-9). Clearly, it is only (A) but not the negation of (B) that is reduced *ad absurdum* by the single case. But one can repeat the process at will, and indeed, as Dancy rightly points out, not only with substance words (*op. cit.*, pp. 107-114). Consequently, one should not distinguish with Dancy between an essential and a non-essential argument in Aristotle here. Dancy takes the first to proceed by means of a strong claim to unity of meaning, in the sense of univocal conditions for the use of a word, against the real negation of PNC (i.e., against the negation of B). The second he takes to proceed by means of a weak claim to (minimal) unity of meaning in the sense of the negation of identity (of meaning) of any word with all (words or) things, and would simply refute the "most bizarre" statements of the opponent (i.e., (A)). One can be fair to Aristotle, though, only if one treats as secondary what Dancy treats as the main argument. Dancy's "clincher" (see n. 59 above) is in reality only an appendix to the real, i.e. the purely pragmatic, argument.

This appendix uses logical means which only someone who was already convinced by the previous pragmatic considerations would accept. The "clincher" argument (1006b 28-34) does not by chance follow the pragmatic considerations, to which II refers back in the text of I (1006a 31-b 28). For it is not directed against an opponent, but only to a convert. In other words it is only an exposition (*via expositionis seu judicii*) of that which was previously shown, as it were, *via inventionis*. So for Aristotle's defense of PNC the proof of the necessity of one meaning, which does not extend to everything (to all other meanings), suffices, irrespective of where its limits may peter out. To determine this in individual cases would perhaps be the task of a science proceeding according to definite criteria, but not the task of first philosophy. It is wrong to think that Aristotle regarded as insufficient a minimal distinction of meaning, which for the sake of a defense of PNC can dispense with detailed precisions. The contrary view may perhaps be engendered by Aristotle's reasoning from a substance expression such as "man". But Aristotle could just as well have reasoned –as Dancy has in dispute with Anscombe convincingly shown (*op. cit.*, pp. 107-114)– from an expression for an accident. He would thereby simply have made his task easier from the beginning. The *a fortiori* argument would then have been impossible, but also unnecessary. For accidents have themselves no accidents (1007b 2 f.; cf. 1007b 14 f.). Thus for them no accidental real properties in the sense of *accidens praedicamentale* (ὂν κατὰ τὰ σχήματα τῆς κατηγορίας) need be considered, but only another meaning of συμβεβηκὸς (cf. 1007b 15: ἀλλ'ὅσα ἐκεῖνος). Where there is no substance such as Callias, Socrates, or Christ, in order to bind *accidentia praedicamentalia* together as their real properties, every accident fits together with every other or with none. Both possibilities are equally fatal to communication. The pragmatic argument, which concludes from meaninglessness as negation of a *minimal* distinction of meaning to the impossibility of mutual understanding, would have arrived at its end. Within the total argument this is the situation in III, where the *a fortiori* argument has its continuation and completion. But this can't be shown in detail here (cf. the papers referred to in n. 5 above). To sum up (cf. also the end of n. 21 above), whereas I and II show the unavoidability of postulating differences in meaning, III shows the unavoidability of accepting substances as subjects or bearers of some meanings (attributes) but not of others. We could label I and II a "transcendental deduction of different categories" (without specifying which ones). Then we would have to label III a "transcendental deduction of the category of substance" (as opposed to accidental categories). So, it is not until III that one can speak of "οὐσία" as "ὑποκείμενον" as well as, correspondingly, of "συμβεβηκὸς" as property. Even at the beginning of III "οὐσία" is still to be taken as a synonym for "τί ἐν εἶναι" in the sense of (abstractly defined) meaning. And it is precisely because different meanings which do not belong definitionally together have nothing to do with each other that we must accept different subjects with which some meanings (now conceived as real properties) are compatible and others are not. Otherwise there would not be any order in the world or regularity (rules) in the language. In other words, communication would then be impossible. But even then (at the end of III) Aristotle has not yet "deduced" (in the transcendental, not the ordinary, sense of this word) the necessity of accepting οὐσία as τί ἐν εἶναι in the sense of essential as opposed to accidental properties. The substances "deduced" in III are still mere *hypokeimena* ("bare particulars"). The "deduction" of οὐσία as essence (and as a result of necessary as opposed to accidental properties) must wait until *Metaphysics*, VII, 3.

CHAPTER 3

AQUINAS ON ARISTOTLE: SOME EXAMPLES
(EXCLUDED MIDDLE, SUBSTANCE AND GOD)

In what follows I shall be confining myself to three interrelated examples. The first concerns the first principles of demonstration, especially the Principle of Excluded Middle[1] (1), the second the doctrine of substance (2), and the third that of the relationship between God and the world (3). The examples are so chosen as to show why the answer to the Aristotelian question of whether it falls to one and the same science to deal with the principles of demonstration and of substance must be a positive one. This question has already been addressed in the first ἀπορία of Book III of the *Metaphysics*[2]. The choice of these three examples is intended to explain why a positive answer to the question is also important for Aquinas. It is also intended, at least indirectly, to expose some misinterpretations of Aristotle.

The choice of those three examples is meant to explain why the positive answer to this question is also important as far as Aquinas is concerned. It is also meant to uncover, at least indirectly, some misinterpretations of Aristotle.

---

[1] *Editor's Note:* For the terminological hesitation in the Principle of the Excluded Third or Middle see the Foreword and the Chapter 1.

[2] Aristotle, *Metaphysics*, 995b 7 ff.

1

In his Commentary on Aristotle's *Metaphysics* Aquinas introduces the Principle of Excluded Middle as complementary to PNC in the following way: "After having argued against those for whom both contradictory propositions can be true, Aristotle argues against those for whom there can be a middle between the contradictories: for them not always either part of the contradiction is true"[3]. If so, then it is the conjunction of both principles that yields the meaning of propositional negation: if p is true, then not-p is false, and vice versa. But inasmuch as modern logic bases both principles on propositional negation, it must define them differently. Let us explain the difference by beginning with some historical considerations.

The origin of the Aristotelian discussion of the first principles is to be found in the disputes which Plato waged against those Protagoreans who had denied the very possibility of saying something false. Plato demonstrated the possibility of saying something false by having Socrates state that Theaeteus is flying while he was actually sitting. In arguing thus, Plato was applying his fundamental discovery of the distinction between reference and predication. For if we fail to make such a distinction, we would, in attempting to attribute "flying" to Theatetus, have to attribute it to the flying Theatetus, and Plato would not yet have made his case. In other words Plato's discovery is that the predicate does not share in the constitution of the subject. And it is precisely by applying this discovery to the proposition "Theatetus is flying" uttered under the given circumstances that Plato succeeded for the first time in establishing the case for PNC, as Aquinas was later to formulate this principle. For in so doing Plato had not yet said that if the original proposition is false its negation ("Theatetus is not flying") must be true, nor indeed that, in general, contradictory propositions cannot both be false, as he ought to have said, had he in fact presupposed the validity of the definition of propositional negation. In order to take this additional step the Principle of Excluded Middle is required, as Aquinas pointed out. This can, in turn, be established without having recourse to

---

[3] Thomas Aquinas, *In libros Metaphysicorum*, n. 720.

the meaning of propositional negation but simply –as in Aristotle[4]– with reference to the predicate "false"[5]. Therefore it is not the definition of propositional negation which is presupposed by both PNC and Excluded Middle, but rather that definition presupposes the two principles individually. For, if according to PNC, *at most* one of two contradictory propositions can be true, and according to Excluded Middle *at most* one can be false, then only by invoking both –and only then– can one say that if one of them is true the other must be false and vice versa. So in connection with each of the two principles taken separately, which is how Aquinas takes them, negation should not yet be understood to mean propositional negation in the sense defined by propositional logic, nor should either of the two principles be understood truth-functionally. They are not equivalent but rather complementary to each other. So it is not surprising that on Aquinas' construal far from depending on the foundations of formal logic they provide them.

In defining the two principles independently of truth-functionality and distinguishing each so sharply from the other, Aquinas is only following Aristotle. Whereas Aristotle considers not only the Protagoreans but Protagoras himself[6] and Heraclitus as well to be the main opponents of PNC, insofar as both of them make "everything true"[7], it is for Aristotle above all Anaxagoras, who, in holding that "there is something in the middle of the contradiction", "makes everything false"[8]. For "when things are mixed [as in Anaxagoras] the mixture is neither good nor not-good, so that one cannot say of any thing that it is true"[9].

That contradictory propositions cannot both be false does not yet imply that if one is false the other must be true. This stipulation, viz. that at least one of the two must be true, follows only under presupposition of

---

[4] Cf. Aristotle, *Metaphysics*, 1011b 23-27.
[5] Thomas Aquinas, *In libros Metaphysicorum*, n. 721. For details see note 18 below.
[6] Cf. Aristotle, *Metaphysics*, 1009a 6 ff.
[7] Cf. Aristotle, *Metaphysics*, 1012a 24 ff.
[8] Aristotle, *Metaphysics*, 1012a 26f.
[9] Aristotle, *Metaphysics*, 1012a 27 f.; ROT. More on this in section 2.

the so-called Principle of Bivalence. But here, too, one must be careful not to mistake the modern variant of Bivalence for its Aristotelian or Thomist counterpart. Only the former may perhaps be, and indeed often has been, taken as identical in meaning with the truth-functional definition of negation[10]. The confusion of Aristotelian Bivalence with propositional negation, though, can easily be avoided –if only because in the former, unlike the latter, only one proposotion is involved (either p or, alternatively, not-p, where "not" in "not-p" is, of course, not yet to be understood truth-functionally). Aristotelian Bivalence does not rest on the fact that there are only two possible truth-values linked with each other by means of propositional negation. It is based rather on the fact that, for any proposition, there are only two possibilities of making a claim about it, viz. either by affirming or denying it (be this p or, separately, not-p): if in affirming p the claim succeeds, then p is true, whereas if in affirming p the claim fails, then p is false, and correspondingly –but separately– for not-p. Likewise, if in denying p the claim succeeds, then p is false, and if in denying p the claim fails, then p is true and correspondingly –but separately– for not-p. This is the genuinely Aristotelian form of Bivalence. Here "p" and "not-p" have not been directly confronted with one another. It has merely been stated that "p" can be true as well as false and that, when seriously uttered, it has to be either true or false. But this is not the same as to say that if "p" is true then "not-p" is false and *vice versa*, since so far nothing has been said about "not-p". And similarly for "not-p"[11]. The fact that any seriously

---

[10] For one example among many others cf. H. Weidemann's commentary on Aristotle's *Peri Hermeneias* (Berlin 1994, p. 229).

[11] Here is to be found some similarity with intuitionist logic, but only inasmuch negation there does not mean "it is proved that not-p" but "it is not proved that p". Accordingly, as far as negation is concerned, truth-functionality runs in intuitionist logic as follows: (1) if p is true, then not-p is false; (2) if p is false, then not-p is true; (3) if not-p is true, then p is false; (4) if not-p is false, then not-not-p is true (but not, as in classical logic: (4') if not-p is false, then p is true). In view of this, an intuitionist logician might prefer to speak of "proof-functionality" rather than of "truth-functionality". But either way negation is to be understood functionally and so very differently from the way it is understood by Aristotle or Aquinas in connection with the PNC and of excluded middle (cf. also n. 17 below).

uttered single proposition, be it affirmative or negative, includes either a successful or an unsuccessful claim to truth and the fact that no proposition includes a claim to falsity suffice, in combination with Aristotelian Excluded Middle, to justify the transition from "not both contradictory propositions can be false" to "if one contradictory proposition is false, the other is true"[12]. They do not, however, suffice to exclude the possibility of both being true. To do this is precisely what Aristotle and Aquinas expect of PNC.

One might ask what advantages accrue to such a division of labor between the first two principles. One answer to this question is that on Aquinas' interpretation one would not be compelled to restrict the range of validity of Excluded Middle. This is a far-reaching topic[13]. It can only be touched upon here with a view to examining what advantages it offers for the interpretation of Aristotle. Consider, for example, the vexed question of *futura contingentia*. Aquinas' interpretation turns on the adverb *determinate* and its cognates. He construes them in such a way that it is possible for the one or the other of two contradictories ("tomorrow there will be a sea battle" and "tomorrow will not be a sea battle") to be considered true today, provided one does not specify which one. (This is consistent with the one of the two being considered true and the other false, once again provided one doesn't specify which is which)[14].

This genuinely Aristotelian approach has been severely criticized by both modern classic and modern intuitionistic logicians. The modern classical logician Peter Geach, for example, writes: "People have tried to maintain...that of a pair of contradictory predictions relating to a future contingency neither need be true. (Sometimes they say that neither need

---

[12] In combination with Bivalence what Excluded Middle is intended to exclude is that the truth is to be sought in a *tertium* that is neither p nor not-p.

[13] Suffice it to say that for Aquinas it is never necessary as it is sometimes for the intuitionist to shift from Excluded Middle (or Bivalence) to intuitionist *tertium non datur*.

[14] "Quae sunt de contingentibus, necesse est quod sub disjunctione altera pars contradictionis sit vera vel falsa; non tamen haec vel illa determinate" (Thomas Aquinas, *In Peri Hermeneias*, n. 204).

be *determinately* true; but this qualification, though it may make their doctrine easier to swallow, is quite devoid of sense)"[15]. It is true that Geach does not expressly refer to Aquinas, but the criticism clearly applies to him[16]. The same applies to the intuitionist logician Michael Dummett who in connection with the same doctrine speaks of "philosophical confusion"[17]. Whether or not this criticism is correct

---

[15] "The law of excluded middle" in *Logic Matters*, p. 81.

[16] Of course, in connection with Excluded Middle, Aquinas would not say that "neither need be *determinately* true" but rather that, it being impossible for both to be false, both could be true, though only indeterminately. But the difference seems to be quite irrelevant for the criticism at issue (and perhaps rests on a slip of pen). If understood as referring to the future outcome, the modal expression "both *could* be true" would obviously convey an absurdity, whereas if it is taken to refer to the the time before, it expresses the very definition of "*futura contingentia*" (cf. also the end of the main text).

I take "could" (in "both *could* be true") as corresponding to double possibility. Modern modal logic accepts the equivalence of "Mp" and "MMp" (cf. G. E. Hughes and M. J. Cresswell, *An Introduction to Modal Logic*, p. 44 f.; cf. also *A New Introduction to Modal Logic*, London and New York 1996, p. 52 f.) but is well aware of the fact that implication of the latter by the former is not always intuitively obvious, it being open to the same kind of reservations as the implication of "LLp" by "Lp" from which it derives ("...this is both a disputed question and one of some obscurity", ibid., p. 43 = p. 51 of the new version). To avoid any misunderstanding I shall not use standard modal operators. I take double possibility ("could") as implied by, but not implying, single possibility ("can"); otherwise Excluded Middle would come into conflict with Non-Contradiction. Taken as I do, the expression "both *could* be true" corresponds neither to an inclusive nor (of course) to an exclusive, but just to a non-exclusive, "or". This seems best to catch the otherwise (i. e. in terms of standard logic) indeed elusive meaning of "*indeterminate*". With this proviso I thouroghly agree with the stress laid by H. Weidemann in his commentary on the importance of time-relative modalities for the issue of "*futura contingentia*" (cf. note 10 above and note 18 below).

[17] Cf. M. Dummet, "Bringing about the past" in *Truth and other enigmas*, p. 338 (in connection with the doctrine of divine foreknowledge). As regards the allegedly "curious doctrine according to which a disjunction can be said to be true without its members being true or false" (Mignucci as cited by Gaskin, cf. note 18 below) some have even spoken of "Aristotle's fantasy". And, as long as one clings to

depends, of course, on whether, along with modern logicians, one takes the truth-functional definition of propositional negation as the basis for the first two principles or, following Aristotle and Aquinas, one adopts the opposite stance. Now, even without dealing directly with Chapter 9 of *Peri Hermeneias*[18], one can recognize the advantages of Aquinas's

---

truth- (or proof-) functionality in connection with the two first principles, rightly so.

[18] At the beginning of that chapter 9, Aristotle frames the question of *futura contingentia* in terms of the validity of Bivalence. After a long discussion he rejects in the end only propositional negation (cf. H. Weidemann's commentary referred to in note 10 above). One cannot say (as Weidemann does) without begging the question that by virtue of this fact alone the validity of Bivalence in the case of future contingencies has been rejected as well. In fact, Aristotle's way from Bivalence to Propositional Negation goes through three stages: (a) Bivalence, (b) Excluded Middle, and (*via* (b) along with Non-Contradiction) (c) Propositional Negation. In *Metaphysics*, IV, 7 Aristotle establishes (a) by means of the definition, first ("μὲν"), of "false" and, then ("δὲ"), of "true"; and it is not before *Metaphysics*, 1012b 10-12 that he establishes (b). The connection between (a) and (b) is as follows. "False" is "to say of what is, that it is not, or of what is not that it is" (1011b 26 f.). If so, then, first of all, not all assertions need be false. (The *possibility* of true assertions has been left open). For assuming that one were to say of that which is that it is, then, according to this definition of "false", one would (at the very least) not be saying anything false, and similarly if one were to say of that which is not that it is not. To get from "not all assertions need be false" (the *non-necessity* of all assertions to be false) to "it is not possible for all of them to be false" (the *impossibility* of all assertions being false, which corresponds to (b)) all that is needed is to consider the case of assertive affirmation and negation of the same thing (1012b 10-12). So (b), viz. the impossibility of all propositions being false, has been demonstrated without recourse having been had to (c). As far as I know, the first (and until 1996 only) author known to me who, in connection with the problem of *future contingentia*, questions the possibility of dealing with the Aristotelian principles in terms of truth-functionality is Dorothea Frede (cf. *Aristoteles und die 'Seeschlacht'*, Göttingen 1970, p. 76). D. Frede calls her interpretation "traditional" (cf. *Oxford Studies in Ancient Philosophy*, (III), 1985, p. 31). Cf. now also R. Gaskin, *The Sea Battle*, Berlin 1996, p. 149, and B. Hafemann, *Aristotle's Transzendentaler Realismus. Inhalt und Umfang erster Prinzipien in der "Metaphysik"*, Berlin/New York 1998). A non-truth-functional view of the principles makes the concept of practical truth possible thereby loosening

interpretation for a proper understanding of Aristotle by referring to a related text which has itself been much discussed, if not as often.

If one reads through the entire explanation given by Aquinas in n. 1808 and n. 1809 of his commentary on the *Metaphysics*, one may wonder why there has been so much disagreement among interpreters as what the beginning of *Metaphysics* IX, Chapter 4 means. The Aristotelian text reads: "If what we have is the possible or a consequence of the possible, evidently it cannot be true to say, 'this is capable of being, but will not be', –a view which leads to the conclusion that there is nothing incapable of being"[19]. The controversy turns on the words "'this is capable of being, but will not be'". From Aristotle's rejection of such a statement some interpreters have on the basis of the principle of plenitude ("if p is possible it will sometime occur") inferred that Aristotle espoused a weak form of determinism. But since this would contradict Aristotle's position in the foregoing chapters of the same Book IX, other interpreters have felt obliged to tamper with the text as a whole[20]. However, if one takes into account the genuine Aristotelian meaning of Excluded Middle, as expounded by Aquinas, then Aristotle's point is almost trivial, viz. that in talking about future contingencies one must not say that some event is possible but will not happen; otherwise one would be treating one of the two contradictory alternatives as impossible, viz. the one that will not be actualized. And since, contrary to the tenets of the Megarians, the latter is not less possible than the former, this would amount to confusing 'false' with 'impossible', thereby destroying the distinct meaning of 'impossible' itself ("...concluding that there is nothing incapable of being"). However, the possible, though unrealized, alternative can only *post factum* be deemed "false". At the time that the prediction was made the alternative that only afterwards will turn out false is not less true than the other –but only true only *indeterminate*.

---

the rigid dichotomy between "truth (about the past)" and "freedom (for the future)" (cf. Chapter 11, "Discovery and Verification of Practical Truth", as well as the end of the present chapter).

[19] Aristotle, *Metaphysics*, 1047b 3 ff.

[20] Cf. for the controversy R.T. McClelland, "Time and Modality in Aristotle" in *Archiv für Geschichte der Philosophie*, 63, 1981, pp. 130-149.

Thus, it is only by departing from the genuine Aristotelian meaning of the first principles, as preserved by Aquinas, that one can speak of our text as "the hardest passage"[21] in *Metaphysics* IX.

2

As regards the relationship between substance and accidents, it is possible to detect a departure from Aristotle in Aquinas' early period. Consider, for example, the famous passage on analogy in Aquinas' commentary on the *Libri Sententiarum* of Petrus Lombardus: "Analogy may be spoken of in three different ways: first, with respect to meaning but not with respect to being, for 'being healthy' is to be found only in the animal...; or with respect to being but not with respect to meaning...; or with respect to both..., as in the case of substance and accidents; with respect to these the common nature must have some being in that of which it is said, albeit in varying degrees of perfection". Aquinas is here clearly referring to the no less famous beginning of the second chapter of *Metaphysics* IV. But whereas Aquinas sharply distinguishes between analogy as it pertains to "health" and as it pertains to "being", no such distinction is to be found in Aristotle's text. Accidents *are* no more than, say, the color of urine *is* itself healthy; accidents are only substance in one of its ever-changing manifestations or in one stage of its development. However much it may be in accord with the *Categories* to attribute some kind of being, be it ever so slight, to the accidents, it is assuredly not in accord with the *Metaphysics*[22]. Granted Aquinas did not go as far as Duns Scotus was later to go, for whom substance and accidents partake in the same way of univocal being. Still, at least at the beginning of his career he took a step, however small, in the same direction. *Via* Scotism this would eventually culminate in the brand of

---

[21] Cf. R. Sorabji, *Necessity, Cause, and Blame*, London 1980, p. 136.

[22] Cf. Aristotle, *Metaphysics*, 1030a 25 - b 3, where, with reference to the same examples, Aristotle equates accidents with not-being even more clearly than in 1003a 33-b 10.

modern rationalism later devastatingly criticized by Kant. For, curiously enough, it was Kant, who by subjecting the Scotist-rationalist approach to critique in his First Analogy of Experience, restored the genuine Aristotelian meaning to the kind of analogy known since Cajetanus as "*analogia attributionis*". Had Aquinas gone the whole way, i.e. had he attributed to the accidents being in the same sense that he attributed being to substance, then like Scotus and rationalism he would have been forced to accept a strong parallelism between the ideal realm of concepts and the realm of reality (*ordo et connexio rerum idem ac ordo et connexio idearum*), i.e. in the sense of Scotus' *distinctio formalis a parte rei*[23]. But this was not even the case in Aquinas' early commentary on Petrus Lombardus' *Libri Sententiarum*, let alone in the works that were to follow.

Remarkably, neither in his *Summa contra gentiles* nor in his *Summa theologiae* did Aquinas repeat the threefold division of analogy of his early commentary. Instead he is to be found operating with another division which corresponds exactly to the Aristotelian text at the beginning of *Metaphysics*, IV, 2. In this respect one might perhaps speak of an evolution similar to the one Aristotle underwent in the period from the *Categories* to the *Metaphysics*. Be that as it may, Aquinas now distinguishes between analogy in the sense of the relationship of the many to the one (*plurium ad unum*) and analogy in the sense of the

---

[23] This is the sense criticized by Kant in connection with the relationship between substance and *accidentia*. Since according to Aristotle *accidentia* have no proper being, the distinction and the relationship between the *accidentia* and the substance can only be logical or *secundum rationem*, and the same is true of Kant as well. The restoration of the genuine Aristotelian sense occurred, of course, only within the narrow limits of *substantia phenomenon*. Nevertheless, the similarities are worth noting. Kant writes: "The determinations of a substance, which are nothing but special ways in which it exists, are called *accidents*... If we ascribe a special [kind of] existence to this real in substance... this occasions many misunderstandings... But... it is unavoidable, owing to the conditions of the logical employment of our understanding, to separate off..."; *Critique of pure reason* (Transl. Kemp-Smith), A186 f./B230 f.

relationship of the one to the other (*unius ad alterum*). In both *Summae*[24] the context is that of the names that can be attributed to God. To be sure, in the *Contra gentiles* there is still some trace of a difference between the case of being and that of health. However this time the difference is also to be found in Aristotle. The difference lies in the fact that the analogy of "being" that obtains between substance and accidents now corresponds rather to the analogy or *proportio unius ad alterum*, whereas that of "health" corresponds rather to the *proportio plurium ad unum*. I say "rather", because in the end there is not much difference –either for Aristotle or for Aquinas –between the two kinds of analogy. It seems that with his twofold division of analogy Aquinas is now simply trying to be as faithful as possible not only to the spirit but also to the letter of the Aristotelian text at the beginning of the second chapter of *Metaphysics* IV. For whereas in the case of the word "healthy" Aristotle gives as the point of reference (or "focal meaning") the meaning of health itself[25], in the case of "being" he does not mention being itself but gives rather "substance" (οὐσία) as the focal meaning, and this not just once but several times[26]. In so doing, he only makes more conspicuous the fact that there is no common being of which both substance and the accidents partake. So it is the Aristotelian treatment of "healthy" with reference to "health" –and not his treatment of "being" with reference to "substance"– which, when misunderstood, leads to that reification of abstract concepts so typical of rationalism. For, of course, in the case of "health" it is only the animal itself, which is properly called "healthy" –and not some non-existing abstraction "health". Health, being itself an *accidens*, cannot have any real properties, not even that of being healthy. As Aquinas himself put it, when commenting on Aristotle, there is no *ordo accidentis ad accidens quantum ad rationem subjiciendi*[27], i.e., sub-

---

[24] Cf. Thomas Aquinas, *Summa contra Gentiles*, I, c34, and *Summa theologiae*, I, q13, a5.

[25] Aristotle, *Metaphysics*, 1003a 35.

[26] Aristotle, *Metaphysics*, 1003b 5-10.

[27] Thomas Aquinas, *In libros Metaphysicorum*, n. 635. "There is no accident of an accident". Aristotle, *Metaphysics*, 1007b 2 f.

stance is the only fitting subject of ontological attribution[28]. Thus it is only after the intervention of, or after abstraction by, the intellect –in other words, not *a parte rei* but merely *secundum rationem*– that something may be attributed to that which, like the accidents, has no being of its own. The resulting propositions may be true but they do not concern reality as such but only as it is known to us. It is only in the ideal realm of concepts, but not in the real realm of substances, that a distinction can be drawn between substance and accident or between the accidents themselves. But within this realm the distinction must be consistently adhered to. Otherwise those consequences ensue which, as we saw in section (1), Aristotle[29] ascribed to Anaxagoras, viz. the negation of the Principle of Excluded Middle, and which Aquinas correctly understood to imply that all propositions would then be false. This requires some explanation.

In order to establish the Principle of Excluded Middle it was essential that the two realms of reality and ideality be kept apart. The separation of the two was Plato's great achievement. Even in Anaxagoras' day it was still scarcely possible to do so, and even less possible to distinguish them in the way that Aristotle was later to do, i.e. by allowing substantial and accidental determinations to be mixed together in one and the same substance –the only true subject of ontological predication– while at the same time keeping them apart in the ideal realm of concepts. The former thesis, viz. that within one and the same substance no real distinction obtains between properties, has recently been dubbed "substantial holism"[30]. This is a suitable formula for contrasting the Thomist *distinctio rationis cum fundamento in re*[31] with the Scotist *distinctio formalis a parte rei*. For in the former case, as in that of substantial holism, a distinction within substance can only be acknowledged after an act of abstractive intervention on the part of the intellect. Like the *distinctio rationis cum fundamento in re* substantial

---

[28] "Actiones sunt suppositorum" Thomas Aquinas, *Summa theologiae*, II-II, q58, a2.

[29] Cf. also Thomas Aquinas, *In libros Metaphysicorum*, n. 735.

[30] Cf. T. Scaltsas, "Substantial Holism" in T. Scaltsas *et al.* (eds.). *Unity, Identity, and Explanation in Aristotle's Metaphysics*, Oxford 1994.

[31] The terminology is, though, Suarezian.

holism renders the isomorphism between the *ordo rerum* and the *ordo idearum*, so characteristic of the Scotist-rationalistic *distinctio formalis a parte rei*, impossible. Of course Anaxagoras also thought that all determinations of a thing were mixed together in it, but in addition to this he went on to assert that the things themselves were all mixed together, with the result that his was not only a substantial holism, but also, like Quine's[32], a thorough-going holism. Since, however, Anaxagoras could not as yet have distinguished between the real and the ideal realm, he unwittingly read the universal mixture of real determinations back into the realm of concepts. Concepts which, as a result, are no longer distinguishable from one another, can have no *fundamentum in re* or –to put it the way Aquinas did, when commenting on Aristotle on Anaxagoras– *talia sunt eis* (Anaxagoras' friends) *entia, qualia suscipiunt vel opinantur*[33]. The situation is similar to that of those Protagorean sophists, denounced by Plato, who let predicates share in the constitution of the subject, thereby reducing reality to the changing opinions we happen to hold about it and making all propositions true. But the analogy is only partial. For whereas the deniers of PNC thought that one was entitled to use any concept for any other with the result that one could give any answer to any question and it would still be true[34], the deniers of PET argued that insofar as all things as well as their determinations are mixed together, no distinct concepts exist for which one might claim

---

[32] For the similarity between Quine's and Anaxagorean holism cf., e.g. H. Noonan, *Object and Identity: An Examination of the Relative Identity Thesis and Its Consequences*, Martinus Nijhoff, The Hague 1980, p. 95: "If one thinks of colors in Quine's way, so that one regards 'Red', for example, as naming all the red stuff there is, i.e. the spatio-temporally scattered totality of red substance, then red, like any temporal parts, will *be red*, and so will not only be a color, but will also have a color". This amount to a denial of the impossibility of *accidentia* of *accidentia* and of selfpredication. For Plato's criticism of Anaxagoras in this respect cf. C. Meinwald, *Plato's Parmenides*, Oxford 1991, p. 14.

[33] Thomas Aquinas, *In libros Metaphysicorum*, n. 677; cf. Aristotle, *Metaphysica*, 1009b 25-28.

[34] Cf. the Chapter 2, "Aristotle's defense of the Principle of Non-Contradiction" (especially note 4 on Aquinas).

objectivity, with the result that all we say is false[35]. To this Aristotle as well as Aquinas object that our conceptual distinctions do indeed have a *fundamentum in re* which accounts for the truth as well as the falsity of our propositions, even if this does not take the form of a strict isomorphism between our concepts and the real determinations of the actual world. The *fundamentum in re* which underlies our conceptual distinctions may instead be compared with the typing of two letters, say "A" and "B", one superimposed upon the other. By typing them in this way, both would appear mixed together in an unrecognizable fashion[36]. Nevertheless, if one were to say that in the resulting mixed-up pattern there is an A or a B, one would be saying something true, whereas if one were to say that there is, for example, a C, one would be saying something false. It is by means of these and similar considerations that we are led to the conclusion that it is one and the same science that deals with the first principles and with substance qua being as such[37].

3

One cannot speak of Creation in connection with Aristotle as indeed one must when considering Aquinas. If only for this reason, the question of the relationship between God and the universe must be put differently in each case. And yet the conceptual basis for treating this question is in

---

[35] "Unde illud quod est mixtum, nec est bonum nec non bonum, nec album nec non album. Et sic est aliquod medium contradictionis. Et per consequens sequitur omnia esse falsa". Thomas Aquinas, *In libros Metaphysicorum*, n. 735.

[36] Cf. P. Geach, *Mental Acts* (Appendix). The "abstractionism" criticized by Geach corresponds not just to Scotus' but already to Averroes' position referred to by Aquinas in *Summa theologiae*, I, q79, a3, ad2 ("...(sicut) lumen requiritur ad videndum...ut medium fiat actu lucidum..."). The alternative position ("...(sicut) lumen requiritur...ut fiant (colores) actu visibiles...") lies midway between abstractionism and Geach's outright rejection of abstraction.

[37] Cf. Aristotle, *Metaphysics*, 995b 7 and Thomas Aquinas, *In libros Metaphysicorum*, n. 347.

both cases the same. Let us explain this with respect to Aquinas, starting with one of his most influential interpreters in our century.

In his well-known books on participation[38], Cornelio Fabro's bases this relation on that form of analogy which Aquinas defined in terms of the proportion between the many and the one (*plurium ad unum*) and which he, following Aristotle, attributes to expressions like "healthy" or "medicinal". As was already pointed out in section (2) such terms are more properly treated in a manner similar to the way the term "being" is treated, for though "health" can stand on its own conceptually, only substances like animals *are*, strictly speaking, healthy. Fabro proceeds the other way around: he treats "being" in the same way he does the term "health", the latter being considered in isolation from its subjects of attribution. The result is a markedly Neo-Platonic interpretation of the Thomist doctrine of creation as some kind of falling-off. One has to concede that this is one possible way of interpreting Aquinas. But there are certain philosophical advantages to following the genuine Aristotelian approach, and not least when it comes to interpreting Aquinas' doctrine of creation.

One undesirable consequence of letting the question of creation turn on the analogical relation of the many to the one (*plurium ad unum*), and not on that of the one to the other (*unius ad alterum*), is what I shall call "the onto-theological picture theory". The drawbacks of the epistemological picture theory are connected with representationalism. One sometimes finds such a theory attributed to Aquinas or even to Aristotle. The attribution is made mainly on the basis of the use of the word "similarities" (*similitudines*, ὁμοιώματα) at the beginning of *Peri hermeneias*, where it refers to human concepts. It is nonetheless mistaken. However paradoxical it may sound, similarities (*similitudines*) need not be similar (*similes*). Concepts are *similitudines* of things and of their determinations, but they are not *similes* to either. In that moment, in which one denies an isomorphism between the real and the conceptual realms, one has simultaneously deprived these similarities of any basis upon which they might be judged similar. Rather than go into this again, I refer the reader to my explanation of the non-recognizability of the

---

[38] Cf. C. Fabro, *Participation et causalité*, Louvain 1962.

superimposed letters A and B at the end of section (2). Let us go on instead to explain why the onto-theological picture theory does not leave us any better off than its epistemological counterpart.

If one considers being on its own terms, i.e., without reducing the object of this reflection to something merely conceptual, then the doctrine of participation as the relationship between God and His creatures comes to look very much like the doctrine according to which *substantia* and *accidentia*, in the manner of the relationship *plurium ad unum*, both partake of the same being (though not necessarily univocally as in Scotus). But then the creatures, far from being *similitudines Dei*, would be only similar to Him. In itself one might find this fairly reasonable. But the drawbacks of such an approach are not difficult to see, for it belittles not only God but also His creatures. It belittles God inasmuch as Being itself has thereby been taken as the measure of both God and His creatures. Without such a common measure they could not be adjudged similar to one another. And to claim that the common measure is God Himself would not greatly improve matters but would rather belittle His Creation as well. For then one would be obliged to treat the creatures as an imperfect imitation, if not of Being as such, then of God. To belittle God's creation in this way is unavoidable as long as one has not abandoned the idea that for His creatures to be likenesses of God –as Aquinas argues they must be– they must be similar to their Creator. In comparison to God all things would be, in fact, imperfect, but inasmuch as God is incommensurable with anything else, any such comparison between God and His creatures is out of the question. But, then, what can it mean to be a similarity, if not to be similar?

The key to answering this question lies in the notions of participation and of analogy. To take participation first, it can be understood in two different ways. Following some authors[39], one can distinguish between participation by composition and participation by similarity. Not surprisingly, Fabro's interpretation is almost exclusively based on the former. Fabro understands *compositio* in the sense of the so-called *distinctio realis* between essence and being *(esse)*. In this view

---

[39] For C. Fabro see *op. cit.*, above. Cf. also L.-B. Geiger, *La participation dans la doctrine de S. Thomas d'Aquin*, Paris 1953.

participation implies that the essence, which in itself is only potentially, is actualized by its being (*esse*). The difficulty here is how the process of actualization is to be conceived without at the same time treating the essence as having received its being; for then the essence would predate its creation. One could try to circumvent this by regarding the essence of things as God's own ideas. God and His objects would then very much resemble each other. But since one cannot project something which after all belongs to God straightaway into His creatures, one would have to grant the essences a certain amount of independence from God, if only to avoid pantheism. This corresponds to Duns Scotus' doctrine of *ens diminutum*. Scotus construes creation as the translation of (a part of) the somewhat independent ideal order into the real order[40]. And inasmuch as such a translation implies an isomorphism between the two orders redolent of the *distinctio formalis a parte rei*, Scotus' doctrine represents, as indicated in section (2), an inversion of the Anaxagorean position, which translates the general mixed-up character of the real world into the world of concepts. But even if in the end one were compelled to deny that Aquinas had in *any conceivable case* assumed with Aristotle the weaker *distinctio rationis cum fundamento in re* in connection with the relationship between substantia and *accidentia*, he would still be closer to substantial holism than to any form of Scotist rationalism[41]. For Aquinas, too, the abstract order of ideas is *not* the same as the real order of things.

Much more promising than the *participatio per compositionem* is the alternative offered by the *participatio per similitudinem*[42]. It is here that the notion of analogy comes into play. Since this alternative concept of participation does not presuppose a real being, of which both God and

---

[40] Scotus' formula for this reads "*formaliter ex se, principialiter ab alio (sc. Deo)*".

[41] One may regard substantial holism as incompatible with Aquinas' doctrine of transubstantiation. The incompatibility, though, only arises when one approaches transubstantiation in the extrinsic manner of the Scotist *distinctio formalis a parte rei*.

[42] It is also the one favored by L.-B. Geiger (note 40 above); cf. also John F. Wippel, "Aquinas and Participation" in John F. Wippel et al. (eds.), *Studies in Medieval Philosophy*, Washington 1987.

His creatures partake, the reciprocal relation implied by the *analogia plurium ad unum* no longer enters into the picture; it has been dislodged by the non-reciprocal *analogia unius ad alterum* –not reciprocal, of course, but also not semi-pantheistic, as if God's creatures were some kind of *accidentia Dei*, but in a sense that allows for an immediate relationship between the two while nevertheless recognizing that this relation is only real for the creatures. From this alternative standpoint the Being of the created world is nothing apart from its being created[43]. In this case, since God is not created at all, it is no longer possible to posit a similarity between God and His creatures based on a Being of which both partake. Apart from our need for abstract conceptualization there is no such common measure of God and His Creation. It is precisely in this lack of incommensurability that the sense of a likeness that is not similar to that of which it is the likeness is to be found. If one takes the full doctrine of analogy into account, one will have no difficulty in understanding this. As has already been said, in applying the analogy of the one to the other (*unius ad alterum*) to creatures in their relation to God, one need not think of the former as accidents of the latter. Nevertheless there is also a certain degree of analogy between both sorts of relationship, between that of accidents to substance, on the one hand, and that of creatures to God, on the other. The analogy consists in the fact that Creation does not contribute even the slightest amount of being to God any more than the *accidents* increase the being of a substance. The non-similar similarity which creatures *are* in relation to God thus coincides exactly with the kind of analogy which Aquinas' commentator Cajenatus called *analogia proportionalitatis*. This analogy has the peculiarity that, provided some identity of function between the terms involved is preserved, there need exist no relation of mutual similarity between them. In fact *analogia proportionalitatis* means nothing more than identity of function and does not imply a corresponding identity of content. On the other hand the non-identical content may or may not be similar. It is similar, for example, in the case of equal quotients with different factors, for, however different the latter may be, they must all

---

[43] Cf. F. J. Pérez-Guerrero, *La creación como asimilación a Dios: Un estudio desde Tomás de Aquino*, Pamplona 1996.

be numbers. But the content may vary to the point of incommensurability, as is sometimes the case with metaphors and is surely the case where the relation is that between God and His creatures. Aristotle called this kind of analogy "ὁμονύμια κατ' ἀναλογίαν", and as one can see from *Metaphysics* XII, 5, it already had for Aristotle an important part to play in the progress of human knowledge from the universe to God. One might even say that the world, although not similar to God, is nevertheless a likeness of Him in the sense of being His Metaphor or parable[44]. To be sure, in comparing the world with a parable, one would be ascribing to it a certain mythical character. But given the role which falls to non-being in explaining the world, even this would not be necessarily wrong. It is true that such an approach would more nearly resemble Plato's account of the world in the dialogue *Timaeus*[45] than Aristotle's metaphysics, Plato's "verisimilar" narrative (εἰκός μύθος) in this dialogue being closer than Aristotle's doctrine to that of Creation. But even for Aristotle φιλόσοφός ought to be φιλόμυθος as well[46]. Moreover, according to Aristotle, without God as the only unqualifiedly necessary being, of all the things that are, none would be[47]. The importance of not-being in explaining the world could hardly have been underscored more effectively[48]. Now some have thought that in his theology Aristotle was not up to the high analytical standards set by his own ontology, and that this is bound to be even more the case with Aquinas. But neither of these presumptions corresponds to the facts. As

---

[44] Aquinas often combines the *analogia per similitudinem* with the metaphor of light cf. *Summa theologiae*, I, q4, a2; and Aristotle, *Metaphysics*, 1071a 15-17.

[45] Plato, *Timaeus*, 29A-D.

[46] Cf. Aristotle, *Metaphysics*, 982b 18; Thomas Aquinas, *In libros Metaphysicorum*, n. 55.

[47] Aristotle, *Metaphysics*, 1071b 24 f.; cf. 1050b 19.

[48] "...in se considerata (creatura) nihil est...". Thomas Aquinas, *De aeternitate mundi*, n. 7; cf. also *In II Sententiarum*, d1, q1, a5 ad s.c. 2. Even if the world had been from eternity, it would remain so: "...esset nihil, si sibi relinqueretur: ut si dicamus aer semper fuisse illuminatum a sole". *ibid.*; cf. also *Summa theologiae*, I, q104, a2.

emerges not only from the end of *Metaphysics* IV[49] but also from *Metaphysics* IX and XII, in Aristotelian theology God is dealt with in strict dependency on the two first principles without which no communication, let alone demonstration would be possible. To put it briefly, since God is the only necessary being which cannot not be at all (οὐδαμῶς)[50], it is only in him that the two principles find the unrestricted validity they must have, and so it is only in theology that Aristotle's ontological inquiry, no less than that of Aquinas, can find its completion. Here, too, the analytical principles of argumentation and the ontological principle of substance belong together in one and the same science of metaphysics.

---

[49] Aristotle, *Metaphysics*, 1012b 13-31.

[50] Aristotle, *Metaphysics*, 1072b 8; cf. also, e.g., 1071b 13-29.

Chapter 4

The Unity of Aristotle's Metaphysics

It is quite possibly the obsession with the problematic unity of onto-theology that has obscured our view of the genuine unity which the metaphysics of Aristotle evinces. This unity consists in the interconnectedness of PNC and the concept of substance. At a crucial stage in the argumentation PET is also made to play a key role. PNC and PET must here be understood in terms of their original Aristotelian formulations, which do not correspond at all points to their modern counterparts. In the end it turns out that the unity of metaphysics, insofar as it is based on the interconnectedness of these axioms with the idea of substance, also includes the unity of onto-theology. I shall for the most part be keeping the confrontation with other interpretations of Aristotle to a minimum. Instead I shall be concerned to demonstrate that Aristotelian metaphysics continues to be of more than historical interest for the ongoing philosophical discussion. By this I refer above all to the conflict between process or event ontology on the one hand and substance ontology on the other. Several different schools of thought may be subsumed under the first rubric. They extend from the "process thought" inspired by Whitehead, which has come to enjoy a broad following at least within the realm of American theology, to the poststructuralist thought of, say, a Gilles Deleuze in France, which has been especially influenced by Heidegger. I shall however be confining myself in what follows primarily to the event ontology of Quine, himself a student of Whitehead. In its anti-essentialism it understands itself explicitly as anti-Aristotelian. And not without good reason, since essentialism, construed as the antithesis of holism, represents the heart of the Aristotelian theory of substance. This, in turn, constitutes the heart of his metaphysics and at the same time the bonding agent which joins ontology with theology in Aristotle.

There has hardly been an aspect of this theory which has been so persistently misunderstood as his theory of substance. There have been chiefly two sorts of misunderstanding. The first one reproaches the theory of substance for exhibiting a tendency toward reification that borders on rigidity. This reproach has often been summed up in the handy rubric "substantialism". The second misunderstanding is closely related to this but goes well beyond it, construing metaphysics as a whole and Aristotelian metaphysics in particular as primarily a theory of opposites which tears asunder what belongs together: identity and difference, unity and plurality, above and below... and, not least of all, thing and property, substance and accident. Accordingly post-metaphysical thinking circles in Heidegger around the poetic phenomenon of the oxymoron –of composita like "bittersweet"– which ranges from the doctrine of the ambivalence of emotions to that of the event [*Ereignis*] as evidence [*Er-äugnis*, a placing before the eye (*Auge*)]. For here it is not a question of a circling with center and periphery, or with core and surface, but in the final analysis only a question of a straight line with neither beginning nor end, in short of something which does not so much represent the opposite of substantialism as a total indifference to it. We shall have occasion to see to what extent open doors are being rushed when it is a question of the Aristotelian theory of substance.

Books IV, VII-IX and XII of the Aristotelian metaphysics form a continuous argument; I shall confine myself to them. The path leading to this argument had, however, already been paved at the beginning of Book III with the question as to whether it falls to one and the same science to treat both the principles of all forms of argumentation (ἀξιόματα) and substance (οὐσία), i.e., the principles of knowledge, on the one hand, and substance, on the other[1]. The impetus which

---

[1] Aristotle, *Metaphysics*, 995b 5-10. The comprehensive study by Wilfried Kühn, *Das Prinzipienproblem in der Philosophie des Thomas von Aquin* (Amsterdam

Aristotle by means of his positive reply to this question gives to the inquiry extends all the way to that principle (ἀρχή) which by virtue of its very substance (οὐσία) is activity (ἐνέργεια) and which Aristotle calls God (ὁ θεὸς)².

The subject of metaphysics is being *qua* being and what is attributed to it as such³. This formula cannot in itself be reduced to any of the meanings of 'being' that have customarily been distinguished since Frege. A practical paraphrase might read as follows: What is (such-and-such) insofar as it is (such-and-such) –and not, for example, insofar as it is true (by virtue of being conceived in such-and-such a manner)⁴. The parenthesized expression stands for any essential predicate (e.g., 'man'). A particular exists normally as a such-and-such (e.g,. as a man). Nevertheless the subject of metaphysics includes neither general essences like man nor individuals like Socrates to which they are attributed as predicates; it is at best the everywhere constant relation between the essence and its bearer which proves later on to be an identity relation⁵. Therefore the predicative, existential, and identity meanings of 'being' are all present in the formula. The provisional character of this characterization was already indicated by our having placed in parentheses the variable ('such-and-such') for an essential predicate, which refers to the existence of an individual with which the essence is supposed to be identical. The parentheses mean: not everything exists as an entity expressible in predicate form (= as a such-and-such, a this or that). This applies at least to the very first (highest) substance (οὐσία). God's essence is not this or that (such-and-such). Inasmuch as God is pure activity, what He is can only be expressed by means of a verb; the fact that it is pure activity means that it is not an activity of something (expressible as a substantive), but a self-subsistent activity (and therefore not

---

1982), may on the whole be read as an (failed) attempt to demonstrate that a positive reply to this question was already rooted in conceptual confusion in Aristotle.

2   Aristotle, *Metaphysics*, 1072b 25.
3   Aristotle, *Metaphysics*, 1071b 20 and 1003a 21f.
4   Aristotle, *Metaphysics*, 1027b 29-1028a 4; cf. also 1011b 9-11.
5   Aristotle, *Metaphysics*, VII, 6.

expressible as a predicate)⁶. The same already applies, however, *mutatis mutandis*, to everything else which one may also, apart from the very first substance, address as being: everything which one might designate with the name "substance" –regardless of what this may mean and regardless of everything which may be subsumed under it. But even excluding the very first substance, everything which may be expressed by essential predicates (as general) like "man" represents only a tentative and passing stage in the search for what being as such is.

Significantly, Aristotle opens his *prima philosophia* with an inquiry concerning the question of whether by "Being" or "beings" substance (οὐσία) is always (*inter alia*) intended⁷. With this the meanings of "being true" and "being accidental" are tacitly excluded as not belonging to metaphysics⁸. Only being in the sense of the categories (i.e., of real beings, *Metaphysics,* VII) or in the sense of actuality (activity) and potentiality (*Metaphysics* VIII-IX), where "actuality" must be taken to exclude any connotation of a "real" or nominal predicate, are considered. Here the progress from metaphysics considered as a simple theory of categories to metaphysics as the genuine theory of first principles may be seen to emerge. Every theory of categories runs the risk of imposing conceptual or linguistic structures upon reality or of construing the former as mirroring the latter. In the case of metaphysics considered as a theory of principles this risk is not present. Principles may, however, be either ontological or epistemological. This notwithstanding, there is one single ontological principle: substance, which in the final analysis is to be understood as actuality (either pure actuality or the actuality of something potential). And, precisely because the accidents cannot lay claim to any sort of being (as such), one is *not* entitled to regard the categories as a reproduction of reality. They represent a mere abstraction in which the fact has been disregarded that there are in each case only substances (modified in such-and-such a manner) –and

---

[6] Aristotle, *Metaphysics,* 1071b 20.

[7] Aristotle, *Metaphysics,* 10033a-b 18.

[8] Cf. Aristotle, *Metaphysics,* 1031a 15f.

not substances *and* accidents. Still, metaphysics as the theory of principles also deals with the epistemological principles, PNC and PET. It is to this which the qualification "and what is attributed to being as such in itself" in the opening formula of the object of metaphysics[9] alludes. The interplay between PNC (and PET) and substance as (in the end the only!) ontological principle characterizes the genuine unity of Aristotelian metaphysics, as will be shown in the following. Now, if that upon which everything else depends (ἤρτηται[10]) is substance, then "it is of substances that the philosopher [in *philosophia prima*] must grasp the principles and the causes"[11]. Among these PNC is to be reckoned the first principle.

The key text in this respect, whose influence extends as far as the demonstration of the very first substance, God, is the following[12]: "And in general those who use this argument do away with substance and essence. For they must say that all attributes are accidents, and that there is no such thing as being essentially man or animal. For if there is to be any such thing as being essentially man this will not be being not-man or not being man (yet these are negations of it); for there was some one thing which it meant, and this was the substance of something. And denoting the substance of a thing means that the essence of the thing is nothing else. But if its being essentially man is to be the same as either being essentially not-man or essentially not being man, then its essence will be something else. Therefore our opponents must say that there cannot be such a definition of anything, but that all attributes are accidental; for this is the distinction between substance and accident –white is accidental to man, because though he is white, whiteness is not his essence. But if all statements are accidental, there will be nothing primary about which they (the statements) are made, if the accidental always implies predication

---

[9] Aristotle, *Metaphysics*, 1003a 21f.

[10] Aristotle, *Metaphysics*, 1003b 17, cf. 1072b 14.

[11] Aristotle, *Metaphysics*, 1003b 18f.

[12] Here and in the following I have sought to emphasize only the essential points at issue. For a more detailed exegesis cf. "Die philosophische querelle des anciens et des modernes", as well as Chapters 3 and 4 above.

about a subject. *The predication, then, must go on ad infinitum. But this is impossible; for not even more than two terms can be combined. For an accident is not an accident of an accident, unless it be because both are accidents of the same subject.* I mean, for instance, the white is musical and the latter is white, only because both are accidental to man. But Socrates is musical, not in this sense, that both terms are accidental to something else. Since then some predicates are accidental in this and some in that sense, those which are accidental in the latter sense, in which white is accidental to Socrates, *cannot form an infinite series in the upward direction —e.g., Socrates the white has not yet another accident; for no unity can be got from such a sum.* Nor again will white have another term accidental to it, e.g., musical. For this is no more accidental to that than that is to this, and at the same time we have drawn the distinction, that while some predicates are accidental in this sense, others are so in the sense in which musical is accidental to Socrates; *and the accident is an accident of an accident not in cases of the latter kind, but only in cases of the other kind, so that not all terms will be accidental. There must, then, even in this case be something which denotes substance (οὐσία). And it has been shown that, if this is so, contradictories cannot be predicated at the same time*"[13].

The justification of PNC constitutes nothing less than a genuine transcendental deduction, first of the categories in general and then, however, of the category of substance as the subject of properties (*especially* in the underlined sections of the text). The first step (only briefly summarized at the beginning of our text) consists in showing that words possessing meaning are necessary in order to be able to discourse at all but that this would, on the other hand, be impossible if each word were to mean everything[14]. A minimum in the variety of meanings is therefore indispensable. No meaningful word can denote the same as those other words which are not related to it by definition. If 'man' is to serve as a vehicle for communication, then it cannot mean the same as all other words whose meaning (summed up in the

---

[13] Aristotle, *Metaphysics*, 1007a 21-23, 26-29, 31-1007b 18 (my emphasis).

[14] Cf. Aristotle, *Metaphysics*, 1006a 18-b 34, in particular b 6.

meaning of 'not-man') is different from it. Generally speaking, 'being' ('to be') cannot signify 'non-being' ('not to be'). Thus far substance (οὐσία) has been "deduced" only as an abstract meaning among others (τί ἓν εἶναι in the broader sense[15]). In this sense all meanings (including that of 'man'!) are related *per accidens* to one another, i.e., they do not evince any sort of ordering relation; in other words they do not constitute a logical space. For precisely this reason it is not enough to posit categorial distinctions. Ordering principles must also obtain among them, and with this the second step has already been taken: the 'deduction' of substance, this time as subject. This stands in need of explanation.

Meanings like that of 'man', 'white', and 'educated' exclude one another by definition and thus have nothing to do with one another. Nevertheless our language itself demands connections among such meanings. Otherwise it would exhaust itself in tautologies and so prove itself unsuitable for human communication. It is, however, not possible to establish such relations on the basis of accidents, i.e. here more specifically on the basis of meanings which are accidentally related to one another. For accidents (in this sense as well as in the sense of accidental properties –which still has to be shown) evince as ideal forms (τί ἓν εἶναι in the broader sense) only essential features but cannot possibly possess accidental properties (not even essential properties). Only real bearers of diversely constituted (ideally or significantly different) accidents, which may thus in the process turn out to be real properties, are capable of doing this. And these we term substances. As distinct from accidents (both in the sense of ideal meanings as well as in that of real properties) substances may include within themselves meanings (now considered as real properties) which (like man, white, and educated) are not related by definition to one another. That is why in the absence of substances something approximating to human communication would therefore be impossible. For the transcendental deduction of the category of substance as well as that of the categories in general it suffices therefore to investigate the conditions for the possibility of something like linguistic communi-

---

[15] Cf. Aristotle, *Metaphysics*, 1029b 12f.

cation, and both are inextricably tied up with the justification of PNC as a *reductio ad absurdum* directed against those who deny it: as soon as they speak they have already presupposed PNC and with it the categories including that of substance (*qua* subject).

Now the method of *reductio ad absurdum* depends in the following manner on PET: with the help of PNC it has been shown that not everything can be true, e.g., where the simultaneous attribution of both a meaning and its negation cannot both be true, for one meaning cannot imply every other meaning without negating itself. PET by contrast states that not everything can be false[16]. This would be the case only if one meaning were mixed with every other meaning. Then not only would a single meaning gradually drag all the others in its wake and thus negate itself in the end, giving (in the meantime) rise to the impression that every assertion which had been made by means of it must be true since ever more meanings might be predicated by means of it (and one of them would prove to be correct). They would instead be invalid right from the very beginning and so be incapable of forming a single true assertion ("...ὁ δ' Ἀναξαγόρου, εἶναι τί μεταξὺ τῆς ἀντιφάσεως, ὥστ' πάντα ψευδῆ. ὅταν γὰρ μιχθῇ, οὐκ ἀγαθὸν οὔτε οὐκ ἀγαθὸν τὸ μῖγμα εἰπεῖν ἀληθής"[17]). Now, if two sides of a contradiction cannot both at the same time be true but are just as incapable of being at the same time false, then, given the existence of something that is not possibly true (by virtue of its being a contradiction), its negation (on the basis of PET) will have to be true. The method of *reductio ad absurdum* consists in nothing else. We shall encounter it later at a crucial stage in the argument.

It does not suffice, however, to have demonstrated the necessity of there being at least *one* substance: there must be several substances. Otherwise chaos would continue to reign unchecked, and we would not even be able to speak. This may be traced to the fact that the accidents do not themselves possess any accidents, that they are not subjects for other accidents, that they cannot function as substances for other accidents. For under these circumstances no order may be

---

[16] Aristotle, *Metaphysics,* 1012b 11 f.

[17] Aristotle, *Metaphysics,* 1012a 26-28.

introduced that would be comprehensive enough to include everything that we might meaningfully be able to say by means of a combination of the most varied meanings. A single substance cannot be assumed to exist, but a variety of ordering and regulating factors must be presupposed, at least as many as are necessary in order to sustain linguistic communication of a sufficiently rich and diversified sort. This is, however, only possible if one posits essential properties for those substances which are intended to assume this function. For without such essential properties or, rather, proper substances corresponding to substances *qua* subjects the latter would once again flow into one another and become one, backsliding into a single subject having indefinitely many accidents. Several subjects or bearers of accidents are, however, only possible if each of them has its own proper essence, if each is not to be, or to be capable of becoming, all. Otherwise a *regressus in infinitum* would also arise from this standpoint. The same considerations which guided the "deduction" of substance *qua* subject are therefore still operative as guidelines in the deduction of substance *qua* essence. The transcendental deduction of essence corresponds to the Aristotelian demonstration that in the search for what οὐσία is one cannot rest content with a subject devoid of determinations (ὑποκειμένου)[18]. A thoroughly undetermined subject could only exist by itself. With this the Anaxagorean state of total mixedness[19] would not have been overcome. There would be nothing which would in itself be separated and thus there would also be no substances[20].

With this for the first time in the history of metaphysics a distinct separation of essential from accidental qualities or predicates is introduced. In the preceding it had only been hinted at in one passage (significantly in connection with Anaxagoras), namely in the passage where Aristotle repeats that everything would run together, this time resorting, however, to essential predicates exclusively as expressions for substance: 'trireme', 'wall', 'man' and no longer e.g., 'man',

---

[18] Cf. Aristotle, *Metaphysics*, 1029a 7-30.
[19] Cf. Aristotle, *Metaphysics*, 1009a 27.
[20] Cf. Aristotle, *Metaphysics*, 1029a 28.

'white', or 'educated'[21]. Although before the deduction of substance as essence one cannot distinguish between essential and accidental properties in these two triads, one is compelled in retrospect to do so. This distinction –between accidental and essential properties on the one hand and between substantial entities on the other– proves in fact to be crucial for the further development of this one continuous argument of the *Metaphysics*.

The distinction rests on the fact that a single substance may in fact include different accidents but not different essences (οὐσίαι). The doctrine of the invariance of species has its roots here since 'essence' at this point still means something like 'species' ('εἶδος'). Nevertheless the doctrine of the constancy of species does not in principle stand opposed to that of evolution. It does not rule out the possibility that what was formerly the exemplar of a given species might subsequently become the exemplar of another species. It only rules out the contention that in both cases the same individual might be involved, on the grounds that each individual (each substance) may indeed have different accidents but only a single essence, i.e., its own. Otherwise the Anaxagorean state would once again be reinstated, and everything could be contained in everything.

At the same time the aforementioned distinction points to an important similarity between accidents and essential properties: the former can just as little be transformed into one another as the latter. The two may at most replace one another but may not modify each other. Still the similarity is (as was to be expected) not pervasive insofar as the accidents cannot be modified at all whereas the essential properties (the proper essences concerned) can in fact be modified in some way or other. This could have been predicted from the moment on when the essence in question (εἶδος), as distinct from the accidents, even as a form of essence devoid of matter (τί ἐν εἶναι) in the rigorous sense), itself began to appear as subject[22]. In other words, whereas accidents cannot have accidents (not even essential properties as opposed to essential or definitory marks), essential properties (or,

---

[21] Cf. Aristotle, *Metaphysics*, 1007b 20f.

[22] Cf. Aristotle, *Metaphysics*, 1029a 1-3.

rather, essences) may very well have properties. Here, however, the properties concerned must be accidental properties since other essential properties would destroy the essence in question, leaving behind a single indefinite substance. On the other hand the accidental properties modify the essence (οὐσία) and the substance (οὐσία). Admittedly they do not modify them essentially, but they do modify them accidentally. One must not misunderstand the point of this comparison between essences and numbers –as so often occurs– as being that the (real) essence is as rigid as the abstract numbers, which of course cannot accept within themselves anything without negating themselves (as opposed to altering themselves –numbers are namely just as incapable of change as accidents). The comparison[23] should instead be understood in the following sense: since numbers as abstract essences do not allow of accidental modification, each and every modification of them would prove to be essential and thus, as it were, fatal. It is as if what was initially a human being were later to become a wall (or an olive tree): *this* particular human being would no longer exist. In this sense the comparison is not only very fitting but all the more exact as it does not prevent the accidental modification of real essences, this being only excluded in the case of accidents (they are comparable to numbers in this respect), or of the (accidental) modification and differentiation of οὐσία (substance and essence in one).

This proves that there can be no accidents, that there can only be substances modified accidentally in such-and-such a manner. As soon as one deals with the latter, one has already dealt with the former[24]. Insofar as they exist for themselves accidents are just as abstract as numbers, i.e., they do not exist at all for themselves, thus they fail to qualify as being as such[25]. They have absolutely no being of their own. In this respect the Aristotelian theory of being is to be distin-

---

[23] Aristotle, *Metaphysics*, 1043b 33.
[24] Aristotle, *Metaphysics*, 1028b 6f. "So to speak" (ὡς εἰπεῖν) should not be taken to suggest here that metaphysics treats in principle substance as well as accidents but rather that insofar as it handles the former it already handles the latter as well.
[25] Aristotle, *Metaphysics*, 1003a 33-b19.

guished from the theory of the univocity of being according to which being (*qua* existence) is attributed to both substance and accidents[26], but in the first case in the sense of subsistence and in the second in the sense of inherence[27]. To this one may counter: the accidents *are* only modifications of οὐσία (substance *qua* essence), which alone is what it (as a being) *is*. And the accidents *are* (real) only as such modifications. In and of themselves the accidents have no real being, no existence. They only exist as such for thought, through the act of abstraction; as a result one may attribute being to them only in the

---

[26] Cf. further G. Deleuze: "There has never been more than one ontological proposition: Being is univocal. There has never been more than a single ontology, that of Duns Scotus..."; *Différence et Répétition*, Paris 1969, p. 52.

[27] I know of no better commentary (and all the more valuable as it is oblique) on Aristotle's opposing theory with its explicit rejection of the theory of univocal being than A186f/B230f of the First Analogy of Experience in Kant's *Critique of Pure Reason*. The only difference is that what for Kant only applies to the *substantia phaenomenon* applies for Aristotle to the *substantia noumenon*. The text runs as follows: "The determinations of a substance, which are nothing but special ways in which it exists, are called *accidents*. They are always real, because they concern the existence of substance. (Negations are only determinations, which assert the non-existence of something in substance). If we ascribe a special [kind of] existence to this real in substance (for instance, to motion, as an accident of matter), this existence is entitled inherence, in distinction from the existence of substance which is entitled subsistence. But this occasions many misunderstandings; it is more exact and more correct to describe an accident as simply being the way in which the existence of a substance is positively determined... The correct understanding of the concept of *alteration* is also grounded upon [recognition of] this permanence. Coming to be and ceasing to be are not alterations of that which comes to be or ceases to be. Alteration is a way of existing which follows upon another way of existing of the same object. All that alters *persists*, and only its *state changes*. Since this change thus concerns only the determinations, which can cease to be or begin to be, we can say, using what may seem a somewhat paradoxical expression, that only the permanent (substance) is altered, and that the transitory suffers no alteration but only a *change*, inasmuch as certain determinations cease to be and others begin to be" (Transl. Kemp-Smith).

sense of "being true" (ὂν ὡς ἀληθής), which together with being *per accidens* (ὂν κατά συμβεβηκὸς) is to be excised from metaphysics[28].

The existence of material οὐσίαι is accepted by all parties to the dispute. Only for this reason are they taken as a point of departure, and not, for example, because they realize to a more perfect degree the being of substance[29]. Every material οὐσία (substance *qua* essence, which is itself at the same time subject) continually exists as (accidentally) qualified in such-and-such a manner. These modifications of it are not different from it in any real sense. There is no more difference between them than there is between the road leading from Thebes to Athens and that leading from Athens to Thebes. Otherwise the accidents would once again lay claim to their own being (*qua* inherence), and the substance would have to be understood as a nucleus which remains unaffected by the surrounding accidents. Such reified conceptions of substance are only appropriate to the theory of the univocity of being[30]. They are responsible for substance being regarded as something rigid. The substantialist reproach is based on just this type of misunderstanding (On the confusion of the Aristotelian with the Scotist/rationalist theory of substance contested by Kant cf. n. 33 below.).

The material οὐσία (substance *qua* essence) is always accidentally modified in such-and-such a manner. But each time it is only the substance which is continually changing, and not the substance accidentally modified in such-and-such a manner. With this a point as difficult as it is significant has been addressed. First with respect to its

---

[28] Aristotle, *Metaphysics*, 1027b 33 f.

[29] Aristotle, *Metaphysics*, 1029a 33f. Cf. my article: "Wie aristotelisch ist der Aristotelismus", in *Theologie und Philosophie*, 57, 1979.

[30] If one conceives of substance as a nucleus unaffected by its accidents, then it is in the final analysis dispensable. This is, in fact, what happens in the works of G. Deleuze (cf. above n. 32) or of W. V. O. Quine (see below under n. 65). Symptomatic in this respect are the following words of M. Foucault ("Theatrum Philosophicum" in *Critique*, 1970) vis-à-vis the aforementioned book by Deleuze: "Forego the circle, false principle of recurrence, forego the spherical organization of all that is; it is in a straight line [*sur la droite*] that everything recurs...".

significance: were it in each case an οὐσία accidentally modified in such-and-such a manner which were to become something else –and not simply substance– then we would have arrived at an ontology of process. In this case there would only be spatiotemporal phases or –as Quine would say– "slices" (now Socrates-in-this-state and then Socrates-in-that-other-state), of which what one calls substance (or even a real individual) would be composed, but not substance or the individual proper. This latter would be an *epiphenomenon*, a result of arbitrarily or for purely pragmatic reasons of convenience juxtaposed four-dimensional slices. The perspective peculiar to Aristotelian metaphysics appears inverted in the process ontology. Indeed for the former what is primary, even in the case of material substance, is not matter, not even the juxtaposition of matter and (essential) form but the (essential) form alone[31]. Otherwise one could regard the life of a human being as being shorter or longer –and then proceed to shorten or lengthen it, depending upon the interests of the individual doing the assessment in a given situation– e.g., in one's capacity as surgeon where one might require fresh bodily parts for an organ transplant. In keeping with the apophthegm of Anaxagoras things would be exactly as we choose to perceive them[32].

Secondly, as regards the complexity of the point at issue: among the most difficult sections of the difficult Book VII of the *Metaphysics* must be reckoned Chapters 4 and 5[33]. They prepare the way for the proof that the essence of substance –first substance– consists solely in its form (τί ἐν εἶναι in the narrower sense of essential form), thus in the case of, say, Socrates not in his being a man but in his soul as the actuality of something constituted in such-and-such a manner, namely,

---

[31] Cf. Aristotle, *Metaphysics*, 1029a 29-33 with 1028a 30-b 7.

[32] Cf. Aristotle, *Metaphysics*, 1009b 25-28. If it is not the man Theaetetus who sits or flies but in each case the sitting or flying Theaetetus, then everything must be true (cf. *Sophist*, 263A) –but this would constitute a violation of PNC. It is, however, not the sitting Theaetetus who stands up but Theaetetus.

[33] Cf. my "Für und wider den Nominalismus" in *Philosophisches Jahrbuch*, 96, 1989.

of an organic body[34]. "Man", "horse", etc. (and so forth) denote not a first substance but a compound of matter and form[35], no less than "Socrates" or "white man" (or more generally, no less than "an existing essence (modified) in such-and-such a manner, e.g. man in this or that state"). Something of this sort does not even qualify as something asserted *per se*, and even less would it constitute an essence (τί ἐν εἶναι, essential form)[36]. The first substance can accordingly only be an essential form without (individual or general perceptual) matter (as in the case of Socrates or man) because it would otherwise disintegrate into a series of phases or (spatio-)temporal slices from which an original (prior) unity, as is required by the (extensional and even intensional) equivalence of Being and Unity[37], could no longer be established. To put it differently, in contrast to the processes of event ontology material substances may indeed have spatial parts but not temporal ones[38]. A war, a sound –sheer events or processes– have temporal parts, i.e., they have duration, they are extended in space *and* in time. Now the ontology of events treats temporal and spatial parts as being equivalent. A war is never (i.e., at no point in the course of its being waged) completely there, just as little as a body, a war, or a sound (even if the latter are not bodies) is wholly present in any one of its spatial parts. This is not true of substances *qua* essential or substantial forms. They are everywhere and always whole, for they are composed neither of spatial nor of temporal (and –as we shall soon see– not even of intelligible or definitory) parts. They are, in other words, not to be situated either temporally or spatially (and also not in some conceptual or logical space). Thus far, however, this has

---

[34] Cf. my "Der Begriff der Seele in der Philosophie des Aristoteles" in K. Kremer, ed., *Seele. Ihre Wirklichkeit, ihr Verhältnis zum Leib und zur menschlichen Person*, Leiden/Cologne 1984, pp. 46-55.

[35] Aristotle, *Metaphysics*, 1035b 27-30.

[36] Aristotle, *Metaphysics*, 1029b 15-29.

[37] Aristotle, *Metaphysics*, 1003b 23-31.

[38] Even after their separation the latter might remain substances (cf. e.g. *Metaphysics*, 1028b 1-13). One might, e.g., think of the asexual reproduction of a cedar branch which once planted in the earth grows to become a cedar.

remained only an assertion. Nothing up until now conduces to the opinion that the ontology of events must yield to that of substance. This involves not only a question as to the choice of system but also a historical one.

It might from a historical perspective, to take this first, occasion surprise that I equate such constructions as "white man", "educated man", etc. –these are Aristotle's stock examples– which are necessary in the light of the exigencies of Aristotle's substance ontology, with the temporal parts of event ontology: the individuals belonging to a certain species cannot be built up out of phases (Socrates at time t, Socrates at time t', etc.) which, as units, would be prior to them. This second, historical objection is easily defused: each combination of substance and accident ("white man") includes in principle (i.e., with respect to its possibility), if perhaps not always factually, only a temporal cross-section, a limited phase in the course of an individual's existence (e.g. in the biography of a person). For this reason a comparison and even an identification of the two is completely justified.

The systematic objection is somewhat more difficult to refute. For the sake of brevity I shall take as my point of departure the detailed study, which H. Noonan has made of this question with respect to the respective advantages and disadvantages of the Quinean and Geachian standpoints[39]. Geach may here –with certain qualifications that have yet to be mentioned– be taken to represent Aristotle's ontology of substance, Noonan himself opts for –again not without making certain reservations that will likewise have to be discussed– Quine's ontology of events.

Geach (who argues more in the Thomistic than in the Aristotelian spirit) has raised what amount to two powerful objections to Quine's view: 1. The four-dimensional ringworm in which according to event ontology physical reality is thought to consist excludes any type of change in favor of a consistent determinism; 2. The reduction of individuals to four-dimensional rings (slices or phases) leads to absurd consequences. At the moment only 2. need concern us (in connection

---

[39] H. W. Noonan, *Object and Identity*.

with *Metaphysics* VII). (I shall be returning to 1. in connection with *Metaphysics* VIII and IX). One absurd consequence among others runs as follows: it would not be e.g. McTaggart himself who in 1901 believed in the truth of the Hegelian dialectic and who in 1921 then did not believe in it (any longer) but rather McTaggart-in-1901 and McTaggart-in-1921 respectively (the situation is comparable to that of the white man, who is –instead of the man "M"– alleged to be educated, or with the sitting Socrates, who –instead of Socrates himself– is supposed to stand (up), etc.). But a spatiotemporal slice of a philosopher cannot believe or "disbelieve" anything but only a philosopher, e.g., McTaggart. Now Noonan attempts to circumvent this objection in a manner that comes close to giving up Quine's position in favor of the Aristotelian one (significantly he no longer claims to speak here for Quine but for a "Quinean"): "My rejoinder to Geach's argument, I repeat, is the following: I reject his claim that the predicate 'is a philosopher' cannot be true of the time-slices McTaggart-in-1901 and McTaggart-in-1921, and maintain that in fact every time-slice of McTaggart during his philosophical career satisfied that predicate. Consequently, in order to avoid absurdity, I also hold that McTaggart-in-1901 and McTaggart-in-1921 are *the same philosopher*, despite the fact that they have different properties"[40]. The view that there is no cogent reason to insist that predicates like "is a philosopher" represent absolute equivalence relations may conceivably be adopted by a follower of Quine's[41]. This concession –the (contingent) identity of a temporal part (actually an accidental property: e.g., McTaggart's belief in 1901 in the truth of the Hegelian dialectic) with its subject– already implies, however, the sacrifice of temporal parts in favor of real properties. Accidental properties are

---

[40] H. W. Noonan, *Object and Identity*, p. 94.

[41] This last alludes to a difference in viewpoint between Noonan and Geach which cannot concern us here: The former attempts to circumvent the theory of relative identity espoused by the latter by presupposing only a relation of relative equivalence. Both stand opposed to what has been called "Leibniz's Law". If the law ("(a=b) $\rightarrow \forall F(Fa \leftrightarrow Fb)$") were allowed to apply unconditionally, then one could not have Fa=Fb be true and still have Ga Gb be true (e.g., 1/2 could not be the same rational number as 2/4 and still not be the same ordered pair as the latter).

distinguished from spatial parts insofar as they cannot be separated[42]. But they are also distinguished from temporal parts insofar as they —as opposed to the latter— are in effect identical with substance (not with substance plus a property!). In order to change over completely to the Aristotelian position, however, a second concession is still required (incidentally also from Geach). I can identify and count philosophers just as well as I can people (white tables as well as tables). But McTaggart *qua* philosopher (the table *qua* white) is himself in principle nothing other than a four-dimensional slice of McTaggart *qua* man. And this four-dimensional slice is just as incapable as the earlier one of believing or disbelieving something. The first is no longer a four-dimensional slice but something which exists the *whole* time. And it is this and only this which philosophizes (or not). A philosopher philosophizes just as little as a sitting man sits. To be a philosopher is already to believe (or not to believe) something philosophical, it is constituted by this, this is its essence (τί ἐν εἶναι in the broader sense). A philosopher believes this just as little as some accidental property may itself have accidental properties. A philosopher philosophizes *only* insofar as he is a man. This is not any easier but also not more difficult to understand than the thesis that no motion accelerates and/or that no number changes, even if we insist upon expressing ourselves in this way (i.e., misleadingly). Characteristically Quine has assumed the existence of variable numbers since the number of inhabitants of Berlin —the example is Frege's— (presumably) increases. (Frege himself was, by way of contrast, opposed to the introduction of variable numbers). From a mathematical (and from an Aristotelian) standpoint one would have to say rather: it is, of course, *not* the number of inhabitants of Berlin which increases; when Berlin increases its number of inhabitants, a smaller number of inhabitants is replaced by a larger one, just as when substance changes (e.g., when a train accelerates) the accidents which remain unchanged because they

---

[42] Cf. Aristotle, *Categoriae*, 1a 24 f.; and n. 45 below.

do not as such exist replace one another (and the train gradually assumes different but in themselves unchanged velocities)[43].

According to Aristotle (as opposed to, say, Thomas Aquinas) we still have not therewith (in the case of men, trains, etc., as distinct from philosophers, white men, wars, motions, or moving trains, etc.) reached that stratum at which we hit bedrock and the spade is forced to bend. From the essence or *forma essentialis* (man) we must rather proceed to the essential form or *forma substantialis* (e.g. soul) and –this is the crucial step– understand the latter *qua* act. This step, which corresponds to the transition from *Metaphysics* VII to *Metaphysics* VIII and IX, is indispensable, if the non-processual character of οὐσία is not to evade our attempt at understanding.

The transition to the essential form (the *forma substantialis* of Aquinas) finds perhaps its most acute expression in connection with the problem of definition. If an identity already obtains between the accidental properties and substance, then all the more so in the case of those properties which constitute the essence of substance. In the latter case the identity involved cannot be merely contingent. The necessary identity of essential properties (*genera and differentiae*) with one another implies therefore that substance and definition are only included in the final differentia[44]. Just as there is no substance which would be constituted by its essence plus accidental properties but only a substantial essence differentiated (accidentally) in each case in such-and-such a manner where the accidents are contingently identical with it, in a similar way the final differentia is nothing other than a genus modified by the other differentiae in which the differentia have always already entered into a necessarily real identity with the genus (thus e.g., "two-footed/biped" or "rational" is only a special way of living). It is therefore wrong to conceive of the (real) genus according to a figure of Wittgenstein's as something like a fiber which extends across the entire length of a rope (i.e., here: through all species) toward which the differentia simply flock without modifying it, just as it is

---

[43] Cf. the Kant quotation in n. 33 below as well as the sentences italicized by me in the Aristotle quotation on p. 130 f. above.

[44] Cf. Aristotle, *Metaphysics*, 1038a 19 f.

false to conceive of the essence as a fixed core to which accidents are stuck like chewing gum to a table (Putnam's example). Both amount to confusing properties with parts. The stuck-on chewing gum is just as little a property of the table as the white paint (*pigmentum*) that has been applied to it. Property is only the having of paint (*color*), and this involves not only the part to which the paint had been applied –e.g., the tabletop– but the whole table, it is therefore identical –contingently– with the latter[45]. The same applies to the so-called necessary properties (which in the end, of course, constitute the substance itself as its essential form). Only in the act of abstraction (*ratione*) does a specific difference come to supervene on a genus which remains constant across all species. In reality (*a parte rei*), by contrast, there is no difference between the two (*distinctio rationis ratiocinatae* as opposed to the Scotist-rationalist *distinctio formalis a parte rei*). Here there can be no plurality of essential properties. "A single, final (*differentia*) will be the species and the essence [as essential form]"[46]. We can to be sure distinguish by abstraction several essential properties in a single substance (species) but no distinction corresponds to them *a parte rei* –unless it be, for example, that in plants the genus "living thing" appears modified not as in animals by sensibility but certainly by other, possibly unknown differentia. The schema "(*genus + differentia specifica*) = species (e.g., man)" is for metaphysics just as impractical as the schema "(substance + accident) = (e.g. white man)". Both lack that unity which befits being as such –in the

---

[45] The distinction between *color* and *pigmentum* –cf. L. Wittgenstein, *Philosophical Investigations*, I §57– corresponds, in fact, to that between accidental properties and parts in *Categoriae*, 1a 24 f.

[46] Aristotle, *Metaphysics*, 1038a 25f. Frede/Patzig in their commentary on *Metaphysics*, VII translate instead: "...the final difference [will] constitute(s) a unity..." ("μία ἔσται..." sounds, however, more like the Homeric "εἶς... ἔστο", which closes the unified argument of the *Metaphysics*). Cf. also Ross's translation which in my opinion has been unjustly criticized by Frede/Patzig. (1038 a with its "ὁ ὁρισμὸς λόγος ἐστὶν ὁ ἐκ τῶν διαφορῶν, καὶ τούτων τῆς τελευταίας..." has been passed over by them without comment. This seems to me to offer further confirmation of the fact that they do not exhaust the benefits of their own interpretative approach. Cf. my "Für und wider den Nominalismus").

case of material substance its *differentia* modified in each case in such-and-such a manner. In metaphysical exegesis the essence (man) must yield pride of place to the essential form (rational or rational soul). Chapter 12 of *Metaphysics* VII begins, to be sure, with the logical schema "superordinate genus –sequentially arranged differentiae" in order to end, however, with a single difference, in which no plurality of determinations is discernible *a parte rei*. The latter can as a result not be made to stand to one another in the relation of a series[47]. As actuality the essential form (τί ἐν εἶναι) is the realization of some matter, which exists only as potentiality[48], just as the soul is

---

[47] Aristotle, *Metaphysics*, 1038a 33f. Here too our disagreement with Frede/Patzig becomes evident. They comment (on 1038a 33): "What is meant is not that there could within οὐσία be no system of sequentially ordered differentiae; on the contrary they follow each other in the order dictated by the subject matter (cf. τὸ δὲ ἐχόμενον, 1037b 32). It is only that as far as οὐσία is concerned it is a matter of indifference in which temporal order its components are invoked and listed". In my opinion, however, a plurality of forms and thus a (temporal) sequence exist for Aristotle only in the act of abstraction (*ratione*) and in that of naming but not *a parte rei*. Duns Scotus, by contrast, interprets the passage in conformity with his *distinctio formalis a parte rei (In IV Sententiarum*, d11, q3, ed. Vivès, vol. XVII, pp. 395 ff.). He is obliged accordingly to tamper with the original wording of the text (cf. "...nullo modo potest intelligi, quod tota ratio quidditativa sit in ultima differentia...", *ibid.*, p. 430; "...vult dicere, quod nihil aliud est definitio quam primum genus cum multis differentiis...", *ibid.*, p. 431). This discrepancy may be traced to the fact that according to Scotus each form may have its own being: "...nec soli formae substantiali convenit dare esse...", *ibid.*, p. 432. This corresponds precisely to the distinction between subsistence and inherence attacked by Kant, cf. n. 33 above. The final sentence in Frede/Patzig concerning 1038a 33 seems to strike the right note: "A redundancy, which becomes apparent in the listing of parts in a certain grouping, must therefore be present in every grouping". But for precisely this reason there can be no arrangement *a parte rei*. Here Thomas Aquinas, who in other respects systematically overlooks the culmination of Aristotle's argument concerning material substance in the essential form (*forma substantialis* in his terminology), appears to haver been the only one to have hit the nail on the head. For more on this, cf. my book *Forma formarum*, Freiburg/München 1970, pp. 109-11 as well as 25f.

[48] Aristotle, *Metaphysics*, 1045a 25-33.

the realization of that of which the organic body represents only the potentiality, namely, of this or that manner of living as so modified in each case[49]. "The proximate matter [e.g. the organic body] and the form are one and the same, the one potentially, the other actually"[50].

As has already been pointed out, the crucial step consists, in fact, not so much in the transition from essence (*forma essentialis*) to essential form (*forma substantialis*) as in the fact that the latter comes to be grasped as actuality. This occurs in Books VIII and IX. Only as actuality is a formal determination able to combine in a single form (i.e., in itself) all those forms which exclusively precede it in what is only a purely logical analysis (*ratione*). As actuality, however, the essential form (ultimate *differentia*) is likewise not the unifying factor among other combined essential or accidental determinations of form. Otherwise it would continue to be one form among several, just as a syllable (or a house) would consist of letters (or bricks) and their juxtaposition[51]. If the metaphysical constitution of substance were to involve an amalgam of spatial or temporal parts, then the real or (in a logical definition) ideal compound would never be capable of forming a unity of properties. A part is never identical with the whole. In the case of real properties something else is involved. Here it makes no sense to speak of a compound at all[52].

The importance of comprehending the essential form as actuality makes it understandable even with respect to material and moving substances that the Substance Books of the *Metaphysics* end with a clarification of the concepts of actuality and potentiality, reality and possibility (Book IX), which at the same time prepares the way for the interpretation of the very first substance as genuine being as such. In considering the opposition substance/event ontology it is important to keep in mind the following twofold observation: 1. In light of its dissolution of substance into sheer accidents or into processual (independent spatiotemporal) parts, as distinct from real properties of

---

[49] Cf. Aristotle, *De anima*, II, 1, 421a 13-22. Cf. the article referred to in n. 41.
[50] Aristotle, *Metaphysics*, 1045b 18f.
[51] Aristotle, *Metaphysics*, 1043b 5-7.
[52] Aristotle, *Metaphysics*, 1045a 12-25.

a substance, the ontology of events must culminate in a determinism which amounts to the elimination of any form of real becoming; 2. The aforementioned dissolution renders otiose any sort of distinction between the essential form (substance), which is not a temporal process but a completed actuality, on the one hand, and temporal and therefore uncompleted becoming, on the other. The two points are related to one another. As the outcome of the analysis of PNC and PET at the end of Book IV[53] makes clear, it is just as impossible that everything becomes as that everything rests. For those who allow everything to be and not to be all things might be sooner said to have been brought to rest as to have been set in motion. Everything would already be in everything and so there would be nothing into which something could change. One must prove to them that there is something unmoved[54]. This must be explained further.

If all things belong to a four-dimensional continuum with spatial as well as temporal parts, then everything is, in effect, already given, everything already contained (Anaxagorean-style) in everything, and the only motion that can exist under these circumstances is that of an observer (or of science itself) who explores the continuum (which for inexplicable reasons is pre-existent) but does not, as it would have been possible to do –were he himself not unidirectionally oriented with respect to time– explore it "backwards"[55]. Every object in the four-dimensional continuum is then "simply *the content, however heterogeneous* [my italics], of some portion of space-time, however disconnected and gerrymandered"[56]. As Noonan indicates, this implies that everyday objects "[are] assigned a favoured position in our language and conceptual scheme only because of interest-relative

---

[53] Aristotle, *Metaphysics*, 1012b 21-31
[54] Aristotle, *Metaphysics*, 1010a 34.
[55] Cf. P. Geach, "Some Problems about Time", in *Logic Matters*, pp. 304-307. Cf. also P. Yourgrau, *The Disappearance of Time*, Cambridge 1992, where with recourse to the philosophy of Kurt Gödel it is shown to what extent Einstein, to whom Quine appeals for his conception of a four-dimensional worm (cf., e.g., *Word and Object*, p. 172), does not so much explain time as explain it away.
[56] W.V.O. Quine, *Word and Object*, p. 171.

considerations. Thus not only are there people, there are also temporal parts of people, there are physical objects of which people are temporal parts: for example, that spatio-temporally discontinuous object of which George Washington is the first spatio-temporal stage and the Post Office Tower the second. In addition there are such objects as that which consists of the first three decades of Washington and the last four decades of Reagan"[57]. If, however, there is "in reality" (as *substantia noumenon*) only a single spatiotemporal continuum, which we (or science) regard now this way, now that, then it is only we (or science) which changes. Realism and the repudiation of substances which are at each moment entirely present (i.e., which do not have temporal parts) are incompatible with each other just as, and for much the same reasons, that essentialism and holism are incompatible. If everything is already contained (Anaxagorean-style) in everything, then coming-to-be and perishing as well as becoming in general are only appearances, epiphenomena[58].

---

[57] "...the treating of time on a par with space is no novelty to natural science... There need be no *unchanging kernel* [(!) my emphasis] to constitute me the same man in both decades, any more than there need be some peculiarly Quinian textural quality common to the protoplasm of my head and feet..." (W.V.O. Quine, *ibid.*, p. 171 f.). After all that has been said above it should go without saying that the Aristotelian οὐσία (substance and essence) does not constitute an unchanging kernel (cf. n. 36 above as well).

[58] Quine's "Anaxagoreanism" is very well brought out in the following sentence: "If one thinks of colours in Quine's way, so that one regards 'Red', for example, as naming all the red stuff there is, i.e. the spatio-temporally scattered totality of red substance, then Red, like any of its temporal parts, will *be red*, and so will not only be a colour, but will also *have* a colour" (H. Noonan, *Object and Identity*, p. 95). Cf. C.C. Meinwald, *Plato's Parmenides*, p. 14, on the overcoming already in the works of Plato of Anaxagoreanism, which indiscriminately lumps together properties with parts. It might be objected against my interpretation of temporal parts in Quine that the latter distinguishes beween objects which like paths only cease in a metaphorical sense to exist and those which like persons and sounds cease temporally (cf. Noonan, *ibid.*, p. 85). But this need only denote a distinction among objects whose temporal extension may be either smaller or larger (or under certain circumstances even unlimited) but which are in each case determinable as regards their extent in advance. As for the rest Quine's theory can itself only be

In conformity with this conception present and past would coincide with the future (with the possible exception at best of that of the theories replacing each other) and modality with factuality. Possible is then whatever exists at some particular time, necessarily, or always. Chapters 3 and 4 of *Metaphysics* IX have often enough been interpreted in the deterministic sense of a Principle of Plenitude, which is presumed to be unconditionally valid in Aristotle. To this untenable[59] interpretation corresponds that of Chapters 6-10 of the same book which tends to deny the distinction between the actuality of substances and temporal processes[60]. It is, though, false that you now stand, since you are sitting (facticity), and still it is not impossible but possible (modality)[61]. It is possible because there is a *you* who –unlike an event– enters [*eingehen*] as a whole into each of his states, without, however, ever being exhausted [*aufgehen*] by them; more precisely, because there is an actuality, which is completed in every moment and so guarantees the identity of the subject (e.g. of the person) throughout time, i.e., renders it possible that this (the person) is present as a whole

---

understood in the sense of the Anaxagorean apophthegm (Aristotle, *Metaphysics*, 1009b 26f.): everything is immanent to a theory or interpretation. Only theories change and not things since these, of course, cannot exist apart from theories. There is an ineradicable tension between Quine's mythology in "Two Dogmas of Empiricism": "Physical objects are... comparable, epistemologically, to the gods of Homer", p. 44) on the one hand and the naturalism to which he aspires from *Word and Object* onwards, on the other. The former brings him into the vicinity of the poststructuralism of a Deleuze (cf. n. 32, 36, and 66 above).

[59] For *Metaphysics*, IX, 3 and 4 cf. Alfonso García-Marqués, "Der Begriff von 'Möglichkeit' nach 'Metaphysik' IX 3-4", *Philosophisches Jahrbuch*, 100/II, 1993, pp. 357-65; for IX.5 cf. Josef Stallmach, "Vertritt Aristoteles Metaphysik IX 5 selbst den megarischen Möglichkeitsbegriff?", *Archiv für Geschichte der Philosophie*, 46, 1964, pp. 190-205.

[60] The essay "Aristotle's Distinction between Energeia and Kinesis" by J.L. Ackrill (in R. Bambrough, ed., *New Essays on Plato and Aristotle*. London 1965, pp. 121-141) may be taken as representative of this entire school of thought. Cf. M.-Th. Liske's criticism in his essay "Kinesis und Energeia bei Aristoteles", in *Phronesis*, 1991, 36, pp. 161-178.

[61] Aristotle, *Metaphysics*, 1047b 13f.

in every moment –this would not be possible if it (he or she) were to possess temporal as well as spatial parts in the place of accidental properties as potentially fleeting states with which it (he or she) is in each case contingently identical.

Substances are related to processes as completed to uncompleted actions (or as actualities to actions). Like paths still to be traversed the latter always have their goals beyond them and therefore come to an end as soon as this has been reached, whereas in the case of the former the goal has always already been reached. To know is already to have known[62], just as much as for Aristotle there can be no gradual becoming of the essential form *qua* actuality. It is either there or not without first having to become[63]. Substance, and that means the essential form, is a completed actuality of this type[64]. Still, as long as actuality is only the actuality of a potentiality (as the soul is the actuality of the body), the unconditional validity of PNC has not been established, for everything may then be and not be. Since the entire theory was erected on the basis of PNC, it cannot be an occasion for surprise that at the end of the Substance Books one's gaze is once again directed toward it, and it serves at the same time as a propaedeutic for a discussion of the very first substance. Without it there could, in fact, be no being as such[65], but everything would vacillate indeterminately between being and not-being. "The reason is that every possibility (potentiality) is at one and the same time a possibility for the opposite (contradictory)"[66]. "Whatever is therefore potential can be as well as not be. But what potentially is not is possibly not. And what possibly is not is perishable... In itself perishable is, however what is perishable by virtue of its substance (κατ'οὐσίαν)"[67]. "Now, were there something which did not exist of necessity, then

---

[62] Aristotle, *Metaphysics*, 1048b 22-24.
[63] Aristotle, *Metaphysics*, 1039b 26; cf. 1043b 14, 1044b 21 as well as 1033b 5f.
[64] Aristotle, *Metaphysics*, 1050b 2.
[65] Aristotle, *Metaphysics*, 1026a 27-32, 1027b 25-1028a 4.
[66] Aristotle, *Metaphysics*, 1050b 8f.; cf. 1009a 35.
[67] Aristotle, *Metaphysics*, 1050b 11-14, 16.

nothing would exist"⁶⁸. The reasoning behind this argument will first be given in *Metaphysics* XII and then only in Chapter 6, which binds together most of the elements of *Metaphysics* IX, 8, in its proof of a pure actuality lacking potentiality as the very first substance and thus implicitly as the most authentic sense of being as such. In Book IV as well as in the Substance Books explicit anticipations of Aristotle's theology are to be found⁶⁹. *Metaphysics* IX, 8-9 in particular picks up the thread of argumentation that had been dropped in *Metaphysics* IV, 5-8, sometimes offering an almost verbatim repetition. This includes *inter alia* the fact that as long as potentiality (possibility) continues to exist, contrary (and thus also contradictory) opposites are simultaneously possible –e.g., in the case of future contingents⁷⁰. With this allusion has been made to PET, which in its original Aristotelian formulation states that contradictory assertions cannot both at the same time be false⁷¹. He leaves open the question of whether both may at the same time be true, this being, however, precluded by PNC. Now the passage which was designated above as crucial insofar as PET plays there a key role is the passage in *Metaphysics* XII⁷² in which the transition to theology is executed and through this to metaphysics as the science of being as such (substance) and of that which falls to it by virtue of itself.

At this point in our reflections one might ask why, if *Metaphysics* IV in the course of its elucidation of PNC and of PET explicitly looks ahead to the theology, *Metaphysics* XII does not, conversely, refer back to these principles. The simplest explanation for this apparent inconsistency would attribute it to the fact that Aristotle –unlike us– does not have a handy rubric at his disposal for designating both principles. Besides, *Metaphysics* XII, together with *Metaphysics* IV and VII-IX, did not originally constitute a literary unity. As for the

---

68 Aristotle, *Metaphysics*, 1050b 18-20.
69 Aristotle, *Metaphysics*, 1009a 36-38; 1010a 1-3, 34; 1012b 30 f.
70 Cf. Aristotle, *Metaphysics*, 1051a 10-12, which makes the meaning of 1047b 3-14 explicit, in conjunction with 1009a 35.
71 Cf. Aristotle, *Metaphysics*, 1012b 9-11.
72 Cf. Aristotle, *Metaphysics*, 1071b 13-26.

unity of the subject matter being treated, by contrast, there can be no doubt as to the fact that all these books contribute to the gradual and consistent development of a single argument. For the remainder of my exegesis, I shall be confining myself to the all-important interconnectedness of both principles with Aristotle's theory of substance. I begin with PET.

In his essay "What Price Bivalence?"[73] Quine considered the question of whether the Principle of Bivalence[74] may lay claim to unconditional validity. His reply is that he will hold on to it only for purely pragmatic reasons, namely for reasons having to do with the advantages which accrue to the Principle of Bivalence by virtue of the greater simplicity which it affords. There are certainly cases where there would be no reason to hold on to it: everywhere where the domain over which one quantifies is infinite and a decision for one or the other side of a contradiction is impossible. For example, one could not decide how many tables are (possibly) contained in a table standing before me: possibly more than n, possibly not more than n. This alone suffices to invalidate the Principle. If it is to continue to be valid, then only on the basis of an interest-relative decision in its favor. So long as one remains within the confines of pragmatism this is a consistent position, even if Quine does not hold onto the Principle of Bivalence, for the same reasons that metaphysical realism in

---

[73] W.V.O. Quine, "What Price Bivalence?", 90 ff.

[74] From an Aristotelian standpoint the Principle of Bivalence and PET are interlinked in the following manner: the former states that since every assertion is either true or false, then by virtue of the meaning of 'false' not every assertion need be false (1011b 23-29 taken in conjunction with 1012a 21-28), the latter states on the other hand that given two contradictory assertions both cannot be false (1012b 9-11) so that not all assertions can be false (against Anaxagoras as reported in 1012a 26-28). The difference between it and the modern formulation consists exclusively in the fact that according to the latter PNC and PET follow from the meaning of negation as defined in propositional logic so that they are –by means of a DeMorgan Law– capable of being transformed into one another whereas for Aristotle PNC (not all assertions are true) and PET (not all assertions are false), which are in fact not equivalent but only complementary to one another, when taken together only then yield the type of negation defined by propositional logic.

mathematics does when it rejects finitistic intuitionism, which replaces proofs by *reductio ad absurdum* and the application of the Principle of Bivalence with the construction of examples[75]. Quine did not have recourse to similar reflections with respect to PNC. If all scientific (= philosophical) assertions were empirically falsifiable, then there would be no reason for shying away from such reflections other than the weak one that the principle is not properly analytic but purely formal. For Aristotle the situation is different for several reasons: 1. PNC is for Aristotle not valid relative to our needs (e.g. to science or to communication) but is valid in itself[76]; 2. The fact that PNC does not concern being as being true[77] but being *qua* being becomes apparent at the very latest because of the necessity of having to assume substances as subjects (*Metaphysics* IV, 4) and thus already as essences (essential forms), and regardless of whether we succeed in knowing how many of those different substances which must in any case be assumed to exist are possessed of an existence which cannot be traced back to our manipulatory needs and which ones these are; 3. Since PET is not equivalent but complementary to PNC (not everything can be false/not everything can be true)[78], the difficulties which were mentioned above with respect to the Quinean example of possible tables in a single table do not arise for Aristotle. For even assuming a decision to be impossible this would be consistent with the simultaneous possibility of contradictory assertions –until a decision for one or the other side of the contradiction has eventually been made. PET, considered in itself[79], does not commit one to more than this. And this state of affairs corresponds to the latest stage which we have reached in following the course of the single continuous argument of the *Metaphysics*. As far as the proof of a very first

---

[75] Cf. M. and W. Kneale, *The Development of Logic*, Oxford 1964, p. 675ff.
[76] Cf. my article, "Pragmatistische und pragmatische Verteidigung des Nichtwiderspruchsatzes", in *Giornale di Metafisica*, 13, 1992, pp. 213-230.
[77] Cf. Aristotle, *Metaphysics*, 1027b 29-1028a 6.
[78] Aristotle, *Metaphysics*, 1012a 23-28, 1012b 9-13.
[79] Cf. Aristotle, *Metaphysics*, 1012a 29.

substance is concerned, though, this indeterminateness cannot be allowed to remain.

It is not to our purpose here to show to what extent the first five chapters of *Metaphysics* XII may be said to recapitulate the course which our analysis has taken up to this point[80]. The sixth chapter at any rate recapitulates its main features: "What is potentially can also not be"[81]. If there were no (immaterial) principles whose οὐσία (substance, essence, essential form) were actuality, then nothing of what is would be, since it is possible for something to be potentially without its already having come into existence[82]. This is followed by a reminder to the effect that even an Anaxagoras, despite his "holism", recognized in the form of *nous* the priority of actuality over potentiality[83].

The structure which this closing argument of the *Metaphysics* exhibits makes tacit use of PNC and PET in the following manner: Everything which is not merely actuality can also not be. Whatever can not be –under the assumption of an infinite time already elapsed– was not at one time or other. If everything which is could just as well not be, then nothing which is could be –nothing of that which in keeping with PNC must be false, for it would at once possibly be and not possibly be: the former since *ab esse ad posse valet illatio*; the latter on account of the Principle of Plenitude which would arise not for the potential infinite of the future but for the actual infinite of the past[84]. On the basis of PET, however, the contradictory of this,

---

[80] Cf. my article "Kritik und Metaphysik" in *Wiener Jahrbuch für Philosophie*, 1, 1968, pp. 67-91.

[81] Aristotle, *Metaphysics*, 1071b 19.

[82] Cf. Aristotle, *Metaphysics*, 1071b 20 f.

[83] Up to Aristotle, *Metaphysics*, 1072a 6.

[84] Thomas Aquinas returns in his *tertia via* to this argumentative strategy ("...quod possibile est non esse quandoque non est", *Summa Theologiae* I, q2, a3). Since his faith assures him, however, that there can be no actual infinite with respect to the past, he, unlike Aristotle, may only permit himself to make hypothetical use of it in the matter at hand: even if the world were to exist *ab aeterno*, one would be constrained to postulate a God. When viewed systematically this form of argu-

namely, that not everything which is can also not be, must also not be false. Since, though, by virtue of PNC both (everything can also not be and not everything can also not be) are incapable of being true together, there must be something that cannot not be and so something that can only be pure actuality. Everything else would be something which can be (*qua* activity) or not[85] and –in the case of an actual infinite– which sometimes would not have been (active). Only that which consists in nothing else but activity and, so, lacking in every form of potentiality, is a self-subsistent doing (subject *qua* activity as doing; can be sure of not losing its doing = its being). When viewed from this standpoint it is understandable that the culmination of the theory of substance in a single actuality (initially under exclusion of something like "white man" and later also of something like "man") belongs to the inner logic of that prolonged argumentation in which the *Metaphysics* consists. Everything which is something (such-and-such), even the sun which sustains the various species of living things[86], indeed even the entire universe[87], is something which acts in such-and-such a manner and so may fail in its activity and its actuality. Only in a principle which is nothing but its activity (= its actuality) is such an eventuality excluded[88]. This principle is, strictly speaking, PNC turned positive. Released from matter and potentiality it can as it were enjoy the unconditional validity which had been granted to it from the very beginning.

Heidegger once wrote of the Aristotelian God that one could not kneel before him. Others have thought that this God may be reconciled with the God of the Book of Exodus (3, 14). Among these may be reckoned the Schelling of the *Introduction to the Philosophy*

---

mentation would then have to be interpreted as follows: if the world were to exist *ab aeterno*, then the world would at the same time be an actual and a potential infinite –which is contradictory.

[85] Cf. Aristotle, *Metaphysics*, 1072b 13f.
[86] Cf. Aristotle, *Metaphysics*, 1071a 15f.
[87] Cf. Aristotle, *Metaphysics*, 1069a 19, 1075a 11ff.
[88] Aristotle, *Metaphysics*, 1071b 20.

of Mythology and the *Introduction to the Philosophy of Revelation*[89]. He thinks of him as the coming God, who will be what he will be. One might be inclined to regard this interpretation as a precursor of process-theology. For Aristotle, however, it makes no sense to speak of a divine process. The Aristotelian God is immutable. In order for him to change he would have to be something which acts in such-and-such a manner, a substance which undergoes changing states. But this is precisely what he is not, he being rather a pure activity, a pure action, if you will, which is borne only by himself. The fact that he is not a substance which acts but a pure, self-sustaining or substantial action or activity must not be taken to imply that he may be conceived of as a process. Were this the case he would have to be composed of a series of states (actions) which are borne by no substance (no subject). Now as far as the Aristotelian God is concerned there is, in fact, no such substance which might bear individual states (actions). But he is just as little composed of disparate, unconnected states (actions) which simply follow one another in ordered succession and none of which is identical with substance which in any case does not exist. The activity in which God consists is not the activity of a something. On the other hand it also does not resolve itself into a series of activities. All conceivable activities have their unity in him, and this one activity is indistinguishable from him. If therefore a God of this type acts in such-and-such a manner, he does not alter himself in so doing, since he is nothing other than ("his") acting in such-and-such a manner[90]. To conceive of him as mutable or as a process would be to misrepresent his essence as pure, temporally unextended actuality. One might conceive of him as a God, who, insofar as his activity is restricted by nothing apart from PNC, has on occasion been thought a God of the arbitrary. But this, too, would constitute a misunderstanding, even if it were only because Aristotle conceives of the activity, in which above all his God consists, as knowledge and even

---

[89] Fr. W. J. Schelling, *Werke,* Bd. XI and XIII.

[90] Cf. Aristotle, *Metaphysics,* 1072b 8.

more importantly as knowledge of itself[91], which represents at the same time that which is good for everything else as well[92].

Aristotelian metaphysics begins thus as ontology and reaches its culmination in theology, with which, however, it need not cease as at the end of a process. Nevertheless it remains throughout –from its commencement to its culmination– a theory of substance (οὐσία) *qua* being as such. It is only that substances (even the essential forms of first substances) are subjects of properties whereas the very first substance is a subject-for-itself, a self-subsistent activity, which depends on no other subject.

---

[91] Cf. Aristotle, *Metaphysics*, 1074b 33-35.
[92] Cf. Aristotle, *Metaphysics*, 1075a 11-1076a 5.

CHAPTER 5
METAPHYSICS AND REIFICATION

I must admit that I was long tempted to choose a different title for this lecture –one which seemed to give a better idea of its contents. On the other hand, the title I found so attractive did not seem suited to the note of solemnity which normally accompanies an inaugural lecture[1]. I was forced to suppress it –until today, at any rate; for today I have the opportunity of justifying it, and I hope to make the most of it. The title I wanted to use was "The Thing with the Thing".

"The Thing with the Thing": that has a certain ring of looseness about it, but it is also impossible to fail to overhear a note of reproach, as though someone were up to no good with something called a thing. This is in fact one of the connotations which attaches to the related word "reification". The latter is, of course, a derivative notion; but it has acquired such a well-established philosophical meaning in our time that one scarcely ever pauses to consider its humble origins –very much like that key expression of German New Left philosophy "unconstrained communication" (*herrschaftsfreie Kommunikation*)[2]. (It will soon become apparent that this parallel has not been chosen at random). One can, it seems, be "for" or "against" unconstrained communication, without giving further thought to the simple semantics of this high-flown phrase: "constraint", "dominion", "ἀρχή" (on the one hand "ἀρχή πολιτική", "ἀρχή δεσποτική", of course, but also "principles", or simply "beginnings"). Thoughtless appeal to

---

[1] Inaugural lecture delivered at the University of Münster (West Germany).

[2] The German word "*herrschaftsfrei*", rendered here as "unconstrained", might be translated literally as "dominionless". This would bring out more clearly than "unconstrained" the political connotations of the word as well as the connection, emphasized below, with the Greek ἀρχή.

freedom from dominion could therefore be a call for freedom from principles, freedom which has no beginning –in short, utopian freedom. On the other hand, such appeals for freedom from constraints or dominion are issued in the name of humanity, and thus directed against "alien" forces, which aim to control men's lives from without, rendering them objects, things. The call for "unconstrained communication" and the challenge to reification are thus related to one another. The point at which they meet is their critical or –to put it polemically– their inimical attitude towards the notion of metaphysics; for the word "metaphysics" has traditionally stood for all that which transcends the human realm –those alien principles or powers which must be rebuffed. Consequently, metaphysics is accused of a reifying and alienating tendency which must be challenged in the name of humanity.

Ideological attacks upon traditional metaphysics are generally launched from two quite different quarters, positivism and Marxism. Philosophically, despite all points of convergence, these are nonetheless distinguished by two quite conflicting methods: the analytical and the dialectical. From this methodological point of view the critique of metaphysics seems less gruff, but all the more biting. In the following I shall concentrate upon the analytical method. I am aware of the limitations imposed by this decision, but I believe there are advantages as well.

The advantages and disadvantages of this choice for a treatment of the critique of metaphysics are clearly marked out by Ernst Tugendhat in his comparison of the relations which linguistic analysis and hermeneutics (including dialectical method) bear to metaphysics: "One can view linguistic analysis as a sort of truncated hermeneutics, hermeneutics at the ground-floor level. It lacks historical dimension and a broadly based concept of understanding. Hermeneutics itself, on the other hand, lives precariously perched on the top floor, unconcerned with the stability of the foundations. The hermeneutical criticism... of traditional metaphysics... is directed only against the latter's limitations; the inherited ground-floor structures are placed under a protection order, but one keeps right on building on top of them... Linguistic analysis never got that far. Nonetheless, it is not interested in razing the building, as was positivism, it thinks itself possessed of new means and methods of effecting a more stable renovation"[3].

Forced to choose between the "beautiful risk" and hard work in the cellar I have chosen the latter. Thus, I shall treat the question of reification and metaphysics from the lower perspective of philosophical analysis. At the end of this paper, however, I shall permit myself to climb to the top for a brief panorama.

Since the days of its positivist origins analytical philosophy has altered its attitude to metaphysics considerably. Things have in fact gone so far that analytical philosophers no longer shrink from the name "Metaphysics"[4]. Of course, metaphysical leanings are also evident in works in which the word "metaphysics" does not grace even the subtitle. An example would be Anthony Quinton's book *The Nature of Things*. Quinton certainly claims for himself the right to do metaphysics –provided one understands metaphysics as "the attempt to arrive by rational means at a general picture of the world"[5]. Quinton thinks that both opponents and adherents of metaphysics will be able to agree on this minimal definition –with the simple difference of course that the opponents of metaphysics will consider the programe of constructing a general picture of the world hopeless.

Metaphysicians in the traditional vein will certainly have no quarrel with the minimal definition as it stands: in fact it expresses in everyday language the traditional task of ontology, conceived as the science of beings as such. Nonetheless it is not clear what has become of the second traditional concern of metaphysics, namely onto-theology: who, in other words, is to take over the task of philosophical theology? The above-quoted minimal definition of metaphysics as ontology does not necessarily entail that this question must go unanswered. For theology might still find a place within ontology as

---

[3] "Phänomenologie und Sprachanalyse", *Hermeneutik und Dialektik*, R. Bubner, K. Cramer and R. Wiehl (eds.), Festschrift for H.-G. Gadamer, Tübingen 1970, vol. II, 3f.

[4] Cf. P. Strawson, *Individuals: An Essay in Descriptive Metaphysics*, London 1959.

[5] A. Quinton, *The Nature of Things*, London / Boston 1973, p. 235.

the attempt to construct a general picture of the world. The answer given by implication in Quinton's book is, however, a very different one. For the result obtained in the first, ontological part of traditional metaphysics is thorough-going materialism in a new key[6]. The newness is to be found not so much in the result itself as in the method of obtaining it. Instead of approaching his task through the findings of natural science, as did the classical materialists, Quinton's method is logical. Even such things as abstract entities, numbers, thoughts, values and necessary truth –so intractable to the positivist onslaught– are "materialized"[7]. No room here for an immaterial God, who could be anything more than a projection of unsatisfied material needs. Consistently enough, such a being receives no mention[8]. This ontology of comprehensive materialism seems to have banished all those powers which made "reification" possible. Man and world are left utterly alone with one another. Neither God nor any other principles, ἀρχαι, powers, ideas, or whatever can exercise their alien and alienating dominion over men. General ontology ushers in total enlightenment.

Quinton's position is symptomatic of much of the contemporary intercourse between analytical philosophy and metaphysics, for two reasons. First, his book exemplifies the sort of metaphysics most[9] analytical philosophers who are no longer ashamed of the word prefer. The second reason is indicated by the title of the book itself: *The Nature of Things*. The word "thing" may be viewed as the everyday translation of the philosophical word "substance". This documents anew the long-hidden metaphysical underpinnings of analytical philosophy. At the same time, it shows up a paradoxical phenomenon:

---

[6] "The general result, the author believes, is a comprehensive materialism, one that rests on logical rather than scientific foundations" –as the dust-jacket of the book proclaims.

[7] A. Quinton, *The Nature of Things*, pp. 252-380.

[8] A. Quinton, *The Nature of Things*, pp. 146, 174 and 238, mention the problem of God, but only in referring to the positions of others.

[9] Not all, cf. for example, G.E.M. Anscombe and P.T. Geach, *Three Philosophers: Aristotle, Aquinas, Frege*, Oxford 1961.

despite the initial appearance of, perhaps not a rough rebuff, but nonetheless a sharp philosophical critique of metaphysics, the critique seems to rest upon an everyday interpretation of the concept of substance, and is thus itself threatened by the spectre of reification.

In what follows, I shall attempt to show that the critical attitude of analytical philosophy towards metaphysics embodies a tendency –indeed, an extreme tendency– towards "reification". I propose to justify this claim by discussing three problems which might at first glance seem to have less to do with the grandiose concept of reification than with its more humble ancestor, the notion of a thing: (1) the problem of substance itself; (2) the problem of the soul; (3) the problem of one of the so-called faculties of the soul, the will. That is the negative side of my undertaking. The positive side will be the attempt to show the extent to which classical metaphysics, in contrast to the materialist ontology of certain analytical philosophers, can steer clear of the inconveniences of reification embodied in these three problems. I hope it will be clear at the end that my undertaking is based on something more than a perverse pleasure in turning things on their heads.

1

As regards the problem of substance, I shall be fairly brief. My point of departure is Aristotle's theory of predication: the subject, conceived as that first substance or individual (atom) of which everything else is said, appears at least in the *Categories* to be a thing-like substratum[10], on to which predicates –also thing-like– are attached like labels. Analytical philosophy has long vacillated between accepting and rejecting this paradigm of substance. The reasons for rejecting it are to be found in the empirical heritage, which parted

---

[10] For a criticism of this Aristotelian position see especially K. Flasch, *Die Metaphysik des Einen bei Nikolaus von Kues,* Leiden 1973, I Teil: "Historisch-systematische Exposition des Problems", pp. 3-144.

ways with the notion of a substrate and reduced things to bundles of properties. This tendency reaches its apogee in Russell's theory of definite descriptions, as refined by Quine. The result of the Russell-Quine techniques for the elimination of singular terms is a language which, apart from quantifiers, makes do with only purely predicative, i.e., general terms –thus a sort of Platonic or, if we think of Hegel's "*spekulativer Satz*", a sort of Hegelian language, no longer related to individual substances. In its generalized form Russell's position finds scarcely any advocates these days. The pendulum of analytical philosophy has long since begun to swing back in the Aristotelian direction of individual substances.

According to this view, neither are proper names like "Socrates" simple abbreviations for definite descriptions like "the philosopher who etc.", nor are such descriptions themselves altogether eliminable in favor of general predicative terms. That proper names are not abbreviations for definite descriptions implies that they have no meaning; that is not to say that they have no function. The function of proper names, however, is conceived in this view as purely referential, ostensive. In accordance with this view the notion of substance embodied in the theories of linguistic analysis is characterized by a stronger emphasis on the purely material or spatiotemporal, i.e., "thingish", components of language. Both the individuation and the identification of substances (or, as we might say, of things) depends upon this component, viz. (in Aristotelian terms) upon the ὑποκείμενον, or subject, and, ultimately, upon matter. Once again, Quinton is a most consistent advocate of this species of analytical philosophy: "Substance in its first sense..., as individuator, is position", namely "position in space and time", and matter is explicitly defined as precisely this position in space and time[11]. In this connection, Quinton refers to Aristotle: "Aristotle's view that every concrete individual is a compound of sharable form and individuating matter is the first clear formulation of the positive theory of individuating substance"[12].

---

[11] A. Quinton, *The Nature of Things*, p. 28.

[12] A. Quinton, *The Nature of Things*, p. 4.

Every student of Aristotle will be struck by the apparent self-assurance with which (1) matter is presented here as the principle of individuation and (2) substance is taken to be composite. On the other hand, we can scarcely suppose that Quinton is ignorant of the fact that the principle of individuation cannot be simply identified with Aristotelian matter or that the Aristotelian substance cannot be viewed simply as the composite of form and matter.

The fact that Quinton clings to this particular interpretation of Aristotle might well be explained by the fact that it corresponds more closely to his own materialist position. Quinton certainly knows that matter as such is, taken alone (*materia prima*), quite incapable of providing a basis for individuation. For this reason, and despite his criticisms of Russell's theory of descriptions, Quinton espouses a form of the bundle theory, according to which the sum of the predicates expressing general properties of a thing is a sufficient basis for individuation. Taken in this sense the bundle theory is closely related to the principle of the identity of indiscernibles. According to Quinton, this will be the case when one takes the principle of the identity of indiscernibles in a broad sense, in which one of the properties of a thing is its position. Thus the materialist interpretation of substance remains untouched. This interpretation is characterized by Quinton as follows: "Positive theories of substance explain the unification of these complexes [sets of properties] by their connection with a special additional unifying element". Here, however, the materialist conclusion is directly contradictory to the clearly articulated position of Aristotle –whom Quinton views as the first clear proponent of that positive theory of substance to which he also subscribes with qualifications. For Aristotle explicitly refuses to view the unifying component of substance materialistically as simply one element among others[13].

---

[13] The reism of Kotarbinski is a linguistic version of a strictly materialistic ontology of things. Cf. G. Küng's remarks in Chapter 8 of his book *Ontology and the Logistic Analysis of Language* (Dordrecht 1967). Quinton also refers to Kotarbinski in *The Nature of Things*, p. 245. Since this chapter was written, much work has

That is all I shall say about the complex question of substances and things. In view of the extremely schematic and abstract nature of these remarks one may appropriately ask what relevance they have for my topic "Metaphysics and Reification". I shall attempt to answer this question by looking at the other two problems mentioned at the outset: that of the soul and that of the will.

2

An explicit repudiation of the materialist understanding of the principle unifying the substantial properties of a thing can be found in the Book VIII of Aristotle's *Metaphysics*, in which the notions of δύναμις and ἐνέργεια, possibility and actuality, are introduced. These notions are construed there in such a way that their applicability to the definition of the soul in *De Anima*, Book II, becomes obvious. In *De Anima*, Aristotle considers the possibility that the relation of the body to soul may be understood by analogy with that of a ship to its captain, contrasting this somewhat Platonic image with his own more mature conception. The latter is often expressed in accordance with a proposition sanctioned by the Council of Vienne: *anima forma corporis*. This formula is, however, comprehensible only when we take its suppressed premise into account, namely that form provides the being or actuality of the body (*forma dat esse*).

Were we to content ourselves with the conception of the soul as nothing more than the form of the body, we would merely underline the dualism illustrated in the metaphor of captain and ship. The living substance would still be conceived as a composite, and the form, instead of being the bond holding the whole together, would be one element among others, very much in keeping with the materialist view. In other words, the formula *anima forma corporis*, taken by itself, explains nothing. By incorporating the word "form" it simply

---

been done on the theory of substance in Aristotle by Frede, Patzig, M.-Th. Liske, M.J. Loux, F. Lewis, H. Weidemann, Ch. Witt and others (cf. Chapter 6 below).

provides a verbal cover-up for the latent materialism. Thus it is scarcely surprising that when Aristotle is concerned to be precise, he does not employ the notion of *forma corporis* (εἶδος σώματος) but rather an expression of his own making: ἐντελέχεια σώματος, or more exactly πρώτη ἐντελέχεια σώματος τοιόνδε: the soul is not the form of the body, nor is it the actuality of some body or other, but rather it is the primary actuality of a specific kind of body with specific kinds of characteristics, namely an organic body. This refinement is designed to dispel the dualism of body and soul, with its reifying bent (later to be found in the Cartesian expressions *res extensa* and *res cogitans*). The soul is no longer conceived as one thing in another thing, as some alien "body" in the body, exercising an alien and alienating power over it – a sort of sublimated "clump". (For the sense of this term, see the quotations from Nietzsche below).

The success of Aristotle's repudiation of reification is, however, usually masked by paraphrasing the formula *anima forma corporis* as *anima est forma substantialis materiae primae*. The use of this paraphrase by writers as recent even as Karl Rahner[14] turns the true Aristotelian definition of the soul on its head and renders the ambiguous formula of the Council of Vienne completely incomprehensible. For, understood in terms of the utterly undetermined *materia prima*, a body would be bereft of even that minimal organic structure which is necessary for life. In contrast to this view Thomas Aquinas, whom Rahner takes as an authority, never defined the soul as *forma substantialis materiae primae*[15], but, following Aristotle, as *actus*

---

[14] Cf. for example *Geist in Welt*, München 1957, p. 326; *Hörer des Wortes*, München 1941, p. 154 f.; *Das Problem der Hominisation*, Freiburg / Basel / Vienna 1961, p. 52.

[15] The vulgar notion of substance as an indeterminate substrate from which properties are hung like "hams from a beam" lives on in the neoscholastic conception of the soul. Cf. B. Russell, *My Philosophical Development*, London / New York 1959, p. 161. (Quoted from G. Küng, *ibid.*, p. 71). Küng is certainly right in his criticism of the empiricist conception of substance, but in fact remains himself (*loc. cit.*) committed to the neoscholastic misconception. Bernhard Lakebrink has subjected the neoscholastic conception behind this misunderstanding to a thorough critique: see "Geist und Welt nach Thomas von Aquin", in *Thomas von*

primus corporis organici; for only organs can form the basis for life, the actuality of which is the soul. This is the reason why Aristotle can view the body as the possibility of the soul and the soul as the actuality of the body.

Gilbert Ryle deserves thanks for restoring clarity here, by pointing out that the word "being", interpreted in the sense of "existing", is ambiguous. To talk in one breath about the existence of the soul and the existence of the body is, in Ryle's opinion, to commit a category mistake. The recognition of this mistake enables one better to understand the Aristotelian doctrines of the soul and of substance. For, in the case of the body, Aristotle thinks that "existence" means just "suitable for life" (i.e., possibility, potency, δύναμις), whereas "existence" in the case of the soul means something altogether different, namely the actuality of that possibility. This conception, whereby the soul is seen as the actuality of life and the body as its mere possibility, would have a sound biological basis, if it could be shown that death can occur without organic damage. If one concurs with Aristotle and Thomas in viewing the soul as the actuality (not of a *materia prima* but) of a body whose organic endowment makes life possible, then one will not be tempted to view the relation of body and soul like that stranger in Oxford –the comparison is Ryle's– who after viewing all of the colleges, laboratories, etc., still wants to know where the university is: as though the latter were nothing more than one particularly important element among others, one thing among things. Oxford University is in fact nothing more than the actual life of the colleges, etc., their soul or their being, where "being" (οὐσία) is to be understood as a verbal noun[16].

Aquin im philosophischen Gespräch, W. Kluxen (ed.), Freiburg / München 1975, pp. 38-71. Cf. also my contribution, "Der Begriff der Seele in der Philosophie des Aristoteles", to K. Kremer, ed., *Seele. Ihre Wirklichkeit, ihr Verhältnis zum Leib und zur menschlichen Person.*

[16] In contrast to the German word for οὐσία, "Wesen", the English expression "essence" cannot be taken in a verbal sense. Heidegger has often pointed, in this connection, to such terms as *Staatswesen*, *Verkehrswesen*. "Being", taken verbally, must therefore be strictly distinguished from the traditional concept of essence

5. METAPHYSICS AND REIFICATION

In order to characterize this non-elemental[17] relation between matter and form, body and soul[18], as the possibility and actuality of life metaphysicians since Aristotle have commonly employed an expression the sense of which, like actuality (ἐνέργεια), is more verbal than substantival: namely ἀρχή, dominion, power. The characterization of the soul as ἀρχή, indeed as the ἀρχή δεσποτιχή of the body is, despite appearances, a further safeguard against the reifying tendency of such substantival expressions as "soul" and "body". Of course the notion of an alien domination is unavoidable if one persists in conceiving the soul as *forma substantialis materiae primae*; for the fully indeterminate character of pure materiality has nothing of its own which could be preserved by the dominion of some ἀρχή or other. Every dominion over a *materia prima* would have to be an alien domination or –to use a word from another metaphysical tradition– a *Fremdbestimmung*.

(*essentia*). G.E.M. Anscombe has shown that the concept of *essentia*, which is the target of most of the attacks on so-called Aristotelian essentialism, is not to be found in Aristotle. Cf. G. E. M. Anscombe / P. Geach, *Three Philosophers*, p. 43. Schelling emphasized that the scholastic *forma* is a much more suitable translation of the Aristotelian οὐσία than the scholastic term *essentia*. See Schelling's *Werke*, Bd. XI, 406 (on *Metaphysics*, 1032b, 1-21). The difference which Schelling hints at in the two notions is of course that marked by the scholastic distinction between *forma substantialis* and *forma essentialis*. It can scarcely be denied that Thomas Aquinas had a more sound logical theory of predication than did Aristotle (cf. Geach, *ibid.*, p. 76); on the other hand, whether the resultant emphasis on the so-called *forma essentialis* ("*homo*") as against the *forma substantialis* ("*anima*" or "*vivere*") can be considered an advance in every respect is doubtful (cf. my "Kritik und Metaphysik", *Wiener Jahrbuch für Philosophie*, 1968, pp. 67-91, on Schelling's interpretation of Aristotle with his rejection of *forma essentialis*).

17 See R. Sorabji, "Body and Soul in Aristotle", *Philosophy*, 49, 1974, 78, cf. p. 70.

18 If one takes this verbal side of οὐσία into account, one is no longer confronted with the alternative of either some thing or nothing. Cf. R. Bambrough on Ryle: "Ryle was so concerned to make clear that there is no such *thing* as the mind that he has given the impression to many (and possibly sometimes even to himself) that there are no such things as minds" (*Proceedings of the Aristotelian Society*, 72, 1971/72, p. 66).

This would bring us to our third point: the problem of the will and thus of freedom. But before embarking on that discussion I should like to summarize those points of the first two issues which are relevant to the relation between metaphysics and philosophical analysis. Many analytically orientated advocates and opponents of the notion of substance −be they representatives of the bundle theory like Quinton or of the inherence theory− are inclined to the view that traditional metaphysics is vitiated by so-called "Aristotelian essentialism". This alleged insight is supposed to have shaken the logical foundations of metaphysics, making it necessary to construct a new, and possibly materialist edifice in its place. The objection is based on a general repudiation of the fundamental metaphysical distinction between substance and accident or between substantial and accidental predicates (i.e., humanness as predicated of Socrates on the one hand and his pale skin colour on the other)[19]. Furthermore, on the positive side, analytical philosophers emphasize the distinction between predications and statements of identity. The metaphysical distinction between substance and accidents is said to be possible only if we conflate the concepts of identity and predication, asserting the identity of substantial attributes ("human being") with the possessor of those attributes ("Socrates") and thus committing ourselves to the confusion of two logically very different things[20].

Now it would seem scarcely disputable that there is a fundamental logical difference[21] between statements of identity like "Socrates is

---

[19] For a critique of this standpoint, cf. G.E.M. Anscombe / P. Geach, *Three Philosophers*, pp. 17, 86. Cf. also M.-Th. Liske, *Aristoteles und der aristotelische Essentialismus*, Freiburg / München 1985.

[20] Cf. G.E.L. Owen, "The Platonism of Aristotle", *Studies on the Philosophy of Thought and Action*, P.F. Strawson (ed.), Oxford 1968, pp. 156-163; Aristotle's *Metaphysics*, Books Γ Δ Ε, translated with notes by Christopher Kirwan, p. 100 f. Cf. P.T. Geach as well in *Three Philosophers*, p. 76.

[21] But cf. Lesniewski's *Ontology*. On the latter: Ch. H. Kahn, *The Verb 'Be' in Ancient Greek*, Dordrecht / Boston 1973, p. 5: "In Lesniewski's usage, 'χ ε γ' may take as true substitution instances 'Socrates is wise', 'Socrates is Socrates', 'Socrates is the husband of Xanthippe' or 'the husband of Xanthippe is wise'. Identity (for individuals) is defined as a special case of the epsilon relation, namely the

the philosopher who drank the hemlock cup" and (even substantial) predications like "Socrates is a human being": the order of the former can be reversed, but not that of the latter. However, Aristotle himself seems not to have asserted so flatly the identity of that for which the substantial predicate "human being" stands –even if it is the "essence" of Socrates– and Socrates himself[22]. He seems, rather, to have maintained that the individual (Socrates or whatever) and its οὐσία, as its verbally interpreted being (i.e., as its actuality or soul), are identical with one another. This would of course make the search for some unifying element, which could only be a "thing", superfluous. It is true that we must assume some link between a *forma substantialis* and a *materia prima*. However, no such assumption is necessary to explain the union of a *materia ultima*, i.e., an organic body, with the form or soul of that body. It is for this reason that Aristotle writes in the above-mentioned Book VIII of the *Metaphysics:* ἡ ἐσχάτη ὕλη καὶ ἡ μορφὴ ταὐτὸ καὶ ἕν, δυνάμει, τὸ δὲ ἐνέργεια[23]: the two (the organic body and the soul) are one and the same-the one as the possibility of life and the other as its actuality[24]. The search for some unifying element between the body and the soul is thus misguided (οὐ

---

case where 'χ ε γ' and 'γ ε χ' are both true; and what Russell regarded as 'a disgrace to the human race', the use of a single sign for predication and identity, is thus in part justified".

[22] Cf. the painstaking interpretation of Hermann Weidemann on *Metaphysics*, VII, 6, 10, 11, and VIII, 3 (*Metaphysik und Sprache. Eine sprachphilosophische Untersuchung zu Thomas von Aquin und Aristoteles*, Freiburg / München 1975, pp. 80-102) with a careful survey of the literature (unfortunately, however, without reference to Owen's essay cited in note 20. But cf. in the meantime his critique of Owen's interpretation in his article "In Defence of Aristotle's Theory of Predication" in *Phronesis*, 1980, 25, pp. 76-87).

[23] Aristotle, *Metaphysics*, VIII, 1045b, 18-19.

[24] See E. D. Harter, "Aristotle on Primary Ousia", *Archiv für Geschichte der Philosophie*, 57, 1975, pp. 1-20, who has put the somewhat confused discussion of the notion of οὐσία (Albritton, Lacey, Lesher, Woods) back on the right track, by focusing on the importance of εἶδος as ἐνέργεια (*forma substantialis*) in contradistinction to εἶδος in the sense of species (*forma essentialis*). Cf. also my review of Frede/Patzig on *Metaphysics*, VII "Für und wider den Nominalismus".

δεῖ ζητεῖν εἰ ἕν ἡ ψυχὴ καὶ τὸ σῶμα)[25]; for, among the many senses of being and unity, the highest, the predominant (κυρίως) is actuality. The sentence "the soul dominates the body as does actuality possibility" is indeed a statement of identity, but not a predicative statement like "Socrates is a human being". The theological consequences of this (non-reifying) conception of the relation between body and soul as that between possibility and actuality are perhaps problematic. Nonetheless, they are drawn by Thomas Aquinas in his commentary on the Fifteenth chapter of the first letter to the Corinthians ("Death, where is thy sting?"), where he writes: "without the resurrection of the body it would be not easy (*haud facile*), indeed it would be difficult (*immo difficile*) to prove the immortality of the soul"[26]. In any case, it is by no means clear that a logical confusion between statements of identity and predication is the foundation of Aristotelian metaphysics.

3

As regards my third question, namely the problem of the will, one tends at first, almost of necessity, to conceive the situation in a reifying manner, as though the soul were some sort of inner core about which its faculties are arranged like the layers of an onion. This conception has been the target of a good deal of derisive comment, culminating in Hegel's image of a "soul sack" [*Seelensack*] from which one can pull out all sorts of different things: here's this and that; and here is –thus Hegel– the understanding or the will. Characteristically enough, the direct target of Hegel's mockery is post-Aristotelian philosophy[27]. In contradistinction to genuine

---

[25] Aristotle, *De Anima*, II, 412b, 6.

[26] Edition Vivès of the works of St. Thomas (Parisiis, MDCCCLXXVI), Vol. XXI, p. 33, col. b towards the end.

[27] F. Hegel, *Vorlesungen über die Geschichte der Philosophie*, Bd. III (Jubiläumsausgabe), Bd. 19, p. 574.

Aristotelianism, which Hegel was to rediscover, rationalism and empiricism are indeed marked by a substantialist and reifying tendency, a tendency Hegel attempted to overcome in his doctrine of the speculative (not merely predicative) proposition.

In attacking the *qualitates occultae* (*virtus locativa, virtus dormitiva*), early modern philosophy made no exception of the soul, understood as *forma substantialis*, nor of the will, as *forma accidentalis*. At the same time, however, it greatly augmented the number of mythical entities. In the place of each of those "potencies", dismissed as occult powers, there sprang up any number of "acts", raised to consciousness through introspection. Thus, an act of the will was thought to be caused by some conscious thought, which distinguished free acts from unfree acts and gave prominence to the former[28].

Gilbert Ryle has characterized this theory of volitional acts as "a causal hypothesis, adopted because it was wrongly supposed that the question 'What makes a bodily movement voluntary?' was a causal question"[29]. The Aristotelian query "whether human beings can merit praise or blame was consequently construed as the question whether volitions are effects"[30]. As Ryle has shown, the conception of volitional acts as mental events can be discredited by pointing out that most voluntary actions are in no way "the result of overcoming indecisiveness". Thomas Aquinas expressed the same thought: *dubitatio* –as he succinctly puts it– *non est de necessitate electionis* (for otherwise God would not be free)[31]. These similarities are not pure coincidence. With their distinction between verbs for dispositions and verbs for events, Ryle and Wittgenstein rediscovered an important

---

[28] In his book *Action, Emotion and Will*, London 1963, which is partly dependent upon Ryle but is also critical of his behavioristic tendencies, Anthony Kenny has subjected this theory to sharp criticism. Cf. the same author's "Thomas von Aquin über den Willen", in W. Kluxen (ed.), *Thomas von Aquin im philosophischen Gespräch*, Freiburg / München 1975, pp. 101-131.

[29] G. Ryle, *The Concept of Mind*, London 1949, p. 67.

[30] G. Ryle, *The Concept of Mind*, p. 76.

[31] *Summa Theologiae* III, q18, a4 ("Utrum in Christo fuerit liberum arbitrium"), ad1.

dimension of Aristotelian doctrine, long covered up by the conscious-event theory of volition. Event-verbs like "think about", "wake up", "build", "be in pain", or "itch" always point to temporal processes; verbs of disposition, like "know", "believe", "love", "desire" and "will" do not necessarily do so[32]. The fact that volition, willing, is not always and not primarily a temporal process of either internal or external nature shows how far afield one is of the true meaning of the Latin *actus* (actuality) when one translates *actus voluntatis* by the English "act of will", or "volitional act".

This is not due merely to the fact that the use of *actus* (like ἐνέργεια or ἐντελέχεια) is not limited to temporally determinate events (in analogy to spatially determinate things), much less to objectified conscious processes. It can, for example, signal the fact that a rose really (*actu*) is, or really is red. Even the expression *actus voluntatis* itself, normally understood as a (mental) event, can in fact refer to a tendency and thus be thought of as a dispositional predicate rather than an event-predicate. Once again, Thomas Aquinas puts the point concisely: *actus voluntatis inclinatio quaedam est*[33]. This genuinely metaphysical theory of willing ("volition") does not fabricate some new mechanism, like a further layer of the onion. Rather, the will becomes, in actuality, what it in fact already is (as disposition) –just as the soul is nothing more, but also nothing less than the actuality of that of which the body is the suitable organic structure or possibility. The blanket charge of substantialist reification, raised against metaphysics, seems once again, at least in the case of Aristotle, to be largely concocted.

---

[32] Cf. for example, Wittgenstein, *Philosophical Grammar*, Oxford 1974, §§ 10, 11; and G. Ryle, *The Concept of Mind*, Ch. 5. For the Aristotelian distinction between κίνησις and ἐνέργεια and its unique difficulties, cf. especially J. L. Ackrill, "Aristotle's Distinction between *Energeia* and *Kinesis*", in Renford Bambrough (ed.), *New Essays on Plato and Aristotle*, London / New York 1965, pp. 121-141. Cf. also M.-Th. Liske's recent critique of Ackrill in "Kinesis und Energeia bei Aristoteles" in *Phronesis*, 1991, pp. 161-178.

[33] Thomas Aquinas, *Summa Theologiae*, I-II, q6, a4. The entire sentence is quoted and interpreted by A. Kenny in "Thomas von Aquin über den Willen", p. 109 ff. (cf. n. 27 above).

5. METAPHYSICS AND REIFICATION

As directed against the logical and linguistic foundations of metaphysics, the sharpest formulation of this charge can be found in the work of Nietzsche (where it also serves as a meta-critique of linguistic analysis). Nietzsche's challenge is relevant to each of the levels we have considered thus far. (a) First, at the level of substance: "Every judgment contains the whole, full, profound belief in subject and predicate, or in cause and effect (namely, as the affirmation that every effect is an activity and that every activity presupposes an actor); and this further belief is in reality nothing more than a special case of the first, so that the one fundamental belief is that there are subjects, that everything which happens stands in a predicative relation to some subject or other"[34]. (b) Secondly, at the level of the body: "Psychological history of the notion of 'subject': the body, the thing, the whole as constructed by the eye suggests the distinction between an act and an actor; the actor, the cause of the act, conceived in ever more refined fashion, is finally reduced to the 'subject'"[35]. (c) And finally at the level of soul and volition: "As regards the superstition of the logicians, I shall never tire of emphasizing one tiny fact which these superstitious persons do not like to admit –namely that a thought comes when 'it' wants to, and not when 'I' want it to; which means that it quite simply flies in the face of the facts to say: the subject 'I' is the condition for the predicate 'think'. It thinks: but that this 'it' should be precisely that famous old 'I' is –to put it mildly– nothing more than an assumption, an assertion, certainly not an 'immediate certainty'. [Here one may note that Nietzsche is really gunning for the modern theory of conscious acts.] Indeed, even this 'it thinks' is too much: for the 'it' embodies an interpretation of the process without itself being a part of that process. One draws a conclusion based on grammatical habits: 'Thought is an activity, every activity presupposes one who is active, thus–.' In much the same way the Atomists, in contemplating the 'power' which caused, sought the small 'clump' of matter, in which that power resided, from which that power exercised its causal potency, in short the 'atom'; clearer heads

---

[34] Fr. Nietzsche, *Werke*, ed. Schlechta, Bd. III, p. 501.

[35] Fr. Nietzsche, *Werke*, Bd. III, p. 485.

eventually learned to do without this 'bit of earth', and perhaps some day even the logicians will get accustomed to doing without that small 'it' (in which the honest 'I' of old has taken refuge)"[36]. "We created thingness in the image of the subject". "The modes of expression given in language are useless...; it is one of our insatiable needs...to create an ever coarser world of... things". And immediately following: "There is no such thing as the will"[37].

The foregoing remarks will, I hope, have made clear at least one negative aspect of my suppressed title "The Thing with the Thing": a metaphysics of either external or internal "clumps" is precisely what Aristotle himself was trying to avoid by shifting from the substantival understanding of οὐσία in the *Categories* to the verbal interpretation found in the *Metaphysics*. This shift is an attempt to replace the weak, reifying foundations of metaphysics with something more durable.

Aristotle's new foundations were taken over not only by Thomas Aquinas but also by Hegel and, at the close of the era of German Idealism, by the later Schelling, a careful student of the Philosopher. All four thinkers found it necessary to reinforce their metaphysics against the pressures towards reification exerted –as Nietzsche rightly points out– by the predicational structure of ordinary sentences. Indeed, a system of counter-pressures was necessary to erect such an edifice at all. This is true not only in the case of the doctrines of substance, the soul, the will and freedom but also –and especially– in the case of the doctrine of God. Nevertheless, there are significant differences among the four thinkers. Aristotle leaves the level of predication, the ground-level of Indo-European languages, intact; his analyses take their departure λόγικος, i.e., from the level of linguistic usage. He transcends this level, however, at decisive points in his discussion and reverts to another. At this non-predicative level he can, for example, say that God is understood as pure actuality or *actus purus* (οὐσία ἐνέργεια), not as hypokeimenon, i.e. not as a passive subject of predication. In contrast to this, the linguistic foundation of Hegelian dialectic, namely the *"spekulativer Satz"*, which Hegel

---

[36] Fr. Nietzsche, *Werke*, Bd. II, p. 580 f.

[37] Fr. Nietzsche, *Werke*, Bd. III, p. 540.

ordinarily explains in terms of the reversible identity "God is Being", is laid amidst the ruins of the Indo-European declarative sentence. Hegel writes: "the very nature... of the sentence, which contains the distinction between subject and predicate, [is] annihilated by the speculative proposition, and the statement of identity, which the former becomes, [contains] the counterthrust to that relation"[38]. The price paid for this increased radicality is that Hegel, unlike Aristotle, leaves metaphysics unprotected against the charge of a confusion between predicative and identity statements. The result is obvious: whereas the exchange between linguistic analysis and Aristotelian metaphysics has proved increasingly fruitful, it is almost impossible for analytical philosophy, living in the ground-floor, and dialectical, living dangerously in the top-floor, to understand one another. Communication has degenerated here pretty much to an exchange of taunts: the accusation of irredeemable logical confusion against the accusation of shallowness. On the other hand, Aristotle's move beyond the Indo-European predicative structure is the foundation for all Aristotelian varieties of ontotheology, in contrast to the merely ontological metaphysics of the analytical tradition. Despite this fact, one often hears it said that metaphysics and its allies (e.g. theology) are completely compromised by the predicative structure of the Greek language and thus inexorably bound up with Western culture (including its tradition of colonialism). To discredit this thesis[39] one need not even point to the fact that the God of metaphysics is expressible in no predicative sentence. Even the "is" of such identity

---

[38] "Formally, what has been said can be expressed thus: the general nature of the judgement or proposition, which involves the distinction of Subject and Predicate, is destroyed by the speculative proposition, and the proposition of identity which the former becomes contains the counter-thrust against that subject-predicate relationship". G.W.F. Hegel, *Phenomenology of Spirit*, trans. by A.V. Miller, Oxford University Press, New York 1977, p. 38 § 61. The form of the predicative proposition is, Hegel says, "one-sided and therefore false". *Enzyklopädie*, Ausgabe Nikolin Pöggeler, Hamburg 1959, p. 62, § 31 Zusatz.

[39] Cf. the well-balanced remarks of Ch. H. Kahn, in *The Verb "Be" in Ancient Greek*, Chapter 1 ("The Verb 'Be' and the Question of Linguistic Relativism", Dordrecht / Boston 1973.

statements as "the soul is the body (namely as its actuality)" or "volition is the will (namely as its actualization)" cannot –in contrast to the reifying copula of the predicative sentence– be properly expressed in our ordinary language. As Schelling points out in his profound interpretation of Aristotle, one would have to say something like "the soul is [transitive] the body [direct object]". Schelling notes that something like this may be said –ironically enough– in Arabic, though not of course in Indo-European languages[40].

4

As I said at the outset, I intended to confine myself to the ground-floor level of the problem of reification and metaphysics. I fear I have carried out my threat all too literally. However, I did promise one final glimpse from the top.

In classical metaphysics the "political" domination (ἀρχή πολιτική) of the will by the understanding serves to open up the true dimension of freedom. The full development of this freedom, however, requires that the will submit completely to reason (as ἀρχή δεσποτική), as does the body to the soul. This means, in the tradition

---

[40] Cf. Fr. W. J. Schelling, *Werke*, Bd. XIII, p. 229. As early as 1806 in the *Aphorismen über die Naturphilosophie*, Schelling had pointed to a transitive use of the copula, which is incompatible with predicational structure: "This is precisely the point of the proposition: "God is all things", which would have to be rendered not so much with *est res cunctae* as rather (*invita latinitate*) with *est res cunctas* (...the things [are] converted from the passive to the active case...)" (*Werke*, Bd. VII, p. 205). In order to emphasize this transitive sense, Schelling often capitalizes the copula or italicizes it, or both, e.g. *Werke*, Bd. XI, p. 585. In keeping with the same insight, Thomas Aquinas sometimes pays more attention to the sense than to ordinary grammatical conventions: "*Dicendum, quod non oportet formam, quae est principium essendi rem, esse principium cognoscendi rem per essentiam suam*" (*De Ver.*, q. 8, art. II ad 4). Cf. the author's *Forma formarum*, Freiburg / München 1970, p. 166; *Transzendentale Einbildungskraft*, Bonn 1970, pp. 40-45; *Eindeutigkeit und Variation*, Freiburg / München 1973, pp. 198-201.

of Christian metaphysics, that the individual will comes to be despotically dominated by the will of God. Critics of metaphysics see this view as the culmination of the alleged reifying tendency. The notion that the human will should submit to any alien power whatsoever is seen as a typically "metaphysical" projection of certain social structures (authority, property, etc.) on to the world beyond. Indeed such transfers of reifying models –be they sociomorphic or technomorphic– are seen to form the basis of all metaphysics. This position is not confined to those of Marxist persuasions[41].

As I have no time to discuss this final charge of reification[42], I must content myself with a somewhat dogmatic review of the alternative position of classical metaphysics. Since doubt and indecision play –as we have seen– no part in the metaphysical notion of freedom, there is no conflict between the submission of the will to reason (and that means, at least in the tradition of Christian metaphysics, to the will of God) and human freedom. On the contrary, the freedom of the will is only then fully realized when it is unshakably founded upon reason. For subservience consists precisely in refusing to be thus dominated (ἀρχή) by that which is one's own (οὐσία), indeed one's own in the deepest sense (*intimior me meo*). Thus the refusal to submit is identical with the submission to some other, genuinely alien domination (uncontrolled passions, political ideologies, or whatever): "Since man is precisely that which is in

---

[41] Cf. E. Topitsch, *Vom Ursprung und Ende der Metaphysik. Eine Studie zur Weltanschauungskritik*, Vienna 1958. Cf. also H. Kelsen, "Gott und Staat" und "Die hellenisch-makedonische Politik und die Politik des Aristoteles", both in *Aufsätze zur Ideologiekritik*, edited with an introduction by Ernst Topitsch, Neuwied 1960.

[42] It would be interesting to study the extent to which Anselm of Canterbury, the metaphysician who made the most explicit use of sociolegal terminology in treating the relation of God and man, employed careful linguistic analysis to emphasize the priority of the ontological relation. Cf. for example, *Cur Deus Homo*, München 1970, p. 44.

harmony with reason, he is truly a slave when he is led away from reason by anything alien to reason"[43].

This metaphysical conception of will and freedom is poorly suited to the purposes of some future mode of communication free of dominion and of principles (ἀρχαι) ("*herrschaftsfreie Kommunikation*"). Thus, it most certainly represents a challenge to the spirit of the times. The theological attempt to shirk the challenge by dropping metaphysics and taking refuge in the Bible would be of little help; for the Bible –like metaphysics– is full of "despotic" relations, some of which are in fact presented as the will of God[44]. Of course one could write off such Biblical views as belonging to the social conditions of the *Urgemeinde*. But it is also possible to meet the challenge in the way of metaphysics, i.e., by maintaining that sociomorphic models cannot be used to judge states of affairs which transcend the order of "things" and cannot, therefore, be reifying. In the same way the virtue of justice, the ἀρχή πολιτική, which serves to regulate the property relations between married couples –or, for that matter the legal relations between strangers– cannot completely replace the ἀρχή δεσποτική of love, no matter how enlightened family laws may be. What Aristotle says of happiness is also true of love, as an essential aspect of every happy human life: inasmuch as happiness is the actualization of virtue and thus of freedom, it cannot be a κτῆμά, i.e., a thing, which one could simply possess[45]. The same is true of the ἀρχή δεσποτική upon which the metaphysical happiness of *amor Dei intellectualis* is founded; this authority is concerned less with the domination of "property relations" than with the majesty of the Lord[46]. For this reason the attempts on the part of theologians to

---

[43] Thomas Aquinas, *In Epist. ad Rom.*, c. 6, leet. 4, ed. Vivès, Bd. XX, Rome 1876, 469, col. a. For Thomas's doctrine of freedom, cf. especially A. Zimmermann, "Der Begriff der Freiheit nach Thomas von Aquin", in *Thomas von Aquin 1274/1974*, L. Oeing-Hanhoff (ed.), München 1974, pp. 125-161.

[44] Cf. for example *I Peter*, 2, 15, 18-19.

[45] Aristotle, *Ethica Nicomachea*, IX, 1169b 30.

[46] Cf. Hans Urs v. Balthasar, *Herrlichkeit. Eine theologische Ästhetik*, Bd. III, 1. Teil ("Im Raum der Metaphysik"), Einsiedeln 1965, p. 21: "Before the object domain

distance themselves from metaphysics –whether theologically sound or not– seem, at least philosophically, a trifle surprising. Perhaps "The Thing with the Thing" might have expressed this surprise more fittingly.

---

proper to aesthetics as a science came to be delimited in the era of late rationalism (Baumgarten) and critical philosophy (Kant), it had-provided one survey the tradition in its entirety-been a component of metaphysics conceived as the science of the Being of beings, and, insofar as "Being" was taken to denote the final ground of the world's manifoldness, metaphysics was also considered to be indistinguishable from theology. Now, just as it was found necessary to anchor what was true and good in the world, albeit fleeting and only partially recoverable, in something that was enduringly and integrally true and good, if only to make it more comprehensible, so that beauty which was event-like in its flashing intensity, had to be embedded in a permanent, absolute beauty that had its home in the preserving [*heil*] ἀρχαι of being –with the 'divinities,' with the 'divine,' with 'God'".

CHAPTER 6
ON ARISTOTLE'S THEORY OF SUBSTANCE

In the following I shall be offering an interpretation of the theory of substance in the series of chapters from Book VII, Chapter 4 to Book VIII, Chapter 6 of "the Substance Books" of the *Metaphysics*. The main standpoint from which I shall be regarding Aristotle's theory is given by his statement in Book IV to the effect that no accident can be the accident of another accident[1], a statement which I have already interpreted in Chapters 1 and 5 of the present book without, however, having expressly referred there to the chapters of the *Metaphysics* just mentioned. Special emphasis will be laid on those interpretative aspects which bear on the problem of time. Much work has been done on Aristotle's theory of substance in the last ten years or so, and I shall also be giving an account of how my own interpretation relates to this work.

1. The realm within which the search for "οὐσία" is to be conducted

Chapter 4 of Book VII begins in a rather linguistic (or logical) fashion by attempting to determine the realm in which the sense of substance as τί ἐν εἶναι or essence is to be found. The answer is, in any case, not to be sought in the realm of accidents but rather in that realm in which a thing is (said to be) something else by virtue of itself (καθ'αὐτὸ)[2]. Thus you as a person are not by virtue of yourself that

---

[1] Aristotle, *Metaphysics*, 1007b 2 f., 14 f.
[2] Aristotle, *Metaphysics*, 1029b 13.

which is (said) to be musical[3], but the surface is by virtue of itself or –according to another interpretation[4]– white is by virtue of itself (in) a surface[5]. The important thing to bear in mind is that something is (said to be) by virtue of itself something else only if it cannot exist without the other. This is, however, not to say that "to be a surface" is (said) "to be white" nor is it to say –according to the other interpretation– that "to be white" is (said) "to be surface". In other words, the definition of "surface" is not the definition of "white" (even if "white" is taken in a broad sense)[6] nor is the definition of "white" (however it is taken) that of "surface" –which again is not to deny that the one is never without the other. This rider is important. For in such cases it is precisely the fact that the two (white and surface)[7] are always and necessarily together which accounts for the kind of infinite regress that one would invite were one to allow an accident to be an accident of another accident or were one to allow the essence of something to fall without further qualification within the realm of the καθ'αὐτό (cf. Section 2 below).

But although the καθ'αὐτό by itself denotes the kind of accident (i.e. a necessary accident) the elimination of which no substance could survive, it denotes an accident all the same, i.e. something that does not belong to the definition nor, by virtue of the very same fact, to the essence of something. Accordingly, it is crucial to distinguish between being καθ'αὐτό (or just necessarily) and being essentially or by definition, or, to put it more precisely, to distinguish, within the realm of being in its own right (καθ'αὐτό), the more restricted realm of essence

---

[3] Aristotle, *Metaphysics*, 1029b 15.

[4] Cf. M. Frede and G. Patzig, *Aristoteles 'Metaphysik Z'. Text, Übersetzung und Kommentar*, München 1988, Vol. 2, p. 62.

[5] In my opinion both interpretations amount to the same thing. If the Greek "λευκόν" is taken in the broader sense of shining, then surface is on its own λευκόν since each surface reflects or is capable of reflecting light. White on the other hand can only exist as a white surface.

[6] Cf. note 5 above.

[7] In the broad sense of "white" a surface is always white, and white (in whatever sense) is always in a surface.

or definition. Otherwise we would be encouraging the kind of infinite regress[8] that results from the pseudo-possibility of connecting in the course of our communicating with one another (the meaning or definition of) any word with (the meaning or definition of) any other word; this includes connecting words with one another whose meaning or definition –because of their being connected to one another at most in the manner of καθ'αὐτό accidents– can only be connected at random (*per accidens*), i. e. which are not connected at all[9].

However, the kind of infinite regress just outlined is not the only one with which we shall be concerned. Once it has been shown[10] that, in order to halt a threatening imminent infinite regress, we must acknowledge the existence of substances which, due to their specific essences, do not admit all but only some types of accidents (be they καθ'αὐτό accidents or contingent accidents) and so exclude others, there is still another regress which must be addressed. It is the regress that would follow were one to allow for the possibility of accidents (of whatever sort, contingent or not) admitting other accidents –even on the basis of already acknowledged substances. The accidents involved here would be those we normally call the properties of things (*accidentia praedicamentalia* as opposed to *ens per accidens*). The question to which I shall now turn is the question of why the possibility of such accidents admitting other accidents should lead to an infinite regress. It is not enough to point to the fact that one would in so doing be piling accidents one on top of the other like an enormous heap on

---

[8] Treated in Chapters 1 and 3 above.

[9] The equation of "being connected only at random" with "not being connected at all" is valid only insofar as "connection at random" is understood to mean "not to be connected at all in a rational way for purposes of communication". However, this does not imply that no form of communication is possible at all by means of words connected only at random with one another. It only means that communication would collapse were we to try to communicate exclusively with words connected in that way. This is the core of the "transcendental deduction" of substance (cf. note 8 above).

[10] Cf., again, note 8 above.

the ground of some substance. In Section 2 I would like to explain why the problem is a bit more subtle than that.

2. Infinite regress of substances

The key to the explanation lies in the distinction already hinted at between the realm of essence and that of accidents (contingent or necessary –καθ'αὐτό). To put it more precisely, the key to the explanation lies in the distinction to be made within the realm of the καθ'αὐτό between the essential and the καθ'αὐτό itself, i. e. between the essence of something (substance) and its accidents however necessary they may be. But to take –following Aristotle himself[11]– the καθ'αὐτό accidents first has the advantage of making for a clearer exposition. For even if the contingent accidents are equally incapable of existing independently of some substance or other, the connection with substance is more intimate in the case of necessary accidents. In the case of καθ'αὐτὸ accidents the connection is not only a necessary one but it is in fact essential or definitory; not, of course, in the sense that the accidents καθ'αὐτό (*per se*) belong to the essence of a substance nor in the sense that their definition belongs to its definition in the way that *animal rationale* as the essence of *man* belongs to the definition of "man" (this is what the Scholastics called *per se primo modo*); but rather, the other way around, in the sense that the definition of a substance belongs to their own definition in the same way that *animal rationale* belongs to the definition of *risibilitas*, i. e. in the same way that the essence of man belongs to the possibility of laughing (what the Scholastics called *per se secundo modo*)[12]. But this suffices to explain why the advisability of approaching substance by first speaking of the accidents is more perspicuous in the case of the καθ'αὐτό or *per se* accidents than in that of the contingent accidents. It is by considering this special kind of necessity that one can grasp more easily

---

[11] Aristotle, *Metaphysics*, 1029b 18 ff.

[12] Such distinctions were, of course, made after *Analytica Posteriora*, I, 4.

the precise sense in which the infinite regress would take place, were it possible for accidents of accidents to exist.

So it is not surprising that in Chapter 4 of *Metaphysics* VII Aristotle hints at this regress[13] in the midst of an explanation of the difference between essence (τί ἐν εἶναι or *per se primo modo*) and necessary accidents (*per se secundo modo*). Nor is it surprising that, in *order* to make the regress plain, he shows (in Chapter 5) so much interest in an expression for a necessary or καθ'αὐτό accident, viz. "snub" employed (in English) as an attributive adjective. Taken in this sense "snub" denotes a form –say, hollowness or convexity ("σιμότης" or *"simitas"* in contrast to the abstract form denoted by "κοιλότης" or *"curvitas"*) of another thing, in this case of a nose. Nevertheless, the complex structure thereby alluded to is the same as the complex structure of contingent accidents, when considered in conjunction with some substance or other. But before I go into more details I would like first to anticipate the point of the argument. As has already been mentioned, it is an argument designed to show the necessity of defusing the kind of infinite regress that would take place were one to allow accidents to be attached to accidents –even were one to assume that at the bottom of them all there must be some substance or other. The regress which we are concerned to hinder does not consist simply in the fact that, say, the peg is attached to the wall (taken as the substance) and that on the peg hangs a coat and in the coat is a pocket and in the pocket something else, and so on. Even supposing that one could imagine an endless progression along these lines, it would not help to clarify the situation. To catch the gist of the argument, one has to realize that it is not so much a question of the proliferation of accidents as a question of the proliferation of one and the same substance.

The proliferation of one and the same substance (exemplified by a wall, the ground, a nose, or whatever) follows from the fact that each accident (regardless of kind) is in its own right (καθ'αὐτό) the accident-of a substance. In other words, it is not so much that the accident is attached to a substance but rather, the other way around, that a sub-

---

[13] By means of the expression "ἐκ προσθέσεως" (Aristotle, *Metaphysics*, 1029b 30).

stance is necessarily, as it were, attached to it; and in the case of the necessary accidents the substance is attached essentially or by definition to them in the manner of the *per se secundo modo* –all of which serves to make the connection more conspicuous but does not imply more than that. For, given the fact that a substance is always attached to an accident or –to put it more precisely– that no accident can exist without a substance, the attempt to predicate another accident of the substance not directly but *via* some other accident would –insofar as that very substance is also involved in the second accident– result in something like "the (second) accident-of a substance is accident of another (the first) accident which is itself accident-of a (the very same) substance being thereby the (second) accident not only accident-of a substance but accident-of an-accident-of a-substance".

If we take the second accident to be *musical*, the first *white*, and the substance *man*, then the result would be, first "musical-of man which is musical-of white man", and, since *white* in this case is itself *white-of* man (generally, *-of some substance*), then "musical-of man which is musical-of white man (or of whatever substance, but always of the very same substance)". This way of explaining the example already shows that, in order to get an infinite regress going, one need not consider the existence of further accidents: the regress can already be set in motion by considering a single accident. In other words, there cannot in the end be a duality of substance *and* (even one) accident. For, since an accident is always an accident of a substance, "accident *and* substance" means "accident of substance and substance" (where "accident", again, means "accident of substance", and so on). Generally speaking, accidents are nothing more than the changing states in which a substance may exist. The importance of this fact for the interpretation of the "Substance Books" beginning with Book VII will appear in due course.

One need only consider the consequences of taking more than one accident in order to realize why one cannot predicate an accident of a substance together with another accident, e. g. "musical" of whiteman, but must predicate it of the substance only, "musical" of man alone, even if it should happen that the man under consideration is, in fact, white. This, too, will constitute an important step in the Aristotelian quest for substance or οὐσία. Nevertheless, it is important to realize that the infinite regress is derived by taking the example of just one accident of a substance. This is shown in Chapter 5 of Book VII, where the example chosen is that of the expression "snub nose".

The disturbing feature of his argument is the fact that Aristotle seems unduly to switch from "snub nose" to "hollow nose" and back again in the midst of one and the same argument[14]. There is, however, no impropriety in doing so. The reason for this was already hinted at shortly before, when we spoke of the structural identity which obtains between contingent and necessary accidents. Were one to ignore this structural identity, the regress would stop before it had even begun. True, since "snub" means "hollow nose", "snub nose" is "nose which is a hollow nose" ("hollow nose nose"). But it seems as if we could not go further than this, for, unlike "snub" which is an expression for an accident καθ'αὑτό, "hollow", as an expression for a contingent accident, does not refer to a nose. However, with "hollow" something else (ἐκ προσθέσεως)[15] is also being referred to –not, of course, necessarily a nose, but at least some substance or other. So, from "hollow" alone one could not derive "hollow nose", but only, say, "hollow something". Now, "hollow something" does not yet lead to the specific regress targeted by the Aristotelian example, i. e. it does not lead to the regress "hollow nose nose", let alone to an infinite regress, but it does at least lead to the regress "hollow something something". The two questions which now pose themselves are, first, what entitles Aristotle to shift from one of the two regresses to the other and, secondly, how is the regress to be kept going[16], once it has been started one way or the other.

To answer these two questions one has to realize two facts: first, the fact that "snub nose" and "hollow something" (as well as "snub nose nose" and "hollow something something") are structurally identical, and, secondly, the fact that the "something" or substance referred to in this particular case of hollowness is a nose, so that the hollow-

---

[14] Cf. Aristotle, *Metaphysics*, 1030b 33 - 1031b 1.

[15] Cf. Aristotle, *Metaphysics*, 1030b 14 f, 16, 1031a 3, 4 f. with 1029b 30.

[16] Aristotle, *Metaphysics*, 1030b 35 (εἰς ἄπειρον εἰσιν).

ness involved is itself snubness. So one can understand why Aristotle feels entitled to switch from one of the two accidental forms, i.e. that of snubness, back to the other, i.e. that of hollowness, and back again[17], even if one knows that "snub nose" is not the same as "hollow nose", since "snubness" does not mean the same thing as "hollowness"[18]. With this in mind we can reconstruct the argument as follows: "snub nose" means "hollow nose nose", which, in turn, means "hollow something nose nose"; but the something that is hollow is a nose, so that the hollowness in this case is snubness; as a result, instead of "hollow something nose nose", one can also say "hollow nose nose nose" (this step may be omitted); and since the hollowness involved is snubness, one is also entitled to say "snub nose nose nose" and, hence, "hollow nose nose nose nose" and, for the reason just given, this can be converted into the expression "snub nose nose nose nose", and so on.

3. Searching within the realm of the substance

One might think all this to be idle reasoning, but the conclusion Aristotle draws from it has far-reaching consequences. The conclusion is that there can only be a definition of essence (οὐσία)[19], but not of such compounds as "snub nose" or "hollow nose", nor indeed of any category besides that of substance (οὐσία)[20]. The generality of this conclusion together with the way Aristotle chooses to illustrate it confirms our interpretation. For, on the one hand, the only examples he uses are those involving compounds of substance and accidents καθ'αὑτό like "snub nose" ("female animal", "odd number"), but, on the other hand, he treats these compounds as being on a par with acci-

---

[17] It is not possible to answer the further question of whether he *is* entitled to do so or not on purely formal grounds. I shall refer to this below.

[18] Cf. Aristotle, *Metaphysics*, 1030b 28-30..

[19] Aristotle, *Metaphysics*, 1031a 1 f.

[20] Aristotle, *Metaphysics*, 1031a 2-8.

dental compounds[21], even ones like "hollow nose", or such simple accidents as quality, odd[22], and so on. None of these examples has a definition[23] that would offer an account of its essence[24], nor for that matter an essence[25]. Without modifying this conclusion Aristotle then goes on to weaken it in a relatively insignificant respect, one to which he had already alluded in the last part of the previous chapter[26], namely by distinguishing between a proper and an improper sense of definition as well as of essence. It is only in the improper sense that one can say that accidental compounds of whatever sort have definition (ὁρισμός) as well as essence (τί ἐν εἶναι). "Improper" means here that it is only after abstracting *conceptually* from the substance, from which accidents cannot *really* be separated, that it is possible to define accidents in general (i. e. including compounds of substance and accident) as if they have an essence of their own. Scholastics (from Suarez on) spoke in this connection of *distinctio rationis cum fundamento in re*. The application of this distinction to the relationship between substance and accidents has important consequences[27]. But the consequences to which I have been referring are more far-reaching, for they concern the realm of essence itself, that we had already demarcated within the broader realm of the καθ'αὑτό; to speak

---

[21] I borrow the expression from Frank Lewis, *Substance and Predication in Aristotle*, Cambridge 1991.

[22] "οἷον ποιοῦ καὶ περιττοῦ". Aristotle, *Metaphysics*, 1031a 3.

[23] Aristotle, *Metaphysics*, 1031a 1-6.

[24] Aristotle, *Metaphysics*, 1031a 12 f.

[25] Our interpretation is also borne out by Aristotle's own remark to the effect that in all these expressions the same thing is said twice (Aristotle, *Metaphysics*, 1031a 5). In the context just explained this remark can only mean that the forbidden plurification is that of substance, and hence that the infinite regress originates with substance, once one attempts to define a random chosen accidental compound (of substance and accident).

[26] Aristotle, *Metaphysics*, 1030a 17 - b13.

[27] But even Thomas Aquinas did not apply it to the relationship between substances and accidents. In this respect he began to depart from Aristotle (s. for this Chapter 3 above and Chapter 9 below).

again in Scholastic terms, they concern not the *per se secundo modo* but the *per se primo modo*. But even this is not enough, for, as we shall see, it is necessary to draw within the realm of essence still another distinction. This will take us far beyond the next chapters of Book VII (Chapter 6) and even into Book VIII.

A recurrent theme from Book VII (Chapter 6), onwards concerns the question of the identity of something (ἕκαστον) and its essence (τί ἐν εἶναι). After the analysis we have given of the relevant parts of Chapters 4 and 5, it should come as no surprise to see Aristotle rejecting the identity of normal accidental compounds like "white man" with their own essence, always assuming that they have an essence[28]. On the other hand, it is surprising to see Aristotle generally affirming the identity of things said καθ'αὐτό and their own essence[29]. To explain this it is necessary to take into account the hypothetical nature of the main section of this chapter[30]. Aristotle is here arguing under the assumption that things said καθ'αὐτό exist in the sense of the (Platonic) theory of Forms. This means that the relevant predicates are not accidental compounds in the proper sense of καθ'αὐτό ("snub nose" and the rest), but rather simple predicates (like "animal") including those Aristotle himself would not have accepted as substances ("good" and the like). So the realm in which the οὐσία as τί ἐν εἶναι is to be sought is the narrow one of essences within the broader realm of the καθ'αὐτό, but, for the time being, also that of accidents in general. Given the hypothetical nature of the argument, there is nothing surprising in this[31].

---

[28] Aristotle, *Metaphysics*, 1031a 20-28.

[29] Aristotle, *Metaphysics*, 1031a 28 - b 22.

[30] Aristotle, *Metaphysics*, 1031a 29 ff. Not all interpreters agree on this (cf. my article "Für und wider den Nominalismus", p. 368).

[31] Nevertheless, immediately after having developed the main argument, Aristotle points out that the identity thesis as regards accidental predicates such as "white" and "musical" only holds in the sense of forms abstracted or separated (Plato-like) from their own subject. Cf. Aristotle, *Metaphysics*, 1031b 22- 26.

There is a danger in not sufficiently taking into account (or not taking into account at all) the hypothetical nature of the argument[32]. It is the danger of considering its result to be definitive. Of course, none of his interpreters has attributed to Aristotle a Platonic stance in this chapter. The danger is rather that of taking the chapter as a confirmation of the thesis according to which the primary meaning of οὐσία sought for in the whole of Book VII is to be found in Aristotelian essential compounds of form and matter, which are expressed on the general level by words such as "man" (or their definitions, e. g. "*animal rationale*"). It would not be surprising to find this misunderstanding in interpreters for whom such compounds (whether singular or general) do in fact embody the primary sense of οὐσία[33]. It is more surprising to find this thesis defended by interpreters[34] who adhere to the thesis that the individual form alone is first substance. Since this is a thesis I myself am strongly inclined to accept[35], I would like to

---

[32] Cf. note 30 above.

[33] Such is the case of interpreters who tend to interpret Aristotle along Thomistic lines, as for example Horst Seidl does (cf. his valuable comments on his revised edition of Bonitz German translation of the *Metaphysics*, Hamburg 1980). But the same applies to Marie Louise Gill's interpretation which is based on a hitherto (even in Moerbeke's translation used by Aquinas) neglected reading of *Metaphysics*, VII, 3, 1029a 5-7 with "τὸ ἐξ ἀμφοῖν πρότερον" for "τοῦ ἐξ ἀμφοῖν πρότερον" (cf. her *Aristotle on Substance: The Paradox of Unity*, Princeton UP 1989, p. 16). On the other hand, Gill grants that it is not before Chapter 16 of Book VII that the priority of the compound of matter and form over the form alone is given unequivocal expression. His interpretation is very much in line with that of John Duns Scotus, for whom it is illegitimate to take the form alone as the first substance (or the specific *differentia* alone as its definition as in VII, 12) and at the same time hold (as in Book VIII, chapter 6) that matter and form are the same thing taken in its potentiality and its actuality respectively (cf. *Ordinatio*, IV, d. XI, q. 3, Vivès num. 47 ff.).

[34] As Frede and Patzig do in their commentary on Book VII (cf. note 4 above).

[35] Even if one has to admit that the only text unequivocally advocating the existence of individual (substantial) forms is not to be found in the so called "Substance Books" of the *Metaphysics* (1071a 28; cf. the review of the commentary of Frede/Patzig included in the article referred to in note 30 above).

elaborate a little on it before returning to the question of the identity of something with its essence.

4. The dispute about individual forms

As far as I can see, the most recent Anglo-Saxon interpreters of the "Substance-Books" of the *Metaphysics* agree in rejecting the existence of individual substantial forms, even if for most of them the form alone has pride of place over the compound of form and matter. They mostly explicitly take issue with Frede and Patzig[36] on this point, some of them even independently of the Frede/Patzig commentary, since its main thesis had already been advanced by Frede in English[37]. Their interpretation has been seen as nominalist. As a matter of fact, Frede and Patzig not only consider the individual form to be the first substance of the *Metaphysics*; they point out that the *Categories* had already taken something individual to be substance in the primary sense, viz. individuals like Socrates. On the other hand, according to Frede and Patzig there is in *Metaphysics* VII no more room for the role of secondary substances played in the *Categories* by the species and the genus of an individual substance. So there would be no room for universals at all. Where the critics disagree is on what positive doctrine should replace that advocated by Frede and Patzig. In order to introduce some order into the different positions I should like to begin by taking two of them, the first standing at the opposite extreme from that of Frede and Patzig's allegedly positively nominalist interpretation and the other lying in the middle of the spectrum. The first is that of Gill[38] and the second that of Frank Lewis[39]. But since I have already outlined the general position of Gill I shall be concentrating first

---

[36] See note 4 above.
[37] Cf. e. g. Michael J. Loux, *Primary Ousia: An Essay on Aristotle's Metaphysics Z*, Ithaca 1991, p. 12, note. 4.
[38] Cf. note 33 above.
[39] Cf. note 21 above.

on that of Lewis before turning to the other two and then proceeding to yet other interpreters.

Chapter 13 of *Metaphysics* VII is of special significance for Lewis just as it is for Frede and Patzig. It contains the strongest arguments against universals as substances (and not only as first substances). But, unlike Frede and Patzig, Lewis still holds out the possibility of interpreting its main thesis in a straightforwardly non-nominalist way. This possibility offers in addition a way out of a *prima facie* contradiction between the tenets of VII, 13 and those of the other chapters of VII, in which Aristotle seems to accept the possibility of universals as substances, indeed as primary substances, albeit not directly but *via* the (substantial) forms of substances. In his attempt to unravel the puzzle Lewis first lists three apparently inconsistent propositions, all of which have some backing in the text of *Metaphysics* VII:

(1) No universal is a substance[40].

(2) Forms are primary substances[41].

(3) Forms are universals[42].

Lewis proceeds to eliminate the inconsistency by distinguishing between an absolute and a relative sense of "substance"[43]. In the absolute sense a substance can be universal (as in (2) and (3) taken together), but not in the relative sense (1). With this the problem can be elegantly solved. For then a substance must be denied its own (absolute) universality only in the sense that it is not universal relative to or in connection with that of which it is the substance. So the form (soul) is the primary substance of the man, but it is not universally spoken of men (one cannot say "Socrates is soul": whereas one can say "Socrates is man": "soul" can be predicated of no man). But the form can universally be spoken of the matter of man. Lewis calls this "metaphysical predication" and opposes it to such "normal" predications as

---

[40] This is the thesis argued for in *Metaphysics*, VII, 13.

[41] Cf., e.g., *Metaphysics*, 1035b 21 f., 1035b 27 ff. u. v. a. 1037a 5.

[42] Aristotle, *Metaphysics*, 1029a 23 f., 1036a 28 f., 1038b 4-6, 1043a 5 f. and 1049a 27-30.

[43] Loux has proposed a very similar interpretation (cf. note 37 above, pp. 207 ff.).

"Socrates is (a) man". To predicate metaphysically is not a matter of linguistics. What the soul does is to make out of these pieces of matter an individual of this kind (e. g. by making these bones and sinews into a man). Accordingly, the only thing one has to do to dissolve the inconsistency is to modify slightly or, rather, expand (1):

(1') No universal is a substance with respect to that of which it is substance.

So the form is the substance of the individual, but it is universal only with respect to its matter, whereas the species is universal with respect to those individuals of which it does not constitute the substance.

The way in which Lewis construes his own dissolution of the inconsistency is designed to overcome the threat of nominalism which results from interpreting VII, 13 out of context. Accordingly, he calls his a "reductive" interpretation in order to contrast it with the "eliminative" interpretation of Frede and Patzig. That means that whereas the latter eliminate the possibility of universal substances altogether, the only thing that his own theory claims to do is to reduce the linguistic to the metaphysical predication by tracing the former back to its real origins in the latter, i. e. the relationship between the individual and its essence to that between the matter and the form. In other words, one can legitimately say "Socrates is (a) man" due to the fact that the matter out of which Socrates is made is transformed by the form into a man. But although this interpretation succeeds in overcoming the allegedly positive nominalism of Frede and Patzig, it can only do so by paying a certain price. The price is that of blurring the distinction between the εἶδος as form and the εἶδος as species[44]

---

[44] Without recourse to individual forms the distinction between εἶδος as species and as formal cause had quite convincingly been stated (against G.E.L. Owen and M Woods) by John A. Driscoll ("Εἴδη in Aristotle's Earlier and Later Theories of Substance", in O'Meara, *Studies in Aristotle*, Washington 1981). W. Mesch ("Die Teile der Definition (Z10-11)" in Ch. Rapp, ed., *Aristoteles. Metaphysik. Die Substanzbücher*, Berlin 1996, p. 154, n. 8) and Ch. Rapp ("Kein Allgemeines ist Substanz" (VII, 12, 14-16)" in ibid. p. 183) dismiss any strict distinction between εἶδος as form and εἶδος as species for the reason already given by Woods ("I

(what the Scholastics called *"forma substantialis"* and *"forma essentialis"* respectively). The reason for this is that Lewis is as little prepared as Gill and others to accept the individuality of the form. However, it is not easy to understand how a universal form is capable of transforming matter into an individual, and there are still more drawbacks to Lewis's interpretation[45]. So, since accepting the individuality of the form does not lead by itself to nominalism, I shall try to retain the positive aspects of Lewis's interpretation while at the same time trying to avoid its drawbacks.

---

must already regard things as possessing the form before I can think of objects as a genuine plurality", "Problems in *Metaphysics*, VII, Chapter 13" in *Aristotle: A Collection of Critical Essays* edited by J. M. E. Moravcsik, London 1968, p. 237); cf. my article "Wie Aristotelisch ist der Aristotelismus?" in *Theologie und Philosophie*, (54) 1979, p. 98. But this only proves that *considered in themselves* the (sychronically or diachronically) different parcels of matter cannot be regarded as individuals of a given species; it does not prove that they do not owe their *being* such (functional) matter to the form.

[45] Compare for example the tension or even contradiction between the straightforward rejection of individual forms on page 320 of Lewis' book (with explicit reference to Frede, Patzig and others in the long note 25 of the same page) and the following sentence on page 329 of the same book: "Some universals, forms, for example, are not suches but thises". Were one to deny the individuality of such thises (and *Metaphysics*, 1017b 25 f. acknowledges –substantial– forms to be thises), then one would rather be inclined to see in the famous final passage of *Metaphysics*, VII 8 conclusive evidence against the acceptance of individual (substantial) forms in *Metaphysics* VII. Through their straightforward distinction between εἶδος as form and εἶδος as species –but not even as second substance!– Frede and Patzig (as well as Bonitz/Seidl at least in the above-mentioned translation, are in a position to avoid such conclusions by taking the first occurrence of εἶδος in this passage (1034a 5-8) to mean the form and the last two occurrences to mean the species. Consequently they need not take refuge in matter to explain the individuality of substances. What the matter (even, e. g., in Thomas Aquinas) accounts for is not the *individuatio* proper but only the *plurificatio* of individuals below the universal level of a species (cf. on this my book, *Forma formarum. Strukturmomente der Thomistischen Seinslehre in Rückgriff auf Aristoteles*, Freiburg-München 1970, pp. 134 and 156).

This can be done by taking the form to be universal not with respect to the matter belonging to all individuals of the same species but with respect to the matter belonging to each one of them separately. This amounts to understanding the multiplicity of the matter not in a spatial but rather in a temporal sense. It is not just the case that the form is to be called universal insofar as it applies in the same way to the various scattered pieces of matter which make up several spatially and/or temporally separated individuals. It is also universal in the sense that it remains one and the same throughout the lifetime of each of these individuals and so causes the changing matter of every single one to become the matter of individuals of the same species. Obviously, in order to be capable of doing this, the form must itself be an individual. True, the temporally changing pieces of matter of one and the same individual are in themselves not exemplars of a species like the spatially or temporally scattered pieces of matter of several individuals; they are, e. g., not men but at most a-man-now and a-man-later. Since the Aristotelian ontology is not a Quinean one, the kind of universality attributed here to the form cannot contribute anything to eliminating the arguably nominalist bent of at least Frede and Patzig's interpretation[46] –nor need it do so. For, first, the individuality of the form does not rule out its universality, whether construed in Lewis's sense or in our sense, which is indeed perfectly compatible with it, and, secondly, as we shall see, there are still other means of avoiding a nominalist interpretation while at the same time stressing the indi-

---

[46] Other interpreters, though accepting the individuality of the (substantial) form like, e. g. Charlotte Witt, cannot in any way be charged even of nominalist overtones. In the case of Witt this is due to the fact that she does not see the Aristotelian form as guaranteeing the identity of the individual substance over time but rather its actual unity: "I believe there is very little evidence for the Frede-Hartman proposal that the issue is substantial identity. Rather, the essence is the cause of being of a substance; the central function of essence is to explain the actual existence of a unified substance". C. Witt, *Substance and Essence in Aristotle: An Interpretation of Metaphysics VII-IX*, Ithaca and London 1989, p. 142 f, note 1. As regards E. Hartman cf. his *Substance, Body, and Soul*, Princeton 1977. Cf. also *Unity, Identity and Explanation in Aristotle's Metaphysic*, edited by T. Scaltsas, D. Charles and M.L. Gill.

viduality of the form even more than Frede and Patzig have chosen to do. More difficult is the question concerning the evidence for the identity of the substance over time[47]. But the necessity of distinguishing even more strongly than Frede and Patzig[48] do between "essence" and "form" may also be of some help here. With this I mean the necessity of making distinctions not only within the realm of the καθ'αὑτό but also within that of essence itself. To this question we shall now return (cf. section 3 above) so as to make it clear why it is not possible to consider the results of *Metaphysics* VII, 6 to be as definitive as Frede and Patzig would like them to be or –which amounts to the same thing– why it is necessary to stress the hypothetical nature of the relevant passages of Chapter 6 more than they themselves have done. We might express the same thing by saying that our next task consists in criticizing Frede and Patzig in order to make their own interpretation stronger.

5. The identity of substance with its essence as individual form

Symptomatic for Frede's and Patzig's not having exhausted the possibilities of their own interpretation is the fact that they skip without comment over the final passage of *Metaphysics* VII, 12 in which Aristotle states beyond any doubt that the whole account of οὐσία is to be found in the *differentia specifica* (διαφορά) so that –to take his own example– the definition of man is simply "two footed" (in contrast to "two footed animal"). I shall not dwell too much on this specific thesis[49]. It suffices to point out that the reasons given to sustain it follow

---

[47] Cf. note 46 above.

[48] Let alone than Witt.

[49] The book of mine referred to in note 45 is for the most part devoted to this Aristotelian thesis and to its consequences for Thomas Aquinas. In "Die Einheit der Aristotelischen Metaphysik" (in *Philosophisches Jahrbuch*, 101, 1994, pp. 13 and 14 along with notes 14 and 15 = Chapter 4 above) I tried to show the weaknesses

the same pattern analyzed above with respect to accidental compounds in general[50]. What is of interest for us here is to note that the corresponding analysis is carried out by Aristotle this time within the realm of essence itself. That is why Frede and Patzig's omission is so characteristic. For it turns out that in their comments on the resumé offered at the end of VII, 11 concerning the question of whether there is something identical with its own essence they express themselves as if the positive answer Aristotle had given to this question in the case of the substance and its essence had remained unchanged since the end of VII, 6[51]. If one takes the central part of VII, 6 not hypothetically but at face value one might be tempted to think that such things as animal or man (considered at first on the level of generality but, by implication[52], applicable also to that of singularity) are in fact identical with the content of their definition, i. e. with their essence or τί ἐν εἶναι. But this impression must be adjusted in light of the fact that it is only the form, when considered apart from matter, that is identical with its τί ἐν εἶναι.

In order to demonstrate why this is so, one may argue in three interconnected ways: first by tracing the pattern of the proliferation of matter (which stands in the same relationship to the form as the substance to the accident)[53], this pattern being analogous to the proliferation of substance which would take place if one were to add accidents to accidents of a substance; secondly, by explaining the way in which matter becomes by virtue of the form the matter of an individual be-

---

in Frede's and Patzig's interpretation of the other (shorter) passage (1038a 33) in which Aristotle states this thesis.

[50] This includes also the fact that it is the genus that would proliferate were one to take "*animal rationale*" (or, for that matter, "*animal bipedum*") to be the definition of "*homo*"; for, since "*rationale*" (or "*bipedum*") refers to "*animal*", the definition would yield "*animal animal rationale*". In this connection it is to be borne in mind that matter, represented here by the genus, is to form just the same as accidents are to substance (cf. section 7 below).

[51] Cf. M. Frede / G. Patzig, *Aristoteles 'Metaphysik Z'*, II, p. 218.

[52] Cf. M. Frede / G. Patzig, *Aristoteles 'Metaphysik Z'*, II, p. 87.

[53] Aristotle, *Metaphysics*, 1029a 23 f and 1048b 8 f.; cf. *Physics*, I 7, 191a 7 ff.

longing to a determinate species; finally and above all, by working out the temporal implications of the first two arguments. In the following I shall begin by considering as briefly as possible the first two points so as to spare some space for the third and most important point –most important, that is, insofar as it promises to yield some perhaps unexpected evidence as to the identity of substance over time or at least to compensate for the scarcity of such evidence.

First. There is no essence (εἶδος as *forma essentialis*), say, of man, without some matter (sinews, bones and so on), which in the end must be singular matter. So if one were to define "man" one would have to say something like "(this) in some way or other organized material something" or, simply, "something (e. g. animal rationale = man) material"; but since in "something" some matter or other is implicated (just as in the case of "nose" some nose or in the case of "white" some, as it were, "surfaced" body[54]), the same kind of regress is involved as in the case of accidental compounds, viz. "something (e. g. man) material material", and so forth. Given the structural identity (or analogy) between the relationship accident-substance and the relationship matter-form this should be no cause for surprise[55]. But here "form" ("εἶδος") still means εἶδος in the sense of *species* (matter and form), and the resulting redundancy ("matter matter and form"), because it leads to an infinite regress, is precisely the kind of thing to be overcome by arriving at the εἶδος in the sense of the form alone (*forma substantialis* in contrast to *forma essentialis*; one may also say, essential form as opposed to essence). It is only at this juncture that the regress preventing the identity of something with its τί ἐν εἶναι (or "essence" generally speaking) as the content of the ὁρισμός (or definition) is brought to a standstill. Nothing less has been achieved with the result obtained at the end of VII, 11. But this result is got at in a roundabout way which includes, among other things, some consid-

---

[54] To elaborate, this does not mean that the surface itself (something in the category of quantity) is white; it is the body (in the category of substance) alone that is white and extended and so on or, for that matter, changes in color, just as it is not the white man, but only the man, that is or becomes musical, even if he is white.

[55] Cf. note 53 above.

erations concerning the way in which the (substantial) form makes of some pieces of matter the matter of an individual of precisely this or that kind. This is our second point.

Second. We may introduce this topic by pointing to, as well as correcting, a misconstrual of Aristotle's definition of the soul as the (essential) form (*forma substantialis*) of animal. This misconstrual was very common in Scholasticism. According to it, the soul is the substantial form of the primary matter ("*forma substantialis materiae primae*")[56]. This has, of course, little to do with Aristotle's definition, according to which it is not the *materia prima* but the *materia ultima*[57] of which the form as its (first) actuality is the form. Between primary matter, if there is one, and ultimate matter one has to distinguish still other kinds of matter, but they too are out of the question here. "*Materia ultima*" means organic matter, i. e. matter capable of performing specific functions of vegetative life or of animal life. No intermediary matter (let alone the primary one) is capable of doing that, the reason being that they lack the kind of integration or unity needed for the job. Take the flesh (sinews, muscles, etc.) and the bones of some animals like man. If they were not integrated by the soul, they would not even be capable of, or have the potential to, perform the functions with which they would seem to be endowed, given their outward form or organization. "Outward form or organization" means here the material disposition of their parts. Lacking the inward form or soul[58] they are only material parts[59] external to each other and would sooner or later fall apart and disintegrate as, indeed, they do completely after the death of the animal. But the process of disintegration begins even earlier. Following Gill, who develops her terminology in the course of

---

[56] Cf. among many others, Suzanne Mansion, "Soul and Life in the *De Anima*, in G.E.R. Lloyd and G.E.L. Owen (eds.), *Aristotle on Mind and Senses*, *Proceeding of the Seventh Symposium Aristotelicum*, p. 12.

[57] Cf. Aristotle, *Metaphysics*, 1045b 18.

[58] But here, as always (see Chapter 2 of this book), the reifying image of two separate pieces (of matter!), one inside the other, is to be held in abeyance. Even the inside piece would be outside (the other).

[59] Incidentally, a redundant expression.

her fine analysis of VII, 10 and 11[60], we may call this elemental matter so as to contrast it with the functional matter as the integrated ultimate one. Between the functional matter and the soul as its form there is only a modal difference, which means that the former is only potentially the same thing which the latter is actually, namely life of some kind or other, whereas with respect to the appropriate elemental matter it, the functional one, is the actuality of its outward form or organization. So the way in which the form transforms the matter into an individual substance is by causing the elemental matter to become functional matter. Without the form flesh and bones would not be organs or instruments for living; they would remain flesh and bones and sooner or later not even this but would degenerate into matter with an even lower degree of integrating or uniting form. Now, the question of the integration or unity of substance is perhaps more intimately connected with that of its identity over time than has sometimes been suspected both by those who recognize individual forms and those who do not. As far as I can see, the reason is that in both cases insufficient attention has been paid to the fact that, in the end, Aristotle only adheres to the thesis of the identity of something with its essence in the case of the form considered on its own[61]. With this I return to the third and main point.

Third. It is at first sight rather surprising that Aristotele seems not even to answer the very question he himself had raised in VII, 6, i.e. whether something is identical with its essence (τί ἐν εἶναι) or not, or at most to answer it only in the negative. For, at least in the case of material things, the form cannot exist on its own. Consequently, if only the form is identical with its essence and if the form *is* (or, according to other interpretations, belongs to) the essence (τί ἐν εἶναι) of anything, be it living or not, then nothing (i.e. no substance) would seem to be identical with its essence nor with itself either. As far as Aristotle is concerned, this would, however, be too strange a consequence for its premises to be true. So we must look more closely at the

---

[60] Cf. note 33 above.
[61] Cf. Aristotle, *Metaphysics*, 1036a 1 f., 1037a 21-b7, 1043b 2 f.

reasons why he nevertheless chose to identify the form, and only the form, with its essence so as to dispel all such doubts.

6. Atom and primary substance

It is here that attending to the temporal dimension of one and the same substance turns out to be momentous. It is true that in the case of material things the form cannot exist in isolation from matter. But it is also true that one may consider one and the same compound of form and matter either from the point of view of its matter or from that of its form, materially or formally, i. e. according to its potentiality or according to its actuality. To consider it materially is to consider it in terms of its (spatial or temporal) extension. To view it as extended in some parts of space is not to consider it as a unity but as a diversity of parts different from, even if connected in a more or less continuous fashion with, each other. Continuity is in itself a kind of unity. But the unity of continuity found in spatially extended parts is not sufficient to enable these parts to perform the functions they are intended to perform. In other words, to consider substance materially in the sense of a unity of mere continuity is to view it as elemental matter rather than as functional or ultimate matter. It is akin to viewing a body from the anatomical but not the physiological standpoint or to judging a machine not in the light of its functioning but according to its visual aspect. From this standpoint neither the parts of the body nor that of the machine are regarded as organs or instruments, but they remain mere parts. Now, as soon as one begins to pay attention to the functional aspect (mechanical, physiological or otherwise) of something, one has already acknowledged its temporal dimension.

A characteristic feature of the temporal dimension is its lack of parts. One can excise at least some of the parts of an extended body but one cannot perform the same operation with respect to its temporal extension without interrupting, and thereby putting an end to, its existence. To that extent, temporal continuity is subjected to stronger conditions than its spatial counterpart. Outside our calculating mind there is no possibility of conjoining two periods of time contiguously or indeed of subjecting any of them to a form of organization looser than that of continuity such as would be possible in the case of distinct spatial parts that have been put together[62]. What in the spatial dimension of material substances constitutes their parts corresponds in the temporal dimension to the changing states[63] in which the substances find themselves[64]. And, if only because of the uninterrupted passing of time, the substances undergoing such "changing" states may be said, even under hibernation conditions, to be continuously changing (in the proper sense of "continuous"). But despite these differences both spatial parts and temporal states coincide in being purely material or, as one might also put it[65], accidental aspects of substance. In this sense there is not as great a difference between the question of unity and of that of identity as there may at first appear. To explain this let us have a closer look at the difference hinted at above between the *Categories* and *Metaphysics* VII.

Just as Frede and Patzig tend to maximize the differences between these two works their critics tend to minimize them. I should explain here why I myself am inclined to go along with the former rather than with the latter, and I propose to do this by way of a comparison between the individual substance of the *Categories* (ἄτομον) and the οὐσία σύνθετή of the *Metaphysics*[66]. To a certain extent, comparing

---

[62] Cf. Chapter 9 below.

[63] "Changing" in the sense of appearing and disappearing while remaining the same substance which, consequently, is the thing that can properly be said to change (there are as few changes of states - or, for that matter, of changes - as there are accidents of accidents, viz. not even one).

[64] I leave aside the question of substantial change in light of which some might be tempted to admit the possibility of two states (of what?) succeeding one another contiguously.

[65] Metaphysically considered, matter is the index of the (of course, only accidental) variability of the substance.

[66] Since the accidents, as already explained, are strongly tied to the matter in the sense that both taken together represent the indices of changeability of substance, there is not much difference in the end between οὐσία σύνθετή and σύνολον. The former refers to the matter inside substance and the latter to its accidents (which,

them already amounts to equating the two of them, viz. to the extent that in the *Categories* nothing is said about the individual substance (Socrates) being the primary substance which would exclude the accidents or its matter. Indeed one may even go so far as to say that delving deeper in *Metaphysics* VII, into the structure of this alleged primary substance than was done in the *Categories*, i.e. analyzing it into its component parts, form and matter, and in the end taking the (individual) form alone to be the true primary substance was to liberate the true primary substance from the shackles of both accidents and matter. This is, of course, not to say that there is such a thing as a primary substance (the form) existing independently of any accidents or matter. Just as the material substance is always embodied in some matter or other, it is always found in some accidental status or other. But in whatever material or accidental status a compound substance (οὐσία σύνθετή, σύνολον or ἄτομον) may at whatever time be found, the decisive thing is that it *is* always the same substance and that it remains the same as long as the changes do not go beyond certain limits and become essential changes. The limits within which changes are allowed to take place without detriment to the integrity of the substance are marked by the εἶδος in the sense of the specific kind (*forma essentialis* or *species*), whereas the εἶδος in the sense of individual form (*forma substantialis* e. g. Socrates' soul) is that whose existence ensures that some pieces of matter (flesh or whatever) do not transgress the very limits of the variability of substance[67]. So the individual substantial form is nothing mysterious or superfluous. It is not a thing hidden inside another thing let alone inside other things, which would make it something universal. We have already seen why the latter does not explain anything, least of all the emergence of functional matter from elementary matter, i. e. the making of parts into mechanical instruments, biological organs and so on. The whole point of admitting individual forms is that there is an obvious difference between the

---

though, are not to be regarded as somewhere "outside" it). This is precisely the reason why neither the accidental compound nor the compound of matter and form can be identical with their own τί ἐν εἶναι.

[67] Cf. my book *Eindeutigkeit und Variation*.

substance in some accidental status or other and the substance itself or the substance as it is in itself. The latter is nothing separated from the former, it is the former inasmuch as the individual substance (ἄτομον, οὐσία σύνθετή, σύνολον) remains the same throughout its actual or potential changes[68].

Far from thinking that since there is no form of material substance that can exist separately (with the possible exception of the *nous* of man), the move by which Aristotle restricts the identity of something with its essence (τί ἐν εἶναι) to the form alone would actually make impossible the identity of anything with its own essence, one must, on the contrary, acknowledge that it is precisely this move which explains how substance can remain the same throughout its changes, it being the only thing that changes. It is only because one must distinguish between the changing substance and the substance in itself or καθ'αὐτὸ in the strictest possible sense of the word (τί ἐν εἶναι) that one is compelled to recognize not only individual forms but also the fact that only these can be identical with their own essence. This by no means implies that the individual substance and its individual form are two different things. They are the same thing viewed from two different angles –first from the angle of the materiality of substance (with the result that the compound substance is then taken as the primary

---

[68] But any actual change must continuously take place, at least with respect or relative to some other change in the world (think again of the case of hibernation), without which the world would not exist. So, even if some substance should *per impossibile* remain unchanged in the absolute sense, one would still be obliged in the case of an actually unchanged substance to make the distinction between the οὐσία σύνθετή and the εἶδος as individual form, for the substance could in principle always be otherwise, i.e. it is always possible that the substance might change. So the distinction between the individual substance and its individual form might be only a modal distinction, but it is a distinction that one must always observe. This is the reason why, contrary to so many (from Duns Scotus to, say, Gill) I do not see any incompatibility between *Metaphysics* VII (1-15) and *Metaphysics* VIII (culminating in Chapter 6). All one has to do to ascertain their compatibility is to take seriously the fact that, in the end, it is only the forms that are identical with their essence (τί ἐν εἶναι).

substance)[69], and then from the angle of its pure formality. But are we not, in making the distinction between individual substance of some kind or other and its form a purely modal distinction between two different points of views, falling back into a nominalist interpretation?

7. The issue of nominalism

The clearest explanation I have found of why Frede's and Patzig's interpretation should be considered nominalist also raises the strongest criticism the two have had to face. It runs as follows: "Frede and Patzig attribute to Aristotle the position that the substantial form is particular. This is incompatible with Aristotle's claim that the substantial form is definable and, hence, universal. So, they aim to resolve the incompatibility by attributing to Aristotle a nominalist theory of definition. It is not, they say, that definition is *of a universal*; rather, definition is *predicated universally* of many particulars"[70]. After quoting the original German the author, Scaltsas, continues by assuming that Frede and Patzig "are employing a nominalist theory of predication, as we understand it in contemporary philosophy, according to which an account in terms of a linguistic entity, the predicate, is true of the referent of the subject. But there are no grounds for attributing such a theory to Aristotle"[71]. What should we make of these charges in light of our previous remarks?

Like Frede and Patzig, Scaltsas, too, does not seem to believe that much progress has been made on the way from the first appearance of the problem of how a substance can be identical with its essence in VII, 6 to the final results as they are presented in VII, 11[72] and in VIII, 3[73]. In his book Scaltsas does not even refer to the corresponding pas-

---

[69] As is the case with Gill and with most scholastics.
[70] T. Scaltsas, *Unity, Identity and Explanations in Aristotle's Metaphysics*, p. 93.
[71] T. Scaltsas, *Unity, Identity and Explanations in Aristotle's Metaphysics*, p. 94.
[72] Aristotle, *Metaphysics,* 1037a 21 - b7.
[73] Aristotle, *Metaphysics,* 1043b 2-4.

sages[74]. But on the basis of in his explicit criticism of Frede's and Patzig's position one might be able to draw out an implicit criticism of my own interpretation of these two passages as it might be raised by an imaginary objector. One could, at any rate, counter that the form which in both passages is claimed to be identical with its essence must be understood to be universal on the grounds that an individual form would cease to be at the same moment in which the individual itself ceases to be, whereas, if the form is to be scientifically cognizable –as it undoubtedly is for Aristotle– it must be universal and imperishable like the species[75]. If, in this case, the form is to contribute to the transformation of the elemental into the functional matter and one is still to distinguish between εἶδος as individual form and as species[76], the universality of the form will have to consist in the fact that it is one and the same form which together with matter participates in the constitution of the spatially as well as temporally distinct individual substances. The individuality of these substances would then be due to the differences in their respective matter[77]. But this would not be of much help in denying the attribution of a nominalist stance to Aristotle. The imagined critic would be obliged to take the form not as being universal in the strict sense but rather as being universal in the limited sense of its being common to several individuals[78].

This, however, does not amount to a definitive objection on my part to my imaginary critic as far as the issue of nominalism is concerned. The interpretation of the universality of the form, which construes it as being as the one and the same with respect to various temporally changing pieces of matter belonging to individuals of the same kind, can with even less justification purport to answer the question of

---

[74] Nor to Aristotle, *Metaphysics*, 1038a 25-30.

[75] Scaltsas himself makes this point; cf. *Unity, Identity and Explanations in Aristotle's Metaphysics*, p. 95.

[76] Cf. section 5 above.

[77] That would correspond to the position of Gualterius Burleus (cf. the article referred to in note 30 above, pp. 385 and 392).

[78] Cf. Frede's and Patzig's criticism of this notion as applied to *Metaphysics*, VII in *Aristoteles 'Metaphysik Z'*, I, p. 50 f.

nominalism in Aristotle than Lewis' interpretation from which it is, in fact, derived. Lewis' metaphysical predication is not predication in the normal sense. In a proposition like "the matter of Socrates and of Plato, etc., is the common rational soul" the "is" is not predicative[79]. Similarly the matter-of-Socrates-now has even less claim to be a man than Socrates-now[80]. Rather, the issue of nominalism is directly related to the question of whether in the *Metaphysics* every residual trace of the secondary substances (*genus* and *species*) of the *Categories* has been eliminated, this form of predication being, as has already been said, the usual one linguistically ("Socrates is (a) man"). Nevertheless, Lewis' distinction between a metaphysical predication of the form with respect to its the matter and a linguistic predication is relevant for an understanding of the aforementioned criticism of the present interpretation.

This interpretation comes very close to that dubbed by Theodore Scaltsas "substantial holism"[81]. But there is still a difference between the two of them. The difference concerns the issue of nominalism. It is important to be clear about the similarities as well as about the difference. Scaltsas writes, "That a substance is not composed of distinct elements does *not* entail *nominalism*"[82]. With this I agree. But inasmuch as he does not acknowledge individual (substantial) forms at all, Scaltsas is not entitled to apply this dictum to them, but only to the accidental forms and the parts of a substance (in accordance with the

---

[79] In Schelling's interpretation of Aristotle this "is" had been made the subject of an explicit analysis (cf. my "Metaphysik und Kritik. Zur Synthese von aristotlischer Metaphysik und Transzendentalphilosophie", *Wiener Jahrbuch für Philosophie*, (1) 1968, as well as Chapter 7 below; but cf. also H. Weidemann, "Schelling als Aristoteles-Interpret", *Theologie und Philosophie*, 54, 1979, pp. 20-37).

[80] Socrates-now (white or educated or whatever) cannot be the subject of attribution of any accidents. (Cf. in this respect Geach's criticism of Quine in "Some Problems about Time", *Studies in the Philosophy of Thought and* Action, selected and introduced by P.F. Strawson, Oxford 1968; included also in *Logic Matters*).

[81] In his book Scaltsas does not use this expression, but see his contribution to the book edited by him and others (cf. note 46 above).

[82] T. Scaltsas, *Unity, Identity and Explanations in Aristotle's Metaphysics*, p. 127.

so-called "homonymity thesis")[83]. The substance does not contain the former as distinct elements because, in their distinctness, the accidental forms are merely the products of our abstracting thought. With this I, again, agree. It is the thesis which Scholasticism (Suarez) had called *distinctio rationis cum fundamento in re* but here applied solely to the accidents, the changeability of the material substance being understood as the *fundamentum in re* of the distinction. But as far as the substantial and the essential form are concerned (the εἶδος being understood either as the individual form or as the species, *forma substantialis* and *forma essentialis*) things are a little more complicated. On the one hand, according to the present interpretation, the *forma essentialis* or *species* is just as little an element of the substance as its accidents are. It, too, is but a product of our abstracting thought. But, on the other hand, according to the same interpretation, this need not imply a form of nominalism any more than it did in the case of the accidental forms and the parts of substance. In this respect, the present interpretation seems to depart from Scaltsas substantial holism. In keeping with the interpretation defended here, the *forma substantialis*, understood as individual form, must in some sense be prior to the individual substance (ἄτομον, οὐσία σύνθετή) as well as to the εἶδος as species (σύνολον), i. e. in the sense of being primary substance –and this regardless of whether, along with so many authors, we are inclined to admit species and the like at least as secondary substances in the *Metaphysics* or not, i.e. of whether we follow Frede and Patzig or not.

The following example may help to clarify the situation. The example is that of two letters (say A and B) superimposed on one another so that they become unrecognizable. Despite their being irrecognizable, it would be true to say that each one of them is contained in the resulting mixture whereas it would be false to assert the same of, say, the letter C. This fact may be used to develop an analogy to the theory of predication advocated by Frede and Patzig and rejected as nominalist and hence non-Aristotelian by Scaltsas. In order to deter-

---

[83] This is a stipulation to the effect that any parts detached from the living whole retain only the name of what they had previously been all along.

mine to what extent Scaltsas's assessment is correct we have to distinguish three different forms of substantial holism, first with respect to the relationship between substance and accidents, second with respect to the relationship between the universal form (εἶδος) as species and the individual substances falling under it as its specimens, and, finally, with respect to the relationship between the (individual) form (εἶδος) and the individual substance "in" which it is "contained". Let us consider the three in that order.

As far as the first case is concerned there is no discrepancy (at least between Scaltsas's and the present interpretation). Take again the example of the letters. Scaltsas has rightly placed much emphasis on the Aristotelian example of how the letters form a syllable[84]. But note that my example was different. In it the letters did not form a syllable at all. For this reason it more accurately corresponds to another example which Aristotle himself contrasted with that of the syllable, viz. that of the segments of a circle (as well as to the acute angles contained in a right angle). The difference is that the letters define the syllable and are, therefore, primary with respect to it, whereas in the case of the segments (as well as that of the acute angles) it is the other way around[85]. Now, in our example the resulting mixture cannot be defined in terms of the letters. Since they are unrecognizable, it is possible to recognize within the one picture a variety of other (mostly unnamed) patterns which together would make up the original including the letters A and B. This means that the whole pattern is prior to the individual patterns (letters or whatever). And that is why the other examples (the Aristotelian ones having to do with angles and segment but also mine concerning the mixed-up letters) only function when accidents are considered in their relationship to substance and not when it is a question of understanding individual substantial form as primary substance. For, unlike the substantial form, accidental forms are secondary with respect to substance. Now, the other examples exhibit an interesting peculiarity when compared with that of the syllable: the parts of a syllable do not stand in a relation of continuity to each other.

---

[84] Aristotle, *Metaphysics*, 1034b 25 f., 1035a 14 f.; cf. 1041b 12 ff., 1043b 5 ff.

[85] Aristotle, *Metaphysics*, 1034b 21-28.

It is irrelevant here whether their relationship is construed as one of contiguity or merely, as Aristotle calls it, one of ἐφεξῆς (such as obtains between two detached houses standing next to each other). Important is only the fact that, as has already been emphasized above, two accidents, understood as two different states of the same changing substance, are themselves continuous with each other (and hence are not in the proper sense "succeeding" each other), so that they represent the temporal analogues of the non-contiguous letters in the mixture –as opposed to the use of the same letters in the syllable BA. This peculiarity shows clearly that the "changing" or "succeeding" accidents (inaccurate expressions for substance which is itself involved in a process of *continuous* change) only exist in substance in the same way that segments exist in a circle or acute angles in a right angle, viz. potentially (and actually but then only after the intervention of the abstracting mind)[86]. So Scaltsas was correct to point out that, in the case of accidents, substantial holism does not entail nominalism at all. But what about the essential or the substantial form (*forma essentialis* and *forma substantialis*)?

As far as this question is concerned it is my contention, first, that in the case of the essential form and in that of the substantial form substantial holism does not lead to a nominalist stance, and, second, that the predication theory attributed by Frede and Patzig to Aristotle, while nominalist by contemporary standards, is not necessarily so by Aristotelian standards[87]. So, if one were to take, as I think we should, the individual substantial form as substance in the primary sense, then one would obviously be forced to modify the example concerning the

---

[86] In contrast to Scotus' *distinctio formalis a parte rei* (*"a parte rei"* means precisely "before the intervention of the abstracting mind").

[87] Mario Mignucci does not rule out the possibility of a development in predication theory from the *Topics* to the *Peri Hermeneias* in the sense of an increasing approximation to the mereological theories of today (cf. his "Aristotle's Theory of Predication" in *Studies on the History of Logic*, edited by Ignacio Angelelli and María Cerezo, Berlin 1996). But even if this were the case, it is impossible to exclude another further development, this time away from contemporary standards (cf., e. g., P. Geach, "History of the Corruptions of Logic" in *Logic Matters*).

mixed-up letters, perhaps along the following lines: The two letters superimposed upon one another represent an individual substance whose belonging to some kind or other is due to the individual (substantial) form. When I first I introduced the example, its essence was defined, as it were, by absence, i.e. set off against the presence of the pattern contained in the letter C. We may now suppose that the substance undergoes different states, losing in the process some properties and acquiring others. Now, as long as it does not manifest any property corresponding to the letter C (or the letter C itself) one will be obliged to say that it still belongs to the same species (the same *forma essentialis*) and thus remains the same individual substance, albeit in another (i.e. in a "changed") accidental status. If the species, as I contended, is that which marks the boundaries going beyond which the sameness of the individual substance can no longer be preserved, one could hardly argue otherwise. Does this represent a nominalist stance? One will be tempted to answer in the affirmative only if one conceives of the universal essence in the (somewhat mereological) sense of a thing (the universal essence or compound of form and matter on the level of generality)[88] being inside another thing. This seems to be suggested by certain expressions such as "ἔνυλον εἶδος"[89]. However, the argument according to which it is only the form (without the matter, that is to say, the *forma substantialis*) that is identical with its own essence (τί ἐν εἶναι), and not the accidental compound ("white man") or the compound of matter and form ("man")[90] –is precisely designed to offset this suggestion. To see how, one must first address the question of the individual substantial form directly.

The substantial form (*forma substantialis*) can with just as little justice be compared to a thing inside another thing as the essence (*forma essentialis*). It cannot even be considered a form (*formalitas*) within substance as a whole. This corresponds rather to the stance

---

[88] Cf. Aristotle, *Metaphysics*, 1035b 27 ff.

[89] Cf. *Physica*, IV, 3, 210a 21.

[90] Both of which, as we have seen, amount to the same thing, i. e. to the substance viewed from the standpoint of its materiality and therefore as still possessing some contingent status; cf. Aristotle, *Metaphysics*, 1037b 3-7.

taken by Scotism whose impact on modern philosophical rationalism was indeed substantial before the critique launched by Kant. And even after Kant such ideas survive more or less uncontested in Aristotelian new-Scholasticism. But they are not genuinely Aristotelian. Now, to say that the essence (e. g. *homo* as the *forma essentialis* of Socrates) does not exist as such, i.e. actually *a parte rei*, but only potentially, that is to say, that it exists actually only after the intervening abstraction of the mind or –what amounts to the same– that its *distinctio* vis-à-vis the individual substance is only *secundum rationem ratiocinatae seu cum fundamento in re* does not conflict with genuine Aristotelianism. In this respect, genuine Aristotelianism lies between the doctrine of the *distinctio formalis a parte rei* on the one hand (and the related conception of predication as an isomorphism between the real realm of things and the abstract realm of ideas) and genuine nominalism, on the other. This is why, by Aristotelian standards, there is no need to attribute a nominalist theory of predication to those who like Frede and Patzig think that a definition is always of something universal, but that the universal need not always be actually out there (but only potentially). Accordingly, to say that *"homo"* is predicated universally of several particulars without having a corresponding *formalitas a parte rei* need not imply a nominalist theory of predication. However, if one proceeds from the *forma essentialis* (man) to the *forma substantialis* (soul), things are different. For, independently of whether we deliberately decide to classify *species* and *genera* as "second" substances, as occurs, for example, in the *Categories*, or not, as occurs in the *Metaphysics*, the substantial form cannot be universal in the sense that it may be predicated universally of many individuals of the same kind in the same way as *genera* and *species*. This would be incompatible with the individual form being *primary* substance. But though the charge of nominalism has already been dismissed with respect to the *forma essentialis*, the sense in which the *forma substantialis* is to be considered prior to the individual substance ought to be further explained, all the more so if one regards the two of them as being neither universal in the proper sense nor common (in the sense already explained) but individual.

The crude representation of a thing within another thing might here be suggested by the fact that, as has already been indicated, it is only the individual form which is identical with the content of its definition or τί ἐν εἶναι. The sense in which the *universality* of an *individual* form may nevertheless be upheld has already been explained in connection with the temporal modification which Lewis's notion of metaphysical predication was made to undergo. The notion, once so modified, may also be of help here. The individual form is not something different from the individual substance but the same as the latter inasmuch as it remains the same throughout its career. Remaining the same throughout its career does not mean remaining unmodified. Otherwise the individual form would be a thing within another thing in the same way that a hidden kernel remains untouched by the accidental changes of the individual substance as the container of such a hidden kernel. Now, although the difference between the individual substance and its individual form is not real in this reified sense, it is not fictitious either. The difference is rather a modal one in the sense that the substance that *actually* remains the same as long as it continues to exist is nevertheless *potentially* many as yet unrealized accidental forms. These forms are the states through which it may or actually will pass before ceasing to be. True, in this case the individual form will also cease to exist. But since its universality, unlike that of the *species*, is not such as to be related to individuals belonging to one kind but rather is related to the matter of a single individual, this should not be understood as constituting an objection but at most as a sign of the fact that in the "Substance Books" of the *Metaphysics* Aristotle had moved farther away from Platonism than ever before. The explicit acknowledgment of individual forms in Chapter 5 of Book XII of the *Metaphysics* shows that they are, at the very least[91], not incompatible with Aristotle's metaphysical theory. In addition one might point to the philosophical advantages of this view[92]. I shall

---

[91] Cf. M. Frede "Acerca de la noción de sustancia en Aristotleles, otra vez", *Methexis*, 5, 1992, p. 97.

[92] In this context cf. also my article "Für und wider den Nominalismus", pp. 92 ff.

close with some remarks regarding the temporal aspect of substance as it relates to Aristotle's physics as well as to his theology.

Like the *Metaphysics*, the *Physics* also ends with theology. On the other hand, much of the *Metaphysics* is physics and seems at times[93] to be merely preparing the way for theology. So the boundaries between physics, ontology and theology are not easy to draw. Besides, there is some analogy between the theory of temporal continuity developed in the *Physics* and the view presented here as the metaphysical theory of substance. When I say this, I am thinking of the analogy which obtains between the many instants of time and the many accidents of the particular substance. Substance passes through many states, conditions and situations which continuously "succeed" one another. But, of course, inasmuch as they do this continuously, they remain one and the same (substance) and therefore do not stand in a relationship of succession to one another[94]; in the same way there is really only one instant of time that we are able to divide into several instants in our mind, setting as we do, dividing lines of time for whatever purpose we want –something we must in fact do if we are to survive as scientists, physicists, historians or just rational beings. Now, what corresponds in metaphysics to the one instant of real time is the substance. They alone, in contrast to accidents, actually exist, but they exist in continuously "changing" accidental states which are themselves nothing else than the changing substance itself. Inasmuch as the latter is grasped as changing it is the individual substance *tout court*, but inasmuch as it remains the same throughout, and indeed because of, its changes it is the primary substance and the very subject of change from which it only differs *secundum rationem*, i.e. in the sense of the distinction between its potentiality and its actuality, its materiality and its formality. So there does not seem to be any incompatibility between *Metaphysics* VII, 4-16, on the one hand, and *Metaphysics* VII, 16 through *Metaphysics* VIII, 6, on the other. For material sub-

---

[93] Cf., e.g., Aristotle, *Metaphysics*, 1037a 10 ff.

[94] As already said, continuity excludes the possibility of two items (either instants of time or contingent states of substance) being in the relationship of either contiguity or ἐφεξῆς to one another.

stance always has the structure exemplified by the expression "snubness"[95], and the fact that we must leave such a compound structure behind in order to arrive at the primary substance only means that in order to do so we must adopt the standpoint of pure formality, i. e. of the whole substance considered in terms of actuality as its most important aspect[96]. This complex and at the same time simple structure had been worked out in *Metaphysics* VII, 12 with the same result but at the universal level of *species*. The *differentia specifica* is in itself the whole of the *species* considered from its most important aspect. And in *Metaphysics* VIII as well as in *De Anima* it turns out that this most important aspect is the aspect of its function or actuality. With this the way has been paved toward the pure actuality of God. It is the way of analogy, defined as the identity of function despite differences in content and leading from Book VIII through Book IX to Book XII of the *Metaphysics*.

---

[95] Still referred to at the end of *Metaphysics* VII (1037a 27 - 34), this time in connection with the body and the soul of the living being.

[96] Compare *Metaphysics*, 1045b 18 f., with *De anima*, II, 1, 412b 6-9.

CHAPTER 7

SCHELLING ON ARISTOTELIAN METAPHYSICS
AND KANTIAN CRITICISM

"Jede Ausscheidung ist Krisis"
("*Purification means crisis*")
Schelling, *Werke*, XIII, p. 68

Metaphysics does not deal with any specific subject –to use the Scholastic terminology for what some would rather call "object". According to Schelling metaphysics tries to understand what "subject" means and to arrive at a subject that remains subject without becoming object. But whereas Aristotelian metaphysics would understand "subject" in the sense of (organic) substance, Kantian transcendentalism would understand the same word rather in the sense of *ego* as knowing subject. This gives us a hint as to the difficulties Schelling had to overcome in trying to bring about a synthesis between the two traditions of Aristotelianism, on the one hand, and transcendentalism on the other. In some respects, Leibniz had already tried to anticipate such a synthesis. According to him, the double meaning of the word "subject" is by no means purely incidental, as one can realize by considering the double meaning of the word "*repraesentatio*". On the one hand, *repraesentatio* means some subjective idea, while, on the other, it means something that, like a general essence (οὐσία), is representative of (goes proxy for) many things of the same kind[1]. And just as the *ego* is able to unify many ideas in one concept, so the essence of anything is able to unify a multitude of determinations into one individual. Nevertheless, the Leibnizian synthesis of *ego* and substance *via*

---

[1] Schelling sees the conjunction of both meanings in the German word "*Verweser*" (cf. Fr. W. J. Schelling, *Werke*, XI, p. 417; cf. note 5 below).

the concept of representation was soon to be dissolved by Kant into the non-substantial *ego*, on the one hand, and the non-essential or phenomenal thing of the *Critique of Pure Reason*, on the other.

Following the path of the *Critique of Judgment* the earlier Schelling had already been able to recapture in his philosophy of organism the essentials of the Leibnizian monadology and also, though indirectly, of the Aristotelian metaphysics of substance. But the later Schelling set out to demonstrate that the same kind of criticism that had led to Kant's destruction of traditional metaphysics, when pursued to its ultimate consequences, can recapture the Aristotelian stance of a thoroughly independent (ἁπλῶς χορισμένον) subject which, being only itself[2], is at the same time the representative unity of all that is, thus becoming the guarantee of metaphysical knowledge.

The unity of the concepts of χωριστόν and critique, crisis and metaphysics, is as old as metaphysics itself. For Parmenides all one can know depends on something that in no way cannot be known, and this is the separation –the "crisis", as it is called by Parmenides (fr. 8)– between being and not being, being such and such and not being such and such. To put it in a more Aristotelian way, if something is or is such and such, it cannot in the same respect be and not be or it cannot in the same respect not be such and such. But as soon as the question about scientific decidability becomes, as in Kant, independent of any metaphysical insight into what is in itself, or in advance, decided, then the quest for the most reliable knowledge gives way to the question about the possibility of such an insight and the fundamental reliability of first theoretical principles is replaced by an equally fundamental unreliability of all that may theoretically be known: it is not the case either that bodily substances need theoretically or in principle to have three dimensions or that the *ego* need to have precisely such and such categorical endowment. All one (the *ego*) can know with some reliability is only appearances, i. e. things that are marked by the possi-

---

[2] I. e. that remains as a subject; cf. W. Schulz, *Die Vollendung des Deutschen Idealismus in der Spätphilosophie Schellings*, Stuttgart 1954; cf. Aristotle, *Metaphysics*, 1060a 26 f.; XII, 1073a 4; 1075a 12 ff.

bility of not being as well as of being otherwise³. As Schelling was to show, this puts at risk, but at the same time obliges to the reconsideration of, the virtualities of the very first PNC.

As regards the question of a critically decided subject that does not become object but always remains subject and can, therefore, neither possibly not be nor be otherwise, it is indifferent whether things *qua* appearances are, as in Kant, denied or, as in Aristotle, given a representative essence in the sense explained above. The reason for this is that all we can know, be it three-dimensional bodily substances or subjects that only can be known as objects, is but a possibility of being⁴ which is liable not to be or to be otherwise⁵. This means for Schelling that, in the end, one has to overcome the level of essential contents (of *what* something is or of Platonic εἰδέ) in order to arrive at something reliable that can pass the critical test to which Kant subjected all knowledge in his first critique. But this does not represent any novelty on Schelling's part. Even in Aristotle it was not possible to arrive at the very first substance (οὐσία) without having overcome the Platonic level of forms (εἰδέ) attached to some content or other. It was precisely only by a sustained critical process of getting rid of, or critically eliminating, all ideal or specific contents still to be found in living beings that Aristotle was able to arrive at the very first beginning of a principle (τοίαυτη ἀρχή) which, being nothing but its own activity (ἧς οὐσία ἐνέργεια), could not in any possible way (οὐδαμῶς) not be.

Now it seems as if, by this critical elimination of any content in order to get a principle which in itself is devoid of any εἶδος or content, the representative unity of reality as well as the possibility of knowing it is gone for ever. For that unity seems to rest on the hierarchical organization of nature into genera and species (εἰδέ) that has always

---

3   Cf. Fr. W. J. Schelling, *Werke*, X, p. 6 (with respect to modern philosophy from Descartes on).

4   Schelling says "*Seinspotenz*".

5   In connection with the organisms which, according to Aristotle, are given their proper essence ("*Eigenwesen*") Schelling expresses the liability to not-being by means of the verb "*verwesen*" (to decay) (cf. *Werke*, XI, p. 417).

proved so convenient for knowledge. Nevertheless, were the unity of the whole of being based upon such hierarchical contents that never are nor can be identical either with their many activities or with their very actuality, then nature and being as such would totally lack that very decisiveness, i.e. the complete separation between being and not-being, by which metaphysical knowledge stands or falls. The situation would be like that of a body which, due to the shape and content of its organs is, according to Aristotle, only capable of living without being able to transform on its own this capacity or possibility into the actual activity of living. And since, according to Aristotle, for living things to be means for them nothing other than to live, we must take this analogy as a serious warning against any attempt to cling on to a realm of εἰδέ which stops short of an activity that, having been critically purified of all generic and specific contents, is the only thing by means of which we might attain some absolutely reliable or metaphysical knowledge.

Only something like activity can be a candidate for that actuality of being that, not being mingled with any mere possibility or capability, *is*, without wavering between being and not being, actuality and possibility, and so can unconditionally satisfy that complete separation between being and not-being required by the unconditionality of the truth of PNC. The reason for this is that, whereas any performing activity undoubtedly is or exists while the mere concept of an activity undoubtedly does not exist nor is in any way active, the content of which any active thing, be it a living or a thinking thing, consists without being identical with its own activity remains the same independently of whether it actually or only possibly (conceptually) exists. As Kant put it: "if I take the concept of anything, no matter what, I find that..., whatever it may be that exists, nothing prevents me from thinking its non-existence"[6]. What one might call the decisiveness of metaphysics, i.e. its purely rational decision to separate in an unconditional way being from not-being is thereby given up. According to Schelling this happened because Kant was only prepared critically to separate the subject of metaphysics, i.e. the thing-as-it-is-in-itself (the

---

[6] I. Kant, *Critique of Pure Reason*, B 643 f.; translat. N. Kemp Smith.

being as such or the subject as such), from the world of nature and to some extent also from the *ego*. What he was not prepared to do was also to separate it from the embodiment ("*Inbegriff*") of all possibilities, predicates or concepts (from all contents or εἰδέ: *omnitudo realitatis seu possibilitatis*). It is at this juncture that the later Schelling, in order to bring to completion Kant's critical task, falls back on Aristotle.

Kant's embodiment of all realities only represents the prolongation of a continuous line along which, starting from individual substances, one rises up to their universal predicates. Schelling speaks in this connection of a "purely abstract totality of possibilities"[7]. Such a continuous line is that of λόγος by means of which we say *what* things are. It is a continuous line, because it is not yet interrupted by any kind of critical elimination of contents. Now, if, argues Schelling, one clings on to such a continuous line then one cannot take the last step on the way of a thoroughly critical purification of reason. Kant only envisaged this step, without being able to take it. This last step would take one away from the universal embodiment of all general realities or possibilities ("*omnitudo realitatis*") to the highest individual substance as the ideal of pure reason, i.e. from mere ontology to the Aristotelian ἐπιστήμε θεολόγικη as well as from, as in Schelling, the negative to the positive philosophy[8], so as to bring fully to light the otherwise hidden motive in transcendental philosophy[9].

By means of the λόγος, i.e. of predicating something of something else ("man" and "living being" of Socrates) one only deals with general concepts of genera and species. But, according to Schelling, the generality proper to those concepts falls doubly short of the universally representative unity sought by Aristotle's first philosophy as well as by Schelling's own positive philosophy. In saying something universal of something particular, e.g. being a man of Socrates as well as of Plato, one is touching only superficially upon the essence in which

---

[7] Fr. W. J. Schelling, *Werke*, XI, p. 488.
[8] Cf. Fr. W. J. Schelling, *Werke*, XI, p. 286 ff., XII, pp. 70-93.
[9] Cf. also W. Schulz, *Das Problem der absoluten Reflexion*, Frankfurt a.M. 1963, p. 21.

both of them share. It is as it were a condescending way of speaking that does not bother about particularities. Particular or individual distinctions are viewed as unimportant or incidental. But the fact that any man comes from some other man does not yet explain why Achilles stems from Peleus[10]. On the other hand, such abstract characteristics in which several individuals may agree with one another are restricted to single specific or generic domains. Along these lines the most one can arrive at is an accumulation of all single domains, but not their internal unity. In order to clear the way to a truly representative unity of all domains of being the most important thing to do, therefore, is to replace the progressively continuous line of predicates having univocal contents, each one restricted to a single domain, with the line of analogical concepts going through and transcending them all or, to put it another way, to replace the line of abstract (or modal) concepts (so to speak "what-concepts") with that of concrete concepts (which, in contrast to "what-concepts", one might call "how-concepts"). At first, the latter includes the modal concept of possibility no less than that of actuality. But since possibility goes together with univocally abstract concepts ("what-concepts") none of which in themselves need to represent anything actual[11], the shift from univocal contents to modal concepts indicating analogical functions must end by abandoning even the concept of possibility.

Such is the path followed by Aristotle for reaching the theological unity of reality as a whole[12]. For him "actuality" ("ἐνέργεια") means

---

[10] Cf. Aristotle, *Metaphysics*, 1071a 20-22.

[11] They are real, but "real" does not here mean "actual" but rather a possible content ("what") or, as Kant put it, a "*Sach-heit*" (from "*Sache*" meaning both "*res*" and "content"). Whereas "*Realität*" ("*Sachheit*") always means an "*ali(ud-) quid*", "*Wirklichkeit*" means an actuality that may be devoid of any content.

[12] Cf. Aristotle, *Metaphysics*, XII, 4 and 5. Independently of the differences in specific content between beings living respectively in water or on earth or in the air, the *modus* or way that such diverse things as, say, fins, feet or wings function remains the same throughout; they all are, actually, for the sake of locomotion. The same applies to the way in which the four Aristotelian causes –independently of their different constitution according to the different domains involved– behave in respect to one another in order to fulfill the unitary task of making life possible

a *modus* ("how", "way") that absorbs into itself the function of "reality" in the sense of "what"¹³. Such a modal concept denotes in fact something completely different from any abstract essence in the sense of a Platonic (or Platonist) εἶδος. Understood in this way "actuality" (or "actual") would stand, for example, for "rational" (or "soul") in contrast to "man" or "animal". An abstract essence is a species (or a genus), what scholastics would have called *forma essentialis*. It is not pure form (the *forma substantialis* of scholastics) devoid of any matter or –which in this context amounts to the same– devoid of any content. *Forma essentialis* is rather form+matter (as, to borrow the Aristotelian example, in "snubness")¹⁴. "Man" is soul+body taken in general

---

and keeping it going. The case of the sun is especially illuminating for the way Schelling views Aristotelian philosophy as an ongoing process toward pure functionality or actuality. The sun lies midway between living things and God's pure actuality or functionality (νόησις νοήσεως). The sun has no specific or generic community whatsoever with plants, animals or men (it is not ὁμοειδές, cf. *Metaphysics,* 1071a 16 f.); it is rather, as Aristotle put it, that through the function of its ecliptic movement originating the changes of seasons that the sun makes sublunar life possible and keeps it going. This, of course, is a piece of Aristotle's obsolete cosmology, but it illustrates pretty well the importance attached by Aristotle to the increasing purification of all contents by means of the shift from univocally abstract concepts to analogically modal ones, as developed in the chapters 4 and 5 of *Metaphysics* XII and picked up by Schelling in order to complete Kant's critical task and rehabilitate traditional metaphysics. Along with the shift from specific and generic concept to modal concepts goes the shift from univocity to analogy, where "analogy" ("ὁμονύμως κατ' ἀναλογίαν") means identity of function in spite of diversity of content.

¹³ Cf. note 12 above.

¹⁴ Cf. Aristotle, *Metaphysics,* VII, 5; as well as Chapter 6. The method of generalizing corresponds to the *forma essentialis*, whereas the method of formalizing corresponds to the *forma substantialis*. Scholastic philosophers spoke of "*abstractio totius*" (the Aristotelian "χωριστόν κατά τὸν λόγον") and "*abstractio formae seu partis*" (the Aristotelian "ἀφαίρεσις") respectively. "*Totius*" means here that both forma and matter are taken at the level of generality, whereas "*partis seu formae*" means that only the form is taken without matter. Formalizing (ἀφαίρεσις) was originally the method of mathematics by means of which the numbers of arithmetic as well as the abstract geometrical forms (e.g. of concavity

(καθόλου, *in communi*). By contrast, actuality as *forma substantialis* or, in living things, as soul is –like concavity or hollowness without a nose– pure form, though, unlike concavity, not accidental, but substantial form. For this reason it represents the whole substance in a more comprehensive and unitary sense than the *forma essentialis*. This is why one can predicatively (καθόλου) say of Socrates that he is (a) man or, more generally, (an) animal, but not that he is soul. Such impossibility is not to be considered a disadvantage. *What* "man" means or *what* "Hector" is, remains the same thing independently of whether one is speaking of a living or of a dead man, i.e. of something that can or of something that cannot function or behave as a man. A generalizing abstraction or abstract definition says nothing about the actual capacity for functioning or behaving according to the specific essence of anything; it touches only the anatomy, so to say, at the level of generality. By contrast, formalizing modal concepts such as "living" (i.e. having a soul, whether rational or not) or "rational" do not denote an abstract content but a concrete way of being or living. They concern not only the anatomy but also the physiology of the body. With respect to them it is not the same thing whether Hector is alive or not. Both the living man and the dead body dragged by Achilles around Patroclus's tomb are called "Hector" or said to be a man, but they only have the (individual or general) name in common; the dead body, however recognizable its anatomy may have been, *is* neither Hector's nor a man's body. The body and the soul of a living thing that can still function or behave as a man are the same thing; not, however, in the sense in which Socrates and man are the same composition of matter

---

or hollowness) are derived. Interestingly, mathematics is for Aristotle nearer to metaphysics than physics (cf. *Physics,* II, 2, 193b 36 ff.). Aquinas's *separatio* as the method of metaphysics and theology as against the *abstractio* of both physics and mathematics is but the transformation of *abstractio formae* from the realm of accidentality into the realm of substantiality. As late as the 16th century Cajetanus was still able to write that the formalizing *abstractio* of mathematics was nearer to the metaphysical *separatio* proper to the ἁπλῶς κεχωρισμένα than was the generalizing *abstractio*: "propter quod metaphysicalia ut sic non comparantur ad physicalia per modum totius universalis..., sed ut formalia ad materialia, sicut et mathematicalia. Et hoc est valde notandum" (*In de ente et essentia, proemium*).

and form taken at the level of individuality (Socrates) and of generality (man) respectively. They are rather the same thing in the manner in which the soul, though being only form, represents the whole of the living man viewed from the strongest side of his being, i.e. from his being actually alive, whereas the body, though it is only matter, also represents, like the soul, the whole living man, but only as viewed in his weakest aspect, i.e. in his mere possibility or his capacity to be actually alive[15].

Now, what the bodily organization is to the living being, such is the *omnitudo realitatis* as the embodiment of all material contents to the being *tout court*. It is, that is to say, the mere possibility or capacity to be in general, but not the actual being itself which is something individual. To reach the latter it is not enough to stop at the level at which the differentiation of the modalities into possibility or potentiality, on the one hand, and of actuality, on the other, takes place. What is needed is a final purifying crisis by which the complete elimination of

---

[15] Cf. end of *Metaphysics*, VIII, 6 and of *De anima*, II 1. Schelling praised scholastic philosophers for having translated "εἶδος" in the sense of οὐσία not by *"essentia"* but by *"forma"* (cf. *Werke*, XI, p. 406). *Forma substantialis* corresponds to individual essence, whereas *forma essentialis* corresponds to specific essence. Schelling was well aware of the fact that essence, meaning a mere content ("what") which, because of its generality, represents only a possibility of being (in the case of animals a mere possibility of living), corresponds to the bodily organization of living things rather to their souls. Even general contents are more easily known than individual souls; to some extent they can even be seen with the eyes (cf. *Physics*, II 1). To know substantial form requires a deeper kind of knowing and seeing which Schelling compares to artistic insight: "The content ("what") is always for us the first thing known; it never represents an original seeing but is always presupposed. The painter depicting Callias sees first of all *what* Callias is, whether dark or pale, thick-haired or bold, etc. But all this is not Callias. Those are characteristics Callias has in common with many other men. Put together they would only represent a mere material similarity to Callias. But the artist goes further than this into something that (being ἐνέργεια actively) *is* all these things, something to which they relate as its mere presupposition. This way he is able to depict Callias himself". (*Werke*, XI, p. 403 ff.; for Schelling's interpretation of Aristotle's τί ἓν εἶναι as ἐντελέχεια cf. XI, p. 403 ff.).

all material contents and so, too, of the last remnants of possibility can be effected. This amounts to a thoroughgoing formalization which, even if it shows some important similarities with that of mathematics, goes far beyond it[16]. The result of such a move is an actual principle (ἀρχέ), an actual beginning that is not anticipated by any possibility; that is to say, a true principle that is not dependent on anything but on

---

[16] Mathematical formalizing (ἀφαίρεσις or scholastic *abstractio formalis*) functions in many ways according to a pattern following which one can arrive at the ἁπλῶς κεχωρισμένον searched for in metaphysics –provided one ultimately gets rid of the materiality mathematics only abstracts from without ever being completely free of it. So the result of mathematical formalizing is some kind of abstraction after all, never what Aquinas (*in Boethii de trinitate*) called *separatio*. Mathematical entities cannot subsist on their own. Nevertheless, they can pave the way for metaphysics by leaving aside matter –though only in this abstract way. The generality arrived at in geometry is not the abstract one of polygon in general, for example, but the concrete one of triangle. Now this gives a pattern for metaphysically grasping the relationship between the different ways of life in living things (cf. *De anima*, III, 414b 28-32). The relationship between Socrates, man and animal corresponds to that between this triangle, the general content triangle and the even more general content polygon, whereas the relationship of the vegetative, the sensitive and the intellectual soul to one another in Socrates corresponds rather to that obtaining between the single polygons. Just as the triangle is not outside or –in the vertical order of species and genera– below the quadrangle and so on but inside them all, so the θρεπτικόν is contained in the αἰσθητικόν and the λογιστικόν. But that means that the relationship between them is not that of univocity. Unlike the genus animal which remain the same in content throughout all its subordinate species and individuals, the vegetative soul or θρεπτικόν is not the same in plants, animals or men. The relationship is not to be called "κατ' ἕν" (where "κατά" indicates direction from above to below) but "πρὸς ἕν" (cf. *Metaphysics*, 1003a 33-b 19; πρὸς ἕν was called by Cajetanus *analogia attributionis*). In the same way, whereas the logical genus animal is predicated univocally of the species, which are constituted by so called specific differences joining the genus from outside without modifying it, is the metaphysical genus nothing other than some species or other, while each species (cf. *Metaphysics*, 1057b 35) is, again, nothing other than or beyond its own *differentia specifica*. This is why, metaphysically speaking, the *differentia specifica* represents the whole οὐσία (cf. *Metaphysics*, VII 12; cf. on this chapter my book *Forma formarum*; cf. also, more generally, as *Eindeutigkeit und Variation*).

which all things depend. Such a principle must be unique and, because devoid of any nameable content beside its own actuality, cannot not be compared with anything else. As long as a given actuality consists in something or other –in being either animal or man, sun, world, *ego* or even all this together (the "*omnitudo realitatis*")– it still presupposes some possibility, something that can be as well as not be, and so is not yet pure actuality but, at most, reality. The actuality of a presupposed possibility is nothing other than a hypothesis turned real. It is, only *if* the presupposition has been actualized. But then it is, to put it in Kantian terms, not thing-in-itself but appearance and so is subjected to the principle of sufficient reason, i.e. it needs something else in order to be. Just as anything which is something or other –for instance, the sun or the universe– can possibly not move or not act, since it only has the possibility of doing it ("everything having a power needs to activate it"[17]), so the whole possibility of being or "*omnitudo realitatis*" might not have been, even if for Aristotle it, like the universe, has always been: "It is possible that something can be but does not be"[18]. It is because the vault of heaven is not identical with its however long lasting movement that it is not necessarily moving. Now, just as the everlastingly moving universe remains the mere possibility of its own movement, so, too, anything, including every possible thing, is nothing else than its own possibility. And should it eternally exist as such a possibility yet it would, nevertheless, eternally exist in the way that Kant's transcendental philosophy calls an appearance, i.e. both in the way of possibly being otherwise as well as of not being at all[19]. But if the only beings are appearances, i.e. if being as a whole is only the possibility of being, then PNC cannot have the unconditional validity

---

[17] Aristotle, *Metaphysics*, 1071b 17.

[18] Aristotle, *Metaphysics*, 1071b 25 f. Neither this nor similar passages (above all *Metaphysics*, 1050b 3-19 and 1071b 24-26) have, of course, anything to do with a theory of creation. Their sense is rather this: there must be something necessarily existing, viz. God, for otherwise the universe would have to be contingent –which it cannot be.

[19] This is the most important meaning of "appearance" from Kant onwards (cf. my article "Das Problem der Außenwelt im transzendentalen Idealismus", *Philosophisches Jahrbuch*, 76, 1968).

it must have. The principle delimits what cannot possibly be so, viz. that with respect to one and the same thing something can and at the same time cannot be the case. Just this impossibility would be possible, if there were only be being as possibility of being (Kant's *omnitudo realitatis seu possibilitatis* or Schelling's *"Seinpotenz"*) –regardless of whether it actually is or not. For the possibility of being is also possibility of not being[20].

So Kant's embodiment of all realities or predicates cannot represent for Schelling a final critical decision. Embracing as it does all possibilities, including the alternatives to those actualized, the *omnitudo realitatis* rather represents the realm of pure indecisiveness between being and non-being. Schelling interprets this indecisiveness as referring to the subject that, according to Aristotle, is required by contrary and privative opposites, including also the excluded part of the opposition[21]. Such a subject is a presupposed third between the opposites (a something, a content or a "what"), some kind of lead weight that makes impossible a complete critical elimination or separation ("χωρισμός" in the sense of Aristotelian God as "ἁπλῶς κεχωρισμένον"). Still, the indecisiveness concerned is the condition for the possibility of any meaningful predicative ("καθόλου") saying. It is precisely because of the all-including[22] function of the *omnitudo realitatis* which, allowing room (*"einräumend"*) even for the excluded possibility, keeps a final decision still open that there can be meaningful propositions. Without it, i.e. without the possibility for any proposition to be false by true affirmation of its negation, each proposition would be like the allegedly true ones "the voice is not white" or "the stone is healthy" or "the baby is uneducated", etc., the negation of which are all equally devoid of sense. Just as only of what can be sick can it be said that it is healthy and only of what can be dark can it be

---

[20] Cf. Aristotle, *Metaphysics*, 1071b 17 f.

[21] Cf. Aristotle, *Metaphysics*, XII 1 and 2, 1069b 3-9. In order to convey the precise sense of that inclusion Schelling employs the verb *"einräumen"* as a translation of the Greek "χωρεῖν" ("making place for another") (Cf. Fr. W. J. Schelling, *Werke*, XI, p. 305 ff.; cf. also XI, p. 290 ff., XI, p. 428, XIII, p. 96.

[22] Cf. note 16 above.

said that it is bright, etc., so, too, "to be" can only be said predicatively of what can equally not be. And that is the sense of Kant's *omnitudo realitatis* or of Schelling's potency to be (*"Seinspotenz"*)²³. The realm of the principle of sufficient reason ("why is something so and so rather than otherwise? Why is there something rather than nothing?") is like all-embracing privative opposition. Privation is not like unconditional negation ("ἀπόφασις ἁπλῶς") but a negation that is restricted to some or other domain or content ("ἀπόφασις ἀπὸ τινὸς ὁρισμένου γένους"). Excluding the other part of the opposition such a negation nevertheless includes its possibility²⁴. The situation does not change so long as the whole stock of possibilities has not been exhausted. It is not enough no longer to consider the moving, functioning or acting of the sun, of the vault of heavens or of the whole universe or even of the totality of being as something accidental but rather as substantial, being the actuality of them all, if on the other hand the content of the sun or the vault of the heavens or the universe or even the being as a whole is still presupposed to such an actuality just as much as the organic body is presupposed to the soul as the actuality of life of which such a body is only a mere possibility. For all things would only hypothetically be actual as depending upon and conditional to those presupposed possibilities. It is only by resolutely interpreting Aristotelian metaphysics as theology, but not as ontology, that, according to Schelling, any residue of indecisive wavering between being and non-being can be overcome and the unconditional decisiveness of the principle of contradiction achieved²⁵. One can only get rid of the wavering still included in the half-hearted exclusion of one opposite if one is prepared to go forward to something that is not only this or that or even all things actually but actuality *tout court*. "There must be some principle consisting only in its activity and whose essence is therefore nothing but actuality"²⁶. According to

---

[23] Cf. Fr. W. J. Schelling, *Werke*, XI, p. 308 ff.; p. 524 f.; IX, p. 215 f., XII, p. 52 ff.
[24] Cf. Fr. W. J. Schelling, *Werke*, XI, p. 307.
[25] Compare Aristotle, *Metaphysics*, 100b 11-17 with Fr. W. J. Schelling, *Werke*, XIII, p. 161.
[26] Aristotle, *Metaphysics*, 1071b 20.

Schelling one is fully entitled to see in this Aristotelian pure actuality the very first principle of all being the most original thing one can think of. For this must be something the possibility of which cannot be thought of before it is actually there[27].

Having reached the place reserved for an activity which, because it is in advance critically purified of all possible contents, lies before, and is free from, any uncritical indecisiveness, the next task on the path of a metaphysics which will complete Kants's critical endeavor is to point to the kind of activities that are not qualified to occupy the place of a truly first principle or ἀρχέ that cannot dispense with, abandon or put behind itself its own beginning. Unfitted for being an activity that does not presuppose any essence but is its own essence are all activities which require a subject as some kind of support in order to be in the first place. Such are all activities falling into the category of movement, for movement always presupposes some moving thing as its subject and cannot, therefore, itself be something substantial. So this second stage of metaphysics consists in the critical separation of the concept of movement (κίνησις) from that of activity (ἐνέργεια). In contrast to any such movement having an end outside of itself, ἐνέργεια always has its end (its τέλος or perfection) within itself. As Aristotle says, when one lives one has already lived and when one thinks one has already thought[28], but the laying of the foundation stone does not mean that the building is already there. In the case of any truly substantial activity the beginning should therefore be sufficient for the whole, it must not be conceived of as going on toward an end in order for it to arrive at its fulfillment. Now even an animal has to go on living in order not to cease to live. By contrast, a fully actual (and hence also truly original) life, since it would be complete from the start, need not go on living like the soul of a body which, because of its specific organs, is not life itself but only the possibility of life. By contrast, the very first principle is never in danger of not living nor is it in need of any effort in order to keep on living. For the same reason, in trying to bring Kant's transcendental philosophy to its comple-

---

[27] Cf. Fr. W. J. Schelling, *Werke*, XIII, p. 263 and XIV, p. 187.
[28] Aristotle, *Metaphysics*, 1048b 33-35.

tion, Schelling (like Fichte before him) was compelled critically to purify the first principle of being as well as of reason from all objective ingredients, i.e. from the idea of a merely general being as the content of reason itself. Otherwise such a principle could not stand on its own but would be dependent upon, and indecisively hanging from, some presupposition which would only unduly weaken it. For thus it could not be the first principle upon which all things depend[29]. Schelling has also to recognize that one cannot stop at the soul, even were one to take it generally as the actuality of all living things like Plato's world-soul: "For this concept of an essence that is itself activity, but activity of something else, the language has a very convenient name, namely "soul"... Also Aristotle, on whom we ought to fall back for every definition, encountered the same concept. He explained it as actuality ("ἐντελέχεια"), not actuality *tout court*, but actuality of some thing that is such and such, i.e. of some thing that is only capable of living"[30].

Closer to a critically decided subject that, remaining subject without turning into an object, can stand on its own, closer to it than the concept of organism in the Aristotelian metaphysics of forms (εἰδέ) as well as that of a Platonic intelligible world of ideas (εἰδέ), this being a not yet completely purified reason, lie therefore for Schelling both the *ego* of transcendental philosophy and the Aristotelian spirit or νοῦς in the sense of an active thinking (νόησις). For only by remaining free from every material content, as Aristotle said[31], can the *nous* take command of and know the whole range of material forms or material being[32]. This represents a further purifying crisis. Pure reason has also

---

[29] Cf. Aristotle, *Metaphysics*, 1072b 14.

[30] Fr. W. J. Schelling, *Werke*, XI, p. 402.

[31] Aristotle, *De anima*, III, 4, 429b 18-20.

[32] To see the connection of this with the necessity of overcoming the Kantian *omnitudo realitatis* one has to take into account that "material" means here any content. In other words, material means also formal, if by "formal" one understands a pure content. The contention of Schelling is then that this content (the whole realm of εἰδέ) is not yet so purified as to be able to stand on its own or, in the sense of Platonic χωρισμός, to be truly ἁπλῶς χωριστόν.

to go through it. It is of this νοῦς that, commenting on the word "spirit" ("*Geist*"), Schelling writes that "its meaning is totally different from that of 'soul', for only the spirit is something that can break free from all being as the matter of thought". And he adds: "Science, for example, is not the work of soul but of the spirit"[33]. Nevertheless, were the spirit, because of its capacity of freeing itself from any objective content, to consider itself to be the unique and incomparable first principle (ἀρχέ) it would be claiming a place which does not belong to it[34]. For in order to become free from all things it has yet to exercise such a capacity, and this means that it is not itself aloof from things which it can only after that operation command (ἀρχέιν).

The subordinate rank of Aristotelian *nous* as well as Kantian *ego*, neither consisting purely in a truly and everlastingly original beginning (ἀρχέιν), is proved by phenomena associated with the spirit or reason such as that of forgetting and remembering. The strain of having to remember in order not to forget is for Schelling but the consequence of the predicament in which the spirit or *ego* finds itself of abstracting from itself in order to know something else and above all of abstracting from its being a subject in order to know itself, but then only as an object.

As long as one does not go beyond the gap between object and subject, essence or substance (οὐσία) and activity (ἐνέργεια), content and mode, "what" and "how", possibility and actuality, matter and form as well as κίνησις and ἐνέργεια, one has everywhere to presuppose some kind of inert weight in the form of a possibility that has not been actualized in advance –be it the body or be it the power of thinking without yet thinking or be it, as in the case of the alleged first principle, an *ens realissimum*. This way one surrenders the critical decisiveness of the commanding principle (ἀρχέ) of knowledge, the one thing presupposed to knowledge of all other things, and with it also the original beginning of anything. The passage in the *Critique of Pure Reason*, from which we quoted an excerpt about the undecidedness between being and not being at the beginning of the present

---

[33] Fr. W. J. Schelling, *Werke*, XI, p. 402.
[34] *Ibid.*

chapter, bears witness of such a loss of a truly original beginning: "There is something very strange in the fact that once we assume something to exist we cannot avoid inferring that something exists necessarily... Thus while I may indeed be obliged to assume something necessary as a condition of existence in general, I cannot think any particular thing as in itself necessary. In other words, I can never *complete* the regress to the conditions of existence save by assuming a necessary thing, and yet am never in a position to *begin* with such a thing"[35].

If the commanding beginning of a true principle is not to be lost by being reversed into a movement of thinking commanding it then the journey toward the true principle both of being and of knowledge ought not, as in Kant, to stop half way. Only through a complete purification of the universal content containing all possibilities of being can the thinking of the spirit be transformed into an absolute knowledge[36] by subjecting it to, and letting it be commanded by, the true principle which is an original activity of pure actuality, the possibility of which cannot even be thought, or believed in, or imagined, until one has been confronted with its actuality (such being, according to Schelling, genuine originality). At this point Schelling's negative philosophy can give way to a positive philosophy (of mythology and revelation) in which as a matter of fact the possibilities of being do come after the pure actuality of a truly original beginning. But, according to Schelling, this is also the point Kant's critical impulse stopped short of. It is because he was seeking for the ideal of reason along the lines of the *omnitudo realitatis* that Kant had to interpret the God of metaphysics as that individual thing that actively *is* all possibilities, i.e. as *ens realissimum*, without being able to consider Him as detached from all of them. And it was precisely because of this that he had to inquire into the very possibility of God without realizing that

---

[35] I. Kant, *Critique of pure reason*, B 643 f.; translat. Kemp Smith.
[36] Fr. W. J. Schelling, *Werke*, XIII, p. 98.

this very question cannot but miss God's pure actuality[37]. Similarly, Kant was compelled to ask about the very possibility of metaphysics, whereas for Schelling positive philosophy, once the critically purifying task of negative philosophy has been completed, has to begin on its own without presupposing negative philosophy[38]. It is only for historical, though also for didactic reasons, that he himself begins with negative philosophy along the lines of, but at the same time beyond the whole range of, Kants's critical philosophy proceeding right to the ultimate issues of Aristotle's metaphysics.

With respect to something which, like the truly original beginning, can in no way be anticipated by anything at all, any question about its possibility comes always too late. As regards any actual thing or content we have to distinguish between its possibility and its actuality. Only with respect to the everlastingly original beginning of pure actuality could we not do it even if we wanted to. That is why from Schelling's standpoint Kant's final theoretical stance, according to which it is because of the peculiar constitution of our subjectivity that we must distinguish between possibility and actuality, contingency and necessity[39], cannot stand up against a sustained critical enterprise like that of the genuinely Aristotelian metaphysics which succeeded where Plato had failed, viz. in establishing a truly critical χωρισμός. Confronted with the very first principle of a ἁπλῶς κεχορισμένον our thinking cannot proceed any more along the lines of abstraction. Such a principle cannot be reached by means of *abstractio* but only, as Scholastics would say and Schelling repeats[40], by *separatio*. Through *abstractio* one is only able to obtain generalities. It is only through *separatio* that one can arrive at the substantial formality of a principle devoid of any content used up, as it were, by sheer actuality. To leave this actuality out of consideration amounts in the final analysis to

---

[37] In "Die philosophische querelles des anciens et des modernes" I have tried to retrace this back to the transformation of Aristotelian metaphysics brought about by Duns Scotus.

[38] Cf. Fr. W. J. Schelling, *Werke*, XI, p. 564; XIII, pp. 92, 155.

[39] Cf. §§ 76 and 77 of the *Critique of Judgment*.

[40] Fr. W. J. Schelling, *Werke*, XI, p. 488 f.

bringing thinking to a standstill. By contrast, the decisiveness of the original beginning is thinking as everlasting living and being (*intelligere, vivere, esse*[41]).

Such an original beginning cannot be called in question by any conceptual thinking. Being definitively decided, it can in no way get lost: αὐτό ἀκίνητον ὄν, ἐνέργεια ὄν, τοῦτο οὐκ ἐνδέχεται ἄλλως ἔχειν οὐδαμῶς[42]. What, like the νόησις νοήσεως, is its own behavior, cannot be otherwise even when it behaves so or otherwise (or behaves this and then that way), for it is not *something that* behaves so or otherwise but is just a behaving so or otherwise. In this beginning of an everlasting subject that always remain subject the critical principle of decision which, in the form of PNC, is something purely negative and abstract finds its own positive fulfillment.

At this point the question returns of how such an ἀρχέ can be something general and intelligible, having got rid of any kind of community grounded in contents like those of genera and species. It is the question of how such a pure activity, being critically purified from all reminiscences of a κίνησις and so, too, of any object, can nevertheless be the God on whom all things depend, as Aristotle would have put it[43], or be the Lord of Being, as Schelling put it[44]. Between the answer given by Aristotle and that given by Schelling to this question lies not so much Kant as Christianity with its own approach to history, different from that of paganism. But the direction in which Schelling seeks the new generality has more in common with Aristotle than with Kant or Hegel. So he attacks both of them and sides with Aristotle when he writes: "The way goes not from the general to the particular, as is usually held today"[45]. "There is nothing general before individuality itself; the general essence does not exist without some-

---

[41] Cf. also Fichte's *Doctrine of Science* from 1804, *Werke* X, edited by I. H. Fichte.
[42] Aristotle, *Metaphysics*, 1072b 8.
[43] Cf. Aristotle, *Metaphysics*, 1072b 13 f.
[44] "*Der Herr des Seins*" or God of Christianity as Schelling conceived Him.
[45] Fr. W. J. Schelling, *Werke*, XI, p. 588.

thing absolute (actively) *being* it", i.e. –in Aristotelian terminology– "without there being something that is the cause of its being"[46].

In contrast to this uncritical procedure of (generalizing) *abstractio* the critical way of *separatio* leads to a generality which, being grounded in an absolute individuality, is genuinely representative. The general pattern of this kind of representation is mathematical formalizing as applied and transformed into a theological metaphysics that has left behind any merely ontological generalizing. So it is not the abstract idea of polygon that functions in a geometry as Aristotle conceived it as the general pattern for all polygons but the concrete idea of triangle. In the same way, for mathematics as a whole it is not abstract mathematics that functions as the general discipline but concrete arithmetic (although not all commentators of Aristotle agree on this). And it is not the later developed *metaphysica generalis* that functions as general theoretical science but the ἐπιστήμε θεολόγικη. Nor is it the abstract concept of art that functions as the general idea of art but it is first of all drama that represents all mimetic arts. In the same way, it is not abstractly objective norms that represent morality but truly excellent men. And the same holds regarding the man himself: it is not a collection of his several powers that is representative of him but, above all (μάλιστα), the highest and most separable of them all, viz. νοῦς; and similarly for the πόλις: it is its most outstanding characteristic that represents the general organizing form (σύστημα) of any given political constitution. Nowhere is generality to be found outside of some concrete form. Generality is everywhere embodied in the most prominent and best part[47], which represents and commands the whole domain involved. Thus and most generally, being as such is not to be found in some pale community of characteristics but in a thoroughly separated individual with respect to which all things are organized[48].

This was the direction in which Schelling was to follow Aristotle. It does not lead from the general down to the particular. It is rather the

---

[46] Fr. W. J. Schelling, *Werke*, XI, p. 586.

[47] Κύριον καὶ ἄμεινον.

[48] πρὸς ἕν ἅπαντα συντέτακται; Aristotle, *Metaphysics*, 1075b 18 f.

individuality which is itself general –a concrete, not an abstract generality. And it is in the unobstructed enjoyment of theory that this concrete and genuinely representative generality can be most distinctively experienced. So we might resume our argument by referring to the Aristotelian doctrine of pleasure. At the end of the long journey of theological metaphysics, after every kind of movement has been removed, pure actuality, that pleasure of which Aristotle says that it emerges like the bloom upon genuine activity[49], shows up also in Schelling's latest philosophy[50].

In contrast to any conceptual content that can be attained by *abstractio*, the actual being of which can always be called in question, experienced sensations of pleasure have the same unique and unquestionable character[51] as the performed activities which they accompany as their perfective bloom. Like seeing, pleasure is something total (τελεία) in each moment. As Eduard Mörike put it, "the beautiful rests blissfully in itself". But inasmuch as common pleasure (either the

---

[49] Aristotle, *Ethica Nicomachea*, 1174b 33.

[50] Cf. Fr. W. J. Schellings, *Einleitung in die Philosophie der Mythology*, lecture XX.

[51] One may consider the following text of Marcel Proust the best translation into the language of modern aesthetics of the gist of Aristotelian metaphysics as developed by Schelling: "I felt... that desire to live which is reborn in us whenever we become conscious anew of beauty and happiness. We invariably forget that these are individual qualities, and, mentally substituting for them a conventional type at which we arrive by striking a sort of mean among the different faces that have taken our fancy, among the pleasures we have known, we are left with mere abstract images which are lifeless and insipid because they lack precisely that element of novelty, different from anything we have known, that element that is peculiar to beauty and to happiness...". Among other things, the difference between *abstractio* and *separatio* is very well expressed here. Then Proust continues in another key: "So is it that a well-read man will at once begin to yawn with boredom when one speaks to him of a new 'good book', because he imagines a sort of composite of all the good books that he has read, whereas a good book is something special, something unforeseeable, and is made up not of the sum of all previous masterpieces but of something which the most thorough assimilation of every one of them would not enable him to discover, since it exists not in their sum but beyond it".

pleasure inherent in sensitive life or that of an *ego* objectifying itself in the process of thinking itself) always occurs in a subject that is not identical with its own blissful activity, such pleasure cannot simply be identified with the pure happiness bestowed by a substantial activity from which pleasure in no way can ever be separated. True, in the second treatise on pleasure in the *Nicomachean Ethics* Aristotle dismisses as irrelevant the question whether it is the enjoyable activity of knowing that is acting or rather its subject[52]. But this is so only as long as the known object and the knowing subject remain dependent upon each other, with activity and passivity (τὸ ποιητικόν καὶ τὸ παθητικόν) being in harmony. In such circumstances, as long as the enjoyable activity lasts, the difference between the perfectly successful activity of true happiness and a partly still inert and strenuous activity of mere pleasure cannot but remain hidden from us. But one is able to notice the difference as soon as the pleasure of an activity, by reason of any small alteration in the balance between activity and passivity, recedes and gives way to some other. As Aristotle points out, the worse the actors are the more the spectators in the theater indulge in eating sweets. The action has been degraded into a mere show[53].

By contrast, it is not possible that the very first ἀρχέ, remaining uninterruptedly in command as it does, ever loses the freshness of its own beginning. Not being a beginning of anything different from its own beginning, i.e. having completely got rid of the quality of κίνησις, it can never either fail or fall behind, either recede or get tired —whereas in order for pleasure to persist it has to be kept going with some effort however minimal. It is behind that need to be kept going that there lurks the possibility both of fatigue or weariness and of shallow habituation to something that, just as it has to keep on going in order to be, it may have been keeping on going for an indefinitely past time[54]. Here, too, pleasure reflects the condition of temporality. It also reflects the process of movement inherent in the life and knowledge of both substances and *egos*. However enjoyable that kind

---

[52] Aristotle, *Ethica Nicomachea*, 1174b 16 ff.

[53] Cf. Aristotle, *Ethica Nicomachea*, 1175b 10-13.

[54] Cf. Aristotle, *Ethica Nicomachea*, 1175a 1-10.

of living and knowing may be, such a condition transform both into something strenuous and tiresome[55]. It is only in the perfect individuality of an ἀρχέ as a purely detached beginning unable to leave its own beginning behind it that everything else is left behind, including getting used to or forgetting anything or ceasing to be in any way. Before it all other things have to recede –"χωρεῖν", as Schelling says–[56] in order to make room for everlasting happiness[57]. Hegel ends his *Encyclopaedia of Philosophical Sciences* with a quotation taken from Chapter 7 of Book XII of the *Metaphysics*[58] and ending with the words: "And this is God". But, in contrast to Schelling, who in the same connection relies more upon Chapter 9 than upon Chapter 7 of the same book, Hegel interprets them as referring to an ἀρχέ that has not got rid of all content of thought[59].

Let us take stock of our interpretation by elaborating on this difference. E. Oeser is the only author known to me who gives any account of the relationship between Aristotle and Schelling[60]. This is surprising, if one realizes how much Schelling's interpretation of Aristotle has been praised by some important scholars. Wolfgang Wieland, for example, while considering the chapters on Aristotle in Hegel's lectures on the history of philosophy to be "the best exposition of Aristotle's philosophy available", still stresses the fact that Schelling's interpretations of Aristotle are in some respects superior to those of Hegel[61]. He refers approvingly to their greater "*spekulativer*" force. In my opinion this greater force of Schelling's as compared with Hegel's interpretations is mainly due to the fact that the latter, unlike the former, do not overcome the dimension of εἶδος. With respect to Hegel's quotation from Aristotle's passage about the νόησις νοήσεως just

---

[55] Cf. Aristotle, *Ethica Nicomachea*, 1175a 1-10.
[56] Fr. W. J. Schelling, *Werke*, XI, p. 428; XIII, p. 96.
[57] Cf. Aristotle, *Metaphysics*, 1072b 24.
[58] Aristotle, *Metaphysics*, 1072b 18-30.
[59] Compare, e. g., 1072b 22 f. in Chapter 7 with 1074b 32-35 in Chapter 9.
[60] E. Oeser, *Die antike Dialektik in der Spätphilosophie Schellings*, Wien-München 1968.
[61] W. Wieland, *Die Aristotelische Physik*, Göttingen 1962, p. 34; cf. also note 16.

given, H.-G. Gadamer has pointed to the limitations of idealist Aristotelian interpretation as a whole. There cannot be any doubt either about the fact that the Aristotelian model for life is not taken from thinking but first of all from the metabolism of living things, or about the fact that Aristotle mainly conceives thinking according not so much to the pattern of the activity of thinking as to that of the content thought, i.e. the εἶδος, received. From this Gadamer concludes: "It is therefore only with respect to the general structure of some self-relationship that Hegel agrees with Aristotle"[62]. With respect to *De anima* III 6, Gadamer comments on this conclusion that "where the opposition of *steresis* is not any more there thinking thinks itself, i.e. *eidos* is present to itself"[63]. In passing from Hegel to Schelling one can recognize an important difference to the credit of the latter as regards the interpretation of Aristotle. For Schelling, unlike Hegel, was able to realize that Aristotle arrived at his theology precisely by overcoming εἶδος. True, drawing, like Hegel, upon Fichte's concept of *Tathandlung* in the sense of intellectual intuition and pure willing[64], Schelling, too, conceives the Aristotelian ἐνέργεια according to the pattern of the self-relationship of pure thinking. But at the same time he was fully aware of the fact that clinging to the dimension of εἶδος would hinder one from arriving at just this self-relationship of pure thinking and willing. The way in which Aristotle had moved on from biology to theology confirms the thesis about the greater reliability of Schelling's as compared to Hegel's interpretation with regard to this important point. Aristotle characterizes the activity of organic life as well as of human thinking only according to the pattern of εἶδος[65], whereas in characterizing God's own activity of living and thinking he lets drop any mention of εἶδος[66]. The dropping out of εἶδος is indeed

---

[62] H. G. Gadamer, "Hegel und die antike Dialektik", *Hegel-Studien*, 1, 1961, p. 196.

[63] H. G. Gadamer, "Hegel und die antike Dialektik", p. 196. Aristotle, *De anima*, III, 6, 430b 20 ff.

[64] Cf. Fr. W. J. Schelling, *Werke*, XI, pp. 480, 369, 419 ff., 453 f., 459 ff.

[65] Cf. Aristotle, *Metaphysics*, 1050b 2 f.; and *De anima*, III, 4, 429a 15.

[66] Compare the passages referred to in the previous note with *Metaphysics*, 1072a 25 f. and 1072b 22.

necessary in order to see the identity of God's activity of thinking with God's substance[67]. To hold on to εἶδος, essential as it is for the duality of possibility and actuality as far as the relation of knowledge in the case of the human νοῦς and even in the case of the νοητόν of God's νοῦς is concerned, would amount to unduly widening the gap between the idealistic interpretation of Aristotle and Aristotle himself –at least as far as Schelling is concerned. From Schelling's point of view the characterization of God's activity of thinking as νόησις νοήσεως is to be preferred to any other use of the expressions "νοῦς" and "νοητόν", both of which indeed suggest something like an εἶδος. For whereas the activity of God's thinking might be characterized as νοῦς, yet the human νοῦς, on the other hand, could not be characterized at all as "νόησις". The reason for this is that, in advance of any act of knowing (νοοῦν), the human intellect is something that may either know or not know, i.e. it is νοητικόν. As such it is in need of something known (νοούμενον) which may be either actually known or not actually known, i.e. which in advance of its being a νοούμενον must be a νοητικόν and as such a mere εἶδος[68]. In other words, as long as one clings to the dimension of εἶδος then the original activity in which, if in anything, God as νόησις νοήσεως consists and whose possibility cannot be anticipated by anything at all, is nowhere to be found. The fourfold splitting up into νοητόν, νοούμενον, νοητικόν and νοοῦν parallels, in fact, that of κινητόν, κινούμενον, κινητικόν and κινοῦν[69]. It is a characteristic of man's intermittent, not of God's everlastingly enjoyable knowledge, in which the first principle of all things as interpreted by Schelling consists. Having arrived at this point along the road of negative philosophy mirroring traditional metaphysics, Schelling's further endeavour is to recapture the dimension of εἶδος. But this is the task of positive philosophy. And this task can only be fulfilled *a posteriori* by taking into account the facts recorded

---

[67] Cf. Aristotle, *Metaphysics*, 1074b 18 -35.

[68] Cf. Chapter 4 of *De anima*.

[69] Cf. Aristotle, *Physics*, II, 3, 202a 12 ff. as well as the overcoming of this fourfold pattern in *Metaphysics*, 1074b 25-1075a 5.

in mythology[70] and revelation. This way Schelling thought to leave behind Hegel's "lazy God" who only emerges at the end of a predictable ideal development, when nothing more and, *a fortiori*, nothing original is left to do.

---

[70] Schelling is well aware of the fact that for Aristotle the φιλόσοφός ought to be also a φιλόμυθος (cf. *Metaphysics*, 982b 18 as well as fragment 668, Rose = fragment 11,1, Gigon).

CHAPTER 8

HEIDEGGER ON HEGEL AND ARISTOTLE:
A STRAIGHT LINE?

About the same time as Martin Heidegger was maturing into a philosopher, Marcel Proust, in his monumental *Remembrance of Things Past*, referred to a professor of history at the Sorbonne by saying of him that "he was out of sympathy with the modern Sorbonne, where ideas of scientific exactitude, after the German model, were beginning to prevail over humanism"[1]. The time to which Marcel Proust referred was, of course, that of *la belle époque*, a century ago. A quarter of a century later the German model of which Proust spoke was firmly established almost everywhere in the academic quarters of the Western world. Whether or not the philosopher Heidegger was ever attached to this model, the fact is that he sought to keep his own work at an increasing distance to it without, however, ever attaching himself to the rival model of humanism. In this respect, the two world wars were undoubtedly of special significance for him.

It was only after World War Two that, in his letter to Jean Beaufret, Heidegger defined his own position towards humanism in a fully explicit way. But in the period between the two great wars of our century he had already touched upon the issue of humanism and culture in a rather dramatic way. This was a period during which Germany, despite its first crushing defeat, was witnessing a revival of her Classical tradition under the heading of "The New Humanism" of which Werner Jaeger's *Paideia* was only one, though an outstanding example. In the purely philosophical field one may think of Ernst Cassirer's *Philoso-*

---

[1] M. Proust, *A la recherche du temps perdu*, Gallimard, Paris 1954, v. II, p. 868. English translation by C.K. Scott Moncrief and Terence Kilmartin in the Penguin Books, vol 2, p. 897.

phy of Symbolic Forms as a similarly outstanding example. And it was in the famous series of disputes between Ernst Cassirer and his junior colleague Martin Heidegger in the Davos of Thomas Mann's *Magic Mountain* that the two attitudes most dramatically clashed with each other when Heidegger reproached Cassirer for inviting man to make himself comfortable in the shelters (*Behausungen*) of culture without realizing that it is the genuine task of philosophy, as Heidegger put it, "to cast man back from the sloth of using the products of the spirit into the hardship of fate"[2]. As is well known, he eventually went so far as to reject the title of philosophy for his own endeavors altogether[3].

Under such circumstances one may ask what the point is of discussing Heidegger alongside two classic philosophers such as Aristotle and Hegel. The scope of this question is not limited to the issue of humanism. It affects not only Heidegger's attitude towards culture in general and philosophy in particular, but it affects his attitude towards the German model of exact investigation or *Forschung* as well. In fact, Heidegger's motives for mistrusting both models can be traced back to the same origin. Their common origin lies in the very nature of metaphysics in the sense given by Heidegger to the term "onto-theology", i. e. in the sense in which metaphysics represents a progressive oblivion of being in favor of beings, of *Sein* in favor of *Seiendes*.

I am not going to give a new interpretation of this real or alleged oblivion nor to repeat other interpretations. Rather, in the introductory part of my exposition, I would like to explain the way in which Heidegger's thesis of *Seinsvergessenheit* is to be considered responsible for Heidegger's persistent attitude towards both humanism and *Forschung*. Then, in the central part of my exposition I shall draw some consequences from this attitude with regard to Heidegger's interpretation of Hegel and Aristotle concerning time, being, and substance.

---

[2] M. Heidegger, "Davoser Disputation", edited as an appendix to *Kant und das Problem der Metaphysik* in *Gesamtausgabe* (*GA*) I 3. Frankfurt 1991, p. 291.

[3] Cf. M. Heidegger, "Das Ende der Philosophie und die Aufgabe des Denkens" in *Zur Sache des Denkens*, Tübingen 1969, pp. 61-81. For his own work Heidegger retained at first the title "*Forschung*", if only in the sense of "*phänomenologishe Forschung*", but he gave this up later on (cf. also note 25 below).

Finally, in a third section, I shall conclude with some remarks in a more general key.

1

Heidegger's attitude to both cultural humanism and exact investigation was rooted in his conviction of the inadequacy of theory vis-à-vis human life in its individual as well as its historical dimension. The word "theory" is here to be taken literally, i.e. broadly enough so as to encompass all connotations of "looking at" including the Biblical "enticing of eyes" or "*Augenlust*" ("lust of the eyes"). But, of course, it is not so much because the Greeks were, as the saying goes, "*Augenmenschen*" ("men of eyes") that they, according to Heidegger, bequeathed the notion of theory to the Western world. Even during the time of the Third Reich Heidegger at least rejected firmly any kind of biologism, naturalism or, for that matter, racism. If the Greeks were "*Augenmenschen*" this was because of their mental or spiritual attitude, i.e. because of the way in which being manifested itself to them and at the same time concealed itself from them. This also holds for metaphysics as interpreted by Heidegger.

What is concealed from metaphysics are its own foundations, i.e. the fact that the essence or sense of being is time. A clear example of this is to be found, according to Heidegger, in what he once –drawing more on the Scholastic tradition than on Aristotle himself– called *analogia entis*. In this tradition substance represents the leading meaning of being, its *primum analogatum*. But whereas at the beginning the Greek "οὐσία" was still understood in the full range of its own connotations, at the end it was reduced to the impoverished notion of *substantia*. What the notion of *substantia* mainly left out was precisely the temporal connotation of "οὐσία" (*Anwesenheit* and *Gegenwart*, presence and the present) on which Heidegger, rightly or wrongly, put so much stress. According to Heidegger, this is already evident in the twist taken by onto-theology into the timeless and eternal when Aristotle set about finding the most primordial sense of "οὐσία" in a unique and –to borrow from Schelling against Hegelian Aristotelianism– idle or lazy God ("*fauler Gott*") who makes his appearance only at the end of the system, when nothing more is to be done[4]. It is the same twist that had already led Aristotle to give pride of place to the world –detached theoretical wisdom over the world–orientated practical wisdom, σοφία over φρόνησις, *theoria* over *praxis*.

In fact, immediately after World War One Heidegger started to scourge what he had been seeking to defend before, viz. the objective and universal validity of eternal truths and values. After such a catastrophe for Europe in general and Germany in particular Heidegger came to see in the belief in allegedly pure objective truths the attempt of human life or *Dasein* to distract itself from its radically contingent condition or, as he put it, its facticity. In this respect no difference in principle is to be found between humanism and *Forschung*. The pretensions to unshakeable results on the part of the latter correspond on the part of the former to the picture of cultural contents hanging, as it were, on the high wall of ideal values as if among them one could choose the fittest ones, as from a collection of clothes, in order to cover one's own existential nakedness. Even Aristotelian virtues, being as they are κτῆματα rather than χρῆσεις, properties and proprieties rather than praxis proper, represent for him some sort of moral code and are by this very fact to be considered but another consequence of the objectifying drive in metaphysics. The same applies, of course, to the whole realm of Hegelian objective spirit, substantial *Sittlichkeit* or public morality. So it is not surprising that just as Heidegger never found the way from the Aristotelian ethics to the Politics, he, similarly, never found the way from the passions of the *Rhetorics* to the virtues of the *Nicomachean Ethics*[5]. Nor is it surprising that, under such circumstances, to deal with metaphysics ought for him to be at the same time to retrace its living origins by patiently

---

[4] Cf. Fr. W. J. Schelling, *Münchener Vorlesungen*, Werke, X, p. 160.

[5] W. Marx (*Heidegger und die Tradition*, Hamburg 1980) is not the only one to find fault with Heidegger about this (cf. a survey in A. Vigo, *Zeit und Praxis bei Aristoteles*, Freiburg / München 1996, p. 227 f, note 69).

removing the sediment laid on them by the sheer passing of time and history. In his view, simply looking back to metaphysics without any destructive intention would have in his view the same deadly effect as the looking back of Lot's wife to the doomed city or that of Orpheus sending Eurydice back to the realm of death as a result of the same sort of idle curiosity or *Augenlust*. Thus the constructive aspect in metaphysics' de-construction –as Heidegger's expression "*Ab-bau*" was to be translated later on as literally as it was appropriately– is not to be taken as objective reconstruction but, precisely, as appropriation, *An-eignung* or, to lean on Heidegger's later keyword, *Er-eignung*. This was not so much because of any incapacity on the part of the interpreter for reaching objectivity as rather because of there not being any objectivity to be reached here after all. For even the now past metaphysics, when still alive, despite its thrust towards reification, was less of a closed actuality like those of Hegel's or even Aristotle's lazy God, than it was an open potentiality like time or history.

Now, supposing one should accept Heidegger's standpoint on this score, the question arises, as to whether there is, as regards our concern with the metaphysical past, any alternative between objective validity, on the one hand, and subjective wilfulness on the other. The answer to this along Heidegger's lines would be to say that, in dealing with its own essential past, philosophy has not so much to bring back (*wieder-holen*) now dead realities as to bring to light precisely those living possibilities hidden in metaphysics itself that, for whatever reasons, were never realized in it. Obviously, such an attitude fits neither the German model of exact investigation nor that of cultural humanism. But it is, as a matter of fact, the very attitude with which Heidegger looked into the metaphysical past. It is something of this sort that I myself intend to do in the second part of my lecture. More precisely, what I intend to do is to try to bring to light some of the possibilities Heidegger himself once detected in Aristotle as well as in Hegel concerning the issue of time and being, time and substance, whitch he himself never further developed. In other words, I am going to approach Heidegger himself in the same spirit in which he approached Aristotle and Hegel or even metaphysics as a whole.

2

In so proceeding, one may be obliged to pay a price: it is the price of unduly simplifying –at least from the standpoint of *Forschung*. This risk has already been hinted at in the expression "a straight line", which appears in the title of the present lecture. And it becomes even more evident in the words of a contemporary French philosopher who, like so many others nowadays in France, has been deeply influenced by Heidegger. I mean Gilles Deleuze. In his book *Différence et Repétition* Deleuze maintains that from Parmenides to Heidegger "there has never been more than one ontological proposition: Being is univocal. There has never been more than a single ontology, that of Duns Scotus..."[6]. Is Deleuze unduly simplifying? He is, at any rate, playing with the word "univocal". From Parmenides to Heidegger ontology has spoken with only one voice: this seems to be Deleuze's contention. And this contention need not be simplistic. For Heidegger's history of being has to do with univocity only in the general sense that what philosophers have said (or voiced) in the past has always been the same (*das Selbe*), where the "same" or "sameness" ("*Selbigkeit*") has "otherness" ("*Andersheit*") not outside but inside itself, just as identity, according to Hegel, encompasses difference; or just as, according to Aristotle, the *differentia specifica*, far from being added to an identical genus from outside, is nothing else than the latter in its own differentiation[7]. So the important thing to ask here is how it is that all three, Aristotle, Hegel, and Heidegger, came to say the same thing, and this not despite but precisely because of their differences. Consequently, rather than making external comparisons, it would be more to the point to attempt to repeat the gist of their thought about being and time in a way that, even if it should fail to coincide completely with the philosophy of any one of the three, preserves the thing that matters, *die Sache*. The more so as Heidegger's original intention was not to liquidate but to liquidize (*verflüssigen*) or revitalize Aristotelianism in a similar spirit to that in which Hegel had hinted at

---

[6] G. Deleuze, *Différence et Repétition*, p. 52.
[7] Cf. Aristotle, *Metaphysics*, VII, 12.

when shortly before his death he wrote the following words: "If something ancient is to be renewed, (...) then the form of the idea given to it by Plato and much more profoundly by Aristotle, is infinitely worthy of being recollected, also for this reason that the unpacking of it by means of appropriating it (*Aneignung*) to the formation of our thoughts is immediately, not only an understanding of it, but a step forward for science itself"[8]. Hegel went so far as to say that for anyone taking philosophy seriously the best thing to do would be to teach Aristotle[9]. Now, Heidegger's own appreciation of Aristotle is not far from that of Hegel[10] who, however, tended rather to minimize distances, whereas Heidegger, on the contrary, tended to maximize them[11].

As is well known, Heidegger's criticism of the Aristotelian and Hegelian conceptions of time was directed against the idea of a succession of "nows". In this he was, to put it mildly, not exactly attack-

---

[8] G.W.F. Hegel, *Enzyklopädie der philosophischen Wissenschaften*, Werke, 8, Frankfurt 1975, p. 31: Vorrede 1827. For the translation I am indebted to D. Dahlstrom.

[9] "Würde es ernst mit der Philosophie, so würde nichts würdiger, als über Aristoteles Vorlesungen zu halten", *Geschichte der Philosophie*, Werke, 19, p. 148.

[10] As in the case of Hegel the evidence is too profuse to be accounted for here. For the purpose of this paper, centered on the problem of time from the *Physics* onwards, the following words of H.-G. Gadamer on occasion of the discovery of Heidegger's Aristotelian programmatic text of 1922 (the primordial cell of *Sein und Zeit*) are instructive: "Das bedeutet, daß den jungen Heidegger damals mehr als die Aktualität der praktischen Philosophie ihre Bedeutung für die Aristotelische Ontologie, Metaphysik, beschäftigt. Das 6. Buch der Nikomachischen Ethik erscheint in dieser Programmschrift eigentlich mehr als eine Einleitung in die aristotelische Physik". H.-G. Gadamer, "Heideggers 'theologische' Jugendschrift", *Dilthey-Jahrbuch*, 1989, p. 231: "Die Wiederaufgefundene 'Aristoteles-Einleitung' Heideggers von 1922" edited by H.-U. Lessing, p. 266 of the same issue of *Dilthey-Jahrbuch*.

[11] Cf. M. Heidegger, *Logik. Die Frage nach der Wahrheit. GA* II, 21: "philosophisch verstanden wird die durch Aristoteles grundgelegte und in Hegel vollendete philosophishe Logik nicht gefördert durch weitere Sohn- und Enkelschaft, um philosophisch weiterzukommen bedarf es eines neuen Geschlechtes".

ing them on their strongest side. The enigma of time consists already for Aristotle not so much –as for St. Augustine– in the idea that, upon closer examination, the reality of time boils down to a succession of "nows" each one of which is not time or even part of it; rather it consists primarily in the fact that, although whatever is is only now –now this, now that, and so on–, there is, nevertheless, only one now, just as, according to Heidegger, there is only one being voicing itself, as it were, throughout history and, indeed, identical with its own ever differently voiced history, as opposed to an alleged hiding itself merely behind its changing manifestations in history. However, the reason why there is only one now is not that in the putative succession of nows, one immediately following upon another, it represents the limit between past and future nows. Just as there is no such immediate succession there is no such limit either, except by way of abstraction[12]. To be sure, we can mark off as many limits as our historical or physical research or even our everyday orientation in the world may require: for instance, just that moment between Coriscus still being in the Ly ceum and his starting to go to the market place; or between Coriscus still going in that direction and his arrival there. There is no difficulty in accepting as many "now" –limits as one wants as long as one is engaged in practical business or appraisals, including scientific ones– as historians do, when they date, say, the end of a war with the signing of a peace treaty, even though the shooting is still going on, or as physicists do when they dismiss computational errors as being negligible with respect to the purpose in hand. The difficulty with, or rather the very impossibility of objectively pinning down the real "now" (as opposed to any such given abstract "now") only becomes apparent at the philosophical level.

Already in his *Physics* Aristotle had shown the insurmountable difficulties involved in pinning down the instant of change –not only the transition from motion to rest and vice versa, but also more general forms of change. The difficulties are rooted in the very nature of continuity, as distinct from both contiguity and closest neighborhood. If time, like movement, is continuous, then the very notion of contiguity

---

[12] Cf. Chapter 9: "Aristotle and the Reality of Time".

(ἁπτόμενον) –and all the more so that of closest neighborhood (ἐφεξῆς)– is misapplied when what is involved is not a question of practice, scientific or otherwise, but a philosophical or, rather, metaphysical theory of real time. And since real as opposed to abstract or extended time is no magnitude at all, the very notion of succession, even that of a continuous succession, is misapplied here as well[13].

The upshot of all this is that *in rerum natura*, which includes human history in the sense of *res gestae* (not in the sense of recorded history), there can be only one "now". And this is the true enigma of time. For it then seems as if one ought to be able to infer from this that, to take Aristotle's example, the Trojan War is still going on. But it only seems so[14]. Likewise, it is a non sequitur to infer with the Sophists from the fact that Coriscus's being in the Lyceum is not the same as his being in the market place that it is not the same Coriscus who is now here and then there. The analogy drawn by Aristotle here between the only one "now" of real time and the identical substance despite or rather because of the different states into which it itself is continuously changing has been often overlooked. And it is not unlikely that it was Heidegger's own overlooking of this analogy which lay at the root of some of the difficulties he encountered when writing the then pending third section of the first part of *Being and Time* and which ultimately forced him to abandon continuation of that work. One year before Heidegger's death, however, in 1975, a series of lectures were published which he had delivered in Marburg on the same topic shortly after the appearance of *Being and Time*, a series which is also important for the light it sheds on the development of Heidegger's views on Aristotle's and Hegel's treatment of time. Let me explain this.

Less than two years before the publication of *Being and Time* Heidegger could still write that Hegel's treatment of time in the *Philosophy of Nature* "kills (*totschlägt*) the proper content of the Aristotelian interpretation, putting it, as it were, on ice, and leaving purely formal

---

[13] Cf. Aristotle, *Physics*, 206a 33-b2.
[14] Aristotle, *Physics*, 219b 18-22.

and empty results in its place"[15]. But the series of lectures just mentioned of two years later already have a totally different ring to them. Thus, after having raised the question, "to what extent is time itself the condition of the possibility of Nothingness as such?"[16], Heidegger concludes: "In the end (one has to acknowledge) that Hegel was on to a fundamental truth when he said that Being and Nothing are the same thing"[17]. And with a sentence which anticipates further developments in his thought he adds: "We are not sufficiently prepared to enter into this darkness. It is only by going back to (the enigma of) time that it will be possible to cast some light on the interpretation of being"[18]. Heidegger was then about to reverse his first attempt at regaining the original sense of being and, taking time now not as his point of departure but rather as his destination, he set out in a direction that was ultimately to lead to the notions of "*Ereignis*" and of the history of being.

The preceding quotations may suffice as evidence grounding the two-fold contention, first, that even after the *Kehre* Heidegger continued his search for the meaning of being in the direction originally laid down by Hegel's concept of negativity as the identity of being and nothingness and, secondly, that the concept of negativity, once so defined, provides the key to understanding Aristotle's analogy between the one and only ever-changing "now" and the substance (οὐσία) of the Physics, which Heidegger himself interpreted as movement or mobility (*Bewegtheit*) in the sense of an unlimited or imperfect act (ἐνέργεια ἀτελές)[19]. So in his essay on Aristotle's notion of φύσις published in 1958 in *Il Pensiero*, but written already in 1939, Heidegger paraphrases Hegel in order to convey the meaning of φύσις as *Bewegtheit*[20] or limitless actuality by saying: "All living things are in

---

[15] M. Heidegger, *Logik. Die Frage nach der Wahrheit*, GA II 21, p. 266.

[16] M. Heidegger, *Die Grundprobleme der Phänomenologie*, GA II 24, p. 443.

[17] *Ibid.*

[18] *Ibid.*

[19] Aristotle, *Physics*, 201b 31-32.

[20] M. Heidegger, "Vom Wesen und Begriff der Physis. Aristoteles, Physik B,1" in *Wegmarken, GA* I 9.

the process of dying as soon as they start to live"[21]. This is but the sadness which, as Hegel put it[22], haunts the whole of nature. The identity of being and nothing is, in effect, the identity of coming-to-be and passing-away; that is to say, it is not just a passing-away after having come-to-be, but coming-to-be and passing-away coinciding in the one and only one unlimited "now" in which, unlike the many "nows" as mere limits of time, at which nothing occurs, all things do occur. Thus, at the very beginning of the *Science of Logic*, under the heading "Moments of Becoming", Hegel writes: "Becoming is in this way in a double determination. In one of them, nothing is immediate, that is, the determination starts from nothing which relates itself to being, or in other words changes into it; in the other, being is immediate, that is, the determination starts from being which changes into nothing: the former is coming-to-be and the latter is ceasing-to-be. Both are the same, becoming"[23]. Thus, it is not surprising that, when Heidegger –in his efforts to cope with the problems of being and time as well as of time and being, and after a relatively long period in which he had moved from Aristotle to Kant[24]– at last returned to Aristotle in the essay just mentioned on φύσις, he did so as already under the sway of Hegel's notion of negativity[25].

---

[21] *Ibid.*, p. 367.

[22] Cf. G.W.F. Hegel, *Wissenschaft der Logik, Werke*, 5, p. 140.

[23] G.W.F. Hegel, *Wissenschaft der Logik, Werke*, 5, p. 112; *Science of Logic*, I, Humanity Press International, Atlantic Highlands, N.J. 1969, p. 105 f.

[24] "Im Winter 1925/1926 änderte Heidegger in einem dramatischen Bruch den Plan seiner Vorlesung und gab statt weiterer Aristotelesinterpretationen eine Interpretation der Lehre von der transzendentalen Einbildungskraft und der Schematisierung". O. Pöggeler, *Neue Wege mit Heidegger*, Freiburg / München 1992, p. 194. Cf. also D.O. Dahlstrom, "Heideggers Kant-Kommentar, 1925-1936", *Philosophisches Jahrbuch*, 1989, pp. 343-366 as well as D. Köhler, *Martin Heidegger. Die Schematisierung des Seinssinnes als Thematik des dritten Abschnittes von "Sein und Zeit"*, Bonn 1993.

[25] Cf. M. Heidegger, *Hegel. Die Negativität* (1938-1939), GA III. Abteilung. Unveröffentlichte Abhandlungen. In the meantime, if only for one semester (Aristoteles, *Metaphysik*, IX 1-3, summer 1931), he had already lectured on Aristotle's οὐσία in a different mood. Cf. O. Pöggeler, *ibid.*, p. 232: "In jenen Jahren re-

Heidegger regards the eight books of the *Physics* as constituting the original Aristotelian metaphysics in which the burden of onto-theology had not yet become so heavy as to crush pre-Socratic (above all Heraclitean) insights into the essence of nature under its weight. Inasmuch as it preserves those insights, Heidegger's interpretation of this original metaphysics turns on the identity of universal passing-away and universal coming-to-be. Thus, at the end of his essay on the Aristotelian φύσις Heidegger comments on fragment 123 of Heraclitus (φύσις κρύπτησθαι φιλέι) by saying: "Being loves to hide, what does that mean? Usually this has been understood to mean that being is almost inaccessible so that great efforts are needed to bring it out of hiding and to exorcise, as it were, its love of hiding. Quite the opposite: the hiding belongs to being itself and that is why it loves it"[26]. These words represent an accurate explanation of the ἄπειρον-structure proper to time as something from which nothing is merely hidden as is the lost umbrella from the distracted professor (Heidegger's own example) –except itself from itself, since time itself is outside itself. It is, in fact, in real time as the unlimited "now" –as opposed to any given abstract "now"-limit– that the truth of manifestation is originally and inextricably tied to the untruth of concealment. On the other hand, it has to be said that Heidegger never explored this Aristotelian-Hegelian path any further, even after the *Kehre*. Such an exploration would have led to an interpretation of Aristotelian time and substance quite different from that of time as a mere succession of nows or of substance as *primum analogatum* of being in the sense of something hiding behind an alleged veil of accidents from which it

---

vidierte Heidegger seine Rezeption der Analogie des Seins (nämlich der Ausrichtung aller Seinsweisen auf eine leitende Bedeutung) zugunsten der Erfahrung der ἐνέργεια als eines Am-Werke-Seins und somit einer 'Geschichte'... So wollte Heidegger fortan nicht mehr weiter akademische Philosophie, sei es in der Weise Husserls, betreiben". Cf. *Ibid.*, p. 35: "...wenn δύναμις Eignung ist, muß die ἐνέργεια als eine Wirklichkeit, die eine offene Möglichkeit in sich trägt, in ihrer Bewegtheit und mit der Not ihrer Notwendigkeit ein Ereignis sein".

[26] M. Heidegger, *GA* I 9, p. 300.

ought somehow to be exorcised[27]. It must be said as well, however, that even after having reversed the hermeneutical priority of time over being, Heidegger kept on insisting on another genuine aspect of Aristotelian time; it is this, that just as there can be no being without man (no *Sein* without the clearing of *Da-sein* in the wood of nothingness), so there can be no time without man; that, to put it another way, man is not a traveler along a particular path of time but is temporality itself. This, of course, sounds more like *Physics* without *Metaphysics* than Aristotelian metaphysics proper as the science of *ens qua ens*. For as the science of *ens qua ens* metaphysics seems to banish all forms of negativity from being and to relegate them instead to the realm of mere thought or to *ens ut verum*[28]. As a matter of fact Hegel himself had already explicitly protested against the exclusion of negativity from being as such. Again shortly before he died Hegel wrote: "It is therefore said that although nothing is in thought or imagination, yet for that very reason it is not nothing that is, being does not belong to nothing as such, but only thought or imagination is this being... that nothing does not possess an independent being of its own, is not being as such"[29]. The contrary is true according to Hegel. So, just as, according to both Hegel and Heidegger, one must not sever being from nothing, so one must not sever *ens ut verum* from *ens ut ens* or being from man (*Sein* from *Dasein*) either. In this respect both Hegel's and Heidegger's thought is, in fact, Aristotelian philosophy stripped of the doctrine of *ens ut ens* as distinct from *ens ut verum*. Heidegger himself –like Hegel[30]– refused to subordinate the latter to the former right

---

[27] Cf. M. Heidegger, *Was heißt Denken?*, Tübingen 1954, p. 68: "Alles wahrhaft Gedachte eines wesentlichen Denkens bleibt –und zwar aus Wesensgründen– mehrdeutig. Diese Mehrdeutigkeit ist niemals nur der Restbestand einer noch nicht erreichten formallogischen Eindeutigkeit, die eigentlich anzustreben wäre, aber nicht erreicht wurde. Die Mehrdeutigkeit ist vielmehr das Element, worin das Denken sich bewegen muß, um ein strenges zu sein".

[28] Cf. Aristotle, *Metaphysics*, 1027b 25-31.

[29] G.W.F. Hegel, *Wissenschaft der Logik, Werke*, 5, p. 108 f.

[30] Cf. note 29.

from the beginning[31]. But the situation is a little more complicated than that, both as regards non-being and as regards truth. For not only does Aristotle say, in a famous passage, on which Heidegger often commented[32], that truth is the main meaning of being[33]. He also sometimes treated non-being on a par with accidents despite the fact that these are ways of being. And he does it in the very passage in which he explains metaphysics as the science of being *qua* being[34].

Let me make two comments on this. First, if any sense is to be made of the comparison between, on the one hand, time as the simultaneous coming-to-be and passing-away of the only one continuous "now" and, on the other, the essence (οὐσία) of all that belongs to nature (David Ross, for instance, dismissed the whole passage in the Physics as too obviously wrong to be commented on)[35], then this is arguably in the sense in which physical οὐσία is taken to manifest and hide itself in its changing states[36]. Now, this description corresponds not only to the notion of φύσις as developed by Heidegger. It corresponds also to an important aspect of *Ereignis* as appropriation, to which I shall now address the second of my remarks.

At the lecture held in Freiburg in 1957 on identity as the sameness of being and thought ("τὸ γὰρ αὐτό νοεῖν ἐστίν τε καὶ εἶναι") and reprinted in the volume *Identität und Differenz* Heidegger said: "The word *Ereignis* is taken from an already evolved language. *Ereignen* originally read: *eräugen*". Here one can still hear the German for "eye" –"*Auge*"– or even its cognate form, "*be-äugen*", meaning "to eye something" or "to take a close look at something". So Heidegger concludes his series of renderings with "to appropriate in looking" ("*er-blicken, im Blicken zu sich rufen, an-eignen*"). And he adds:

---

[31] Cf. M. Heidegger, "Phänomenologische Interpretationen zu Aristoteles", *Dilthey-Jahrbuch*, 1989, p. 268.

[32] Cf., M. Heidegger, *Logik. Die Frage nach der Wahrheit*, GA II 21, pp. 170-182.

[33] Aristotle, *Metaphysics*, 1051b 1.

[34] Aristotle, *Metaphysics*, 1003b 6-10.

[35] *Aristotle's Physics. A revised text with introduction and commentary by W. D. Ross*, Oxford 1960, p. 599.

[36] Aristotle, *Physics*, 219b 18 ff.

"Understood in this way it is just as incapable of being translated as the key Greek term λόγος or the Chinese Tao"[37]. Perhaps. But, wherever the truth of the matter may lie here, the consideration which allows one to discern an intrinsic connection between Heidegger's *Ereignis* and Aristotle's comparison of "οὐσία" with the identical "now" of time, which only conceptually has "nows" different from each other, is offered immediately after the passage quoted, when Heidegger continues: "Therefore, the word "*Ereignis*" no longer refers here to what we usually describe as some recurrence or happening. It is to be understood as a *singulare tantum*. What it says occurs only once ("*ereignet sich nur in der Einzahl*"), and in fact not even once ("*in einer Zahl*"), but is unique (beyond number)"[38].

As I noted above, Heidegger's interpretation of Aristotelian and Hegelian time as a succession of "nows" treated neither on their strongest side. We have already seen this with respect to Aristotle. The same also applies, however, to Hegel. Take, for instance, Hegel's following contention about time: time "is the being which, in that it is, is not, and in that it is not, is. It is intuited becoming; admittedly, its differences are therefore determined as being simply momentary; in that they immediately sublate themselves in their externality, however, they are self-external"[39]. One may take this contention as a paraphrase of the unlimited "now" which Aristotle compared with the always changing and only relatively resting physical οὐσία of Coriscus or of anything else. Such an οὐσία shows the structure of the unlimited act (ἐνέργεια ἀτελής) which Heidegger interpreted as *Bewegtheit* embracing both movement and resting. For Aristotle's definition of

---

[37] M. Heidegger, "Der Satz der Identität" originally published in *Die Albert-Ludwigs-Universität Freiburg 1457-1957. Die Festvorträge bei der Jubiläumsfeier*, p. 76.

[38] *Ibid.*

[39] G.W.F. Hegel, *Enzyklopädie der philosophischen Wissenschaften im Grundrisse*, Werke, 9, p. 48; *Philosophy of Nature*, transl. by M.J. Petry, vol I, London 1970, p. 229 f.

ἄπειρον does not read, as it has sometimes been translated[40], "that which always has something outside itself". This corresponds rather to the definition of the perfect or limited. The limits (points, lines, surfaces), taken as in contiguity, not continuity, are themselves only outside each other just like those "nows" by means of which we break up the only one continuous "now" into more or less smaller events in an ultimately futile attempt to control the unique *Ereignis* in whose tapestry we are all, as it were, interwoven. Aristotle's definition of the unlimited should,of course, read instead: "that of which some part is always outside" ("οὗ ἀεί τί ἔξω", where "οὗ" modifies "τί", and not "ἔξω")[41]. And it is precisely because the moments are not outside each other, but each individual moment is, as Hegel himself said, outside itself ("*sich selbst äusserliche*", "self-external") that they form a unique and continuous flowing.

So much for potentialities that had perhaps even in Aristotle not always been fully actualized but which a sympathetic reading of Heidegger's interpretations of Hegel and Aristotle could help to bring if not fully then at least a little further to light. Along these lines one might fairly straightforwardly gain a view of the traditional notion of substance more orientated towards a temporal than to a spatial model of substance as conceived under the new-Scholasticism, just as Heidegger once was trying to "liquidize" (but not yet to "liquidate") the concepts of scholasticism. I come now finally to some brief considerations of a more general kind.

3

As radically temporal we too are always outside ourselves and thus vulnerable. To be sure, all things in the world are alike in being somehow composed of that enigmatic stuff which is ecstatic time. But we

---

[40] E.g. as late as 1987 by H. G. Zekl, vgl. *Aristoteles' Physik, Griechisch-Deutsch*, Hamburg 1987.

[41] Aristotle, *Physics*, 207a 1, 8.

alone are aware of the fact, and try to escape our fate by compensatory devices such as computation of time and so on. The result is what we usually call "culture" –from the most primitive burial rites to the most sophisticated technology, be it beneficial to or destructive of mankind. Philosophy as such and metaphysics in particular form a part of such precautionary measures. But inasmuch as we fail to take seriously our radical temporality and historicity, i.e. the fact that we do not merely consist in being something (*bestehen*), e.g. in being a rational animal, but do also properly ek-sist (*ent-stehen*), all cultural precautions, included humanism, are, according to Heidegger, in the end illusory and self-delusive.

"*Ek-sistence*" is always in the process of starting anew, provided one does not succumb to routine. Anything that may be said to consist in being something else, anything that has consistency (*Bestand*), is always a objective content (*Inhalt*). Philosophy, for instance, as a cultural precaution, is full of contents. All that we can grasp with the help of a definition –man or whatever– is a content. But time is not a content nor does man in his historicity consist in anything. *Ek-sisting* rather than consisting beings like ourselves are, of course, always, relentlessly getting older and passing away, but at the same time they are always starting to be in the first place. In other words, man, history, philosophy, being, are, like time, always repeating themselves; but, like time itself, what they are always repeating is not closed realities but open possibilities. The title of Deleuze's book, to which I previously referred, *Différence et Répétition*, was intended to hint at this –only its author completely failed to realize how much of all this is already to be found in Aristotle, whom he has so maligned in his book[42]. Similarly, it would perhaps not be false to say that had Hei-

---

[42] The main shortcoming of this book lies in the inability of its author to grasp why, according to Aristotle, the *differentia specifica* does not merely express a part of but the whole οὐσία. In this he was indeed following Scotus' doctrine of *univocatio entis* in the usual sense of this term (cf. note 6 above). As for Scotus' own inability to cope with Aristotle's doctrine of οὐσία in this respect cf., e.g., "quod finalis differentia erit terminus et definitio, nullo modo potest intelligi, quod tota ratio quidditativa sit in ultima differentia...". *In IV Sent.*, d. 11, q.3, ed. Vivès, n. 47.

degger from the beginning better assessed Aristotle's and Hegel's views on time and οὐσία, then he would have arrived much earlier at his notion of *Ereignis* as appropriation. But this would at best be true in a rather irrelevant way. What matters is not the duration or the length of the way traversed but the traversing itself, a traversing which is always at the same time a transformation. Thus, at the beginning of his lecture on "Identity" mentioned above Heidegger wrote: "In thinking about something that matters it might happen that, on the way, thought undergoes some change. So, in thinking of identity, it is advisable to pay less attention to the content than to the way. The very unfolding of a lecture such as this makes it impossible anyway to dwell on the content"[43]. Here again, you have the overcoming of the misrepresentation of real time as an extended line with points succeeding one upon another in the way Heidegger once interpreted the whole Aristotelian as well as Hegelian notion of time. The overcoming of such a misrepresentation in the last quotation, though, sounds as if a lecture could never stick to just one topic. What, however, was meant was rather the opposite, namely that, if the topic is a dead one, nobody can stick to it for any length of time, except outwardly, whereas if the topic is a living one –not a topic at all, as it were, i.e., not a pure content– it varies continuously so that one cannot simply return to the same spot as one can direct his view back and forth along a straight line. (Etienne Gilson was, incidentally, present at this lecture, having received during the same ceremony an honorary degree from the University of Freiburg. And it was after this lecture that he remarked: "I have only twice heard philosophy spoken aloud (*en haute voix*): once by Henry Bergson and today by Heidegger"). Now, what to Heidegger as well as Deleuze remained hidden in the metaphysical theory of οὐσία –hidden perhaps even to metaphysics itself– was the possibility of viewing οὐσία not only in the sense of substance but even in that of essence, as something transforming itself continuously like time, though, of course, not essentially. One may bring out the appropriate kind of transformation in terms borrowed from Aquinas by saying that the change concerns only the οὐσία as *forma sub-*

---

[43] M. Heidegger, "Der Satz der Identität", p. 69.

stantialis, whereas the οὐσία as *forma essentialis* or εἶδος (in the sense of species) remains unchanged. In this Aristotelian essentialism clearly differs from any kind of holism for which there are no bounds marked by the different species beyond which no individual can change and yet remain itself. This reservation does not go against taking Aristotle's analogy between real time and substance in a strong sense. On the contrary. Let us explain this briefly before ending.

Independently of whether time be considered in terms of the history of being or in terms of the one and only continuous "now", there are two possible mistakes that one may make in dealing with time (and if, as in a statement once derided by Heidegger[44] Hegel thought, time is somehow even the truth of space then there are also two possible errors one may commit in dealing with space): the error of thinking that nothing is old and the error of thinking that nothing is new. Take the example of a straight line which has been drawn on a blackboard. As long as it has not been erased, enlarged, or foreshortened, it seems to remain unchanged as far as its being on the blackboard is concerned. But this is not in fact the case. Only so long as one fails to take into account the lapse of time, i.e. the flowing of the one and only real "now", can one consider the straight line on the blackboard unchanged. For as soon as one has finished drawing it[45] the line is, of course, already there, but at each particular moment in time it is only there then, and not at some later point in time. The line is itself something temporal. As such it is, like everything else, changing. Only when regarded in merely spatial terms can it be said not to have

---

[44] "'Die Wahrheit des Raumes ist die Zeit'... Die umgekehrte These hat Bergson ausgesprochen ... Bergson aber wie Hegel vernichten das, was an echtem Gehalt darin liegt, dadurch, daß sie ihn aufheben, nicht in sicherer Wahrheit, sondern in einer grundsätzlicher Sophistik, von der überhaupt Hegels Dialektik lebt". M. Heidegger, *GA* II 21, p. 252.

[45] Cf. G.E. Owen, "General and Particular" in *Proceedings of the Aristotelian Society*, London 1979/80, p. 18: "an unfinished statue can be a statue, an unfinished circle is not a circle. Aristotle disregards the difference, even in house-building (*Physics*, 201b 11-12)... statements of the form 'A is becoming/making a Y' do not carry in their truth-conditions or entailments any requirement that there must (timelessly) be some particular Y for A to become/make".

changed. However, nothing is purely spatial. In this, Aristotelianism –especially with regard to its critique of Anaxagoras and Empedocles[46]– is Hegelianism and Heideggerianism avant la lettre. A thoroughly unchanging and hence timeless universe is for Aristotle as impossible as it is for Hegel or Heidegger. The fact of the line changing, however, is not limited to a particular period of time. Periods of time are always periods of rest-time frozen, as it were, by the mind, which –by virtue of its retentional as well "protentional" (Husserl) power to extend or stretch the "now"– is able to transform time into space, that is to say, that which represents no magnitude at all into a magnitude. By way of contrast, the fact of the line's changing depends on the fact that real time as the unique "now" does not stop flowing any more than the universe stops moving, whereas any period of time or, for that matter, of history is by definition limited and static. A period of time, like the line drawn on the blackboard, must have a beginning and an end. It is not limitless, ἄπειρον. To put it briefly, then, the first error would be to deny that, regardless of how late in the course of its development it might be at a given point in time, the universe is always new, that in it nothing is ever left behind, i.e., left behind in a past that no longer exists. In this sense, of course, nothing can be said to be old.

The second error is just the reverse of the first. It consists in proceeding from the fact that, to take the same example, the straight line remains unchanged in its career –for, however dull its career, it is like everything else in that it, too, is always starting afresh– to the conclusion that the line that yesterday I saw on the blackboard and that I still see there today is not allegedly the same line at all and, in general, that nothing can be said to be old or aging in any sense whatsoever. This would be tantamount to denying that Coriscus can at any two points which we may choose to select within the ceaseless flowing of real time be the same person, on the grounds that Coriscus-at-the-Lyceum is no longer Coriscus-in-the-market-place, as if the real thing were not the changing Coriscus himself but rather his unchanging abstract states "Coriscus-at-the Lyceum" and "Coriscus-in-the-market-place"

---

[46] Cf. Aristotle, *Physics*, VIII 1.

or as if the real time were not the only one now but rather different nows succeeding one upon another. True, if Coriscus is no longer in the market place, then this state of Coriscus is no longer anywhere, not even somewhere in the past, since the past does not exist. Therefore, one cannot even say that it has been left behind, except of course in the sense that his having been in the market-place has been preserved in the memory of all those who happen to think of Coriscus' displacement. But this does not prevent its being in Coriscus in the sense of having been there. We are so used to the idea of substance as something that solidly remains in space throughout temporal change that we scarcely realize the challenge contained in this second error. Due to a reifying tendency inherent in the spatial representation of substance we are naturally inclined to regard the previous stages in the career of whatever we are talking about as having been left somewhere behind unchanged, like a line which after having been drawn on a blackboard is still there. It costs us not a little effort to realize that they are just as little anywhere as, say, the skull of the young St. Thomas which was allegedly kept in Montecassino while that of the older St. Thomas had been buried at Toulouse. In other words, whereas there is at least some truth in Hegel's dictum according to which time is the truth of space, its converse, viz. that space is the truth of time, has nothing to offer except the coarse representation of real time (or substance) as a straight line. But to throw away the idea of the identity of substances "over time" for this reason, i.e., to abandon the very idea of physical substances altogether, would be but another way of clinging to the same coarse representation. A physical substance is, by virtue of its temporality, analogous to a snail carrying along all its belongings –*omnia mea mecum porto*– or like a tree, which has its annual rings inside it. It is precisely because nothing is left behind that all things, while constantly in the process of starting anew, are at the same time always getting older. Coriscus' now being in the Lyceum is different, simply by virtue of his previously having been in the market-place, from what it would have been, had he not been in the market-place.

The same applies to the notions of *Ereignis* and of the history of being. Just as it is wrong to say that there is nothing new or nothing old since time is precisely both passing away and starting to be at once, so it would be equally wrong to say that, e.g., Aristotle's, Hegel's, and Heidegger's *Sache* –the thing that matters for each of them– was each always the same or always different. Either way we would not be progressing beyond, but rather falling behind, Aristotle's analogy between time and substance. For it would be like saying that physical accidents as well as the happenstance of everyday life or even the different epochs in the history of mankind do not affect either the essence of things or the *Sache des Denkens*; it would be like adding differences to the identical genus from without and getting in the process only the dead content of εἶδος as general species (the *forma essentialis*) instead of the living essence (the *forma substantialis*), the soul, or the heart, of the matter. From this standpoint this would be no less wrong than to say that from Aristotle or even from Parmenides onwards up to Heidegger and beyond the questions or problems of philosophy have remained the same, and only the answers or solutions offered in response to them have been different. Were we to cling to this idea we would still be thinking in rather straightforward terms of a thoroughly unchanged, extended line, i.e. of content rather than of a changing path, relying more on a spatial than a temporal model for viewing philosophy and its history. But the fact that not only the answers, or solutions, but along with them also the questions or problems do change throughout history ought not to deter one from saying that the *Sache des Denkens* is always the same. Otherwise, the history of philosophy would be, as Hegel put it, just a collection of peculiar opinions.

Since the similarities between Aristotle's theistic, Hegel's quasi-pantheistic, and Heidegger's atheistic thought do not reflect the repetition of a closed reality or content but that of an open possibility, the path which leads from Aristotle to Heidegger via Hegel cannot be said to have started with Aristotle or stopped with Heidegger. Surely the fact that neither Aristotle's nor Hegel's metaphysics was atheistic is mainly to be attributed to the fact that neither rejected, as did Heidegger[47], the ultimate truth of PNC. It is true that for Hegel, unlike Aristotle, contradiction is the very soul and essence of anything that is not in itself dead. But contradiction is not the only force pushing forward that process in which –if in anything– being consists for Hegel. Just as vital for the process of being is the striving to overcome that contradiction which lurks in each one of the several stages of a given life-process, be it that of consciousness or anything else –with the result that the validity of PNC is preserved, if not during the individual stages themselves, then at least at the end, i.e. in the process as a whole. Whether pantheistically or not, all forms of productive contradiction, be they in thought, nature or history, find their resolution in God. That is why Hegel can close his system with a quotation from Aristotle without having to take the trouble to comment on it[48]. As Aristotle put it, without the principle called God nothing would exist at all[49]. To place such a great emphasis on the negativity of the world is Hegelianism *ante litteram*. But is it compatible with Heidegger's atheistic thought? His not accepting non-contradiction as a principle at all blocked the way of onto-theology. But perhaps the resulting thought only appears atheistic because Heidegger preferred till the very end to embrace the contradiction involved in accepting only the ultimate Heraclitean φύσις-λόγος in the belief that the miracle of being thus becomes all the more conspicuous; in other words, because he preferred to go on wondering at the fact that there should be something rather than nothing instead of asking why there is something and not nothing, this latter being –as he put it– still a metaphysical question, and the ultimate one at that; because, let us say, he preferred to peer over the abyss (*Ab-grund*) rather than to search for some final ground –lest the source of all philosophy, wonder, should disappear.

Somewhere else in his *Remembrance of Things Past*, with which I started, Marcel Proust wrote: "An artist has no need to express his

---

[47] Cf. M. Heidegger, *GA* II 33, p. 198 f. (taking into account that for Aristotle Protagoras was the main opponent of the PNC).

[48] G.W.F. Hegel, *Enzyklopädie*, par. 577, in *Werke*, 9, p. 395.

[49] Cf. Aristotle, *Metaphysics*, 1050b 19; 1071b 55 f.

thought directly in his work for the latter to reflect its quality; it has been said that the highest praise of God consists in the denial of him by the atheist who finds creation so perfect that it can dispense with the creator"[50]. Heidegger's attitude towards religion is less clear-cut than that. The ambiguity ranges from the almost Satanic lifting of the hand against God, which Heidegger attributed to philosophy even at the time in which he considered himself to be doing philosophy, to something perhaps quite the opposite of this[51]. Who knows whether somehow behind his giving up of any cultural way of transforming the thingness of things into the objectivity of objects including exact research, metaphysics and finally even philosophy as a whole there did not lie something like Hölderlin's complaint, viz. "*zu lang ist alles Göttliche dienstbar schon*", i.e., the sadness about the instrumentalizing of the divine "since long, too long ago", which Heidegger himself reckoned to the *Frömmigkeit des Denkens qua Dankens*, to the piety of thinking qua thanksgiving or gratitude. But this does not remove the ambiguity of Heidegger's thought as regards the issue of atheism, it rather makes it inevitable[52]. On the other hand, I have in no way been claiming that the objectifying method of *Forschung* or research proper to the historiography of philosophy should be forced to yield pride of place to something as questionable (*fragwürdig*) as the history of being. Indeed, were one to forsake the former for the latter, one would be in even less of a position to do justice to *Seinsgeschichte* itself[53]. All that I have been suggesting is that the model called by

---

[50] M. Proust, *A la recherche du temps perdu*, v. II, p. 415.

[51] Cf. M. Heidegger, "Jede Philosophie... muß... gerade dann, wenn sie eine 'Ahnung' von Gott hat, wissen, daß das von ihr vollzogene sich zu sich zurückreißen des Lebens, religiös gesprochen, eine Handaufhebung gegen Gott ist. ...atheistisch besagt hier: sich freihaltend vor verführerischer, Religiösität lediglich beredender, Besorgnis". M. Heidegger, "Phänomenologische Interpretationen zu Aristoteles", *Dilthey-Jahrbuch*, p. 246, note 2. Cf. also the quotation in note 27 above.

[52] Cf. notes 27 and 51 above.

[53] To take just one example: it can be shown that Heidegger's notion of Aristotelian ἐνέργεια is defective inasmuch as it takes into consideration only the aspect of manifestation ("*sich zeigen in Anwesenheit*") and not that of (perfect) activity. But

Marcel Proust the German model of exact investigation represents a more historical than philosophical approach to the history of philosophy and that the concern with the history of being possibly represents, by contrast, a more philosophical than historical approach.

---

as far as Heidegger's reversal of the priority relation between actuality and potentiality is concerned his was at least a productive error.

CHAPTER 9
ARISTOTLE AND THE REALITY OF TIME

According to Heidegger, Aristotle laid the foundations of the notion of time which was to dominate the history of metaphysics down to Hegel or even Bergson. In it time appears as a succession of different nows. Heidegger considers this to be a vulgar notion of time against which he sets his own theory. According to Heidegger, time is something ecstatic in that, in remembering the past and, above all, caring for the future, man is outside himself. Besides, whereas in the Aristotelian notion of time the stress is put on the present, in Heidegger's own theory the stress is put on the future. No doubt, this is an important difference. There are still many others. If one looks carefully, however, into Aristotle's treatment of time in Book IV of the *Physics* –which Heidegger surely did many times before writing *Being and Time*– one sees that in it the idea of a succession of nows appears derivative; derivative, that is, with respect to the more fundamental notion of a now which, being something continuous, cannot be in itself (*ut sic* or *ut ens*) in any relation of succession to any other now, but remains one and the same throughout. On the other hand, taken not in itself but only in the sense of *ens ut verum*, the single now can be rightly considered to be two or more instants following one another. In other words, the idea of a succession of many present nows –now this, now this, etc.– would be false as soon as one leaves its abstract character out of the account.

Here the adjective "abstract", or the substantive "abstraction", is to be understood in the sense in which Thomas Aquinas spoke of *abstractio totius* and *abstractio partis seu formae* (generalization and formalization) as the means by which the sciences of physics and mathematics are respectively constituted. Consequently, we may also say that there are two possibilities of viewing the present now. Metaphysically viewed, the now is one and the same, it is unique; but physically, or even mathematically viewed, one can and indeed must speak of a multiplicity of nows following one another in some way or other, i.e. either in the sense of contiguity or in that of consecutiveness (ἁπτόμενον and ἐφεξῆς respectively). *A parte rei* (or actually, or really) the present now is only one, but there are many nows *secundum rationem* (or potentially, or abstractly). As we shall see, here all depends on Aristotle's analogy between the relationship of the one now to many nows and the relationship of the substance to the accidents.

1. The aporias about the reality of time

To see why this is so and to what extent the analogy is valid, one has to follow the aporias about the reality of time with which Aristotle begins his treatment. There are three of them. The most important is the last. It is the only one to which Aristotle explicitly refers in the answer to all three. Nevertheless, the first two also contain important elements for the resolution. So I shall start with both of them and then concentrate on the third aporia. The first two are closely connected with each other. Each one shows that time consists of what is not, for the past is no more and the future is not yet, whereas, as the second aporia explains, the present which is the only real thing as regards time, seems to be only the limit between past and future and therefore not time or part of it itself.

Now, one important feature of Aristotle's first aporia is that he distinguishes between an infinite time and any finite stretch of time one may choose. Each one of them is composed of past and present, i.e. of what is not. So "infinite time" (ἄπειρος χρόνος) does not mean here the real time which consists of a permanent, though ecstatic, present. Nevertheless, the distinction made in this first aporia between time as something limited and time as something unlimited is important.

As for the second aporia, it contains two important features: first the explicit introduction of the concept of parts in connection with time; and, second, the implicit comparison between instants of time and points on a line. As Aristotle says, "...time is not thought to be composed of nows"[1], any more than a line is composed of points. The comparison between points and nows will be made more explicit in the third aporia. The only reason given in this second aporia for the non-existence of time is that for anything composed of parts to exist at least some of them ought to exist themselves; but the only possible parts of time, viz. past or future (or parts of both) are not real, whereas the only real thing with respect to time, viz. the present now, is not extended time. So much as for the two first aporias.

Let us turn now to the third aporia. It begins as follows: "The instant seems to divide (or limit: διορίξειν) the past from the future"[2]. Here "instant", or present now, does not refer only to the present instant right now but also to the present instants belonging to the past or the future. To borrow some Augustinian expressions, the present instant does not refer only to the *praesens de praesentibus* but also to the *praesens* (or rather, in plural, *praesentes*) *de praeteritis* as well as to the *praesentes de futuris*. They all seem to divide the past from the future. But whereas the absolutely present now (i.e. the *praesens de praesentibus*) is only one (Hussey's "permanent present" in chart II below), there are many abstractly present nows (Hussey's "unrepeatable instant[s]").

The reason for there being only one really present now but many abstractly present nows is that the former (i.e. the *praesens de praesentibus*) is shifting (or changing, in the sense of altering –just as a substance is also, even if at rest, at least relatively altering), whereas the latter (i.e. the *praesentes de praeteritis* or *de futuris*) cannot shift or change at all, since neither the past nor the future really exist. And it is because they do not really exist that, unlike the real now as well as any real substance, the *praesentes de praeteritis* and *de futuris* do not change in the sense of altering while remaining the same, but only in the sense of substituting for, or succeeding, one another. They do it,

---

[1] Aristotle, *Physics*, 218a 7 f. (Hussey's translation in the Clarendon Aristotle Series throughout).

[2] Aristotle, *Physics*, 218a 9.

of course, not of their own (for they do not really exist), but only owing to the abstracting, remembering or expecting, powers of the soul.

Up until now I have only referred to the sentence introducing the third aporia. As for the aporia itself, it consists of a dilemma inside which one can discern other dilemmas (cf. chart II below). The two horns of the whole or main dilemma are the following: first, there cannot be many nows, nor, second, there can be there only one now. And given that according to the first two aporias the present is the only remaining candidate for real time, time seems not to be anything real at all.

Each horn of this main dilemma contains in its turn two parts. Both horns are, as it were, split. In fact, as we shall see, the first horn contains inside it some smaller dilemmas. That is not the case with the second horn of the main dilemma. It is itself split as well, but not in the way of containing in it other dilemmas. Since this second horn is easier to understand intuitively, I shall start with it. It runs as follows: "(...) Yet it is not possible either that the same now should always persist". The first reason given for this runs as follows: "For (i) nothing that is divisible and finite (πεπερασμένου) has only one limit, and it is possible to take a finite time (χρόνος λαβεῖν πεπερασμένος)"[3].

The last words echo the first aporia, in which, as already said, both infinite time as well as time taken as finite (καὶ ὁ ἄπειρος καὶ ὁ ἀεὶ λαμβανόμενος χρόνος) consist of past and future parts, none of which, as the second aporia explains, exists. At this stage of the third aporia, Aristotle concentrates on time as limited or finite, for it is only finite time that needs two limits or nows. But the important concept is that of the infinite or, if possible at all, the infinite limit. True, the concept of an infinite or unlimited limit seems to be paradoxical. But such is also the notion of the unlimited (ἄπειρον) itself. In Book III, chapter 6, the unlimited had been already defined by way of contrasting it to the limited or perfect whole[4]. The limited is that which always has something, namely something else, outside itself. By con-

---

[3] Aristotle, *Physics*, 218a 22-25.
[4] Aristotle, *Physics*, 206b 17 f., 207a 1 ff.

trast, the ἄπειρον is that of which (οὗ) something is always outside[5], viz. outside itself. In other words, the real present is, one might say, ecstatic –a word which Aristotle himself used in other contexts in connection with time[6]. On the other hand, real time is different from magnitude in that it is always ceasing to be[7]. It is, I would say, only by referring to the limited or abstract, but not to the unlimited, ecstatic, or ἄπειρον, present, that the possibility of there being only one now seems to be excluded.

Let us look at the second part of this second horn of the main dilemma. The point here is, perhaps, even easier to grasp intuitively. It is that, if there were only one now, nothing would be either previous or subsequent (οὔτε πρότερον οὔτε ὕστερον) so that events that happened thousands of years ago would be still happening today. With regard to this conclusion one may, I think, put forward two remarks. First, if there were only one absolutely present now in the sense of the ecstatic present, it would not just remain but also shift, i.e. start as well as cease to be at once. In other words, it would not be a *nunc stans* but a *nunc fluens*. This would be fully in agreement with the paradoxical notion of the ecstatic ἄπειρον. Second, events like the Thirty Years War (later on Aristotle speaks in a similar context of the capture of Troy) do not exist as such (or *ut sic*). The Thirty Years War, like any other past war, or more generally, any other past event, extends over some limited time, i.e. over many abstractly present nows of the past. But nothing extended over time, be it past or future, can take place in the really present now. Being outside itself, this real now is not itself extended like a whole having *partes extra partes*, as is the case with any limited or abstract time. Events are processes which (like Hussey's "change[s]") do not exist of their own, any more than accidents do. In fact, events, like movements or changes, are accidents. So, the issue of the reality of events turns, in the end, on the question of the reality of accidents. It is, I think, the most important aspect of the resolution of the whole third aporia. But, before going on

---

[5] Aristotle, *Physics*, 207a 7 f.
[6] Aristotle, *Physics*, 222b 15, 16, 21.
[7] Aristotle, *Physics*, 206b 1-3.

to the resolution, we still have to deal with the first and most complex horn of the main dilemma in which, as I said, other minor dilemmas are contained.

This first horn shows definitively the impossibility of numerically distinctive real nows succeding one another. A little surprisingly, though, Aristotle starts by speaking of parts, but not of nows. "Surprisingly" because the parts of time (past and future as well as, by implication, their own parts) had already been excluded from the present now as the only remaining candidate for real, but not limited, time. Real time, not having *partes extra partes*, cannot be extended, just as an event, being extended over a limited period of time, cannot as such (*ut sic*) be real. Now, Aristotle says that the parts of a limited period of time cannot be simultaneous, except in the sense in which one would say that a smaller extension of time (e.g. the present day) is contained in a greater one (e.g. in the present year). For, since parts, like the past and the future, are not present in any absolute sense of the word "present", i.e. right now, nor were they ever present in this very sense, there are no days or years either in the sense of *ens ut ens*, any more than events exist in the absolute sense of "present".

Before switching from parts of limited times to present instants or nows proper, Aristotle builds a dilemma inside this first horn of the main dilemma –a middle sized dilemma, so to speak. For in the process of switching from parts to nows he builds yet another dilemma inside the middle sized dilemma –a mini-dilemma, as it were.

The middle sized dilemma consists in showing that there cannot be real parts of time, because they would have to stand in a relation either of simultaneity or of temporal succession to each other, neither of which is possible. Aristotle takes for granted the impossibility of simultaneous parts except in the abstract sense mentioned above of smaller parts inside greater parts like days in years. Indeed, it seems intuitively obvious that parts of time ought to be successive. Nevertheless, Aristotle has an argument to prove it. Since time is as such (*ut sic*) infinite, if its parts were simultaneous, they would form an infinite actuality or actual infinitude, like a spatial accumulation or infinite heap, a thing that he never accepted. (In fact, Aristotle did not take into consideration even the possibility of an expanding universe, which would amount only to a potential infinitude).

The second horn of this middle sized dilemma refers to the impossibility not of a simultaneous, but of a successive multiplicity of nows as regards time. It is here that Aristotle switches from parts to instants proper. And in doing so he builds yet another dilemma, the smallest but perhaps the most important of all of them. Both horns of this mini-dilemma turn on the impossibility for each successive now of ceasing to be. First, no now can cease to be while still being (or, as Aristotle express himself, in itself, ἐν αὐτῷ). This seems to be not less obvious than the fact that parts, or even nows, if real at all, ought to be not simultaneous but successive. Provided one leaves aside the possibility of an unlimited, ecstatic or always shifting now, this seems to be not less obvious than the fact that parts, or even nows, if real at all, ought to be not simultaneous but successive.

As for the other horn of this smallest dilemma, the reason given for the impossibility that any now cease to be in a now other than itself is that no instant can be related to any other instant in any kind of immediate sequence. Here the expression "immediate sequence" is a translation of the Greek "ἐχόμενα" which sometimes has been mistaken for "συνεχόμενα" and translated "continuous". Hussey chooses the neutral "adjoining" and translates the passage as follows: "...it is impossible for the nows to be adjoining one another, as it is for a point to be adjoining a point"[8]. I take this to mean the impossibility not, of course, of a relation of continuity, but of one either of contiguity (ἁπτόμενα) or, still worse, of maximal or next neighborhood (consecutiveness, ἐφεξῆς) between the alleged many nows. My fingers, for instance, would be in such a relation of neighborhood if I were to spread them out, because between each two no other thing of the same sort, i.e. no other finger, would be there, whereas, were I to put them together, they would be contiguous to each other not having anything of the same or of a different sort between them. In this case, the edges would touch, but not be identical with each other as in the case of a

---

8 Aristotle, *Physics*, 218a 18 f.

relation of continuity[9]. Now, that is precisely the reason why two nows cannot be in the relation of contiguity or succeed one another. As Aristotle explains in Book VI, chapter 1, of the *Physics*[10], two indivisible items, e.g. points or instants, if they were to touch each other, would merge into one. Being indivisible, each one of them could touch the other only as a whole. In other words, the relation of contiguous succession between nows would collapse in that of continuity, in which the two edges do not merely touch each other but are rather one and the same, as it would be the case with one big finger composed, e.g., of index and middle finger.

Here, however, a difference is to be noticed between two points on a line merging into one and two temporal nows doing the same thing. In both cases contiguity –let alone next neighborhood (conscutiveness)– is excluded. But whereas the line still has parts[11], it is only the abstract or extended time which has parts and is hence divisible in parts. By contrast, real time consists of only one present now and is, in this respect, indivisible. Its continuity or endless divisibility is not like that of an extended line coinciding with Hussey's "ubiquitous point", but rather like that of a continuously shifting point. Since it cannot be detained or interrupted, this continuously shifting point can be only mentally but never actually divided into parts like a line. Therefore, a more adequate analogy to the shifting now or permanent present instant ceasing and starting to be at once, would be rather that of the drawing of an infinite or unlimited line by means of a pencil with an eraser rubber attached to it. Inasmuch as the drawing and erasing takes place at once, there is only one and the same point (Hussey's "ubiquitous point"), but one that is not just permanent (as Hussey's expression "permanent present" suggests) but passing away as well.

Put briefly, the argument about the impossibility of contiguous instants or present nows is as follows: since instants, unlike fingers, or houses put together in a row, do not have parts, any more than points do, they cannot touch one another without melting into one; in other

---

[9] Cf. Aristotle, *Physics*, 226b 34 - 227a 10-14.

[10] Aristotle, *Physics*, 231b 2.

[11] Cf. Aristotle, *Physics*, 231b 5 f.

words, the previous now (which under the already mentioned circumstances –i.e. leaving aside the unlimited now– could not cease to be in itself) cannot cease to be in the next now either, for there is no next now at all. The consequence of this is that between two instants there must be another instant and so forth *ad infinitum*. But then, again, at least with regard to the past, the intermediate instants would form an infinite actuality of simultaneous nows. As Aristotle says: "since the now has not ceased to be in the next now but in some other one, it will be simultaneously in the nows in between, which are infinitely many; but this is impossible"[12].

A consequence of this smallest but most important of all three dilemmas is –as Hussey points out– that "straightforward realism about the past is no longer possible"[13]. This could pose some problems to the view attributed to Aristotle according to which the world exists, as it is called, *ab aeterno*, i.e., that it has been eternally there. On the supposition of a non-straightforward realism with respect to the past, however, the contention that the world has always existed would rather mean that there can be no time at which nothing existed, or nothing was moving, just as there can be nothing, or nothing moving, without time. It is, I think, primarily in the sense of this interconnection between time and movement that both always existed and will indeed always exist, viz. together. This does not necessarily imply that both exist *ab aeterno*.

2. Preparing the resolution of the aporias: movement and time

This brings us to the intermediate passage after the exposition of the aporias before Aristotle goes on to the resolution of the whole difficulty about the reality of time. It is in those intermediate passages that the well known definition of time as counted number of move-

---

[12] Aristotle, *Physics*, 218a 18-21.

[13] Cf. p. XXV of the introduction to his Clarendon Series Translation; cf. p. 157 of the Commentary appended to it.

ment according to before and after is given. This definition applies to the physical time which can be measured by any sort of clock, i.e. to extended time, rather than to the permanent but uninterruptedly fleeting now. Accordingly, it leaves the changing thing out of consideration and concentrates on the change which, taken in itself, is but a product of our abstracting powers. But though the resolution proper turns precisely on the analogy between "the permanent present", "the changing thing" (or substance) and the "ubiquitous point" rather than on the abstract movement (abstracted, that is, from the changing thing) and its *analogata* ("magnitude" and "time"), those intermediate passages are nevertheless important for the resolution itself.

The important thing about the relationship between time and movement as regards the resolution of the aporias is twofold: first, time is never completely detached from nor completely attached to movement; in other words, the difference between the two is relative; and, as a result, secondly, the difference between movement and rest is relative as well. For Anaxagoras as well as for Empedocles, but not for Aristotle, there could have been, and indeed had been, a time in which nothing was in motion, but all things were at rest[14], just as for Newton absolute time could be flowing without anything moving or, indeed, existing. (In Anaxagoras, e.g., all things –or rather qualities of which things are supposed to be composed– had been for some indefinite time completely at rest before starting to move under the influence of the νοῦς in order to build up the things of everyday experience). By contrast, for Aristotle there can be no absolute rest just as there cannot be absolute time either. According to him, rest is relative not only in the sense that only things capable of moving can rest but also in the sense that, were something absolutely cut off from moving things, it would be impossible to consider it resting at all. That means that resting things move as well, at least externally or relatively. In some way, this also applies to a body changing places without itself internally altering. For places, unlike forms, are external to bodies. But it applies no less, say, to a unmoved bottle or to a frozen particle, for they change at least their relative position to things which they

---

[14] Cf. Aristotle, *Physics*, 250b 24-29

themselves do change. For there to be something resting, i.e. remaining in the same state during a period of time, the turning of the potter's wheel, to borrow an example from St. Augustin, would be sufficient, though, of course, not necessary. What is necessary is that, if not the potter's wheel, something else should move in relation to which even the changing thing would change if only relatively or externally.

The fact that nothing in the real world, including the inner world of the soul, can be absolutely at rest is necessary because otherwise real time, as a continuously running away now, would be detained and hence destroyed. Time can and must be stopped, i.e. considered limited, for purposes, e.g., of measurement; but it cannot be in itself stopped. In itself it is limitless, a limitless instant or limit. On the other hand, though time is not completely detached from movement, it is not completely attached to it either. Neither is time the same thing as movement nor is the only one continuously shifting now identical with changing things or substances, any more than, to use an Aristotelian example[15], the number ten is identical with ten horses, for it applies also to ten dogs, etc., or the measuring unity is identical with one horse. This does not mean that one has to take the limitless now as the measure of time or movement. It rather means that one has to take the comparisons summarized in Hussey's table with some precautions. This applies above all to the analogy between time and magnitude. For real, as opposed to abstract, time is in itself not extended; it is not a magnitude proper. For it to be extended, it would have to have *partes extra partes* in the sense of a sequence of contiguous nows. But it has been already shown that that is not possible.

With respect to this there is an important aspect in which the analogy between magnitude and (real) time fails, but not that between substances and the permanent present now[16]. It is this: one can actually divide a straight line into two or more parts. In this case the line would be interrupted, but the parts would not disappear because of that; they would still remain, though no longer as one but as two or more lines. On the other hand, one never can actually divide, or inter-

---

[15] Aristotle, *Physics*, 220a 23 f.; and 220b 8-12.

[16] Cf. Aristotle, *Physics*, 206b 1-3.

rupt, real time; it would be to destroy it altogether. No parts would then remain, for real time has no parts. As already said, the indivisible now is continuous not in the sense of being extended, but in that of being always flowing, i.e. ceasing and starting to be at once –as long as there is something moving in the world. Now, though a substance is not simply composed of parts, any more than real time is, it is in some way composed of properties, which, in any case, is something completely different. To say this, however, is not to criticize Hussey's table. On the contrary. A look at it rather confirms it. For, as long as the line remains the same, it has to remain unaltered as well (at least internally, i.e. not relatively to other changing things), whereas every substance survives the accidental changes that modify it, and it survives precisely because of those very changes or modifications –just as the one and same now survives because of its uninterrupted (and uninterruptable) ceasing and starting to be at once. That means, once more, that real time is not magnitude, and this is rather confirmed by Hussey's table itself, for in it "time" underneath "magnitude" is not real time, any more than, without some changing substance, "change" can be anything real on its own. And now to the resolution itself.

3. Resolving the aporias: the analogy between substance and instant

As I just mentioned, a substance is as little composed of parts as real time is. Instead, a substance has properties changing over time in the way in which real time has nows succeeding one another. But just as the properties are only different *secundum rationem* from each other as well as from the substance, so the nows are only different *secundum rationem* from each other as well as from the permanent present. "*Secundum rationem*" does not mean, of course, that the difference between the properties of a substance, or the nows of real time, is a fictitious one. It only means that there is an identity between them, though a contingent one. Coriscus in the market place –to take Aristotle's own example– and Coriscus in the Lyceum are not really different any more than nows succeeding one another in a relation either of contiguity or neighborhood are really different from one another.

The crucial text in this connection as well as for the resolution of the aporia reads as follows: "Just as the change is always other and other, so the time is too, though the whole time in sum is the same. For the now is the same X, whatever X it may be which makes it what it is". (The Greek expression for "whatever X it may be..." reads "ὃ ποτε ὄν". In his commentary Hussey, relying on other passages of the Aristotelian corpus as well, says that it "is used to pick out the substantial reality beneath a phased sortal concept". With the exception of the word "beneath", as I shall presently explain, I agree with Hussey's paraphrase). The passage continues as follows: "...but its being is not the same"[17]. "Being" (εἶναι) means here the same as the expression "λόγῳ" (dative, i.e. *secundum rationem*") used shortly afterwards, when Aristotle continues: "The moving thing is, in respect of what makes it what it is, the same (as the point is, so is a stone or something else of that sort); but in definition [τῷ λόγῳ] it is different, in the way in which the sophists assume that being Coriscus-in-the-Lyceum is different from being Coriscus-in-the-market-place. That, then, is different by being in different places, and the now follows the moving thing as the time does change". The passage ends by saying: "So the now is in a way the same always, and in a way not the same, since the moving thing too [is so]"[18].

It is to be conceded that in other passages Aristotle seems to be saying something different. This applies above all to the italicized section of the following passage: "For the change and the motion too are one by virtue of the moving thing, because that is one (*not [one] X, whatever X it may be that makes it what it is* –for then it might leave a gap– *but [one] in* definition (ἀλλὰ τῷ λόγῳ))"[19]. The explanation given here (inside the brackets) seems indeed to reverse the situation, as if the unity were this time supposed to be only *secundum*

---

[17] Aristotle, *Physics*, 219b 9-11.
[18] Aristotle, *Physics*, 219b 9-31 with omissions.
[19] Aristotle, *Physics*, 220a 6-9 (my emphasis).

rationem. However, since "definition", like "being" (as shorthand for "τὸ τί ἐν εἶναι"), can refer to different things (definition or being of either the substance or the accidents), I do not think that there is necessarily any inconsistency there. So I shall stick this time, too, to the interpretation I have been suggesting from the beginning. That is to say, Coriscus in a particular state and Coriscus in another state (where "state" can mean "place" but also any other contingent situation), are not really different, since the substance is always the same. If they were different not only *ratione* but also *a parte rei*, then the situation would be rather like that of space-temporal rings of a four-dimensional worm as in Quine. One can picture it like this:

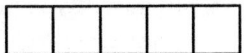

(but without gaps suggesting a relation of neighborhood rather than contiguity). In such a case, there would be only succeeding accidents or nows without any real unity. Yet it cannot be the case either that the unitary substance or now remains unaltered underneath the changing properties or nows respectively –like this:

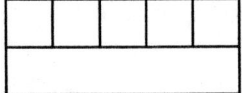

(but, again, without gaps, horizontal or vertical). What is wrong with either way of picturing the relation is that both –like perhaps the word "stage[s]" in Hussey's chart as well as the expression "beneath" in the paraphrase quoted some moments ago– suggest the idea of a discontinuous substituting of accidents one for another instead of that of a continuous altering of the substance or the present now itself –as if properties or nows were some sort of temporal parts that, after lasting for a while in a static or frozen present, would give way to others– the picture suggested by the Zenonian paradox of the flying arrow. To be sure, on the abstract level, one may consider the replacement of universal properties in such a way. Universal properties are placed next, or even outside of, each other in some sort of logical space. However, *a parte rei* there cannot be temporal but only spatial parts next to or outside each other. That is why real, i.e., spatially extended, parts can be cut off and still exist. But, as Aristotle himself pointed out in the second chapter of the *Categories*, this cannot happen with properties, any more than with nows, except in our thinking of them. And so, just as there is no next now to any given now, except by way of abstracting from the one now and making two out of one[20] –as if the end of the past now were a different now from the beginning of the future–, so there is no next contingent state of Coriscus succeeding the previous one. There is only Coriscus continuously changing in the sense of altering, even if we mostly do not notice it.

Coriscus' being in the market place does not succeed Coriscus' being in the Lyceum, nor indeed does Coriscus' starting to leave the Lyceum succeed Coriscus' still being there. There is no moment immediately following, or next, any other in which this could happen. Even the accident called "Coriscus' being in the market place" is an abstraction from the contingent state comprehending it as well as many other accidents. There are no accidents giving way to one another as if some were ceasing to be before others could start to be. It is the substance itself, in this case Coriscus, which bears the whole burden of changing, and its changing is not a discontinuous substitution of contingent states one for another but a continuous altering (not only in the particular sense of qualitative alteration). The accidents or comprehensive states themselves do nothing of their own. There are no accidents of accidents: συμβεβηκὸς οὐ συμβέβηκοτι συμβεβηκὸς, as the key sentence of Aristotelian metaphysics in this context reads, any more than there are, contrary to Quine's theory, variable numbers or movements of movements. It is not the movement itself that speeds up or down but, e.g., the locomotive, just as it is not the number of inhabitants of Berlin that increases or decreases but Berlin itself –a point already made by Frege which Quine, owing to his theory of spatiotemporal slices, felt compelled to disregard.

The impossibility of there being movements of movements or events of events is pointed out by Aristotle in Book V of the *Physics*[21]. This impossibility is, of course, in full agreement with his meta-

---

[20] Aristotle, *Physics*, 220a 12, 18; and 222a 10-20.

[21] Aristotle, *Physics*, 225b 15 f.

physics of substance, according to which accidents do not pile one upon another nor upon the substance –e.g., the quality upon the quantity. It is not the accident white, nor is it the white man, that becomes educated, but just the man, Socrates or Coriscus, and only he remains as well changes throughout changes, just as there is only one now that keeps going indefinitely. Those are standard examples of Aristotle's, but the principle that each accident modifies the substance immediately and not through intermediate stages or accidents applies generally. It is not just that substance alone bears the whole burden of continuous change, it is substance alone which accounts for the continuity of change. So, too, it is not the extension of whatever extended thing, nor is it the thing plus its extension, which becomes white, but the thing itself and nothing else. True, the thing has to be extended in order to be, e.g. colored, but that is a different point. So much for the analogy between substance and real time. But there are also some differences.

An obvious difference between substances and real time is that only the latter exists always, that is, uninterruptedly, whereas the former can cease to be despite the fact that time goes on. But this is only a consequence of the relative detachment of time from change. Owing to the relative detachment of time from movement and the moving substances as well, for real time to be it is not necessary that the same substance always keeps going. Consequently, there may be a discontinuity between ceasing to be and starting to in the case of substances, but not in that of time. In the former, but not in the latter, case both, starting to be and ceasing to be, may be different even *a parte rei*. Similarly, with the exception of circular movement, no change can go on for ever; it has to end somewhere. This does not apply to time. Like circular movement time, as Aristotle says", is always at a beginning and at an end"[22]. In the case of both, time and circular movement, beginning and end are only different *secundum rationem*. To quote Aristotle: "time will be like the circle –the convex and the concave are in what is in a sense the same– so time is always at a beginning and at

---

[22] Aristotle, *Physics*, 222b 4.

an end"²³. This poses the problem of whether, as Aristotle continues, "opposites would hold simultaneously and in respect of the same thing"²⁴. But, of course, the problem is posed generally whenever there is a change of state. For even if, except in the case of circular movement and under the supposition of an expanding universe, there is no movement that goes on for ever, whereas every rectilinear movement has to end somewhere, the question arises as to whether in the moment of changing from movement to rest, however relative those distinctions may be, the changing thing is still moving or already resting. And the same applies to the moment in which a substance starts or ceases to be. Does it already exist at that moment or does it not yet exist?

Those are the same questions Plato asked in the second part of the *Parmenides* after the second section of the first hypothesis. To answer them Plato had recourse to the notion of suddenness (ἐξαίφνης), which appears to be outside time as well as to contravene PET, since, according to Plato, in this extra-temporal instant neither the previous nor the subsequent state of the changing thing occurs. And with such difficult questions Aristotle is still wrestling in Book VI and Book VIII²⁵ of the *Physics*.

One could try to picture the problems involved here by means of two figures, an angular and a round arch. The angular arch means that the changing from one state to another, e.g., from the state of being moving into the state of being at rest, is not thouroughly continuous. Take, e.g., a ball thrown upwards. It cannot go on indefinitely. It has to go downwards somewhere, and the question is what happens then. If the ball were not to stop in between, the two movements upward and downward would be continuous to each other; in other words, they would be one and the same rectilinear movement which, unless the ball stopped somewhere below or above, would be, moreover, potentially infinite. But Aristotle was not prepare to accept even that. So for him, at the point of return, the ball has to rest for some time. The hori-

---

23 Aristotle, *Physics*, 222b 2 f.
24 Aristotle, *Physics*, 222b 4f.
25 Aristotle, *Physics*, 262a 12 ff.

zontal line at the top of the angular arch would stand for that period of rest however short. But this is not the end of the matter. For the question is what happens at the juncture of changing states represented this time not by the straight line at the top of the figure but by the angles. Letting aside the extra-temporal ἐξαίφνης of Plato's, there are two alternative possibilities left: either both states coincide or they do not coincide at that juncture. The first case would be one of continuity, the second one of discontinuity. As regards rectilinear, but not circular, movement or time Aristotle takes sides, naturally, with the latter alternative. But then the question arises as to which one of both states takes place there, that of rest or that of movement. One answer to this question is: only the following, but not the previous, state. But then one might ask again whether the decision would not be arbitrary. Now, one possibility for answering this question negatively would be by having recourse to the following analogy: the first moment of the following state is like being at a given point on a line, whereas the last moment of the previous state is like being at the next point away from the former. For, just as there is no such next point, so there is no last moment of the previous state either. This is the solution favored, e.g., by Richard Sorabji. It, undoubtedly, avoids at least having to accept a succession of nows *a parte rei*. But whatever its merits, it cannot be straightaway applied to the case either of time or of circular movement. For in each case a straightforward continuity is needed, which is not yet warranted by only avoiding either contiguity or next neighborhood. The required continuity would have to be no longer represented by an angular but rather by a round arch. The upshot of this is that, since real time cannot be actually interrupted, this solution cannot be accepted without further qualifications.

But, first, what about the other alternative, i.e. what about the possibility of both, the previous and the following state, taking place at the juncture of changing from one to the other? To say that the continuity of real time, like that of circular movement, compels one to accept that before and after both are at the juncture of changing from one to another seems to contravene PNC. But it is not necessarily so, and this for two reasons: first, PNC is not contravened by simply saying that "F" and "not-F", e.g. being there and not being there, or before and after, take place at the same moment. It is only contravened if one says that "being there" and "being not there", "before" and "after", or, in general, "F" and "not-F" mean the same. For it is only then that one would not only affirm and deny the same predicate of the same subject, which, as in the case not only of movement or time but also in many other cases, e.g. of Christian theology, is all right, but also in the same respect, i.e. *eadem ratione* (κατὰ τὸ αὐτό). In other words, both, before and after, here and there, God and man, one and three, etc., do coincide *a parte rei*, but not *secundem rationem*, which is precisely what Aristotle had said in the key passage of the resolution.

Once the continuity at the juncture of changing states has been thus saved, one might try to see whether this would not provide the qualifications needed for accepting Sorabji's solution according to which there is a first moment of the following state but not a last moment of the previous one. After all, the resolution explicitly said that in one sense, viz. precisely *secundum rationem,* there is truly a succession of moments or a distinctio between before and after, and such a distinctio is by no means a fictitious one. They may be indistinguishable from, or mixed up with, one another, but both, before and after, are nevertheless there. (One might picture this by means of letters typed on one another. Though not longer recognisable, the typed letters, e.g., "A" and "B" are, together with many other shapes, there, but not, e.g., a shape like "C"). Besides, to return to the special case of changing between movement and rest in both possible directions, the difference between movement and rest is not absolute. In fact, the problem of seemingly incompatible states arises not only at the juncture represented by the angles of the angular arch but all along the lines upwards and downwards themselves. On the other hand, the similarity between points and instants is not perfect. True, there are neither next points nor next instants; nevertheless, the points remain unchanged along with the line, whereas no single instant endures for any period of time. And since there are only spatial, but not temporal, real parts, infinite divisibility cannot mean in the case of real time, as in the case of a line and abstract time, that the action of dividing results in smaller parts each time.

One way of giving the gist of the resolution is to say with Aristotle: "time is both continuous, by virtue of the now, and divided at the now"[26]. According to the interpretation given, this means that it is a unity *a parte rei* and divided *secundum rationem* or abstractly. So it is not one and many in the same respect (κατά τὸ αὐτό). Inasmuch as time is continuous there is only one now; but inasmuch as it is divided there are two or many nows, according to the way one chooses to divide it. It could not be otherwise. For, if it were actually divided, then, as Aristotle says[27], time would come to a halt and, as a result, be destroyed in thought as well as in actuality. So time "divides potentially, and qua such the now is always different, but *qua* binding together it is always the same, just as it is the case in mathematical lines: [a point is] not always the same point *in thought*, for if one divides the line it is different in different cases, but inasmuch as [the line] is one, [the point] is the same everywhere"[28]. "...And for that reason it is *thought* always different, for the now is not the beginning and the end of the same thing [αὐτοῦ]; otherwise opposites would hold simultaneously and with respect to the same thing. And so time will not give out, for it is always at the beginning"[29].

4. Final remarks

I started with some remarks about the way Heidegger interpreted Aristotle's theory of time. I would like to finish in the same way. On the one hand, I have stressed the untenability of considering Aristotle's theory of time to be, as Heidegger had it, merely that of a succession of nows, but, on the other hand, I have also stressed the importance of the present for Aristotle, and in this respect, I think, one cannot but be fully in agreement with Heidegger. Now, as far as I

---

[26] Aristotle, *Physics*, 220a 4 f.
[27] Aristotle, *Physics*, 220a 13, 17.
[28] Aristotle, *Physics*, 222a 13-17 (stress of the author).
[29] Aristotle, *Physics*, 222b 2-7 (stress of the author).

know, no one, perhaps not even Aristotle, took the primordial importance of the present now for real time as seriously as Brentano. For him, only the present right now is real, but it is not a empty now. Brentano himself spoke of a πλήρωμα (fullness) with which the present now is endowed. For, as far as the past is real, it is inside the now like year-rings inside a tree. And the same might apply to the necessary aspects of the future inasmuch as they exist already *in causa*. That [together with Wittgenstein's metaphor], could perhaps help to understand how it is that in the only one now there are, nevertheless, many nows different from it only *secundum rationem*. It might also help to understand the relation between the being of the present and the not-being of past and future. In this respect Heidegger, but not Brentano, came once to recognize the paramount importance of Hegel's notion of negativity with respect to time. Before, he had harshly derived Hegel's theory of time based on that of Aristotle's using almost the same words of contempt Brentano had used himself against Hegel's theory. But while still teaching in Marburg Heidegger wrote: "In the end [one has to acknowledge] that Hegel was on to a fundamental truth when he said that Being and Nothing are the same thing"[30]. And referring to time in the same context he asked: "to what extent is time itself the condition of possibility of Nothingness [Hegel's "negativity"] as such?"[31]. Now, against the exclusion of negativity from Being as such, Hegel explicitly protested as forcibly as Heidegger was later to protest. I quote some key words of Hegel in this respect: "it is therefore said that although nothing is in thought or in imagination, yet for that very reason it is not *nothing* that is, being does not belong to nothing as such, but only thought or imagination is this being (...) that nothing does not posses an independent being of its own, is not being *as such*"[32]. For Hegel, on the contrary, being and nothing belong together in thought as well as in themselves. So one is tempted to regard Heidegger's as well as Hegel's thought in this respect as Aristotelian philosophy stripped of the doctrine of *ens ut sic*

---

[30] M. Heidegger, *Die Grundprobleme der Phänomenologie*, GA, 24, p. 443.

[31] *Ibid.*

[32] G.W.F. Hegel, *Wissenschaft der Logik*, Werke, 5, p. 108 f. (stress of the author).

as distinct from that of *ens ut verum*. With this proviso one could take Hegel's following words as a quintessence not only of Heidegger's but also of Aristotle's notion of ecstatic time: time "is the being which, in that it *is* is *not*, and that it is *not*, is. It is intuited becoming; admittedly, its differences are therefore determined as being simply *momentary*; in that they immediately sublate themselves in their externality however, they are *self*-external"[33]. It is a very concise formula for ecstatic time. So much so that one might think that in stressing so much ecstatic time in Aristotle I was more or less unconsciously applaying the method called by Gadamer of "melting of horizons" ("Horizontenverschmelzung") throughout my paper. If so, it would not be perhaps completely disadvantageous. After all, no philosophical question is the property of any single philosopher. In that case, I only would hope that the position of Aristotle has remained recognisable behind the supposedly melted horizons. The resulting pattern would be, too, one of actual sameness (*Selbigkeit*) and differences *secundum rationem*. Undoubtedly, I have stressed the importance of the flying now much more than Aristotle did. He had not even an expression for the corresponding concept. But, besides the analogy between the present now and the substance, there are, I think, at least four reasons which justify speaking of it. The first reason is that, although one can take time also as limited, it is in itself unlimited; the second reason is the definition of the unlimited itself ("οὗ ἀεί τί ἔξω"), which in the case of time is to be taken differently than in that of magnitudes[34]; the third reason is the fact that, while limited time, although it is not a counting but a counted number, depends nevertheless on the counting soul, real time, like movement[35], would exist also if there were no counting souls at all, for it would exist at least as countable number, which seems to apply primarily to infinite time, but does not coincide with the movement even of the last sphere; finally, the fourth reason is that the fact that time is one in definition means

---

[33] G.W.F. Hegel, *Philosophy of Nature*, transl. by M.J. Petry, vol. I, Allen and T. Unwin, London 1970, p. 229 f.

[34] Aristotle, *Physics*, 206b 1-3.

[35] Cf. Aristotle, *Physics*, 223a 25-29.

that it is always the limit of past and future, i.e. an unlimited limit. For this is, once again, the paradoxical concept of ἄπειρον applied to time. Where my interpretation perhaps departed from Aristotle is in that, unlike him, I was trying to see what the metaphysics, but not the physics, of time would be like, taking "metaphysics", as in Heidegger, in the strong sense of a theory of the present or presence. To assess the extent of the departure, if any, one would have to approach the question of the relationship between *Physics* and *Metaphysics* in Aristotle.

CHART I

Third aporia:

impossible
- many
  - simultaneous
  - succesive
    - in itself
    - in other
- one
  - finite time = two limits
  - thousend of years ago = now

CHART II[36]

Continuum	Unifying particular	'Phase' of unifying particular
Magnitude	Ubiquitous point	Located point
Change	Changing thing	Stage of changing thing
Time	Permanent present ('the before and after in change)	Unrepeatable instant

---

[36] Chart II taken from E. Hussey's Commentary on *Physics* III and IV in the Clarendon Aristotle's Series.

PART II

FIRST PRINCIPLES AND THE THEORY OF ACTION

CHAPTER 10
NON-CONTRADICTION AND PRACTICAL TRUTH*

In speaking of "practical truth" I refer not to the truth of propositions about actions (for example, the truth of moral judgments); by it I understand rather the truth of actions themselves. True moral judgments are still theoretical. This extension of the concept of truth to the practical realm had been hinted at as early as Plato in the dialogue, *Euthydemus*. In his confrontation with the Sophists, he once had Socrates ask: "Well, Euthydemus,... I may perhaps be going to say something silly; but forgive me. Here it is: If there is no such thing as speaking false or thinking false or being stupid, surely there can be no making a mistake either, when one does something. For in doing it there is no mistaking the thing that is done. You will state it so, will you?" "Certainly", he said. It was not Plato, though, but Aristotle who first spoke *expressis verbis* of practical truth.

If one accepts the notion of practical truth, then it makes sense to distinguish between right and wrong actions, right and wrong ways of life. But if there is no practical truth, then all kinds of action and all ways of life are in principle equally valid, differences among them being only a function of changing circumstances and consequences. Just as the rejection of PNC amounts to saying that there are no false propositions, so the rejection of practical truth amounts to saying that there are no morally wrong actions. But since the problem of ancient or contemporary moral relativism is a rather general one, I propose to approach it *via* some more particular questions. The concept of practical truth can be useful in at least three different respects: firstly, in order to avoid ethical naturalism without at the same time falling

---

* On Excluded Middle (Third) and Practical Truth cf. Chapter 3, Part 1, note 8 above, as well as Chapter 11, Afterword and Appendix to Chapter 3, Part 1 below.

into ethical formalism, secondly, in order to view the relationship between means and ends in the right light as well as, thirdly, that between understanding and willing in moral action. All three items bear on the disjunction, if there is one, between a deontological or a teleological approach in ethics, which preoccupies a great many moral theologians today.

I shall treat these three points in the order (Sections 2, 3, 4) in which they are listed above and conclude by putting the main results in nonformalized symbolic terms (5). But before doing so I would like to dispose of a preliminary difficulty concerning practical truth by shifting the problem of practical truth from the level of action proper to that of choosing or deciding (1).

1

Notwithstanding those words of Plato quoted above it still seems as if praxis could never be true or false at all. Truth and falsity seem to apply to sentences or to thoughts, never to things or events. But actions should be grouped together with things or events rather than with sentences or thoughts. So it is from the very start not quite clear what the expression "practical truth" could mean. This calls to mind one common objection to the so-called practical syllogism. "Health is to be striven for, light meat is healthy, poultry is light, this is poultry, therefore I will eat this". One cannot derive, so we are told, the conclusion from the premises since one cannot derive an action from propositions.

The same objection has been raised against Kant's distinction between action and cause, between the freedom which characterizes moral causality and natural causality. As a free agent the will acts according to Kant not on the basis of causes but on the basis of the representation or idea (*Vorstellung*) of causes, i.e., on the basis of principles. To quote Kant, "everything in nature works according to laws. Rational beings alone have the faculty of acting *according to the conception* of laws –that is, according to principles, that is, have a will"[1]. And Kant continues with a sentence with which we will have more to do in Section 4 of this chapter: "Since the deduction of actions from principles requires *reason*, the will is nothing but practical reason"[2]. Against this the objection has been raised: "How is it possible that such an obvious mistake [as that of deriving actions from propositions] went for so long unnoticed?"[3]. The objection, though, is out of place. One cannot, of course, derive an action from a proposition. But both, Aristotle and Kant, mean something else, namely: given that someone has truly chosen to act in a certain fashion, then he will do so whenever the circumstances permit it. They are entitled to speak of action rather than of choice because the transition from the latter to the former can be interrupted only accidentally. Whenever the choice is a real choice, a decision, the link between choice and action is an essential link. So, in saying that action derives from some principles or propositions Aristotle, as well as Kant, may, and indeed does, mean by "action" choice or decision (προαίρεσις or *electio, Entscheidung*), from which the action proceeds as it were automatically, provided nothing comes between the two.

But then the question comes down to whether one can derive a decision (or choice) from a principle or proposition or set of propositions or of principles, since the question of action itself plays only an accidental role. Or, to put it in terms more convenient for our problem, the question is not primarily whether an action but whether a choice or decision, like a proposition, can be called true. Since this question is interwoven with our three initial points I shall take up the

---

[1] (Transl. Abbot). "Ein jedes Ding der Natur wirkt nach Gesetzen. Nur ein vernünftiges Wesen hat das Vermögen, *nach der Vorstellung der Gesetze*, d.i. nach Prinzipien zu handeln, oder einen Willen". I. Kant, *Grundlegung zur Metaphysik der Sitten*, Akademie Ausgabe, IV, p. 413.

[2] "Da zur Ableitung der Handlungen von Gesetzen *Vernunft* erfordert wird, so ist der Wille nicht anderes als praktische Vernunft". *Ibid.*

[3] "Wie kommt es, daß ein so offensichtlicher Fehler so lange unbemerkt blieb?" Cf. R. Bittner, "Handlungen und Wirkungen", *Handlungstheorie und Transzendental Philosophie*, ed. G. Prauss, Frankfurt a.M. 1986, p. 22.

first of these forthwith. In so doing I am not, however, arguing that an action could not under any circumstances be deemed true or false. After all one may fairly naturally speak of an action as being either meaningful or senseless as in "what is the sense of doing this?" Now, sense and meaning are all that is required to make possible the attribution of "truth" or "falsity". With these preliminary remarks I was only trying, as I have said, to avoid unnecessary, although important, problems regarding the meaning of "sense" and "true" in connection with "action" or even with "things" and "events" (even with "nature"!).

Nothing has been lost in taking the concept of practical truth to be a question as to the possibility of assuming true or false choices instead of true or false actions[4]. But if nothing has been lost, then nothing, or so it seems at first, has been gained either. For unless a prescription is conjoined with some descriptive content, it cannot be true. On the other hand, if it is so conjoined, the danger of ethical naturalism still looms on the horizon. This corresponds to our first general point: is it necessary to accept ethical formalism in order to avoid ethical naturalism?

2

The question as to the possibility of practical truth has not yet been settled with its transposition from the sphere of action to that of choice or decision. It might still be objected that if there is room for a distinction between choices and propositions or judgments (including moral judgments about choices as distinct from the choices themselves), the former, but not the latter, being practical, this is due to the imperative force which accompanies every real decision. However, an imperative –like any "decisionistic" act of will– is as such devoid of any content. Its content accrues to it by virtue of a

---

[4] This is why Duns Scotus in fact identifies praxis with *actus voluntatis*, cf. *Ordinatio*, Prolog., pars. 5, q. 1-2, ed. Vaticana, I, n. 230.

descriptive judgment, which –insofar as it is true– simply mirrors the nature of things.

Thus, if we are to escape the dilemma –either formalism or naturalism– there must be a prescription that bears as it were within itself a descriptive content. Only inn this way would it be possible to avoid the need of deriving an "ought" from an "is". (The problem, of course, arose only after the process of "de-teleologizing" nature was completed). Now, there are in fact such prescriptions with intrinsic contents: they are commonly called gerundives. As Aquinas has said, and as has been stressed in our time as well (by Grisez), there is a difference between *fac hoc* (do this!) and *hoc est faciendum tibi* (this is to be done by you) in that the former, but not the latter, "admit[s]" –as Theron has written– "of division into Hare's phrastic and neustic". And Theron adds: "In saying an action is to be done (by you) I predicate something of it, as I don't if I tell you to do it"[5].

There is an intrinsic link between truth and gerundives which is lacking between truth and imperatives. Whereas one cannot say "it is true that do this", it is perfectly possible to say "it is true that this is to be done". The "is" in "this is to be done" is in fact the veritative or veridical "is". This applies on the level of superficial grammar to translations of gerundives without "is" as well (in the case of e.g. "this must be done" one can just as well say: "it is true that this must be done"). Thus, whereas the content of "do this" is exhausted by "this" (whatever it may happen to refer to), the content of "this is to be done" does not consist only in the "this". In other words, the content of "this is to be done" is itself prescriptive. The prescriptivity of the content of gerundives points to the fact that practical reason must in some sense be independent. Of course, the formula *hoc est faciendum* derives from *hoc est bonum* and from *bonum est faciendum*, but neither of these two premises may be derived from the other, and the latter is itself practical. Gerundives are also endowed with imperative force. But this force is neither the force of will nor that of reason as such: it is the force of practical reason proper. In other words, this imperative force is, first, not the force of logic, and, secondly, even in

---

5 S. Theron, "Morality as Right Reason", *The Monist*, 66, 1983, p. 29.

those cases where the formulation of the first practical rule contains an imperative of the will, as in the Latin Psalm's *declina a malo et fac bonum* this does not refer –as V. Bourke seems to assume[6]– to man's or God's will indifferently, but only to God's will, and under no circumstances to the will of the agent as conceived by Kant in conformity with the voluntarist conflation of practical reason and will. Thus, when Bourke in commenting on Grisez objects, "To say that 'the first principle is not primarily an imperative, although it is a genuine precept', is simply to confuse the issue"[7], this is at least just as confused as the view he is criticizing. Another question one might raise in this context is whether gerundives derive their prescriptive force from God's commands alone or rather, as Aquinas claims, from eternal law. Even in the latter case no naturalistic fallacy would be involved. But I cannot go into this further here. As regards human reason we may now say: it must by nature be both practical and theoretical –theoretical because reality is given to it and practical if only because reality or nature as a whole as well as human nature are not given to human reason as thoroughly perfect but as perfectible, an expression of this being the natural tendencies of man as a sensible, living, and rational being. Inasmuch as these tendencies (to survive, to procreate, to know) are purely natural, they are morally neutral[8],

---

[6] At least in his "The Synderesis Rule and Right Reason", *The Monist*, 66, 1983, pp. 71ff.

[7] *Ibid.*, p. 74.

[8] This, however, should not be understood to mean that they are indifferent to morality. On the contrary, even if they are not themselves moral, the natural tendencies, as opposed to non-natural, purely ideal values, set the standards for morality. "Neutral" here does not mean "indifferent", if by "indifferent" one understands either "irrelevant to moral choice" or "ambivalent between good and evil". This ambivalence is first introduced by the exercise of reason (and hence of the will too). In the absence of these neutral tendencies moral life could not get started. For moral life presupposes the possibility of (knowingly) deviating from natural tendencies in which the standards of morality are more or less manifest (or more or less hidden, depending upon one's point of view): "secundum ordinem inclinationum naturalium est ordo praeceptorum legis naturae". Thomas Aquinas,

neither good nor evil. (As Plato himself once had occasion to ask, of what use would knowledge be, if it itself did not participate in the Good?). But as soon as natural tendencies are apprehended by practical reason with a view to doing something, they become ambivalent between good and evil on account of the use which the will[9] must make of them in a teleological or intentional order of means and ends. This is nothing more than an application of the general principle, *natura determinata ad unum, ratio ad opposita*. Accordingly the principle of synderesis does not simply run *bonum est faciendum* but "*et malum vitandum*".

But just as the first theoretical principle is intended to overcome the ambivalence between being and not-being, the first practical

---

Summa Theologiae, I-II, q94, a2. The *ordo praeceptorum* is not the *ordo inclinationum*, but it is in accordance with it.

[9] It is on this level, and not on that of the natural tendencies, that the indifference or ambivalence of reason and the will, which manifests itself in the possibility, firstly, of deviating from some natural tendency or other and, secondly, in the possibility of the will's following the deviation disclosed by reason, comes into play. Thus the word "indifference" here is not intended to suggest that both the natural tendency and its deviation are equally valid but rather that they are equally possible. Without the possibility of deviation meritorious behavior (and hence morality) would have been deprived of its point. To that extent morality requires that there be something like *libertas indifferentiae* in addition to autonomy or self-determination. The error consists merely in taking autonomy to be something positive rather than ambivalent or indifferent. This corresponds to the error made by Kant. In equating autonomy not with that openness to contrary determinations which constitutes the very possibility of morality but with positive morality Kant was destroying the very foundations of morality he wanted to lay (cf. n. 18 below). In this he was anticipated by some late Scholastics. But precisely because their views on morality are founded on this error they can offer no compelling reason for denying the necessity of this ambivalence or indifference to morals. Only insofar as one refuses to accept this indifference on the part of the natural tendencies as the basis of morals can later stipulations mandating freedom of belief be viewed as involving a break with tradition, whether it be the Thomistic tradition or any other. More on this in my article "Kontingenz und Willensfreiheit. Bemerkungen über den Begriff der Menschenwürde", *Neue Hefte für Philosophie*, 24/25, 1985, pp. 106-146.

principle is intended to overcome the initial ambiguity between right and wrong. To take an example of Plato's, just as it is not settled from the very start whether a eunuch is or is not a man, or a pumice is or is not a stone, or a bat is or is not a bird, or a reed is or is not wood[10], so evil is not in every case clearly different from the good. A total ambiguity, though, would rule out the possibility of PNC as well as the rule of synderesis being valid, i.e., it would render theoretical as well as practical truth pointless insofar as it would under these circumstances be permissible to assert truly of any subject any predicate, as well as to pursue any course of action and any way of life. Now the only alternative to theoretical relativism is to accept the existence of some propositions (viz. contradictions) that could never be true[11]. Similarly, the only alternative to ancient or modern practical relativism is to accept the existence of some kinds of action which could never be good.

According to traditional morality there are four such essentially forbidden courses of action. Interestingly, all four correspond to one or other of the three fields in which, according to St. Thomas, the fundamental inclinations of man may be detected: to the drive to self-preservation as a sensible being corresponds the unconditional precept not to kill innocents; to the drive to procreation as a living being corresponds the prohibition of some sexual practices; and to the desire to know as a rational being corresponds the prohibition of lying as well as of torture. It is not to my purpose to defend traditional morality here. I am only saying that insofar as one fails to admit one or the other absolute prohibition morality becomes to that extent meaningless, just as the rejection of PNC has as a consequence the meaninglessness of any proposition or any form of verbal behavior or even –as Aristotle stressed– of any behavior at all.

If there were no absolute prohibitions there would also be no point in asserting that *bonum est sequendum et malum vitandum* because there would be be in principle no difference between good and evil, just as if there were no absolutely false propositions there would be no

---

[10] Plato, *Republic*, 479B 3-C 5.

[11] Aristotle, *Metaphysics*, 1007a 21-b 18.

difference in principle between truth and falsity. If the first principle of practical reason is to have any point, the ambiguity between good and evil must come to an end somewhere. But if there are no absolute prohibitions, all ways of life are in the short or in the long run interchangeable or equally valid from an evolutionary standpoint. So the distinction between good and evil implies that only one way of life, i.e., only one last end of life, is morally possible. As we shall presently see, this should not be taken to imply a lack of variety.

For practical reason the natural inclinations are ambiguous between good and evil because it views them in the light of the use to which the will might put them. But at the same time and by the same token practical reason introduces into natural inclinations an intentional or teleological order of means and ends which may itself be either good or bad. This constitutes our second general point: practical truth as involving a correct relation between the means and ends of life.

3

In the realm of technical instrumentality practical truth comes down to the suitability of means to independent ends. Here the stress lies on "independent", any means being considered good which conduces to these independent ends. Since such means insofar as they are purely technical are also morally neutral, there is no need to justify them[12]. Once the end has been chosen and fixed in advance –its independence consisting in nothing other than this– any means are permitted provided they conduce to it. In the realm of technical instrumentality, however, not only are all means suitable to achieving an end interchangeable with one another, provided, of course, that they are all equally capable of completing the task appointed them, but

---

[12] To maintain that all forms of action are morally neutral, which amounts to rendering all courses of action pre-moral, obviates of course the need for justifying means in terms of ends. Cynicism has thus been defeated, but only at the price of sacrificing morality itself.

the ends themselves are also interchangeable. Ends are in this connection even less necessary than means. Means may at least lay claim to a hypothetical necessity whereas technical ends are not necessary at all. Their existence depends exclusively on whether they have been chosen as ends or not. In the realm of instrumentality one must in fact fix in advance the end to be pursued; it must be worked out, and it is sometimes even necessary to draw a diagram of it. That is why the means need here only be effective, i.e., why they are really only means. In the realm of morality, on the contrary, one is never free to choose one's end. One cannot even make a sketch of it. The only end which man is not capable of choosing since it does not lie in his power to reject it is the final one: happiness. But although happiness cannot be rejected, one can very well fall short of it or lose it, for it can never be perfectly known in advance. There is no possibility here of choosing the end independently of the means.

Moral practical truth implies precisely (or at least additionally) this same interdependence of means and ends, and not simply the suitability of means to ends which are fixed independently of them. This serves to explain why the model of the practical syllogism does not completely satisfy the requirements of moral practical truth. It is not possible to derive prior to the conclusion (which corresponds to the means, i.e., to the action itself) even one, much less both, of the premises, which correspond to the end[13]. The interdependence of

---

[13] Cf. E. Ricken's review of Anselm W. Müller's *Praktisches Folgern und Selbstgestaltung nach Aristoteles*, Freiburg-München 1982, in *Philosophische Rundschau*, 31, 1984, pp. 269ff.: "According to Aristotle practical truth may be predicated of προαίρεσις. But to which criteria should one appeal in determining the truth of the conclusion, which ascribes to human beings a *telos* (and hence to us as reasoning beings and agents) and upon which practical reasoning is based? This question is in fact a crux of Aristotelian interpretation... One may legitimately question whether in taking the practical syllogism as the model for Aristotle's practical philosophy one has opened the way to a proper understanding of it or whether despite the textual support to which it may claim this approach has not rather served to block further access to it. There can be no doubt as to the fact that practical thinking for Aristotle is directed toward an end; problematic is only whether this end may yield the premises of a practical syllogism... When Aristotle

means and ends also explains why moral knowledge (*prudentia*) has to be genuinely practical, whereas a good technician may refrain from exercising his skill or may even intentionally –i.e., in accordance with his own true (albeit furtive) end– make "mistakes". Praxis here involves the disclosure rather than the mere application of previously known principles. As Aristotle had argued, if one is to know what one intends to do, one must (try to) do what one intends to know[14].

Is it possible to accept a plurality of morally different forms of life, here understood to be modes of behavior which are optional and therefore interchangeable in the sense that one may, and even must, choose among them?[15]. If our previous statements were correct, this is not possible. To answer this question in the affirmative would be to confuse morality once again with technique. In the technical sphere not only are the means interchangeable with other means, and the ends with other ends, but the means are even interchangeable with the ends, for the same course of action may be an end or a means depending on our choice of action. In the realm of morality, on the other hand, there is no such interchangeability, either among means and ends respectively, or between means and ends. Insofar as there is only one

---

claims that the proper starting point for practical reasoning reveals itself only to the good, this is redolent of his doctrine of the correct means, and so to be understood primarily in terms of its negative implications: The good cannot be identified with some *telos* possessing a definite content".

[14] Cf. Aristotle, *Ethica Nicomachea*, II, 1, 1163a 32 ff.

[15] The fundamental choice of one way of life as opposed to another can signify either a decision between good and evil, it being very unlikely, however, that one would opt for an alternative which one views as evil, or a decision between equally valid or good last ends. Either way the decision would be devoid of objective content. It could only be "free" in a voluntarist and subjectivist sense. An objective and rational justification would have to be given on another level, i.e., either by defining "morally" right (as distinct from "morally" good) choices as those which would have the best consequences for oneself or by consistently adhering to the choice originally made. In the following I shall be concentrating on, and in the final analysis rejecting, the thesis of a plurality of different ways of life, all presumed to be equally good, which follows from the technical model of action.

final end –happiness, i.e., true happiness–, some restrictions must attach to the means of attaining it but this need not imply some sort of rigidity in the choice of one's means. Above all this should not be understood to mean that there is only one way all men have to behave or one culture everybody ought to accept.

To begin with, the non-interchangeability of means and ends only applies to absolute prohibitions. Thus the uniqueness which characterizes the truly moral way of life does not exclude, but rather includes, a great variety of alternative modes of behavior and even of cultures[16]. The variety which the unique moral way of life evinces is, though, totally different from the plurality of equally "good" ways of life. In the former case choice does not range *among* several permissible, even if incompatible, forms of life but only occurs *within the confines of* a single morally acceptable way of life. The many morally compatible forms of behavior or cultures are here all reducible to one other since they are all simply different implementations or anticipations of the unique last end, viz. of true happiness. Accordingly one need not, in choosing one, reject the other, as in the technical model of morality.

The important thing to bear in mind here is that the technical model does not allow for the possibility of moral wrongness. As Plato and Aristotle had already emphasized, it makes no sense to speak of a mistake in those cases where the alleged "mistake" has been made in the pursuit of another (higher) end. As a result the man who intentionally makes mistakes is from the technical point of view a better human being than the man who unintentionally makes them. Now, the possibility of deviating from norms without doing wrong must obviously come to an end at the highest level of the hierarchy of means and ends. But if there is no unique last end, it always remains open to one to justify one's decisions simply by freely (i.e. gratuitously) exchanging the last end, which had only been chosen provisionally, for some other. A parallel may once again be drawn in this respect with attempts to negate the necessity of the first principle of theoretical reason. The root of the analogy lies in the resulting

---

[16] Very roughly speaking, all cultures which accept human rights.

impossibility of there being either theoretical or practical falsity. In both cases it would be meaningless to speak of "truth" since the truth would have become readily accessible to all and it would have become impossible to make a mistake. Thus, in neutralizing the moral relevance of means or of kinds of action, such theories as voluntarist prescriptivism are instrumentalizing morality and hence destroying the kind of truth peculiar to it, namely, practical truth. And with this I proceed to the third and last general point, viz. the relationship between understanding and the will in moral life.

4

Aristotle characterizes practical truth as an agreement between the understanding and the will, or more precisely between right reason and right desire (which for him means willing in some sense of βούλησις). Now, if reason is by nature practical in the sense outlined above, then the difference between it and the will will have been rendered negligible. This is to some extent the case in Aristotle but even more clearly the case in Kant. Yet this would result once again in the dissolution of morality.

According to Aristotle, βούλησις as effective will or decision, as distinct from ineffective wish, is nothing but desire in harmony with reason: whenever man's desire (ὄρεξις, appetitus) is in harmony with his reason, his desire is not concupiscence (ἐπιθυμία) or anger (θυμός) but will (βούλησις)[17]. Still, if the will is by definition nothing

---

[17] "ἡ γὰρ βούλησις ὄρεξις, ὅταν δὲ κατὰ τὸν λογισμὸν κινῆται, καὶ κατὰ βούλησιν κινεῖται), ἡ δ' ὄρεξις κινεῖ καὶ παρὰ τὸν λογισμόν· ἡ γὰρ ἐπιθυμία ὄρεξίς τίς ἐστιν". Aristotle, *De anima*, 10, 433a 23-28. True, the *logismos* may or may not be in the service of the good. But Aristotle is at the same time stressing the rightness of reason (433a 26 taken in conjunction with 433a 23). Be this as it may, the important thing to keep in mind is that if the will must by definition act in accordance with (right or wrong) reason, there can no longer be any room for freedom of the will.

other than desire in accord with reason, i.e., nothing but (right) desire, then the result is something very close to Socratic intellectualism: wrong-doers are either ignorant or patients in need of medical treatment, never sinners deserving blame or condemnation. Kant arrives at a similar conclusion but in a more straightforward fashion. Indeed the main purpose of the *Critique of Practical Reason* is to show that reason can be rendered immediately practical. But here, too, there is no freedom to do evil but only freedom to do good[18], the main difference between Aristotle and Kant being that the latter reduces practical reason to the will rather than the other way around.

One way or another, it would seem, then, one cannot do evil knowingly (or consciously) so that everything that one does in accordance with the dictates of one's own conscience would therefore be good. In particular there is here no possibility of *peccata ignota*. Now, in order to restore responsibility (or even culpability) for one's own actions one must first reject the conflation of the will with practical reason. This can only be achieved, and in Christian doctrine has in fact been achieved, by undoing the semi-identification of both in Aristotle as well as the thorough-going identification of both in Kant and reversing the relationship of priority which Aristotle assumed to obtain between reason and the will as regards practical truth[19].

---

[18] Hence Kant's equation of freedom with autonomy and of autonomy with morality. Cf. G. Prauss, *Kant über Freiheit als Autonomie*, Frankfurt/M. 1983.

[19] In his remarkable book (cf. n. 14 above) A.W. Müller has succeeded in effecting this reversal. Thus, strictly speaking, A. Graeser (*Sophistik und Sokratik, Plato und Aristoteles*, München 1983, p. 312, n. 121) is correct in observing that Müller is no longer interpreting Aristotle's theory of practical truth. Since I have dealt with these matters not only in the article "Theoretische und praktische Wahrheit" (in *Rehabilitierung der praktischen Philosophie*, ed. by M. Riedel, Freiburg, 1974) to which Graeser (*loc. cit.*) refers, but also in "Die Theorie der Praxis als praktische Theorie. Zur Eigenart der Aristotelischen Ethik" (in *Zur Theorie der Praxis*, Walberberger Studien, ed. P. Engelhardt, Mainz 1970), "Praktische Wahrheit. Bemerkungen im Anschluß an Aristoteles" (in *Wahrheit und Begründung*, eds. V. Gerhardt and N. Herold, Würzburg 1985), and "Kontingenz und Willensfreiheit", I shall not be dwelling on this here.

Even granting the fact that practical reason has to do with means whereas desire has to do with ends, the entire content of moral or practical truth cannot be exhausted by simply adapting the former to the latter, viz. in the suitability of means to independent ends. As we saw, this would be to reduce practical to technical truth. It is equally important or even more important conversely that the will conform to, but not be identified with, practical reason. This acknowledges the possible objection, and in fact overcomes the danger, that the will might knowingly decide against reason. In other words, man is indeed free to choose among several ways of life. But this is in turn just another way of saying that he can knowingly decide to do wrong or to act badly. It should not, however, be understood to mean that all last ends or ways of life are equally good and hence interchangeable in the course of individual or collective human evolution as decisionistic or voluntaristic prescriptivism is obliged on pain of inconsistency to maintain; otherwise morality would once more have been reduced to a technique and the possibility of moral wrong-doing negated.

The naturalism which lies behind the conception of a plurality of equally valid forms of life which due to their mutual incompatibility compel one to choose among them comes most clearly to the fore in the distinction between good and evil, on the one hand, and "moraly" right and wrong, on the other, which may be traced at least as far back as D. Ross. Since it is beyond dispute that the good is to be chosen (if only because the concept of the good is held to be devoid of content and the criteria for its application are considered to be lacking), the only possible rules for judging are to be found on the side of rightness or wrongness. But rightness here is simply a matter of a choice's having the best consequences for the person or society making the choice and hence of its being among all possible choices the best suited to future eventualities, either for the individual or for mankind as a whole. Of course even here one may discover rules or norms for telling right from wrong but the point here is that they are only temporarily or factually valid. These rules cannot even in the negative and restricted sense of prohibitions be timelessly valid nor can they remain identical through time. What is now right may later be wrong; otherwise it would make no sense to alter continuously one's moral decisions in order to adapt to changing circumstances. Just as potentially, i.e., with the passing of time, contradictions may arise[20], so incompatible or contrary forms of life may in a single lifetime or over generations be chosen, one after the other, by the same person or by the same collectivity respectively.

The parallel between the rejection of the first principle of practical reason and that of theoretical reason consists in the fact that the latter amounts to a denial of things (or persons) remaining the same through time, whereas the former amounts to a denial of the possibility of speaking of the same rightness or wrongness through time. Just as according to Euthydemus it is not Cleinias himself who changes from ignorant to wise, but only the ignorant-Cleinias-now and the wise-Cleinias-later (i.e., Quine's four-dimensional slices), so according to consequentialism there is no rightness or wrongness but at most only rightness (or wrongness)-now, rightness (or wrongness)-later etc. In other words, just as the rejection of PNC eliminates all essence and reduces all things to accidents, each of which may be related to any other and thereby making the concept of rightness senseless as well as rendering discourse impossible, so the rejection of rightness-through-time makes even incompatible forms of life interchangeable and hence moral discourse senseless.

Neither on the theoretical nor on the practical level can an alternative to essentialism be found apart from that of a holism according to which any rule regarding individuality and morality must be settled conventionally or at least pragmatically in view of the best possible results for survival in light of the changing circumstances. However, not even the concept of rightness (or wrongness)-at-time-t could be maintained on consequentialist lines since there is here no criterion for judging which consequences are to be reckoned as forseeable at any given time. It would be possible *a limine* to regard all the consequences of a given action, even the most remote, as having been foreseeable, if one so chooses. Hence any course of action may be viewed as being either right or wrong, depending on how many of its consequences are considered to have been

---

[20] Aristotle, *Metaphysics*, 1009a 35.

foreseeable. As was the case when the validity of the first principle of theoretical reason had been denied, so here, too, the rejection of an overriding moral principle leads to a thorough-going factualness in judging. Insofar as it presupposes the necessity of some definitive rules for distinguishing rightness from wrongness, essentialism constitutes the only possible alternative to holism in the theoretical as well as in the practical field. Holism, if it is not to be thrown into thorough disorder, must also admit definitions[21]. But according to one of its leading adherents, W.V.O. Quine, one may be compelled in the short or the long run to part with any particular rule since each logical or practical principle (even the first ones) is subject to empirical refutation. His pragmatism allows the holist to talk coherently. He is not condemned, as is the sophist of Aristotle's *Metaphysics* IV, to be silent like a plant but is even credited with the faculty of being able to behave like a (perhaps higher) animal. What he cannot do is speak as a moral being. A consistent holist cannot accept any essential difference between man and animal[22].

---

[21] "But if one does that, there is no discussion. Those who say this entirely eliminate substance [οὐσία] and what it is to be. For it is necessary for them to maintain that all things are coincidences and that there is no such thing as just what to be a man or to be an animal [is]". Aristotle, *Metaphysics*, 1007a 19-23 (Transl. Kirwan).

[22] Aristotle, *Metaphysics*, 1010a 1-4. "Still the German word "*Handlung* " [action] is not used to refer to every form of natural activity. One usually uses it when speaking about what human beings do but even here not in all cases. To bleed is not a *Handlung*, to whistle is, to yawn is a dubious borderline case. But this is a peculiarity of the German language which does not point to a real distinction... I am not suggesting here that such peculiarities of the language should be ignored when using the word "*Handeln*". Rather I am suggesting that we abandon the view that more than a linguistic peculiarity is involved. And of course I am not denying that what reasonable beings do differs from what other animals do. But they only differ from one another in the sense that what birds do is different from what elephants do... Why should Nature have to be guided, why should it not be Nature which gives birth to the beautiful? Reason is on this view something which may legitimately be expected from the kind of animals that we are and indeed only from us". R. Bittner, *Moralisches Gebot und Autonomie*, Freiburg-München 1983, p. 24, n. 3. Under these circumstances the most consistent thing to do would

5

I would like to close this chapter by expressing the upshot of all this in non-formalized symbolic terms. Investigations into the meaning of symbols have established that the triangular and quadrangular forms employed in ethics as well as in the arts, have different symbolic values. Whereas quadrangular forms, as they are used e.g. in hermetic thought, like circular forms, symbolize the attempt to cope with evil by integrating it into human life, triangular forms (upwards-pointing forms) are symbolic of the effort to cope with evil by overcoming it through asceticism, etc. Now, suppose we have a cube and a pyramid, each having a quadrangular base congruent with that of the other, and suppose we take each base to symbolize the plurality of modes of behavior or of cultures. The difference between the two is then expressed vertically and corresponds to two different modes of ordering means and ends, i.e., to two different intentional or teleological hierarchies, depending on whether or not there is a plurality of last ends or of legitimate ways of life. If there is, then there is no convergence in a single point at the top of this hierarchy, as in the case of the pyramid, but only a horizontal plane, as in the case of the cube[23].

---

be to deny the appropriateness of applying the concept of morality to human beings. Cf. also R. Bittner, *Moralisches Gebot und Autonomie*, p. 14.

[23] W. Wieland expresses this idea in the following manner: "In the end the real point of contention must always revolve around the question of whether the whole of human action may without remainder be subsumed within a single teleological order or whether there is a point at which man stands before the choice of several teleological (world-)orders, among which he can no longer choose by orienting himself with respect to a superordinate teleology. Thus what is at issue here is the question of whether an absolute goal has been prescribed for human action in its entirety, in which case human action would no longer lie fully within the agent's sphere of influence, or whether the opposite is not in fact the case". *Platon und die Formen des Wissens*, Göttingen 1982, p. 268. Among those who have opted for a plurality of final ends must also be reckoned E. Tugendhat: "In reflecting we come to a highest point where we can no longer objectively ground our decision but where rather that which corresponds to my highest good is itself first consti-

A cube has neither apex nor base so that one usually plays dice with a cube, but never with a pyramid. Symptomatically enough quadrangular forms are fundamental for that type of thought which, like Heidegger's (*das Geviert!*), sides with Protagoras against PNC, the playing of dice here corresponding to Heidegger's thorough-going facticity. In keeping with this evil is not to be rejected but to be integrated as a whole[24]. In keeping with this approach there is no single way of life, regardless of how multifaceted it might be; there are only synchronically or diachronically incompatible ways of life, among which we are not always able to choose, if only because history or socialization (Heidegger's *Seinsgeschichte* or Wittgenstein's *Abrichtung*) have already for the most part and as a matter of concrete fact chosen for us.

According to cubically symbolized thought there are apexes or bases only within the confines of individual cultures, whether one calls them *Menschentümer*, *Lebensformen*, *Sprachspiele*, or whatever. Within these individual ways of life it is, of course, possible to distinguish between right and wrong, higher and lower, but each individual form of life is in itself right. All forms of life are in principle equally valid; each of them may in due course rise to prominence. The cube reflects the lack of any comprehensive

---

tuted by my will". *Selbstbewußtsein und Selbstbestimmung*, Frankfurt 1979, p. 238.

[24] As Rilke put it in one of his sonnets to Orpheus: "Many a rule of death, rose with deliberate rightness,/onwardly-conquering man, during your hunting past:/better than trap or net known to me, fluttering whiteness,/they were wont to hang down in the cavernous karst./Gently letting you in, as were you a token/publishing peace. But then: vassal would twitch at your thong,/Night would cast from the caves pallid handfuls of broken flight doves to the light... Not even that, though, was wrong./Far from the gazer remains every emotion but gladness,/nor from the hunter alone, gathering, watchful and keen,/that which his suns have matured./ *Killing merely is one form* of our wandering sadness.../ Pure in the spirit serene's/all we ourselves have endured" (Transl. Leishman, Rilke's emphasis). Cf. D.B. Linke, "Heideggers Mandala", *Philosophisches Jahrbuch*, 1986, pp. 286-300.

overriding objective hierarchy, which has been displaced by the complete interchangeability of ends.

In an illuminating article in *The Monist*, from which I have already quoted, Stephen Theron writes: "I do not think there is any appearance of satisfactoriness in a dismissal of the question [about the common justification of theoretical and practical reason] by retreat into conventionalism, of a type which appears to emerge in... some of Wittgenstein's utterances as when he says that justification is a language-game based on a shared form of life, that to have exhausted the justifications to the point of saying 'This is simply what I do' [i.e., my form of life] as equivalent to reaching bedrock". Thus, on one interpretation of Wittgenstein "common sense views... can be regarded as the true basis –hough by no means the justification– of rational belief and discussion". To this Theron objects: "Yet common sense as such is not sacrosanct before the exigencies of inquiry... In fact without a guarantor common sense could be common illusion"[25].

This is, in fact, the main question: whether we should abandon the rational way of life, blurring again the borderline between dream and waking life, myth and λόγος. The only alternative to this is metaphysics, since it is based precisely on the conviction that it constitutes a question of fundamental importance whether man is seeking after truth or rather after illusions, on the theoretical as well as on the practical level[26]. That is why even Kant, like Aristotle, "was trying to overcome scepticism, in his [i.e. Kant's] case by searching for a transcendental deduction of categories as well as of moral law". As Aristotle saw, as soon and so long as the sophist is engaged in argument, he ceases to be a sceptic as regards the first principle of thought. Similarly as soon as one is engaged in ethics one is committed to some form or other of inconditional practical truth.

---

[25] S. Theron, "Morality and Right Reason", p. 32.
[26] Aristotle, *Metaphysics*, 1010b 7-14.

CHAPTER 11
DISCOVERY AND VERIFICATION OF PRACTICAL TRUTH

Practical truth refers to the truth of actions, not to that of judgments of value about actions. The *aporetic* nature of practical truth lies in the fact that it seems to be at the same time necessary and impossible: necessary for discriminating right from wrong actions; impossible because actions resemble propositions, which can be true, less than they do things or events, which apparently cannot be true or false independently of our appraisals.

One could try to dissolve the ἀπορία by asserting either the necessity or the impossibility of practical truth. The semblance of impossibility can be made to disappear provided one takes "truth" broadly enough so as to include things and events as well as propositions and appraisals. Within as well as outside philosophy this has not been uncommon. To take just a few examples, the expression *veritas rerum* was a familiar one in Scholasticism; Heidegger's construal of ἀλήθεια as some kind of primordial appearing or openness (*Offenbarkeit, Unverborgenheit*) cannot be dismissed *a limine*; the *Vulgata* translates ἀληθεύεντες ἐν ἀγάπῃ[1] into *veritatem facientes in caritate*, which sounds like a paradigm of practical truth; and actions performed in accordance with the virtue of ἀλήθεια (sincerity) were dubbed true in classical Greek[2].

Alternatively, one can deny the possibility, to say nothing of the necessity, of practical truth by taking "truth" instead narrowly enough so as to exclude things, events, and actions. In this case one could still

---

[1] *Ephes.*, 4, 15.
[2] Cf. Aristotle, *Ethica Nicomachea*, 1108a 19 f.

speak of any defective thing, natural catastrophe, or misguided action as not being as it ought to be so that one would not even be called upon to renounce some form of natural teleology. All that would be required is not to use "true" or "false" for something that would better be called "good" or "bad".

Either way, the problem of practical truth would have been dealt with as if it were a pseudo-problem. To raise it again would only be to squabble about the best use of words, to engage, so to speak, in linguistic philosophy of a rather poor sort.

In the following I wish to show that in speaking for the first, and indeed almost for the last, time *expressis verbis* of practical truth Aristotle was dealing with serious philosophical problems (I), with which Plato had already been concerned (II). At the end (III) I shall briefly hint at the importance of these problems in connection with issues disputed by modern as well as contemporary philosophers.

1. Discovery (I)

At the *locus classicus* for Aristotle's theory of practical truth can be found the following: "...since moral excellence is a state concerned with choice, and choice is deliberate desire, therefore both the reasoning must be true and the desire right, if the choice is to be good, and the latter must pursue just what the former asserts. Now this kind of intellect and of truth is practical; of the intellect which is contemplative, not practical nor productive, the good and the bad state are truth and falsity (for this is the form of everything intellectual); while of the part which is practical and intellectual the good state is truth in agreement with right desire"[3].

Taken by itself this passage does not provide much justification for speaking of practical truth as the truth of actions. In it truth is directly identified only with intellect or reason, not with desire or choice; with

---

[3] Aristotle, *Ethica Nicomachea*, 1139a 22-6 (ROT throughout).

that with which one thinks and deliberates, not with that with which one carries out an action or wishes it to be done. Desire is not called true but right, nor is προαίρεσις ("choice"), as a result of right desire and true deliberation, called true but good (σπουδαῖα). Elsewhere it is said straightaway: "choice is neither true nor false"[4]. And since choice normally leads to action, this again seems to speak against the possibility of a truth of actions. The same thing appears to be the case in the treatise about truth in the *Metaphysics*, where it is said: "the end of theoretical knowledge is truth, while that of practical knowledge is action"[5]. In the sentence immediately preceding, however, it is stated without any restriction that philosophy, and hence practical philosophy too, "should be called knowledge of the truth". And shortly afterwards one source for the scholastic doctrine of the *veritas rerum* turns up ("as each thing is in respect of being, so is it in respect of truth") as well as for the infamous degrees of truth theory ("that which causes derivative truths to be true is most true")[6].

In order to speak rightly of practical truth in Aristotle one need not go so far perhaps as to accept some kind of *veritas rerum*. Out of context the sentence introducing practical truth could be *prima facie* understood as follows: if a good choice is to be made, one must discover the means most suitable for arriving at that good end toward which right desire is (always) directed. If reason states that these are the means appropriate to such and such a good end, and if as a matter of fact things really are so, then we have a piece of practical truth. Whereas a command ("do this and that") cannot be true, a gerundive statement like "this is to be done to get that" can. And if the means-end relation is unambiguous because the end is easily arrived at, then one need not wait for the result in order to be able to issue a true judgment, since the outcome is normally fixed in advance.

This interpretation is in accord with the usual meaning of "truth". To this extent it is not necessarily false. Understood thus, practical truth does not essentially differ from theoretical truth, whose status is,

---

[4] Aristotle, *Ethica Eudemia* 1226a 4.
[5] Aristotle, *Metaphysics*, 993b 20 f.
[6] Aristotle, *Metaphysics*, 993b 26 f.

so far, uncontroversial. In either case, should the course of future events not correspond to expectations, i.e., to that which normally should obtain, then the events concerned are to be dismissed from consideration and regarded as casual exceptions. On the other hand, since practical truth would still be about actions, its qualification as "practical" would not be unjustified. However, although the interpretation need not be false, it is surely insufficient. It only takes into account cases of purely instrumental relations between means and ends, i.e., the kind of action in which Aristotle was scarcely interested when he introduced the notion. This is sufficiently conspicuous from the wording of the *locus classicus* but appears more clearly from the context. In this connection attention should be paid to the structural identity between practical philosophy, practical reason, and practical truth.

To begin with, the point of ethics as a practical science is, according to Aristotle, not the acquisition and growth of knowledge but to become good[7]. Knowing something means here knowing how to do it. The acquisition as well as the growth of such knowledge obtains only through practice, at the very least not without it. This is why ethics as the science of practice (as opposed to sophistical rhetorics) is truly practical science. (In "science of practice" the "of" is not only *genitivus objectivus*, like the *"de"* in *science de moeurs,* but *subjectivus* as well). And this is also why inexperienced men cannot learn, let alone teach, ethics[8]. Max Scheler's famous self-justification, in which he (borrowing from Schopenhauer) compares the function of moral philosophers to that of sign-posts which indicate the right direction but need not themselves follow it, cannot be taken seriously. In this respect, though, practical philosophy only mirrors its subject matter: "the things we have to learn before we can do, we learn by doing"[9]. This applies to crafts as well as to moral excellencies or

---

[7] Aristotle, *Ethica Nicomachea,* 1103b 26-30; *Ethica Eudemia,* 1216b f.; *Ethica Nicomachea,* 1179a 35-b 4.

[8] Aristotle, *Ethica Nicomachea,* 1095a 2f.

[9] Aristotle, *Ethica Nicomachea,* 1103a 32 f.

virtues[10]. Nevertheless, the difference between both is important. Having already learned some technique one need not himself put it into practice, unless perhaps in order not to forget it. As long as one has not forgotten it, one remains a good technician regardless of whether or not one practices one's skills or knowledge. It is not by chance that in the last sentence cited above, which refers directly only to craftsmanship, the stress is put on the process of learning. A master may leave the execution of work to his apprentices. In moral affairs, where the connection between knowing and doing is as close as possible, this would of course be absurd.

Properly speaking a technique (τέχνη) is only some kind of knowledge. To master a technique or to be a good technician is to know how to do something irrespective of whether one actually does it or not. The execution, indeed, as we shall presently see, even the good execution, lies outside the technique; it only supervenes upon it. So far there is no difference between technique and theory. The difference with respect to morals comes to the fore in connection with wisdom as a moral virtue or excellence (φρόνησις), where the question of truth again comes into play. It is precisely because the relationship between knowledge and moral praxis is closer than the relationship between knowing how to do something artfully and doing it (let alone the relationship between theoretical knowledge about some action and the action itself as its subject matter) that practical truth in moral matters *is* the truth of (*genitivus subjectivus*) actions.

According to Aristotle there are five different manners of achieving truth[11]. Two of them, viz. art (τέχνη) and moral wisdom (φρόνησις), are practical. Both are called either dispositions with true reason (λόγος) or else true dispositions with reason[12]. Nevertheless, only the latter (φρόνησις) corresponds to that true reason to which the description of practical truth in the *locus classicus* refers. According to it in order for practical truth to obtain not only is a true assessment of the appropriate means to some end required but also good desire or

---

[10] Cf. also Aristotle, *Ethica Nicomachea*, 1103a 34-6, 1105b 12-18.

[11] Aristotle, *Ethica Nicomachea*, 1139b 15 f.

[12] Aristotle, *Ethica Nicomachea*, 1140a 10, 1140b 20 f.

desire for good ends. But the end of any art as such is indifferent to right or wrong, good or bad. Art only seeks the means to an end upon which it itself neither reflects nor deliberates. All that matters is to achieve the end whatever the latter may be, provided only that one wish it. This is so much so that the more voluntarily a technician makes mistakes so as not to achieve some end or other the better he is as a technician and the less voluntarily he makes the same mistakes the worse a technician he is: "in art he who errs willingly is preferable"[13].

What that proves is not only that the master in any art, in contrast to the morally acting man, may refrain from putting his knowledge into practice but also that he may put it wrongly into practice so as to thwart his (immediate) end, provided this is more suitable for his further purposes or higher ends. He also can lay the conventional rules of art aside without changing his purpose, and without detriment to his art, if, e.g., in unusual circumstances, or even in normal ones, this would lead to the same result. Here there is no necessary link between end and means, purpose and definite course of action. The more a physician masters the art of medicine the better and more discretely he can harm as well as heal, destroy as well as preserve life. He can also, whether rightly or wrongly, refrain altogether from any treatment without being by virtue of this omission a worse physician as such or, as Plato put it (see below), according to the strong definition. And, of course, he may also apply methods of his own invention.

In all these respects (except perhaps the last, for which too see below) the true disposition in which moral wisdom consists differs totally from the true disposition in which any art as know-how consists in that the former but not the latter requires both knowledge and practice, which means that the arts do not constitute praxis proper. For this reason practical truth also does not apply to them. The most concise way to summarize the difference is to say: art, but not moral wisdom, needs (the complement of) virtue (τέχνης μέν ἐστιν ἀρετή, φρονήσεως δ'οὐκ ἐστίν, "while there is such a thing as excellence in

---

[13] Aristotle, *Ethica Nicomachea*, 1140b 22 f.

art, there is no such thing as excellence in practical wisdom")[14]. This means: art is not in itself a virtue (of character), it does not require its own implementation, let alone guarantee that the knowledge in which it consists will be put to good use. On the other hand, practical wisdom as such *is* a virtue or disposition of character which not only requires the implementation of its purpose but also ensures the good use of the knowledge in which it too consists. In other words, φρόνησις, as opposed to art, is truly practical and indeed thoroughly effective. Aristotle himself expressly draws the conclusion that φρόνησις is not an art but a virtue[15], which, despite the fact that φρόνησις is being treated in Book VI of *Ethica Nicomachea* along with the intellectual virtues, in harmony with the context, cannot but mean ethical virtue. Accordingly, Aquinas translates the premise, cited some lines above, of this conclusion, substituting "virtus" for "prudentia" as follows: *virtutis non est virtus* to be supplemented by: *sed artis est virtus*[16].

To sum up, it is true that practical *truth* is not impossible, its possibility being due primarily to the intervention of *reason*, which correctly prescribes what has to be done in order to achieve the end toward which right desire aims. It is also true that the nature of this prescription is gerundive rather than imperative and therefore can be true (or false). But it is not true that the form of the gerundive ("this is to be done"), in contrast to the imperative ("do this"), is merely instrumental so as to delineate the means for achieving an end which could exist and be recognized independently of what one would have to do in order to achieve it, i.e., independently of the means themselves. Were this the case, then the true reason (λόγος) governing moral deliberation would be an art or technique among others. Just as with respect to moral virtue one cannot really (πράγματι) distinguish, let alone sever, knowing how to act from implementing this

---

[14] Aristotle, *Ethica Nicomachea*, 1140b 22 f. The best translation I know is Duns Scotus': "artifex eget virtute ad recte agendum". *Ordinatio*, Prol. pars 5, q. 1-2, num. 231.

[15] Aristotle, *Ethica Nicomachea*, 1140b 34 f.

[16] Cf. Thomas Aquinas, *Summa Theologiae*, I-II, q57, a3, 2.

knowledge, so too with respect to moral wisdom one cannot sever, as opposed to simply distinguishing notionally, the application of the means from that for the sake of which they are to be applied. *What* is to be done (τί) is not really (*a parte rei*) distinguishable from the purported end itself (ἥνεκα τινὸς). Only the intellectual virtue of φρόνησις, i.e., only moral wisdom, enjoys the kind of infallibility that Socrates was prepared to claim for all kinds of knowledge of virtue, so that according to Aristotle infallibility characterizes only that knowledge of virtue (*genitivus subjectivus*) in which practical wisdom, as distinguished from mere wisdom about praxis, consists. The morally wise person does not act well because he has certain pieces of true information concerning what must be done in order to achieve some end or other. Nor does he act well because these pieces of information enable him to know what would be the right end to achieve. Rather, he acts well because his knowledge *includes* the right desire towards that which is truly good, each desire being in principle effective. In other words, he acts well because his knowledge, being itself an effect of desire, is truly practical or effective. For this reason practical truth, like moral wisdom, is infallible. It is the privilege of the man of wisdom, the φρόνιμος; whether there has ever been a man who by virtue of his moral wisdom had attained practical or effective truth is another question, a question belonging rather to the problem of verification. The distinctive trait of both moral wisdom and practical truth is infallibility in carrying out by means of action the right insights of reason, this infallibility not being independent of right action itself; unlike Plato, Socrates did not take this into account. Action always takes place under changing circumstances. So practical truth, as the truth of actions, is itself always changing. But may it change limitlessly? I shall return to this point.

Φρόνησις and practical truth both arise, rather laboriously, from good choices, which under normal circumstances lead to good actions, and they lead, in their turn, rather effortlessly to good choices and actions. Without a tradition of political culture including parents and pedagogues as well as legislators this of course would amount to a vicious circle. Such choices, as *Ethica Eudemia* has it[17], are in themselves neither true nor false but only insofar as they are good (σπουδαῖα) or bad (φαῦλη). Contrary to φρόνησις, προαίρεσις is not, indeed cannot be, infallible. It is not only the case that προαίρεσις (purpose and choice) is as such indifferent to right and wrong but to good and bad action as well. Without effective moral wisdom the acting person can deviate from his purpose as is plain in the case of weakness of the will. The incontinent has a purpose (προαίρεσις)[18] which does not lead him to action.

2. Verification (I)

Although the man of moral wisdom is infallible in the sense that his having the right purpose and making through good desire the right choices rules out the possibility of incontinence as well as, of course, vice, this does not imply that practical truth can easily be ascertained. The difficulties have much to do with the concept of rightness (ὀρθότης) which is central to the concept of practical truth but has not yet been explained. In connection with practical matters "rightness" (or "correctness") can indeed be used as a synonym for "truth". Thus,

---

[17] Aristotle, *Ethica Eudemia*, 1226a 4; cf. above.

[18] Since προαίρεσις can also mean choice, uncertainty sometimes arises as to whether the incontinent has it or not. The right thing to say is, I think, as follows: the incontinent has προαίρεσις (purpose) but his action is not "prohairetic" or characterized by an effective choice (προαίρεσις again). A. Kenny (*Aristotle's Theory of Will*, London 1979, p. 93) seems not to agree with this. In any case, it is not true that there "can be practical truth in the reasonings of an evil man" (*ibid.*, 94). Consistency is not sufficient for practical truth. In order for there to be practical truth προαίρεσις has to be good (σπουδαῖα), and this requires moral virtue (cf. Aristotle, *Ethica Nicomachea*, 1145a 4f.). The truth of practical reason must be in accord with right desire. Similarly, art (τέχνη) as such or according to the strong λόγος (Plato, *Republic*, 341 B), even if it is always perfect (cf. *ibid.*, 340 E), has nothing to do with practical truth. It is infallible, but it can willingly make mistakes (*ibid.*, 340 C, 341 D-342 B). (More about this below n. 25).

in defining φρόνησις, Aristotle can substitute "right" for "true"[19]. In keeping with this, Scholasticism usually defined *prudentia* not as *vera* but as *recta ratio agibilium*. In the heyday of rationalism this was considered redundant, *ratio* being always understood to mean something "right". However the case may stand with *ratio*, nothing could have been more opposed to *rectitudo* or ὀρθότης. Its genuine sense can best be grasped from a remark Aristotle makes in connection with εὐβουλία or good deliberation as part of moral or practical wisdom: "(*theoretical*) knowledge does not need rightness since it does not make mistakes" (ἐπιστήμες οὐκ ἐστὶν ὀρθότης, οὐδὲ γὰρ ἁμαρτία[20]). This remark seems to attribute to theoretical knowledge the infallibility that was previously attributed to moral wisdom. Aside from the fact, however, that the infallibility of theoretical knowledge does not pertain to action, practical infallibility is not incompatible with, and in some sense even presupposes, the possibility of error in knowledge.

Theoretical reason can err only *per accidens*, viz. insofar as one can use it in the wrong way. As in the case of technical knowledge –as opposed to moral wisdom– this wrong use can, and indeed must, be intentional, i.e., an intentional mistake. Not surprisingly ἐπιστήμε in Plato is often just another word for τέχνη, as is still the case in *Ethica Eudemia*. At the beginning of the last book of *Ethica Eudemia* the contrast between moral virtue and ἐπιστήμε, including τέχνη, is emphasized in order to show, against Socrates, that moral virtue is an ethical virtue: if all the virtues "are kinds of knowledge, one may use justice also as injustice"[21]; just as a dancing artist can "wrongly" use his hands like feet in order to walk[22], "so one would do unjust actions from justice, as ignorant things may be done by knowledge" [ἐπιστήμες]. But if this [the doing of unjust actions for the sake of justice] is impossible, it is clear that the virtues are not species of

---

[19] Cf. Aristotle, *Ethica Nicomachea*, 1144b 27 f.

[20] Cf. Aristotle, *Ethica Nicomachea*, 1142b 10.

[21] Aristotle, *Ethica Nicomachea*, 1246a 35-37.

[22] Cf. Plato, *Hippias Minor*, 374 C.

knowledge"²³. Moral wisdom is, of course, also some kind of knowledge and something true (ἀληθής τί). But inasmuch as it is the highest kind of practical knowledge, it cannot be made subject to an even higher one; it cannot be used in such a way that, as in the case of the arts, from an intentionally wrong use there may arise a true or right one²⁴. On the other hand, to any truth in the sense of rightness or correctness belongs intrinsically a tendency in the opposite direction to rightness or correctness²⁵. Hence moral wisdom must be corrected by itself. *Recta ratio* is, as it were, *correcta ratio, ratio seipsam corrigens*.

The possibility of making mistakes belongs intrinsically to any kind of practical knowledge. But while in any art rectification amounts to justifying any intentional mistakes for the sake, or from the point of view, of some superior art, the φρόνησις must have inside itself its own capacity for self-correction in which its justification consists. In it knowledge and good use must coincide. That too proves its character as πρᾶξις proper in contradistinction to the arts, where, e.g., the saddler knows how to make the things which are to be used, not by himself, but by those who know how to ride and so on up the ladder of arts, i.e., of means and ends. In the same way the physician as such (or according to the strong λόγος) knows only how to heal but he does not know when it would be better not to heal rather than to heal²⁶. If moral wisdom were an art, it would be the

---

[23] Aristotle, *Ethica Nicomachea*, 1246a 37- b 1.

[24] Cf. Aristotle, *Ethica Nicomachea*, 1246b 4-13.

[25] Here too Duns Scotus grasped very well the point at issue: "ubicumque contingit in praxi errare et recte agere, ibi est notitia necessaria ad dirigendum", *Ordinatio*, n. 275; "Beati ergo licet non possint errare, non sequitur quod non habeant habitum etiam directivum, quia eo per impossibile circumscripto errare possent", *ibid.*, n. 279; "poneret necessitate naturali voluntati inesse, ita quod ibi non contingeret eam errare et recte agere", *ibid.*, n. 301. For him even propositions like '*Deus est trinus*' or '*Pater generat Filium*' are examples of *veritas practica* (cf. *ibid.*, n. 317). I cannot go into this. It suffices to say that the fifth part of the Prologue of the *Ordinatio* (*De Theologia quatenus Scientia Practica*) is built around the *locus classicus* for practical truth in Aristotle.

[26] Cf. Plato, *Laches*, 195 C.

supreme art, in which, according to Plato, doing and knowing as well as knowing and using coincide[27]. Socrates was looking for such a supreme form of practical knowledge, but he failed to find it precisely because he did not distinguish between art and moral virtue. Thus, if practical wisdom is nothing other than the supreme kind of knowing-how or art, then just as in any art it is better to make mistakes intentionally than to make them unintentionally, so it is better to act unjustly with knowledge than without it. This is the ἀπορία at the end of *Hippias Minor*[28]. Not only is moral wisdom *gubernatrix artium* (Plato's τέχνη βασιλική in *Euthydemus* and *Politikus*) but it is also *genetrix virtutum*[29] and, as such, supreme virtue.

It is the intrinsic possibility of mistakes and the consequent necessity of correction that makes the task of ascertaining truth in moral matters difficult. This intrinsic possibility derives, in its turn, from the fact that moral rightness consists in the location of a mean which can as a matter of fact only be achieved by correcting the tendency inherent in every relevant kind of action to exceed the mean in opposite directions so as to do too much or too little. And this, of course, is a difficult task if only because there are no clear-cut boundaries between the mean and the extremes which would enable one to tell right from wrong. The only certain thing is the existence of some boundaries regardless of where they may be situated. Without such boundaries each course of action could in principle be called right in which case practical truth would be itself boundless and *eo ipso* self-destroying. This indeed is the basic problem of practical truth, in whose vicinity the concerns of practical and theoretical reason begin to converge. In this connection it would not be exaggerated to speak of a practical PNC.

---

[27] Cf. Plato, *Euthydemus*, 289 B.

[28] Contrary to the end of *Ethica Eudemia*, 1246b 33-36: "the Socratic saying that nothing is stronger than moral or practical wisdom is right. But when Socrates said this of knowledge he was wrong. For moral or practical wisdom is a virtue and not a species of knowledge, but another kind of cognition" (ROT, slightly modified; cf. *Ethica Nicomachea*, VI, 13).

[29] Cf. Aristotle, *Ethica Nicomachea*, 1145a 1f.

According to PNC not all that we are able to say is true. Given two propositions one of which is the negation of the other it is clear that both cannot be true. Some people, dubbed by Aristotle Protagoreans, refused to accept this as a matter of principle. If they were right in maintaining that one cannot *say* anything false, then it would have been equally correct for them to have argued that one cannot *do* anything false since all we purposely do is in accord with some hypothetical (instrumental) or categorical gerundive proposition. In the first case there would be no possibility for theoretical error, in the second no possibility for practical mistakes, and in either case truth would be boundless[30]. Nor would it make any sense to bother about anything at all. Boundless practical truth is as self-destructing as its theoretical counterpart. Sense would be lacking altogether. But this would make communication impossible, forcing us back to the status of a plant.

In order for communication to be possible the words we use to convey something cannot mean everything. They too must have some boundaries in meaning or range of application, independently of where the boundaries are set[31]. True, in stating this PNC has not yet been established. All that has been established so far is that contradiction (the coincidence of being and not-being, so and otherwise, right and wrong) cannot be necessary, unavoidable, or all-embracing, not that it is impossible as is required by PNC. But that is the right way to start in dealing with it.

To approach the question of PNC Aristotle begins with purely pragmatical considerations. That is all that is needed at the start in the field of practice, of which communication is but an aspect. But this does not mean that in this field truth amounts to some sort of suitability. A theory of practical truth is to be distinguished from a pragmatist theory of truth. In the same way, to say that without PNC we would be unable to communicate does not mean that the entire truth of PNC is to be found in its suitability for communication. This would blur the distinction between appearance and reality. The defense of PNC

---

[30] Cf. Plato, *Euthydemus*, 287 A.
[31] Cf. Aristotle, *Metaphysics*, 1006a 34-1006b 17.

would have to start all over again. The reason why the principle has to be retained has nothing to do with our need either to communicate or to survive, nor with a need to survive through communication. The reason lies in reality itself, i.e., in its opposition to appearance. In other words, the validity of PNC is not relative to us. It is not relative but unconditional, not hypothetical but categorical. For, in order for reality to be, there must be some kind of difference between being and not-being regardless of where the boundaries are.

The same applies to practical truth as well. If the reason why we must distinguish between right and wrong lay in our need to make this very distinction for purposes of survival or communication, the difference between technical and moral praxis would collapse. The question of where the limits between the two are to be located is a secondary one. The whole field of action represents a continuum[32], and there are arts upon arts. Some resemble morals more than others, e.g., medicine and the art of shipping more than carpentry. The nearer some art is to moral praxis the less prescriptions are of any use for it and the more relevant the individual case becomes[33]. In each individual situation the mean, which is the target of right reason, must be fixed differently. And in no one case can it be thoroughly designed in advance, save in the most technical arts. Morals lie clearly on the other side of the gamut. In morals, if anywhere, the mean as the truth of right reason is not a mean in itself but only for each of us in our individual situation[34]. This does not amount to subjectivism, but objective prescriptions are here no more than rules of thumb. One must put up with vague approximations[35]. General assessments apply more widely, but those which are particular to the case are truer (ἀληθινώτεροι[36]).

Among the rules of thumb are the so-called cardinal and other virtues. They are abstract concepts to which nothing distinctively corre-

---

[32] Cf. Aristotle, *Ethica Nicomachea*, 1106a 26.
[33] Cf. Aristotle, *Ethica Nicomachea*, 1104a 7f.
[34] Aristotle, *Ethica Nicomachea*, 1106a 30 f.
[35] Aristotle, *Ethica Nicomachea*, 1104a 1.
[36] Aristotle, *Ethica Nicomachea*, 1107a 31.

sponds *a parte rei*. To say this is not to advocate any sort of nominalism. Even the difference between the several virtues is a matter of *distinctio rationis* (*ratiocinatae*) with continuous transitions like colours in the spectrum. But the comparison fails insofar as the colours can be considered as parts of a spectrum, whereas the virtues, being properties but not parts of individuals, merge with each other as soon as they are no longer considered *in abstracto* but *a parte rei*. (Incidentally, this means more than simply extensional identity with intensional difference, such an identity being at the heart of the *distinctio formalis a parte rei* as well). In the case of virtues one cannot even say, as in that of colors, where the mean lies in which each one of them, considered in its absolute purity, would consist. But if there is no possibility of saying across the board where the mean is to be located, so there is likewise no possibility of saying what is to be reckoned as a departure from it. The reason for this underdetermination is not to be found in the limitation of our capacity of knowing but in the nature of things. Virtues are not spiritual mechanisms by virtue of which individual persons are virtuous. They are rational, not purely natural capacities[37], and as such open to development in directions that are in themselves mutually contradictory (τῶν ἐναντίων, *ad opposita*[38]). Departures from a mean that cannot be observed nor even exist in advance of the action that realizes it belong to correctness *qua* correcting reason *per se*, not *per accidens* as is the case with theoretical knowledge (ἐπιστήμε) as well as with nature and natural virtues. In nature too there are contraries. Light is not the same thing as shadow, warming not the same as cooling, etc. But when the sun fails to spread light or warmth, some obstacle must have been there in between. The not-seeing of an eye, capable of observing, in the daytime must be traced back to some hindrance or illness. Now, the usual parallel between health and moral goodness ends here. Insofar as it arises from correct reason moral virtue is not something from which departures take place but consists itself in correcting deviations, like a captain continually steering. With regard to virtue proper, as opposed to

---

[37] Cf. J. D. Scotus, *Ordinatio*, n. 301.

[38] Aristotle, *Metaphysics*, 1046b 5 f.

natural virtue, possibility follows actuality. It is as if we could see because we often had actually seen[39]. If being original refers to that whose possibility can only have been believed in after its actuality, then moral virtue is original.

On the other hand, according to Aristotle, nature and theoretical knowledge are in themselves perfect, and so is τέχνη as well[40]. There is no need here for self-correcting, whereas moral virtue informed by *recta qua correcta ratio* is like wood that has to be straightened out in a direction opposite to that in which it tends to expand[41]. That means that techniques can be reproduced without any modification: "the products of the arts have their goodness in themselves, so that it is enough that they should have a certain character"[42], but the case of the virtues is "not similar"[43]. There is no set of rules waiting only to be applied. In morals the application and constitution of rules are not two distinct and successive processes. The only exceptions are either abstract concepts of the virtues or particular men. Consequently, while morally there is no possibility of bluffing, bluffing pertains to the very essence of the arts. The only thing that matters in the arts is to be effective in either one of two senses of the word: we say this is the effect of that as well as this gives a good effect, meaning by this that it makes a good impression (on somebody). In contrast to this, to effect an end is not the only important thing in morals but also to effect it well, that is, with intrinsically good means or actions, whereas according to the instrumental relationship between means and ends it is possible to do wrong to achieve good. So, if someone having, say, a bad ear were able to imitate, as sometimes happens, a foreign accent, to say of him that he is bluffing would be preposterous –however surprising the performance is. Effectiveness being what all arts are about, the difference between bluff and genuineness fades away. Virtue too can, of course, be imitated but is not a matter of imitation or effective-

---

[39] Aristotle, *Ethica Nicomachea*, 1103a 30 f.
[40] Cf. again Plato, *Republic*, 340 E, 342 A-E.
[41] Aristotle, *Ethica Nicomachea*, 1107b 6 f.
[42] Aristotle, *Ethica Nicomachea*, 1105a 27 f.
[43] Aristotle, *Ethica Nicomachea*, 1105a 26.

ness[44]. Here there is, unlike in art, a gap between being and showing, appearance and reality. The best account of this is to be found in the first two books of Plato's *Republic* as well as in the *Gorgias* (see II).

Right action cannot simply flow from principles. It is also needed to arrive at the principles of action[45]. The more often one acts well, the better one can in principle know what one ought to do. Actions have a disclosing force. That is why practical truth is not only not impossible but necessary. It is not only that knowing what we ought to do is not sufficient for doing it; in order to know it we ought to do it –not blindly, but also not without any kind of risk.

Take by way of contrast the case of future contingent events. If while it is still winter someone says that it will be cold this year during the dog days and another person simply denies it, then, even if that year the dog days were not cold, the latter would not be any more right than the former, had he not had reason for his denying it. And inasmuch as the former could appeal to the normal course of natural events he would indeed have more of a claim to being right[46]. To say this is not simply to reject verificationism but, in a certain sense, to adhere to it, since it appears here that being in a position to know something is a necessary condition for the truth of at least some statements. However, this is not a case of future contingency proper, since according to the ancient Greek view of natural events knowledge or truth is not concerned with accidental causality. More to the point is the question of whether tomorrow there will be a sea battle since its obtaining or not is a matter of decision on the part of the admirals. But it still does not involve the question of practical truth, the decision being of a technical nature. If the prospects were good and the battle necessary for victory, it would be foolish to refrain, provided political considerations do not interfere. Technical truth is comparatively easy to ascertain, since technical ends are by definition (i.e., *ratione*, but not always *a parte rei*) well delimited. But since the end of moral decision is nothing but the general good of life, i.e., well-being in a

---

[44] Cf. Aristotle, *Ethica Nicomachea*, 1105a 17ff.
[45] Cf. Aristotle, *Ethica Nicomachea*, 1140a 33f.
[46] Cf. Thomas Aquinas, *In Peri Hermeneias*, n. 172.

comprehensive sense, practical truth requires not only the applying of good means to good ends but also the weighing of different ends or goods against each other. To positively ascertain what to do morally is under these circumstances a difficult task. In order to act rightly in those cases where means and ends are not to be kept apart all circumstances must be taken into account. That is why "men are good in but one way, but bad in many"[47]. Inasmuch as virtues have to do with what is best, there is reason to doubt whether some human person has ever embodied practical truth. But if there are no well-defined positive or absolute prescriptions to do the good, there are yet some limits to the difficulties regarding verification. Without limits in the weighing of alternative goods there could only be metaethics as well as ethics in the sense of a *science de moeurs*, i.e., descriptions of changing social conditions but not ethics as practical philosophy. The task of locating the mean of virtue may be so difficult as to constrain one to put up with the second best journey[48], viz. to avoid the greater evil. Still, there are cases in which the question of right or wrong is settled from the outset. These are negative cases or unconditional prohibitions.

As a rule of thumb we have to avoid the unlimited expansion of desire in that direction to which we most tend, i.e., the agreeable. In the realm of the practical the agreeable plays the same role as appearances in that of theory. To raise the agreeable to the status of a principle of practice is like raising appearance to the status of a principle of theory. Both lead to the blurring of the difference between true and false, right and wrong. As a result all we say or do would be theoretically or practically true. It is not by chance that Aristotle opposes the principle of the agreeable (τὸ ἡδύ) to that of the true (τἀληθές[49]). To the latter belong that of the good (ἀγαθὸν) as well as the morally fine (καλόν).

The parallel between practice and theory with respect to principles can, accordingly, be put as follows: as has already been said, without an absolute limit to its meaning, no word could have any sense. It had

---

[47] Aristotle, *Ethica Nicomachea*, 1107a 1.

[48] Aristotle, *Ethica Nicomachea*, 1109a 35.

[49] Aristotle, *Ethica Nicomachea*, 1108a 12 f.

also been said that this alone does not yet result in the impossibility but only in the denial of the necessity of contradiction. The latter follows, though, from repeating the same consideration for each word. PNC is unconditionally true, but its truth is only negative. Not to reckon with the difference between being and not-being is impossible. But it is possible not to know where to draw the line or set the limits. The doctrine of categories is designed to do the job. But any categorial division draws more or less on linguistic conventions. Similarly, without some absolute limits, there can be no morality. The limits vary from that which may under no circumstances be done to that which more or less depends on convention. Where the line is to be drawn is again mostly a matter of convention or tradition. But not all conventions are on an equal footing; there are some ways of acting whose badness is not a matter of degree. They do not have means or extremes. "such like things imply by their names that they are themselves bad, and not the excesses or deficiencies of them. It is not possible, then, ever to be right with regard to them; one must always be wrong"[50]. "As there is no excess and deficiency of temperance and courage because what is intermediate is in a sense an extreme, so too of" some kind of actions, "there is no mean nor any excess and deficiency, but however they are done they are wrong" (ὡς ἂν πράττηται, ἁμαρτάνεται[51]). Circumstances do not matter, although some can make things worse[52] and others arouse compassion as well as understanding[53], but never approval, even if the most appalling sufferings (τὰ δεινότητα) are at stake. Correction (ἐπανόρθωμα[54]) is not possible in such cases nor a mistake (ἁμαρτία) in the assessments made. This implies that no man, in appealing to his all-embracing φρόνησις, may under any circumstances have recourse to means intrinsically bad, though φρόνησις usually does rectify as well as justify departing from the normal ways to achieve some end.

---

[50] Aristotle, *Ethica Nicomachea*, 1107a 11-18.
[51] Aristotle, *Ethica Nicomachea*, 1107a 21-28.
[52] Aristotle, *Ethica Nicomachea*, 1110a 22.
[53] Aristotle, *Ethica Nicomachea*, 1110a 24 f.
[54] Cf. Aristotle, *Ethica Nicomachea*, 1137b 12 f.

3. Discovery (II)

I have already touched upon some Platonic anticipations of Aristotelian tenets. In what follows I would like to deal more specifically with these anticipations. I shall restrict my attention to a few Socratic dialogues starting with the *Euthydemus*. The *Euthydemus* is important for us for two reasons. First because it explicitly draws a comparison between theory and praxis in connection with denying the possibility of falsity. Secondly because it is, with the exception of the *Politicus*, the only dialogue to deal with the regal art (τέχνη βασιλική), which is the main forerunner of Aristotelian moral wisdom. The first item concerns rather the problem of verification[55]. So I shall start with the second one. Its significance lies in the fact that the mastering of the regal art enables one to use other goods rightly, including arts, so that it is directly relevant to the construal of practical truth as right action.

After some not too serious deliberations Socrates addresses in *Euthydemus* the question of the right use of goods[56]. For in order to be or do well[57], or to be fortunate, the acquisition of, say, riches, health, and virtue is not sufficient. They must be used as well[58]. But, again, using them is not sufficient. They must be rightly used[59]. Otherwise it would be better, because less harmful, not to use them at all. Now, to do anything well one must not be ignorant but wise "so that wisdom everywhere causes men to be fortunate (εὐτυχεῖν): since I presume she would never err, but must needs be right in act and result; otherwise she would be no longer wisdom" (οὐκ ἁμαρτάνοι ἄν ποτέ σοφία ἀλλ' ἀνάγκη ὀρθός πράττειν καὶ τυγχάνειν. ἦ γὰρ ἂν οὐκέτι σοφία εἴη[60]).

---

[55] See Section 4 below.
[56] Plato, *Euthydemus*, 277 D-E.
[57] Lamb: "prosper", Plato, *Euthydemus*, 278 E.
[58] Plato, *Euthydemus*, 280 D.
[59] Plato, *Euthydemus*, 280 E.
[60] Plato, *Euthydemus*, 280 A.

Apparently, wisdom (σοφία) as here defined enjoys the infallibility of practical truth that Aristotle attributes to moral wisdom (φρόνησις). It, therefore, cannot be understood as being one type of τέχνη or ἐπιστήμε among others. Plato is well aware of the fact that σοφία, unlike any ordinary τέχνη, would not be what it is were it either to abstain from work or to do it wrongly. What will later be called royal art is here still called wisdom, but it is practical wisdom just as much as Aristotelian φρόνησις.

Owing to its infallibility wisdom is not in need of good luck (μηδὲν προσδεῖσθαι εὐτυχίας[61]). That does not, of course, mean that wisdom can cope with all contingencies of nature. In this respect wisdom too is well in need of, or desires, luck[62]. What it means is rather that, not being an ordinary τέχνη, wisdom is not in need of the good fortune which consists in having a good character. For a wise man is always a man of good character who does the things needed and does them well. In other words, the connection between wisdom and good fortune or character is not a matter of coincidence or good fortune since wisdom involves moral character. It is a moral excellence, i.e., a virtue, just like the Aristotelian φρόνησις.

If this interpretation is correct, then in this Socratic dialogue Plato is already on the verge of overcoming the Socratic view according to which virtue is nothing but knowledge. On the other hand, Plato is here saying that the good use of anything, including virtue, depends on knowledge (ἐπιστήμε) but that this cannot be purely technical knowledge. Now, that the interpretation which is substantially in accord with, and in its turn confirms, the interpretation of *Ethica Nicomachea*[63] is correct can be confirmed by the fact that the key term "to be in need of" (προσδεῖσθαι[64]) occurs several times in significantly similar contexts within Book I of Plato's *Republic*[65].

---

[61] Plato, *Euthydemus*, 280 B.
[62] Cf. Aristotle, *Ethica Nicomachea*, 1140a 19 f.
[63] Aristotle, *Ethica Nicomachea*, 1140b 22 given above, 1 and n. 1).
[64] Plato, *Euthydemus*, 280 D.
[65] Plato, *Republic*, 342 A, B, C.

The general context there is the discussion of the definition Thrasymachus gives of justice as "the advantage of the stronger"[66]. By this is meant the obedience paid by the ruled citizen to the laws issued by the rulers of each city for their own advantage. Thrasymachus is not at pains to deny that this behavior is unjust on the part of the rulers since his main thesis, and the main target of Socrates' attacks, is that injustice pays more than justice.

At first Thrasymachus does not distinguish between appearance and reality, knowledge and ignorance, truth and falsity. Not to distinguish between the two means reducing reality to appearances, i.e., to the illusion of reality with no possibility of error. Here we still have a parallel to the negation of PNC on the level of action. The picture that emerges from this negation is, as it were, two-dimensional. The third dimension and with it the possibility of a difference between reality and illusion reappears as soon as the possibility of error is taken into account. And this Socrates does by asking whether it is not possible that the rulers are mistaken about their own advantage in urging laws the observation of which would be detrimental for them. In this case justice could no longer be considered the advantage of the stronger. To this Thrasymachus replies by introducing a distinction between those rulers and, in general, craftsmen who act in accordance with the rules of their art and those who do not. Only the first are truly rulers or craftsmen. In making this distinction Thrasymachus attributes to all manner of arts the type of infallibility that Aristotle ascribes only to moral wisdom (and Socrates to wisdom). "No craftsman errs" (οὐδεὶς τῶν δημιουργῶν ἁμαρτάνει[67]). And Socrates' question "whether the rulers in the various states are infallible" (ποτερον ἀναμάρτητοί οἱ ἄρχοντες[68]) is at last answered in the affirmative.

It is important to realize two things; first, that in so answering Thrasymachus is returning to his main position according to which things are, to employ again the same image, two-dimensional, and secondly, that Socrates is only tactically taking up Thrasymachus'

---

[66] Plato, *Republic*, 338 C.

[67] Plato, *Republic*, 340 E.

[68] Plato, *Republic*, 339 C.

position which is incompatible with Aristotle's account of practical truth and implies the autonomy of each art. Both points are intimately connected with each other. Thrasymachus is denying by implication any overall ordering of human affairs both for individuals and for the community and thus ruling out the possibility of a final good as well as of a single end in human life. And by so doing Thrasymachus is also ruling out the possibility of any difference between right and wrong that transcends particular aspects of life. As a matter of fact, by dismissing as irrelevant those who commit error in their speciality Thrasymachus is also eliminating the difference between true and false within each particular sector of life. For him only those are worthy of consideration who are capable of living their desires to the full, whatever the latter may be. In the realm of politics this means first and foremost the tyrants and, more generally, those who practice injustice on a large scale[69]. That which is not worthy of consideration includes in any case ordinary people and their doings –these are for Thrasymachus no more worthy of consideration than Herr Krug's pen for Hegel[70].

Socrates' acceptance of Thrasymachus' stance is *ad hoc* inasmuch as it is conditioned by the possibility of rebutting the latter's definition of justice. If, because of the indefectibility of any technique, each real technician is perfect, then no one is in need of anything or anybody else. So the real ruler will rule for the advantage of the ruled like the doctor for that of his patients, the shepherd for that of his sheep, and the ship's captain for that of his passengers. The fact that each of them may earn money for this does not refute but rather confirm the self-sufficiency that "according to the strong definition" is characteristic of any technique. The art of earning money too is an autonomous technique. It is precisely because lack of selfishness is part of any tech-

---

[69] Cf. Plato, *Republic*, 344 B and *Gorgias*, 491 D.

[70] Herr Krug was a philosopher who challenged Hegel to deduce the pen with which he was launching his attack against him. Hegel's answer –the pen of Herr Krug is not worthy of being deduced - was not simply a joke. Since only what is rational or perfect is for him real, indeed God himself, then error does not matter nor even exist. At most it is material to be sacrificed on the altar of reason.

nique that an additional reward can and in many cases must be granted. So justice cannot be identified with the advantage of the ruler.

In accepting for the sake of argument the unselfishness of any art Socrates is not affirming its infallibility. Only wisdom, the regal art, is infallible. The other arts are fallible not only insofar as, owing to a lack either of character or of skill, the execution in general as well as the good execution can be frustrated, but also to the extent that, not being autonomous, each can be defective vis-à-vis the requirements of the next higher art and all of them vis-à-vis those of the highest or ruling art. Both these conditions represent limitations absent from the Thrasymachean (as well as Calliclean) arts. True, these too are in the service of men, but of men whose only purpose is to live their desires to the full. Conflicts among desires are at any one time resolved through capitulation to the strongest desire in whose service the appropriate technique (i.e. instrumental reason) has to be deployed, without any limitation.

In regal art, as with moral wisdom, reason is not instrumental to those desires left unconstrained by other desires but is itself constraining. It is reason which ought to rule over the spontaneous desires as well as over the techniques designed to satisfy them; reason which "showed the way to the right use [ὀρθῶς χρῆσθαι] of those advantages and rectified their conduct [κατορθοῦσα πρᾶξιν]"; reason which "supplies mankind not only with good luck, but with welfare"[71].

4. Verification (II)

In the *Euthydemus* Socrates draws a parallel *expressis verbis* to the alleged impossibility of thinking or saying something wrong. The parallel concerns the corresponding impossibility of doing something wrong. It is designed to be a two-fold *reductio ad absurdum*. Firstly, since denying the possibility of practical falsity would be absurd, we

---

[71] Plato, *Euthydemus*, 281 A-B.

cannot deny the possibility of false thoughts or sentences either. The key passage runs as follows: "if there is no such thing as speaking false or thinking false or being stupid, surely there can be no making a mistake either, when one does something. For in doing it there is no mistaking the thing that is done" (ἄλλο τί οὐδ' ἐξαμαρτάνειν, ὅταν τις τί πράττειν[72]). Secondly, any effort whatsoever would, as a result, be in vain, for instance, the endeavors of the two sophists Euthydemus and Dionysodorus at the beginning of the dialogue to teach young Cleinias so as to make him wise.

To this one of the two sophists replies by pointing out the inappropriateness of recalling something said in the past in order to settle something in the present[73]. This reply helps to make the parallel between the possibility of falsity in the theoretical and in the practical realm more precise. The episode in which this exchange takes place had been prompted by the remark of the same sophist according to which trying to make some youngster (Cleinias) wise is like trying to kill him[74]. Protagoreans like the two Sophists of the dialogue[75] are the main deniers of PNC[76]. They do not take into account the difference between substance and accidents nor that between necessary and contingent predicates. According to them to lose a property, whatever its nature, is *eo ipso* to cease to be; to acquire a property, whatever its nature, is *eo ipso* to become another thing or person; any change is substantial. If to be is, as for Protagoras, to be for someone[77], to whom it appears to be or so to be, then it could not be otherwise. Appearances being as it were two-dimensional, there can be no question of something beginning or ceasing to exist without someone to whom it appears to be so. To speak anachronistically, if, in order to make some sort of organ transplants possible, it should be convenient to fix the

---

[72] Plato, *Euthydemus*, 287 A.
[73] Plato, *Euthydemus*, 287 B.
[74] Plato, *Euthydemus*, 283 D.
[75] Plato, *Euthydemus*, 286 C.
[76] Cf. Aristotle, *Metaphysics*, 1009a 6-16.
[77] The ethic dative in 285 B ("Let them destroy the lad for us (ἡμῖν)" may be intended to recall this doctrine).

moment of clinical death at a comparatively early stage, there would be for the Protagoreans no difficulty in so doing. It is up to us, either as theoreticians or as practitioners, to decide on the issue; not necessarily in a wilful manner, but always according to our individual or collective needs. Similarly, deciding when, in a discussion, it is permitted to recall something said before and when not, is completely up to the (strongest of the) disputants. Euthydemus and Dionysodoros behave accordingly[78]. The same thing applies to moral matters in general. Protagoreans exclude any principles whose validity, like unconditional prohibitions of the sort referred to above[79], applies independently of changing times and circumstances. If there happen to be some such prohibitions, then this is only because, as a matter of fact, it would seem to all men in all times on whatever grounds to be the most convenient thing to do –for the time being, even if a change of mind should never be forthcoming. True, the validity to which such principles could lay claim would not necessarily be of a temporal nature. Still, this would not be sufficient to save morality. For its validity would not be that of necessity either, unless one reduces the meaning of "necessarily" to that of "always". The principles would still have purely instrumental relationships to some external ends.

The interesting thing about the parallelism between PNC and the principles of morality is that none of them is relative to anything else, so PNC is not simply relative to our need to communicate. Granted, Aristotle attempts to justify it in this manner, viz. pragmatically, but this has nothing to do with pragmatism, which reduces truth to suitability or effectiveness. If the principle cannot be justified except pragmatically, this is precisely because it itself is not in need of justification. Insofar as it is possible to have doubts as to its unconditional validity, it is not the principle itself which has thereby been rendered dubious but it is rather we who find ourselves in the position of doubting. That is why it cannot be justified except pragmatically. If it could be proved from something else, e.g., our needs, it would not be a first principle at all.

---

[78] Cf. Plato, *Euthydemus*, 283 G, 286 A.

[79] Sectio 2 end.

Does the same thing apply to the principle(s) of morality? And would this mean that man is for the sake of the sabbath? The answer is yes to the first question and no to the second one. No, because the question of the sabbath being a ritual and thus instrumental is not at issue here. Yes, because of some aspects of the parallel to PNC which have still to be explained.

The conflation of substance and accidents, necessary and contingent properties, on the part of the Protagoreans only succeeds in upholding the possibility of first saying or thinking and then doing something false. The argument proper is aimed, however, at another conflation, the conflation of what one says or thinks about something with the thing that is spoken or thought about[80], that is, referent and statement or subject and predicate. But, as Plato discovered, the two are not only different but can actually diverge as in the case of false statements[81]. In rebutting Protagoreans and the like Aristotle too draws on this distinction[82]. If the predicate of any proposition enters into the constitution of the subject matter, then no falsity is possible. If "Theaetetus flies" were not about Theaetetus but about a flying Theaetetus, the proposition could of course not be false. True, the argument does not work for essential predicates. But this does not matter. For Aristotle does not draw on the distinction between essential and accidental predicates in order to justify PNC[83]. In this too he is in accord with Plato.

In the next exchange with Euthydemus and Dionysodorus[84] the discussion turns from falsity to contradiction proper. If contradiction were impossible PNC would by implication not be necessary. On the other hand the actuality of people contradicting each other as well as themselves shows that the necessity of justifying PNC is only a neces-

---

[80] Cf. Plato, *Euthydemus*, 284 C 8f.
[81] Cf. Plato, *Sophista*, 262 E-263 D.
[82] Aristotle, *Metaphysics*, 1005b 14-17.
[83] When at the end of his main argument he proves the necessity of distinguishing between οὐσία and συμβεβηκὸς (*Metaphysics*, 1007a 31) the former does not have the meaning of essence but of substance as subject.
[84] Plato, *Euthydemus*, 285D-286C.

sity for us. Only in itself, but not for us, is PNC the most knowable thing, just as we should want only what is according to its nature good, and not what is good according to subjective appearances (see below). Contradiction is here to be understood in the sense of two interlocutors making incompatible statements on the same subject matter. Obviously, if the statement partakes of the constitution of the subject matter, there can be no such thing as the same subject matter about which it would be possible to have different opinions. Since it is now suitable for his present purpose Dionysodorus himself recalls that the principle had been established before[85]. And he gives four special reasons for the impossibility of two interlocutors contradicting each other[86], shortly before Socrates draws the general conclusion we started out from according to which no mistakes could then be made at all[87]. The *reductio ad absurdum*[88] involved in this conclusion parallels that employed by Aristotle in vindicating (for us) PNC. I cannot go into the details of this vindication here but must concentrate instead on its application to morality. The hints included in the *Euthydemus* have been developed in the *Gorgias*, both dialogues being intimately related to each other. So it is the latter upon which I shall rely.

The *Gorgias* addresses expressly the issue of contradiction, but this time in the form of self-contradiction. First on the part of those who try to defend rhetoric as seeking persuasion but not truth about justice, second on the part of those who regard injustice as bringing more benefits than justice and act accordingly. They are represented by Gorgias, Polos and Callicles. Like Thrasymachus they, too, but most patently Callicles, think that it is not being truly but only being apparently just that is really good for man. That is why rhetoric is so prominent. Characteristic is the way they interpret themselves collectively. Each time Socrates seems to have caught someone in a contradiction someone (in the case of Callicles, Callicles himself) comes forward in his (own) defense, appealing to his good manners which prevent him

---

[85] Plato, *Euthydemus*, 286 A.
[86] Plato, *Euthydemus*, 286 A-B.
[87] Plato, *Euthydemus*, 287 A.
[88] Plato, *Euthydemus*, 287 E-288 A.

from revealing his true state of mind. According to Socrates Gorgias stated on the one hand "that the rhetor might actually use rhetoric unjustly"[89] and at the same time (though a bit later) "that the rhetor is powerless to use rhetoric unjustly and to be willing to do injustice"[90]. (The translations are T. Irwin's). The overzealous Polus rushes to his aid[91]. Attack and defense are not quite clear, but at least in Polus' opinion Gorgias, out of shame, is taking recourse to the conventional esteem of justice and putting up with contradicting himself. That would not be so surprising coming from someone who himself esteems apparent justice more highly than the real one.

With Callicles it is slightly different. Socrates acknowledges this in addressing him: Gorgias and Polus are "short of free speaking, and more prone to shame than they should be... they are so far gone in shame that because of his shame each of them dares to contradict himself in front of many people, and on the most important questions. But you have the things the others lack... And as for being the type to speak freely without shame, you say it yourself and your speech a little earlier agrees with you"[92]. But later on, Callicles too shows consideration for shame and convention. After Socrates has pointed to the pleasures of catamites[93], Callicles protests: "Aren't you ashamed to lead the discussion to such things, Socrates?"[94]. But then he goes so far as to admit the possibility of shameful or bad pleasures[95], which possibility indeed undermines his previous and, for his cause, fundamental identification of pleasures with goods. The denial of their sameness means the rejection of the way of life Callicles recommends. It consists in living one's own pleasures to the full. That, of course, need not indicate a change of mind. "Well, so that I don't leave my

---

[89] Plato, *Republic*, 460 E.
[90] Plato, *Republic*, 461 A.
[91] Plato, *Republic*, 461 C.
[92] Plato, *Republic*, 487 B-D.
[93] F. Schleiermacher translates κίναιδος with "child molestor" [*Knabenschänder*]. ("isn't that strange and shameful and wretched?", Plato, *Republic*, 494 E).
[94] *Ibid*.
[95] Plato, *Republic*, 495 A.

argument inconsistent, if I say that they're different, I say they're the same"[96]. Neither Gorgias nor Polus nor Callicles are Protagoreans. For them reality is not two-dimensional, it is more than reality as it appears to some individual or collective body. But as rhetoricians they are more interested in appearance than in reality. Even Callicles who professed to speak his mind and so allow nature to speak through him against convention cannot bring himself to fully disregard his own feelings of shame. For some type of action to be shameful it is not necessary for it to be, according to him, really bad. And this applies to theory as well as to practice. Callicles bothers less about consistency than about appearances[97].

Consistency is necessary, though not sufficient[98] for practical truth. Practical truth requires consistency with regard to right or just desires.

---

[96] Plato, *Republic*, 495 A.

[97] "I accuse you", says Socrates to him, "of never saying the same about the same things" (*Republic*, 491B). But when inconsistency threatens to come to light, he can withdraw even on pain of falling into another inconsistency, as long as the latter still remains hidden. Only by sticking to the principle of maximizing pleasure as well as saving appearances can he maintain consistency. But such a precariously sustained consistency is always in jeopardy. Just as in pragmatism PNC remains only conditionally valid (viz. through consistent inconsistency as in Quine's philosophy, cf. *Word and Object*, § 3 n. 5) so that it could be empirically refuted (for instance, through the disappearance of science or the death of anyone whose survival depended on it), so too for rhetoricians like Callicles there is no type of action (be it that of the *Knabenschänder* or whatever) which could not only at any point in time but also unconditionally be called unjust. To decide whether the validity of PNC is or is not unconditional also requires a decision as to whether its defense is to be carried out in pragmatistic terms, as it is in the pragmatism of Quine, or merely in pragmatic terms, as it is in the metaphysics of Aristotle. As far as ethics is concerned the question is whether morality could exist without negative prescriptions (prohibitions) whose validity is unconditional and *a fortiori* omnitemporal. For the sake of brevity I shall stick to Socrates' discussion with Callicles. This is not equivalent to adhering to Plato's claim to be able to ascertain wherein the good that is to be positively achieved consists. Only in this manner can Plato establish a political strategy (a technique) in order to achieve that goal (cf. *Gorgias*, 521 A).

[98] See Section 1, with n. 18 above.

Callicles' inconsistency in admitting bad (injust) pleasures is only apparent since his admission too is only apparent. His overall view requires the sameness of good and pleasure. This implies not only the need for maximizing pleasure, and hence courage as well, but also the need for avoiding any restraint, so that temperance has to be dismissed[99]. Here the next inconsistency threatens, since not all pleasures are compatible with each other. But that inconsistency too can easily be overcome. Normally it is the strongest pleasure which imposes itself. And if external circumstances do not permit it, a prudential calculation still makes temperance unnecessary. So, only natural virtues (prudence in the sense of Aristotelian δεινότης as well as natural courage) –but neither natural temperance as a sign of weakness nor indeed natural justice– are required, but by no means their moral counterparts. Justice, as normally understood, whether natural or moral, is the first virtue to be slighted. For since justice, as normally understood, is always for the benefit of others, it is among all virtues the most difficult one to justify when our own benefit, interest, or good is at issue.

Indeed, the gist of Plato's moral question as well as that of the issue of practical truth is whether justice, which in a second, non-ordinary sense also means virtue in general, pays and is thus even on purely egoistic grounds practical or effective. In other words, the main question is why I should act justly. For if there are compelling reasons why I should act justly, there are also compelling reasons why I should act virtuously in general, i.e., justly in the second or philosophical, but still not Platonic, sense. Justice in a third, Platonic, sense constitutes, though, the upshot of the argument.

The main presupposition of the argument for the practical character of justice and hence for its practical truth is that with respect to one's own good no one puts up with appearances[100]. That is why sophistic rhetoric misses the point from the outset. Only the real good –call it happiness, good fortune (εὐτυχία), or whatever– is beyond question. Now, the reason why justice in the first or ordinary sense and in the

---

[99] Plato, *Republic*, 492 A.

[100] Cf. Plato, *Republic*, 505 D.

second or philosophical sense pays is that it brings about in us justice in the third or Platonic sense, viz. consistency or harmony in the soul and of the will with itself, i.e., happiness, and conversely in the case of injustice.

Against this the obvious objection is that, contrary to Plato's contention, acting unjustly need not bring about any physical or psychic disease or even political disarray. As Kant put it, even in the case of a nation (*Volk*) of devils the problem of how the state is to be organised can be solved, provided they have ("prudential") reason (Aristotelian δεινότης). True, it might perhaps be the result of self-deception that we are (or *feel!*) individually or even collectively happy. But that could mean that the appearance of good is after all sufficient for happiness. On the other hand this counterobjection cannot withstand Plato's account of the myth of a last judgment. The argument (λόγος[101]) is decisive for Plato as well as for practical truth in the general (and not only moral) sense[102]. But first, its implications for Plato. Not coincidentally, the *Gorgias*, the *Republic*, and the *Phaido* conclude with similar myths. It would not be an exaggeration to say that it represents the climax of Plato's philosophy.

Like the biography of Sherlock Holmes, a biography of the fictional Socrates should be attempted. In it the *Apology* would do proxy for the missing dialogue concerning the philosopher which was to complete the announced trilogy that had begun with a treatment of the sophist and the politician[103]; for at the end of the *Theaetetus*, which is apparently intended as an introduction to the trilogy, Socrates is made to leave in order to respond to the accusation of Melitos[104]. So the third dialogue is there after all, the philosopher, as it were, in action against the rhetoricians. Only the account of Socrates' imprisonment and death remains to be told, the whole story ending with Socrates requesting the offering of a cock, the herald of a new day, to Aescu-

---

[101] Cf. Plato, *Republic*, 523 A.

[102] See Section 5 below.

[103] Plato, *Sophista*, 217 A.

[104] Plato, *Sophista*, 210 CD.

lapius, the god of health[105], this request having been preceded by the last speech of Socrates, again on the last judgment. It is the beautiful risk spoken of at the beginning of the dialogue. Why should the risk of hoping for an afterlife of realized justice be beautiful (ἐλπίς *kale*[106])? Does it not rather bespeak of wishful thinking and the will to self-deception?

To begin with, the myth is a true account. It represents the missing link in the argument for the goodness of justice[107]. If there were judges who could not be deceived by appearances[108] and who had the will to judge and punish justly, then the question of whether justice or rather injustice pays would be settled once and for all. But would morality not in any event have been destroyed by the motivational problem having been solved or the *principium executionis* having been arrived at in this way? For then refraining from injustice as well as doing justice would seem to be instrumental to receiving rewards and thus non-moral. Another way of putting it is to say that the first principle of action (*bonum est sequendum et malum vitandum*) is not yet moral. As a matter of fact, the necessity of acting *sub ratione boni* applies to moral as well as immoral actions. To make things worse, refraining from injustice, if not doing just things as well, would be –together with the knowledge of the necessary instrumentality of virtue for happiness– a non-free outcome of our natural desire for happiness. On the other hand, the connection between virtue and happiness would not be a necessary (or natural) one but would depend upon the will of the judges (or their master, Zeus) and so be arbitrary.

True, the whole system would have to be set up by a judge who has the will to punish or reward. But the objection of arbitrariness on the part of the rewarding judge could only be raised by those for whom, like Callicles, virtue is in fact a bad thing. For those for whom virtue

---

[105] Plato, *Phaido*, 118 A.

[106] Plato, *Phaido*, 70 A.

[107] The best interpretation of the *Gorgias* that I know of is P. Stemmer's, "Unrecht Tun ist schlechter als Unrecht Leiden", *Zeitschrift für philosophische Forschung*, 39, 1985. Stemmer, though, leaves out the account of the myth.

[108] Plato, *Gorgias*, 523 C, 524 CD.

is good the dispensation of the judge is everything other than arbitrary. For them it is rather something natural, whether it derives from a free and good will or of necessity. This is in accord with the natural (as opposed to the mythical) theology of the *Republic*. But if God's dispensation is just in the ordinary sense of justice, then the objection that it is destructive of morality fails as well. And since that objection followed from the apparent instrumentality of virtue vis-à-vis the good, this one fails too. Since virtue is according to the myth good, seeking one's own good need not prevent one from seeking justice for the sake of justice. Nor need the pursuit of happiness be immoral. So the first principle of action can and, since morality would be necessary for the good life, indeed must, after all, be accorded a moral significance. In the non-moral sense *bonum est faciendum et malum vitandum* merely indicates that we always act for the sake of the good; only in its moral sense does the gerundive come to acquire the full bearing of practical truth.

To argue in favor of the hope that it is not injustice but justice that pays is, of course, not without risk since the fulfilment of that hope is not thereby guaranteed. Such a hope would only be warranted if there in fact existed a highest power endowed with the capacity to judge justly. But the narrative of a last judgment does not prove that much. It does not prove that morality is good but that, if morality is to be good (and followed), there must be some power of great might usually called God that dispenses rewards. The risk of things being otherwise is still there. True, the risk is a beautiful one for, contrary to first appearances, the decision made in taking the risk and thus possibly being wrong is a decision in favour of justice itself. But it is still a risk, ultimately the risk of losing one's integrity by indulging in self-deception. So it is necessary to see what the argument does prove and what it does not.

It proves in any case that to put up with the mere appearance of justice would be under the circumstances described irrational. If justice were really good, the way of injustice would be closed even for those who take their decisions only from the standpoint of the good and not of the just. So the question as regards the *principium executionis* –the most difficult one if one starts out from the common understanding of justice and its unconditional prohibitions– is definitively settled. Those who would already have made their decisions with regard to what is just were not in need of the argument. As for the others, even after having been convinced, the relation between justice and the good would still be an instrumental one and their motivation, consequently, not a moral one. But they too would realize the irrationality of opting for injustice. Only if there is such a judge can the immoralist be defeated on his own ground. The argument is a true ἔλεγχος. In this respect as well it parallels the "justification" given for PNC insofar as neither God nor PNC itself stand in need of justification. If there is a God, injustice, even assuming the existence of a divide between justice and the good, is prohibited, that is, it is prohibited under any circumstances. But would it not be possible to object that the argument does not prove God's existence and hence that it fails to prove that justice is truly good?

5. Verification (III)

Since the possibility of error belongs intrinsically to practical as opposed to theoretical truth, the argument proceeding from a last judgment is a paradigmatic case of the former. Socrates' account could perhaps be simply a myth, it could be false. And yet, it could not turn out to be false. The special thing about that myth is that its falsity could not be verified but its truth could. It is on this asymmetry that Pascal's argument *du pari* is based.

In essence the argument states that because of this asymmetry we have nothing to lose in the case of its being false, whereas in the case of its being true we have everything to gain. So on the whole we would be wise to believe in God. The decision is purely rational. Unlike Plato's argument, Pascal's has no moral content. It considers only happiness, not justice as well. That is why it has been so often scorned. William James e.g. writes: "If we were ourselves in the place of the Deity, we should probably take particular pleasure in cutting off believers of this pattern from their infinite reward"[109]. In this verdict he was not thoroughly consistent. His reception is mainly polemical and dwells on things like masses and the uses of holy water, in which neither James nor his Protestant audience in Providence believed and which are for the argument equally unimportant. Those who are disappointed by the purely eudemonistic approach of the argument ought to take into account that, as in the case of the Platonic myth, the argument does not, as James was aware, give Pascal's own motivation for believing in God. His addressees are persons, as yet morally uncommitted, who are more concerned with their happiness than with anything else. They could only be moved by fear of the Lord (which after all is alleged to be the beginning of wisdom). It would be not farfetched to compare them with Aristotle's beginners in the moral life who under the guidance of parents, pedagogues, and laws, only come to know what ought to be done by doing the things they are instructed to do.

As for the structure of the argument, James, no less than Pascal, is implicitly trying to demonstrate its validity. Provided some religious feeling or other is still alive in the individual he or she is right in deciding to believe in its content. As a matter of fact, this is practical truth stripped of its moral as well as its religious content. However, rather than being practical or even pragmatic, what remains of truth in James, contrary to Pascal, is a form of pragmatistic truth, which means a truth that has been made to fit pragmatism. Truth appears here as a function of our needs, psychological as well as social. Our decision to believe something, including the decision to believe in truth, "what is [this] but a passionate affirmation of desire, in which our social system backs us up? We want to have a truth"[110]. Truth has been reduced to verification. It is a truth which we make. "The truth of an idea", writes James elsewhere, is "the process namely of its verifying itself,

---

[109] W. James, "The Will to Believe", quoted from *The Writings of William James*, edited by J.J. McDermott, Chicago 1977, p. 720.

[110] *Ibid.*, p. 722.

its veri-*fication*"¹¹¹. The main difference between (James's) pragmatism and (Pascal's, or, for that matter, Plato's) metaphysics lies in the fact that the former, but not the latter, rules out the possibility of truth without veri-fication by identifying verification with the making of "truth".

This, of course, applies according to any thoroughgoing pragmatism to all theoretical truths, including PNC, whose necessity is but a function of our need to communicate just as its truth is but a function of our need for self-preservation. But it also applies to morality. The difference between right and wrong, no less than that between being and not-being, is thus not conventional or arbitrary, if for no other reason than because it itself is necessary for there to be any conventions at all. For any given convention necessity will be relative to this distinction. No convention is possible unless there is a difference between right and wrong. This distinction, however, is not sufficient, but only necessary for morality in the ordinary sense of the word, insofar as this sense acknowledges the difference between true and false as well. Otherwise there could be no objective decision among different forms of life but only a decision on grounds of appearance. It is not by chance that James understands verification as a series of smooth transitions from one piece of experience to another, which "come to us from point to point *as* being progressive, satisfactory, harmonious. This function of *agreeable* leading is what we mean by an idea's verification"¹¹². That is why the moral character of practical *truth* is so important –and why pragmatistic truth shares some but not all the features of practical truth proper. The moral character is lacking.

So there are two sorts of moral necessity in pragmatism, both of which fall short of morality: a necessity for convention and a conventional necessity, neither of which is unconditional. Thus for pragmatism all moral conventions are on an equal footing. There could not be a moral convention whose validity would itself be more than conven-

---

¹¹¹ W. James, "Pragmatism's Conception of Truth", *The Writings of William James*, p. 430.

¹¹² *Ibid.*, p. 431 (my emphasis).

tional. The choice is in each case a matter of the intensity of feelings on which, as in James, blind will supervenes.

In metaphysics, on the contrary, the abstract difference between right and wrong either in theory or in practice is not the only one to escape conventionality, just as little as the fact that we cannot, unless out of confusion, doubt the validity of PNC means that any categorial difference has to be a conventional one (or that only that between substance and accident, the only one following from PNC, is not conventional). There is much convention in categorial distinctions, but conventions too can be true. The abstract difference between right and wrong calls for a search to locate where the boundaries are, including those between the purely conventional and the moral proper. This is, first of all, a matter of detecting possible unconditional prohibitions. As far as positive attitudes are concerned, though, there are no limits to be detected. Here unrestricted originality is called for. The restriction just hinted at regarding the necessity of first principles in theory and practice accounts for the way James himself distinguishes between pragmatism and metaphysics ("we" and "the scholastic" –the expression would sound less pejorative in Charles Peirce): "The strength of his [the scholastic's] system lies in the principles, the origin, the *terminus a quo* of his thought; for us the strength is in the outcome, the upshot, the *terminus ad quem*"[113]. True, first principles in metaphysics are valid relative to nothing, but they are few. So the field of agreement, however fundamental the difference between metaphysics and pragmatism, would be greater than one would at first think. It extends even to theoretical truth, at least insofar as the latter too is practical and creative. As for this, some final remarks may be added.

"There would have been no triumph in success, had there been no hazard of failure; it is no triumph to Euclid, in pure mathematics, that the geometrical conclusions of his second book can be worked out and verified in algebra"[114]. These words of J. H. Newman could be a paraphrase of Aristotle's concise phrase cited above "ἐπιστήμης οὐκ

---

[113] W. James, "The Will to Believe", p. 726.

[114] J. H. Newman, *Grammar of Assent*, 5th ed., p. 278.

ἔστιν ὀρθότης, οὐδὲ γὰρ ἁμαρτία"[115]. But there is a difference, implicit in the past tense of the quotation. Newman had before applied to mathematical physics ("when the planet Neptune was discovered, it was deservedly considered a triumph of science..."), as opposed to abstract mathematics, what Aristotle seemed to reserve for practical reason, viz. the intrinsic possibility of error. This intrinsic possibility belongs in fact also to modern, as opposed to Aristotelian, science. If there could be any sort of infallibility it would be only –as is the case in Aristotelian moral wisdom (φρόνησις)– in the sense of correcting at least latent errors. It is not the sort of infallibility Protagoreans and the like would accept as the only possible one, viz. an infallibility without any risk of error. Such immunity was due to a failure to distinguish between subject and predicate. If opinions take part in the constitution of the subject matter, there can be no objective knowledge (as opposed to subjective opinion); there can only be continuously changing boundaries between what is right and what is wrong. As applied to moral matters this sort of infallibility was to be given its classic expression by Hume: "...the opinions of men, in this case, carry with them a peculiar authority, and are, in a great measure, infallible. The distinction of moral good and evil is founded in the pleasure and pain, which results from the view of any sentiment, or character; and as that pleasure or pain cannot be unknown to the person who feels it, it follows, that there is just so much vice or virtue in any character, as every one places in it, and that 'tis impossible in this particular we can ever be mistaken"[116]. Such infallibility is in agreement not only with Hume's moral naturalism but also with the extension Socrates made (by way of a *reductio ad absurdum*) of the Sophistic negation of PNC, and hence of the distinction between substance and property, to action or practice. But it does not much differ from the sort of infallibility to which any pragmatism must adhere as soon as it is stripped of its realistic background. If William James' contention that "the risk of being in error is a very small matter when compared with the blessings

---

[115] Aristotle, *Ethica Nicomachea*, 1142b 10.

[116] D. Hume, *A Treatise of Human Nature*, Vol. II, III.ii.8, ed. A.D. Lindsay, London 1960 [1911], pp. 246-7.

of real knowledge"[117] is to make any sense, then neither our feelings, however intense, nor our will can have the last word. Otherwise the decision between, say, Huxley's and Newman's beliefs[118] would have nothing to do with truth. Similarly, even granted that "the question of having moral beliefs at all or not having them is decided by our will"[119] a decision as to the truth of different or even incompatible moral beliefs cannot depend on feeling or will any more than one about the course of Neptune can. Inasmuch as pragmatism does not accept this Socratic parallel between theory and practice, it is obliged to abandon practical truth altogether. So James resorts to a distinction between science on the one hand and morality on the other to the effect that as regards the former but not the latter one has to distinguish between truth and verification[120]. In so doing he is not thoroughly consistent with his unrestricted plea for deciding to believe. For the prerequisite for this plea ought to be the connection between deciding to believe and the possibility of truth, i.e., practical truth. But it turns out that this connection in James's pragmatism can only be retained in the case of theoretical science. As regards morality and religion there is no hope for any true decision. But then deciding to believe in these areas threatens to be either impossible or amounts to a lack of integrity; Socrates' beautiful as well as Pascal's somewhat less sublime risk would be nothing but wishful thinking.

In a paper entitled "Deciding to Believe" Bernard Williams differs from James in drawing this conclusion. In this Williams is being more consistent than James. In another respect, however, greater consis-

---

[117] W. James, "The Will to Believe", p. 727.

[118] "Huxley belabors the bishops because there is no use for sacerdotalism in his scheme of life. Newman, on the contrary, goes over to Romanism, and finds all sorts of reasons for staying there, because a priestly system is for him an organic need and delight". W. James, "The Will to Believe", p. 722.

[119] W. James, "The Will to Believe", p. 722.

[120] Cf. his critical remark: "Science has organized this nervousness (lest she become deceived) into a regular technique, her so-called method of verification; and she has fallen so deeply in love with the method that one may even say she has ceased to care for truth by itself at all". W. James, "The Will to Believe", p. 729.

tency may be said to lie on James's side. James does not explicitly deny the possibility of objective religious or moral truths, so that the resulting ambiguity allows him to avoid having to infer a lack of integrity on the part of those who believe in either or both of these areas. On the other hand, Bernard Williams draws his conclusion only after having considered cases whose truth or falsity could be empirically proved. The inconsistency lies here in the hope that his argument could also be made to apply to the cases of morality and religion[121]. For then it would be necessary either to consider these cases as being also empirically verifiable or falsifiable –which obviously is not even possible– or else to adhere to empiricism –which is perfectly possible but would beg the question of practical truth in those areas.

Both James's and Williams's conceptions allow for objective truth only in the realm of science, not in that of religion or morals. That means that practical truth could at most apply to science. For religion and ethics there could at most be truth in James's sense of verification, that is "truths dependent on our personal action"[122]. Regarding such truths, James adds, "faith based on desire is certainly a lawful and possibly an indispensable thing"[123]. This empiricist stance would be just as little capable of satisfying a true believer as the reduction of truth to verification would be of satisfying a scientist who had not already opted for empiricism. In other words, James's pragmatism is only non-empiricist with respect to science. Either way James, no less than Williams, misses the point of practical truth, although all the elements necessary for it are there. It would be necessary to combine his acceptance at least of the possibility of objective truth in science with his insights into the practical structure of belief in order to reach again the level where the question of practical truth had been put forward by Aristotle or even Plato.

---

[121] Bernard Williams's reasons for rejecting the moral integrity of deciding to believe in any area whatsoever is reminiscent of the schoolboy's definition of belief reported by James: "Faith is when you believe something that you know ain't true". W. James, "The Will to Believe", p. 734.

[122] W. James, "The Will to Believe", p. 731.

[123] *Ibid.*

CHAPTER 12
NATURA AD UNUM - RATIO AD OPPOSITA: ON DUNS SCOTUS' TRANSFORMATION OF ARISTOTELIANISM

The period marking the transition from the 13th to the 14th Century is generally characterized as a time of great upheaval of philosophy and theology. On this point there exists widespread agreement, even among those who harbor views that would otherwise seems irreconcilable –for example on the issue of whether this development represented a boon or bane for succeeding generations. Another point on which a broad consensus has evolved concerns the decisive role that this epoch is believed to have played –for good or for ill– in setting medieval thought on its historical path toward modern philosophy and theology. In what follows I shall be discussing only one aspect of this spiritual and intellectual transformation, the one which is most easily recognized as having paved the way for Kant. But I shall be concentrating here on the *terminus a quo* of this development, and not on its *terminus ad quem*. Both the concept of nature as external determination and that of freedom as self-determination –those twin pillars of Kantianism– are part of a general transformation which Aristotelianism underwent in the hands of Duns Scotus and which brought it into the proximity of voluntarism.

At any rate, it is clear that once the capacity for self-determination came to be accepted as the main characteristic of *ratio*, as it did after Scotus, the will was destined to become the true rational power. But for this to be possible, its rival, the intellect, had first to be dethroned from its traditional place above nature and reduced to something purely physical, a mere piece of nature, as it were. This change in status was reflected in many elements of the Franciscan tradition from 1277 onwards, and it is still at work in Duns Scotus. Indeed, in the case of Scotus one can discern with special clarity how voluntarism arose in the late Middle Ages as the result of a profound transformation in the role assigned to the intellect. The transformation was as important for the overcoming of Greek necessitarianism as it was for a new and distinctly modern conception of freedom as lying beyond the bounds of nature.

Still, it would be going too far were one to ascribe to Scotus the kind of pragmatism according to which the concept is built up out of judgments and thus ultimately out of decisions of the will. It is not as if Scotus had wanted to argue that our concepts emerge from the changing convictions reflected in those propositions which we at any one time consider to be true. For him it is not the use of words that decides their meaning, but rather their meaning which determines their use. In this respect, Scotus still has his feet planted firmly on Aristotelian ground where the concept is prior to the judgment and it is the sense of the individual words that governs the truth of a proposition[1]. Consequently, PNC owes its validity in Scotus exclusively to the compatibility or incompatibility of the meanings of the concepts involved. And no matter how often a word may change its meaning, this never occurs as a result of our having changed our convictions. Behind the concepts with their unchanging meanings lies the reality of things as well as the objectivity of certain *a priori* possibilities, each laying claim to a firmness or steadfastness (*ratitudo*)[2] which is independent of our personal need to communicate with, and understand, one another. The fact that this need would remain unfulfilled, were PNC to be invalid, is thus not the reason why Scotus considers it valid. The reason is rather to be found in the *formalitates*, or contents of reality itself, as well as in the *a priori* conditions of its possibility, which belong to the realm of ideality. To be consistent, an alternative interpretation would have to substitute a reading of *res* derived from

---

[1] Cf. Chapter 2 above.

[2] For more on the corresponding two-fold concept of *ratitudo* cf. L. Honnefelder, "Die Lehre von der doppelten ratitudo entis und die Bedeutung für die Metaphysik des Johannes Duns Scotus" in *Deus et homo ad mentem Johanni Duns Scoti. Acta Tertii Congressus Scotisticus Internationalis (Studia scholastica-scotistica,* vol 5), Rome 1972.

reor, reris –a reading expressly rejected by Scotus– in place of one derived from *ratus* and actually approved by him. In effect, such a reading takes away from reality and from the ideal conditions of its possibility the last vestiges of their firmness and steadfastness and makes both dependent on our more or less fleeting opinions or –at best– on our more abiding convictions.

Although Scotus still clung in this respect to the Aristotelian doctrine of abstraction or concept-formation and did not subscribe to a rival theory, be it voluntarism or pragmatism, he did in other respects depart from Aristotle, and in ways that could not but facilitate a subsequent movement in that very direction. For him the concept of abstraction no longer means, as it did for Aristotle, that the intellect sees the *formalitates* of reality in, and sets them apart from, the matter of sensory perception and imagination. Abstraction now means that the intellect (*intellectus agens*) reproduces at the level of universality the forms along with the corresponding matter, which is to be found in the sensory imagination at the level of the particularity of *phantasmata*. At this other, higher level the resulting *species intelligibilis* does no more than represent reality –copy it and function as token or proxy for it.

Such a reinterpretation obviously diminishes the value of abstraction. Thus *cognitio abstractiva* no longer signifies something positive; it is merely a substitute (*pro statu isto*) for the lack of *cognitio intuitiva* and so resembles more nearly a privation. The acknowledged starting-point for epistemology has become the distance between the subject and the object, to be bridged by knowledge. And any progress in knowing is now to be understood in terms of an approximation to, rather than a penetration into, reality. For, even if the expression "for the present state" need not be construed as alluding to original sin, it clearly has a negative connotation. This fundamental shift in the role of the intellect must continually be borne in mind when assessing the voluntarist transformation brought about by Scotist philosophy. It constitutes the basic framework within which Scotus, having started from the Aristotelian distinction between the active natural and the active rational powers, arrived at his theory of freedom of the will as the spontaneity of self-determination[3]. We must consider this transformation in more detail.

On the whole, Duns Scotus agrees with Aristotle in assigning the criteria of "*ad unum*" and "*ad opposita*" to *natura* and *ratio* respectively, but he places a greater emphasis on understanding exactly how this ascription is to be made[4]. According to Scotus both the rational and the non-rational powers are simultaneously related to the two sides of a given opposition. But whereas the former –and, above all, the will– are endowed with the capacity for self-determination, the latter are not; they are always compelled by external causes in one direction or the other. And since the intellect is just as incapable of deciding on its own whether to be active or to remain passive –i. e. to know or not to know– as it is of deciding of its own accord whether to know this or that, in this way or otherwise –to say nothing of knowing

---

[3] It is not coincidence that in both Scotus' *Quaestiones subtilissimae super libros metaphysicorum Aristotelis* (lib. IX, q. XV) and in his *Quaestiones quodlibetales* (q. XVI) the discussion of the difference between *natura* and *voluntas* follows the discussion of passivity or activity with respect to the *intellectus agens* and *the intellectus possibilis* (q. XIV, again, in the *Quaestiones subtilissimae* and *quaestiones* XIV and XV of the *Quaestiones quodlibetales*). The *Quaestiones subtilissimae* are somewhat aporetic in nature; they often do not take a clear decision between alternatives. This does not apply, though, to the *quaestio* XV of *liber* IX, which its early date of composition notwithstanding, seems to represent the definitive statement of its subject. My quotations are taken from this *quaestio* (cited in conformity with Wadding's numbering). As regards the extent of the intellect's activity, and conversely of its passivity, the passivity of the intellect is clearly much more pronounced in Scotus than in Aristotle. Not only did the latter stress the compatibility of activity and passivity in the case of the *intellectus possibilis* but in the end he was even prepared to remove every trace of passivity from it: it is δεκτικόν but at the same time ἀπαθές. In his book *Der Wille als reine Vollkommenheit bei Duns Scotus* (München 1962) W. Hoeres argues that "Scotus' concept of *receptio* introduces an entirely new category beyond the alternatives 'active' and 'passive'" (p. 283 f.). However the case may stand with Scotus, Aristotle has, in the final analysis, eliminated passivity from the intellectual reception of forms.

[4] "tenendo differentiam esse bene assignatam, primum videndum est quomodo sit intelligenda" (num. 2).

what is true or false– it has to be reckoned among the natural powers[5]. In each case, the determining factor lies outside the intellect, normally in the will itself, but in the case of knowing in this way or otherwise in the object known. The will, by contrast, is always a self-determined principle: the reason for its acting or not acting, acting in this way or otherwise, never lies outside itself. Rather, it resides in the will itself[6], and is, in fact, nothing other than the will. The will is therefore its own reason, but inasmuch as a cause is always (*natura*, if not *tempore*) different from its effect, the will as, so to speak, "self-causing" can, in a certain sense, have no cause at all. While it is, of course, true that each type of reason represents a kind of cause –and in this sense the will *is* a kind of cause–, the converse does not hold. In this latter sense reason differs from other causes in being autonomous or self-causing, and with the already noted exception of reason or will itself no cause can be self-causing. Thus, in *ratio*, as opposed to *causa*, some form of self-foundation is always involved[7].

In this respect one can already detect in Scotus a reversal of the Aristotelian position. For him, the natural power is no longer univocally fixed on one part of a pair of opposites, so that the rational power is no longer the only power capable of entertaining both opposites of its own accord. Assuming, then, that the natural power were able to activate itself, it would have to actualize both members of a pair of opposites at the same time. Since the two sides of an opposition cannot both be true, the natural powers would, however, remain

---

[5] "Sic intellectus cadit sub natura: est enim ex se determinatus ad intelligendum, et non habet in potestate sua intelligere, et non intelligere, sive circa complexa (sic!), ubi potest habere contrarios actus. Non habet etiam illos in potestate sua assentire, et dissentire" (num. 6).

[6] "...quare voluntas illud volet? Nulla est alia causa, nisi quia est voluntas" (num. 5).

[7] If Scotus nowhere concludes *expressis verbis* that reason or the ground is always self-grounding, that *ratio* is always *autodeterminatio*, this is because he considers the will to be the genuine rational power whereas he sometimes reckons intellect with *ratio*. Thus he can say, "Ratio enim non est determinativa, cum sit oppositorum, respectu quorum se non posset determinare" (num. 9). It is not *qua* will, but only *qua* intellect, that *ratio* is incapable of determining itself to action.

as stymied in their ability to act as, say, Buridan's ass[8]; clearly, they must be activated from without, ultimately by a self-causing rational power. The assignment of this role to a natural power leads to an *aporia*: by embodying both sides of a given opposition, the natural power would become entangled in a contradiction; on the other hand, if the rational powers are consistently to avoid contradiction, they must remain inactive indefinitely. This aporia can only be resolved through recourse to the notion of a self-determining will. (*Ratio* –insofar as it is distinguished from the will– is no less a part of *natura* than the intellectus itself). This, too, represents an inversion of the original Aristotelian teaching[9]. In any case, it has become evident that the activation of any given natural power, be it within man or outside of him in nature, must ultimately derive from a self-determining will.

The preceding argument has made it possible, in turn, to identify two distinct, albeit interrelated, presuppositions that underlie Scotus' notion of self-determination. The first presupposition relates to the ability of the will as self-determining to mediate or choose between two opposing tendencies –i. e. toward acting or non-acting and toward acting in this way or that–, a necessary assumption if the active power is not to end up being determined by nature, above all by its own nature. With this the second presupposition has already been addressed, namely, that the active power not be construed as having been determined, not even by its own nature. In point of fact, Scotus does acknowledge a natural tendency on the part of the will, but he also insists on its remaining free *vis-à-vis* this natural tendency –even in the

---

[8] "Vel ergo ambo aget, vel nihil" (num. 13).

[9] Depending on one's point of view both rational and natural powers can be either *ad opposita* or *ad unum*. The difference in the way these terms apply to the respective power depends on whether the transition from the former to the latter is effected by the power itself or not. Given that this is the case, one is equally justified in arguing for or against the thesis that Duns Scotus is here a basic reversal of the Aristotelian position. As far as the intellect is concerned there is undeniably a reversal, for it has now come to be reckoned among the natural powers. But with respect to the natural powers one cannot legitimately speak of a reversal, since they are still being viewed as *determinatae ad unum*, albeit from without or externally.

case of eternal bliss or *beatitudo*. To express the same thought differently –but in terms that are essentially those of Duns Scotus– self-determination presupposes an absence of determination, i. e., a certain degree of non-determination. This non-determination corresponds, as it were, to a lack of "naturalness", which, despite the implied privation, should be regarded as a positive characteristic. It is only by virtue of this non-determination –or lack of naturalness– that one is able to say afterwards that it would have been equally possible to have taken a decision other than the one actually taken. Non-determination is not overcome through the agency of an external cause but there is a reason for its determining itself, and that reason lies in the power itself or, to put it more precisely, it is the power itself. When understood in this sense reason signifies nothing other than self-determining power. Behind it there is no other reason for acting[10]. Indeed, from this standpoint a rational power is no less *ad unum* than a natural one. Whereas the latter, however, is directed toward the choice of a particular alternative by something different from itself, the former is directed to it by itself. Furthermore, it may equally well be said of both powers that they are directed to this choice *ad opposita*: the natural power by virtue of its very nature or on its own (*ex se*)[11]; the rational power, by

---

[10] "Si ergo huius differentiae quaeritur causa, quare scilicet natura est tantum unius, hoc est, cuiscunque, vel quorumcumque sit, determinate ex se est istius, vel illorum: voluntas autem est oppositorum, id est, ex se indeterminate huius actionis, vel oppositae; seu actionis, vel non actionis: Dici postest, quod huius nulla est causa" (num. 4).

[11] When referring to the hetero-determination of nature, Scotus often writes simply "*determinatio*" or employs one of its cognates. Similarly, when referring to the self-determination of the will, he often writes "*indeterminatio*" (in the sense of "*indeterminatio sufficientiae superabundantis*"). Instead of "*determinatio*" (or "*determinata*") he may sometimes write "*determinatio ex se*" (or "*determinata ex se*"). Here "*ex se*" does not, of course, imply some kind of self-determination but is, as a term, indifferent both with respect to self-determination and to hetero-determination. This is borne out by the fact that "*ex se*" can also be used in connection with "*indeterminatio*" or its cognates (cf. n. 10 above). In such cases it signifies self-determination ("*se determinare*"). In other words, "*ex se*" stands for a neutral "considered in itself", and "nature, considered in itself, is *determinata*"

contrast, not on its own (*ex se*) or in virtue of its very nature, but in such a way as to be capable of being free from itself[12]. Thus both the natural and the rational powers are capable of entertaining opposites but only reason, insofar as it is identified with the will, can determine itself to choose one of a particular set of opposites, the natural power being reconciled to this particular one from outside and in a predetermined fashion. Duns Scotus himself conceptualizes their relationship in the following manner: the natural power as belonging to nature is already determined (deterministically, as it were) and so cannot determine itself, whereas the rational is undetermined and is thus free to determine itself. In keeping with this distinction he refers to the kind of non-determination that can determine itself as an *indeterminatio superabundantis sufficientiae*, to which he opposes an *indeterminatio insufficientiae*[13].

Consequently, the main question for Scotus is not so much whether the natural powers are directed to the choice of one particular alternative and the rational powers to the consideration of opposites but why this should be so[14]. And the short answer is that to be a natural object is to have a cause in the sense of an external cause whereas to be rational (as is the case with the will) is to have a reason in the sense of a reason for and of itself. Viewed in this way the rational power is no less directed toward a particular alternative than the natural, and the latter is no less capable of entertaining opposites than the former. But the rational is only by and through itself directed to the choice of one alternative, whereas considered on its own (*ex se*) the natural power is bound to opposing alternatives and has therefore to be directed toward

---

stands for "nature is on its own hetero-determined", just as "the will, considered in itself, is *determinata*" stands for "the will, considered in itself, is self-determined".

[12] Freedom *qua* freedom from one's own self plays an important role in the last phase of Schelling's philosophy, in which he sometimes refers to Scotus and Scotists (cf., F. W. J. Schelling, *Abhandlung über die ewige Wahrheiten*, Werke, XI, p. 759 f.).

[13] Num 5; cf. note 23 below.

[14] "Quare scilicet natura est tantum unius... voluntas autem... oppositorum" (num. 4).

one particular opposite, i. e. determined to act by something other than itself. It is thus no exaggeration to say that one can already find in Scotus the Kantian opposition between nature and freedom. Both identify nature with a thorough-going external determination (hetero-determination) consisting in an unlimited chain of causes, each lying beyond or outside of the other, just as both construe freedom to imply self-determination both in the sense that it is an end in itself or a self-justifying reason and in the sense that it is capable of initiating of its own accord a theretofore non-existent chain of events.

As we have seen, the chief distinction that Scotus draws between the natural and the rational is that the former is on its own (*ex se* or naturally) determined, whereas the latter is on its own (*ex se* or naturally) undetermined. On the basis of this non-determination (which allows for the possibility of embracing or actualizing opposites) the rational is able to determine itself to one of two opposites, i. e. to action; conversely it is on account of its prior determination by causes external to it that the natural cannot determine itself to the choice of a particular opposite. The rational is "not unequivocally oriented toward a particular one" in the sense that the rational is not determined, or bound, to anything but has to determine itself to whatever it may become. At the same time this needs not preclude the possibility that it may naturally tend more toward one of two opposing alternatives, e. g., to the *beatitudo* rather than to its opposite[15]. Being rational in the sense of not being oriented toward a particular one means, however, being able to decide against one's own nature; in other words, there is as yet no place in Scotus for the so-called *libertas indifferentiae*. To the extent that the intellect, considered on its own (*ex se*), is something purely natural, the will is –in this regard– something clearly distinct from the intellect and so not completely without its own nature. From this consideration alone it may be seen how far Scotus still is from recognizing a form of self-determination that would be entirely independent of nature[16].

---

[15] Cf. Chapter 13 below.

[16] "Sola enim (sc. voluntas) est non talis, nec ideo negandum est eam esse talem" (num. 8).

As a result, the will, as Scotus conceives it, is not exhausted by its own factual decisions; it is not pure facticity[17]. On the other hand it is impossible to gainsay a certain tendency toward facticity on the part of the will in Scotus. This tendency is inherent in the voluntarist strain of Scotus' philosophy. As soon as the schism between the will as self-determination and nature as external determination has been made to run through the whole realm of Being, as is the case in Scotus, the actual content to be decided upon pales in importance beside the question of whether the decision itself was self-determined or not. Under such circumstances nature can easily cease to be considered something rational in the sense of being governed by some kind of form or reason (λόγος) and thus become relegated to a place beyond any predetermined order[18]. Still, regardless of whether something determines itself in conformity with its own nature (or not) or whether it is determined in conformity with (or against) its own nature –i. e., regardless of whether something is assigned to the realm of nature or to that of reason– the decisive question is that of self-determination or external determination, and not that of maintenance of some order or

---

[17] Significantly, in setting up his basic dichotomy *natura* and *voluntas*, Scotus draws on the Aristotelian distinction between chance in the realm of nature and chance in the realm of of intentional behavior: "Unde prima divisio principiorum activorum est in naturam et voluntatem. Iuxta quod Aristoteles in 2. Physic. duas ponit causas moventes per accidens: casum iuxta naturam, et fortunam iuxta propositum sive voluntatem" (num. 4).

[18] The idea that efficient causality is synonymous with uninterrupted hetero-causality is at odds with the doctrine of natural teleology. It is entirely non-Aristotelian but is consistent with Ockham's doctrine, as set down in the *Summulae in libros physicorum* as well as in his *Super sententias* and *Quodlibeta*. In all these works nature, because of its lack of reflection, is thoroughly non-teleological. On the other hand, the *Expositio in libros physicorum*, attributed to Ockham as well, is wholly in accord with Aristotle's conception of natural teleology. However the question of attribution is ultimately to be decided, the important point for us to note here is how far the deteleologization of nature had already been carried out within a short period after Scotus's death, and very much along the lines which Scotus had originally laid out with his conception of nature as *determinatio ad unum*.

other. The question as to the existence of a preestablished order is also important but in the end secondary, because it no longer yields –as it did in Aristotle– the main criterion according to which something is judged to belong to nature or not[19]. The main criterion is now given by the question of whether the order was maintained through self-determination or not. Only to the extent that one has failed to take this into account, can one find it surprising that the intellect should now be made to side with the "irrational" as the purely natural[20].

For Aristotle nature and reason belong somehow together. From his standpoint what occurs within a certain order is something natural and at the same time rational. Accordingly, what is against nature also goes against reason. But with the primacy of the will as self-determination over the intellect as something natural and with the characterization of nature as hetero-determination the importance of the Aristotelian idea of order was strongly relativized. To be in agreement with some order or form (λόγος) is no longer determinative either of nature or of reason, and even less so of a final free will. Unlike the intellect, the will is not constrained either to act or not to act, to act in this way or to act otherwise. Indeed, it is the intellect which is constrained by the will: the will moves the intellect not only to know or to refrain from knowing but also to know one thing or to know something else. That is why Scotus considers the intellect or, for that matter, the reason to be natural and not in the usual sense rational.

Thus the question which Scotus repeatedly raises prior to treating the will as self-determining, i. e., whether it is permissible to view the intellect as something passive[21], is easily answered. Although the

---

[19] Following in the footsteps of Duns Scotus, Fonseca, the teacher of Molina and Suarez, was to submit the Aristotelian criterion to an intensive examination (cf. *Petri Fonseca Commentariorum in Metaphysicorum Aristotelis Stagiritae libros*, lib. IX, cap. II, q. I, sect. I; in the Cologne edition of 1615 this corresponds to the page 556 b of the vol. III).

[20] "Voluntas, quae indeterminata est ad actum proprium, illum elicit, et per illum determinat" (num. 7).

[21] Cf. n. 3 above and, especially, the num. 13 of the q. XIV of lib. IX of the *Quaestiones subtilissimae*.

question may be answered in the affirmative. It would be a mistake to infer from the intellect's passivity that it remains inactive during the process of knowing. This would in fact directly contravene the letter of that Aristotelian doctrine to which Scotus always tries to remain as faithful as possible. What it is legitimate to infer is that the intellect, in order to be moved into action and so come to know, requires the causal agencies of both the will and the object to be known: it is dependent on the will so that the intellect can emerge from its state of non-knowing and on the object so that the intellect can know that particular thing which it comes to know and no other. Only the will is, however, purely active so that the intellect is, at least, in relation to it, wholly passive[22].

Scotus emphasizes the dominant role of the will among the active principles so often that he sometimes seems on the verge of losing patience. To him it seems almost ludicrous to want to apply general statements about the active principles to the will. But even more than this he is concerned to highlight the will's independence and lack of prior determination –a putative fact he regards as a token of its pure perfection. The more independent an active principle is, the more perfect it is[23]. Similarly, the significance attached by Scotus to non-determination extends so far that even that contingency which is the inevitable concomitant of a lack of determination is valued more highly than the necessity inherent in nature[24] –an unthinkable state of affairs from a genuinely Aristotelian viewpoint. Independence, lack of determination, and contingency, all three belong in a unique way to the will. The absence of determination on the part of the will should, however, not be considered evidence of an underlying passivity as in the case of the intellect but rather as sheer activity. Indeed it is the very opposite –and intentionally so– of that particular inability to de-

---

[22] "Voluntas est principium activum, distinctum contra totum genus principiorum activorum, quae non sunt voluntas, per oppositum modum agendi" (num. 8).

[23] "Quis enim negat activum esse perfectius quandto minus dependens, et determinatum, et limitatum, respectu actus, vel effectus?" (num. 8).

[24] "Haec enim nobilior est contingentia, necessitate" (num. 8).

termine itself[25] which is characteristic of the passive intellect with its indecisiveness *vis-à-vis* opposing options and its patient reliance on a decision of the will and the casual intervening of the object. More generally, one may even say that the reason for the intellect's lack of determination with respect to a choice of opposites as well as that of nature, considered as a whole, is ultimately to be found in the will's capacity for self-determination. In short the progression toward ever higher ends or goals must come to an end in the will. The harmony of doing (i. e. making or producing) and using that had been postulated by Plato occurs –*pace* Plato– in the will and is not effected by any form of knowledge[26].

---

[25] "Est quaedam indeterminatio insufficientiae, sive ex potentialitate, ex defectu actualitatis, sicut materia non habens formam, est indeterminata ad agendum actionem formae. Est alia (indeterminatio) superabundantis sufficientiae, quae est ex illimitatione actualitatis, vel simpliciter, vel quodammodo. Primo modo, indeterminatum non reducitur ad actum: nisi prius determinetur ad formam ab alio: secundo modo, indeterminatum potest se determinare... Indeterminatio autem quae ponitur in voluntate, non est materialis, nec imperfectionis, inquantum ipsa est activa; sed est excellentis perfectionis, et potestatis non alligatae ad determinatum actum" (num. 5).

[26] "Si intellectus per eandem notitiam, est aliquo modo oppositorum, ut ostendens; ergo potentia activa indeterminatior potest esse excellentiori modo oppositorum, scilicet ut ipsa una existens possit se ad utrumque illorum ostensorum determinare: alioquin frustra videretur data fuisse potentiae prima oppositorum: quia ipsa sine secunda in nullum illorum posset; ita quod argumentum fit a minori: non autem a causa propria: scientia enim non est causa propria differentiae praedictae" (num 8). The last words refer specially to the example of the sun introduced by the opponents of Aristotle in order to refute his distinction between natural and rational powers (cf. num 3): the sun, too, seems to have opposite effects (*per se* hit, *per accidens* cold) just as much as science has, for, e.g., medicine is *per se* related to the *habitus* (of health) but *per accidens* to its *privatio* (illness) (cf. num. 2 end). Now, Scotus contends that this all has to be subjected to a further analysis, for the ambivalence of science (or art) is rooted in the fact that without the self-determination of the will, the ambivalence itself would be useless. In other words, one has to go behind the *prima facie* distinction nature/reason (*ad unum/ad opposita*) to the distinction nature/will (alien-determination/self-determination).

According to Scotus, the intellect owes its passivity to its being a part of nature. And it is mainly owing to its place within the natural realm –and only secondarily to the passivity deriving from that place– that the intellect is ambivalent between conformity and disconformity or non-conformity with nature. But this claim would seem to involve a contradiction. For at the very last it seems odd to say that nature itself is characterized by an ambivalence between conformity and disconformitiy with itself. However, this objection presupposes for its validity that this ambivalence toward itself is the most fundamental characteristic of nature. But this is not, in fact, the case. Even more fundamental than that ambivalence which nature shares not only with the intellect but with the will as well is another characteristic which nature also has in common with the former but not with the latter. This more fundamental characteristic may be likened to a kind of forerunner of the modern principle of *inertia*, viz. that, if left to itself, nature always remains in that state in which it previously found itself. As far as this principle is concerned, it is a matter of secondary importance whether that state is itself in conformity with nature or not. In light of the priority which Scotus grants *inertia* over ambivalence as a characteristic feature of nature, one is obliged to distinguish between a broader and narrower concept of nature, and it is just this distinction which enables one to circumvent the aforementioned contradiction. The broader conception of nature leaves open the the non-conformity with nature precluded by the narrower conception. The latter, narrower view coincides with the Aristotelian concept of nature; the broader view signals from afar the coming of the modern conception of nature. This, in turn, arises either from the complete removal of rationality from nature and its ascription solely to the will –a spirit, so to speak, severed from its links with nature– or from the circumscription of reason within nature to a purely instrumental or technical rationality. It is this notion of the limited rationality of nature that was to receive its classic expression in Kant's *Critique of Pure Reason*. Beyond nature, so construcd, there is only the will in its being as non-determination and so, by implication, as self-determination[27]. Crucial for this extended no-

---

[27] "Aut enim potentia ex se est determinata ad agendum, ita quod quantum est ex se,

tion of nature is thus that it be subject to an *inertia* –like principle which makes it impossible for it to alter its own state, regardless of whether this state itself happens to be in accord with nature or not. With the elevation of this principle to a superordinate role the significance of being in accord with nature has been relativized to such an extent that the way is now clear for a deterministic and rationalist conception of nature so encompassing as to include all things that are capable of acting upon one another. At the very beginning of this conceptual evolution it was still possible to detect some effort on the part of exegetes to remain faithful to Aristotle[28], but then as the distance from his original standpoint steadily increased, the divergence finally led to open confrontation. Indeed no greater opposition can be imagined than that between Aristotelian nature in which the principle of activity lies within nature itself and a nature so conceived that the principle of movement lies wholly outside the things moved. In Scotus the reversal is already almost complete. Thus in Scotus' interpretation of Aristotle it is only by virtue of the fact that nature is determined, i. e. hetero-determined, that it is in the end unambivalent and unequivocal in its orientation (*determinata ad unum*). In Aristotle the same result would instead have been adduced as proof of a thing's unnaturalness. For since in nature the same species always perpetuate themselves (e. g. *homo generat hominem*), it is impossible for nature to entertain relations to anything other than itself. The numerical difference to be found among individuals of the same species does not be-

---

non potest non agere, quando non impeditur ab extrinseco; aut non est ex se determinata, sed potest agere hunc actum, vel oppositum actum: agere etiam, vel non agere. Prima potentia communiter dicitur natura, secunda dicitur voluntas" (num. 4).

[28] "Sed quomodo faciunt praedicta ad intentum Aristotelis, qui differentiam dictam non ponit inter naturam, et voluntatem, sed inter irrationalem potentiam, et rationalem, per rationalem intellingens solum intellectum...? Respondeo, intellectus, et voluntas, possunt comparari ad actus proprios quos eliciunt; vel ad actus aliorum potentiarum inferiorum, in quibus quandam causalitatem habent: intellectus ostendendo, et dirigendo: voluntas inclinando, et imperando. Prima comparatio est essentialior... Secundum hanc primam comparationem non videtur loqui Aristoteles" (num. 6).

long to nature per se, i. e. by virtue of its essence. Not surprisingly, then, the increasing distance from Aristotle is reflected in a growing rejection of species-essentialism in favor of individual-essentialism.

As a result, *determinatio ad unum* comes to mean something very different in Scotus than it did in Aristotle. For Aristotle it means a nature closed in itself; for Scotus, on the contrary, it implies an open-ended nature. Scotus' nature does not act for its own sake nor does it have its meaning or sense within itself: whereas the objects of nature have their *raison d'être* in each other, i.e. in other physical objects, nature as a whole has its *raison d'être* in something completely outside itself. Thus, when considered in its entirety, nature is alienated from itself. So conceived, it is completely vulnerable to exploitation by the active powers of mankind; at any rate there has been a marked tendency, historically, to interpret its passivity or *inertia* along these lines.

What I have been calling the *inertia* –like principle of nature applies equally well to the intellect in its radical opposition to the will. The intellect, too, would remain indefinitely in the same state of knowing or not-knowing, were nothing external to it –be it the will or the object to be known– to effect a change in it. The intellect follows the affecting will and the affecting object without putting up any resistance of its own. Unlike the (finite) will, the intellect cannot stand, as it were, in its own way or resist its own insights. Being itself no more than a product of nature and so incapable of self-determination[29], the intellect cannot deliberately err, as the will can. Scotus differs importantly in this respect from Aristotle but also from Kant. For, unlike Kant's *Vernunft*, the intellect is not identical with the will: when the intellect is possessed of some insight, it cannot deny or disown it[30].

To be absolutely clear on this point, it is not that the intellect's passivity precludes the possibility of error, as if the task of the intellect consisted simply in receiving impressions from external things which

---

[29] Cf. n. 5 above.

[30] "Non habet etiam illos (actus suos) in potestate sua assentire, et dissentire" (num. 6).

it then raises to the appropriate level of generality. If that were so, then the intellect would, indeed, always know things exactly as they are, and its errors would, at best, be errors *per accidens*, attributable to the (precipitated) intervention of the will. In Scotus this is not yet the case. While it is true that Scotus distinguishes between *realitas objectiva* and *realitas formalis*, between the intellectual image (*species intelligibilis* as *intellecta*) and reality itself, the *realitas objectiva* is of a lesser degree of being than its formal counterpart: the *ens cognitum* is an *ens deminutum*. And although the image is not the thing itself nor is the known idea to be confused with reality itself, the subject is in the process of knowing not only brought into relation to the former but also in relation to the latter. The criterion for truth has not yet been identified exclusively with the clearness and distinctiveness of the intellectual idea: a discrepancy between such an idea and the reality it represents is still conceivable. Thus the intellect's infallibility can only be explained in terms of the fact that it is incapable of opposing anything into which it has an insight or at least into which it believes it has an insight. The intellect differs from the will in not being able to decide against its own insight or act against its own better judgment[31]. Scotus even goes so far as to deny the intellect the role of power in relation to external objects[32]. The will, by contrast, is in relation to itself a power to the utmost degree[33]. Thus the very possibility of there being a capacity for entertaining opposites –the ultimate explanation for the ambivalence inherent in reason– lies alone in the will itself[34].

---

[31] Cf. n. 5 above.

[32] "Tunc voluntas est proprie rationalis, et ipsa est oppositorum...: et non oppositorum modo naturae, sicut intellectus non potens se determinare ad alterum: sed modo libero, potens se determinare. Intellectus autem proprie non est potentia respectu terminare. Intellectus autem proprie non est potentia respectu extrinsecorum, quia ipse si est oppositorum, non potest se determinare, et nisi determinetur, nihil extra poterit" (num. 7; cf. also note 19 above).

[33] "Voluntas autem actionis suae, sive circa hoc oppositum in quod potest, sive circa illud, non est principium ex se determinatum sed potestative determinativum sui ad alterutrum" (num. 8).

[34] "Tota ratio potentiae ad opposita formaliter est in voluntate" (num. 9).

As a result, the fallibility of the will is actually two-fold: firstly, that fallibility that can be traced back to that of the intellect and, secondly, that fallibility which is incurred when the will detaches itself from the intellect and decides against the insight –or alleged insight– proferred by the latter. By deciding against a presumed insight on the part of the intellect, the will may unwittingly hit upon the truth, but this would only have been a fluke, and so the will cannot be credited with actually having known what was correct. Whereas the intellect is compelled to assent to either a genuine insight or a merely putative one –whatever may happen to be the case– the will may or may not assent to it. And this is possible because, unlike the intellect, the will is fettered neither by its own nature or insight nor by any alien nature or externally derived insight. As long as preferential choice or προαίρεσις did not fall within the exclusive domain of the will[35] but was –as in Aquinas but already in Aristotle– a matter of the will and the intellect acting conjointly, it was difficult to allow for the possibility that one might decide against the better or superior reason. The doctrine of *libertas indifferentiae* could, however, only be developed after those ties, binding the will to the intellect or reason, had been completely severed –something that only happened after Scotus. Even with the dissolution of this bond, though, there is no reason to surrender that ethical maxim according to which one always decides for the sake of something good (*sub ratione boni*), for *sub ratione boni* is not equivalent to *sub ratione maximi boni vel optimi*. Indeed it would be wrong to try to play this principle off against that of *libertas indifferentiae*. *Malum* can, but need not, consist in the choice of a lesser good against a greater one: to choose badly or to make a bad choice, even if it is against one's better judgment, is not necessarily to choose something bad. It is clear that this is not only consistent with, but actually

---

[35] "Non sic autem de voluntate: si enim est oppositorum virtualiter, simul est eorum, sed non eorum simul, quia non est eorum modo naturae: sed potens se determinare ad alterutrum ante alterum, et ideo sic faciet" (num 10). Shortly later Scotus mentions the reason for attributing preferential choice only to the will: "quia (contraries) non repugnant absolute, nisi ratione privationis talis, non autem rationis volibilis: ut videtur, quia utrumque inquantum positivum, videtur volibile" (num. 11).

follows from, the concept of will as self-determination[36]. Since the intellect can incite itself neither to the act of knowing nor to the knowledge of a particular this or that, it must in each case first be moved by external influences, like any other natural object, if it is to know[37]. As a result, its knowing is always limited to a single opposite or alternative –the one which brought it about–, and the knowledge acquired is thus necessarily of a piece with the nature that caused it. The will, by contrast, is contingent and remains so even during the actual moment of choice where it is still free to choose or not to choose, to choose this or to choose that[38]. For Scotus, unlike in Aristotle (and later Ockham), the contingency is so radical that it is not confined to the period preceding the action itself.

Let us sum up: it was not Scotus' purpose to argue that the criterion which Aristotle proposed for distinguishing between nature and reason, or, more specifically, between the natural and the rational active powers or principles (*natura est determinata ad unum/ratio ad opposita*) has become obsolete. His contention was rather that this criterion, correct as far as it goes, is not logically or philosophically primitive: its validity depends on a previous distinction. Natural active powers are focused toward a one (*ad unum*), because they are incapable of determining themselves. Duns Scotus subjects this criterion to yet another modification, however, insofar as he allows the natural active powers to entertain opposites as well, even if the manner in

---

[36] "Patet, quod potentia rationalis, prout dicitur voluntas est contrariorum, non simul fiendorum: sed potest se determinara ad alterutrum, non sic intellectus" (num. 13).

[37] "Si autem arguitur de intellectu cognoscente opposita, tunc verum est, quod respectu extrinseci non potest aliquid, nisi determinetur aliunde: quia ex se est illorum per modum naturae, non potens se ad alterutrum determinare: vel ergo ambo aget, vel nihil" (num. 13). The fact that it cannot make any choice neither to nor in the exercise of knowing means that the intellect is no more –as in Aristotle– an ingredient of προαίρεσις (νοῦς ὀρεκτικόν or ὄρεξις διανοετική). The προαίρεσις belongs only to the will.

[38] "Si arguitur de voluntate, dico quod illa potest in actum nulla determinatione in ipsa praeintellecta actui: ita quod prima determinatio, et tempore, et natura, est in positione actus: et si tunc de ipsa accipiatur, in nihil potest, nisi prius determinata: falsum est" (num. 13).

which, for example, will and intellect confront alternatives is different. Indeed it is precisely because the natural powers are also in a sense *ad opposita* but without the ability to choose between either of a pair of opposites (*ad unum*) that they are thought to be in need of an external cause in the first place.

CHAPTER 13
ARISTOTLE AND SCOTUS ON PRACTICAL TRUTH:
A COMPARISON

As far as I know it was not until John Duns Scotus that the Aristotelian concept of practical truth once again became relevant for Western thought. Of course, any one wishing to comment on the *Nicomachean Ethics* would have had to have dealt with it. But this is not to say that the concept had been of much further relevance; only with Scotus does it come to acquire a different status. The reason for this reversal lies in his conception of theology as a practical science.

"Practical science" is an expression of Aristotelian coinage. It means that ethics is not simply for the sake of knowledge, but primarily for the sake of action[1]. In learning to do ethics properly one also improves one's behavior. Precisely for this reason, theology is for Duns Scotus not a theoretical but a practical science –notwithstanding the fact that the object of theology, God, is not the same as the object of ethics, viz. our actions, and that God is necessary whereas our actions are contingent. This qualification amounts to an objection against the practical character of theology[2]. It may in turn be elaborated upon, as Duns Scotus does in one of his *objectiones*, to

---

1 Aristotle, *Ethica Nicomachea,* 1095a 5 f.

2 "Praetera, practica ponitur esse contingens, *De Anima*, III (433a 26-30) et I *Ethicorum* (1094b 7, 21-22); rei objectum huius, scientiae non est contingens, sed necessarium; ergo"; J. D. Scotus, *Ordinatio*, Prolog. *Pars quinta*, num. 218, ed. Vaticanum I 151. In the following when referring to individual passages I shall simply give the numbers ("num.") and the page in volume I ("I") of this edition. - Parallel discussions are to be found in the *Lectura* (prol. *pars* 4, qq. 1-2) translated into English by Allan B. Wolter, *Duns Scotus on the Will and Morality*, Washington D.C. 1986, pp. 117-143 with the original text.

yield three arguments against the priority of theology over the other sciences: if theology were for the sake of praxis, it would not be the highest science, first, because the contingent seems to rank below the necessary; secondly, because theory is for its own sake, viz. for the sake of knowledge or contemplation, whereas, as has already been said, practical science is not for the sake of knowledge itself but for the sake of action; thirdly, because theology would be less certain than metaphysics[3]. Despite these and other objections, Scotus holds on to his view concerning the practical character of theology. True, the authorities to whom he here appeals in support of his own thesis are not taken from Aristotle[4]. But this does not hold against the above mentioned points of convergence. It only proves that Scotus' theology follows the pattern of Aristotle's practical, but not that of his theoretical philosophy[5]. This is, however, not to deny that alongside the similarities there are characteristic dissimilarities which have still to be discussed. On the whole one may say that Duns Scotus' disagreement with Aristotle is expressed mainly in the *objectiones* whereas his agreement is expressed mainly in the *responsiones*.

Since the concept of practical truth is intimately related to Aristotelian practical science, it is not surprising that it also plays a prominent role in Scotus' theology. In this respect, too, there are differences to be noted which, however, need not preclude the possibility of even more basic similarities. Whether the differences are in fact decisive or, whether, on the contrary, the similarities are more basic is a matter of some controversy as well as the issue of whether

---

[3] "Item, omni aliqua est nobilior; nulla nobilior ista [sc. theologia]; ergo etc. Probatio primae: tum quia speculativa est sui gratia, practica gratia usus, tum quia speculativa est certior, ex I *Metaphysicae* [982a 14-16, 25-28]" (num. 220, I 152).

[4] "Contra: Rom. 13: Finis legis est dilectio. Item, Matth. 22: In his duabus mandatis universa lex pendet et prophetae. Item, Augustinus De laude caritatis: 'Ille tenet quidquid latet et quidquid patet in divinis sermonibus qui caritatem servat in moribus'" (num. 222, I 152).

[5] "Hae autemauctoritates probant quod ista scientia non est praecise propter speculari, sed speculativa nihil quaerit ultra speculari, secundum Avicennam I *Metaphysicae* II" (*ibid.*, I 153).

the Aristotelian or Scotist conception is more consistent with itself and with the facts. Questions regarding the first principles in their bearing on the theories of action and of substance ultimately turn out to be crucial here as well. I propose to approach these questions by starting with the second of the two *quaestiones* of the Fifth Part of the Prologue to the *Ordinatio*. The two *quaestiones* (first, whether *theologia* is a practical science; secondly, whether a science is called practical with respect to praxis as an end) are intimately related to one another. This is evident from the fact that two of the three objections Scotus quotes against his own theory in this second *quaestio* had already been handled in connection with the first *quaestio*[6]. Only the third and last objection in the second *quaestio* takes the concept of truth explicitly into account. Thus I intend to concentrate on this third objection. It reads: "Besides there is the authority of *Metaphysics* II, according to which the end of theoretical science is truth, whereas that of practical science is action"[7].

Scotus' answers are often of such complexity that it is not easy to grasp their philosophical point. In attempting to come to grips with them, I shall start with Plato[8]. In Plato's *Euthydemus*, one may read: "If it is impossible to say or think something false... then it is equally impossible to do something wrong"[9]. Here you have in a nutshell the problem of, as well as with, practical truth. Practical truth is not the truth of sentences but rather the truth of the actions themselves, *veritas actionum* so to speak, viz. some sort of *veritas rerum* –just as much as

---

[6] The two first objections in the second quaestio read: "III *De Anima* dicit philosophus: 'Intellectus extensione fit practicus, et differt a speculative fine' (433a 14-15)"; and: "Item, I *Metaphysicae*: 'Practica est minus nobilis quam speculativa, quia gratia usus' (982a 14-16). Hoc argumentum non teneret nisi usus esset per se finis illius habitus" (num. 223 and 224, I 153).

[7] "Item, II *Metaphysicae*: 'Finis speculativae (scilicet scientiae) est veritas, finis autem practicae est opus' (993b 20-21)" (num. 225, I 153).

[8] I am here following and enlarging upon the oral presentation of my contribution to the Scotus conference mentioned in the Foreword. The original paper has appeared in German in the proceedings of the conference.

[9] Plato, *Euthydemus*, 287A.

practical science is not a science of actions but, as it were, performative science (sometimes, in fact, loving science[10]) as opposed to a science which would make only true assertions about actions. In other words, practical science is not for the sake of knowledge, but, again, for the sake of action, viz. for the sake of becoming a better person, or virtuous, or more perfect. That is why the aim of theory is knowledge, whereas the aim of practical science is praxis (*opus*). But granted that practical science is truly practical, is it a science at all? Scotus is here quoting from the *Metaphysics* by way of objection. The quoted words ("finis speculativae est veritas, practicae autem opus") seem in fact to make truth (*veritas*) and praxis (*opus*) mutually exclusive. If so, obviously, practical truth would be impossible, a mere oxymoron.

However the appearance of impossibility persists only as long as one understands "praxis" merely in the sense of factual activity, i.e., of whatever one happens to be doing, as we just saw was the case in the *Euthydemus*. Then, of course, whatever one happens to do would be the right thing to do simply by virtue of its having been done. Or as Plato puts it, "whatever one does, he cannot be mistaken (ἁμαρτάνειν) in doing it". Now practical truth, which according to Scotus is like prudence only more general[11], can only exist where there is the possibility of right and wrong, ὀρθότης and ἁμαρτία, *rectitudo* and *peccatum*. That is why, according to Scotus, the *theologia Dei* –either as *theologia necessariorum* or as *theologia contingentium*, and as distinct from *theologia hominis*– cannot be regarded as a proper practical science. God's will cannot be in discord with his intellect. If it could, then God would be capable of sinning[12]. The possibility of right and wrong is not only a precondition for human as opposed to divine praxis, it is also constitutive of practical as distinct from theoretical science. As regards Aristotle this appears most concisely in the dictum that the notion of correctness (ὀρθότης, *rectitudo*) is foreign to theoretical science insofar as error (ἁμαρτία) is

---

[10] Cf. n. 4 above.

[11] Cf. num. 351, I 227 f.

[12] "Quia non potest ei dissentire; tunc enim posset peccare" (num. 325, I 212).

also unknown to it[13]. As Plato would have put it, right reason is corrected, or even correcting, reason[14]. In Aristotle it is only corrected, in Scotus correcting reason. In this respect, the latter is more voluntaristic, and at the same time more intellectualistic, than the former. The reason for this is that in Scotus intellect and will are distinguished from one another in a way that they are not in Aristotle, viz. *formaliter a parte rei* (cf. the end of this chapter). The upshot of this difference is that in Aristotle both practical reason and will are likewise threatened by error, whereas in Scotus this applies only to the will –to reason only inasmuch as the will is rational power itself.

According to Scotus, reason as such, i.e., not as will, is intellect which is a purely rational power[15]. As a purely natural power, it cannot reflect on or behave to itself in a way which would enable it to assent to error[16]. On the other and, the possibility of assenting to error belongs to the very rationaly of the human will. For this reason the human will has to be directed and corrected by the *ratio*. And it is precisely for this reason that in Scotus *ratio* is rather *corrigens* than *correcta* as it is in Aristotle. This is also the reason why of the two Scotus is the more intellectualistic but at the same time also the more voluntaristic, since under such circumstances the will is able to oppose the correct dictates of reason from beginning to end. In fact, by means of a characteristic *si per impossibile* argument Scotus attempts almost

---

[13] Cf. Aristotle, *Ethica Nicomachea*, 1142b 10. Cf. J. D. Scotus, *Ordinatio*, num. 237, 274, 275, 298, 301, 302, 310, 312, 322, 329, 330, 333, 336, 344, 354, 361. In the appendix to my contribution to the Scotus conference mentioned above I quote from these texts.

[14] Cf. Plato, *Euthydemus*, 281B.

[15] Cf. Chapter 12, "Natura ad unum - ratio ad opposita. Zur Transformation des Aristotelismus bei Duns Scotus".

[16] The intellect can *judicare de actus suo* (cf. num. 233, I 158) and thus can also err. What it, unlike the will, cannot do is to diverge from right judgment.

desperately to preserve the power of the will to diverge from the correct dictates of reason even in the case of the blessed in heaven[17].

The fact that Scotus ascribes to the will a greater independence from the intellect than does Aristotle is also reflected in Scotus' conception of how prudence is related to the moral virtues. For the latter to exist the former is necessary, precisely because the human will is not bound by nature, not even in its pursuit of eternal happiness (*beatitudo*)[18], but not vice versa. On the other hand, the thesis that prudence is capable of existing independently of the moral virtues requires some qualifications[19]. It is all the more necessary to recognize these qualifications if one intends to bring out the similarities and differences between Aristotle and Scotus. In this context I would like to concentrate on the following passage of Scotus: "praxis is an act which lies in the power of the knower. This can be proven by drawing on Book VI of the *Ethica Nicomachea*[20], for according to Aristotle the artist is in need of some virtue in order to act correctly; but the artist does not need any virtue with respect to that which does not lie in his power, therefore the artist has in his power the making of the work; the man endowed with practical reason [the *prudens*] has even more power over his actions, for he is actually

---

[17] "Beati ergo licet non possint errare, non sequitur quod non habeant habitum etiam directivum, quia eo per impossibile circumscripto errare possent" (num. 279, I 188).

[18] "Si dicas quod si voluntas nec necessario velit beatitudinem... dico quod ut in pluribus habet actum volendi, sed non necessario aliquem actum. Unde potest suspendere se ab omni actu" (*Ordinatio*, III, d. 49, art. 2). I owe this reference to H. Möhle who is graduating from the University of Bonn with a dissertation on the fifth part of Scotus' prologue to the *Ordinatio*. Cf. the English translation in *Duns Scotus on Will and Morality*, p. 195.

[19] Cf. the papers of M.E. Ingham, M. McCord-Adams, and H. Möhle distributed at the above mentioned conference in Bonn. Cf. also S. Dumont, "The Necessary Connection of Moral Virtues to Prudence according to John Duns Scotus –Revisited", *Recherches de Théologie Ancienne et Médiévale*, 1988, pp. 184-206.

[20] Aristotle, *Ethica Nicomachea*, VI, 1140b 22: "artis quidem est virtus, prudentiae autem non est".

("formally") virtuous"²¹. Two interpretations of this passage are possible, depending on whether one takes the reference to Aristotle at face value or not. In the latter case the passage should instead be read in a Platonic mood, assuming Plato had not already arrived at what is commonly regarded as the Aristotelian distinction between art and virtue or art and prudence (where "art" is but another term for "technique" or "specialization"). While it is true that prudence on this view turns out to be the highest art, it still represents only an art and not a moral virtue. This un-Aristotelian interpretation corresponds to Plato's stance in, e.g., the *Hippias Minor*, a dialogue within whose confines the paradox that knowingly doing wrong is superior to unknowingly doing wrong cannot be resolved. For normally²² those who intentionally do wrong, although they know how to act correctly, are better than those who have committed errors without knowing or intending, but better only as regards some art or technique, and not as regards virtue or morality²³. This first interpretation is in accordance with Scotus' thesis to the effect that moral wrongdoing is still possible despite the intervention of prudence.

However, the letter of the Scotist text just quoted would seem to be in conformity with the Aristotelian text to which it refers. For the latter²⁴ prudence is not an art but a virtue. This ensures that in the case of prudence knowing what is the right thing to do and doing it do not come asunder. That is why Aristotelian prudence is not merely technical but truly practical. To *do* what reason recognizes as the right thing to do means nothing more than deciding to do it for as soon as one has decided to do it, only an external hindrance can prevent one from doing it. In this latter respect there is no difference between

---

²¹ "Praxis est actus qui est in potentia cognoscentis. Quod probatur ex VI *Ethicorum*, quia artifex eget virtute ad recte agendum; non autem indiget virtute respectu illius quod non est in potestate sua; igitur artifex in potestate sua habet factionem: multi magis prudens habet in potestate sia actionem, quia est formaliter virtuosus". J. D. Scotus, *Ordinatio*, num. 231, I 156 f.

²² But cf. Chapter 10 above.

²³ Cf. Chapter 7 above.

²⁴ Cf. also Chapter 7 above.

Aristotle and Scotus[25], but only in this latter respect. The difference becomes evident in the fact that, according to Scotus, the human will always remains free to decide in harmony or disharmony with right reason or prudence. The ultimate reason for placing such a great emphasis on liberty of will is that for Scotus the will is not, as for Aristotle, a natural power with a natural inclination to beatitude but rather the sole truly rational power subject to contrary inclinations ("*natura ad unum, ratio ad opposita*"), which are ultimately either right or wrong. Thus, although Scotus in the quoted passage contended that the prudent man is "formally" virtuous, this does not have the same practical weight as in Aristotle.

True, according to Scotus, practical wisdom or prudence not only shows the will which course of action it ought to follow but may also influence the will's decisions. Still, it influences the decision only as a partial cause. The decision always lies in the end with the will. Accordingly what ought to be understood literally in Scotus' text, which ends with the declaration that the prudent person is formally virtuous, is the parallel which it draws between the morally wise man, i.e., the *prudens*, and the morally neutral technician. Each has the power to do or to make things respectively, but far from excluding the possibility of refraining (*non velle*) from doing or making the right thing –or sometimes even of doing or making the wrong thing (*nolle*)– this even includes it. We shall presently try to assess what implications this clear departure from Aristotle's position has for Scotus. But in spite of that one should be careful not to overlook the underlying agreement. For both Aristotle and Scotus, human praxis, as opposed to theory, includes as *conditio sine qua non* the possibility of wrongness independently of whether this possibility belongs specifically to practical reason, as it does in Aristotle, or to a will which in Scotus is set apart from intellect (*distinctio formalis a parte rei*).

On the basis of such similarities and dissimilarities, I shall try to show how Scotus manages to cope with the objection taken from Aristotle's *Metaphysics* II, which, as we saw, seemingly threatened the very possibility of practical science as well as of practical truth. The

---

[25] Cf. J. D. Scotus, *Ordinatio*, num. 234 f., I 159 f.

objection was found in the second and more difficult *quaestio* of the fifth part of the Prologue of the *Ordinatio* (*utrum ex ordine ad praxim ut ad finem dicatur per se scientia practica*). Scotus' thesis here is that human theology is practical insofar as praxis or action is taken not as an end but as an object. What does that mean? The easiest way to see the point of this contention, which is intended as a response to the objection previously raised against the very possibility of practical truth, is to refer again to the issue of ultimate beatitude.

To be sure, God is the ultimate object of blessedness. Nevertheless, one might object that it is also the ultimate *end* of action as well. One could with all the more justification object to it on the grounds that man can both arrive at as well as fall short of his ultimate end and that the tension between success and failure, acting rightly and wrongly, is, as we saw, an integral part of the very possibility both of practical truth and practical science. Nevertheless, Scotus is committed to considering God as well as actions not as ends, which they, in fact, are for practical truth and practical science, but rather as objects. The reason for this seems to be that to speak of God (or of beatitude) as an end conveys the connotation of something natural –as if the will were by nature inclined to, and so in its liberty of indifference, were bounded by its own natural end, whereas for Scotus, as has already been said, the will is not a natural power at all.

In contrast to "end", "object" has another connotation, viz. that if the will chooses an object, it does so freely, i.e., not for its own sake but for the sake of the object itself, be it God or whatever else. Here another concept of freedom emerges, freedom as radically opposed to nature. And that is why Scotus has been praised as the harbinger of a new era in philosophy and theology, the era of modernity being considered by some to be more in tune with Christianity than the previous one because more detached from paganism and the bounds of nature. It is the era in which Fénélon's doctrine of *amour pur* was already paving the way for Kant's doctrine of a good will untarnished by any taint of selfishness but also the era of Diderot, who, incidentally, wept at Fénélon's grave, as well as of Rousseau, who first defined man as *animal liberum* in a somewhat Scotist sense[26]. Of course, God is only the ultimate object of action, whereas Scotus' contention is that, in order for science to be practical, action itself must be taken as an object but not as an end. But the important thing in any case is to keep open the possibility that right and wrong decisions may be made, either by the will as an independent power, as in Scotus, or by the person as a whole as in Aristotle. If action itself and as such were the last word on the matter, as it is for the Protagorean sophists in Plato's *Euthydemus,* then everyone, irrespective of what the person happens to be doing, would always be right. But then precisely what is needed for practical truth to emerge in the first place would be lacking altogether, whereas if we do not fix on the external activity, i.e., on the factual performance as the end of the matter, but look instead at the object, the tension between rectitude and mistake can be restored and with it the practical character of truth as well as –for Scotus– human theology. And so it is that the text of *Metaphysics* II turns out to offer no evidence at all for the mutual exclusion of *opus* and *veritas* as if the first belonged only to praxis and the second only to theory[27]. With this the imminent danger of practical truth and theology proving to be impossible has been averted. As far as Scotus is concerned, the way is now free to consider even such sentences as "Deus est trinus" or "Pater generat filium" to be instances of practical truth[28] by virtue of the gerundive implicit in

---

[26] For other links between Scotus and Kant in the same vein cf. Chapter 12 above. In other respects one can see Kant as the vanquisher of rationalist metaphysics, which had itself been influenced by Scotus. (Cf. my review mentioned in the Foreword and my closing remarks in the present chapter).

[27] The objection is posed in *Ordinatio,* num. 225 (I 225), but not definitively answered until num. 358 (I 231 f.) where Scotus refers back to num. 252-255, 259, 265-266. My interpretation is borne out by the fact that according to Scotus *theologia divina* "non est practica, quia... [voluntas divina] vel naturaliter tendit in illud [intellectum], vel si libere, nullo modo est de se quasi indifferens ad rectitudinem" (num. 330, I 215), "tunc enim posset peccare" (num. 325, I 212). In short, without the possibility of error or of wrongdoing there can be neither practical science nor practical truth. In this respect Scotus does not depart from Aristotle.

[28] Cf. J. D. Scotus, *Ordinatio,* num. 317, I 209.

them[29]: God is not to be loved only as one person as he is in Islam, etc.

Let me make some attempt at assessing the merits and demerits of the two different positions. It has sometimes been maintained that Scotus has a more general concept of prudence than, e.g., Thomas Aquinas insofar as prudence for the latter only comes to bear on the choice of means in the pursuit of a given end. Whatever the case may be with respect to Aquinas, the fact is that the restriction of the efficacy of prudence to the selection of means does not apply in every respect to Aristotle. Aristotle does not always restrict prudence in the manner attributed to him by Scotus[30]. True, for Aristotle, as for Aquinas, the will is a natural power (ὄρεξις, *appetitus naturalis*) with natural tendencies, as it is not for Scotus. But this does not imply either for Aristotle (or even for Aquinas) that the will is so fixed on happiness as not to be in danger of making the wrong choices even with regard to the true end of life. This may be attributed to the fact that for Aristotle practical reason can be influenced by bad moral habits so as to mistake the wrong course of action for the right one and thus lead the will astray. In this sense moral virtues and prudence are much more intimately connected in Aristotle than they are in Scotus. For in the case just referred to, according to Aristotle there would be no prudence involved, i.e. such a man would not be a prudent man at all. The difference between the two of them in this connection is not based on the impossibility of wrong choices even with regard to the right ends on the part of the Aristotelian approach. It is rather based on the fact that the connection between prudence and the moral virtues in Aristotle cuts both ways: there can be no moral virtue without prudence, as is the case in Scotus as well, but also no prudence without moral virtue, whereas Scotus not only tends to sever the moral virtues from each other but also prudence from the virtues. It is in this

---

[29] Cf. Chapter 6 above.

[30] Cf. Aristotle, *Ethica Nicomachea*, 1142b 33 in conjunction with J. D. Scotus, *Ordinatio*, num. 353 (I 229): "si autem philosophicus possuisse aliquam praxim circa finem".

sense that prudence is for Scotus already on the way to becoming a technique again as it had once been in Plato[31].

One of Scotus' reasons for disconnecting the virtues from each other may be sought in the different possibilities for developing them separately, just as one reason for his disconnecting prudence from the virtues may be sought in the fact that the prudent occasionally make bad choices, despite the fact that Scotus, as we saw, called the *prudens formaliter* virtuous. "In this way, it is easier to understand the moral expert or virtuous person who, though not vicious, is not always virtuous"[32]. One is, in fact, inclined to agree with her in considering this a more realistic approach whose advantages she describes thus: "In this way, Scotus allows for a higher level of moral objectivity than does Aquinas, and still accounts for moral error or sin"[33]. Nevertheless, one can also see the rationale of Aristotle's stance, provided one does not fix on separate faculties, *habitus*, and even actions as *formaliter* different from each other *a parte rei* –the view Aquinas himself was perhaps moving towards with his *analogia secundum intentionem et esse* as distinct from that of the *secundum intentionem tantum*[34]. Therefore I would like to conclude the present chapter with some remarks concerning the advantages which the Aristotelian approach might offer in this respect.

From the point of view of *ens ut ens* accidents do not exist except as modifications of individual substances, though from the point of view of *ens ut verum* (*veritas propositionis*) one can and indeed must consider them as abstractly or conceptually different entities which may truly be ascribed to some individuals. The problem concerning the relationship between the virtues goes back to Plato's *Protagoras*. The thesis to be found there concerning the unity, or indeed, identity

---

[31] Plato was well aware of the problems involved (cf. *Sophista*, 246D). For further developments cf. B. Wald, *Genitrix Virtutum. Zum Wandel des aristotelischen Begriffs der praktischen Vernunft*. Münster 1986.

[32] M.E. Ingham, "Practical Wisdom: Scotus' Presentation of Prudence", *John Duns Scotus. Metaphysics and Ethics*, Leiden / New York 1996, p. 568.

[33] M.E. Ingham "Practical Wisdom", p. 569.

[34] Cf. Chapter 1, section 1 above.

of the virtues sounds paradoxical only if one takes sentences like "Justice is courageous" as normal predications. However, if one takes them, following Gregory Vlastos, in the sense of the so-called Pauline predications ("love is patient", etc.), the paradox disappears. For then this sentence is only shorthand for "Socrates (or whoever) is now (or for whatever time) in some condition or total state or other which can be truly characterized as one of his being just and courageous", and similarly for other sentences. Here one encounters for the first time the real identity of conceptually non-identical determinations (like the road leading from Athens to Thebes and that from Thebes to Athens or the concave and the convex, viz. the μῖξις (*mixtura a parte rei*, but by no means *ratione*) of which Aristotle speaks in his treatment of PET[35]. The same *distinctio rationis cum fundamento in re* applies to the two-way connection between prudence and the moral virtues. In fact, it is not very plausible to assume that bad decisions would are not capable of somehow ruining man's prudence along with his natural orientation to the end of true happiness. Besides, one has to take into account that in the Aristotelian approach to the will nature is not a merely animal instinct unconditioned by historical traditions and the like. This applies also to the Aristotelian conception of natural law, i.e., of that which is by nature right. Classical natural law differs, in fact, very much from the modern conception of human rights[36].

The model of how the virtues are connected with one another which M. McCord-Adams credits to Ockham[37] turns out to be very similar to the Aristotelian one provided one gives up the picture of the relationship between substance and accidents as one involving a fixed

---

[35] Cf. the end-appendix on PET.

[36] Cf. my article "Naturrecht oder Vernunftethik?", in *Rechtstheorie*, 18, 1987, Heft 3, pp. 291-31.

[37] "In a normally varied life, upper level virtue of one kind will not long survive without 'parenting' others". M. McCord-Adams, "Scotus and Okham on the connection of the Virtues", *John Duns Scotus. Metaphysics and Ethics*, p. 521. Cf. also B. Wald's *Genitrix Virtutum* referred to in n. 31 above.

core with accidents moving around it[38]. Nevertheless, the Aristotelian model does not entail those difficulties to which M. McCord-Adams alludes when she asks: "are we to envision the same habit with a series of intensional objects, or a series of numerically distinct habits over time?"[39]. From a genuine Aristotelian standpoint the answer is: over time it is only substance that remains numerically one, as it is only substance that changes over time. "Numerically distinct habits" or, for that matter, "acts"[40] can only mean different total states which the human person continuously undergoes, becoming in the process more or less virtuous. For this reason, there is for Aristotle no point in speaking of moral development, as in Ockham, "in terms of a succession of numerically distinct habits in the agent"[41]. Abstracting from *ens ut ens* or reality as such we can, of course, and indeed must distinguish between different acts as well as between different habits in themselves (i.e. precisely "abstractly"). But between such conceptual distinctions ("*ratione*") and alleged entities in the reality of the morally acting person no one-to-one correspondence may be established.

---

[38] It is true that this picture was inspired by Aristotle's *Categories*, but it is also true that, at least as far as *prima philosophia* is concerned, this work is to be read critically in the light of *Metaphysics* IV, VI-IX and XII, and not, as so often, vice versa (cf. Chapter 5 above).

[39] M. McCord-Adams, "Scotus and Okham on the connection of the Virtues", p. 502.

[40] "According to Scotus, numerically the same act of alms-giving may be contingently virtuous, and indeed first virtuous and then vicious because first done in the right circumstances and then not (or vice versa)". M. McCord-Adams, "Scotus and Okham on the connection of the Virtues", p. 502 (with reference to John Duns Scotus, *God and Creature: The Quodlibeta Questions*, trans. Felix Alluntis and A.B. Wolter, Princeton 1975, secs. 18.8.400: 18.15-23. 403-400). It is difficult to conceive of an act that might be numerically the same over time. Aristotle left such questions unanswered in *Physics*, V, 4 (cf. 228a 19). From a metaphysical point of view there can be no doubt, however, as to how they are to be resolved.

[41] Cf. M. McCord-Adams, "Scotus and Okham on the connection of the Virtues", p. 502.

In the rejection of any sort of *distinctio formalis a parte rei* Ockham, would, of course, acquiesce. As McCord-Adams put it in her book *William Ockham*: "Ockham thinks his really invincible weapon is the principle that it is impossible for contradictories to be simultaneously true about one and the same being –that, in effect, the Indiscernibility of Identicals is the criterion of distinction for real beings"[42]. But the principle has been interpreted in a way that precludes the possibility of distinguishing between *distinctio rationis* and *distinctio a parte rei,* as is apparent from the rider "in every way" which I have stressed in the following quotation: Scotus, "too, was sensitive to the fact that often in philosophy or theology there is reason to deny that x and y are really distinct things (*res*) and yet apparent cause to affirm that x is F and y ist not F. But the Indiscernibility of Identicals, which unquestionably applies to everything that exists in reality, implies that nothing real that is *in every way* the same can be both F and not F"[43]. "In every way the same" means also conceptually or intensionally the same, i.e., *secundum rationem* or κατά τὸ αὐτὸ = τῶν *auton logon*). In other words, the rider precludes the possibility of Socrates, man and white being the same *a parte rei* while differing *secundum rationem* as in Aristotle's treatment of PNC[44]. The rider thus deprives the question posed by McCord-Adams of sense, i.e., whether it is "possible to distinguish within what is really one and the same thing [*res*] nonidentical or distinct property-bearers"[45], by rendering a positive answer impossible from the outset. According to Aristotle there is only one property-bearer, viz. the continuously changing substance in which properties, be they virtues or whatever else, may only be distinguished rationally [*ratione*] from each other and from substance. But the very possibility even of such a minimal *distinctio* has been *a limine* excluded by Ockham. M. McCord-Adams herself implicitly acknowledges this when she writes: "surprisingly, he [Ockham] is

---

[42] M. McCord-Adams, *William Ockham*, Notre Dame University Press 1987, p. 68.
[43] M. McCord-Adams, *William Ockham*, p. 24 (my emphasis).
[44] Cf. Chapter 3 above.
[45] M. McCord-Adams, *William Ockham*, p. 24.

most successful in making this charge [viz. that the view he discusses runs counter to the Indiscernibility of Identicals in one way or other] against one of his most distinguished opponents, viz. Scotus. Most of the others are more imaginative than Ockham fully appreciates in circumventing violations of this principle"[46]. And so, too, I may add, was Aristotle.

As already noted, my last remarks on the relationship between substance and accidents have been made from the metaphysical point of view of *ens ut ens*. This point of view is transcendental in the sense that no empirical confirmation is to be expected from it. It seems to me that moral experience is also in agreement with this state of affairs. For in the end no one can pass moral judgment on persons; one can only, by way of abstraction, pass judgment on modes of behavior, not on tokens as it were but only on types, since in this respect tokens, viz. concrete moral actions (individual accidents) are nothing more than the total condition in which all the accidents that constitute the human person at each stage of her life are *a parte rei* identical with each other and with the person him or herself. Expressed in Christian terms, only God can judge persons[47]. Although this does not, strictly speaking, correspond to the Aristotelian way of putting it, it is not as regards content distinctly un-Aristotelian either. For, according to Aristotle, it is neither reason nor will that decides rightly or wrongly but man himself, just as it is only Nureyev who dances and sweats and not some entity like the dancing Nureyev or his dancing which is presumed to be in Nureyev himself[48].

---

[46] M. McCord-Adams, *William Ockham*, p. 68.

[47] Christianity "came in startlingly with a sword, and clove one thing from another. It divided the crime from the criminal. The criminal we must forgive unto seventy times seven. The crime we must not forgive at all". G.K. Chesterton, *Orthodoxy*, London 1943, p. 158.

[48] Cf. Chapter 1, section 2.

CHAPTER 14
FURTHER DEVELOPMENTS IN THE PROBLEM OF PRACTICAL TRUTH

Before Aristotle practical truth had never been made the subject of philosophical discussion, after him hardly ever. And even Aristotle mentioned this concept only once and even then more in passing[1]. On the other hand he more or less explicitly makes use of it in the passages immediately surrounding this one[2]. In what follows I will also be attending less to the concept itself than to those implicit associations which the expression naturally tends to evoke. Above all I will not be undertaking an exegesis of the relevant texts[3]. These are in any event so scanty that one cannot come very far without appealing to auxiliary hypotheses[4]. The following remarks center around the question of whether practical error is possible. The relevance of this question for our topic is suggested by the following consideration: should the possibility of error be constitutive of practical truth –as will in fact emerge– then its denial would weigh more heavily in the case of practical truth than in that of theoretical truth. For if there were no falsity, then theoretical truth would at least still be necessary whereas practical truth would under the aforementioned circumstances not even be possible.

---

[1] Aristotle, *Ethica Nicomachea*, 1139a 25f.
[2] Cf. Aristotle, *Ethica Nicomachea*, 1139a 29f.
[3] But cf. n. 21 below.
[4] The most painstaking textual exegesis known to me is that of A. Graeser, *Sophistik und Socratik*, ed. W. Röd, *Die Philosophie der Antike*, 2. Teil, München 1983, pp. 239-243.

The stronger the inclination to ground knowledge in action or even to reduce theory to praxis, the more urgently is the need to confront the subject of practical truth brought home. This tendency has made itself noticeable on a wide variety of fronts: not only with respect to the priority of ready-to-handedness [*Zuhandenheit*] over presence-at-hand [*Vorhandenheit*] in Heidegger but also, to give just one further example, in the Kantian and post-Kantian endeavour to conceive of reason not so much as a faculty which only retrospectively swings into action but rather as one which is first constituted through the execution of actions. The present chapter represents part of a more explicit confrontation with this form of endeavour. Such endeavours also bear directly on the relationship between understanding and the will. Some reflections concerning this relationship, which originate within the Aristotelian tradition, stand in close proximity to the pragmatic dimension of truth. This will form the starting-point of what follows (1). After the possibility of practical truth has in the middle section (2) been established by means of a proof of the possibility of practical error, an attempt to apply this entire problematic to the question of whether one may decide to believe something will be discussed in the conclusion (3).

1

Within the Aristotelian tradition Thomas Aquinas among others anticipated what has on occasion been termed a pragmatic contradiction: "There are eleven people in the neighboring room but I don't know it for a fact". The source of the contradiction here lies neither on the logical nor on the semantic plane but on the pragmatic level, namely, in the fact that the person does not see himself in a position to ground his assertion. This is indeed a more or less contingent state of affairs, a more or less factual circumstance. In the germane passages in Aquinas[5] the ability to ground one's own assertions does not in itself constitute a sufficient condition for their being true. Thus one cannot speak in connection with Aquinas of a verificationist theory of truth. Nevertheless the following view espoused by Thomas would seem to grant the pragmatic, and hence verificationist, component priority over a semantic component based on mere correspondence: if, for example, in the case of a prediction, one were with one's statement to have hit upon the truth without, however, having had something to go on (*Anhaltspunkte*), say criteria, then the result can hardly be deemed true. One who had in proceeding from certain criteria failed to arrive at the truth would still have come closer to asserting the truth than one who had haphazardly hit upon it[6]. This seems at first glance to argue in favor of the order of priority already mentioned –subjectivity over objectivity, pragmatics over semantics. If one examines the examples which Aquinas proffers more closely, however, then the verificationist aspect of this conception of truth would seem to recede into the background. Here Aquinas is invoking something akin to the classic example which Aristotle borrows from metereology to explain contingency: whoever erroneously prognosticizes warm weather for the dog days says something true in comparison to someone who correctly maintains the opposite since even if the former were to lose the wager he may at least give good reasons for his prediction. Aquinas is here, as in the case of restoring health[7], clearly thinking of the uniformity of nature which is seldom disrupted by violations of natural law, so that the objective point of view has once again been granted priority over the subjective, the semantic component priority over the pragmatic. The extent to which

---

[5] Thomas Aquinas, *Summa Theologiae*, I, q16, a3; *De Veritate*, I, 9; *In Peri Hermeneias*, Nr. 83-87, 164-204.

[6] This is implied, for example, by the following passage: "De eo enim quod est magis determinatum ad unam partem possumus determinate verum dicere quod hoc erit vel non erit, sicut medicus de convalescente vere dicit, iste sanibitur, licet forte ex aliquo accidente eius sanitas impediatur". Thomas Aquinas, *In Peri Hermeneias*, Nr. 172.

[7] Cf. n. 6 above.

practical truth figures in these considerations has thus in the end been shown to be rather small. This cannot be explained solely by the fact that the examples chosen (warm weather during the dog days, normal convalescence) were taken from the realm of nature. Nevertheless, it is important to note that Thomas Aquinas always demands from a perfect concept of truth (*ratio perfecta veritatis*) not only conformity (*adaequatio*) but at the same time a moment of reflexivity, which corresponds to the pragmatic component[8].

This reflexivity, which for Thomas is required by the *ratio perfecta veritatis*, brings us one step closer to the realm of practical truth. *Qua* reflexive this reflexivity is initially attributed only to reason, and then only to a reason which has already been conceived as theoretical. The reflexive structure, however, belonging to reason is also characteristic of the will to an extent which could not have been fully appreciated by Thomas[9] and even less so by Aristotle. The will and desire (ὄρεξις) in general, though, play a decisive role in practical truth. Already Aristotle had expressly noted that practical truth, whatever else it might be, must in any event coincide with the correct form of desire[10].

The reflexive character of reason differs from that of the will on one decisive point. This distinction may be so characterized that intentionality belongs only to the reflexive character of theoretic reason. Here intentionality is to be understood not in the sense of purposefulness but simply as that type of identity which is not physical or, more generally, real. To be sure, one may already speak of intentionality in the sense of intentional identity in connection with concepts in which the kind of reflexivity peculiar to truth can of course not yet be found. But the concept corresponds exclusively to the semantic moment of *adaequatio* with the known. Only with the judgment does a reflexive knowledge of this correspondence arise. And it is precisely for this reason that the concept of truth culminates

---

[8] Cf. among other texts *Summa Theologiae*, I, q16, a2 and *De Veritate*, I, 9.

[9] But cf. Thomas Aquinas, *De Veritate*, 24, 3 and above all *De Malo*, VI.

[10] Aristotle, *Ethica Nicomachea*, 1139a 24, 30f.

in judgment[11]. Thus, whereas an identification of the knower with the known has already been brought about during the process of concept-formation, it is only with the formation of judgments that a reflexivity or identification of the knower with himself occurs. However, in the former as in the latter case it is a question, so long as the will remains uninvolved, of detached identification. In neither case does the act of knowing result in a complete identification of the knower with what is known, even if this should be himself.

The case of that which is known being unlike that which knows poses no special difficulties for the understanding of this detachment: simply by virtue of the fact that I know something I do not become it myself nor do I myself become like it. And that is also true of perceptual knowledge. Whoever sees something red does not himself become red just as little as one need oneself become ill in order to be able to diagnose an illness. Plato had already called attention to this fact, which renders the imitation model of knowledge invalid[12]. In this respect Aristotle expresses himself unclearly when he remarks laconically that the knower becomes like the known but does not become the known itself[13]. Obviously the non-passivity and the absence of endurance (*Erleidenslosigkeit*) which Aristotle requires of the knower must extend further. If one is nevertheless entitled to speak of a passivity and a capacity to endure (*Erleidensfähigkeit*) in connection with theoretical knowledge, then at most in the sense that a mirror does not itself become either the mirrored or like the mirrored: i.e., it does not itself become, e.g., a red reflection but a reflection of red –which is something completely different. Indeed intentionality in

---

[11] "Veritas quidem igitur potest esse in sensu, vel in intellectu cognoscente quid est, ut in quadam re vera: non autem ut cognitum in cognoscente, quod importat nomen veri". Thomas Aquinas, *Summa Theologiae*, I, q16, a3. "Cognoscitur autem (veritas) ab intellectu secundum quod intellectus reflectitur supra actum suum, non solum secundum quod cognoscit actum suum, sed secundum quod cognoscit proportionem ejus ad rem... Unde secundum hoc cognoscit veritatem intellectus quod supra se ipsum reflectitur". Thomas Aquinas, *De Veritate*, I, 9.

[12] Plato, *Republic*, 438 E.

[13] Aristotle, *De Anima* 429a 15f.; cf. 424a 24.

the sense of intentional identity, which may already be found in perceptual knowledge, consists in nothing else. And the detachment which one encounters in all cases of theoretical knowledge consists in nothing other than this. This, too, is a form of praxis but considered in itself not a praxis by virtue of which one might really become different, i.e., either better or worse than before, depending upon what has been known, by virtue of which one might, in short, become like the known.

This type of detachment is, however, characteristic not only of the so-called perceptual or intellectual *simplex apprehensio* but also of the judgments of reason through which it not only knows something objectively but in conformity with this also recognizes in the things and facts known its own adequacy in knowing them. Even in the case of this reflexivity, which is required by a purely active principle[14] and hence by a heightened activity or "practicality", the detachment peculiar to theory has still not been abandoned. Without the participation of the will the knowledge of one's own self can, like one's knowledge of another, aspire to no more than an identity which remains both before and afterwards purely intentional. Although in the process of knowing the subject turns back completely upon itself[15], it remains uninvolved the whole time. Even in the case of self-knowledge one remains at a distance from oneself. One does not in so doing become more or less oneself. But this is not because one is already oneself. The identification with oneself in which the turning back upon oneself consists is not without result: it brings about something. It constitutes, in fact, a praxis but this praxis does not change the knower himself and is in this sense unchanging. The accumulation of knowledge is what this praxis consists in; all it brings about is knowledge. But this knowledge is not such that I myself

---

[14] Thomas points this out in the intermediate phrase which had been omitted in the last quotation (n. 11), "quae cognosci non potest, nisi cognoscatur natura principii activi, quod est ipse intellectus". Thomas Aquinas, *De veritate*, I, 9

[15] "Reditione completa", as Thomas Aquinas says a little further in the same passage.

become different, i.e., better or worse. For this to happen the active intervention of the will as distinct from the intellect is necessary.

Thomas Aquinas has himself called attention to the fact that theoretical judgments of knowledge are despite their reflexivity actually non-subjective and unchanging in the sense just mentioned[16]. He does this every time the question of whether the will represents a higher faculty than that of the intellect arises. In and for itself, Thomas replies, (*simpliciter*) the intellect is the higher faculty but not with respect to becoming better or worse. It is in this latter respect that the will is of more importance for the agent. As far as his becoming better or worse is concerned it is worth more to him than his intellect or reason since this depends more on the will than on reason. In a crucial respect the will may be said to be even more properly ours than reason, and not simply because we can do nothing to alter the fact that we are endowed with reason. In a certain sense we can in fact do something about it, namely, we can determine in each case how much reason and thus how much generality we may lay claim to. But even then only to a limited degree. And this is once again an affair of the will. For regardless of how much effort we devote to extending the boundaries of our reason, we can never pass beyond them. They are in effect bestowed upon us by nature whereas those of the will, which most certainly exist, have at least not been fixed in every respect. With this we stand already before a crucial respect in which the will is more properly ours than reason so that it must be worth more to us than reason since as far as we are concerned more in fact depends on it. We might express this aspect as follows: whereas reason or the intellect belongs to our natural equipment, the will is not necessarily given to us in every aspect by nature. The Scholastics speak here of a double will. The terminology which they, including Thomas Aquinas, employ is somewhat confusing for our purposes. They speak on the one hand of a *voluntas ut natura* and on the other –and this is the source of the confusion– of a *voluntas ut ratio*[17]. This terminology is confusing

---

[16] Cf. Thomas Aquinas, *Summa Theologiae*, I, q82, a3 and *De Veritate*, 22, 11.

[17] Thomas Aquinas, *Summa Theologiae*, III, q18, a3; Thomas notes that this terminology reflects common usage among the Masters.

insofar as one might be tempted to infer that the will as *voluntas ut ratio* is in fact in every respect identical with reason, in other words that we are here standing before the common origin of theory and praxis, at the root of subjectivity as it were.

In order to avoid possible misunderstandings I would like to adopt here another terminology. Thus, rather than speaking of *voluntas ut natura* we should like to say on the one hand that the will can be a faculty of man, or if one prefers, of the soul. And it is doubtless this as well. I say, however, "can be" in order to retain at least this much of the scholastic distinction between *voluntas ut natura* and *voluntas ut ratio*: namely, that this distinction involves not the will *qua* faculty –as such it is one and may in no way constitute a duality– but only the will as act[18]. As distinct from this we would like, on the other hand, to speak of the will as not being a faculty at all and so as not being something that might have been conferred by nature. In this sense the will is only that for which it decides in each case. It is what it does in each case or –to put a more paradoxical gloss on it– that which it makes of itself in each case; still more paradoxically expressed: it is only the use to which it puts itself in each case. That this does not imply the absurdity of a *creatio ex nihilo* is explained not only by the fact that man consists of more than just will but also by the fact that the will is *itself* a faculty.

With this qualification in mind –which would have to be developed further if the whole of subjectivity were to be reduced to praxis and hence the distinction between reason and will were to be eradicated altogether– it would be advisable to retain the notion of a will which exhausts itself in the use to which it puts itself[19]. Here two points are to be found commingled which are immediately related to practical truth. The first has to do with the fact that there can be no use of the will such that it would turn the will against itself. At the same time this implies that since will and use are identical here, the errors of the

---

[18] "Haec autem diversitas actus non diversificat potentiam". *STh.*, III, q18, a3.

[19] In this connection the Scholastics sometimes spoke of *voluntas ut voluntas*. Although Thomas Aquinas himself, as has already been said, did not, Petrus a Bergamo in his *Tabula Aurea* on Thomas surely did.

will cannot, like the errors of reason, simply be attributed to misuse; to put it differently, that the will cannot err *per accidens,* (which is the only form of error open to reason) that its erring is an erring *per se* and thus again a self-erring. With this the question of the will's capacity for truth has already been raised. Again the second point touches upon the specifically practical (and as such not only non-theoretical but also thoroughly non-natural or even unnatural) character of such a will where the use is thought to engender its own possibility. These points are intimately related to one another.

2

Reason is not in itself immediately practical. Insofar as it constitutes part of our natural equipment it requires the stimulus of both objects and the will in order to be roused into activity; it is no different from the senses in having first to be stimulated by physical objects. We are made capable of seeing –says Aristotle[20]– not by virtue of our having seen many things but rather it is because we are endowed with organs of sight that we also see in actuality. And that according to Aristotle applies to all things that are ours by nature and not *by virtue of ourselves*, i.e., to all those things with which we are neither fully identified nor with which we can fully identify ourselves. Moreover reason is not in itself practical but essentially a natural capacity because it does not bring about changes either in the world or in us, and least of all changes of the sort that would make of us better human beings.

In the case of the will the situation is at least partially reversed. Insofar as the will exhausts itself in use, actuality precedes capacity –as with all things, according to Aristotle, that subsist independently of or not only with respect to nature, as in the case of the ethical virtues[21]. Thus here it is conversely the function that first engenders

---

[20] Aristotle, *Ethica Nicomachea*, 1103a 28-31.

[21] Cf. Aristotle, *Ethica Nicomachea*, 1103a 26ff.

the organ. To be sure this circumstance, namely, that actuality precedes possibility, application acquisition, activity disposition, and use possession, is paradoxical. But it is presumably no more paradoxical than the phenomenon of freedom itself. Now, again unlike reason, the will, insofar as it is constituted by this paradox, cannot err merely through misuse. There can be a misuse of reason which first gives rise to the possibility of theoretical error, but insofar as the will exhausts itself in use there can be no misuse of the will through which it would first be capable of erring. A will that does not subsist by nature may of course also err but not in the way reason does, i.e., simply *per accidens*. A will that does not simply subsist as part of pure nature –and something like this belongs to the very essence of a free will– is not only capable of error, it, and it alone, must in fact be so *per se*. Now when an interpreter like Wolfgang Wieland denies this will every capacity for error[22], then only because he is assuming the Platonic standpoint, only half-heartedly corrected by Aristotle[23], according to which the will is totally lacking in autonomy with respect to reason. In so doing, however, one obscures the distinction between a *per se* error and a *per accidens* error. From the Platonic point of view there can be only a *per accidens* erring, i.e., only errors arising from subsequent misuse, i.e. a use that runs counter to a previously constituted nature: either (as in Plato) the use of reason against itself

---

[22] Wieland speaks in this context of a purely factual will (which is to be rejected from that standpoint which he on this point apparently shares with Plato): "One can of course define away all moments of an action which are susceptible of error as belonging to its boundary conditions. A factual will which would to be sure be capable of accepting norms but would no longer be capable of error would then remain as the core of the action. Between that which one should not do and that which one "actually" does not want to do there would arise an opposition which one might attribute in a number of cases at most to errors of the agent as to the existence or non-existence of a certain state of affairs. Where such reductions are no longer possible one would then be confronted with a will which is now purely factual and no longer capable of error". W. Wieland, *Platon und die Formen des Wissens*, p. 265.

[23] With the exception of Book VII of the *Ethica Nicomachea*. Cf. *De Anima*, 433a 24f.

or (elsewhere) the use of the will against itself. Where there is, however, no nature –as in the case of the will as a self-creating function– contrary to which one might act, it is not the case that every capacity for error would be excluded. On the contrary, here with the possibility of erring *per se* a new aspect of the capacity for error comes into view. On account of this new aspect one may no longer, strictly speaking, refer to erring but only to an erring of one's self or a falling short of one's self, not to detached deciding –which would apply just as well to reason and theory– but to a personal choosing between possible alternatives, i.e., of a decision by one's self for one's self.

That the will cannot be used in opposition to a nature which it does not, in fact, possess (i.e., that there is no *willenswidriger Gebrauch des Willens*) does not imply that a *voluntas ut voluntas*[24] is incapable of error. Whoever is of this opinion presumes with Plato that the will must always choose for itself the Good. But only he can choose *for himself* the good who may also choose for himself what is evil. But only he can choose for himself what is evil, and is capable of choosing it knowingly. This is according to Plato impossible for human beings. They must obey the dictates of reason. It follows, then, that for him there can be no practical error. And this in turn implies that man is not brought to err by himself but that he is misled by reason, or more precisely, by a misuse of reason. Therefore there are, once again, no *per se* errors. Even in Plato there are indications[25] that the misuse of reason may itself to some extent be traced back to the will but they amount to no more than that. The subject was, however, actively taken up by the late Scholastics[26]. We cannot pursue this further here. We

---

[24] Something of the sort has been –in accordance with principles laid down by Thomas– called *libertas indifferentiae*. Here what is at issue is the freedom of decision (*liberum arbitrium*) characteristic of finite, or more precisely, of contingent rational creatures. One might also speak here of a "contingent will". Cf. my essay "Kontingenz und Willensfreiheit".

[25] Cf. Plato, *Sophist*, 246D.

[26] Walter von Brügge, for example, regards the desire not to know as the paradigm of moral shortcoming (cf. E. Stadter, *Psychologie und Metaphysik der menschli-*

need only keep in mind the distinction between theoretical and genuinely practical errors. Only in the case of the latter is it a question of errors about which (and that means also against which) one could have *in principle*, disregarding some isolated cases, done something. Only here does subjectivity together with personal responsibility come fully into its own as a reflexivity which can in principle, in contrast to the mere intentionality of reason, lead to a freely chosen *identité assumée* with oneself. What becomes evident here is the moral dimension of praxis and simultaneously with it praxis as such in its opposition to theory but also to τέχνη. Before we consider this more closely, let us already call attention to the following at this point: from the fact that the will has proven itself to be capable of error –and this to an especially high degree– it may reasonably be inferred that this will have direct consequences for the concept of practical truth. Error and truth are in fact correlative concepts. If the practical erring of the self differs so greatly from theoretical error, practical truth will also evince features substantially different from those of theoretical truth.

The distinction between theoretical and practical error may be blurred by proceeding from one of two mutually opposed extremes: either intellectualistically as in Plato or voluntaristically[27]. In both cases the peculiar character of practical truth as well as of practical error falls by the wayside. In the case of theoretical error one stands at least ideally before an alternative: either one arrives at one's goal or one falls short of it, whereby the goal is to be conceived as an objectively univocal state of affairs. The falling short of and the failure to arrive at one's goal are here viewed as states of non-knowledge[28] –and even more so, the very absence of an attempt. In both respects practical error is different: first, one is usually concerned with more than a single alternative, and secondly, the shortfall (but also the absence of an attempt) need not always be purely negative and so morally irrelevant. Both points, which correspond to the

---

chen Freiheit. Die ideengeschichtliche Entwicklung zwischen Bonaventura und Duns Scotus, Paderborn/Vienna 1971, pp. 78-81). Cf. also Chapter 10 above.

[27] See n. 35 and 43 below.

[28] Cf. Plato, *Republic*, V as well as Aristotle, *Metaphysics*, IX, 10.

distinction between *libertas specificationis* and *libertas executionis* respectively (to act in such-and-such a manner, on the one hand, and to act or not to act on the other) are important in connection with practical truth.

In the case of a "theoretical decision as to whether or not" one is only concerned with a single alternative because all possibilities apart from the correct one are regarded as comprising a single whole: as a falling short or false alternative. Here it does not –ideally, as we have said– depend on us which one qualifies as the correct one, rather, we are absolved from having to make a decision by the subject-matter itself. When correctly viewed that which in theory corresponds to the *libertas specificationis* reduces to that which in praxis corresponds to the *libertas exercitii*. Here it is a matter of secondary importance whether one does not attain truth by falling short of it or by failing to carry through the attempt. In the realm of praxis (i.e., of "personal decision for or against"), by contrast, a failure to decide may have grave consequences. Whoever fails to choose for himself here has already by virtue of this very fact chosen. And through his abstention he may just as easily have hit upon what is correct, which is in itself revealing enough, as, which is even more revealing, have done something wrong. This implies that a very different sense accrues to "falling short" here. It is not neutral, it is not situated beyond or even at the margins of praxis, but just like hitting upon what is correct it is to be found in the center. Again this does not imply a leveling of the distinction between correct and incorrect, true and false, good and bad, or even evil. On the contrary, the fact that falling short of what is correct cannot be excluded, that, even in those cases where it rests on a failure to decide for oneself, it stands in the center of the domain of praxis as one of its possible alternatives just like the decision which hits upon what is correct, may be attributed to the fact that here the possibilities do not already lie in waiting, ready for use, but are themselves first constituted through praxis as such. This is no more paradoxical than something which we have already encountered, it is indeed a necessary consequence of it: namely, that in the case of all things which are not given by nature and thus in the case of practical truth and of practical error as well, possibility does not exist before actuality but rather first comes into being after it, just as ability follows upon deed, organ upon function[29].

If, however, the possibilities do not already lie ready but as it were await our decision in order to come into existence, then it is in a certain sense a matter of indifference whether they are the right or the wrong possibilities. In a certain sense they are all on a par with one another: they are all *my* possibilities, possibilities for the person who decides such-and-such for himself, even by not deciding. In this sense none of them is to be distinguished from any other –not even the correct decision, let alone the ones which fall short of it. The situation is very different in the case of theoretical knowledge where it is usually meaningless to speak of false knowledge. Knowledge in the ordinary sense of the word is either true knowledge or no knowledge at all. In praxis, by contrast, this disjunction is not valid: It is not simply that a failure to decide here may still constitute a decision, but even a decision which falls short –regardless of whether it owes its existence to abstention or not– is a decision; although not the correct one, it is without a doubt genuine. One may also express this as follows: the possibility of a shortfall is immanent to praxis but not to theory. This is but another way of saying that whereas reason can err only *per accidens*, namely through misuse, the will can also err *per se*, and insofar as it is *qua* contingent will endowed with a *libertas indifferentiae*, it can only err *per se*. Irrespective of whether it decides correctly or incorrectly for itself, it does not decide against its own factual "nature" since there is no nature against which it might be turned (and hence no use of the will that might be deemed "*willenswidrig*").

A consequence as well as a question follows from the preceding. The consequence is that if the possibility of falling short is constitutive of praxis, then the right praxis –and, insofar as it also represents a reasonable praxis, the right reason– must be a corrected praxis, the *recta ratio* a *correcta ratio*[30]. Under these circumstances,

---

[29] Aristotle, *Ethica Nicomachea*, II, 1.

[30] In response to a previous attempt on my part to define practical truth A. Graeser (*Sophistic und Sokratik*, p. 312, n. 121) had written partly in approval, partly in

however, since right and wrong have drawn so close to one another, the question, what is meant by right and wrong, successful and misguided, true and false, acquires a certain urgency. Is error possible at all in the realm of praxis?

The problem of practical truth is closely related in Aristotle to that of the practical syllogism. There is, however, a technico-practical and an ethico-practical syllogism. We intend to consider the otherwise sufficiently well-known distinction between τέχνη and praxis only insofar as it is able to shed light on the problem of practical truth. The distinction is already essential to our last question, viz. to what extent one can with respect to praxis speak of right or wrong, indeed whether error is at all possible here. At the same time it will allow us to

---

reproof: "The identification of practical truth with ὀρθός λόγος (φρόνησις) is certainly dubious and finds no support in the text itself. The second idea, however, touches upon an extremely important perspective which deserves to be pursued further". This second perspective is the one developed in the text above. This entire chapter is, if you like, an attempt to "pursue it further". In another earlier article it had been somewhat more fully worked out than it was in the passage of the essay from which Graeser had excerpted it: "Theorie der Praxis als praktische Theorie. Zur Eigenart der aristotelischen Ethik", see p. 61 in addition to the rest). As regards Graeser's critical comments I would like to note: 1. The scholastic definition of *prudentia* as *recta ratio agibilium* certainly represents an extremely loose adaptation of 1140b 5 but finds literal support in 1144b 27f. 2. My identification of practical truth with a *recta ratio*, which if it coincides with anything then only with the ὀρθὴ ὄρεξις, with the right form of desire" (cf. my essay "Theoretische und praktische Wahrheit", p. 164) is to be sure hypothetical. But the investigations of Kenny and of Graeser himself have shown that practical truth will at any rate have much in common with the means-ends relationship. So, without entirely abandoning the realm of the purely hypothetical I should like to add here the following remarks which are developed further in the main text above: right reason as defined by the technico-practical syllogism must, if one is to be able to speak of practical truth, first be brought into alignment with a form of correct desire. On the other hand right reason in the sense of the ethico-practical syllogism, if one is to speak here of practical truth as well, must always, already as far as the selection of means is concerned, be in conformity with right desire, since one cannot of course separate means from ends here.

remove some doubts which naturally suggest themselves after the preceding remarks.

There can be no doubt that much of what has in the preceding been discussed under the rubric of "practical error" or "practical truth" would apply equally well to science and thus to theory. We need only think of the experimental sciences. Aristotle's dictum, "In the sciences there is no such thing as correctness or error, and the correctness of opinion is truth"[31], does not apply to them. In a science conceived as purely theoretical, correctness and incorrectness lie far apart. It was no accident that we have up until now as far as the concept of science has been concerned focused on the ideal case of pure theory. But this is not the only type of science possible. This, however, does not imply that the basic distinction between theory and praxis should be abandoned nor that the one should be reduced to the other. To appreciate this one need only recall that what is meant with the practical features of a theory are really technical features. With Aristotle τέχνη came to be considered an intermediate realm which combined in itself the characteristics of theory as well as of praxis in the strict sense of morality. In order to answer the question, what in praxis, at least in moral praxis, "correct" and "incorrect" mean, and so to arrive at the concept of practical, as opposed to theoretical, truth we must therefore eliminate all technical features from it. In order to do so we will take as our point of departure the general question, whether error is at all possible.

This question was first raised with respect to both the theoretical and practical realms in sophistic circles. As far as the former was concerned the sophists answered the question in the negative: there can be no false knowledge. Plato, however, struggled not only against this sophistic thesis but independently of it explicitly posed the question of whether in the realm of action there could be something like exemption from error or even infallibility. In the case of an affirmative answer correctness and incorrectness –which in the case of moral praxis at any rate lie extremely close to one another insofar as the morally good would not be possible without the freedom to choose

---

[31] Aristotle, *Ethica Nicomachea*, 1142b 10f.

evil or the possibility of the morally wrong– would completely coincide.

Plato's entire confrontation with the sophists as regards the possibility of exemption from error and infallibility within the realm of action finds its most succinct expression in the sentence: *virtutis non est virtus*. The sentence itself first appears in Aristotle, but the sentiment may be found as early as Plato[32]. It should be supplemented by *artis, sed non virtutis, est virtus*, although in Aristotle "φρόνησις" stands in the place of "*virtutis*" ("*prudentiae*")[33]. Still that is of no consequence here. More important –and more difficult– is the second occurrence of "*virtus*" ("ἀρετή"). Often it has been translated, and not badly, as we shall see, by "perfection"[34]. At first glance this supplementary phrase may be understood to have at least two meanings: first that whoever is able to do something, i.e. has a skill at his disposal, need not, simply because he has it, put it to use, and secondly, he need not, simply because he has it, act in comformity with it in his capacity as an expert. Already here the affinity between theory and τέχνη becomes apparent. Both are activities or types of praxis –only that τέχνη is oriented toward activity or praxis in the specific sense of change whereas this is inapplicable to theory. The fact, however, that τέχνη is oriented toward change means only that whoever has this skill at his disposal *may* in conformity with it bring about this change. With this, though, nothing has been said as to whether he will do it. This is chiefly due to two factors, both of which lie outside τέχνη as such: first, whether he who is able to do something also *wishes* to do it, and secondly, in the case of his being able to or wanting to, whether he also intends to execute it in conformity with rules of practice.

---

[32] Cf. Plato, *Republic*, 342A-E. In this passage when read in conjunction with the *Hippias Minor* are to be found the origins of the Aristotelian claim which one may loosely translate as follows: virtue, as distinct from technical skill, need not be supplemented by virtue.

[33] Aristotle, *Ethica Nicomachea*, 1140b 22.

[34] E.g., in O. Gigon's translation.

A deviation from the rules of practice need not in the case of τέχνη already constitute a professional blunder but it must be justified. The technical is never an end in itself but is always the means to something else. This makes deviation possible in principle. Its justification must, then, be vouchsafed by this other, i.e., by an extra-technical, goal. To be sure, he who intentionally makes a mistake is a better technician than he who allows one to creep in unawares, but not therefore a better human being. For it is possible that under the then prevailing circumstances the mistake could not be justified by any superordinate goal. Still the question as to justification is as far as τέχνη is concerned in principle always appropriate. This has ramifications that extend to vital issues. The physician is committed to curing the patient but the preservation of life is not always the best thing that could happen to a patient –a decision as to which, however, never falls within the competence of the physician *qua* physician. But he who undertakes such a separation of means from ends in the realm of morality as well makes of ethics a technique. Everything which one does is then, as in the case of a technique, only necessary insofar as it is expedient. Everything which one does in a given case thus becomes a means from which one may always deviate as the need arises and from which one in fact must deviate if another, perhaps contrary but more effective means presents itself. The result is that there can be neither absolute prescriptions (*Gebote*) nor absolute prohibitions (*Verbote*). Certainly errors are still possible according to this finalistic conception of morals and this in the double sense of a subjective and of an objective erring. Errors in the sense of an objective erring are namely possible when the consequences of the measure taken are poorly suited to the goal for whose sake it had been adopted. This is the consequentialist side of the finalistic conception of morals. Again according to this conception mistakes in the sense of a subjective erring of self are possible, if the correct subjective attitude is lacking, namely because one did not choose the good as the guiding principle for action. Both correspond roughly[35] to the two moments on the basis

---

[35] Only roughly because it is precisely the intertwining of means and ends in moral action which forbids both a purely objectivistic-intellectualistic and a subjectivistic-voluntaristic solution. Cf. also Chapter 8 above.

of which Aristotle distinguishes an ethical from a technical praxis[36]. But whereas the correct subjective attitude for Aristotle –just as it was for the classical conception of moral theology– was also merely a necessary condition for the morality of an action, it is for the opposing position, which is sometimes advocated in moral theology, already a sufficient one. This is a necessary consequence of the uncoupling of means from ends. Through this uncoupling the means –which are nothing other than that which one in each case does– become morally neutralized. From now on any type of action at all, including the murder of innocent human beings, even of one's own mother[37], is in principle allowed. The only limits which are henceforth acknowledged to be moral are no longer set by that which moral theology had once called "the object of the act" (what one does) but from an attitude which has itself been cut loose from every form of *a priori* bond. This then assumes the form of a perfect conscience free from error. Conscience as the only binding authority no longer allows –as is the case in Thomas[38]– for the possibility that one could in following this conscience, which for the agent is binding, incur guilt[39]. In other words conscience here has in fact become absolute[40]. Precluded is above all the possibility of the so-called *peccata ignota*[41]. The only type of guilt still possible would be that of ignorance. If, however, conscience can no longer orient itself with respect to a moral

---

[36] Cf. Aristotle, *Ethica Nicomachea*, 1105a 26-1105b 12.

[37] Aristotle himself gives this example (cf. *Ethica Nicomachea*, 1110a 23-29). It is consistent with his point of view that he generally assigns limits to the application of the principle for assessing goods or weighing them against each other (cf. *Ethica Nicomachea*, 1107a 8-25).

[38] Cf. Thomas Aquinas, *De Veritate*, XVII, 4, A.

[39] Cf. my essay "Freiheit" in *Persönliche Verantwortung*, P. Geach, F. Inciarte, R. Spaemann (eds.), Köln 1982, p. 93 ff.

[40] Cf. my "Theonomie, Autonomie und das Problem der politischen Macht", *Theologische Revue*, Münster 1982, Column 95f.

[41] Cf. n. 44 as well as "Autonomie und Theonomie des Gewissens", in L. Elders, F. Inciarte, P. Rodriguez, *Die Person im Anspruch sittlicher Normen*, St. Augustin 1981, pp. 18-53. Cf. also Chapter 15 below.

authority, since the latter in fact no longer exists, then the possibility of ignorance is ruled out from the very start: conscience (*Gewissen*) here is tantamount to certainty[42] and certainty (*Gewißheit*), in turn, to truth. In keeping with this, however, it would likewise be precluded that the peculiar character of practical truth, as distinct from theoretical truth, might consist in a concept of correctness (*rectitudo*, ὀρθότης) which would at the same time be constituted by the possibility of incorrectness. In those cases where, due to the strict exclusion of every form of *libertas indifferentiae*, freedom *qua* autonomy only allows for a choice of the good the concept of morality itself has already been abolished[43].

The advantage that is to be obtained by uncoupling the realm of means and thus that of action from that of ends is at first glance very great but reveals itself upon due deliberation to be negligible. Admittedly, with the instrumentalization of the means-ends relation finalistic ethics succeeds in circumventing the chasm of cynicism. Insofar, however, as it sees itself by virtue of the moral neutralization of every type of action relieved of the necessity of having to assume the principle according to which the good sanctifies all means, it also, in doing away with the possibility of a distinction between technique and praxis, dispenses with the possibility of morality. This elimination consists not simply in the elimination of evil but more precisely in the fact that the possibility of evil is set off in a radical way from that of good. To be sure, both good and evil still remain as possibilities. And both possibilities are also realized. But they are realized independently

---

[42] Cf. n. 40.

[43] Here the theorems of a utilitarian (or consequentialist) ethics overlap with those of an antiutilitarian ethics in the Kantian sense. To point to contradictions in the Kantian position, however, does not in itself constitute a justification of the utilitarian position. All the less so when objective utilitarianism is bound up with an ethics of conscience or conviction (*Gesinnungsethik*). For more on this cf. the discussion surrounding R. Spaemann's essay "Verantwortung" in the anthology cited in n. 39: *Herder-Korrespondenz*, November 1982 - February 1983. I have treated this topic under the aspect of extortionability in a lecture which has since appeared in print, *Ethica della responsibilità ed etica della convinzione*, Documenti CRIS, Rome 1983.

of one another. Whoever has decided for himself to have a good attitude is incapable –as long as he persists in this attitude– of moral failure. And conversely for whoever has chosen the contrary maxim; only a conversion might save him. The exclusive orientation with respect to these two extremes –which borders on the Calvinist *praedestinatio gemina*– leaves the genuine moral realm unexamined.

This intermediate realm, from which incidentally the bestowal of grace need not be excluded, is the realm of what Aristotle had called continence (ἐνκράτεια) and incontinence (ἀκρασία). In the beginning the two mutually opposed possibilities of good and evil lie side by side in this realm, and the separation of the two can only occur subsequently on the basis of decisions which may at any time be overruled. To this extent the *rectitudo* of the *recta ratio* (ὀρθός λόγος) and of the *appetitus rectus* (ὀρθὴ ὄρεξις) is the result of a more or less strenuous, depending on the moral steadfastness involved, overcoming of the contrary possibility. The *rectitudo* itself is then to be understood as a correction and the *recta ratio* as in fact being a *correcta ratio*. Otherwise the realm of the specifically moral vanishes. Where, however, there can be no practical error, there can also be no practical truth. To retain this concept one must therefore eliminate those technical features from praxis which are determinative of a consequentialist ethics. This implies that the concept of a (moral)-practical truth is irreconcilable with consequentialism. The repudiation of practical error by consequentialism runs parallel to the sophists' repudiation of theoretical error –with the exception that the consequences for the concept of truth are perhaps even more momentous in the former case than they are in the latter: on the one hand elimination of practical truth, on the other the exclusive validity of theoretical truth. Some brief comments concerning these partial parallels may be of help[44].

To the sophistic denial of the possibility of error in the realm of knowledge, Plato opposes his distinction between that of which we speak and that which we say about it. From this point on it was no

---

[44] A more exhaustive presentation would have had to have worked out, among other tasks, the holistic components of sophistic and of consequentialism.

longer possible to question PNC, i.e. to deny the possibility of contradictory opinions of which at least one would have to be false by appealing to the thesis that such opinions, insofar as they are distinct from one another, cannot refer to the same thing. In order to refute the sophistic position it was thus not absolutely necessary to reject the other thesis of the sophists which equates knowing nothing with not-knowing and knowing something with producing it. One will, however, always tend to favor this other means of refuting the sophistic position over the Platonic one if one fails to distinguish between knowing and acting by reducing the former to the latter. To be sure, one may then go on interpreting knowledge in terms of intentionality but the latter will from now on be understood as an intention to be realized. If the intention is realized, then the cognition is true, otherwise it is false. Truth now signifies the success, falsity the falling short of an intention. Here the distinction between truth and appearance need not as with the sophists have been annuled. The distinction between "true" and "false" can in fact be preserved (as in Gerold Prauss)[45]. The question is only: at what price?

In these circumstances the distinction between "true" and "false" must at any rate be subjected to a radical reformulation with respect to the Platonic position. Insofar as the semantic dimension is made to recede behind the pragmatic, truth in particular becomes verification and this in turn becomes the realization of possibilities that did not formerly exist. Does this not reduce truth to practical truth as well? Certainly not to the Aristotelian conception of practical truth insofar as it is not voluntaristic nor can it be conceived according to the categories of success and failure. As far as a voluntaristic interpretation of practical truth is concerned, only one of the components distinguished by Aristotle –the right reason (ὀρθός λόγος) and the correct form of endeavor (ὀρθὴ ὄρεξις)– namely the latter, can in the final analysis remain. The distinction between correctness and incorrectness can after this only be arbitrary. Such an interpretation is inevitable if the exemption of technical reason from error presupposed

---

[45] Cf. among other texts Prauss's *Einführung in die Erkenntnistheorie*, Darmstadt 1980.

by Plato and Aristotle is transferred to the realm of ultimate ends, i.e., to the moral realm. As a result of this exemption from error the expert, when he makes what seems to be a mistake, does not realize his original intention, as we have seen, but pursues in reality a different and superordinate one. This must, of course, come to an end with the good life as the ultimate end –unless one assumes a plurality of such absolute ends or life-projects[46].

---

[46] "In the end the real point of contention must always revolve around the question of whether the whole of human action may without remainder be subsumed within a teleogical order or whether there is a point at which man stands before the choice of several teleological (world-)orders, among which he can no longer choose by orienting himself with respect to a superordinate teleology. Thus what is at issue here is the question of whether an absolute goal has been prescribed for human action in its entirety, in which case human action would no longer lie fully within the agent's sphere of influence or whether the opposite is not in fact the case". W. Wieland, *Plato und die Formen des Wissens*, p. 268. E. Tugendhat (*Selbstbewußtsein und Selbstbestimmung*, p. 238) has expressed himself in favor of a plurality of goals: "In reflecting we come to a highest point where we can no longer objectively ground our decision but where rather that which corresponds to my highest good, is itself first constituted by my will... If this were not the case, the willing [*Wollen*] might still without further appeal be able to support itself with reasons, but the will would in this way lose its gravity, as it were, its seriousness, and this means: it would no longer constitute my having taken a stand [*Stellungnahme*]". Even assuming there to be a single goal in life, however, one may still speak of one's own decision, i.e., when one (necessarily) desires the goal but not the means (necessary) to reach it. In this case it is precisely the correspondence required by Aristotle between ὀρθός λόγος and ὀρθὴ ὄρεξις that is lacking. Now, if the means are the constitutive elements of the goal itself, then not to choose the means to an end means to miss the end. This is, however, always the case as far as moral praxis is concerned. The Aristotelian expression for "means" (τὰ πρὸς τὸ τέλος) does not preclude the possibility that what is at issue here are the constitutive components of the goal itself. Indeed the ethical means are of just this sort which can thus never be pure means in the normal sense. For more on this cf. A. Kenny, *Aristotle's Theory of Will*, London 1979, p. 149f. as well as A. Graeser, *Sophistik und Sokratik*, p. 237. Both treat in this context the so-called practical syllogism with which the concept of practical truth in Aristotle is closely conjoined. - In his book *Plato's Moral Theory* (Oxford 1977) T. Irwin shows how

3

After having proven that practical truth is possible by establishing the meaning of practical error we shall in closing discuss one example of how the concept of practical truth may be applied, namely in the case of deciding to believe.

In an essay published under the same title Bernard Williams has defended the thesis that a decision to believe is possible only under very unusual circumstances[47]. Under these circumstances it would, however, violate the dignity of the human being. He distinguishes between truth-centered motives for such a decision and non-truth-centered motives. Only a motive of the second kind could lead without inconsistency to the decision to believe; it would, however, render such a decision morally dubious. Williams adduces the example of a man whose son has to all appearances been lost in a disaster at sea. Naturally he would like to believe that his son is alive. Now he can only bring himself to do this by taking drugs, going to a hypnotist, or something of the sort. But then what is important to him is not primarily that his son be alive but that he believe it. If for no other reason than on account of this nonchalance with respect to the truth "most of us would have a very strong impulse against engaging in a project of this kind"[48]. Were one, on the other hand, to understand the father's desire to believe that his son is alive in the following sense, i.e., that he wants his son to be alive, thus implying in effect that he wants the belief so engendered to be true, then he would in conformity with such a truth-centered motive abstain from the very attempt. For this would neither help his son nor help make the desired state of affairs come true.

    Plato increasingly turned away from an instrumental understanding of the happiness-virtue relationship toward an ethical understanding of it.

[47] "Deciding to believe", *Problems of the Self, Philosophical Papers*, 1956-1972. Cambridge 1973, pp. 136-151.

[48] B. Williams, "Deciding to believe", p. 150.

Williams explicitly confines himself[49] to such fact-based examples, whose truth or falsity may in principle be ascertained empirically. Still he expresses the hope[50] that his remarks might also be of significance for, e.g., religious questions pertaining to belief. Before I go on to examine this more closely in light of an example drawn from this realm I should mention the philosophical conclusion which Williams draws from his discussion of our question: belief is something which overcomes us and about which we can do nothing, unless it be at the cost of our own sincerity. Under these circumstances it is understandable that he criticizes Hume's thesis according to which the incompatibility of belief and decision is purely contingent. The fact that one cannot sincerely decide to believe is not analogous with the contingent fact that one cannot decide to blush. It is at least conceivable that someone could decide to blush just as it is conceivable that each of us could decide to stop breathing; but it is not conceivable, except, as has already been said, in cases of extreme insincerity, that someone could decide not to believe, or, for that matter, to believe.

In my opinion it is no accident that Williams only adduces such atypical examples as going to the hypnotist and the like. By confining himself to empirical types of belief (whether it is raining, etc.) where verification is always in principle possible (and often easy) he is able to make do as far as the question of truth is concerned with the Principle of Excluded Middle and that of Bivalence. The decision to believe can under these circumstances all too easily cross over into "the project of trying to get oneself to believe the false"[51]. In those cases where no such easy decision as to the truth or falsity of an assertion is possible, however, it is of course an entirely different matter. Here the question has been displaced from the semantic level of truth-conditions to the pragmatic level of truth-criteria. This occurs, however, when, as in the case of practical truth, the possibility of falling short of it is constitutive of its correctness, i.e., when the *recta*

---

[49] B. Williams, "Deciding to believe", p. 136.
[50] *Ibid.*
[51] B. Williams, "Deciding to believe", p. 151.

ratio is at the same time a *correcta ratio*. It is perfectly possible to conceive of examples along these lines –different from those to be found in Hume (but also from those in Williams)– in which believing and deciding do not belong together contingently but rather necessarily. The examples would simply have to be constructed in a manner markedly different from that of Williams[52]. I shall presently be offering an example which satifies this condition.

The possibility of challenging belief is as much a part of it as the overcoming of such challenges. When considered together both help to explain why a decision to believe is not only possible but is even constitutive of belief. The overcoming of such challenges is, however, not simply a characteristic of religious belief, nor even of belief as such: it represents an essential characteristic of practical truth. The latter is situated in the realm of correctness. Still practical truth would have nothing to add to theoretical truth if it did not include the possibility of incorrectness. The fact that the *recta ratio* is at the same time a *correcta ratio* implies that the possibility of a shortfall has been overcome –although it is a possibility which cannot, without remainder, be overcome. But the correctness of practical truth not only differs from the *adaequatio* of theoretical truth; it also differs from the justification in which the reflective-epistemological components of theoretical truth consist. In the case of theoretical truth the possibility that one may arrive at definitive results is not ruled out: this or that is such-and-such and not anything else; or even simply: either it is so or (exclusive "or") it is not so. Should it prove possible one may abandon the field marked out by criteria of truth and press on as far as truth itself. Justification, then, passes over into correspondence. In this respect as well, the correctness of practical truth has much in common with the justification of theoretical truth. Only with this difference,

---

[52] Of a sufficiently different variety is also M. Dummett's example of a tribal chief who in order to protect the young men of his tribe during their initiation hunt performs his ritual dances not only after the hunt must already have occurred but even, due to the occasional unreliability of reports concerning the activities of the young men, after the hunting party has returned. Cf. "Bringing about the Past", *Truth and other enigmas*, pp. 333-350.

that in the case of practical truth the main burden of proof has been shifted *entirely* to the side of the criteria. This is the only difference but it is an important one. I will clarify this by means of an example.

Let us imagine a man still in his youth. Let us say for the sake of argument that he has read Spengler's *Decline of the West*. This and his own observations have led him to doubt the chances of Christianity's survival and hence the probability of its being true as well. Still according to his own estimates the situation with respect to this religion is not so far advanced that he might, despite his youth, expect to witness its eventual demise. A shimmer of hope remains. This hope, however, if it rests on anything, is founded only on the fact that in comparison with the putative end of this religion his own death is as it were impending. On the basis of other considerations as well he regards a theoretical decision concerning this (for him) vital question to be impossible: both one affirming the truth of Christianity as well as one denying the truth of Christianity. To be sure he can allow things to run their course and observe them from a detached standpoint. But he would of course like to come to a decision, if it at all possible. Now let us assume that he decides in this situation to devote his life in some form or other to the Christian cause –in some form or other, which for whatever reason allows him to say to himself: This religion has a chance of survival, if at all, only in some such manner. His commitment, however, would remain ineffective were he to pursue his doubts further. Thus he decides to set these aside once and for all. We ask ourselves: what kind of decision is this? Is it sincere? Was it ill-considered? Was it at all possible, i.e., was it really a decision?

For the moment only one thing is certain: here neither a theoretical decision nor a decision which is intended to give rise to this kind of decision is involved. He will not know after his decision, and even less so during or before it, what is the case with respect to the truth of Christianity, whether it is true or not: this much he knows, or at least believes he knows, in advance. Indeed his decision arises from the conviction that he will neither now nor in the future come to a decision as to the "true" or "false" of the matter. That it is here a question of a practical decision is of all things the least doubtful[53]. Nevertheless Christianity cannot by means of it, regardless of how practical it might be, become untrue or even truer. Thus the practical character of the decision is, on the other hand, not total. Only if we were to make the truth ourselves or if it were in some way to create itself could it be of an all-encompassing character. Thus our young man has not decided that Christianity is true but rather that it *shall be* true, provided this "shall be" is not understood to denote in turn a truth in the process of becoming[54]. But what else then? Simply a wish, the wish that Christianity might prove to be true? Then we would be in the realm of wishful thinking and so at least in the proximity of insincerity. But there is another possibility. A wish –yes, certainly. But not simply the wish that Christianity might be true. There is, to be sure, nothing disreputable about that; one might adduce reasons for such a wish. But the point of the decision is not to be found in the wish, rather the wish is already there. On the other hand the decision also does not originate with the wish that Christianity might be true; we cannot do anything about that. Nevertheless the decision does

---

[53] The practical character is well brought out in M. Dummett's essay (see n. 52 above). "The chief no longer thinks that there is any evidence as to whether the young men had been brave or not, the strength of which is unaffected by whether he intends subsequently to perform the dances"; "he will cease to think it pointless to perform the dances after having received such an adverse report"; "In fact, it seems likely that he will come to think of the performance of the dances as itself a ground for distrusting...), or even for denying outright,) the adverse reports of the observers" M. Dummet, "Bringing about the Past", p. 348. Dummett goes on to write: "The attitude of such a man seems paradoxical and unnatural to us, but I cannot see any rational considerations which would force him out of this position" (*Ibidem.*, p. 350). And he concludes: "I do not know whether it could be held that part of what people have meant when they have said, 'You cannot change the past', is that, for every type of event, it is in principle possible to know whether or not it has happened, independently of one's own intentions. If so, this is not the mere tautology it appears to be, but it does indeed single out what it is that makes us think it impossible to bring about the past" (*Ibidem.*, p. 350).

[54] This is, again, the difference between "deciding as to whether or not" and "deciding for himself for or against".

correspond to the wish that its truth *be* more probable, and the desire to which the subordinate clause gives expression is also aimed at this: "that Christianity *be* true". For here "verisimilar" and "veridical" are related in the same manner as truth-criteria to truth. This implies that the decision is not directed at a truth which we could not in any event alter but rather at possible criteria in support of such a truth. With the decision that Christianity *be* true "be" comes to denote not the desire that Christianity might finally prove itself true, but rather the desire that the criteria for assessing its truth might –for oneself or for others– be multiplied. Now this certainly lies in our hands or at least could in principle lie in our hands. At the end of the experiment (with an all-out effort, i.e., at the end of one's life) the signs pointing to the moribundity of this religion might well have decreased. The situation depicted is in this respect not much different from that of the Calvinist, who in his pursuit of success is intent only on gathering criteria pertaining to his status as one of the chosen. Even more to the point here would be a comparison with Newman's *Grammar of Assent*.

Under circumstances different from those envisioned by Williams a practical decision to believe evinces, so it would appear, a very complicated structure. Still its basic pattern may frequently be encountered elsewhere, even where the decisions are of a simpler nature. Thus, e.g., in the case of someone who is not quite certain as to whether he can satisfactorily hold an office: only assumption of the office can decide the matter. In so doing he has already effectively warded off fatalism, even if he should later fail. In order to risk taking the first step, be it ever so hesitantly, he must decide in favor of optimism. And it is no accident that common parlance here appeals to divine grace: "He upon whom God confers an office". Thus the decision has in itself something of the experiment, even of the wager. The spectrum of such more or less ordinary cases ranges in fact from Pascal's wager all the way down to such reflections (or replies) as: I still don't know why I will do this or that but I'll do it. This is indeed the place where something akin to grace might well intervene. The common pattern consists therefore in the active repudiation of fatalism. In this both the standard and non-standard cases acquiesce.

The young man of our story need not have ignored the fact that according to Christian teaching a universal apostasy must already have taken hold. He need only, in conformity with the belief upon which he has decided, repudiate fatalism. An important difference remains nonetheless. In the case of religious decisions a final confirmation cannot be obtained, at least not before one's death at any rate. It remains a decision to be maintained throughout life and so is always subject to revision. The difference reveals itself to be two-fold. 1) In the non-standard case, as distinct from the standard empirical cases, a transition from criteria to truth is out of the question. The transition is effected without our intervention, it does not lie in our hands. 2) Although the truth for which we wish to find criteria will in the non-empirical cases remain inaccessible to us all our life, its existence is not thereby precluded. We cannot in this case bring about truth itself but only criteria for it. Here both remain incommensurable with one another. And even though the generation of criteria lies in our hands, they are nonetheless genuine criteria. Now where the truth cannot be reduced to criteria because the latter cannot be rendered in terms of the former its content is specifiable solely by giving the truth-conditions of the sentences in which it may be expressed. Here, if anywhere, the realism associated with the classical concept of truth, which rests on the PET and the Principle of Bivalence, is at home. In this case at least truth can in no way be dependent on our being able to know it. In all other cases the truth, insofar as it may be rendered in terms of criteria, may be dependent on our being able to know it and on our coming to know it. "All other cases" should be understood here very broadly. It includes all cases which involve contingency and so time in general. Thus the eternal is presupposed only in the sense of something having been decided absolutely (*per se*, in itself). From God's standpoint everything would already be decided. To be sure, this does not imply that one may not conceive of God as being free. But it does imply that from His standpoint the Principle of Bivalence is necessarily valid. For Him it cannot simply be a question of criteria but it can only be a question of truth itself. This is, however, not our standpoint.

In all other non-empirical cases in which, by contrast, temporality plays a role the opposite decision would have been just as possible. Do we stand then with our example before a case of groundless decision? Williams is committed by virtue of his own presuppositions to saying this and indeed he says as much: with respect to the only case of deciding to believe which he assumes to be possible (going to the hypnotist, taking drugs) he writes: "However, even if it is granted that there is something necessarily bizarre about the idea of believing at will, *just like that*"[55]. But indications, if nothing else, in favor of the one or the other decision are normally available. Of course they do not offer conclusive evidence but they are genuine criteria just the same. Criteria usually offer something to go on. In theology such criteria, insofar as they apply to belief, are called *motiva credibilitatis*. To what extent motives will force the decision in one direction or other depends on many factors (character, experiences, etc.). But in the final analysis the decision will have been made by ourselves. But not, *pace* Tugendhat[56], completely without reason, for, as has been said, criteria are already available. Only the weight that we wish to attach to them is dependent on us. A final grounding of the decision is just as impossible as one of freedom in general. Kant saw this. But this does not imply that either the decision or freedom in general is fully ungrounded as has been argued by Tugendhat, who makes out a case –in analogy with Williams' example of deciding to believe by hypnosis– for this being ultimately essential for every decision when he writes: "if the will were still able without further appeal to support itself through reasons, then the will would as it were lose its power"[57]. This irrational trait is not necessary even in those cases where a decision to believe is involved. Criteria do not cease to be genuine criteria simply by virtue of the fact that they in this case happen to be only hints and remain so until the very end. Even motives based on considerations of plausibility are genuine motives, if not proofs. There are also inductive reasons which one is not entitled to ignore simply

---

[55] B. Williams, "Deciding to believe", p. 149 (my emphasis).

[56] Cf. n. 46 above.

[57] B. Williams, "Deciding to believe", p. 238.

on the grounds that they do not suffice to constitute a deductive argument. The preceding applies not only to the special case of deciding to believe. Indirect proof of a thesis which one cannot prove directly through refutation of the objections to it is reckoned among the traditional *motiva credibilitatis*. Kant regarded this strategy as the only adequate one in the case of freedom in general[58]. And rightly so to all appearances[59].

Appendix on Deciding to Believe

It has been said that one ought not to decide to believe, that it would be dishonest, that it would violate the moral integrity of the individual. Whoever is of this opinion presupposes that it is at least possible to do something of the sort. Where knowledge is involved, however, the question as to the integrity or lack thereof of the individual cannot even be raised. For one can under no circumstances decide to know. One can of course set off on the way to knowledge but it does not lie in our power to influence whether we reach our destination or not. Where it is a case of knowing one is ultimately at the mercy of what is known. One may not know something or one may not want to have known it or one may turn one's eyes away or wish one had, but if one knows it, and insofar as one knows it, one is obliged to accept it. This implies that knowing as such, even in the case of self-knowledge, does not lie in our hands and is to that extent not our affair: it is not by virtue of us but by virtue of something else, namely, by virtue of what is known. Belief is a different matter altogether. This is the reason why Kant was able to claim that belief is

---

[58] I. Kant, *Grundlegung zur Metaphysik der Sitten (Foundations of the Metaphysics of Morals)*, Akademie Ausgabe, 4, p. 458ff.

[59] Cf. also my essay "Freiheit und Determinismus. Logische und metaphysische Aspekte" *Persuasione e libertà nel mondo contemporaneo* (ed. Moutsopoulos, Tilliette, Prini, Dummett, Inciarte, Rosado, Riondato, Pareyson, Incardona) Palermo 1979, p. 73ff.

a meritorious type of holding to be true[60]. This applies generally but first and foremost to religious belief.

In contemporary philosophy the problem of belief in the general sense of "conviction" has been extensively discussed. Here allusions as to the possibility of applying general questions and results to the problem of belief in the more specific sense have not been lacking. The possibility of establishing a connection seems all the more obvious to English-speaking philosophers insofar as "belief" may connote both "conviction" in general and "faith" in particular. Particularly revealing –both in the positive as well as in the negative sense– is Williams' treatment of the matter. In his essay "Deciding to believe" Williams comes to a negative conclusion[61]. As we shall have occasion to note, this corresponds to the inadequate side of his deliberations, which on account of the manner in which the result has been obtained is nevertheless instructive. Instructive is also the manner in which he works out the distinction between knowledge and belief. Williams argues that "there might be *some* machine to which we could properly ascribe beliefs"[62]. "The point", Williams continues, "is that a machine to which we properly ascribed knowledge could be a lot more primitive than one to which we properly ascribed beliefs"[63]. The reason for this lies in the fact that in order for the machine to believe it would also be necessary to equip it to turn out assertions that were insincere. Normally, the machine must know or at least be familiar with whatever it has said but it need not believe it.

It is debatable to what extent the expressions "knowledge" and "belief" are appropriate in connection with a computer[64]. This, however, does not really address the point at issue. The point is: knowledge is sincere; belief may be sincere or insincere. And the reason for this is to be found in the fact that it belongs to the nature of belief that

---

[60] Cf. I. Kant, *Critique of Judgment* (§ 91); and *Preisschrift über die Fortschritte der Metaphysik*, Akademie Ausgabe, XX, p. 298.
[61] B. Williams, "Deciding to believe", pp. 136-151.
[62] B. Williams, "Deciding to believe", p. 146.
[63] *Ibid.*
[64] Cf. B. Williams, "Deciding to believe", p. 146.

it be constituted by something akin to willing. "So in a sense", Williams himself writes[65], "we need the will" in order to believe or to arrive at conviction. Why only "in a sense" is not explained. In another context apart from that of the computer the restriction, as we shall presently see, could have been dropped.

Thus far sincerity or insincerity had been identified —and as far as this aspect of Williams' argument is concerned will continue to be so later— with whether the assertions correspond to belief or not, not with how one comes to believe. In this respect the thesis which Williams advances is a two-fold one. 1) Insincerity is present wherever one decides to believe. 2) Such cases are quite rare and atypical. This second part of his thesis reveals quite clearly the limitations of Williams' approach. Thus we shall make it our point of departure. The first point is in any event closely related to the second.

The second part of this twofold thesis does not follow from any premises that Williams had previously proved or posited. On the contrary. Admittedly Williams himself writes: "Indeed from what has already been said it seems that we have some rather good reasons for saying that there is not much room for deciding to believe"[66]. Still if one is to take his cautious reference ("in a sense") to the will seriously, one would have to say instead: if it belongs to the nature of belief —as distinct from that of knowledge— that it be in some sense (as Williams claims) "of" the will or if (as I have argued) the will is even constitutive of belief, then the decision must likewise belong to it. The dispute may in fact be reduced to a choice between "in some sense" or "constitutive". Williams has recourse to the will only in retrospect: once one has independently of any act of the will arrived at a conviction, one may afterwards decide whether to express it or not. The meaning of "in a sense" was after all not so ambiguous as it at first appeared: it means "in retrospect". This being the case, if one continues to subscribe to Williams' point of view, then it is not clear in what the distinction between belief and knowledge might be thought to consist. If the machine has been so constructed that it is incapable

---

[65] B. Williams, "Deciding to believe", p. 147.
[66] *Ibid.*

of *expressing* itself in opposition to its true state of "mind", then it is a case of knowledge, otherwise it is a case of belief. The state to be expressed, though, remains the same throughout. Williams also speaks in the first case of a "B-state" where "B" stands for belief in an unqualified sense. The qualification applies, however, not to the state itself, as has already been remarked, but to something which has been added, namely the inability on the part of the machine to express itself in a manner contrary to its true state of knowledge or, for that matter, of belief. In short, belief proper is for Williams knowledge (B-state) + something else. The distinction between belief proper and knowledge is purely quantitative, not qualitative, external, not internal.

Now there are in fact cases in which one need not distinguish between knowledge and belief insofar as the will does not belong to the nature of belief constitutively but, if ever, only retrospectively. These are generally speaking cases of empirical belief, i.e., cases in which one knows or only believes one knows a given state of affairs. And Williams confines himself to precisely these cases and appears to do so intentionally[67]. It is evident that in such cases little room remains for decisions proper, i.e., for personal decisions for or against something, as distinct from theoretical decisions in which no alternative is involved. The cases involved would have to be of a very select nature. And in fact Williams only considers such cases, i.e, only those cases that are, as we have said, rare or atypical. We shall soon have occasion to observe what sort of examples are here involved.

This is also of relevance to the question currently under discussion, whether the distinction between belief and knowledge is not an internal one, whether it applies only to the retrospective possibility of concealing one's beliefs. The question may also be formulated as follows: Is it not the case that the will is much more intimately related to belief than reason is? We have seen that Williams answers this question in the affirmative. But by virtue of his initial decision to confine his examples to empirical convictions (the belief that it is

---

[67] He intentionally confines himself to "cases of more straightforward factual belief" (B. Williams, "Deciding to believe", p. 136). The question is to what extent this one-sided diet affects his results.

raining outside, etc.) he obstructs unnecessarily a view of the full implications of his answer. This may be explained by reference to the fact that in the most relevant cases in which the distinction between belief and knowledge is constitutive one cannot avoid deciding for or against a certain conviction, e.g., for or against a confession of faith. These are the cases in which one *cannot* –with varying degrees of impossibility– know with certainty[68] where the truth lies, where in other words the decision for or against a belief is not trivial, in short, where the decision lies ultimately with oneself. Williams appears to exclude them from the very outset from his attempts at clarification when he remarks that he will not be speaking of such things as religious and moral beliefs although "many of the most interesting questions in the philosophy of belief are concerned with beliefs of this type"[69]. Nevertheless he himself expresses the hope that his remarks will also "have some relevance" for such questions although those cases in which a personal decision is not precluded *a priori* have been excluded from consideration. The key word here is "grace".

What within the confines of the purely empirical cases considered by Williams can only appear, if at all, as the exception (e.g., the decision to believe) must in those cases where the distinction between belief and knowledge is an internal one be the rule. The exceptions must in each case be of an extraordinary nature: in the one case something akin to the closing off of one's self from an evident state of affairs, in the other something akin to a supernatural bestowal of grace. As far as the former is concerned Williams may continue to be of assistance to us. In this respect his remarks lead in the right direction. At the end of this path lies a recognition of the insincerity of such a decision to believe (i.e., of a decision to believe what is false or what is held to be false). Although this result may already be anticipated, it repays the effort –with regard to the non-empirical cases– to proceed here as well step by step.

---

[68] Important here is the question of whether knowledge and belief may exist alongside one another (cf. Thomas Aquinas, *De Veritate*, XIV, 9).

[69] B. Williams, "Deciding to believe", p. 136.

It is no coincidence that Williams compares his own conception of belief with that of Hume. For both belief is a passive phenomenon –with the exception that for Williams passivity is not, as it is for Hume, purely contingent. Thus Williams is of the two the more radical. For Hume the example of belief is on a par with that of blushing. While one cannot decide not to blush as one can, for example, decide not to breathe, the corresponding ability, namely that of deciding to blush, cannot be precluded *a priori*. Williams observes in this connection that Hume "seems to think that it is just a contingent fact about belief that it is something that happens to us"[70]. Williams, on the other hand, is of the opinion that belief is something which happens to us *as a matter of principle*. The explanation which he gives indicates that he distinguishes belief from knowledge only to the extent that the content of the former but not that of the latter may be false. In other words, the distinction is a merely external one, it depends on the content and not on the state itself, it is objective, but not subjective as well. One can just as little deny for oneself, unless it be externally for the sake of appearance, that one hold something to be true as one can deny that one knows something. The distinction boils down to the claim that that which one believes may be false. It is a completely objective distinction. There is no longer any conceivable distinction between belief *as a state* and a B-state.

One would, in proceeding from the uncontested circumstance that the objective content of belief may just as well be false as true, still have to preserve the subjective quality peculiar to belief, i.e., one would still have to be able to accomodate adequately the equally uncontroversial claim that belief, as Williams himself remarks, is more intimately related to the will than knowledge. It suffices for this purpose to exploit fully the ambivalence which attaches to something ("p", e.g., the belief that Christianity is true) when it is taken as a content or object of belief and which disappears when the same content is taken as an object of knowledge. It is especially true in the case of a reflexive belief that is aware of its being something distinct from knowledge that p might be false. Williams, however, has already

---

[70] B. Williams, "Deciding to believe", p. 148.

allowed the opportunity to escape from the trivial realm of irreflexive belief to slip by him insofar as he has lost sight of this ambivalence (i.e., that p might just as well be false as true). He only takes into account the (purely theoretic) alternative, "either p is true or false", but not the genuinely practical alternative, "p is possibly true", which of course includes "p is possibly false". Here the use of the word "possibly" does not remain confined to the future as is evidenced by the case of the father who *prays* for the salvation of his son although he might possibly have already drowned in a shipwreck. This case, which is also considered by M. Dummett in his essay "Bringing about the Past"[71] in the context of a verificationist conception of truth, presupposes at the very least –which, however, is not Dummett's chosen topic– that the father wants to believe in the continued existence of his son. This, however, does not in itself imply that he already believes it. Similarly, the circumstance that the victim of a nocturnal assault calls for help need not necessarily be taken to imply that he believes the police to be within hearing distance of his cries; but notwithstanding this he must first want to believe it and secondly he must really believe in the possibility of his being heard. In the absence of these two conditions his cries would be pointless. The fulfilment of both conditions, on the other hand, enables one to speak of belief in the reflexive sense. In any event belief presupposes a relation to possible truth. And it is at most only in certain trivial cases where its distinguishability from knowledge, as has been pointed out, depends entirely on the objective state of affairs that the relation which a given belief bears to truth is one of belief to unmodalized truth or falsity. Williams fails to take this into account. As a result, for Williams the only possible alternative to p (that which one believes to be true) is the falsity of p. One cannot, however, believe in something, which one takes to be false –as long as one takes it to be false– and it is only with patent insincerity that one could leave no stone unturned in an effort not only to forget it, i.e., to forget that it is false, which might for several reasons be understandable, but in order to believe it, i.e., in order to believe that it might nevertheless be true.

---

[71] M. Dummett, "Bringing about the Past", pp. 333-350.

Such an extreme case of insincerity would, for example, be at issue if the father in the above case were to seek escape in drugs, hypnosis, or something of the sort in order to be able to believe that his son is alive. This would in fact be an extremely atypical case. It is, however, the only type of decision to believe that Williams considers. The insincerity of such an attitude lies in the wilful disregard of the truth. If the experiment were to succeed, then the result of this decision would amount to a holding to be true of something that is false and which one knew to be false when one decided for oneself to undertake the experiment. It is a case of *ignorantia affectata*, which, of course, does not remove but rather increases the guilt.

Irrespective of the question whether this experiment may possibly succeed[72], such a result would in fact constitute one, but not the only possible, case of a successful "decision for oneself to believe in something". Williams refers to "two applications of the notion of 'wanting to believe' something"[73]. In the case of the first application truth-centered motives do not play a role. This would correspond to the case of the father as thus far developed. In the case of the second application such motives do in fact come into play. William correctly points out that this is "the more plausible" meaning of "he wants to believe that his son is alive". This is to be understood in the sense of "what he essentially wants is the *truth* of his belief"[74]. The shift here from "deciding to believe", which corresponds to William's original problematic, to "wanting to believe"[75] is not as innocuous as it initially appears. It is namely by means of this shift that the practical dimension has been obscured. Only insofar as it takes place in this dimension may one be assured, first, of the very possibility of "a decision for oneself to believe", and secondly of this decision's not being from the very outset insincere.

---

[72] Can one, for example, in a dream or under similar circumstances, where the effect of the will has been suspended, perform such reality-oriented acts as believing, referring, etc.?

[73] B. Williams, "Deciding to believe", p. 149.

[74] B. Williams, "Deciding to believe", p. 150.

[75] *Ibid.*

In order to bring the practical dimension back into view, one would have to alter the details of the case so that the father does not simply desire that his son be alive but that he wants to be of assistance to him –which, of course, requires some decisions on his part. Theoretical decisions are in the very nature of the case out of the question. A practical decision, on the other hand, would be for the father to pray, for example, for his son. I propose to set aside here the logical problems involving temporality, which are posed by the adoption of this attitude, although they are among the most interesting and in fact occupy in M. Dummett the center of attention. I will continue to confine myself to Williams' essay. The latter is only able to dismiss the possibility of the father deciding for himself to believe in the continued existence of his son as "impossible and incoherent" because, as we have said, he has obscured the practical dimension. The practical dimension, regardless of whether it refers to the future or even to the past, is that of "what could have been otherwise". In order to be able to draw practical conclusions it suffices, however, that one not regard "what could have been otherwise" as being out of the question. An example of such a conclusion would be the decision to pray. Admittedly this decision does not in itself constitute a decision to believe in the continued existence of his son, still the latter decision is presupposed by the former. With the father's decision to pray for the life of his son it is not simply the belief in the possibility of his continued existence which has been presupposed. Belief does not aim at possibilities. The question thus arises, what this object of belief could be in favor of which one might make a personal decision. For the undecidability of p's truth-value need not imply the falsity of p.

It could not perhaps have been anticipated from the course of his entire argumentation that Williams in his closing remarks would encapsulate the results of his inquiry in the question of whether one might decide to believe what is evidently false[76] and that he would consider such a decision, where truth-centered motives are involved, to be impossible and, where such motives are not involved, to be

---

[76] Twice on B. Williams, "Deciding to believe", p. 151. Cf. also p. 149 above: "believing things that they know are false".

possible, albeit insincere; but it is on the other hand not simply coincidental. The reason is that Williams fails to take into account the possibility that the person concerned might in the moment of choice not be convinced of p's falsity but might simply be in doubt as to its falsity, and that means at the same time in doubt as the truth of p. The person involved considers both to be possible. From this follows, however, not the disjunction "p is true or p is false" but "it is possible that p is true or it is possible that p is false". The first alternative, taken for itself, would not constitute an object of belief but of hope. But that there still be a glimmer of hope is nothing more than the prerequisite for one's reasonably being able to decide for oneself to believe p –and also for one's reasonably being able to hold p to be true. To decide for oneself in favor of p does not mean that one has decided for oneself against the possibility of not-p but only against not-p. This would, in fact, be out of the question if the possibility of not-p had already been ruled out.

The question as to what that object of belief might be in favor of which one might for oneself decide, and this in all sincerity, can be answered negatively: it is in any event not the falsity of p but also not the truth of p as such; nor is it the sheer possibility of p, which constitutes instead the object of hope. Positively expressed the answer would run: the object of belief for which one oneself decides is p itself, i.e., the content of p, e.g., that the son is alive. But insofar as belief, as distinct from knowledge, is a meritorious holding-to-be-true it is a holding of p to be true whereby the possibility of not-p remains open. It belongs to the very nature of belief that it allow of being challenged; it can only sustain itself in the overcoming of such challenges. One need not decide for oneself to believe what one already holds to be true, but one must in any case continually –as long as there is reason to hope– affirm it. If one disregards the religious undertone, the same might be said to apply even to the most trivial empirical examples, those to which Williams confines himself, at least theoretically. For doubt as to the truth of even the most uncontentious of our everyday convictions is in this respect never ruled out. The only genuine counterexample would be the conferral of grace (or obstinacy) where every form of challenge has been preempted. In the positive sense (in the form of grace, namely) this applies to religious belief. But even here the normal case is expressed in the exclamation, "I believe, help my unbelief" (*Mark,* 9, 24).

We might summarize as follows: As far as the relation to truth is concerned which is necessary if the decision to believe is to remain sincere the very possibility of truth suffices. Were one to emend the meaning of Williams' protasis ("If in full consciousness I could will to acquire a 'belief' irrespective of its [possible] truth") along the lines suggested by the bracketed word, then the apodosis with which Williams concludes would be rendered superfluous: "it is unclear that before the event I could seriously think of it as a belief, i.e., as something purporting to represent reality"[77]. In this passage "[possible] truth" does not assimilate belief to hope; it simply stands for the possibility of the opposite being true. Thus the possibility of deciding proves to be not only contingently, as in Hume, related to it; it is even less true to say, as Williams does, that this possibility is not even contingently related to it, which only serves to emphasize the passivity of belief to a point that it becomes indistinguishable from "pure knowing". Williams writes: "he [Hume] seems to think that it is just a contingent fact about belief that it is something that happens to us"[78]. Belief, when it comes, overcomes us inevitably, without our being able to resist it. Surely, an assertion that permits of a profoundly religious interpretation[79]. To this end one would have to treat it not as

---

[77] B. Williams, "Deciding to believe", p. 148.

[78] B. Williams, "Deciding to believe", p. 148.

[79] Williams's essay begins as follows: "When the subject of belief is proposed for philosophical discussion, one may tend to think of such things as religious and moral beliefs, belief in the sense of conviction of an ideological or practical character... However, this is not in fact what I shall be talking about, though what I say will, I hope, have some relevance to issues that arise in those areas". B. Williams, "Deciding to believe", p. 136. This hope has only been realized with regard to that built-in grace which which we have here described as being characteristic of religious belief. The consensus on this point appears, however, to be purely coincidental. The practical-existential cases together with subjectivity as such all remain incidental to Williams's treatment of the matter. But these are the cases in which theoretical detachment proves to be insufficient. Far from violating the integrity of

the rule but rather as the great exception. In any event our discussion has led to the conclusion that in the normal cases that lie beyond the reach of empirical decidability, one must decide to believe. Thus belief –as distinct from purely theoretical knowledge– is truly a meritorious or blameworthy holding-to-be-true that may, insofar as the will is involved in such practical decisions, change the moral condition of the believer for the better or for the worse. A decision in favor of religious belief is not necessary for human dignity. But it may just as little be said to be inconsistent with it, all the less so as the root of human dignity is to be sought in personal freedom.

---

the individual the decision, to believe something may offer a possible means of preserving the dignity of man, which accrues to him by virtue of his free will.

CHAPTER 15
PECCATA IGNOTA: ON MORAL OBJECTIVISM AND MORAL SUBJECTIVISM

1

Conscience is often viewed as the last court of appeal in matters of morality. This view of course goes against traditional ethics, for which conscience is at most only the ultimate authority in a subjective sense. But even taking this restriction into account, the appeal of the other view (conscience as the ultimate authority whatsoever) is still great. For, since morality attaches rather to the attitudes (to the so-called *Gesinnung*) than to the actions themselves or to their results, the transition from conscience as merely subjective to conscience as the absolute arbiter of morality is a very easy one. So, not surprisingly, the appeal to conscience seems to be the most common way of interpreting the teaching of the *Humanae Vitae*, but sometimes perhaps also of wakening or, even, circumventing it. This, at any rate, is the thesis I would like to defend. To be more precise, I would like to show that, even if morality attaches, as it undoubtedly does, more properly to attitudes than to actions and results, nevertheless conscience cannot yield the guiding principle of morality. In this connection the issue of *peccata ignota* becomes relevant.

"Conscience", of course, has more than one meaning. In a certain sense "conscience" may be taken to mean something infallible, viz. in the sense that even the greatest rascal cannot help but perceive its most fundamental signals. But this is a matter of psychology rather than of ethics, of facts rather than of norms. The ethical question is whether conscience is still binding even when it is mistaken. To this question the traditional answer is clearly yes. This answer has several implications. But, first of all, it presupposes the very possibility of an erroneous conscience. The possibility of a *conscientia erronea*, though, is no reason why conscience should be less than absolutely binding. The very fact that traditional ethics insists on the obligation to follow even a mistaken conscience points rather in the opposite direction; it implies that, according to traditional ethics, conscience is indeed absolutely binding. (In what sense "absolutely" is to be understood here will be discussed later). But the absolute obligation to follow one's own conscience, be it right or wrong, mistaken or not, does not justify the transition from conscience as the ultimate moral authority in a subjective sense to conscience as the ultimate authority whatsoever in moral matters –or to put it in traditional terms, from *conscientia qua regula proxima* to *conscientia qua regula ultima* of morality. The illicit character of this transition could be better seen if mistaken conscience were considered binding in cases not only of guiltless but also of culpable error (not only of *ignorantia vel error inculpabilis* but also of *ignorantia vel error culpabilis*). In my opinion, this view, however extreme, corresponds precisely to the traditional view concerning the manner in which conscience is binding. In this case, even were one to go so far as to say that conscience is absolutely binding it would still make perfectly good sense. I shall come back to this later.

That even a guilty erroneous conscience is binding represents, though, a rather extreme view with even more extreme implications. Not surprisingly, it has been denied on different grounds by both opponents as well as adherents of traditional morality. By opponents because they often do not admit the existence of a guilty erroneous or even of a merely erroneous conscience, continuing to ascribe to conscience the leading role in the interpretation of moral law; by adherents, because they sometimes refuse to acknowledge some of the consequences which follow from the obligation to obey the dictates of even a guilty erroneous conscience, that is to say, which follow by implication. Perhaps the most extreme implication of the obligation to follow even a guilty erroneous conscience is the fact that, according to the traditional view, the possibility of being condemned for having followed one's own guilty erroneous conscience cannot be excluded from the outset. If there were a duty to follow it, one could in fact be condemned for doing one's duty. And that, the possibility of condemnation through the fulfillment of duty, is, of course, paradoxical. My main concern is not with this paradox, but in order to remove some misunderstandings concerning *peccata ignota*, it may be of some help to start with it.

Since I have been accused both verbally and in writing of taking an objectivistic stance on this issue I would like to make it clear from the start that I am not affirming the likelihood of one's being condemned on account of one's having followed a guiltless erroneous conscience, as if God's judgment took into account only what is objectively right or wrong while thoroughly disregarding the attitudes on the subjective side, that is once again, the *Gesinnung*. In fact, not only have I never said or writte such a thing: I have explicitly denied it[1].

Two things seem to me worth noting in this connection, one more important than the other. The less important one is the paradox referred to above. I still believe that it follows as an inexorable consequence of the view which maintains the absolute necessity of following one's own conscience. But if the word "condemnation" sounds odd, as it sounds to me and as it possibly sounds to everyone else, we may drop it. All that I wanted to hint at by means of it can also be rephrased in connection with issues that are more important or –since nothing could scarcely be more important than condemnation or salvation– with issues more central to our purpose. This is the issue, if you will, of the charge of objectivism itself. Here one must proceed with some care. If the charge of objectivism is flung without the needed precautions, the very possibility of *peccata ignota* must *a limine* be denied. Now, not only the Old Testament[2], as well as the

---

[1] Cf. my essay "Freiheit" in *Persönliche Verantwortung*, P. Geach, F. Inciarte, R. Spaemann (eds.), pp. 93-97) as well as "Grenzen des Utilitarismus in der Moral" (written against one of my critics) in *Verantwortung. Festgabe für Johann Mader*, Vetter, Pöltner, Kampits (eds.), Wien 1987, pp. 89-102, "*Anmerkung*".

[2] "O cleanse thou me from my secret faults", "*ab occultis munda me*", *Psalm*, 19, or even in the *De profundis* Psalm.

New Testament[3], stresses that possibility but also the Christian experience in general does so. Indeed, even from the point of view of natural law or of common morality it is not at all a matter of indifference whether there is sense in admitting the possibility of *peccata ignota*. Not being myself a theologian I propose to deal with this theme, first, from the point of view of Christian experience in general (2), and, secondly, from the point of view of natural law (3), setting aside exegetical matters concerning Aristotle or others.

2

In order to appreciate the existence of hidden sins and hidden guilt in Christian experience in general, I propose to take an example drawn from real life. True, it is not an everyday example, but it is nevertheless, I think, characteristic. And inasmuch as it touches upon the question of having children or not, the example is connected with the issue of *Humanae Vitae*. In order to achieve sterility, non-natural, artificial measures must be taken. For that reason alone, voluntary, freely chosen sterility must clearly be rejected in accordance with the standards of *Humanae Vitae*. Still, one can imagine situations in which, because of the intrusion of nobler intentions, its evil remains hidden to the agent or agents: think of cases of illness and of a reasonable fear of transmitting it. There are even more obvious cases: cases, I mean, in which the evil is more evident but nevertheless contrives to remain hidden. One such case was described by an Episcopalian convert after the death of his young wife. In a letter to the author, C.S. Lewis called her death "a severe mercy". And this remark gave the book, *A Severe Mercy* by Sheldon Vanauken, its title. The reason why the young couple chose sterility was, beside their worries about overpopulation, their wish, as two lovers, to avoid anything which could threaten their intimacy –what they called *The Shining Barrier*. In the same letter, Lewis hinted at the wrongness of

---

[3] "I am not conscious of any guilt, but I am not therefore justified", 1 Cor., 4, 4.

the Shining Barrier on several levels: "Begin at the bottom. What would the grosser Pagans think? They'd say there was excess in it, that it would provoke the Nemesis of the gods; they would 'see the red light'. Go up one: the finer Pagans would blame each withdrawal from the claims of common humanity as unmanly, uncitizenly, uxorious. If Stoics they would say that to try to wrest part of the Whole... into a self-sufficing Whole on its own was 'contrary to nature'. Then come to Christians. They would of course agree that man and wife are 'one flesh'; they would perhaps admit that this was most admirably realised by Jean [his wife] and you. But surely they would add that this One Flesh must not (and in the long run cannot) 'live to itself' any more than the single individual. It was not made, any more than he, to be its Own End. It was made for God and (in Him) for its neighbours –first and foremost among them the children it ought to have produced. (The idea behind your voluntary sterility, that an experience, e.g. maternity, which cannot be shared should on that account be avoided, is surely very unsound...)"[4].

After his own conversion and even after having received the "severe mercy", this husband and young widower was still far away from true Christian attitudes. So, Lewis went on in the same letter: "She was further on than you, and she can help you more where she now is than she could have done on earth. You must go on. That is one of the many reasons why suicide is out of the question". And then: "There's no other man, in such afflictions as yours, to whom I'd dare write so plainly. And that, if you can believe me, is the strongest proof of my belief in you and love for you. To fools and weaklings one writes soft things. You spared her (very wrongly) the pains of childbirth: do not evade your own, the travail you must undergo while Christ is being born in you". The addressee "promised to think deeply about all he [Lewis] had said". And he did. As a result, he came to realize gradually the possibly hidden sinfulness of his and his wife's life-project before as well as after conversion despite the shining sides of it. The more sublime some aspects of the common project were, the

---

[4] S. Vanauken, *A several Mercy: C.S. Lewis and a pagan love invaded by Christ, told by one of the lovers*, London 1977, p. 212.

more hidden was this sinfulness. The author writes: "in so far as the Shining Barrier meant closeness, dearness, sharing, and, in a word, love, it must, surely, have been sanctified by God. To avoid creeping separateness in the name of love was simply being true to the sacrament of marriage"[5]. But the more this was the case, the more easily the shortcomings of such a sublime relationship could be overlooked. For "the Shining Barrier", as the author himself points out, "was more than that. In its Appeal to Love –what is best of our love– as the sole criterion of all decisions, it was in violation of the Law; for what was best for our love might be not in accordance with our love and duty to our neighbor. And the Shining Barrier contained an ultimate defiance of God"[6]. On which our author remarks: "We had thought our love invulnerable; and so perhaps it was to the world, as long as the Barrier stood. But God [by virtue of her having been converted earlier than he] had breached it, after which our love was vulnerable to any menace". How much of this went into Lewis' own writings is difficult to say. As he says in *The Four Loves*, published some years after this happened: "To love at all is to be vulnerable. Love anything, and your heart will certainly be wrung and possibly be broken. If you want to make sure of keeping it intact, you must give your heart to no one, not even to an animal... It will not be broken; it will become unbreakable, impenetrable, irredeemable. The alternative to tragedy, or at least to the risk of tragedy, is damnation"[7].

In the case of the Vanauken couple, the real danger was rather more subtle. It lay in the unconditionality of the dedication of the lovers to each other. For, since unconditional dedication is only due to the One Who Is Love as well as Law Himself, as soon as one transfers it to somebody or something else the door has been lain potentially open to any wrongdoing. This too is, no doubt, why Lewis wrote after the death of young Mrs. Vanauken: "One way or another the thing had to die. Perpetual spring time is not allowed. You were not cutting the wood of life according to the grain. There are various possible ways in

---

[5] S. Vanauken, *A several Mercy*, p. 212.

[6] S. Vanauken, *A several Mercy*, pp. 212-213.

[7] C.S. Lewis, *The Four Lovers*, London 1989, pp. 111-112.

which it could have died tho' both parties went on living. You have been treated with a severe mercy"[8]. These words express the author's (Vanauken's) thoughts on the way to overcoming his sublime self-deception and coming at last to see that the death had in fact been a mercy –"a severe mercy", which under the given circumstances comes close to "a merciful punishment". The author asked himself: "What would have resulted from them [the breached Barrier and the jealousy towards God, since she had already surrendered her will to God], if she had recovered? That is the question I must ask"[9].

The answer was not reached without a thorough examination of the real situation, and it apparently took some years to arrive at it. Vanauken's analysis in this connection is a rigorous confirmation of the existence of *peccata ignota* as well as a good example of the difficulty of discovering them. So it is not surprising that they are so often overlooked in real life as well as in theory. To theory I shall turn presently in connection with natural law (3). But first still more excerpts from this example drawn from real life in order to get a glimpse at some other aspects of the matter: "If my judgement of myself –that the jealousy [towards God] would survive– is correct, there are, I think", Vanauken says, "three possibilities to be examined: 1) I should, somehow, have become as wholly committed –mind and heart– as she... As Lewis rightly saw, I had moved from 'us' to 'us-and-God' but was still lightyears from 'God-and-us" in my pagan heart. I, therefore, conclude that –unless God had compelled me by grace– I should not have become as wholly committed as she. 2) I should have attempted, with some success, to damage or lessen *her* commitment to God, not admitting of course, even to myself, that I was doing it... I might, in fact, have succeeded in reducing her devotion to a 'comfortable' level... But I think I should have failed. She was too far gone in God's service... 3) I should have come to hate God –or [her]. If I have not become as committed as she and cannot weaken her faith, what remains? My jealousy of God remains: it will revive... And in the end, I should have come to a hatred of God who

---

[8] S. Vanauken, *A several Mercy*, p. 211.

[9] S. Vanauken, *A several Mercy*, p. 213.

had stolen my love though she still lived. The hatred of course would have been concealed as ceasing to believe. Nobody admits to hating God. But, then, with Jean quite lost to me —would I not come to hate her, too? Her holiness would, more and more, appear to me as hypocrisy. Or fanaticism...". Vanauken's formal conclusion from these reflections runs: "If 1 doesn't happen, if I attempt 2 and fail then 3". And this meant for him: "If my reasoning —my judgement— is correct, then her death in the dearness of our love had these results: It brought me as nothing else could do to know and end my jealousy of God. It saved her faith from assault... If her death did, in truth, have these results, it was, precisely, a severe mercy. —Our love *had* to perish, Lewis says. Perish in its earthly form, at least, or perish utterly in hate or indifference. Perish unless it could be redeemed"[10]. Here is the main point of the story, the real though not everyday story, which I wanted to recall. But there are still two particulars that might be of some interest for the following.

First, the author himself stresses the difference in time between the events recorded and their intellectual as well as existential reappraisal. As I said before, it took several years to pull through. In the meantime they were almost two different persons. "Contemplating these dreadful possibilities [namely 2 and 3] I cry", so Vanauken "even as I write: 'No, no! My God! It could not have happened! Never!' [So, the only sound alternative was her death]. But the I that cries out is not the man who knew her death in that winter dawn and all that followed"[11]. In a word, time was needed to bring light into the events. So much so that even as the author was writing his book some light was still lacking. In the only footnote of the book, he writes: "Now, some years after writing this book and its Afterword, I have been troubled that my book omitted one tiny incident"[12]. This tiny incident had to do with the question of voluntary sterility, about which the author at the time of writing still had some reservations. The first one is quite plain. "If, indeed, we had broken the Law —by attempting perpetual springtime,

---

[10] S. Vanauken, *A several Mercy*, pp. 214-216.
[11] S. Vanauken, *A several Mercy*, p. 216.
[12] S. Vanauken, *A several Mercy*, p. 219, n.

by being 'us-sufficient', by rejecting the children we might have had–then, no doubt, her death might be seen by some of the grimmer sort of religious folk as a richly deserved divine punishment"[13]. In assimilating "severe mercy" to "merciful punishment" above I was, by the way, not thinking of that; I was thinking rather of his (not her) medicinal punishment in being severed from her. Anyway, regarding the question of guilt, Vanauken will not play the role of a judge in his own case. He writes: "It is with the Law I must begin. The Law of God. But not, though, all the Law that we may have violated. If somebody expects a *mea culpa* for our rejection of children, she will not get it. I do not know whether it is illicit to refuse children; it is for the theologians to decide, whether anyone listens or not"[14]. As far as the Catholic Church is concerned, theologians, i.e., the Magisterium, have already judged in the same sense as Lewis in his letter. But that is not my main concern here. So I turn to the general question of hidden guilt in connection with natural law rather than with Christian attitudes. But I should like to point out again the importance of the passage of time for becoming fully aware of sins which would otherwise remain hidden from us. One need only think of the question of resistance against some political systems like Hitler's and others. How sincerely do many lament their connivance only after the nightmare is over. Nevertheless one cannot say the connivance itself was in all these cases, because of an initial absence of full awareness, guiltless.

3

The fundamental aspects of natural law on the level of theory were already pointed out by Aristotle. And his teaching has been taken up by philosophers as varied as, for example, Aquinas, Pascal, and Hegel. Indeed Aristotle's views may on the whole be considered to be

---

[13] S. Vanauken, *A several Mercy*, pp. 211-212.

[14] S. Vanauken, *A several Mercy*, p. 212.

consonant with traditional ethics and common morality. They are all the more important for us as Aristotle developed them in an attempt to overcome the tragic view of life as it had been depicted in classical Greek tragedy. For since the tragic view of life is the classic manifestation of objectivism in morality, in dealing with Aristotle's critique of it we are brought back to the objection with which we were confronted at the beginning of this chapter. The question was whether the critique of objectivism, in itself justified, would not, if too readily appropriated, lead to denying the very existence or even the possibility of sins unknown to their doers. Here "too readily" means: without taking into account the difference between culpable and guiltless ignorance or error concerning the evil supposed to have been done.

A tragic conception of life overlooks precisely this difference. As Hegel put it, the tragic hero assumes responsibility for the full extent of the action; that is to say, regardless of the possibility of his having known what he was doing as well as of foreseeing the consequences of his action –as, say–, in Oedipus. Only after weighing the tragic consequences for his own son did Creon, to take another example, begin to rethink his own behavior towards Antigone –too late, alas. Until this moment, no bad conscience disturbed him, there having been no consciousness of evil or wrongness. Was he, Creon, by that very fact immune to guilt for the time being? Of course not. For there is such a thing as guilty ignorance, and in some cases the ignorance increases the guilt, as in the case of the so-called *ignorantia consequens seu affectata*.

With reference to Pascal, to Aristotle, and hence, indirectly, to Aquinas too, the upshot of the question of *peccata ignota* was put by Hegel himself as follows: he asks whether an action can only be called bad if it has been performed with a bad conscience, i.e., with a developed consciousness of the contradiction between the general law and the particular willing. In Hegel's own words: "At one time great importance was attached to the question whether an action was evil only in so far as it was done with a bad conscience, i.e. with explicit knowledge of the three moments just specified: (α) knowledge of the true universal, whether knowledge in the form merely of a feeling for right and duty, or of a deeper cognition and apprehension of them; (β)

volition of the particular which conflicts with this universal; (γ) conscious comparison of both moments (α) and (β), so that the conscious subject is aware in willing that his particular volition is evil in character"[15].

According to Hegel, Pascal saw very well the untenable implications of answering this question in the affirmative, i.e., of maintaining that an action can only be bad if performed with a bad conscience in the above sense. And he quotes Pascal: "All those half-sinners will be damned who still have some love of virtue left in them. But as for the real sinners, the hardened sinners, sinners without exception, fully and irredeemably, hell cannot hold them: they have given themselves over to the devil so completely that even he has renounced them"[16]. True, Pascal's views are not always free of subtle Jansenist tones. So, when speaking of those who had crucified Jesus, he says that they would have been in need of pardon even if they, had they but known what they were doing, had not done it. It may be that this is in agreement with St. Paul, as Pascal thinks: "Is it not enough to read in the Gospel that those who crucified Christ were in need of that forgiveness which he sought for them, although they knew nothing of the malice of their deeds and indeed, according to Paul, would never have committed them, if only they had known?"[17].

In any case, according to Aristotle, the only case in which ignorance acquits voluntariness, and hence guilt, is the case which Aquinas dubs *ignorantia antecedens*, i.e., the case in which the ignorance itself is the cause of the action and, accordingly, the

---

[15] G.W.F. Hegel, *Philosophy of Right* (translated with notes by T. M. Knox), Oxford 1967, § 140, p. 94.

[16] *Ibidem*. B. Pascal, *Les Provinciales*, 4ᵉ lettre, *Oeuvres*, IV, Paris 1914, p. 256. Pascal's own text runs somewhat differently: "...I had always believed that the less one thought of God, the more one sinned. But, as I now realize, once one has found one's way to not thinking of Him at all, the future can hold only pure things in store. No more half-sinners who still have some love of virtue left in them; they will all be damned, these half-sinners. But as for the real sinners...".

[17] B. Pascal, *Les Provinciales*, 4ᵉ lettre, p. 260.

corresponding knowledge would lead to abstaining from the action[18], But since this ignorance applies only to the particular facts of a given case and not to the general principle being invoked, there is perhaps no difference between St. Paul and Aristotle in this respect. This implies that if those who crucified Jesus had not known that they were crucifying an innocent man, they would not have been in need of pardon. Only insofar as they were in error about the principle "You must not kill innocent people" would they require Jesus' pardon. Accordingly, as regards the distinction between "l'ignorance du fait" and "l'ignorance du droit" Pascal himself quotes Aristotle's own words: "all wicked men are ignorant of what they ought to do and refrain from doing, and that this error is the cause of injustice and of vice in general. But the term 'involuntary' does not really apply to an action when the agent is ignorant of his true interests. The ignorance that makes an act involuntary is not ignorance displayed in moral choice (that sort of ignorance constitutes vice) –that is to say, it is not general ignorance (because that is held to be blameworthy), but particular ignorance, ignorance of the circumstances of the act and of the things affected by it; for in this case the act is pitied and forgiven, because he who acts in ignorance of any of these circumstances is an involuntary agent"[19].

On the other hand, as Hegel himself rightly points out, as soon as questions of awareness –be it of facts or of principles– are involved, psychology too is involved: "How determinate is the consciousness of these moments [*l'ignorance du fait et l'ignorance du droit, de la loi ou du principe*] in distinction from one another, or to what extent it has developed or failed to develop in clarity so as to become a recognition of them, and to what degree an evil action has been done with a conscience more or less downright evil –all these questions are the more trivial aspect of the matter, the aspect mainly concerned with

---

[18] In a note to the same paragraph (§ 140, cf. n. 14) Hegel distinguishes in the Aristotelian text between *ignorantia antecedens* and the other types of *ignorantia* as between οὐκ εἰδὸς *and* ἀγνοῦν. Instead of "ἀγνοῦν" he ought to have written "δι' ἄγνοιαν".

[19] B. Pascal, *Les Provinciales*, 4ᵉ lettre, p. 288.

the empirical"[20]. Accordingly, matters of degrees of awareness of guilt are usually to be banished from ethics. They do not belong to the fundamentals. Since only God knows fully our intentions, ethics has to do more with law than with factual consciousness. Usually we can only judge about the principles. But just as the principles here include the difference between ignoring the principles and ignoring the facts, so the facts here include the degree of knowledge of both, principles and facts, from zero to full awareness. And so whether someone may deny some moral principle without having a bad conscience, only God knows after all. The bounds of the realm of moral principles or of natural law may also be hidden from us. I shall not go into these matters here[21]. All I wanted to show is that the appeal to conscience in moral matters, because of the possibility of *peccata ignota* on the level of principles as well as of facts, is not of much help and that, accordingly, the charge of objectivism should at least be refined. Since conscience is absolutely binding, the appeal to it is always justified, but the question concerning the moral quality of the conscience has not yet thereby been answered. The reason for this is that the way in which a conscience that is in agreement with moral law is binding is not the same as the way in which a conscience that is in disagreement with it is binding. Conscience in agreement with the law is always binding; conscience in disagreement with it is only binding as long as the error (ignorance or whatever) lasts ("*si talis duret conscientia*"). In this sense, St. Thomas says that erroneous conscience is binding *secundum quid*, right conscience *simpliciter*. A person is obliged to follow even an erroneous conscience, not *qua* erroneous but *qua* conscience. There is in other words the moral obligation to overcome

---

[20] G.W.F. Hegel, *Philosophy of Right*, p. 95.

[21] Cf. also the end of Chapter 13. In the example of the crucifixion to which both Pascal and Hegel have recourse the judges, soldiers, etc. may be thought to require exoneration insofar as they did not know of Jesus' being the Son of God or of His not being innocent but perhaps also insofar as they did not know of such principles as "it is not permitted to kill innocents" or "it is not permitted to kill the son of God". Quite possibly the only principle that cannot be extirpated from man's conscience is the first principle of synderesis (cf. Thomas Aquinas, *De veritate*, XVI, 3: "utrum synderesis in aliquo extinguatur").

an erroneous conscience[22]. So, not to act against one's own conscience is a necessary, but not a sufficient, condition of morality. With this in mind, the sense in which conscience (even erroneous conscience) is absolutely binding has been made more precise than at the start.

Inasmuch as action in agreement with conscience is only a necessary condition for morality, i.e., inasmuch as an erroneous conscience is only absolutely binding as long as it lasts, morality is more than a matter of subjective attitudes. Call the other side, the rest, if you want, objectivism or even legalism. If by this someone were to understand the thesis that a guiltless erroneous conscience could nevertheless be culpable, he would surely be right to reject it. Objectivism would on this view be inconsistent. But its rejection would not be very instructive. If the charge has any point, objectivism has to imply the thesis that the culpability or guiltlessness of error is not always a matter of awareness on the part of the acting person. But then its rejection would come very close to the rejection of any objectivity in moral matters apart from the objective ascertainability of the consequences of some actions. To recognize this is, or so it seems to me, to recognize the priority of being over thinking as it must be recognized even in connection with Descartes' *cogito ergo sum*. If I am thinking, feeling etc., that I am guiltless, I have not yet, by virtue of this fact alone, been justified in so thinking, feeling. If I think something is evil and I do it, I am sinning, even if it was not evil. I may be justified in doing it, but not because I did not think it was evil. To infer from *cogito* (*me peccare*), i.e., I am truly conscious of my sins, *ergo sum* (*peccator*), i.e., so I really am a sinner, that *non cogito* (*me peccare*), *ergo non sum* (*peccator*) is a well-known fallacy. In

---

[22] Cf. Thomas Aquinas, *De veritate*, XVII, 4: "utrum conscientia erronea liget". St. Thomas also refers to the terminology of *per se* and *per accidens*: "Et haec solutio potest accipi ex verbis Philosophii in VII *Ethic.*, ubi quasi eamdem quaestionem quaerit, utrum scilicet dicendus sit incontinens qui abscedit a ratione recta, per accidens autem a falsa. Et voluit quod incontinens per se recedit a ratione recta, per accidens autem a falsa; et ab una quidem simpliciter, ab alia quidem sedundum quid. Quod per se est, simpliciter est; quod autem per accidens, secundum quid".

addition to considering the law being appealed to, we need to examine, whether the error was culpable or not. But only a knowledge of the former, and not of the latter, is always in principle possible for us. So, the right balance regarding *peccata ignota* lies somewhere between objectivism and subjectivism. If I remember correctly, the absolution formula used in the ancient rite of confession ran: "*Ego te absolvo a peccatis tuis in quantum ego possum et tu indiges*". Here, it seems, the weights were well balanced. The hope is that there might be more *beneficia ignota* than *peccata ignota*.

The above reflections would still be pertinent even were man to have a natural interest in truth. Even more so, if –as those such as Nietzsche and Heidegger (*contra* Aristotle) seem to allege– he has not.

AFTERWORD

> There are people who never make a mistake because they never undertake anything sensible.
>
> Opinions we dare to form are like draughts which we move forward on the board: they themselves may be lost, but they have started a game which will be won.
>
> Goethe, *Maximen und Reflexionen* (342, 413).

The chapters of Part II were written without taking into consideration the interpretation of the first principles developed in Part I. In fact, with the exception of Chapter 13, they were all written before those of Part I apart from Chapter 5, which is the oldest of all. At the time Chapters 10 to 15 were written I was not interested in proceeding according to a preconceived scheme. Nor am I interested in doing so now. Nevertheless, it seems to me that one can detect more connections between the two parts than may be obvious at first sight. To explain this is the first, but not the main, purpose of these final remarks. The main purpose is to hint at some issues which might be worthy of further development, both from a historical and a philosophical point of view.

Questions relating to the necessity of restricting the validity of the first principles may already be raised in connection with Plato's *Parmenides*. The first and second sections in the first of the two hypotheses of this dialogue ("if the One is") seem to contradict each other since in them the very same predicates are successively denied of and attributed to the same subject, viz. the One, which in the context of the dialogue is equivalent to anything. Moreover, the predicates denied of as well as attributed to any thing are often of such generality (e.g., "identical with itself (or with others)", "different from itself (as from others)") that the negative results in the first section ("neither identical nor different", etc.) seem to run up against PET, whereas the positive results in the second section ("both identical and different", etc.) seem to run up against PNC. However, the respect in which the predicates are attributed or denied is not the same in both cases. On the one hand, the predicates negated in the first section refer to the attributes in terms of which the concept "one" is defined; in other words, they are not predicates proper but, rather, mere concepts. This accounts for the fact that the results of the first section do not run counter to PET. For not even such general attributes as "identical with itself" belong to the definition of the One. On the other hand, in the second section the predicates ascribed refer to the properties of the One, not to the attributes of its concept; in other words, here they function as predicates proper. This accounts for two facts, viz. that the first and the second sections do not contradict each other, and that the second section does not necessarily run counter to PNC since its results do not state, for example, that the concept "identical-with-itself" means the same as its negation. This implies that the foregoing results do not relate to the conceptual level but to that of judgment. It is as if someone (Hegel, Engels, or whoever) were to say "the moving thing is and is not here at the same time". In saying this one is in no way claiming that "here" means "not-here", e.g., "there". But, although, (*pace* Hegel, etc.) there is no danger of formal contradiction involved, there are still some problems left. These are the problems which prompted Aristotle to develop his theology in such a manner as to reverse the priority of potentiality over actuality in general as well as in the realm of contingency. But instead of going further into these I shall point to some related problems in connection with the concept of movement as well as with that of time. These are the problems which in the case of PNC Kant was at pains to banish from consideration by suppressing the phrase "at the same time" in its formulation, thereby rendering it of purely formal relevance. But these are also the problems with which Plato was dealing in the third section of the first hypothesis of the aforementioned dialogue. This third section (in reality, an appendix to the second) refers to the connection between temporal things and their non-temporal forms as well as to the instant in which any change, be it substantial or (like the change from movement to rest and vice versa or from any one state to another) accidental, begins or ceases to be.

Whatever either Plato or Kant may have thought in this connection, it is only possible for the moving thing to be at the same time there and not there because the present instant in which all things really take place is not a resting but a flowing or, rather, fleeting now, not something eternal but temporal. It is such a now that accounts for the continuity of time. It is, therefore, not to be confounded with the several nows of mathematical physics. Insofar as the latter constitute the limits of time by which we measure and try to control the changes in the world, it is they which first introduce discontinuities into the flow of time. And it is because real time, as opposed to physicalist time, is, in fact, continuously flowing that we can, and indeed must, hold the nows which may *via* abstraction (*ratione*) be distinguished in it to be numerically identical with each other, viz. one and the same now, without thereby assuming that, say, the Pelopponesian war is still going on now. Only if one fails to take into account that the continuous, i.e. the one and only, now does not abide in the present moment, would one be obliged to assume this. In other words, in order to control changes in the world we must split the one and only continuously flowing now and regard it as two contiguous nows, i.e. as the end of the past and the beginning of the future. It is only in this sense that the now is a limit of time in which nothing (neither movement nor rest) can occur. Taken in itself, however, the now is in itself not a limit nor has it any limit, and it is within this neither limiting nor limited now that every change takes place.

The similarities and differences between time and substance come here to the fore. The similarities may aptly be conveyed by pointing out that Coriscus here is numerically the same as Coriscus there but different in meaning. However, there are also important differences. True, movement and time are, like the essence of Coriscus, themselves acts. But the former are never complete, whereas the latter is always complete from the beginning to the end of his career. As soon as a substance, owing to its essential form (the substantial form of the Scholastics), comes into existence it may at any time cease to exist without detriment to its substantiality. Being complete from the very start it behaves indifferently as to its further existence so that its ceasing to be can only affect it accidentally. Being as completed act always means having been. In this sense substance may be said to transcend time. By contrast time, like movement, is never complete –and not only for the reason that even after the time required for, say, Coriscus to arrive at the Lyceum has already elapsed Coriscus may still keep on going; but rather for the more fundamental reason that there can be no time without movement nor movement without something moving. It is precisely because time is continuous and therefore unlimited, i.e., always incomplete, that it, unlike substance, cannot begin or end. It is always something different from time which begins and ends, just as it is not the movement of Coriscus that starts or ceases to move but Coriscus himself.

In all this one may detect significant similarities with respect to Kant's treatment of the relationship between time and substance in the *First Analogy of Experience* as well as in the *Refutation of Idealism*, only that Kant was there still under the spell of Newton's conception of an absolute time. For Aristotle, on the contrary, where there is no moving body, there is no time either. Once stripped, however, of Newton's influence Kant's conception turns out not to be in disagreement with Aristotle's. This may be extended to include the Kantian thesis that time is neither finite nor infinite without thereby infringing upon PET, since the reason for this "neither-nor" is the fact that the world as well as the objects in it are not things-in-themselves. This does not necessarily mean that they depend for their existence on consciousness but only that they are not determinately so or otherwise, e.g., do not extend either in time or indeed in space up to a certain point and no further; what does depend on consciousness for its existence are, rather, events, as well as those stretches of time extending from some abstract now to another abstract now without which events could not exist. On the other hand, such products of consciousness are not to be confused with the one and only flowing now. However, it is fair to say that neither Aristotle nor Kant took much trouble to make this distinction explicit. The reason for this might be that the thesis according to which reality or being means the same thing as the present (or presence) represents, as Heidegger has pointed out, an unquestioned presupposition throughout the history of Western metaphysics. One way to confront such a presupposition would be to question metaphysics as a whole: that is Heidegger's way. Another possibility, however, is to make the presupposition explicit. To put it paradoxically, in comparison to human beings animals are the better metaphysicians, since they do spontaneously what we can only get at by the roundabout means of metaphysical reflection, viz. they live in the ever-flowing present without creating events by way of setting limits on and controlling time which is itself unlimited. This does not speak against but rather in favor of the open finitude of man and world upon which Heidegger has laid so much stress. Where he parts company with (Aristotelian) metaphysics is, again, with the thesis of the priority of potentiality over actuality. One can view modern as opposed to Aristotelian metaphysics as involving a shift from the domain of being as such to that of being as truth, the ultimate consequence of this shift being the substitution of the ontology of events for that of substances. In this respect even Heidegger, notwithstanding his rejection of subjectivist idealism, follows the paths of modern philosophy.

With regard to the links between theoretical and practical philosophy, Aristotle himself made explicit the connection between action and PET. Indeed the middle part of Chapter 9 of *Peri Hermeneias* deals with almost nothing else. The most famous part of this famous chapter is the example of tomorrow's sea battle. It is not a matter of indifference whether you view this example from the inner or the outer perspective. The former is the practical perspective, the perspective, say, of the admirals involved. If one admiral decides to engage in battle, his decision is some kind of wager. He bets in favor of the truth of the corresponding proposition. It is a practical truth which means that as long as tomorrow has not yet passed the possibility of failure has not yet been ruled out. But even were the battle not to take place, the sentence expressing the decision to wage it would not be the expression of an irresponsible or arbitrary decision as would be a bet made by some thoroughly uninvolved spectator. There are, of course, degrees of well-informedness between the admiral making the decision and an outsider's pseudo-betting in a thoroughly arbitrary way. (The latter would be the analogue of a bogus assertion). But such degrees of probability must not be considered to be on a par with the ultimate outcome, i.e., they must not be taken to lie on the level of truth values. The ultimate outcome makes the sentence true or false, *tertium non datur*. But it is the sentence at the very time of its utterance that (in retrospect, as it were) is made true by the outcome, not the same sentence at any later time, just as it is already at the time of betting that one is deserving of the fruits of one's wager even though one may only properly be said to have won the bet later. In any case, in order for the sentence to be true it would have to have been asserted at that time with some degree of probability. That is the reason why, to take another classical example, a sentence asserting that it will be hot this year during the dog-days –even if it should turn out not to be the case– has a greater claim to truth than one which without any reason whatsoever asserts the contrary. One may even say that it is μᾶλλον ἀληθής (*potius vera*), more likely true, but not truer (*verior*) than the other.

The example shows the rationale for considering the truth of both alternatives to be a real option, provided neither represents from the very outset a bogus assertion. What the example does not show is the necessity of assuming three or more truth-values corresponding to the various degrees of probability. Probability is analogous to doubting in that doubting is not the end of the matter but a provisional state. In asserting something we always aim at truth, never at falsity nor at doubt. But failing to get at it (i.e., failing to get it) results in falsity, not in doubt. And having realized the failure, one realizes by the same token that by negating the same thing one would have succeeded in one's assertion. Such a negative assertion is not equivalent to propositional negation nor does it operate on the level of truth-functional values. Denying p need not be the same as affirming not-p, any more than affirming and denying p need be the same as affirming p and affirming not-p. Only by smuggling in propositional negation would one be in a position to equate the two. But this amounts to a *petitio principii*. The fact that asserting p must be either true or false is not the reason why not-p must itself be either true or false. In other words, not even the "or" of Bivalence need be exclusive. To treat Bivalence (PB'; cf. the appendix to the Final Appendix) without further ado as being equivalent to the meaning of propositional negation is but a way of begging the question against the possibility of taking the "or" of PET as non-exclusive. Nevertheless the fact that both the affirmation and the denial of p might be true only implies that one must be false if one proceeds by means of truth-functions and hence by presupposing propositional negation. In the case of Bivalence, however, one is, strictly speaking, confronted with only one proposition, i.e., strictly speaking there is no room for truth-functionality at all.

One can pose the question of truth from the point of view of the content expressed in an assertive sentence. The latter either does or does not correspond, then, to reality. The alternative here is between truth and falsity: if the content is true, then it is not false and vice versa. This possibility corresponds to the modern Principle of Bivalence inasmuch as it amounts to the definition of propositional negation. However, one may also pose the question of truth from the standpoint of our uttering the content. If the utterance is sincere, then one aims by means of it only at truth, never at falsity. Falsity here appears as the failure to reach the truth aimed at. It is here that the analogy to betting is illuminating. In betting both parties are equally concerned with winning. Similarly, the initial position of both contenders with respect to a contingent event in the future is itself not that of a mere contradiction. True, they cannot both win. They know that, at the end of the day, exactly one will have won and exactly one will have lost. Nevertheless, both bet, as it were, on truth. And it is precisely because the outcome is not fixed in advance that both could be right. Here "could" is to be taken in the sense of double possibility (PPq, where "q" stands for "p or not-p" with non-exclusive "or", which is just another way of saying that the corresponding truth tables in the appendix to the Appendix below should not be read truth-functionally).

Now, if the question is whether or not, at the time of betting, the contradictory assertions of the contenders are, or even can be, true or false, the answer will differ depending upon the standpoint taken. From the standpoint of mere contradiction (= definition of propositional negation) the answer is, evidently, negative. For nobody knows nor can know at the moment which one is true or false. From the standpoint of the saying or the betting itself, however, the answer is not as clear-cut. And this not only because at the starting-point both contentions could be true. After all, the possibility of being true is not the same thing as unmodalized truth. If this time the answer is not as clear-cut as it was before, this is due to the fact that although only afterwards does one content turn out to be true and the other false, the quest for truth had already been initiated at the time of utterance (i.e., of betting) –when both contenders had reason to hope that they might win the contest. As responsible agents, both know in advance, first, that both could not be false and, secondly, that, since affirming and denying the same exhaust the range of possibilities of getting to truth, one must be true. Now, simply to say at this juncture "one and only one" or "exactly one is true and exactly one is false" would be to take again the purely theoretical, i.e., detached or uninvolved, stance of deciding whether or not, instead of taking the practical one of responsibly deciding for oneself for or against; in other words, it would rule out the very possibility of practical truth. Where practical truth is concerned one has to refrain from operating with the purely theoretical device of truth-functions based on propositional negation. The theoretical point of view is one which arises only in retrospect. But even in retrospect the only appropriate thing to say, as far as future contingents are concerned, is that, although it did not turn out to be the case until later on, it *was* my (or whoever's) personal utterance, i.e., my (or whoever's) wager, not an impersonal as well as intemporal proposition that *won* the competition. It is precisely because the problem of future contingents is, in the end, to be posed in temporal terms, that it cannot be posed in advance in terms of propositional functions which are themselves based on the meaning of propositional negation. It is in this sense that I agree with the traditional interpretation of the problem espoused by, say, Thomas Aquinas. For this interpretation is based on the assigning of truth-values (and indeed of the positive one) not to the single contradictory propositions involved but only to the whole of the non-exclusive alternative. In fact, neither Aristotle nor Aquinas spoke in this connection of the truth, but rather of the necessity, of the alternative as a whole. Its necessity implies, of course, its truth –provided one does not bring in the concept of a propositional truth-function which itself depends on the definition of propositional negation. (With this, incidentally, the usual objection from Cicero onwards falls by the wayside, I mean the one according to which, as Quine put it, it is only "Aristotelian fantasy" to ascribe a truth-value to the whole disjunction and not to its parts).

Given the connection between the issue of Excluded Third and that of practical truth, it only stands to reason that the problem of the contingent future cannot be treated without regard to time-relative modalities, taking time here dynamically, i.e., *a parte ante* as not fully anticipatory or calculable, in the sense of that which is about to happen (τὸ μέλλον), but not statically, i.e., *a parte post* in the sense of that which had been, was, or, as something predictable, is unavoidably in the future (τὸ ἐσόμενον). To put it otherwise, if there be implicit in this a correspondence theory of truth at all, it is a theory of weak correspondence which does not restrict the truth-relation to those cases in which one can be certain about which of the two truth-values is to be assigned. Both members of the contradiction ought, of course, to have a chance, however minimal, of being true. But the corresponding degree of probability is of no relevance, since it does not share in the constitution of either truth-value. What counts is that neither member be necessarily false. This already follows from the definition of "false", just as it follows from the definition of "true" that neither is necessarily true. Thus far the Aristotelian Principle of Bivalence, as explained in Section 1 of Chapter 3 as well as in the Appendix below, undergoes no restriction even in the case of practical truth. The Principle of Bivalence only becomes equivalent to the meaning of propositional negation at that point in time when exactly one of the two alternatives has been ruled out, i. e. when there is no more a matter of future contingency. The reason which Aquinas gives for answering in the affirmative the Solonian question posed by Aristotle, i.e., whether someone can be considered happy before he dies, given the possibility of intervening adversities, might help to clarify the matter. The reason given is that the truth of a proposition about the past is grounded in the truth of the corresponding proposition about the present: *Ideo enim aliquid verum est fuisse, quod verum fuit esse* ("now it is true that it was the case because it was true that it was the case"). True, this statement was made with a view to the past, but it also applies to the future in the sense of what is about to happen, i.e. as an example of the contingent future. Not even virtue suffices to guarantee happiness until the end or, to put it in a Christian way, to guarantee final perseverance. Nevertheless, the fact that verification can occur only afterwards does not imply that the earlier assertion corresponding to the factual outcome had not already in the past been true.

But, one might ask, what about the other assertion? Is it not fair to say of it in retrospect that it *was* false? The answer to this question is: yes, but, again, only in the purely theoretical sense connected with truth-functions. In the sense of practical truth explained in Part II the answer must instead be no. As was shown, the possibility of error is an indispensable constituent of practical truth. We may take the most disadvantageous variant of the case just considered, viz. the case in which, according to the most reasonable expectations but contrary to someone's prediction, the virtuous man remains happy until the very end on account of his virtue so that the corresponding assertion can in retrospect be considered true at the time of utterance. This is the most disadvantageous case since if the wrong prediction had been to the effect that the man would persevere until the very end, it might still have been accorded the status of "more likely true at that time" (*potius tunc vera*). This case would be similar to the one of wrongly predicting cold weather for the dog-days. But in the most disadvantageous case the wrong prediction could not have been accorded even this status. This, though, does not make much of a difference. The point is that the fact that, independently of the degree of probability, one cannot in retrospect unqualifiedly accord the predicate "true" to the wrong prediction does not imply that one may retrospectively call it "false". To do so would be just to blur the practical, prospective, and contingent character of the truth in question. And this applies to either case. As can easily be seen, it is only this version of Bivalence that is consistent with the Aristotelian PET explained in the final Appendix above. What was dubbed Aristotelian Bivalence amounted to the claim that no single assertion (the affirmation or denial of p) must *qua* assertion necessarily be false. As long as one does not take the usual formula for Bivalence ("p is true or false") to be equivalent to propositional negation, i.e., as long as one does not take the "or" in this formula to be exclusive, there is no need to depart from it in order to remain faithful to the Aristotelian PET. What is excluded by this principle is the possibility of fulfilling the truth-claim of each sincere assertion other than *via* the affirmation or the negation of p. It is perhaps no accident that Aristotle, after having questioned Bivalence at the beginning of *Peri Hermeneias* 9, explicitly rejects at the end of the chapter only propositional negation[1]. To say that by virtue of this very fact Bivalence has been implicitly rejected seems to amount to nothing more than a *petitio principii*.

The advantages, though, of severing Bivalence from propositional negation and connecting it with practical truth are not restricted to the Aristotelian treatment of Excluded Third. They are also consistent with the fact that Aristotle does not justify Non-Contradiction formally but only pragmatically. In severing Bivalence from propositional negation one deprives it, to be sure, of the precision necessary for it to serve as an appropriate tool in deciding for or against anti-realism. This loss of precision is perhaps to be regretted in light of the fact that in this form Bivalence seems in the end, *pace* M. Dummett, to be indispensable for dealing with the question of truth-values, even in an unlimited domain of discourse. But conjoining Bivalence instead with practical truth also has its advantages. The most obvious of these, as far as the contents of the present volume are concerned, is that it helps one to understand why one should not bring in considerations stemming from formal logic when treating the Aristotelian justification of Non-Contradiction. As was stressed in Chapter 3, though, the justification on purely pragmatical grounds does not amount to saddling Aristotle with a pragmatistic stance on this point. It would not be wrong to consider Nietzsche the main ancestor of pragmatism. For him Non-Contradiction is but another

---

[1] Cf. Aristotle, *Peri Hermeneias*, übersetzt und erläutert von H. Weidemann, Berlin 1994, p. 299.

useful way of getting things wrong, which is another way of saying that anything we can say is false, i.e., of denying both Aristotelian Bivalence and Aristotelian Excluded Third. Now, with reference to the Aristotelian PNC Nietzsche once remarked that "our belief in things is the presupposition for our belief in logic". Substitute "substances" for "things" and you have the reversal of the second half of the transcendental deduction effected by Aristotle in his attempt to justify Non-Contradiction pragmatically. Some pragmatists are prepared in the face of recalcitrant experiences to give up Bivalence or even Excluded Third but not Non-Contradiction, although both are from the formal (as opposed to the analytic) standpoint equally true, i.e., equally devoid of content. Aristotle need not draw a distinction here.

Appendix to Chapter 3, Part 1

On the Aristotelian Principle of Excluded Third (PET)

The main purpose of this appendix is to bring out the genuine meaning of PET. In trying to do so nowadays one cannot avoid comparing PET with modern principles which might easily be mistaken for it: above all the Law of Excluded Middle[1] (LEM = $p \vee \neg p$) of classical (not Aristotelian or even traditional) logic, but also its semantic counterpart, the Principle of Bivalence (PB'), as well as the Law of Excluded Third (LET = $\neg\neg\neg(p \vee \neg p)$) of intuitionistic logic along with its semantic counterpart, the *principium exclusi tertii* (*pet*) (section 1). Secondly, I wish to show how PET can cope with problems which have sometimes led to the substitution of LET and *pet* for LEM and PB' (section 2)[2]. Finally, I shall try to test my results by interpreting *Metaphysics*, 1047b 9-14 and showing how much of recent controversy on this passage has arisen from not taking PET into account (section 3).

In *Metaphysics*, 1012a 21-28 Aristotle for the first time directly contrasts, as does *Metaphysics*, 1012b 5-13 later on, PET with his own PNC, which again ought not to be confused either with the Law of

---

[1] I shall follow M. Dummett's terminology in *Truth and other enigmas*; see also the appendix below listing and explaining the abbreviations. The only reason for speaking of the Aristotelian Principle of Excluded *Third* instead of Excluded *Middle* is that the expression "Excluded Middle" has often been reserved for LEM.

[2] Unlike LEM and PB', PET makes the substitution unnecessary. In showing this I shall indirectly be explaining why, as Kirwan correctly notes, Aristotle does not "share the inclination to regard PEM as more doubtful than PNC". C. Kirwan, *Aristotle's Metaphysics Book Γ, Δ, and E*, p. 116.

Non-Contradiction (LNC) – (p&-p)³ (or its semantic counterpart PNC') or with the meaning of negation or contradiction in modern classical logic (if p is true, then -p is false, and if p is false, then -p is true = "Principle of Negation" (PN) or "Definition of Propositional Negation" (DPN)). It ought also to be distinguished from the Aristotelian "principle" or meaning of contradiction (= (P)C). I shall take these two passages as my main point of reference throughout. Although I shall occasionally refer to other texts, the picture that I am going to develop here is one that emerges from an analysis of the passages mentioned above. As to whether the emerging picture leads to inconsistencies elsewhere in the Aristotelian corpus, this is a question to which I am not here prepared to give a comprehensive answer. Among the modern interpretations of *Peri Hermeneias* 9 the one that is most consistent with PET is the so-called "traditional" or "standard" interpretation. I shall not try to add a new interpretation of this difficult chapter to already existing ones⁴. Nor do I wish to saddle the modern defenders of the traditional interpretation with PET. But there is at least agreement in not treating the Aristotelian principles truth-functionally.

Some preliminary remarks may be of help. I take "assertion" (ἀπόφανσις), or "to assert", to involve the claim that the content of a proposition (the propositional content p) obtains. I shall call this the "truth-claim" of an assertion (to be distinguished from its "truth-value"). An assertion is true or false depending on whether the propositional content it employs does or does not obtain (exist). The distinction between propositional content p and its assertion Ap corresponds to the scholastic distinction between *oratio* and *usus assertivus* (*indicativus, suppositivus*) (or indeed *interrogativus, imperativus*, etc.) *orationis*⁵. ("Oratio", as distinct from "proposition", has the advantage of not suggesting a third realm of ideal entities at

---

3 With this nothing has been said against regarding PNC as a law of thought in the vein of *Metaphysics* IV, 3.

4 Cf. most recently Aristotles, *Peri Hermeneias*, übersetzt und erläutert von H. Weidemann, especially pp. 300-324.

5 Cf. Thomas Aquinas, *In Peri Hermeneias*, n. 83.

all. The scholastic distinction corresponds roughly to that between propositional content and illocutionary act introduced by Searle in *Speech Acts*). The important thing here is to distinguish between "A(p or not-p)", where neither p nor not-p has been asserted, and "Ap or Anot-p". Where desired, one may mentally add "A" to "p" and "not-p" (as in the case of Frege's assertion sign or *Behauptungszeichen*), but not in the case of PET ("A(p or not-p)"). This has not always been sufficiently taken into account. –To affirm and to deny the same propositional content (= to assert both p and not-p) is a contradiction (ἀντίφασις)[6]. (Here as elsewhere I follow the practice of omitting "at the same time" where obvious). On the other hand, while every assertion has to be either affirmative (κατάφασις) or negative (ἀπόφασις), no affirmative or negative propositional content (*Sachverhalt*) makes an assertion[7]. In stating A(p or not-p), unlike

---

[6] Cf. Aristotle, *Peri Hermeneias*, 17a 33-37.

[7] The negation of p (or of not-p) can be called "denying p (or denying not-p)", which is equivalent, of course, to asserting not-p (or asserting p). But there is no such thing as "dis-asserting", i.e., as denying assertion. This would amount to an impossibility, viz. to raising a claim to falsity. In other words, there can be non-assertive p (= positive propositional content or *oratio* in Aquinas's sense) as well as non-assertive not-p (= negative propositional content or *oratio* in Aquinas's sense), but there cannot be "dis-assertion" as well as assertion. This *is* important in order to get the right sense of PNC and PET. Both answer the same set of questions: first, the question as to whether Ap and Anot-p can both fulfill the truth-claim of a given assertion and, second, the question as to whether Ap and Anot-p can both fail to succeed in claiming the truth. To answer "no" to the first question is to state PNC; to answer "no" to the second, PET. Otherwise one cannot correctly answer the question as to what excluded third (middle) we are speaking about. The answer to this question is: the truth-claim can only, and indeed must be fulfilled either by asserting p or by asserting not-p, there is nothing else to be sought for, no third possibility. With this, of course, it has not yet been stated that the truth-claim could not be fulfilled in both cases. To state this is the job of PNC. Both principles can, and indeed should, be stated independently of each other. As we shall see, this is the basic difference with respect to modern logic. The truth-claim is the tacit, since natural, presupposition of any assertion. For this reason, Kirwan's first comment on *Metaphysics*, 1011b 23-25 ("he cannot really mean to exclude the further possibilities") is beside the point. My remarks in section 2 be-

low concerning Geach's understanding and criticism of PET (in accordance with the customary reading of LEM) apply to Kirwan too, and indeed to most modern commentators known to me, as well as to such authors who, like Quine (and indeed Dummett), prefer to treat Bivalence as the basis for realism rather than LEM (cf. part 2). In what follows, I shall treat Bivalence only in connection with PET (or LEM), and not as it is in itself. Accordingly, I shall distinguish between the Aristotelian and modern variants of Bivalence (PB and PB') only where necessary. Some general remarks, though, may be allowed: Bivalence can be viewed either in connection with affirmation and negation (affirmative and negative assertion) or with respect to the truth-values, true and false. In the latter connection, to reject Bivalence means to accept the possibility of at least another truth-value besides these two. Inasmuch as A himself might have accepted such a possibility (cf. N. Öffenberger, *Zur Vorgeschichte der mehrwertigen Logik in der Antike*, Vol. IV of *Zur modernen Deutung der Aristotelischen Logik*, Hildesheim 1990), it is more appropriate to consider not only PET but PB as well in connection with affirmation and negation, viz. in the sense that the truth-claim of each genuine assertion cannot be fulfilled apart from either affirming or negating p, since these are the only possibilities of asserting or claiming truth. There are only two possibilities of fulfilling a truth-claim (TC), viz. either by affirming p or by denying it, affirming and denying being the only possibilities of asserting p. And similarly for not-p. Now, just as fulfilling TC (as regards either p or not-p) amounts to the positive truth-value (T), falling short of it amounts to the negative truth-value (F). In all this there is no justification to be found for reading PN=DPN into PB (or even PB'). In fact to do so would amount to begging the question to the detriment of PET as in H. Weidemann's commentary on *Peri Hermeneias* (Berlin 1994, p. 299). As already stated by D. Frede, the Aristotelian principles are not to be understood truth-fuctionally (cf. *Aristoteles und die 'Seeschlacht'*, p. 76). One last remark: I am treating the Aristotelian PB only in connection with the definition of "false", and not in connection with that of "true" as well, since taken in itself PET amounts to nothing other than the impossibility of Ap and Anot-p (affirming and negating the same) both being false. For all these reasons, I shall distinguish throughout between PET and its modern rivals, but between the modern and Aristotelian variants of the PB, as already said, only where necessary. Where Aristotelian Bivalence (PB) comes into play is in going from "p and not-p cannot both be false" to "at least one of the two must be true" (double possibility, cf. n. 28 below), whereas modern Bivalence (PB'), if interpreted as equivalent to PN=DPN, would result in "exactly one of the two must be true and the other

stating A(p&¬p), one is neither asserting p nor asserting not-p. But contrary to LEM, PET together with PB states that the truth-claim raised by each pair of contradictories (p, not-p) ought to be fulfilled either by asserting p or by asserting not-p. In saying this (i.e., under *non-exclusive disjunction*) nothing has been settled as to whether the truth-claim could be fulfilled by asserting both. This is the distinctive feature of PET *vis-à-vis* LEM. PET precludes the possibility that in the case of any pair of contradictories the truth-claim could remain unfulfilled, i.e., that Ap and Anot-p could both be false. But, then, of course, it is also precluded that Ap and Anot-p could both be neither true nor false –if only because either Ap or Anot-p (under non-exclusive disjunction) must be true. The denial of the possibility that Ap or Anot-p could both be neither true nor false is reminiscent of *pet*, but it is not the distinctive feature of PET. It results from PNC no less than from PET. –PNC is the complement of PET in that the former, but not the latter, precludes the possibility of Ap and Anot-p both being true. Then, again, of course, it is also precluded that Ap and Anot-p could be neither true nor false –if only because this time either Ap or Anot-p (under the non-exclusive "or") must be false[8]. Thus it is not surprising that the impossibility of Ap and Anot-p being neither true nor false should be treated by Aristotle in connection with PNC[9] no less than with PET[10]. Finally, the conjunction of PNC and PET results in PN, for if, due to PNC, the assertion of *at least* one of the two contradictories p and not-p must be false, and, on the other hand, due to PET, the assertion of *at least* one has to be true (i.e., if *at most* one of the two cases can be true –PNC– and *at most* one of the two can be false –PET–), then Ap is true if and only if Anot-p is false, and vice versa. This is the main difference between Aristotelian (as well as

---

false". Further exploration of the difference between PB and PB' is not needed in order to explain PET.

[8] Cf. the end of n. 7.
[9] Cf. Aristotle, *Metaphysics*, 1008a 3-6.
[10] Cf. Aristotle, *Metaphysics*, 1012a 6f.

traditional)[11] and modern classical logic: In the former PN follows from PNC *and* PET (i.e., from the two taken together), in the latter it is presupposed by the modern substitutions for PNC as well as for PET. Not to be aware of that can easily lead to confusion. On the other hand, inasmuch as traditional logic accepts PET as well as PNC, it is based on the truth-table for propositional negation. On this (important) score there is no difference between it and modern classical logic.

1

I now turn to *Metaphysics,* 1012a 21-28. The text (cited throughout in the ROT) reads here: "the starting-point in dealing with all such people is definition. Now the definition rests on the necessity of their meaning something; for the formula, of which the word is a sign, becomes its definition. The doctrine of Heraclitus, that all things are and are not, seems to make everything true, while that of Anaxagoras, that there is an intermediate between the terms of contradiction, seems to make everything false; for when things are mixed, the mixture is neither good nor not-good, so that one cannot say anything that is true".

"Such people" refers to those who reject PNC as well as to those who reject PET. The refutation of both parties has to start with the definition of words. In other words, the starting-point has to be sought on the semantic level of meaning (concept) and not on the level of truth and falsity (judgment), if the charge of begging the question is to be avoided[12]. This applies to PNC[13] as well as to PET[14]. Any word

---

[11] Cf. Thomas Aquinas on *Metaphysica* IV, 7 and 8: "Postquam disputavit contra ponentes contradictoria simul esse vera hic disputat contra ponentes esse medium inter contradictionem: hi enim dicunt non semper alteram partem contradictionis esse veram", *In Metaphysica,* n. 720.

[12] Cf. Aristotle, *Metaphysics,* 1008a 34-b2.

[13] Cf. Aristotle, *Metaphysics,* 1006a 18-26.

[14] Cf. Aristotle, *Metaphysics,* 1012a 21-24 with 1012b 3-8.

may serve as the word to be defined: "being" or "not-being", "man"[15] or "not-man"[16], etc. The only thing required is that no word mean everything (e.g. "man" may mean neither "white" nor "educated", etc.), which would amount to no meaning at all[17]. Still the fact that Aristotle chooses to define just the words he does, i.e., "true" and "false", has special advantages with respect to distinguishing PET from LEM as well as PNC from LNC insofar as both taken together result in PN without either presupposing it. These advantages can be inferred from the first[18] and, together with 1012b 5-12, main argument for PET[19].

Aristotle begins by defining "false". The reason for not beginning with a definition of "true" is that from 1005b 35 onwards he had already been dealing with objections to PNC, whereas he is now turning to PET. Defining "false" is sufficient to show that no pair of contradictories can both be false just as defining "true" is sufficient to show that no pair of contradictories can both be true, but having finished with PNC Aristotle must now turn to its complement (PET).

The definition of "false" runs as follows: "false" is "to say of what is, that it is not, or of what is not that it is"[20]. If so, then, first of all, not all assertions must be false. The *possibility* of true assertions has been left open. For assuming that one were to say of that which is that it is, then, according to this definition of "false", one would at any rate not be saying anything false, and similarly if one were to say of that which is not that it is not. To get from "not all assertions must be false" (the *non-necessity* of falsity) to "it is not possible for all of them to be false" (the *impossibility* of all assertions being false, which corresponds to PET) all that is needed is to consider the case of

---

[15] Cf. Aristotle, *Metaphysics*, 1006a 30-31.

[16] Aristotle, *Metaphysics*, 1007a 1f.

[17] Cf. Aristotle, *Metaphysics*, 1006b 5f.

[18] Cf. Aristotle, *Metaphysics*, 1011b 25.

[19] I shall not treat the other arguments explicitly but after having treated the first argument proceed directly to the general remarks quoted above. See also n. 30 below.

[20] Aristotle, *Metaphysics*, 1011b 26f.

assertive affirmation and negation of the same thing[21]. For if to affirm of some x which is P that it is not-P or to deny of some (the same or other) x which is P that it is P constitutes (one half of) the definition of "false" (the other half being to affirm of some x which is not-P that it is P or to deny of some (the same or other) x which is not-P that it is not-P), then to deny of some x that it is not-P, where affirming that it is not-P is false, *can* at any rate *not* be false, just as to affirm of the some (the same or other) x that it is P, where denying that it is P is false, *can* at any rate *not* be false. In other words, it is possible, but not necessary, to say something false. Now, the possibility of saying something false according to the definition of "false" is actualized as soon as it is the same P that is being affirmed and denied (e.g. the same predicate that is being affirmatively and negatively asserted) of the same subject. This, of course, amounts to the impossibility of saying something false when it is a matter of simply affirming of something that is P that it is P or of simply denying of something that is not-P that it is P. So (b), viz. the impossibility of all propositions being false, has been demonstrated without recourse having been had to (c). But note that simply by virtue of having said this nothing has as yet been decided as to the (necessary) truth of these assertions. As to whether both sides of the contradiction could be true or not, as well as whether one must be false, this depends on the definition of "true" under consideration. The important thing to realize is that PET, viz. the impossibility of all propositions being false, has been demonstrated without recourse having been had to PN. In fact, appealing to it would have led to LEM as well as to PB', not to PET or PB. It turns out that Aristotelian contradiction, (P)C, is not modern contradiction *qua* negation in propositional logic (PN). The only tools we needed to get at PET were the Aristotelian (P)C, which just means affirming and denying the same thing, *and* the definition of "false". By demonstrating the *non-necessity* of falsity Aristotle has established the genuine Aristotelian PB, which operates with only one assertion. ("Ap is either true or false" means that it *can* be both, i.e., that it is *not necessarily* either; and similarly for "Anot-p is either true or false"). It

---

[21] Cf. Aristotle, *Metaphysics*, 1012b 10-12.

is only by showing the *impossibility* of both Ap and Anot-p being false (e.g. of saying something false by affirming as well as denying the same predicate of the same subject) that one can establish PET proper. Accordingly, Aristotle does not attempt this explicitly until 1012b 10f. Here too, of course, he is drawing not on statements but on definitions (i.e., meanings) of words[22]. Having already implicitly stated PNC by means of his definition of "true", Aristotle can here draw upon PN[23]. But it is noteworthy that immediately afterwards Aristotle still treats the two principles separately, first PET and then PNC[24].

2

Some problems relevant to LEM arise in connection with vague predicates. In his paper "The Law of Excluded Middle" P.T. Geach borrows from Wittgenstein an instructive picture, instructive not only in itself but also with respect to its limitations as a device for illustrating PET:

"To represent a vague predicate P, we draw two concentric boundary-lines, A and B; P will be definitely true of what lies inside the inner boundary, and the negation of P, of what lies outside the outer boundary. 'There would be an indeterminate zone left over; *the boundaries A and B are inessential to the concept defined.* The boundaries A and B are as it were just the walls of the forecourt. They are drawn arbitrarily where it is still possible to draw the firm line. –It is like walling off a bog; the wall ist not the boundary of the bog, it merely surrounds it while itself standing on firm ground. It shows that there is a bog inside, not that the bog is just as large as the walled-off

---

[22] Cf. Aristotle, *Metaphysics*, 1012b 5-8.
[23] Cf. Aristotle, *Metaphysics*, 1012b 8-10.
[24] Aristotle, *Metaphysics*, 1012b 12-13.

area'. The two boundaries would thus stand concentrically on the firm ground, the bog of vagueness lying wholly between them"[25].

Take the sorites-paradox: putting grains together one after another, how can I proceed from "this is not (yet) a heap" to "this is (already) a heap", since no single grain is in itself capable of constituting a heap? Again, from what point up can I judge a man to be tall? –To begin with, the problem with boundaries is not a problem with (the definition of) concepts. Provided they do not belong καθ'αὐτὸ or *per se* (e.g., by definition) together like *man* and, say, *biped animal*, or *surgeon* and *man* (not the other way around), but are coincidental (κατά συμβεβηκὸς, *per accidens*) to each other like *man* and *white*, *white* and *educated*, *surgeon* and *butcher*, etc., concepts cannot be said to mix with one another; indeed far from being connected, they are so sharply distinguished that the question of boundaries between such concepts does not even arise. In order to appear together, they must belong to a third or middle, to something else, viz. to a subject, call it "substance"[26]. And this applies to the meaning (*forma*, εἶδος, τί ἐν εἶναι) of "white" and "surgeon" no less than to the meaning of "man" and "finger" or "bat"[27]. It is in the realm of reality, not of ideality or conceptuality, that mixtures take place, all the more so insofar as, firstly, the meanings of concepts (*formae*, εἰδέ) are situated in reality not as such (i.e., as abstracted or defined) but as properties, and, secondly, insofar as properties are distinguished from parts[28]. Although a black man may have parts that are only white (*pigmentum*), the property of having them (*color*)[29] pertains to the whole man. And this applies even to so-called relative concepts such as *tall*, *more*, etc. The concepts of relations are not relative concepts.

---

[25] P. Geach, *Logic Matters*, p. 86. (The sentence I myself have stressed contains the most useful aspect of Wittgenstein's picture).

[26] Cf. Aristotle, *Metaphysics*, 1007a 30ff.

[27] Cf. Plato, *Republic*, 479c ff.

[28] Cf. Aristotle, *Categoriae*, 1a 24f.

[29] Cf. L. Wittgenstein, *Philosophical Investigations*, I, p. 57.

They are no less clear-cut than such concepts as *man* and *finger*. And in this respect the concept of heap is no different[30].

---

[30] According to *Metaphysics*, 1012a 21-28 cited above, the reason for Anaxagoras' denying PET is some kind of mixing. The question as to whether this refers to a mixing of properties or of concepts doesn't arise in this context. In Anaxagoras' doctrine as understood by Aristotle here there is no such alternative: there are neither properties nor concepts ("λόγοι" in 1012a 23 means concept, but not in a24 or a26, and in a21 it means something else again). Concepts which are not related to each other *per se*, but only *per accidens via* substances as the bearer of properties (1007a 33-b16), cannot exist together. But on the conceptual level there are no such things as substances (in contrast to the concept of substance), therefore no properties either, but only their *pure* contents, i.e. their meanings (e.g. the content of substance or the meaning of "substance"). However, where, as in the case of Anaxagoras' philosophy (at least according to 1012a 21-28), all "things" are mixed, nothing can be pure, i.e., nothing can be a concept (meaning, definition). And there being no concepts, nothing can be a predicate of anything. So there can be no truth. The claim to truth cannot be fulfilled. To ask what "things" (truly) are is to ask nothing, for there is no such thing as "what is" (nor, of course, as "thing"). As has already been said, I am referring to Anaxagoras only within the context of the Aristotelian PET. Nevertheless the attribution of mixing to concepts (which therefore cannot be viewed as concepts proper) could also be sustained by considerations other than those suggested by 1012a 21-28. As J. Brentlinger writes: "It is true that *kinds* of quality are not separable for Anaxagoras, since every part of space contains every kind of quality as a matter of metaphysical necessity. Yet the *individual* parts of a substance are separable from one another and the whole", "Incomplete Predicates and the Two-World Theory of *Phaedo*", *Phronesis*, 1972, p. 72f. Cf. also M. Schofield, *An Essay on Anaxagoras*, Cambridge 1980, p. 13 *et passim*: "It is clear that 'everything' in 'a portion of everything' means 'every *kind* of thing'". For Aristotle, Anaxagoras' doctrine is the complement of Heraclitus's (and Protagoras's) doctrine in the same sense in which PET is the complement of PNC. Both do away with concepts (meanings, definitions), but this occurs for different reasons, viz. either through expanding or through contracting, adding or mixing. One might speak here of an "accordion"-effect. If the sharp boundaries between the concepts were to disappear, then each word (say "man") would have its own meaning *plus* the meaning of any other word with which it were not *per se* related or, alternatively, it would, as it were, absorb the meaning of any other such word. In the first case, one would, in saying what is such and such (e.g., man), at the same time be saying

The possibility of saying something true depends even in borderline cases on whether the entities involved manifest properties which correspond to well-defined concepts or not, irrespective of how much the corresponding boundaries may be blurred in a given physical instance. In reality the boundaries between the properties (as opposed to those of the parts) are somehow always blurred. All things in reality are in some degree borderline cases, cases of being (such and such) and not being (such and such)[31], whereas even concepts like *degree, more false than*, etc.[32], are always definable. In contrast to the realm of reality, the realm of ideality, i.e., of (contents of) concepts, meanings, or definitions, excludes intermediate cases by definition, as it were. (Nevertheless, this is not an uninformative statement). As a

---

> what is not *per se* or by definition the same thing (e.g. white) and so, in applying a given predicate, one would be applying the others *as well*. But then the claim to truth would always be fulfilled (1012a 25). And that is what PNC denies or asserts cannot possibly be true; in general, given two contradictory propositions the claim to truth can be fulfilled *at most* by one of them. This is not LNC. Similarly in the second case. A. now takes as his example the predicate "good". There can be no such thing as good if "good" does *not even* have *its own meaning*. And it could not even be said to have goodness, if its meaning were mixed with, or as it were absorbed in, all other meanings. The mixture would then be neither good nor not-good (1012a 27f.). It is immaterial whether A. (or Anaxagoras) is here referring to properties of things or to concepts since there is properly speaking neither the one nor the other. According to this doctrine, in using words one could only refer to something that is neither reality nor ideality, viz. mere possibilities without actuality (cf. 1009a 30-36 with reference to Anaxagoras and Democritus). This, of course, applies generally. Anyone using a predicate, regardless of which one, would not be able to say anything true (1012a 28) but only something false (1012a 27). The truth-claim could not be fulfilled by either of the contradictories. This is the negation of PET, since it means that, if anywhere, truth should be sought in some third thing between affirming and negating (1012b 26f.). And that is precisely what PET rejects. But here again the question arises as to what exactly it is that PET is rejecting. The answer is: in rejecting the philosophy of "Anaxagoras" Aristotle is rejecting the priority of potentiality over actuality. Here the problem of contingency is involved (see section 3 below).

[31] Cf. Aristotle, *Metaphysics*, 1007a 10ff., 16ff.
[32] Cf. Aristotle, *Metaphysics*, 1008b 31-1009a 5.

result even the most tricky borderline cases do not in the least require that one allow for exceptions to PET, as we shall presently see. On the other hand, whether or not exceptions are called for in the case of LEM is, as is well known, at least a matter of controversy. Even modern classical logicians like Geach are in doubt as to whether a logic of so-called vague predicates, i.e., of predicates relating to borderline cases in reality, would require such exceptions. He ends the paper I was referring to by saying: "I am not prepared to anticipate whether the allowing of exceptions to the Law of Excluded Middle would here turn out to be useful"[33]. Had he taken PET into account, his doubts would have disappeared, and he would have answered the question in the negative. He came, though, very near to PET when, for example, he wrote: "I cannot see that there is any advantage in such formulations" as "For any predicate P and any object x, P is either true of x or false of x" and "Every statement is either true or false"[34]. There is indeed no advantage in them –provided one does not reckon as an advantage the fact that in such formulations the difference between LEM and PET appears in the open. "Every statement is either true or false" refers to PB'. It precludes the possibility that the assertive affirmation or negation of p could be both true and false, i.e., it also precludes the possibility of both (p and _p) being true. The "either/or" of PB' is openly exclusive, whereas in LEM, which Geach prefers to PB', it is only in a hidden way exclusive; in itself it is, in fact, inclusive, but the PN presupposed in LEM ("(A) For any x, either x is F or x is not F"[35]) makes it behave like an exclusive "or"[36]. That is why any chance of PET resurfacing in the semantic counterpart (B)

---

[33] P. Geach, *Logic Matters*, p. 87.

[34] P. Geach, *Logic Matters*, p. 76.

[35] P. Geach, *Logic Matters*, p. 74.

[36] Compare "pv¬p", where "v", despite the fact that it presupposes PN, is in itself inclusive, but the "¬" attached to p makes it behave like an exclusive "either/or". By contrast, the "either/or" in PET does not presuppose PN, but only (P)C in which the built-in "or" is neither in an open nor in a hidden (or indirect) way exclusive, and the built-in "not" is not defined by PN. That is why one must distinguish "not-p" as belonging to PET from "¬p" as belonging to LEM/PB'.

of (A) ("(B) For any predicate P and any object x, either P or its negation is true of x"[37]) disappears as soon as it appears. Since, for the reasons given, there is here too a hidden exclusive "either/or"[38], any chance of keeping open the possibility, characteristic of PET, that both the affirmation and denial of the same thing might be true vanishes altogether. So, the difference between LEM ((A) or (B)) and PB' is after all not so great as it might at first sight appear, and as it certainly appears to Geach. Just as one "cannot see that there is any advantage in such formulations" which favor PB' over LEM ((A) or (B))[39], so one cannot see that there is any more advantage in favoring LEM ((A) or (B)) over PET. The reason is, again, that PN is included in LEM, whereas it is not PN, but (P)C, that is included in PET. Now, (P)C only means asserting p on the one hand and denying it (i.e., asserting not-p) on the other without referring to the fact that "true" and "false" mutually exclude each other and, in fact, without referring to truth-values at all, but only to truth-claims.

In the case of vague predicates too Geach is nearly about to get at PET, but he is also well aware of not having gone the whole way. As already said, the final sentence in his paper runs: "I am not prepared to anticipate whether the allowing of exceptions to the Law of Excluded Middle would here turn out to be useful"[40]. "Here" means "in developing a logic of vague predicates". In connection with Wittgenstein's picture of walling off a bog he writes: "It may appear that second-order vagueness arises over the drawing of the boundaries; but this is not so"[41]. So Geach rightly rejects any type of mixture whatsoever on the conceptual or "second-order" level and admits that to know where exactly to draw the boundaries on the real level is not the main issue, the mixing of properties (as different from parts) being on this level not wholly unavoidable. But, then, Geach goes on: "If x is even doubtfully inside the inner boundary, P will be true of it; if x is

---

[37] P. Geach, *Logic Matters*, p. 74.
[38] See n. 36 above.
[39] P. Geach, *Logic Matters*, p. 76.
[40] P. Geach, *Logic Matters*, p. 87.
[41] P. Geach, *Logic Matters*, p. 86.

even doubtfully outside the outer boundary, the negation of P will be true of it... This conclusion really ought not to shock us. Even if "oak" and "elephant" are both vague predicates, it is perfectly clear and certain that no oak-tree is an elephant; something that has even a doubtful claim to the predicate "oak" is certainly no elephant"[42]. This is indeed perfectly clear, but it is not the main issue. It is not a borderline case at all, a case, where one cannot help doubting whether some thing is P or not-P. In keeping with PET, i.e., without taking PNC, and therefore PN, into account from the very beginning, the relevant question can only be, could Px and not-Px both be true? The example concerning "elephant" and "oak" does not pose a problem either for PET or LEM. (Similarly, one may doubt whether some band of the spectrum is red or rather orange, but not whether it is red or rather blue. To take yet another example, in the issue of organs transplants one may doubt whether brain death is the true definition of man's death or not, but no one would take, say, blindness as such a definition). The boundary-lines A and B in Wittgenstein's picture and its interpretation by Geach aptly show that there must be a boundary which divides, say, baldness from non-baldness, but they do not show where exactly the boundary actually runs *in rerum natura* or whether such a question can be decided in the first place. Only questions such as those cited could pose serious problems. With this in mind I now go on to those cases which touch upon the point in question.

Nothing can be both elephant and oak. Similarly, no tree on the border between USA and Mexico could belong to Canada, but those on the border of Canada could. So one could ask: is the number of maples in Canada odd or even? The question could arise either (a) because the border with the USA passes right through the middle of

---

[42] P. Geach, *Logic Matters*, p. 86 f. As a matter of fact, all predicates become in some sense vague as soon as they are applied to reality since their corresponding properties are all combined in their subject; whether combined as mixed with each other or not depends on whether one adheres to the *distinctio rationis ratiocinatae* or to the *distinctio formalis a parte rei*. In keeping with Aristotle I adopt the stance implied by the first alternative (cf. my article "Die philosophische querelle des anciens et des modernes", pp. 329-352).

some maples or (b) because of uncertainty as to where the border lies or (c) because of the impossibility of counting them for whatever reason. In Wittgenstein's picture, (a) corresponds to the x's located on A or on B; (b) to those located in the bog zone; (c) is a more general and difficult case. The difficulties concern, though, only LEM or PB', not PET. For even if the cases were truly undecidable, insofar as one could perhaps construct an undecidable case (c), this would be no objection to PET, the reason being that PET allows for the possibility of saying both "'the number of... is odd' is true" and "'the number of ... is not odd but even' is true"[43] which both LEM and PB' do not. (In those cases where, as with odd and even numbers, the contradictories involved are *per se* contraries as well the contraries cannot both be false, as is the case with ordinary contraries; cf. n. 13 below). With this, the main thing concerning (a) and (b) has already been said. But it is worthwhile to elaborate a bit more. A decision in the case of (a) and (b) ought to be reached by convention or agreement. This is also the case with the sorites paradox. As Quine writes: "Where to draw the line between heaps and non-heaps... remains an open option"[44]. Now, for PB' (as well as LEM) to remain in force, a decision has to be made. But the decision being more or less arbitrary, PB' rests on

---

[43] Cf. Aristotle, *Metaphysics,* 1012a 9-12.

[44] W.O.V. Quine, "What Price Bivalence?", p. 90ff. Cf. n. 64 below. Insofar as he chooses to concentrate on PB' instead of LEM, does not even manage, as Geach had done, to cover half the distance towards PET, but his examples, unlike Geach's, give rise to serious doubts and hence to real questions. - The reader might wonder how it is that I come to deal so extensively in section 2 with Quine's article since, according to its very title, it concerns PB' but not LEM. The reason is that Quine takes PB', as have so many others, to be equivalent to DPN and thus to entail LEM. (On the other hand, the acceptance of LEM is generally considered not to entail that of PB'). Consequently, when one considers that LEM, but not PB', remains unaffected by such issues as that of the truth of statements about the contingent future (in *Peri Hermeneias,* 9), it seems to me that LEM has been implicitly identified with PET. If this is, in fact, the case, then what modern interpreters have been calling the "standard" or "traditional" interpretation of *Peri Hermeneias,* 9 and my construal of the Aristotelian and traditional PET's would, after all, not exclude one another.

shaky ground. This is even more obvious with respect to both (a) and (b). Both countries, USA and Canada, could more or less arbitrarily agree as to which maples belong to which country (a) or as to where the border exactly lies (b)[45]. But what if they do not? Then PB'/LEM founders, but PET does not (nor indeed PB), for as far as it is concerned nothing hinders one from ascribing the disputed trees to both countries. PET can afford to wait, as it were, and see[46]. Nevertheless,

---

[45] Because of the arbitrariness or at least conventionality of any decision as well as the possibility of *continuum a parte rei*, the decision could always be revised. - It is interesting to note that for M. Dummett the question leading to anti-realism "was not whether the reality that rendered our statements true or false was *external*, but whether it was *fully determinate*" (*Truth and other enigmas*, p. 356f). Much could be said about this in Aristotelian terms, but not here (cf. n. 43 above).

[46] In the meantime, since PET neither (unlike LEM) implies nor contradicts it, PNC has not been contravened. Besides, the claim to ownership of the disputed trees or zones is not the same for both countries. The reasons for ascribing the disputed trees to one country are not the same as those for ascribing them to the other, since the tree-halves falling on both sides of the fixed border in case (a) are different as well. But note that the belonging of part (half) of a tree to it is not itself a part of the tree but a property which concerns the whole tree. That is why the whole tree and not only half of it can belong to the two countries and does belong to both as long as an agreement (in case (a) or (b)) has not been reached. Otherwise neither the conflict nor the question would arise. - Similarly for the sorites paradox (see below): each time one adds a grain one may say that the result is or can be a heap and not a heap in that it is more of a heap than the previous results but less than the subsequent ones (cf. Aristotle, *Metaphysics*, 1008b 31-1009a 5). A decision as to where the borderline should be drawn need not be made any more than in the conflict about the country-border (b). PET/PB, but not LEM/PB', survives even the impossibility of deciding, conventionally or otherwise. - The problem is *a parte rei* more general than the sorites paradox would suggest. Where does one draw the boundaries between man and not-man (eunuch), finger and not-finger, bad and not-bad, etc.? (cf. Plato, *Republic*, 478 ff.: μεταξὺ τῆς οὐσίας καὶ τοῦ μὴ εἶναι). "The paradox", says Quine, "is engendered by vague terms generally". ("What Price Bivalence?", p. 91). That is true, but badly expressed. If all general terms (concepts) are vague, there are no vague terms (as opposed to not-vague ones). "Small" and "smaller" are in principle not vaguer then "man" and "white". It is only because of the indeterminateness ("mixedness") of reality that we can speak of vague terms in the first place. *A*

the possibility of an agreement, however conventional it may be, is always given independently of whether it is realized or not. This is sufficient to avoid having PET come into conflict with PNC.

Once the decision has been made, PET does not fail to take effect either. (Whether the decision is that all the disputed trees or zones should belong to Canada, or all to the USA or some trees or zones to one and some to the other is immaterial). But what if the decision should be impossible either as a matter of fact or because there is no fact of the matter? The former case corresponds to (c), the latter has no analogue in our example. I shall presently take up another example of Quine's to illustrate it. Meanwhile, Quine's example ((c')) corresponding to (c) is whether "there was an odd number of blades of grass in Harvard Yard at the dawn of Commencement Day, 1908" (c'). If we were realists we would "declare that it is either true or false" that c'[47]. To be a realist or not is then a matter of arbitrary decision, which would compromise the validity of PB' (and LEM). For Aristotle, to be a realist[48] no such decisions are necessary. Even if no decision has been, or (because of the supposed impossibility of counting) can be made, PET loses none of its force.

Behind questions like (c) lies, as Quine says about (c'), a "robust" matter of fact[49] –despite the fact that the latter at least is clearly undecidable. But these are, as already hinted, not the most difficult

---

parte rei there is in principle always the possibility of a *continuum* with borderline cases everywhere. On the contrary, different concepts, i.e., concepts which are accidental (*per accidens*) to each other (cf. 1007a 30 ff.), cannot be thought of as a *continuum*. Otherwise they would overlap at some parts, i.e., they would not be *per accidens* to each other. The reason why they cannot mix with each other is that they don't belong to any οὐσία as their subject. Different concepts (*man, white, educated*, etc.) could at most be thought of as being in contiguity, not continuity (cf. Aristotle, *Physica*, 227a 10-17), with each other. There is for A. no all-embracing logical space (more on this in the article referred to in n. 43).

[47] W.V.O. Quine, "What Price Bivalence?", p. 91.

[48] Contrast *Peri Hermeneias*, 18b 38-9 with Anaxagoras' apophthegm reported in Aristotle, *Metaphysics*, 1009b 26-28.

[49] W.V.O. Quine, "What Price Bivalence?", p. 93.

cases for PB'/LEM. The most difficult are those regarding which there is neither the possibility of arbitrary decision as in (a), (b), or the paradoxical sorites case, "nor a matter of inscrutable but objective fact" like (c') and perhaps (c) too. Such is the case ((c")) with respect to questions of the form, "when is a table not a table". The question is wholly undecidable in spite of the fact that one can, as Quine put it, "diminish a table, conceptually, molecule by molecule"[50] and –as I would like to add– with the remaining ones build conceptually (or even really) an indefinite number of other tables. This slight modification would seem to make things even more difficult than they were in Quine's example. For granted that in a substance there cannot be "actually" (as Aristotle would say, or, as Quine says, "as a matter of fact") more than one substance ("tables are mutually exclusive, only one is present"), one cannot help but ask, in introducing with Aristotle the concept of potentiality, how many tables are contained potentially in a single table[51]. This is exactly the sort of question Aristotle would ask. However, what seems to make things still more difficult is the

---

[50] W.V.O. Quine, "What Price Bivalence?", pp. 92-94.

[51] Quine himself suggests this modification of his own example: "A table contains a graded multitude of nested or overlapping physical objects each of which embodies enough of the substance to have qualified as a table in its own right, but only in abstraction from the rest of the molecules. *Each of these physical objects would qualify as a table*, that is, if cleared of the overlying and surrounding molecules, but should not be counted as a table when still embedded in a further physical object that so qualifies in turn", W.V.O. Quine, "What Price Bivalence?", p. 92 (my emphasis). However, while suggesting a multiplicity of tables, Quine is not inquiring, as Aristotle might have done, as to the possibility of a substance (supposing a table to be a substance) being potentially more than one (cf. *Metaphysics*, 1039a 3-17, 1040b 5-1041a 5, 1009a 34-36). According to Quine, one is committed "to treating the table as one and not another" (*ibid.*, 94). This is true as long as one does not put the question in terms of potentiality. So while Quine is presupposing an exclusive "either/or" Aristotle is not. The reason for this is Quine's preference for the modern variant of PB. (Cf. *ibid.*, 91: Bivalance requires "at each stage that the statement that a heap remains, or that the man is bald, be univocally true or false"). The same thing applies to LEM, but not to PET (nor to the genuine Aristotelian PB which states the non-necessity of all assertions being false; cf. section 1 above).

real solution according to PET. The relevant question for LEM as well as for PET is whether sentences such as "there is only one table" (p) and "there is not only one table" (not-p) could both possibly be true (alternatively, for PB', whether affirming and negating p could at the same time possibly be true). As far as this question is concerned the answer of LEM/PB' is definitely no, and this leads to difficulties. But in the case of PET the situation is not quite comparable. This requires explanation.

Quine knows that to state that there is in actuality only one table is no solution: "*Yet* we are committed, *nevertheless*, to treating the table as one and not another of this multitude of imperceptibly divergent physical objects. Such is bivalence"[52]. And such is LEM. But such is not PET. The possibility remains that there could be potentially many tables in this one table, and then the question arises, how many, exactly n or not exactly n? The only threat to PET would then be the possibility of both contradictories being false. But the possibilities which must be taken into account in answering this question do not include this one. They may be summed up as follows:

(1) "It is possible that there are no more and no less than, i.e., exactly n tables in this one table and it is possible that there are not exactly n tables in this one table" ($\lozenge p \& \lozenge \neg p$). This is the only case in which both sides of the proposition could be false, but here the alternatives involved are not mutually exclusive, i.e., they are not true contradictories[53];

(2) "It is possible that there are exactly n tables in this one table and it is not possible that there are exactly n tables in this one table"

---

[52] W.V.O. Quine, "What Price Bivalence?", p. 94 (my emphasis).

[53] From Plato's *Parmenides* to Kant's *Critique of Pure Reason* there had been a clear awareness, firstly, of the impossibility of two contradictories both being false and, secondly, of the fact that it is only when some condition necessary for the contradiction to obtain is lacking that both sides can be false. For Plato, cf. the first section of the first hypothesis as interpreted by C. Meinwald in *Plato's Parmenides*, pp. 76-94 and for Kant, cf. A 503 f./B 531 f. on the mathematical antinomies with reference to Plato and Zeno in A 502/B 532; A 503 f./B 531 f. in particular offers a clear parallel to case (1) above.

($\Diamond p \& \neg \Diamond p$). Here again there are two possibilities to be taken into account: (2a) one side of the proposition ("it is impossible that there are exactly n tables") is true and the other false (perhaps because of the continuity of matter); or (2b) it is not the case that (2a) so that the only option which remains open is that both are true, it being impossible that both could be false. To these one might add still another possibility:

(3) there is nothing here to be decided upon because there is no fact of the matter at all –neither an empirically underdetermined one nor any other kind.

In none of the (three or four) possibilities entertained here has PET been put at risk.

Even assuming that the example is not decidable either by convention or, like the blades of grass example, as a "robust matter of fact", i.e., even in the form originally intended by Quine[54], this would

---

[54] Having suggested the possibility of dividing a single table into a multiplicity of individual tables, Quine continues: "Yet something remains of Unger's point [cf. "What Price Bivalence", p. 92: 'Peter Unger has lately argued that the problem runs deeper (than the heap-paradox). Diminish a table, conceptually, molecule by molecule: when is a table not a table? No stipulations will avail us here, however arbitrary']. There remains the question of how much to include in the table in the way of superficial or hovering molecules... we are at a loss to frame a convention for the molecular demarcation of the surface of a table", W.V.O. Quine, "What Price Bivalence?", p. 93. "It is neither a matter of convention nor a matter of inscrutable but objective fact. Yet we are committed, nevertheless, to treating the table as one and not another of this multitude of imperceptibly divergent physical objects. Such is bivalence" (*ibid.*, p. 94). In the main text this passage had been quoted only in connection with the modified example. But the real problem is the same here as in the unmodified example. For, as Quine further writes, "It is in the spirit of bivalence not just to treat each closed sentence as true or false; as Frege stressed, each general term must be *definitely* true or *false* of each object, specifiable or not. If the term "table" is to be reconciled with bivalence, we must posit an exact demarcation, *exact to the last molecule*, even though we cannot specify it. We must hold that there are physical objects, *coincident except for one molecule*, such that one is a table and the other is not" (*ibid.*; my emphasis). I emphasize "definitely" in order to stress the difference between Quine's "definitely true or

false" and the "indeterminately true or false" corresponding to the traditional interpretation (cf. n. 73 and the end of n. 62; as for the modern view, see once again Quine, who argues that bivalence requires that the statement "be univocally true or false", *ibid.*, p. 91). Again, I emphasize "exact to the last molecule" as well as "coincident except for one molecule" in order to stress the relevant similarity between the unmodified and the modified example. In both cases the alternatives are "exactly n" and "not exactly n", i.e., whether exactly n potential tables or exactly n molecules are needed to make up this one actual table. (For Aristotle at any rate "n" cannot be infinit - not even potentially - since he does not admit, as Quine does, variable numbers). In both cases the question, whether exactly n or not exactly n, can be meaningfully put, even though it is impossible to answer it. But the impossibility of giving an answer applies only to PB'/LEM, not to PB/PET. And since it applies to them not only in this one case but in all such cases where there are, evidently, no objective facts to decide upon, one is forced, if one wishes to save PB'/LEM, to take refuge in extreme cases as in Geach's interpretation of the picture of walling off a bog. In the unmodified table example, though, there is no room for such extreme cases, but only for real borderline ones. On the other hand, the fact that each general term is not without some vagueness, would only come as a surprise to those who were not prepared to accept the fact that no general term, regardless of how clear-cut it is *qua* concept, can prevent the appearance of real borderline cases as soon as it has been applied to reality as a predicate *via* judgment - not because concepts which are not connected *per se* have been mixed but because properties are always mixed in reality. For A. all concepts are clear-cut in a way that no real property is; otherwise he would automatically be an adherent of the theory of *distinctio formalis a parte rei*. With regard to its applicability to reality, each predicate is on a par with so-called vague predicates (see n. 47). At the end of his article Quine writes: "What we now observe is that bivalence requires us further to view each general term, e.g. 'table', as true or false of objects even in the absence of what we in our bivalent way are prepared to recognize as objective fact" (*ibid.*, 94). It is in this respect that the table example, in whatever variant or according to whatever interpretation, may legitimately be compared with the example of vague predicates. A human head with only one hair is just as surely bald as it would be a full head of hair, were it to have billions of hairs, but this does not preclude there being real borderline cases. The only difference here is that the unmodified table example concerns only those cases in which a decision according to some fact of the matter has been rendered impossible but not the very decidability of the question itself. Further differences between Aristotle's and Quine's ways of viewing the question of indeterminacy or underdeter-

not alter the main point. For it belongs to the very essence of PET never to rule out the possibility of such wholly undecidable cases, whereas PB' and LEM[55] (as well as *pet*[56]) rule them out from the very beginning. That is Quine's predicament. And it was also Geach's tacit predicament. The only reason why it did not appear in the open was because –as we saw– Geach had only gone half-way in drawing the consequences of Wittgenstein's picture, i.e., eschewing those borderline cases in which serious doubts and real questions arise as to whether the latter are decidable or not. Potentially there can be undecidably many tables in one table. What cannot be is for a table to be potentially, say, a man[57]. For "man" and "table" are both names for essences. Rejecting as he does the Aristotelian distinction between essence and accident as well as any form of *modalitas de re* Quine himself would not find much point, though, in making such a statement.

3

If my interpretation has been faithful to Aristotle, then a long-standing controversy surrounding 1047b 3 ff.[58], becomes obsolete as

---

minacy respectively do not alter the main issue concerning PB or PET. In Quine it is not always clear whether behind the undecidability of the one-table example there is a fact of the matter which could be decided upon. If not, the example would fall under case (3) (cf. the main text corresponding to this note), otherwise under (2b) (insofar as it is empirically underdetermined).

[55] More on this in section 3.

[56] Cf. Appendix (5").

[57] Cf. Aristotle, *Metaphysics*, 1007a 20f.

[58] "The hardest passage" (R. Sorabji, *Necessity, Cause, and Blame*, p. 136). The passage runs as follows: "If what we have is the possible or a consequence of the possible, evidently it cannot be true to say, 'this is capable of being but will not be', a view which leads to the conclusion that there is nothing incapable of being" (a comparison with the incommensurability of the diagonal follows; cf. 1012a 26-28 with 31-33). For the controversy itself see R.T. McClelland, "Time and Mo-

soon as one reads this passage in the light of PET. For a future event to be contingently possible means: already now (actually) it is false that neither p nor not-p will be; both can (possibility) now (actuality) be at the same time (then, actually) in the future[59]. *Metaphysics*, 1047b 4 f., says this *expressis verbis*: "It cannot be true to say 'this is capable of being but will not be'". Contrary to the common assumption on both sides of the controversy, this sentence, when understood in its entirety, does not endorse the principle of plenitude ("p is possible iff it will sometime occur"). What the sentence states instead is that even in the case of future contingents it is already true now that both parts, p and not-p, can in the future occur, notwithstanding the fact that only one side of the contradiction will take place. And since the sentence "this is capable of being but will not be" has in this context nothing to do with, and hence is not negating, the principle of plenitude, its denial does not imply this principle any more than any other kind of determinism –the assumption which necessitated ascribing the whole sentence under discussion to the

---

dality in Aristotle" in *Archiv für Geschichte der Philosophie*, 1981 (63), pp. 130-149, who sides with G.E.L. Owen, M. Kneale, and others, (as does J. van Rijen in a later article, "The Principle of Plenitude" *ibid.*, 1984 (66), p. 63 n. 7) against D. Ross, J. Hintikka, and others. For an interpretation differing from both interpretations as well as from the present one, see H. Weidemann, "Das sogenannte Meisterargument des Diodoros Kronos und der Aristotelische Möglichkeitsbegriff", *ibid.*, p. 35 n. 44. For the interpretation of 1047b 3-6 expounded in the main text I am indebted to A. García-Marqués. His interpretation of *Met.* IX.4, discussed 1989/90 in a seminar in Münster, has in the meantime appeared in *Philosophisches Jahrbuch*, 100, 1993. In light of his interpretation one may say that only from the standpoint of LEM does the passage appear to be as difficult as it has been made out to be. As a matter of fact its point is almost trivial: one should not, in dealing with future contingents, say that some event is possible but will not happen for one would thereby be treating the one possibility as if it were impossible, viz. the possibility that will not be actualized. In other words, one would have destroyed the meaning of "impossibility" by confounding it with one of the two possibilities associated with a future contingent. So understood, the passage is arguing against the Megarians, and it is not necessary to look for some other known (or unknown) opponent.

[59] Cf. Aristotle, *Metaphysics*, 1009a 35ff. and 1011b 21ff.

Megarians as well as changing the meaning of the next one[60]. Some event is now possible despite the fact that it will not happen or (contrary to the principle of plenitude) perhaps never will happen. It is not any less possible than its contradictory. Both possibilities are already now equally true. "That you are standing now is false, but not impossible"[61]. He can just as easily remain seated as get up.

---

[60] "A view which leads to the conclusion that there is nothing incapable of being", i.e., impossible. The rest of the present paper interprets this sentence as well as its explanation by means of a mathematical example (cf. n. 66 below) according to the main lines laid down in sections 1 and 2 above, without having to change its meaning (see n. 59 above).

[61] Aristotle, *Metaphysics*, 1047b 13f. For Aristotle (contrary to D. Scotus) the present (actuality) cannot be contingent. Nevertheless, the wording of 1047b 13 (which is still concerned with the incommensurability of the diagonal) does not completely exclude the contingency of the present, as *Peri Hermeneias*, 19a 22 ff. does: for the present (actuality) and the past, the false and the impossible coincide, but not for the contingent future. In a recent discussion of *Peri Hermeneias*, 9 one may read: "With this characterisation of necessity, we are now in a position to evaluate the indeterminist results that Thomason derives from his logic of nonlinear time, a logic that, he says, 'puts these alternatives [the possible futures] into the ontological structure of time' and succeeds 'in developing a rigorous form of traditional popular view that 'future contingent' statements can be *neither true nor false*' [my emphasis]". (P. Yourgrau, *The Disappearance of Time: Kurt Gödel and the Idealistic Tradition in Philosophy*, Cambridge 1991, p. 86). The words emphasized show that, in some respect, this view does agree with the Aristotelian one, but not in that respect which is relevant to our concerns. It is true that in the case of future contingents, as Aquinas, for example, put it, here agreeing with Aristotle. (cf. n. 74 below), neither member of the contradiction is already determinately true or false. Where the words emphasized diverge from the traditional view of Aristotle, Aquinas, and others is in treating "true" and "false" in connection with statements about future contingents as both being on an equal footing. For in the Aristotelian view the statements could both be true, but not both false, which is precisely what PET says. I know of no traditional interpretation of Aristotle where the question of future contingents puts PET at risk (or indeed PB in the Aristotelian sense, explained in section 1 above, of the non-necessity of affirming or denying p to be false). As far as the traditional interpretation is concerned it would be manifestly inconsistent to maintain this. Yourgrau does not

Possibility in general means that nothing impossible results if (when) a particular possibility is supposed to occur. This applies both to necessary and to contingent future events. Contingency means

---

seem to notice this. When a few pages before (*ibid.*, p. 82) he had cited, directly from *Peri Hermeneias* itself, the wording of the passage ["Clearly, therefore, not everything is or happens of necessity: some things happen as chance has it, and of the affirmation *and* the negation, *neither* is *true* rather than the other" (*ibid.*, 19a 7; my emphasis)] was at any rate significantly different from the version he later (*ibid.*, p. 86) quotes from Thomason. The words of Aristotle's emphasized by Yourgrau show clearly the contrast to the "traditional popular view" ("can be *neither true nor false*"). Unlike these bracketed words Aristotle's own words do not exclude (nor indeed include) that affirmation and negation of the same proposition (which is not, as Yourgrau seems to accept, genuine Aristotelian PB, but PET) could both be true (neither do they include that both could or must be false, which would be the only way of running up against PET or Aristotelian PB respectively). I cannot go into the details of modern interpretations of *Peri Hermeneias*, 9 (or indeed the details of *Peri Hermeneias*, 9 itself). Suffice it to say that Yourgrau (or Thomason) is not the only interpreter who reads the text in connection with PB'/LEM rather than with PET and with the genuine Aristotelian PB, disregarding in the process Aristotle's very wording. In Yourgrau the founder of intuitionistic logic and mathematics, L.E.J. Brouwer, is quoted as having said the following: "expected experiences... are true only as anticipations and *hypotheses; in their contents* there is *no truth*" (my emphasis). This fits in perfectly well with the Aristotelian and traditional view. But then Yourgrau adds: "Brouwer, of course, is critical of classic logic - especially of the principle of excluded middle (which, as we have seen, so vexed Aristotle)" (*ibid.*, p. 166). I suspect Brouwer, like Yourgrau, was only acquainted with PEM, not with PET. (Incidentally, what, in Yourgrau's words, "so vexed Aristotle" was not "the principle of excluded middle" but, according to Yourgrau, of bivalence, for, in his attempt to interpret Aristotle, Yourgrau had written (*ibid.*, p. 82): "2. *Excluded middle* holds, necessarily, for all propositions. 3. *Bivalence* does *not* hold for *all* (especially future-tensed) propositions". One is tempted to see therein a symptom of the confusion which still prevails with respect to the topic of my paper). On the other hand, the fact that according to Brouwer (as cited by Yourgrau) "the criterion of the truth or falsehood of a mathematical assertion [is] confined to mathematical activity itself" also fits in perfectly well with the fact that for PET the truth-value has to be attached not to the "content", but to the affirmative or negative truth-claim inasmuch as it succeeds or fails.

nothing else than the truth (now) of the possibility of both sides of a contradiction (in the future). Here nothing differs significantly from the previously discussed cases, which would at most have led to restricting the validity of LEM and PB but in any case not that of PET. This is so because, unlike the former two, the latter leaves open the possibility that both sides of the contradiction are true[62]. But as soon as the one or the other, but not both, takes place, PET, as it were, gives way to LEM and PB, i.e. it is no longer needed with respect to that in which it differs from LEM and PNC[63]. If someone insisted on

---

[62] Neither PB nor PN applies here, but still only (P)C. For this reason it would be begging the question against PET to operate with "-p". Similarly, the connective "and" (in "p and not-p"), as far as PET (or PNC) alone is concerned, must not be taken to signify "&", which presupposes PN, but rather a non-exclusive "either/or". Thus, regarding future contingents the important thing is to leave open the possibility of either contradictory being true without saying in advance which one, i.e., to posit neither Ap nor Anot-p as being determinately true (see n. 74 below). That is the bone of contention, not $\Box(p \& \neg p)$ or even $(\Box p \& \Box \neg p)$, which must not be allowed at this point to intervene. To think of either in this connection would be again to beg the question against PET: in the case of the former, because the actualization of the supposed possibility ($\Diamond$) would result in an impossibility; in the case of the latter, because it does not represent a contradiction in the sense of P(C) (nor indeed in that of PN).

[63] This does not imply any restriction on PET's validity. Restricting the validity of PET would only mean allowing for the possibility that both contradictories may be false. But this is not the case here. When the conflict is settled and the question answered, then one side of the contradiction is at any rate true (PET) and the other must be false, not because of PET, but because of PNC. Once the question is settled (if only by the passage of time) things return as it were to normality. To put it another way, contingency is not normal in that PNC does not fully bear upon it (Aristotle, *Metaphysics*, 1009a 35), as in the case of a conflict that has not yet been settled. But note that contingency doesn't come into conflict with PNC any more than PET does. It would come into conflict with it only if all things were contingent. But because of the unrestricted validity of PNC as well as of PET this is impossible. Since the notion of all things being contingent is for Aristotle self-contradictory, there must be something which cannot possibly not be. The argument is a *reductio ad absurdum* (cf. *Metaphysics*, 1071b 25f.). Under PET the contradictory of the contradiction cannot itself be false, and under PET along with

applying it in this respect once the event had occurred, this would result in an impossibility[64]. This does not suggest any restriction on its validity, since the impossible was never included in the range of the application of PET. So the move from LEM and PB to LET and *pet* is thus far unnecessary (and the move from realism to Dummett's antirealism too). "Thus far" means "as long as PET is available".

At first sight, it might seem strange that Aristotle should explain possibility (*qua* contingency) by means of a mathematical example. But that is no stranger than recourse to mathematical examples in

---

PNC it must be true. In connection with the *reductio* some variant of the principle of plentitude does apply. In the case of an actually infinite past consisting of events, all of which could have been as well as not have been, the individual possibilities of their not having been would all have to be actualized at sometime or other, so that nothing of that which now is would have come into existence (There has been much discussion on related passages. For some of the most recent, cf. R. Sorabji, *Time, Creation and the Continuum*, London 1983, p. 277f., as well as L. Judson, "Eternity and Necessity in *De Caelo* I.12", in *Oxford Studies in Ancient Philosophy*, Oxford 1983, pp. 217-255). On the other hand, in Aristotle, as in Greek mathematics generally, the applicability of PET is not restricted to the (actual) infinite. His mathematics is finitistic in the sense that it does not recognize an actual infinite. Nevertheless PET remains valid, as it does in Greek mathematics as a whole. Hence the possibility —contrary to the tenets of intuitionistic finitism— of proving theorems not by the construction of examples but by *reductio ad absurdum*. For a treatment of the incommensurability of the diagonal insofar as it bears on *Anal. Pr.*, I, 41a 26-28, cf. T. L. Heath, *History of Greek Mathematics*, I, Oxford 1921, p. 91.

[64] What about the impossibility of rendering the diagonal commensurable (cf. Aristotle, *Metaphysics*, 1047b 6-12)? In terms of PET the case is no different from that of necessary future events or, for that matter, of present or past ones. Here too PET gives way to LEM and BP' (with respect to that in which it differs from both as well as from PNC) without sacrificing any of its validity. But this is not because of any advantage the former two may have over PET but because PNC, in its specificity, then intervenes and, together with PET, results in PN, from which LEM/BP' as well as LNC follow. (A comparison with the diagonal is also to be found in 1012a 31-33).

intuitionistic philosophy of logic. The comparison[65] illustrates very well the applicability of PET to contingent future events. But it illustrates as well its undisputed applicability (along with PB/LEM) to those cases in which there is no question of the possibility of p and not-p both being true. (As examples of such cases I am thinking, in addition to examples like Geach's concerning elephants and oaks[66], of past and present as well as necessary future events. These examples involve problems whose theoretical solution might have required PET had they not already been solved). Now, the point of the comparison is as follows. The impossibility of finding a common unit for measuring both the side and the diagonal has already been proved. Nevertheless, like all disturbing mathematical hypotheses (Goldbach's and the like), it could just as well not yet have been proved. This is, of course, in the case of the diagonal, counterfactual, but matters of fact are not the same as matters of impossibility (nor of necessity nor, indeed, of possibility). Concerning this there is for the moment no disagreement between Aristotle and his present non-Megarian opponent. Both agree in rejecting up to this point the principle of plenitude so that they need not bother too much about it in this connection as those modern interpreters are forced to do who presuppose LEM and PB instead of PET. However, under the pretext that the principle of plenitude is so far false, as for Aristotle as well as his present opponent it really is, Aristotle's opponent is treating the impossible as if it were possible, necessity (impossibility that such-and-such is necessity that not such-and-such) as if it were contingency, past and present events as if they were future ones. But note that he is not so much treating both as if

---

[65] "Suppose, for instance, that a man (one who did not understand the meaning of 'incapable of being' [i.e., impossible]) were to say that the diagonal of the square is capable of being measured but will not be measured, because a thing may be capable of being, or coming to be, and yet not be or be about to be. But from the premises this necessarily follows, that if we actually suppose that which is not, but is capable of being, to be or have come to be, there will be nothing impossible in this; but the result *will* be impossible, for the actual measuring of the diagonal is impossible. For the false and the impossible are not the same; that you are standing now is now false, but not impossible". Aristotle, *Metaphysics*, 1047b 6-14.

[66] See section 2 above.

they were alike as he is reducing the former to the latter. What he is saying is, first, that the fact that the (hypothetical) possibility of commensurability has not yet been proved does not prove anything –as, as a matter of fact, it (really) does not. But from this true premise the present opponent then wrongly infers that commensurability could be possible and proceeds as if it were possible. Now, this contradicts the definition of possibility Aristotle had already given[67] and is repeating here[68]: possible is everything which upon becoming actual does not result in impossibility. However, precisely this would happen if the possibility of rendering the diagonal commensurable were to become actual[69], for (as a matter of fact) it is not possible to render the diagonal commensurable. This sounds like a case of begging the question, but it is not. For, as a matter of fact, the incommensurability has already been proved. The question has already been settled and so it is no longer a matter for the future to decide, but one belonging to the present and the past; not a case of contingency but of necessity and therefore of impossibility as well; PET, in its specificity, need no longer be concerned with it, as it would have been called upon to do before the case had been settled.

Before I elaborate on this, note that there can be present and past events that have been or once were possible[70] ("possible" in the relevant sense of contingent), no less than there can be future events that are necessary (will necessarily occur). This does not change anything about the (special kind of) necessity of the past and the present. It only means that questions about now present or past things are by now settled; it does not decide anything about whether the things themselves (events or whatever) were or are contingent or necessary. It is all a matter of a changing point of view. Viewed from an ever-passing, ever-different 'now' even the events which, viewed from a by now past 'now', were then future contingent ones (τὰ

---

[67] Cf. Aristotle, *Metaphysics*, 1047a 24-26.
[68] Aristotle, *Metaphysics*, 1047b 9-11.
[69] Aristotle, *Metaphysics*, 1047b 11f.
[70] Cf. Aristotle, *Metaphysics*, 1047b 10.

μέλλοντα) are now (and, of course, were from the point of view of any other now posterior to them) necessary (τὰ ἐχόμενα).

To elaborate, it is not that Aristotle is begging the question by saying that this type of commensurability is impossible and thus concluding that it cannot be possible. It is rather that the present (non-Megarian) opponent is treating the impossible as if it were possible under the pretext that the principle of plenitude is as a matter of fact (really) false. He is acting as if the incommensurability had not yet been proved (which anyone is perfectly justified in doing if he wants to) and then on this hypothetical basis treating impossibility like possibility, necessity like contingency, questions already settled not so much as if they were not yet settled (which he is perfectly correct in doing in hypothetical discourse), but as if they could be settled otherwise, i.e., in the sense of the commensurability of the diagonal. In other words, he is treating by now settled questions as not yet settled, *and then* acting as if the outcome would not be an impossibility. To put the matter still differently, he is not taking his supposition hypothetically but is asserting its content or at least still asserting the possibility that its content is true, i.e., asserting, even after the outcome to the contrary, the possibility that p is true and hence asserting the possibility of asserting p (= Ap). True, according to PET, the assertion of the possibility of Ap and of Anot-p ("p" stands here for the commensurability of the diagonal) is possibly true, but the possibility of Anot-p is not the impossibility of p –otherwise the possibility of counterfactual as well as *si per impossibile* reasoning would not be given. Once the impossibility of p has been proved, one may assert p or not-p, i.e., A(p or not-p) but not just p, unless one is affirming p hypothetically, which is tantamount, of course, to not asserting it[71].

In insisting on applying PET to questions already settled in just that sense in which it differs from PNC as well as from LEM, the present non-Megarian opponent is treating the past and the future as if they were symmetrical. (As already pointed out, there can be present

---

[71] Cf. related (critical) remarks on Aristotle's *De Caelo*, 281b 19ff. in R. Sorabji, *Time, Creation and the Continuum*, p. 278.

or past events that have been or once were contingent, without this changing anything about the necessity of present or past events. It only means that on Aristotelian terms one must not regard past and future as being symmetrical. I shall, though, set aside the issue of the ever different nows). PET is a revised version of LEM insofar as it shares with it the realistic approach. Hence it does not allow for the possibility that assertions about forgotten (but not irretrievably forgotten or never perceived) events may, like assertions about contingent future events, become true. Contrary to LET/*pet*, the "revised version of LEM" (PET), in spite of the ever-changing nows, does not allow the possibility of viewing past and future as symmetrical, *in casu* of viewing the past as a contingent future event. LET/*pet* must keep this possibility open, e.g., in the event that a not irretrievably forgotten event were to be recorded again. Here one would indeed, in some sense, be "bringing about the past" –not necessarily in the idealistic sense of causing past events, but in the non-realistic sense of letting the corresponding statement, which had been in the time preceding, though not irrevocably[72], neither true nor false (= negation of unrevised LEM/PB'), be true again. This is not permitted by PET, which constitutes a revised version of LEM, i.e., the LEM of genuine traditional logic.

The impossibility of there being a symmetry between past and future events has its parallel in the logical, i.e., atemporal, necessity of certain mathematical truths such as the impossibility of rendering the diagonal commensurable. With this I do not mean to say that Aristotle is comparing the incomparable, contingent events with non-contingent (though perhaps not already acknowledged) truths; such a distinction has by no means been blurred here. Rather, he is comparing

---

[72] M. Dummett, *Truth and others enigmas*, p. 364. By presupposing PN instead of PET, it might be thought that in those cases where an issue about the past that has not yet been decided is afterwards decided the past is after all thus far symmetrical with the (contingent) future. Now, PET always applies in cases of contingency, but the decision here under consideration concerns not the past event but the future decision. So there is no room for such a symmetry. Cf. my paper "Freiheit und Determinismus" in M. Dummett et al, *Atti del IV Convegno di Studi Settimane Mediterranee*, Palermo 1979, pp. 73-89.

mathematical propositions with propositions about events precisely in order to show that the incomparable must *not* be compared, viz. past with future, necessity with contingency. According to Aristotle either one must not treat the impossible as if it were possible, or –if one insists on doing so– one must put up with the consequences, i.e., with running at last into an impossibility. Least of all is he begging any questions.

To sum up, in *Metaphysics,* 1047b 3-16 Aristotle is neither maintaining the principle of plenitude, as some, e.g. Hintikka, would have it, nor –like some of his other leading interpreters such as G.E.L. Owen– trying desperately to avoid it, but proceeding in the manner required by PET. One is prevented from proceeding in this manner if one presupposes PN, as both sorts of interpreters, otherwise opposed to one another, do. It turns out that far from future contingents having restricted the validity of PET, they are subject to PET as the dominating principle, whereas everywhere else, i.e., in the realm of actuality, not potentiality, PET gives way to PNC as the main principle. Such an outcome is only from the point of view of LEM/PB a paradoxical one[73]. Above all, it restricts neither the validity of PET

---

[73] If one starts, as modern logicians do, from PN, then the traditional approach to *Peri Hermeneias* 9 (cf. Aquinas, *In Peri Hermeneias,* n. 204: "quae sunt de contingentibus, necesse est quod sub disjunctione altera pars contradictionis sit vera vel falsa; non tamen haec vel illa determinatae"), which stresses the non-exclusiveness of "*vel*", must appear at the very least to be "devoid of sense" (P. Geach, *Logic Matters,* p. 81) and in fact a form of "philosophical confusion" (M. Dummett, *Truth and other enigmas,* p. 338). (Neither of the two is referring explicitly to Aristotle or to Aquinas, each of whom, incidentally, speaks not of the truth but of the necessity of a non-exclusive disjunction). *Peri Hermeneias,* 19b 23 ff., where Aristotle is clearly stating his own position, says in terms of "necessity" the same as PET says in terms of "possibility". It is perhaps no accident that Aristotle, after having questioned Bivalence at the beginning of *Peri Hermeneias,* 9, explicitly rejects at the end of the chapter only propositional negation (cf. H. Weidemann, *Aristoteles Peri Hermeneias,* p. 299). To say that by virtue of this very fact Bivalence has been implicitly rejected seems to amount to nothing more than a *petitio principii* (*ibid.*). The difficulties in taking PET into account accrue to the use theory of meaning which is common ground for many classical as well

nor that of PNC; it only implies that neither is a sufficient condition for dealing with specific problems, PET being needed for problems concerning not yet decidable issues at least as much as PNC is for issues already decided, but neither comes into conflict with the other.

As to whether a philosophy based on PET is a confused one, it should not be forgotten that Aristotle's philosophy is based on PNC too, which, so long as it is not confounded with LNC, yields, together with PET, PN. As a result, Aristotelian logic need not be different from modern logic, although they are based on different principles. On the other hand, one should also keep in mind that in *Metaphysics,* XII, 6, 7[74] PET and above all PNC are still being used, separately or conjoined, as tools. PET cannot therefore be regarded as confused philosophy –unless the metaphysics of Aristotle is itself confused. It is true that a sharp distinction between PNC and PET cannot be drawn in modern classical logic, which in fact allows each to be transformed into the other by means of De Morgan's Laws. Such a distinction, however, was needed, if only because Aristotle saw himself confronted with philosophers whom he took to be separately denying either PNC or PET.

---

as intuitionist philosophers of logic. If meaning depends not on truth-conditions but on verifiability-conditions, then it depends also on the possibility of asserting p and of asserting not-p separately or determinately, (cf. M. Dummett, *Truth and other enigmas,* p. 339) as against Aristotle and Aquinas; similarly on a realist basis, if concepts more or less nominalistically reduce to the use (applicability) of words in judgments, as in Geach and Quine (contrast 1006b 14-18). On the priority of concept and meaning over judgment and use in Aristotle, s. my "Aristotle's Defense of the Principle of Non-Contradiction" in *Archiv für Geschichte der Philosophie,* 76, 1994, pp. 129-150. Cf. also B. Janssen, '*Kants wahre Meinung*'. *Freges realistischer Objektivismus und seine Kritik am erkenntnistheoretischen Objektivismus,* Phil. Diss. (Münster 1994), published, Münster 1996.

[74] Cf. n. 64.

Appendix (to the appendix to Chapter 3, Part 1)

The treatment of the principles in Book IV of the *Metaphysics* is not logical or semantical but dialectical. What justifies symbolization in dealing with them is not so much the attempt to convey their genuine meaning nor the need to set them apart from their modern counterparts but, rather, the attempt to compare the two sorts of principles. The danger here consists not only in demanding perhaps more precision than might be needed but in sometimes stretching the comparison to the breaking-point (cf. the bracketing of some of the lines in the truth-tables of the Appendix). In general, it is to be borne in mind that the tables for the Aristotelian principles are not meant to be truth-functional nor hence genuine truth-tables. To repeat, they are only given to make the difference to the modern appoach more conspicuous. However, the real difficulties for a mind trained in modern logic are not limited to matters of symbolization. This already applies to "(0)" and "(1)" in the Appendix. If "A" were to cause more obscurity rather than increase precision as regards the central point that in asserting "p or not-p" one assert neither "p" nor "not-p", it would not suffice simply to abandon the symbolization. The general point in introducing "A" is that "asserting" means claiming truth and that just as "PNC" states only that the corresponding truth-claim ("TC") cannot be fulfilled by "p and not-p", "PET" states only that the truth-claim cannot remain unfulfilled by both members of the pair "p" and "not-p". *Via* PB this results in "at least one of both ought to be true", but *via* PB' taken as PN=DPN it would result in "only one ought to be true and the other false". Thus far the point is a perfectly clear one, and this independently of whether it is fair to Aristotle, as I contend, or not. And yet, the syntax of "A", if compared with that of Frege's assertion-sign, could pose difficulties –especially when, in stressing the point behind "TC" and "Ap", one is trying to avoid modern debates[75] by proposing to read "p" not as proposition but as *oratio* (from *os, oris*), or, alternatively, as propositional content. In the latter case "Ap" seems to require that "p" function not as a variable for names of

---

[75] Cf. W.V.O. Quine, *From A Logical Point of View*, pp. 71, 108, 118.

propositions (thoughts) nor as a schematic letter for the sentences (or the statements) themselves but rather as a schematic noun-phrase, i.e., as an abbreviation for "that p" so that "Ap" may also function as a schematic noun-phrase, "the assertion that p." But then "A" would appear to be a name-forming operator on names, unlike Frege's assertion-sign, which is a sentence-forming operator on sentences. Since I have been confronted with this objection, I would like to add some remarks here. The difficulty, if there is any, could not be disposed of simply by dropping either the symbolization or the comparison with Frege's assertion-sign. The point of this comparison is that in our case as well one may think of "p" as being equipped with built-in assertion and omit the assertion-sign with its special emphasis on TC. "A" is employed merely for the sake of expository convenience. The difficulty disappears as soon as one realizes that "that p is true" or "the assertion that p is true" are not less reasonable than such phrases as "'p' is true". Frege himself sometimes (e.g. in the *Begriffsschrift* §2) rendered his *beurteilbarer Inhalt* ("judgeable content") with the phrase "*der Umstand, daß*" ("the circumstance that"). Later on he substitutes for "*beurteilbarer Inhalt*" or "*Sachverhalt*" the term "*Gedanke*", which is, of course, equally capable of bearing truth-values[76]. Problems concerning the ontological status of *Gedanken* or propositions have haunted philosophers since Henry of Ghent's *esse essentiae* and Duns Scotus' *esse intelligibile seu objectivum*. They can be rendered less threatening by substituting with Thom as Aquinas "*oratio*" for "proposition" as well as "*usus orationis*" for "_ p" and the like. However, behind such formal considerations lies a philosophical question which one cannot circumvent even at the dialectical level. It is the question that leads some authors to consider PET a senseless or else confused way of interpreting such a much debated principle as PEM[77]. Even were one to concede this for the sake of argument, one ought still to see whether such an allegedly senseless or confused interpreta-

---

[76] Cf. B. Janssen, '*Kants wahre Meinung*'. Searle, too, treats propositional contents such as "that I will come" as being on a par with propositions (cf. J. Searle, *Speech Acts*, Cambridge 1970, p. 31).

[77] Cf. n. 2 and 74 above.

tion of the principle is in accordance with the aforementioned texts of Aristotle; and, if so, whether the charge is, as is my contention, only due to having overlooked the fundamental differences between the Aristotelian and the modern principles.

I now give a list of abbreviations contrasting, wherever possible, Aristotelian (n) with modern (n' and n") principles (in a broad sense of "principle"):

(0) TC = Truth-claim = asserting = A

(1) (P)C = (Principle of) Contradiction = Asserting p = (Ap), Asserting not-p = (Anot-p) = Asserting the affirmation of p, Asserting the negation of p[78].

(1') PN = Principle of Negation[79] = DPN = Definition of Propositional Negation:

$$\underline{p, \neg p}$$
T / F
F / T

(2) T = True = Ap and p, Anot-p and not-p

(3) F = False = Ap and not p, Anot-p and p.

(4)(a) PNC = Principle of Non-Contradiction = On any interpretation of "p", "p" and "not-p" are not both true.

(4)(b) the corresponding truth-table would be:

$$\underline{p, \text{not-p} \quad PNC^{80}}$$

---

[78] (P)C remains undefined in terms of truth or falsity. To make a claim to (to aim at) truth is not yet to succeed in the claim nor yet to fall short of it either. And, of course, there is no sincere claiming to be false.

[79] As stated in the main text, for Aristotle it follows from PNC and PET, not vice versa.

[80] The appropriate connective between p and not-p is for PNC as well as for PET (or their corresponding logical laws) a non-exclusive "either/or" (compare n. 63 above). In the case of PET this amounts to "$\Box\Box \, (p \wedge \neg p)$", which does not imply (but is implied by) "$\Box \, (p \wedge \neg p)$". Otherwise PET would come into conflict with PNC. Modern modal logic accepts with some misgivings the equivalence of "$\Box\Box p$" and "$\Box p$" in the form of a law.

$(T / T / F)^{81}$

T / F / T

F / T / T

F / F / T

(ba) if Ap is T, then Anot-p is F[82]

(bb) if Ap is F, then Anot-p is T or F

(4')(a) LNC = Law of Non-Contradiction = $-(p\&-p)$ = It is not the case that p and -p:

<u>p, -p / LNC</u>

(T / T / F)

T / F / T

F / T / T

(F / F / F)

(4')(b) Semantic Principle of Non-Contradiction (PNC') = No proposition is true or false.

(5)(a) PET = Principle of Excluded Third = On any interpretation of "p", "p" and "not-p" are both not false (and by PB at least one of the two must be true). The corresponding truth-table would be:

---

[81] In the following: bracketed lines serve only to stress the contrast between (4) and (4'), on the one hand, and (5) and (5') on the other.

[82] (4)(ba) plus (bb) is not the same as (1') nor as (1). (1') = (4)(ba)(bb) plus (5)(a)(b); (1) says nothing as to whether the truth-claim (0) has succeeded or failed, hence nothing about truth-values either. - "Not-p" is not the same as "-p" since (1) does not say anything about truth-values. - (4)(a) or (b) are just as little definitions of "T" or "F" as (5)(a) or (b). Aristotle could not defend either PNC or PET on the basis of PN without begging the question. That is why he begins each time on the level of conceptual definition, first (in the case of PNC), with the definition of "man", and then (in the case of PET) with that of "false".

p, not-p / PET

T / T / T[83]

T / F / T

F / T / T

(F / F / F)

(5)(b) PB = (Aristotelian) Principle of Bivalence: On any interpretation of (positive or negative "p") "p" is true or false (non-exclusive "or"; i.e. no p must be false (and no p must be true)).

In (5)(a) PET is to be read as "A (p or not-p)" just as in (5)(b) "p" as "Ap", i.e., as claiming, but not guaranteeing, truth (TC).

(a) if Ap is T, then Anot-p is T or F

(b) if Ap is F, then Anot-p is T

(5')(a) LEM = logical Law of Excluded Middle = $pv\neg p$ = It is the case that either p or -p:

p | ¬p / LEM

(T / T / F)

T / F / T

F / T / T

(F / F / F)

(5')(b) PB' = semantic Principle of Bivalence: Each proposition (p, not-p) is either true or false. "Either/or" is here openly exclusive. However, inasmuch as this exclusive "either/or" means that the assertion that p must be either true or false and that the assertion of not-p must be either true or false hold independently of one another —and not that if the assertion that p is true, then the assertion of not-p must be false and viceversa — strictly speaking PB' should not be taken as equivalent to PN = DPN.

(5")(a) LET = (logical) Law of Excluded Third = $\neg\neg(pv\neg p)$ = It is not the case that neither p or not-p =[84] (5")(b) *pet* = (semantic)

---

[83] Not to be understood truth-functionally.

principium exclusi tertii = No proposition is neither true nor false. Consequently no third truth-value is needed even in intuitionistic logic, *pet* rules out the possibility that any proposition could irrevocably be declared neither true nor false.

---

[84] Here "=" is not quite exact, for although "acceptance of the semantic principle normally entails acceptance of the corresponding logical law, the converse does not hold (M. Dummet, *Truth and others enigmas*).

INDEX OF NAMES

Ackrill, J. L., 149n.
Anaxagoras, 17, 30, 31, 32, 61, 107, 116, 117, 133, 138, 152n., 154, 264, 280, 472, 477n., 478n., 484n.
Angelelli, I., 213n.
Anscombe, E., 102n., 162n., 169n., 170n.
Anselm of Canterbury, 179n.
Augustine, 252

Balthasar, H. U. v., 181n.
Bambrough, R., 149n., 169n., 174n.
Barnes, J., 21n., 86n., 94n., 96n.
Beckmann, J. P., 8n.
Bergson, H., 262, 271
Bittner, R., 298n., 312n., 313n.
Bourke, V., 301
Brentano, F., 291
Brentlinger, J., 477n.
Brügge, W. v., 405n.
Bubner, R., 161n.

Cassirer, E., 245, 246
Cerezo, M., 213n.
Charles, D., 198n.
Chesterton, G. K., 394n.
Code, A., 34, 83n.
Cramer, K., 161n.
Cresswell, M.J., 21n., 110n.

Dahlstrom, D., 251n., 255n.
Dancy, R., 37-40, 42, 44, 75-78, 80-84, 86n., 88-93, 95-101
Descartes, R., 221n., 452
Deleuze, G., 125, 136n., 137n., 149n., 250, 261, 262
Diderot, D., 387
Driscoll, J. A., 196n.
Dummet, M., 110n., 422n., 506n.
Dumont, St., 384n.
Duns Scotus, J., 9, 31, 32, 52, 93n., 94n., 113, 114, 118n., 120, 121, 136n., 145n., 193., 207n., 213n., 236n., 250, 262n., 299n., 323n., 327n., 359-390, 392n., 393n., 491n., 503

Einstein, A., 174n.
Elders, L., 414n.
Empedocles, 264, 280
Engelhardt, P., 309n., 409n.

Fabro, C., 119, 120
Fénélon, 387
Fichte, J. G., 233, 237n., 242
Flasch, K., 163n.
Foucault, M., 137n.
Frede, D., 52
Frede, M., 144n., 145n., 166n., 171n., 184n., 193-200, 205, 208, 209, 211, 213, 215, 216n., 470n.

Frege, G., 17, 18, 33, 127, 142, 285, 487n., 469, 502
Furth, M., 37n., 38n., 75n., 77n., 78, 97n.

Gadamer, H.-G., 161n., 242, 251n., 292
Gaskin, R., 110n., 111n.
García-Marqués, A., 149n., 490n.
Geach, P., 25, 26, 31, 32, 67, 109, 110, 118n., 140-142, 147n., 162n., 169n., 170n., 210n., 213n., 413n., 441n., 470n., 475, 476n., 479-482, 488n., 489n., 495, 499n., 500n.
Geiger, L.-B., 120n., 121n.
Gerhardt, V., 309n.
Gill, M.-L., 193n., 194, 197, 198n., 202, 207n., 208n.
Gilson, E., 73, 262
Gödel, K., 147n.
Graeser, A., 309n., 395n., 409n., 418n.

Hafemann, B., 111n.
Haldane, J., 72n.
Harter, E. D., 171n.
Hartman, E., 198n.
Heath, T. L., 494n.
Hegel, G. W. F., 8n., 9, 67, 68, 164, 172, 173, 176, 177, 237, 241, 242, 244-247, 249-251, 253-260, 262-267, 271, 291, 292, 339, 447-451, 456
Heidegger, M., 8n., 9, 28, 125, 126, 155, 168n., 245-264, 266-269, 271, 290-293, 314, 317, 396, 453, 459
Heraclitus, 30, 107, 256, 472, 477n.
Herold, N., 309n.

Hintikka, J., 24, 26, 91n., 490n., 499
Hoeres, W., 362n.
Hölderlin, Fr., 268
Honnefelder, L., 7n.-9, 94n., 360n.
Hughes, G. E., 21n., 110n.
Hume, D., 355, 356, 419, 420, 431, 436
Hussey, E., 273, 275, 277-279, 281-284, 294n.

Inciarte, F., 7n., 413n., 414n., 426n., 441n.
Ingham, M. E., 384n., 390n.
Irwin, T. H., 7, 83n., 84n., 345, 418n.

Jaeger, W., 245
James, W., 352-358
Judson, L., 494n.

Kahn, C. H., 170n., 178n.
Kant, I., 50-52, 55, 114, 137, 215, 220-223, 229-231, 233, 235-237, 256, 297, 298, 301, 302n., 308, 309, 315, 348, 359, 373, 374, 387, 388n., 425-427, 456-458, 486n., 487n.
Kelsen, H., 179n.
Kenny, A., 173n., 174n., 325n., 409n., 418n.
Kierkegaard, S., 38, 81, 88, 92n., 95
Kirwan, C., 38n., 42, 43, 75, 77-80, 90, 96n., 170n., 312n., 467n., 469n., 470n.
Kluxe, W., 168n., 173n.
Kneale, W., 153n.
Kneale, M., 24
Knuuttila, S., 91n.
Köhler, D., 255n.
Kotarbinski, T., 165n.

Kremer, K., 139n., 168n.
Kühn, W., 126n.
Küng, G., 165n., 167n.

Lakebrink, B., 167n.
Lear, J., 84n.
Leibniz, G., 28, 141n., 219
Letzl, W., 52
Lewis, C. I., 95n.
Lewis, C. S., 442-447
Lewis, F., 166n., 191n., 194-198, 210, 216
Linke, D. B., 314n.
Liske, M.-Th., 149n., 166n., 170n., 174
Llano, A., 29n., 72n.
Lloyd, G. E. R., 202n.
Lombardus, P., 113, 114
Loux, M. J., 166n., 194n., 195n.
Lukasiewicz, J., 44, 86n., 98n.

Meinwald, C., 117n., 148n., 486n.
Mann, Th., 246
Mansion, S., 202n.
Marx, W., 248n.
McClelland, R. T., 112n., 490n.
McCord-Adams, M., 384n., 391-393
Mensch, W., 196n.
Mignucci, M., 110n., 213n.
Möhle, H., 384n.
Moravcsik, J. M. E., 197n.
Müller, A. W., 305n., 309n.

Newman, J. H., 354-356, 423
Noonan, H., 65n., 117n., 140, 141, 148, 149n.
Nietzsche, F., 9, 167, 175, 176, 453, 466

Ockham, W., 368n., 377, 391-394

Oeser, E., 241
Öffenberger, N., 470n.
Owen, G. E. L., 24, 170n., 171n., 196n., 202n., 263n., 490n., 499

Parmenides, 220, 250, 266, 287
Pascal, B., 352, 353, 357, 424, 448-451
Patzig, G., 144n., 145n., 166n., 171n., 184n., 193-200, 206, 208, 209, 211, 215
Peirce, Ch., 93n., 354
Pérez-Guerrero, F. J., 122n.
Plato, 17, 58, 59n., 62, 91, 106, 116, 117, 123, 124, 148n., 192n., 224, 233, 236, 251, 287, 288, 296, 297, 303, 307, 318, 322, 324-329, 332n., 333, 336-339, 341-349, 352, 353, 358, 371, 381-383, 385, 388, 390, 399, 404-406, 410, 411, 416, 417, 455-457, 476n., 483n., 486n., 487n.
Pöggeler, O., 255n., 256n.
Prauss, G., 298n., 309n., 416
Protagoras, 58, 107, 267n., 314, 342, 477n.
Proust, M., 239n., 245, 268, 269
Putnam, H., 144

Quine, W. V. O., 18, 19, 26, 27, 30, 39, 40, 47-49, 60, 65, 67, 83n., 92n., 94, 95n., 117n., 125, 137n., 138, 140-142, 147n.-149n., 152, 153, 164, 210n., 284, 285, 311, 312, 346n., 347n., 463, 470n., 482-489, 500n., 502n.
Quinton, A., 161, 162, 164-166, 170

Rahner, K., 167
Rapp, Ch., 196n.
Ricken, E., 305n.
Riedel, M., 309n.
Rilke, R. M., 314n.
Röd, W., 395n.
Rodriguez, P., 414n.
Ross, D., 21, 22, 24, 26, 75n., 77n., 78n., 80n., 144n., 258, 310, 490n.
Rousseau, J. J., 387
Russell, B., 164, 165, 167n., 171n.
Ryle, G., 168, 169n., 173, 174

Scaltsas, T., 116n., 198n., 208-213
Scheler, M., 320
Schelling, F. W. J., 9, 35, 156, 169n., 176, 178, 210n., 219-221, 223, 230-239, 241-244, 248, 366n.
Schleiermacher, Fr., 346n.
Schofield, M., 477n.
Schrimpf, G., 8n.
Schulz, W., 220n., 223n.
Searle, J., 502n.
Seidl, H., 193n., 197n.
Sorabji, R., 24, 113n., 169., 288, 289, 490n., 494n., 498n.
Spaemann, R., 413n., 414n., 441n.
Spengler, O., 421
Stadter, E., 405n.
Stallmach, J., 149n.
Stemmer, P., 349n.
Strawson, P. F., 161n., 170n., 210n.
Suarez, F., 94n., 191, 211, 369n.

Theron, St., 11, 300, 315
Thomas Aquinas, 8, 9, 15-19, 22-26, 28, 29, 32, 35, 41-43, 47, 50-52, 71, 75n., 105-124, 143, 145n., 154n., 168, 169n., 172-174, 176, 178n., 180n., 191n., 193n., 197n., 199n., 226n., 228n., 263, 271, 300, 301, 323, 333n., 376, 389, 390, 396-402, 413n., 430n., 447-449, 451n., 452n., 462, 463, 468n., 469n., 472n., 492n., 499n., 500n., 502
Tugendhat, E., 160, 314n., 417n., 425
Topitsch, E., 179n.

Vanauken, S., 442-447
Vigo, A., 248n.
Vlastos, G., 391

Wald, B., 390n., 391n.
Weidemann, H., 9, 82n., 91n., 108n., 110n., 111n., 166n., 171n., 210n., 465n., 468n., 470n., 490n., 500n.
Whitehead, A., 125
Wiehl, R., 161n.
Wieland, W., 241, 313n., 404, 417n.
Williams, B., 357, 358, 418-420, 423, 425, 427-436
Witt, Ch., 166n., 198n., 199n.
Wittgenstein, L., 55, 143, 144n., 174, 291, 314, 315, 475, 476n., 480-482, 489
Wippel, J., 121n.
Wolter, A., 379n.
Woods, M., 171n., 196n.

Yourgrau, P., 147n., 491n., 493n.

Zimmermann, A., 180n.